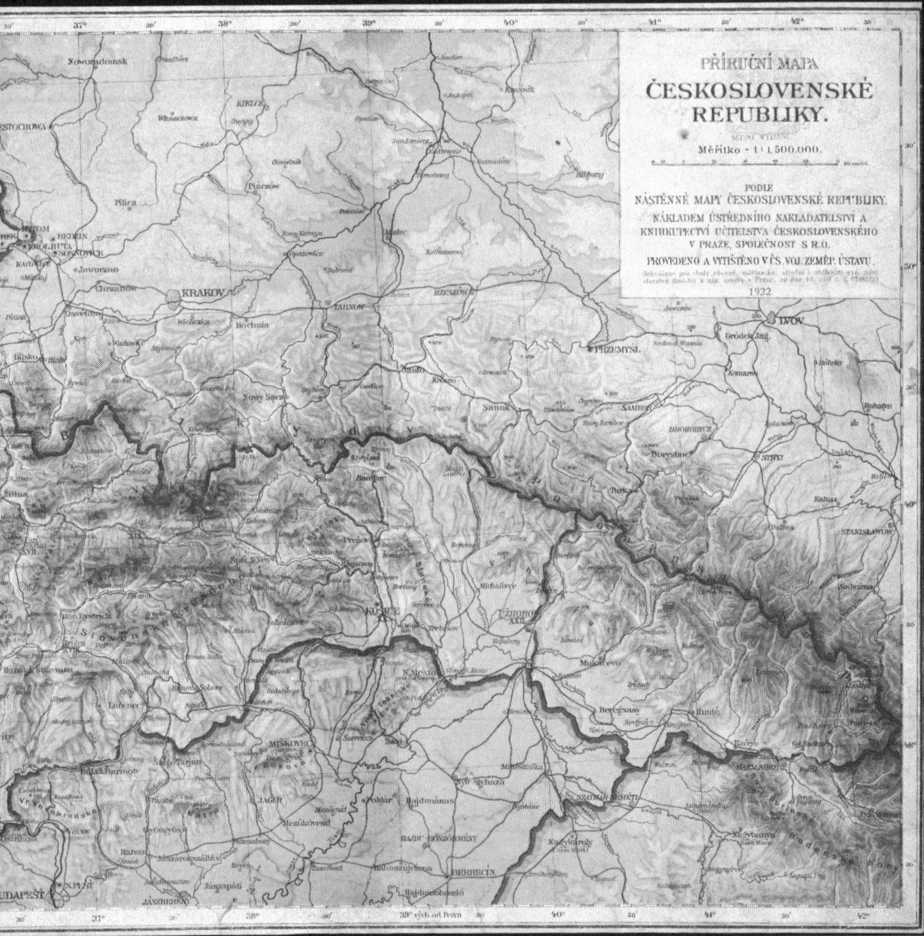

PŘÍRUČNÍ MAPA

ČESKOSLOVENSKÉ REPUBLIKY.

SEDMÉ VYDÁNÍ

Měřítko = 1 : 1,500.000.

PODLE
NÁSTĚNNÉ MAPY ČESKOSLOVENSKÉ REPUBLIKY.

NÁKLADEM ÚSTŘEDNÍHO NAKLADATELSTVÍ A KNIHKUPECTVÍ UČITELSTVA ČESKOSLOVENSKÉHO V PRAZE, SPOLEČNOST S R.O.

PROVEDENO A VYTIŠTĚNO V ČS. VOJ. ZEMĚP. ÚSTAVU.

1922.

החכמה תחיה בעליה קהלת ז
WISDOM PRESERVETH THE LIFE OF HIM THAT HATH IT
EX LIBRIS מספרי
Gift of
Milton A. Glaser
In memory of Esther Glaser

THE JEWS OF CZECHOSLOVAKIA

THE JEWS OF CZECHOSLOVAKIA

HISTORICAL STUDIES AND SURVEYS

VOLUME II

5732–1971

THE JEWISH PUBLICATION SOCIETY OF AMERICA
PHILADELPHIA

SOCIETY FOR THE HISTORY OF CZECHOSLOVAK JEWS
NEW YORK

By The Jewish Publication Society of America
and the Society for the History of Czechoslovak Jews

First Edition

Library of Congress Catalog Card Number: 67–12372

Manufactured in the United States of America

Designed by Sidney Feinberg

THE SOCIETY FOR THE HISTORY
OF CZECHOSLOVAK JEWS

expresses its gratitude and appreciation to the following people and organizations who, through their financial support, contributed to the publication of this book

The Helman Foundation, New York

*

Mr. and Mrs. Max Low, Mamaroneck, New York

*

Mr. Alfred Loewy and the Loewy Family in New York

*

The Petschek and Gellert Families, New York

*

Mr. Lewis Weiner, Hollis, New York

*

The Eli Wishnick Foundation, New York

*

The Gustav Wurzweiler Foundation, Inc., New York

*

The Joseph Popper Lodge and Chapter, B'nai B'rith, New York

DEDICATED

TO THE MEMORY OF

DR. OSKAR K. RABINOWICZ

PREFACE

It is with great satisfaction that we are presenting Volume II of *The Jews of Czechoslovakia.* We wish to express the hope that it will find the same warm acceptance by our members and friends, as well as by the professionals and the general public, as did Volume I. The considerable success of Volume I was gratifying indeed. The present volume continues the remarkable story of the Jewish Community of Czechoslovakia, both as an integral part of and participant in the life and development of the Czechoslovak Republic and as a significant segment of the Jewish people. The essays contained in this volume add to the mosaic which the first volume started to assemble, larger and smaller stones of different colors and shapes, dependent on the different professional backgrounds of the contributors. In this connection we might repeat what was said in the Introduction to Volume I: "While the Editorial Board is thus fully aware that level and approach differ widely from one essay to another, it also feels that these differences are of minor significance when viewed against the unquestionable valuable contribution which each article makes in bringing to light a great amount of historical fact and detail in its own field, and which no future historian of Czechoslovak Jewry can afford to overlook." Thus this volume brings us nearer to our goal of preserving for future generations the heritage of a thousand years of our history. Much still has to be done, and we are pledged to devote all our energies to this task. We hope that the many friends we have won through Volume I—and through the Millennium celebrations which took place under our aegis in 1968—will be ready to help. The present volume could not have been completed without the untiring and devoted work performed by two men in the most dedicated and selfless manner: the late Dr. Oskar Rabinowicz and Mr. Ludovit Sturc, the president of the Society for the History of Czechoslovak Jews. To them goes the expression of our gratitude. We also gratefully acknowledge the continued cooperation on the part of The Jewish Publication Society of America.

***

This volume is dedicated to the memory of Dr. Oskar K. Rabinowicz, who died June 26, 1969. He was the Society's leader and teacher. The last months of his life were mostly devoted to the preparation of this volume and, in particular, to the completion of his essay on Czechoslovak Zionism. He had hoped to see this book published; fate decided otherwise. Our Society's work will forever be connected with his name. In his honor, we have included in this volume a eulogy by his friend, the late Professor Cecil Roth, and a study of his works by his son, Professor Th. K. Rabb.

Dr. Kurt Wehle
Chairman, Board of Directors
Society for the History of Czechoslovak Jews

NEW YORK, AUGUST 1971.

Contents

3. ORGANIZATIONAL LIFE

4. RELIGION, WELFARE, EDUCATION

Illustrations

INTRODUCTION

In the Introduction to Volume I we outlined in detail the aims and aspirations of the Society for the History of Czechoslovak Jews. We listed the many prominent aspects of Jewish life in Czechoslovakia for the years 1918–1939, and our intentions to continue the story of Czechoslovak Jewry in a second and possibly third volume; a list of essays to be published was presented. This present volume contains all those essays and some additional ones as far as they relate to the period 1918–1939, with the exception of the article on Youth Organizations. In addition, it contains four articles leading up to the World War II period.

This volume is divided into six parts. The first part, entitled *In Memoriam*, contains two essays in honor of Oskar K. Rabinowicz, to whose memory the volume is dedicated: an excerpt from a eulogy by his close friend and collaborator, the late Cecil Roth, under the title *My Friendship with Oskar K. Rabinowicz*; his literary legacy is annotated by his son, Theodore K. Rabb, in the study *The Oeuvre of Dr. Oskar K. Rabinowicz*.

The second part, *Movements*, contains four articles. Oskar K. Rabinowicz's *Czechoslovak Zionism: Analecta to a History* is at the same time an overview and a detailed chronicle on Czechoslovak Zionism on the home front and the world scene. The emergence of Czechoslovakia's Jewish women on the Zionist scene is depicted by Irma Polak in *The Zionist Women's Movement*—a history of WIZO (Women's International Zionist Organization) in the Czechoslovak Republic. In *The Czech-Jewish Movement* Egon Hostovsky writes of the assimilated faction which opposed Zionism and Jewish nationalism, and whose members emphatically declared themselves to be Czechs not only by citizenship but also by nationality, and Jews by religion only. Orthodox Jewry was organized in the Agudath Israel or in the Mizrahi movements. The latter is dealt with in Oskar Rabinowicz's article on Zionism. Gertrude Hirschler's study *The History of Agudath Israel in Slovakia* gives a survey of the Agudath Israel movement, which stood for the preservation of the historic concept of the Jewish people as the *'Am HaTorah*, the people of God's Law.

The third part bears the title *Organizational Life*. It contains five articles on aspects of Jewish organized life other than those described in the preceding part. After the collapse of the Hapsburg monarchy much of the spirit of militant Jewish nationalism that had characterized Jewish student life at the University of Vienna during the three decades preceding 1918 shifted to the institutions of higher learning in Czechoslovakia. This phenomenon, which assumed political significance in the 1920s, is discussed by S. Goshen in his study *Zionist Students' Organizations*. In his article *Sports*, Joseph C. Pick not only deals with the political significance of Jewish sport organizations but recounts the internationally noted achievements of Czechoslovak Jews in such sports as swimming, skiing, tennis, table tennis, and other aspects of physical education. At the other end of the spectrum of organized Jewish life are the lodges and fraternal organizations; they are described in Meir Färber's article *Jewish Lodges and Fraternal Orders Prior to World War II*.

The participation of Czechoslovak Jewry in the country's public life, the activities of Jews within the various political parties and factions in the Republic, and the role of individual Jews in Czechoslovakia's legislative and governmental bodies are the subjects of *Jews in Political Life*, by J. W. Brügel. In *The Jewish Party* Aharon Moshe K. Rabinowicz presents the story of the political party which embraced all those Jews who had availed themselves of the right to declare themselves Czechoslovak citizens of Jewish nationality.

The fourth part, under the heading *Religion, Welfare, Education*, combines five articles. Hugo Stransky's study *The Religious Life in Slovakia and Subcarpathian Ruthenia* represents the counterpart to his essay on Jewish religious life in Bohemia and Moravia-Silesia, published in the preceding volume. Chaim Yahil, in the study *Social Work in the Historic Lands*, discusses the philanthropic communal and governmental agencies and the international organizations which worked to alleviate the plight of the Jewish poor and the victims of anti-Jewish discrimination. Within a short two decades the Jews in the eastern sector of the Republic had built a modern Hebrew educational system up to and including the high school level. In *Modern Hebrew Education in Subcarpathian Ruthenia* Aryeh Sole describes these Jewish nationalist-oriented schools, where religious and secular subjects were taught and to which the government gave official public school status and some financial support. Included in this chapter are two articles which deal with some psychological and philosophical aspects of Jewish life in various sectors of Czechoslovakia. The article *Realism and Romanticism* by the late Felix Weltsch, edited for this book by the author on the basis of his previous writings on the subject, is a unique analysis of the characteristics of Bohemian and Moravian Jews. Jan Ehrenwald's *On the So-called Jewish Spirit* is the author's first presentation in English of the results of studies and analyses which he had published earlier on Jewish spiritual crises and anti-Semitic reactions from his vantage point in pre-Second World War Slovakia.

The fifth part, under the title *Art*, adds to the section on *Music*, published in the first volume, six articles on other aspects of Jewish participation in the field of art. Hana Volavková, in her article *Jewish Artists in the Historic Lands*, writes an illustrated study on the visual art created by Jews in the Historic Lands, depicting its modest beginning in the early nineteenth century and the subsequent growth culminating in world acclaim at the beginning of the twentieth century. Frank Reichenthal contributes an illustrated essay entitled *Jewish Art in Slovakia*. Not all cultural achievements, especially in the fine arts, can be classed strictly in terms of a given historical period, but their timeless character assumes particular significance whenever people become aware of the continuity of their cultural heritage. This is true especially of two examples of classic architectural beauty in the Historic Lands: Zdenka Münzer contributes an essay entitled *The Old-New Synagogue in Prague: Its Architectural History*, reporting the results of her studies on the history of the famed *Altneuschul* in Prague, taking into account the most recent research concerning this seven-hundred-year-old edifice. Richard Teltscher writes on *The Altschul Synagogue of Mikulov*, a subject to which he has devoted years of research. S. J. Harendorf's article on *The Yiddish Theater in Czechoslovakia* evaluates the influence of the Hasidic stage in Czechoslovakia on its audiences and on drama in general. Also, Eugen Bárkány's pictorial presentation,

Jewish Cemeteries in Slovakia, recapturing the magic of graveyards going back to the fifteenth century, belongs in this category.

The sixth part, *Transition*, brings us nearer to the tragedy of Czechoslovak Jewry under Nazi rule. Kurt R. Grossmann, in his essay *Refugees to and from Czechoslovakia*, recalls the relief work in Prague in the 1930s in which he himself played a leading role. *Refugees in Prague, 1933–1938* by the late Manfred George, is a firsthand report containing previously unpublished factual information. The part which Czechoslovak Jews played in the practical realization of Zionism, the building of the Jewish homeland, is the subject of the late Fini Brada's essay *Emigration to Palestine*, describing the early "conquest" of the homeland by Jewish pioneers from Czechoslovakia. Aaron Zwergbaum's article on *From Internment in Bratislava and Detention in Mauritius to Freedom* is a thorough report and analysis and a moving story of the fate of that group of Jewish refugees who were stranded on the isle of Mauritius.

With regard to the overall principles and rules which guide the Society in its work, the reader is respectfully referred to the Introduction to Volume I. For purposes of clarity, however, we consider it necessary to quote from that Introduction the following passage: "The Editorial Board was not guided by, nor did it intend that the authors should advance any particular ideology or outlook. Each author expressed his or her own views and opinions on the subject. The members of the Editorial Board perused all articles carefully, and in many cases had pertinent suggestions to make to the authors. However, the essays covered so many widely differing fields that even a larger Editorial Board with a more varied membership could not have included persons familiar with every subject. Consequently, it is the authors alone who must bear sole responsibility for their contributions."

For the benefit of those who are not familiar with Volume I it was decided to reprint the "Note to the Reader" from Volume I, containing explanations helpful for the understanding of this book.

The present volume contains name and subject Indexes covering both volumes.

It is the hope of the Society for the History of Czechoslovak Jews that this volume will constitute yet another building stone in the lasting memorial raised by research and scholarship to the Jews of Czechoslovakia.

NOTE TO THE READER*

In a volume which covers such varied topics and areas as the present one, some technical and methodological explanations are necessary.

1. While this book is limited to the history of the period from 1918 to 1938, this time span could not always be strictly adhered to. For history is a fluid process of development, and problems and events can rarely be understood in isolation. A number of essays, therefore, reach back to the period prior to 1918 (for instance those on literature, the religious congregations, and so on). Readers who wish to acquaint themselves more thoroughly with the issues in both periods should find the bibliographies at the end of each essay helpful.

2. In a historical work of this nature which treats a number of broad and comprehensive areas, it is inevitable that more than one author will deal with the same event, viewing and studying it from his particular vantage point. For instance, the Parliamentary elections in 1920 had a special meaning for the Jewish Party, a different meaning for the sociological and political situation of the Jews in Subcarpathian Ruthenia, and still another significance for the general problem of minorities in the Republic. Therefore, these elections were examined in a number of articles from these different viewpoints. In order to present the reader with a comprehensive picture of this or any other broad problem, cross-references have been introduced into the text by the editors. All such cross-references appear in brackets and are signed (Ed.).

3. The differences in terminology employed in Czechoslovakia, a Central-European country, and in the Anglo-Saxon world, require some special explanation. Thus, for example, "nation" in this volume means a "state," while "nationality" means an "ethnic" nationality. A "Bohemian" is a German, Czech or Jew by nationality, living in the Province of Bohemia. "Bohemian" and "Czech" are thus not identical terms. Nor

* Reprinted from Vol, I, pp. xxi–xxiii.

are the terms "Hungarian" and "Magyar"; the former applies to a citizen of the State of Hungary, the latter to a member of the Magyar nationality.

"Community" refers to the entire Jewish community in the Republic, in a province or in cities; the legally organized sector of the Jewish community in cities and towns (known in German as *Kultusgemeinde* or in Czech as *náboženská obec*) is termed "Jewish religious congregation"; the politically organized Jewish community (with its own mayor, police, etc.) which existed in sectors of certain cities (mostly in Moravia) is termed "Jewish municipality."

4. Hebrew words were retained and transliterated according to the Sephardi pronunciation as practiced in Israel. (The term "Sephardi" has two different meanings in this volume: when employed linguistically it refers to its usage by Spanish-Portuguese Jews, in Hebrew called "Sephardim"; when used religiously it denotes the rites of the religious-social movement founded in the eighteenth century, the Hasidim.) The transliteration is phonetical. The majority of the *consonants* sound exactly as they do in English with a few exceptions: h sounds like the h in "ah" (as in exhaling a sigh), Kh like the ch in "character," and tz like the ts "Tsar." A word should be said about the pronunciation of the *vowels:* a—is like the a in "far" or in "father"; e—is like the e in "end" or the a in "crane"; i—is like the i in "sin" or the ea in "lean"; o—is like in "God" or "for"; and u—is like the oo in "good" or "bloom."

Hebrew books and articles have been listed according to their English titles, followed by the word Hebrew in parentheses.

Some Hebrew names were not transliterated according to the above principles, but retained in the transliterated form if that form had been used by their bearers (e.g., Bar Kochba instead of Bar Kokhba).

5. German words were retained in their original form. The *consonants* are mostly as they are in English, but note the following: c—is like the ts in "Tsar"; j—is like the y in "yes"; sch—is like the sh in "shine"; tz—is like the ts in "Tsar"; v—is like the f in "follow"; and w—is like the v in "victory." The pronunciation of the *vowels* is as follows: a—is like the a in "far"; e—is like the e in "delta"; i—is like the i in "inform"; o—is like the o in "obey"; and u—is like the o in "to." The *modified vowels* are: ä—like the a in "anguish"; ö—like the u in "further"; ü—like the y in "Libya." *Prolonged vowels:* aa and ah—are like the a in "blast"; ee and eh—are like the ee in "née"; ie and ih—are like the ee in "teen"; oo and oh—are like the o in "rose"; and uh is like the oo in "loom." Finally, ei reads like the i in "fine."

6. Czech words were also retained in their original form: c—is like the ts in "Tsar"; č—is like the ch in "child"; š—is like the sh in "shoe"; ž—is like the j in "jealous" (usually transliterated "zh"); ř—is like "rsh" or "rj"; and in the following three consonants the y is like that in "yes": t'—as ty; ň—as ny; d'—as dy. Czech *vowels* sound like those in German

(see above). For the *prolonged vowels:* á—as in "blast"; é—as in "men"; í—as the ee in "teen"; ó—as in "for"; ú and ů—as the oo in "loom."

7. The names of all cities and towns in the Republic were rendered in the official Czech or Slovak languages. Only Prague was retained in the English version, as were the foreign cities of Vienna, Munich, and Warsaw; these names have passed into common language. Where authors preferred to use the additional German or Magyar place names, these appear in parentheses after the German or Magyar name.

8. Some persons have changed their names, and where this is the case the name used in Czechoslovakia was retained and the new name follows in parentheses.

In other cases where the spelling of names in the same family varied (e.g., Schulhoff and Schulhof), the rendition employed by the bearer was used.

9. Persons are listed in a separate Index of Persons. Full names are given insofar as they were ascertainable.

10. In Volume II there is an Index of Subjects, which is also helpful as a cross-reference.

I. In Memoriam

MY FRIENDSHIP WITH OSKAR K. RABINOWICZ

by Cecil Roth

One day, I think in the fall of 1940, when the opening of the German air offensive on London had driven large numbers of persons to find refuge in safer areas and in consequence Oxford had become the wartime Jewish capital of England, I received a letter from one Dr. O. K. Rabinowicz saying that he would like to make my acquaintance and enclosing by way of introduction a copy of his German book on the problems of Shehita. He added in a postscript that he thought he should make it plain that he was not in need of material assistance — which was justifiable enough, in view of the fact that this was not the case with a very large proportion of the continental refugees then in England. On the other hand, on the basis of manifold experiences I imagined that he desired to solicit my assistance in bringing out the work as an English edition. I replied courteously (as I hoped), suggesting an appointment. Dr. Rabinowicz subsequently came to see me in my study and remained for an hour without touching on the matter that I had anticipated.

This proved to be the beginning of a cordial friendship. I imagine that it was I who introduced him to the Jewish Historical Society of England: before long, he became a member of our council and one of our most trusted supporters.

When in 1943, as president of the Society, I convened the representative Conference on the Restoration of Continental Jewish Museums, Libraries and Archives (a hazardous enterprise, with the guns still rumbling in our ears) he not only assumed the duties of honorary secretary but had my opening address published and circulated and took on himself the burden and not-inconsiderable expense of administration as long as we continued in existence. He was also active in a dozen other British organizations, where he brought into play a high, and sometimes unique, cultural standard. When the tercentenary of the return of the Jews to England was celebrated in 1956, he was named co-treasurer of the commemoration jointly with Lord Rothschild. I doubt if any other foreigner made such a mark in Anglo-Jewish life in such a short period.

When I became editor-in-chief of the *Encyclopedia Judaica*, I found myself in ever-closer contact with Oskar, both in the United States and in Jerusalem, where, after he acquired his apartment there, he became as familiar and ubiquitous a figure as he was in his American environment. His wide knowledge of the entire fields of Jewish scholarship and of the specialists in the various aspects made us turn to him constantly. He was inevitably a trustee of the *Encyclopedia Judaica* Research Foundation and at the same time departmental editor for the History of the Jews in Czechoslovakia. I do not think that there was any other person who collaborated both in the organizational material and scientific aspects of our work. To replace him will be impossible.

His principal characteristic, perhaps, was his appearance of entire effortlessness. He always had time for others and never appeared to be entirely absorbed by any one of his manifold occupations — financial, scholarly, organizational, or personal. He listened almost detachedly and then, in his characteristic voice, was immediately prepared with cogent advice which took into account every relevant circumstance and was probably as good as any advice on the subject could be.

He had a facility for friendship combined with a faculty for leadership, which was never sought but always thrust upon him. Wherever he went there soon gathered about him a circle of friends — scholars, businessmen, artists — who before very long were confiding their difficulties and perplexities to him. Persons who came into contact with him in the most diversified ways and with the most diversified objects ended by making him their confidant and seeking his advice on their most intimate personal affairs — advice which was always forthcoming. Jacob Epstein executed a bust of him, and from that time on he was the great sculptor's constant confidant and adviser. This personal persuasiveness permeated the whole of his life and activity in every aspect. Few persons were able to obtain access to private and sealed archives in England and America as this newcomer was through sheer persuasive force of personality.

No man ever pushed himself less — but no man probably served on more committees and councils, to which he always pressed to lend the authority of his name. Yet this was not nominal service on his part: he took his responsibilities seriously, attended all meetings, and was always listened to with deference.

It is amazing that, with all these effortless preoccupations — personal, public, economic — he was able at the same time to devote himself to sheer scholarship. This was not only in the sphere of Zionist history, in which he had his own very definite point of view and for which his unrivaled memory and his systematic files provided him with sufficient guidance (as is demonstrated in his remarkable work *Fifty Years of Zionism*, in which Chaim Weizmann's autobiography was submitted to a searching examination). When, because of some mental association, he became interested in a matter of purely antiquarian history — as in the seventeenth and eighteenth century English army commissioner Sir Solomon de Medina, simply because he was so closely associated with the first Duke of Marlborough, Winston Churchill's ancestor — he brought the same powers of industry and systematic research to bear. On the history of the Jews in his native Czechoslovakia he was, of course, the recognized authority. When he published his bibliography of my own writings in 1966, I found that he had many entries that had long escaped my own memory.

His activity was aided by his remarkable linguistic range. He knew Czech, German, and Yiddish from childhood. A fervent Zionist such as he could not fail to master modern Hebrew, which he spoke effortlessly and well. When he had to leave his native country in 1939 he became so well acquainted with English that it was not easy to discern that he was not a native. In addition, he had a sufficient knowledge of the classical tongues and of the language of the countries where he stayed for any time on his travels, and in all the languages that he knew well he was an effective platform speaker.

If one looks for the reason for the influence he exerted in so many fields of activity it was, I think, basically this: he spoke out of profound knowledge. It was not only that he was personally generous and that his approach was always so balanced and so sound, but also that his knowledge of the world — especially the Jewish world, past and present — was so extensive and so intimate. While among economists he was an economist, among Judaic scholars he was a scholar; and the two qualities merged, each reinforcing the other. It was a combination such as one seldom meets.

THE OEUVRE OF DR. OSKAR K. RABINOWICZ

by Theodore K. Rabb

The two abiding passions of Oskar Rabinowicz's writings were for Zionism and historical accuracy. In his first substantial work, a small book of verses written between the ages of fifteen and nineteen, there is a poem entitled "Ahasuerus" (the traditional name for the Wandering Jew), inspired by Jeremiah 31:15 and 16. The biblical passage contains the famous promise of the Lord to Rachel, weeping because her children find no comfort: "Refrain thy voice from weeping, and thine eyes from tears; for... they shall come back from the land of the enemy." The poem pursues this theme in bitter tones. As one verse puts it:*

> He travelled many dusty streets,
> In strange cities and lands alone . . .
> The dogs were barking at his feet . . .
> And often, too, the boys threw stones . . .

And the refrain runs:

> Oh, Mother Rachel, mourn, cry, and plead,
> I am still not on my way back to the Homeland!

In these early years Oskar Rabinowicz was already deeply committed to the ideal of bringing his fellow Jews back to their homeland. It was a cause to which he devoted all his efforts in the 1920s and 1930s, writing countless brief articles and delivering innumerable speeches across Czechoslovakia. His earliest publication, completed

* *Gedichte* (Vienna & Brno, 1924), p. 25

while he was still at school in his home town of Boskowitz in Moravia, was a translation from German into Hebrew of *Instructions for Gym Classes*, put together for the Hebrew School in Jaffa. The pamphlet was an ephemeral undertaking, but its appropriateness lay in its assistance for the pioneering settlers in Palestine.

Following the doctoral dissertation on Spinoza's concept of God that he completed at the University of Prague in 1924, he turned his attention to Jewish history. His first major work was published in 1929: *The History of the Jews of Aussee*, a small town in Moravia. In this meticulous study of the vacillating fortunes of a tiny community, he displayed not only his love for research into the past but also his enjoyment of the pursuit of precision and accuracy. Carefully documented, it is a model local study.

During the early 1930s his first important Zionist publications appeared. He was by now a leader of the Revisionist movement and a close associate of Vladimir Jabotinsky. Both men were particularly pleased with the achievements of the Jewish Legion, founded in 1917, because it had revealed the prowess of the Jewish soldier, who had been a virtually nonexistent figure for millennia. The legion's activities offered hope that the Jews could defend themselves in the treacherous situation in Palestine. In 1932, therefore, to mark the fifteenth anniversary of its founding, Oskar Rabinowicz edited *The Jewish Legion*, a pamphlet published by the Tel Chaj Fonds in Berlin. He wrote the introductory essay, surveying the previous fifteen years, and suggesting that the legion had won new respect for the Jews in the gentile world. Jabotinsky had two articles in the pamphlet, one of them a reprint of his original 1915 proposal for the establishment of the legion; and there were also contributions by Meir Grossman and various British commanders (including Allenby), whose views of Jewish soldiers were printed. It was a proud, hopeful publication to appear on the eve of Hitler's assumption of power.

Two years later Oskar Rabinowicz published a pamphlet entitled *When Nations Awake*. Dedicated to Jabotinsky and published by the Union of Zionists-Revisionists of Czechoslovakia in Prague, it was ostensibly a general survey of the meaning of national sentiment. It examined such subjects as the influence of music and popular songs, and described the various elements that between them had stimulated Czech nationalism. In each case, however, he found an equivalent for the Jewish people, and thus built up a powerful case

A Jewish Cyprus Project: Davis Trietsch's Colonization Scheme (New York, 1962) Rabinowicz drew a pointed moral from his investigations. A German living in America, Davis Trietsch, believed that by starting Jewish settlement on the fringe of "Greater Palestine" he might eventually be able to colonize the entire area. He received no support from the Zionist movement and made little progress with the British government. Eventually he was offered a few hundred acres of land at thirty dollars an acre, but this, too, was of little consequence. Though he was also involved in the early stages of the East Africa scheme, his contribution had been made, and he soon slipped into obscurity.

Rabinowicz's study printed the main documents of the episode and traced the fluctuating fortunes of Trietsch's activities. Its purpose, however, was revealed only in its final paragraphs, where Trietsch was contrasted with Herzl. Both men, as Rabinowicz pointed out, "negotiated at the same time with the same political authorities regarding the immediate future of their unhappy brethren" (p. 91). But Herzl insisted that Jewry be treated as a nation, with "national and cultural autonomy in concentrated compact territory," whereas Trietsch sought only "scattered settlements" in Cyprus, with no recognition of their national aspirations (p. 92). Here, in this contrast between "political" and merely "practical" Zionism, Rabinowicz saw the key to Herzl's success and the failure of the other schemes of this period.

The towering hero of these years was Theodor Herzl, a figure to whom Rabinowicz returned time and again, not only to point a moral about the Zionist movement but also to explain its success. He was the touchstone by whom all personalities and developments were measured. As a result, in Rabinowicz's words, it was important to "understand the man in all phases of his spiritual growth and in all aspects of his activities." These words are taken from an article which took this lesson very much to heart: "Herzl the Playwright," *Jewish Book Annual*, 18 (1960–1961), pp. 100–115 (p. 100). Analyzing this seemingly insignificant stage in the career of the founder of modern Zionism, during which he wrote twenty-eight plays and sketches, Rabinowicz found a number of suggestive pointers for the future.

The two themes of the plays were the importance of the family as the basic unit of society and the corrupting influence of money. What emerged was the wish for a new kind of society, where family life was upheld and the power of money destroyed. Jews figured prominently among his characters, both as heroes and as villains, but the most prominent feature of the plays was the burning idealism, the hope for a better world than the one he saw. The implications of these views for Herzl's later activity in the Zionist movement were obvious. Among his first principles was to be the insistence that the Jewish state could be founded only on hard work—the charity of the rich was corrupting, and one of his characters cries: "We are not beggars: we are workers!" (p. 113). Similarly, speculators and careerists—the chief villains in his plots—had to be excluded from the new state, and he hoped that its society could rest on the virtues represented by the best kind of Jewish family life.

Rabinowicz made no claim that his article provided the full treatment this subject deserved but, as so often, he was determined to open a neglected area of scholarship. A similar purpose animated his many studies, published over the space of sixteen years, concerning Herzl and England. England was his adopted country, a country that had given him refuge from persecution; Herzl was his chief interest as a historian of Zionism; and between the two themes an important contribution was to be made to modern Jewish history.

The first essay, "Herzl and England," in *The Jewish Monthly* (November 1951), pp. 1–24, outlined the negotiations of 1902–1903 that were to lead to the East Africa scheme (a subject he explored more fully in the article mentioned above). It was an exhaustive account which printed all the relevant documents from the Foreign Office files. Eight years later, in an article with the same title, published in *Herzl Year Book*, 3 (1960), pp. 37–47, he took a larger view, and examined the quality of Herzl's various negotiations with the British government. His conclusion was that the great Zionist had shown remarkable skill, for he had used the East Africa scheme, not to abandon Palestine (as his critics asserted), but for a much larger purpose. All that he sought was recognition of the Jews' nationalist aspirations. The scheme would fail, he knew, but out of it would come "the first recognition of our people as a Nation" (p. 46). In Rabinowicz's opinion, Herzl had sown the seed of the later successes of the Zionists in England.

This theme was taken further in one of his last publications, "Zionist-British Negotiations in 1906," in *Essays Presented to Chief Rabbi Israel Brodie on the Occasion of His Seventieth Birthday* (London, 1967), pp. 311–333. As he proved, by extensive citation of various Foreign Office documents and letters in the Central Zionist

Archives, contacts by no means ceased after the collapse of the East Africa scheme. Herzl's old associate Leopold Greenberg continued his efforts, and the Zionist leadership now attempted to negotiate for a colony in the Sinai Peninsula. As the Protocols of the Eighth Congress (1907) were to put it, they had "maintained the connections which Herzl created" (p. 332).

Once again, Rabinowicz's hero dominated events, a dominance which was explored at greatest length in his book *Herzl, Architect of the Balfour Declaration* (New York, 1958). In this work, the case for Herzl's primacy in the foundation of Zionism, and even in the first moves toward the creation of the State of Israel, was firmly established. The thesis of the book was an elaboration of arguments raised in the articles that have just been described. The evidence was overwhelming that the East Africa negotiations amply fulfilled Herzl's long-term expectations — they brought the British government to recognize the Jews' legitimate aspirations, and the lesson was never forgotten.

With painstaking documentation, Rabinowicz proved that each of the crucial figures in British politics gained his introduction to Zionism from Herzl. Chief in importance was Balfour himself, who, according to Weizmann and his followers, first heard of Zionism when he met Weizmann in 1906. Rabinowicz demonstrated beyond all doubt that Balfour's understanding of Zionism was no different after this conversation than it had been for the previous four years, ever since he had encountered the movement during his government's negotiations over East Africa. A similar conclusion was reached with regard to Lloyd George, Lord Milner, Lord Cromer, Sir Edward Grey and Sir Henry Wickham Steed, all of them central figures in the issuance of the Balfour Declaration of 1917. The vital groundwork had been prepared by Herzl, who fifteen years before had brought these men into contact with the principles which ultimately were to be endorsed by the momentous declaration. Here Rabinowicz's admiration for Herzl blended with lifelong devotion to historical accuracy. His hero's contribution had been slighted by Weizmann and his followers; it was only right to restore him to his true place as the architect of one of Zionism's greatest triumphs.

The same purposes animated what was perhaps his best-known book, *Fifty Years of Zionism. A Historical Analysis of Dr. Weizmann's "Trial and Error"* (London, 1950; second edition, 1952; Hebrew edition, Tel Aviv, 1952; summary printed at the end of the French edition of Weizmann's autobiography). It was clear that *Trial and Error* would become a major document of Zionist history, and Rabinowicz was appalled by its inaccuracies and its blatant distortions, particularly its repeated injustices to Herzl. With telling force, he exposed the old personal antagonism that led Weizmann to minimize and falsify Herzl's contributions to the movement. Again and again he showed that the ideas for which Weizmann claimed all the credit had in fact come from Herzl, and that in earlier years the debt had even been acknowledged.

More serious was the attempt to denigrate the "political" aims of Herzl's Zionism. Weizmann asserted that these were impractical and gave credit instead to his own reliance on the effects of settlement and economic growth. Rabinowicz shows how this interpretation simply turned the facts on their heads—without the insistence on political recognition, the early successes would have been impossible, the Balfour Declaration inconceivable, and the establishment of the state unattainable. In addition, Herzl had advocated a major effort to stimulate immigration, whereas Weizmann had wanted to leave potential settlers to "their own devices" (p. 40), a contrast in which the superiority of the first over the second was once more inescapable. Above all, in accord with his more detailed studies of the East Africa scheme and events in England, Rabinowicz revealed a consistent belittling and misunderstanding of Herzl's aims and achievements in bringing the British government to an appreciation of Jewish hopes and thus preparing the way for the Balfour Declaration.

In the remainder of *Fifty Years of Zionism* a series of lesser, but still significant, shortcomings were brought to light. The harsh treatment of Brandeis was shown to have stemmed from an old personal animosity and to have been based on a misrepresentation of the American justice's position. Similarly, Weizmann overestimated his own influence during the Morgenthau "peace mission" of 1917, and on the development of the Technion in Haifa, particularly during the important strike of 1914. He was revealed as a one-time admirer of the *Hilfsverein* schools who now, for unknown reasons, decided to launch an unfair and inaccurate attack on its founders and proponents.

The Seventeenth Congress (1946), when Weizmann resigned his presidency of the Zionist Organization, was a vital turning point which, once again, failed to receive its due in *Trial and Error*. As Rabinowicz pointed out, Weizmann had long been associated (at least since 1930) with the view that there was no necessity for a Jewish state in Palestine. Events had now left him behind, and the congress turned against him because of a fundamental cleavage of opinion—not, as he wished us to believe, because of personal hostility. Finally, Rabinowicz disclosed a succession of errors and unwarranted slightings in the treatment of Moses Gaster, Leopold Greenberg, Vladimir Jabotinsky, Max Nordau, Nahum Sokolow, Menahem Ussishkin, and David Wolffsohn. The record was set straight, and in the process Rabinowicz served not only the cause of historical accuracy but also Zionism itself, whose leaders were restored to the stature they deserved.

It was exactly in this spirit that, a few years later, Rabinowicz turned his attention to the problem of the Arab refugees in the Middle East. Here was a matter which was both a concern to the State of Israel and also a subject of wildly varying interpretations. What he wanted to do was at least to establish the basic facts in the case, to achieve maximum accuracy as a basis for further discussion. The result was an article, "The Jews and the Arab Refugees," in *Jewish Social Studies*, 21 (1959), pp. 238–245, which examined the appropriate census returns and concluded, with impeccable documentary substantiation, that there could not have been more than 350,000 refugees. By using this figure as a starting point, instead of the usual exaggeration of one million, he felt that a new start could be made toward solving the problem of the homeless Palestinians. The article was a notable example of his efforts for his people and the quest for precision that inspired everything he wrote.

The double aim of all of Rabinowicz's work was equally evident in the investigation into the work of Arnold Toynbee that occupied much of his time during his last years. Not only was Toynbee a distinguished Englishman and a famous historian, but during the 1910s and 1920s he had been an enthusiastic advocate of Zionism. Much of Rabinowicz's scholarship had concerned itself with the importance of English non-Jews to the success of the movement, and he was thus particularly anxious to understand the virulent anti-Zionism that began to characterize Toynbee's writings in the 1930s. In 1968 he published an article, "Toynbee's Pro-Zionism in World War I," in *Herzl Year Book*, 7 (1968), pp. 1–14, which documented the historian's important and helpful advocacy of Jewish aims while in an influential position in the Foreign Office and Chatham House.

It left no doubt as to his complete commitment to the cause. As for the reversal, that was analyzed in a book that is being revised and will be published posthumously, to be entitled *In Service of Prejudice*.

A very different atmosphere pervaded Rabinowicz's studies of the place in Jewish history of another Englishman, Winston Churchill. He wrote a number of articles about the statesman's activities, but his principal publication was *Winston Churchill on Jewish Problems: A Half-Century Survey* (London, 1956). This was an account of all subjects except Zionism. The latter, which was to have been treated in a second volume that was never completed, was covered more briefly in an article which appeared in the *Transactions of the Jewish Historical Society of England* (1970).

In Churchill, Rabinowicz found a figure second only to Herzl in attractiveness and interest. From the time of his first contacts with Jewish matters, during the East Africa scheme and the debates on the aliens' bills of 1904 and 1905, Churchill had been a consistent enemy of anti-Semitism and advocate of Jewish rights. After the defeat of the Aliens' Act of 1905 he received a letter tendering the official "thanks of the Jewish Community for the service which you have rendered it by your eloquent championship of its persecuted co-religionists" (p. 81). This stand was maintained throughout his long career, intensifying as the Nazi regime undertook its campaign of hate and atrocity.

The only solution Churchill saw to the constant persecution was the Zionist solution. In 1906 he wrote of his hope for "a safe and settled home under the flag of tolerance and freedom" (p. 190), and two years later he stated: "I am in full sympathy with the historical aspirations of the Jews. The restoration to them of a centre of racial and political integrity would be a tremendous event in the history of the world" (p. 195). From this position it was but a few steps to the declaration, made in 1954: "I have been, am, and intend to remain an unfaltering Zionist." Rabinowicz followed this progression with his customary meticulous research. Allowing Churchill's words to speak for themselves in lengthy quotations, he laid before his readers the record of a remarkable friendship for the Jewish people by one of the giants of the twentieth century.

The article on Churchill's Zionism received its final touches only a few days before Rabinowicz's death. It had been delivered in London a few months before as the first Winston Churchill memorial lecture, sponsored by the Jewish Historical Society of England and the Friends of Bar-Ilan University. He even made a few suggestions for its footnotes during his last stay in the hospital. As it is, the documentation will not be as he would have wished it to be. Nor will the mammoth, multivolume history of Zionism,which he had planned and prepared for over three decades, ever be finished. The first four volumes were almost ready when he died, and the manuscript, together with his extensive notes for the remainder, will be deposited in an appropriate archive so that they, like the rest of his life's work, can be of use to future generations of scholars.*

* [In the Library of the Hebrew University in Jerusalem (Ed.)]

2. Movements

CZECHOSLOVAK ZIONISM: ANALECTA TO A HISTORY

by Oskar K. Rabinowicz

With the establishment of Czechoslovakia, the building of a completely new Zionist organizational structure became inevitable. The territorial composition of the new Republic required that the Zionist movement, too, transcend the political boundaries within which it had developed in the prewar years. Prior to 1918, Bohemia and Moravia-Silesia constituted separate, and in many respects autonomous, districts within the West Austrian Zionist Organization,[1] while Slovakia and Subcarpathian Ruthenia were integral parts of the Hungarian Zionist Organization with no form of local or regional organizational activity.

More significant by far than these external prewar differences in the Zionist organizational structure among the various areas, which from 1918 on constituted the territory of Czechoslovakia, were the spiritual and ideological contrasts which separated them and which were the result of disparate internal Zionist developments.[2] As to Bohemia and Moravia-Silesia, the Zionist movement in these Historic Lands had long before the outbreak of World War I ranked among the important Zionist territorial groups and left its mark on the spiritual leadership of the world Zionist movement.

I. IN THE HISTORIC LANDS AND IN THE EAST

(A) BOHEMIA

In Bohemia, in particular, under the impact of the evolution which had taken place in Zionism after Herzl's death (1904), with its emphasis on cultural and political activities in the Diaspora (*Gegenwartsarbeit* — present-day activity in addition to the hope for a future National Home in Palestine), an important ideological center emerged in the Prague students' society *Bar Kochba.*[3] As assimilated Western Jews, these students were seeking a "homecoming"[4] to Jewry and Judaism through the acquisition of a knowledge of Hebrew and a familiarity with Jewish spiritual treasures, and by establishing close ties with the cultural renaissance of Eastern European Jewry and the new reality of Palestine.

From 1908 on, they came under the influence of Martin Buber. Adopting his philosophy, because of its affinity with their own ideology, they became the bearers of what was generally described as the *Prager Richtung im Zionismus* (The Prague Orientation of Zionism). By raising the spiritual aspects to a primacy in Zionist thinking, this trend had a deep ideological impact on the Zionist movement, particularly in the West, before as well as after 1918. Many *Bar Kochba* members who left Czechoslovakia at the time of or subsequent to her establishment contributed importantly between the two world wars to the crystallization of a clearly discernible trend in World Zionism, not only culturally but also, to a high degree, politically. This applied in the first place to men such as Drs. Hugo Bergmann, Leo Herrmann, Siegmund Katzenelson, Hans Kohn, and Robert Weltsch. Numerous other members of *Bar Kochba* made their influence felt on the development of Czechoslovak Zionism.[5] While *Bar Kochba*, however, was definitely on the decline after 1918, its Czech sister society *Theodor Herzl* was able to make considerable contributions to Zionist activities in Czechoslovakia in all its aspects.[6]

If a pre-World War I division in World Zionism (practical versus political Zionism) can be applied here, both *Bar Kochba* and *Theodor Herzl* identified themselves with "practical" Zionism as propagated by the opponents of Theodor Herzl and David Wolfssohn, Herzl's successor to the presidency of the World Zionist Organization.

The students' fraternity *Barissia,*[7] too, made important contributions to prewar and postwar Zionist developments in Bohemia and Czechoslovakia. It rejected *Bar Kochba's* primacy of the spiritual aspect of Zionist ideology. While reckoning with the realities of the existing situation it strove for the improvement of the Jewish national character and the ultimate establishment of national Jewish independence. It was less concerned with a deepening of Zionist ideology than with expanding the organizational framework of Zionism. *Barissia* endeavored to educate its members to become conscious and self-disciplined Jews, able and prepared to defend Jewish national rights and honor in the society in which they lived. They were *couleur* students (wearing special caps and ribbons) and embraced the principle of the *Schlagende Verbindungen* (dueling fraternities) which flourished in prewar days at German and Austrian universities. They also fostered the study of Jewish history, literature, and Hebrew language, and insisted on a personal Zionist commitment. From their midst emerged Zionist workers and leaders who attained prominent positions and exercised considerable influence on Czechoslovak Zionism.[8] After 1918, *Barissia* — in contrast to *Bar Kochba* — developed great vitality, particularly in the field of Zjonist propaganda and organizational reforms.[9]

There was, finally, a third important students' group in Prague, the *Jüdische Akademische Lese- und Rede-Halle*[10] (Jewish Academic Reading and Lecture Hall, called *Halle* for short), which was satisfied with neither the preeminently spiritual work, as adhered to by *Bar Kochba*, nor the strictly disciplined organizational activities of *Barissia*. It chose instead a middle path, neither *couleur* nor concerned primarily with its spiritual make-up, but seeing as its purpose the acquisition of as much knowledge of Judaism and Zionism as possible in order to spread it both among students and the general public. It produced a number of outstanding Zionist leaders who made valuable contributions to the Zionist movement as a whole.[11] It affiliated with the *Hallen* in Brno and Vienna.

It would, however, be misleading to leave the reader with the impression that Zionism in prewar Bohemia was and remained a students' movement. There existed also other very active youth organizations formed prior to 1918 and active in the Republic, as for instance the *Tehelet Lavan* (Blue White) scout movement or the *Maccabi* sports organization.[12] The inroads of assimilationism and the growing detachment from religious practice notwithstanding, there were also prior to 1918 a great number of Jews of all ages, classes, and categories who joined the Zionist Organization and remained its ardent adherents in new Czechoslovakia. Wherever possible, they formed Zionist societies in their cities and towns and performed Zionist activities, often amidst great difficulties. Thus the *Volksverein Zion* (People's Society Zion) in Prague was both before and after 1918 one of the Zionist strongholds in Bohemia.[13] There were other *Zion* societies in other towns also — for instance, in Budějovice, Dobříš, Karlovy Vary, Kolín, Kutná Hora, Most, Písek, Plzen, and Teplice Šanov; an *Ahavat Zion* society existed in Cheb, and an *Aschrei Zion* in Chomutov.

A great number of individuals who subsequently emerged as leaders of the organization put their talents at the disposal of these students and general societies and greatly contributed to the spread and strengthening of Zionism, both before and after the emergence of Czechoslovakia.[14]

In 1907 Bohemian Zionists established their own weekly (in German), *Die Selbstwehr* (*Self-defense*),[15] which, as the years passed, became the foremost Zionist periodical in Czechoslovakia. For a while (1913–1914) there appeared a fortnightly in the Czech language, *Židovské Listy* (*Jewish News*),but it was only in 1918 that the weekly *Židovské Zprávy* (*Jewish News*) appeared.[16]

(B) MORAVIA-SILESIA

In Moravia-Silesia, as in Bohemia, students took a prominent part in the organization and propagation of Zionism from the very beginning. Indeed, Moravian students in *Veritas* (Brno) were the first in the Historic Lands to respond to Herzl's call, due to the initiative of its members Berthold Feiwel and Robert Stricker.

There were two permanent students' societies in Brno, *Veritas*[17] and the *Jüdische Akademische Lese- und Rede-Halle*.

The basic concept of *Veritas* was similar to that of *Barissia* (Prague), while the *Halle* pursued the same ideas and practices as her sister *Hallen* in Prague and Vienna. In contrast to Bohemia, however, the Moravian students' societies had the great advantage that, long before 1918, in towns where there was a gymnasium (high school), there had existed Zionist societies formed by students[18] (*Mittelschüler-Verbindungen*). After completing their studies there and on entering universities or technical colleges, their members joined either *Veritas* or *Halle*[19] as a matter of course, as already convinced Zionists.[20]

All these continued their activities with undiminished enthusiasm after 1918. Apart from this, there existed in Moravia-Silesia, in contrast to Bohemia, so-called *Ferialverbindungen* (Vacation Societies), organized by university students who attended institutes of high learning, apart from Brno, in Prague and, primarily, in Vienna. During the terms they were active as Zionists in these places — as, for instance, *Ivriah* (Vienna), which was a society most desired and sought-out by Moravian students. At vacation time they returned to their home towns and utilized their free time to work for the dissemination of Zionism, and did so with marked success. Among the more active of these vacation societies were those in Boskovice (*Latitia*), Hodonín (*Gamalah*), Hranice (*Massadah*), Jihlava (*Hasmonaea*), Moravská Ostrava (*Hessaniah*), Olomouc (*Geulah*), Prostějov (*Giskalah*), Přerov (*Massadah*), and Uherské Hradiště (*Achiwah*),[21]

The influence of members of the students' societies had made itself felt long before the outbreak of World War I and long before Bohemian Zionism assumed its important position. But, again, it would be misleading to create the impression that in Moravia-Silesia only students joined the Zionist ranks and spread the idea in the land. There were other very active Zionist youth organizations,[22] and there arose permanent groups and societies throughout the area, headed by men from all walks of life; these made Moravia-Silesia into an important Zionist stronghold. Among the most active societies were *Zion* in Brno (there existed also two smaller societies, *Emunah* and *Zefirah*), Kojetín, Kyjov, Olomouc, Opava, Prostějov, Uherské Hradiště; while Jihlava had a *Theodor Herzl* society. As in Bohemia, a host of individuals bore the brunt of Zionist activities in Moravia-Silesia as well, both in the Austrian period and in new Czechoslovakia.[23]

It was also in Moravia-Silesia that the ideas of political and cultural activities in the Diaspora, known as *Gegenwartsarbeit* ("work for the present"), were originally formulated. These were submitted by Berthold Feiwel to the Conference of Austrian Zionist in Olomouc (March 1901) and were to have a lasting influence on Zionism and Jewish national Diaspora policies. They were, no doubt, the result of the impact that Karl Renner's talk on Austrian nationalities — given to the Brno conferənce of the Austrian Social Democrats (1899) — had exercised on Zionist thinking with regard to the nationality problem in the monarchy. The actual decision regarding *Landespolitik* (political activities in the Diaspora) was finally adopted at the meeting that followed the Austrian Zionist Conference in Cracow (Poland) in 1906.[24] Again, it was in Moravia that the Zionist-Socialist synthesis found its first adherents within the area that later was to become Czechoslovakia. Out of *Emunah*, *Verein jüdischer Handelsangestellter* (Society of Jewish Trade Employees), mentioned before, which was formed as early as 1898, emerged the first *Po'ale Zion* group in 1907, which later, after 1918, took the initiative for renewing and reorganizing the *Po'ale Zion* movement in Czechoslovakia.[25]

Moravian-Silesian Zionism was greatly enhanced by the appearance of the weekly *Die Jüdische Volksstimme* (in German), founded in 1901 by Max Hickl, the first Zionist periodical to be published in the territory of what later became Czechoslovakia.[26]

(C) SLOVAKIA AND SUBCARPATHIAN RUTHENIA

In contrast, there was no Zionist activity, resembling that in Bohemia and Moravia-Silesia, in the eastern sector of Czechoslovakia, although Zionism had had followers in Slovakia, which was then part of Hungary, since the early days of Herzl's call. On March 22, 1903, the founding conference of Hungarian Zionists, *Magyar Cionista Szövetség*, had already taken place in Bratislava (then Pressburg-Pozsony), and a year later the founding conference of the world organization *Mizrahi*, the religious sector within the Zionist movement, was also held there. Zionism in those areas did not develop a strong organizational basis but relied mostly on individual efforts.[27]

There existed in Slovakia prior to 1918 a number of Zionist societies, but only a few pursued uninterrupted Zionist work, most prominent among them being those in Košice, Nové Mesto nad Váhom, and Prešov, the *Ahavath Zion* of Bratislava (1897) and Nitra, *Beth Jakob* in Trnava (1899) and *Achei Zion* in Kežmarok (1903). Two papers were published there in pre–1914 days, even if only for a short while — the *Pressburger Jüdische Zeitung* and the *Allgemeine Jüdische Rundschau* (a *Mizrahi* organ). However, all the efforts of these and other Zionists in the area did not lead to important and lasting Zionist activities, in spite of the fact that these lands were the home of vast masses of Jewish inhabitants. There were objective reasons for this. In the first place, Slovakia and Subcarpathian Ruthenia were integral parts of Hungary. Their Zionists formed part of the Hungarian Zionist Organization and were not allocated specific district activities (as was the case in Bohemia and Moravia-Silesia).

Second, the struggle of Hungarian assimilationism against Zionism was fought with a bitterness that probably surpassed that found in any other land. The Hungarian assimilationists were extremely strong and influential, particularly in high circles, with the result that the government was greatly influenced by their wishes. Thus, for instance, the statutes of the Hungarian Zionist Organization had not been approved by the authorities for twenty-four years.[28] The only organized Zionist group which maintained itself throughout the period from its inception in 1904 was the *Mizrahi.* It became an independent organization in 1910, when Hungarian Zionists split up at their conference in Košice (May 15, 1910), and *Mizrahi* left the Hungarian Zionist Territorial Federation. This was a severe blow to the entire movement, from which it had not recovered by 1918. It so happened that the bulk of the *Mizrahi* membership resided in Slovakia.

II. DIFFERENT STAGES OF ZIONISM IN WEST AND EAST

The gap between the two geographical sectors of prewar Czechoslovak Zionism proved to be beneficially significant to the leadership of the new era. While the western sector, as indicated above, had by 1918 shaped its Zionist image, the eastern part had no such established configuration. On the contrary, the eastern part was an open field for Zionist penetration, which in the course of the two decades of Czechoslovak independence was accomplished with marked success.

The Czechoslovak Zionist leadership, when it set out late in 1918 to gather the remains of the movement from the ruins of Austro-Hungary, had to contend not only with these geographical, organizational, and intellectual divergencies that had survived the war, but also with decisive events, external and internal, necessitating in no smaller degree the reshaping of both Zionist ideology and practical work.

Among external events, the Russian Revolution must be mentioned as a primary factor. It had made its great impact on the peoples of Central Europe and, indeed, of the whole continent. Everywhere it led to a reassessment of concepts and ideologies in both socialist and nonsocialist camps. This reevaluation reached its climax in the immediate postwar period. In both the defeated countries and the newly created states, a marked shift to the Left took place. This tendency found a fertile soil in the new Czechoslovakia, where large sectors of the country's new leadership and of the political parties, though not explicitly Marxist, became part of the Left.

In addition, the attainment of Czechoslovak independence became an equally important external factor: it gave new impetus to Zionism which recognized in it a lesson the Jewish people would do well to take to heart.

These external influences contributed in no small degree to a general shift in Czechoslovak Zionism toward the Left. This trend, noticeable especially in the first decade of the new State, characterized in particular the youth groups and what later emerged as the "Left Center," a combination of the Zionist National Federation and a Socialist Zionist group in the Republic. This climate notwithstanding, there remained throughout the period a clear demarcation line between the Zionist groupings adhering to organized socialism and the groupings of the Jewish middle classes — adhering to a special brand of liberalism — which formed the majority of the Jewish population and thus also that of the Zionist membership.

The impact of internal Jewish factors was, of course, also very strong. In the first place, the Balfour Declaration (1917), promising Great Britain's assistance in the establishment of the Jewish national home in Palestine, pointed the way to achieving full Zionist success by obtaining independence as had the Czechs and Slovaks. The incorporation of national minority rights into the peace treaties — at which prominent Czechoslovak Zionists such as Drs. Hugo Bergmann, Max Brod, Leo Hermann, Hans Kohn, and Ludvík Singer had worked incessantly — and into the Czechoslovak constitution[29] gave Zionists in the Republic the official basis for a national Jewish policy which was a precondition of national fulfillment in Eretz Israel.

The international postwar situation, moreover, caused a fundamental power shift within the World Zionist Organization. The great influence formerly exerted by Russian and German Zionists had diminished (owing to Germany's defeat) or had completely disappeared (when Russia was cut off from the rest of Jewry), while new forces emerged in the shape of Polish and American Zionism.

Above all, there emerged for the first time in the Zionist Organization's history the concrete possibility of actually establishing an internationally secured national home in Eretz Israel. This constituted a great challenge to Zionism and to each Zionist individually. Czechoslovak Zionists made every effort to support the demand for the establishment of the national home and showed in the first period of Zionist political victories great enthusiasm with regard to personal *'Aliya*.* A report by Cecil Gosling, British chargé d'affaires (on a special mission Prague) to Earl Curzon, acting secretary of state for foreign affairs, records these early sentiments of Czechoslovak Zionists in a dispatch written on July 11, 1919:[30]

> Since my arrival in Prague, I have been in touch with the Jews resident here, amongst whom are a number of Zionists who wish to make their permanent home in Palestine.
>
> Of late, signs of unrest are noticeable among them, especially since the signature of Peace with Germany, and they manifest a strong desire that the Zionist restoration may become effective.
>
> The bulk of the educated Jews in Central Europe are, I believe, loyal to Great Britain, and confident of their just treatment by her. It is, I submit, desirable to afford the genuine Zionists among them facilities to return to Palestine.
>
> Should a belief become prevalent among them that the Jews of Central Europe are to be permanently, or for any considerable length of time, debarred from a restoration of the Jewish Commonwealth, discontent and possibly disorder might well ensue.

The confluence of the external and internal factors, enumerated above, thus caused a basic transformation in Zionist thinking and Zionist *Realpolitik*. The dreams and expectations, which formerly belonged to the realm of propaganda or of hopes, suddenly appeared as capable of practical realization. Zionism in the two decades of the First Republic's existence was, therefore, no longer identical with the prewar methods of propaganda — appealing to the study and understanding of history, dreaming of the future, or referring to the sentimental unity of the Jewish people — but a matter of a clear-cut stand, an alternative of pro's and con's on practical issues, both political and material, which arose from year to year in connection with the progressive upbuilding of the Jewish national home in Eretz Israel and which demanded commitment and, not infrequently, self-sacrifice.

It seems to me appropriate at this point to refer to one additional

* Alas, as time passed on, this enthusiasm had not developed into a mass *'Aliya* before the last one or two years of the First Republic.

factor which had helped to broaden and to spread the Zionist idea, although it cannot be included in either the external or internal factors mentioned above.

Czechoslovakia, from the first year of her existence, became the assembly place of international Jewish national and Zionist conferences. These were attended by leading personalities from all over the world. The problems discussed at these conferences were widely debated in Zionist societies and many a participant at these gatherings subsequently visited important Jewish centers in the Republic and addressed the wider Jewish public. There was thus a continuous flow of Zionist speakers from abroad who enlivened Zionist discussions, pcrticularly in the second half of the period under review, when the various Zionist political parties endeavored to propagate their ideas with the assistance of the world-renowned leaders.

For an illustration of this, a selection of some of the assemblies should suffice. Apart from three Zionist Congresses (1921 and 1923 in Karlovy Vary, and 1933 in Prague) the important meeting of the Zionist Actions Committtee (Prague, 1921) took place, as did the first European conference of all Palestine Offices (the agencies in charge of Jewish immigration into Palestine [Moravská Ostrava, 1921]). Then the world conferences of the various Zionist groupings took place: *HaPo'el Hatza'ir* and *Tze'ire Zion* (1920, Prague); *Mizrahi* (1921, Karlovy Vary); *Radical Zionists* (1925, Brno); *Zionist Revisionists* (1930, Prague); *HaShomer Hatza'ir* (1935, Poprad).

III. ZIONISM AND ASSIMILATIONISM

In this connection the perennial Zionist struggle against assimilation also assumed different forms. Assimilationism was partly paralyzed by the fact that its strong prewar trends toward German nationality in the western areas of Czechoslovakia, and toward Magyar nationality in the eastern sector, became almost completely blocked owing to the new political and national structure of the Republic. Since the centers of the German and Magyar nationalities lay outside Czechoslovakia — actually in hostile lands — to exhibit German or Magyar assimilationist tendencies would have been tantamount to "treason." What remained was, therefore, Czech or Slovak assimilationism. The latter was unknown before the war and remained insignificant thereafter. Czech assimilationism, on the other hand, had existed among Jews in an organized form since a time preceding the emergence of Zionism.[31] It produced, primarily in Bohemia, a press and literature and several serious thinkers and authors who raised the issues of assimilationism to a higher philosophical level.

Based on considerable preparatory work of some forty years prior to 1918, Czech assimilationism expected a great expansion with the emergence of Czechoslovakia. It failed, however. The Zionist-assimilationist controversies in 1918–1938 remained mostly in the realm of theoretical discussions in the press, and only occasionally (mostly on a local level) developed into practical political or cultural struggles. With time, they lost much of the vehemence and bitterness of prewar days, although as late as 1929 the Prague Zionist weekly *Židovské Zprávy* was sued by thirteen Czech-Jewish assimilationists for a reference to assimilationist propaganda in Slovakia, in which former "Magyar" Jews were advised to become "Slovak" Jews. This, the writ maintained, constituted libel, as it shed doubt on the Czech patriotism of these thirteen Jews. The court, however, accepted the defense argument that the patriotism of the thirteen Czech-Jewish assimilationists was not mentioned or implied in the article, which only referred to "German" Jews, who had become "Czech" Jews, and to "Magyar" Jews, who now called themselves "Slovak" Jews. The court rejected the libel suit.[32]

But otherwise no major statewide clashes between assimilationism and Zionism occurred. This was partly due to the fact that the Czechoslovak constitution had recognized a Jewish nationality and the Jews as a national minority, and had thus deprived assimilationism of its primary basis. The linguistic differences in Czechoslovak Jewry, which resulted from the amalgamation of four different geographic and cultural constituents, were an added limiting factor which hampered the development of a Czech assimilationism.

Zionist activities, therefore, did not concern themselves with assimilationism to the extent of pre-1918 days, but concentrated primarily on the dissemination and deepening of Jewish national consciousness in all spheres of Jewish life in the Republic, and on the issues related to the upbuilding of the Jewish national home in Eretz Israel.

IV. ZIONISM DIVIDED BY DIFFERENT TRENDS AND PRACTICES

One of the hotly debated problems following the Fourth Zionist Congress in London (1900) had been whether political, cultural, and national activities in the Diaspora (*Gegenwartsarbeit*) were an integral part of Zionist work or whether Zionism should concentrate its efforts solely on Eretz Israel. In prewar days it had been generally accepted that Jewish national activities in the Diaspora were a corollary of Zionism, even if it proved necessary to organize independent Jewish parties for politico-national pursuits in their respective countries (*Landespolitik*). This applied particularly to Austria and, after 1918, to her successor states. A number of remarkable successes had been chalked up in prewar years in the form of the election of national Jewish candidates to various political, local, and area institutions, as well as to Parliament; but the greatest impetus to *Landespolitik* and its most important achievements came only after the war. Thanks to the peace treaties, with their recognition of Jewish national minority rights,[33] these activities no longer consisted principally of the struggle for the recognition of the existence of the Jewish nationality and its right to be represented in the state legislature by its own representatives. The practical political work, as the results between the two world wars show, had encompassed wide and all-embracing spheres, particularly in Central and Eastern Europe.

Originally, and throughout the period prior to 1918, the initiative with regard to these activities was in the hands of the Zionists, and there it remained while a new order was in the making after the war. Thus it came about that it was the Zionists who represented Czecho·slovak Jewry at the preparatory Conference of Jewish Delegations to the Peace Conference, held in Berne (Switzerland) in March 1919, to discuss proposals to be submitted to the Peace Conference in Paris; they were Norbert Adler, Hugo Bergmann, Max Brod, Max Fischl (all of Bohemia), Berthold Feiwel, Leo Hermann (for Moravia, although both were then working in the offices of the World Zionist Organization in London), Richard Schlesinger (for Slovakia), and Rudolf Kohn (Prague, *Po'ale Zion*).

Zionists also represented the Republic's Jewry at the Paris Peace Conference (Norbert Adler, Hugo Bergmann, Oswald Freund, Ludvík Singer, andM arek Ungar; Hans Kohn acted as secretary of the delegation).

Furthermore, it was the Zionists Max Brod, Karel Fischl, and Ludvík Singer who opened negotiations with the Czechoslovak leaders (*Národní výbor*) Antonín Soukup, Otakar Srdínko, Jiri Stříbrný, and Antonín Švehla in Prague in October 1918, before and during the days of the proclamation of new Czechoslovakia, and presented the demands of national Jewry for equal rights and free development as a national minority.

Finally, it was the Zionists who organized themselves (October 22, 1918) during the revolutionary days of emerging Czechoslovakia as the Jewish National Council (*Jüdischer Nationalrat — Židovská národní rada*), which later expanded into the Jewish party (*Jüdische Partei — Židovská strana*) and became the representative political body of Czechoslovak national Jewry.[34]

Overlapping between the two aspects of Zionist activities was, of course, unavoidable. This was not only the case in Czechoslovakia but also in all those countries (Austria, Latvia, Ljthuania, Poland, and Rumania) in which Jewish National Councils had come into being at the end of World War I, due to Zionist initiative. Therefore, it became necessary to demarcate areas of competence, which was a most complicated task. Even the Twelfth Zionist Congress in Karlovy Vary (1921) was unable to lay down definite principles for this delimitation because of the different political and national structures in these various countries. It decided, therefore, that while political activities in the Diaspora constituted an integral part of Zionist work, the concrete form which these activities were to take in each country was to be left to the discretion of each Territorial Federation (*Landesverband*) and each Separate Union (*Sonderverband*) within the Zionist Organization.[35] This was, actually, the principle which Czechoslovak Zionists had adopted six months prior to the congress.

At the Second Territorial Conference in Brno (March 1921) they had decided to establish at the headquarters of the Territorial Federation (which at that conference was transferred to Moravská Ostrava) a special department for Diaspora activities. This wos to be headed by one of the Zionist leaders who simultaneously was a member of the Jewish National Council and who, for the purpose of heading this department, was to become a member of the Zionist Central Committee. The department was responsible to — and had to report to — the Zionist Annual Conference. On the other hand, it was made a duty of Zionist members in the Jewish National Council to consult the Diaspora Department in matters of policies to be pursued. As a matter of record, the leadership of the Jewish National Council (and later the Jewish party) always had a Zionist majority. Because of this structure, the actual functioning and influence of the Diaspora Department on the political work in the Republic had diminished as years passed by.

In this connection, it should be pointed out that from the outset two wings of the Czechoslovak Zionist movement were not members of the Territorial Zionist Federation: *Mizrahi*, the religious group, and *Po'ale Zion*, the social democratic party.[36] This was consonant with the structure of the World Zionist Organization, in which the parent organizations of the two parties formed Separate Unions. They had the right, in accordance with the directive adopted by the Twelfth Zionist Congress, mentioned before, to make their own decisions with regard to Diaspora activities. *Po'ale Zion*, at the beginning of the period under review, joined the National Council, of which one of the *Po'ale Zion* leaders, Rudolf Kohn, became a vice-president.[37] But soon *Po'ale Zion* reverted to its prewar position and regarded its political work in the Diaspora not as part of joint Zionist or Jewish national ("bourgeois") endeavors. As a Marxist party, it advocated and sought to establish a close link with the other Social Democratic parties in the Republic. So much so that in 1935, when the Jewish party arrived at an agreement with the Czech Social Democrats whereby two national Jewish candidates were to appear on the latter's ballots, the *Po'ale Zion* bitterly protested against this "betrayal" (because of the alignment with "bourgeois" Jewish groups) by their fellow Social Democrats, with whom they had worked for many years. Even after the amalgamation of socialist Zionists in the Republic and the entry in 1936 of the *Po'ale Zion* into Czechoslovak Zionist Territorial Federation, the former retained a free hand with regard to *Landespolitik*. It was only at the April 1938 meeting of the Zionist Territorial Committee (*Landeskomitee*) that the *Po'ale Zion* leader Dr. Chaim Hoffmann (now Chaim Yahil) submitted proposals for a unified Diaspora policy; but by that time this was of no practical value — it was the last year of free Czechoslovakia.

HaPo'el Hatza'ir, too, was a Separate Union in the World Zionist Organization and remained one after the amalgamation with *Tze'ire Zion* under the name *Hitahdut 'Olamit shel HaPo'el Hatza'ir uTze'ire Zion*.[38] Positive Jewish national Diaspora activities formed part of their program, and from the first day of their existence in Czechoslovakia they actively participated in the work of the Jewish National Council (Jewish party), most prominently, as mentioned before, through their leading members Hugo Bergmann and Max Brod. Having had, as a branch of a Separate Union, the right of choice, they decided to join the Czechoslovak Zionist Terrt orial Federation and thus also accepted its position regarding *Landespolitik*. As a matter of fact, at the Second Zionist Territorial Conference (1921) in Brno it was their delegate Moritz Spitzer (Boskovice) who reported on Diaspora activities and submitted a program which was largely adopted, but whose principal part was rejected. (They demanded national political activities not by a separate party but as integral part of Zionist work.) It was at this conference that the abovementioned organizational division between the Zionist Organization and the Jewish National Council in Czechoslovakia was decided upon.

HaPo'el Hatza'ir (later *Hitahdut*) adhered to active participation in Jewish national Diaspora work during its existence in Czechoslovakia, and when in subsequent years its individual adherents formed other Zionist groups (Zionist Realists, Working Association of Socialist Zionists) they continued to adhere to this policy. The Working Association was instrumental, after amalgamating with the Czechoslovak *Po'ale Zion*, in persuading the latter to join the Zionist Territorial Federation, but both groups still retained independence as regards *Landespolitik*.

The Zionist Revisionist Union, a Separate Union within the World Zionist Organization (from 1932 to 1935), did not pursue any independent political Diaspora activity.[39] During the time when they formed part of the Zionist Territorial Federation, Revisionists continued to support Jewish national Diaspora policies as long as these followed an independent Jewish political line. In 1935, when the Jewish party decided not to submit a Jewish list for the parliamentary elections, but entered instead into an agreement with the Czech Social Democrats to secure two candidates on their list — which lacked all reference to Jewish national representation — the Revisionists (then already constituting the New Zionist Organization) refused to support this "anonymity," which they considered contradictory to the basic principles of Jewish national Diaspora policy. A number of prominent non-Revisionist Zionist leaders acted likewise. Thus Norbert Adler, one of the fathers of Diaspora policy in the Republic, resigned his office; František Friedmann, a national Jewish represnetative in the Prague municipality, dissociated himself openly from this "fatal policy"; and Dr. Emil Margulies, president of the Jewish party, resigned from his office in protest.[40] Revisionism equally rejected "anonymous" alignments of any of its members with other Czechoslovak political parties and expelled such members from their organization or insisted on their resignation.[41]

In 1935 *HaShomer Hatza'ir* was recognized as a Separate Union in the World Zionist Organization. Its section in Czechoslovakia did not pursue any Diaspora political activities: it was left to the membership to make their own individual decisions. Some followed the policy of *Po'ale Zion*, others supported the Jewish party.[42]

The Jewish State party was recognized in 1936 as a Separate Union. Having thus emerged after the controversy which arose in 1935 as a result of the agreement of the Jewish party with the Czech Social Democrats, they followed the course of those Jewish national groups and individuals who had rejected the "anonymity" of Jewish candidacies.[43]

It seems appropriate to refer in this connection to the Women's International Zionist Organization (WIZO) which, though not a Separate Union, played an active role in Diaspora political activities. The Czechoslovak WIZO was founded in 1925. It had its representation in the Zionist Territorial Federation from the outset and in Diaspora activities it accepted the guidance of the Zionist Organization and of the Jewish party.[44]

Thus, Czechoslovak Zionism was from the very outset divided on the political aspects of Diaspora activities both in principle (whether or not it was compatible with Palestino-centric work) and in practice (party divisions).

Following the decision of the Second Czechoslovak Zionist Territorial Conference (which was accepted also by Zionists outside the Territorial Federation) not to pursue *Landespolitik* in Czechoslovakia but to leave it solely to the Jewish National Council (later the Jewish party), these political activities no longer constituted any part of the Zionist work in Czechoslovakia. Accordingly, all the aspects of internal political national-Jewish activities during the twenty years of the First Republic's existence, including municipal, territorial, and parliamentary elections, lie outside the scope of this essay, however important a role Zionists played in them.

V. ORGANIZATIONAL STRUCTURE OF CZECHOSLOVAK ZIONISM

In order to function effectively, Czechoslovak Zionism had to organize itself in accordance with the new distribution pattern of the Jewish population in the Republic. Actual Zionist organizational work commenced with the first meeting in Prague of Zionist leaders from Bohemia and Moravia-Silesia (January 5, 1919) on the occasion of the First Czechoslovak Jewish National Congress, which had then been assembled (January 4, 5, and 6, 1919, attended by 340 delegates). At the suggestion of Dr. Emil Margulies, a temporary Zionist Central Committee was set up pending a territorial conference. This temporary leadership consisted of the following: Dr. Ludvík Singer, president; Emil Thein, deputy; Josef Frey, chairman; Norbert Adler, secretary; Rudolf Wodička, treasurer, Viktor Kohn, Jewish National Fund; Paul Grünberg, Palestine Department (all the aforementioned of Prague). The following were members: Dr. Alfred Engel (Brno), Gustav Finzi (Opava, at the time a member of the Zionist Actions Committee), Dr. Leopold Goldschmied (Prostějov), Dr. Hugo Herrmann, Dr. Paul März, Dr. Josef Rufeisen (all of Moravská Ostrava), and Dr. Siegmund Werner (Jihlava). The actual work was in the hands of the Prague members.

This committee laid the foundations for what was later to emerge as the Zionist Territorial Federation (*Zionistischer Landesverband — Zemský svaz sionistický*) of the Republic. As one of its first acts, the committee revised the organization statutes which, prior to 1918, had been those of the West Austrian Zionist Association.[45] Zionism in Bohemia and Moravia-Silesia had been based on local societies, of which any number could exist in each town or city. The new form provided for unified local groups (*Ortsgruppen — místní skupiny*) in each town or city, which would comprise all Zionists, whatever the society they belonged to. All local groups in each area constituted a district. Thus there were Zionist districts in Bohemia (headquarters in Prague) and Moravia-Silesia (headquarters in Moravská Ostrava). In fact, these had existed before 1918. The provisional committee in Prague initiated contact with Slovakia almost immediately. On August 19, 1919, this territory was proclaimed, on the initiative of Bernhard Weiss, a newly created district (headquarters in Bratislava). Its central committee consisted of five to seven members, all residing in Bratislava. The local *Jüdische Rundschau* became the central organ of the district.[46] Some time later, by agreement with *Mizrahi*, a joint Zionist-*Mizrahi* district was temporarily formed in Subcarpathian Ruthenia (head office in Sevluš) and definitely proclaimed on October 31, 1920, at a conference of *Mizrahi* and Zionist representatives. The head office moved to Mukačevo and was iointly headed by Mosche Guttmann (*Mizrahi*) and Dr. Alexander Spiegel (for the Zionist Organization).[47]

Simultaneously with these first organizational steps, the seat of the temporary Central Office in Prague became the focal point regulating all activities. To create the basis for this, the Office registered the Jewish National Fund (*Keren Kayemet*) officially with the authorities; it established a Palestine Commission which, apart from being in charge of matters pertaining to *'Aliya* (immigration into Eretz Israel), was also to concern itself with *Hakhshara* (training) of *Halutzim* (pioneers). It maintained close contact with the Zionist headquarters in Copenhagen and London.[48] The contact with London was particularly close, since Dr. Leo Herrmann, one of the former moving spirits of *Bar Kochba* (Prague), who was general secretary of the World Zionist Executive prior to 1918, had moved from Berlin to the new seat of the Executive in the British capital.

The functions of the provisional Central Committee were handed over to the leadership which was elected at the First Zionist Territorial Conference in Prague (July 26 and 27, 1919).[49] This conference was attended by 97 delegates (47 from Bohemia, 41 from Moravia, and 9 from Slovakia), which indicates the quality of the preparatory work done in a period of internal turmoil and transition in the first six months of the new Republic.

This first Zionist Territorial Conference was chaired by Dr. Gustav Zweig and his deputies: Emil Arnstein (Dobříš), Gustav Finzi (Opava), and Theodor Wister (Bratislava). Kamil Kohn and Julius Kulka (Prague) acted as secretaries. Because of its historical importance it seems appropriate to record at least the headings of the reports presented, and the election of the first Czechoslovak Zionist leadership: Alex Feig (Prague) opened the conference in Hebrew with a talk on "Our Work in Palestine." Emil Kafka (Prague) spoke on "The Jewish National Fund"; Dr. Josef Rufeisen (Moravská Ostrava) on "The Organization Statutes"; and Norbert Adler (Prague) on "Diaspora Activities."

Members of the first Central Committee elected at the conference were:

Bohemia: Herbert Adler, Alex Feig, Dr. Ernst Lebenhart, Hugo Slonitz, Emil Thein (all in Prague); Emil Arnstein (Dobříš); Dr. Hugo Pick (Ústí nad Labem); Dr. Felix Seidemann (Teplice-Šanov).

Moravia-Silesia: Dr. Adolf Grünfeld (Brno); Robert Altbach, Dr. Hugo Herrmann, Dr. Josef Rufeisen (all of Moravská Ostrava); Dr Ludwig Meissner (Olomouc); Dr. Leopold Goldschmied (Prostějov); Gustav Finzi (Opava); Dr. Paul März (Uherské Hradiště).

Slovakia: Siegmund Sametz, Bernhard Weiss (both from Bratislava); Dr. Josef Lövy (Košice); Emil Neumann (Nitra); Richard Schlesinger (Pieštany); Dr. Karl Ferbstein (Prešov); Dr. Frigyes Szillard (Zvoleň and Slovenská Lupča).

Subcarpathian Ruthenia: Dr. Moritz Juskovits (Užhorod).

The members of the Central Committee residing in Prague constituted the Executive of the Czechoslovak Zionist Territorial Federation, with Emil Thein as chairman and his deputies Norbert Adler, Leopold Goldschmied, and Bernhard Weiss.

When, eighteen months later, the Second Zionist Conference assembled in Brno (March 27 and 28, 1921), the first results of the organizational work had become obvious. A total of 66 local groups in Bohemia — 60 in Moravia-Silesia, 55 in Slovakia, and 11 in Subcarpathian Ruthenia — were counted, with a total of 8,685 *Shekel*-(membership dues) paying members. They were represented at the conference by 23 delegates from Bohemia, 32 from Moravia-Silesia, and 18 from Slovakia and Subcarpathian Ruthenia. For the first time also the newly created *HaPo'el Hatza'ir* was represented by five delegates. The adherence of *HaPo'el Hatza'ir* to the Territorial Federation deserves mention at this point because it constituted the first grouping within the formerly unified Zionist territorial organization.[50]

The deeper penetration of Zionism into Slovakia and Subcarpathian Ruthenia, accompanied by a rapid growth of the organization, made it necessary to transfer the headquarters to a place nearer to the areas where the larger Jewish masses lived. The Second Zionist Territorial Conference in Brno (1921) therefore decided to transfer its Executive Committee from Prague to Moravská Ostrava, located on the border between Moravia and Slovakia. Members of the first Executive Committee in Moravská Ostrava were Gustav Finzi, Dr. Hugo Herrmann, Leo Krieger, Dr. Josef Rufeisen, and Dr. Wilhelm Wagner. Each subsequent Territorial Zionist Conference elected the members of the Executive Committee. It testifies to the stability of the organization that the leadership throughout the period under review consisted of a small circle of people who commanded the confidence of the members, and changes occurred mostly because of death, personal, or professional reasons. Josef Rufeisen remained president of the organization from 1921 to 1938, when he resigned.

Dr. Rufeisen exercised great influence on the movement in Czechoslovakia. Although by nature not endowed with qualities of leadership, he acquired a profound knowledge of the economic and human realities in Palestine and understood through untiring labor how to inspire his collaborators to great efforts. In many an important aspect of Zionist work he was familiar with matters of smallest detail and was thus able to conduct concentrated work in all directions, as the need required. In world Zionism he somehow never attained the recognition and/or position which his soundness deserved. His lack of "magic" in a movement of brilliant orators and inspiring leaders was obviously the primary cause of this, but from the point of view of the Czechoslovak Zionist Territorial Federation and of general Zionism he represented stability and serious work.

He was always able to choose collaborators amenable to his ways and methods. Thus, in addition to the above-mentioned members of the first Executive Committee in Moravská Ostrava, the following served on it between 1921 and 1939 for longer or shorter periods: Martha Berger, Leo Eisner, Friedrich Fränkel, Ferdinand Hojda, Dr. Franz Kahn, Leo Kornblüth, Jacques Krieger, Mizzi Löwy, Dr. Paul März (who became president in 1938), Emil Müller, Mila Musil, Siegmund Schmerler, Dr. Siegfried Schmitz, Kurt Thieberger, Felix Winterstein, and Dr. Heinrich Zador.

The organizational statutes which the provisional committee in Prague had prepared were approved by the First Zionist Territorial Conference, approved by the Prague authorities under decree No. S/A 603 1920/177.022, and remained basically the same until 1939. All those departments at the seat of the Executive Committee which had already functioned during the preparatory period were also put on a permanent basis by that conference, and these constituted — until the end of the First Republic — the organizational structure of the Zionist Territorial Federation. New departments were established only if additional activities made their creation necessary — as, for instance, the *Keren Hayesod*, which came into existence on December 8, 1921, some two years after the establishment of the

the Revisionist organization, as a branch of their world movement which in 1932 was recognized as a Separate Union, obtained such a separate status also in Czechoslovakia.[57]

Almost simultaneously, a split developed within the Zionist-Revisionist organization itself, on the question of the relationship to the World Zionist Organization. This led in 1933 to the formation of the Jewish State party which, in Czechoslovakia as elsewhere, retained its separate existence and did not join the Zionist Territorial Federation.[58]

By 1935 the Revisionists established the New Zionist Organization and severed completely their connections with all sectors of the Territorial Federation, as well as with all other constituents of the World Zionist Organization.

In 1928 *Po'ale Zion* renewed its activities in Czechoslovakia. Dissolved in 1920 as a result of the split between the Right and Left wings within their ranks, it now established itself as an independent Czechoslovak Zionist organization. It constituted part of the *Po'ale Zion* world movement, which had obtained recognition as a Separate Union of the World Zionist Organization.[59] *Po'ale Zion* remained outside the Czechoslovak Territorial Federation until 1936 when, as a result of the unification with other socialist Zionists they *eo ipso* became members of the socialist bloc within the Territorial Federation.[60]

In 1935 *HaShomer Hatza'ir* was recognized as a Separate Union in the World Zionist Organization. Its branch in Czechoslovakia did not form a separate group within the Territorial Federation but retained its former organizational structure. Its members who, since the formation of *HaShomer Hatza'ir* as a youth organization, had worked individually within the federation, once they attained the age of eighteen and thus became *Shekel*-payers, continued to do so also after 1935. They adhered to the socialist bloc, which from 1936 on became a unified grouping.[61]

A case *sui generis* was the Czechoslovak branch of the Women's International Zionist Organization (WIZO). It was neither part of a Separate Union nor did it join as a grouping the Czechoslovak Zionist Territorial Federation. Having developed its own program of practical work for the upbuilding of Eretz Israel, lying primarily in the field of women's work (social activities, hostels, mother and infant care, support of *Halutziut*, the Hebrew schools, etc.), it carried out in addition many of the Zionist activities generally pursued also by the other Zionist groupings. Its participation in many of these activities was on an individual basis rather than as an organized group.[62]

As the above bird's-eye survey shows, Czechoslovak Zionism was actually not a unified organization. Many attempts were made to establish an actual Territorial Federation that would comprise every Zionist group in the Republic; but they remained without concrete results. The last such attempt was made at the Tenth Zionist Territorial Conference (July 1932), when a commission was set up to prepare the formation of a federation. Two and a half years later, at the subsequent Territorial Conference (December 1934), the commission had to report its complete failure.

The term "Territorial Federation," in the sense in which it was used in the Herzlian period and as it appeared in the first two or three years of Czechoslovakia, existed in the Republic in name only. In reality it never functioned, even though the Executive Committee in Moravská Ostrava and some affiliated groups used this designation, as did the press right to the end of the First Republic. It is for this reason — its continuous use in public and in print — that I retain it in this survey, fully conscious of its inadequacy.

As a matter of historical fact one must add that at the last pre-World War II Zionist Congress, the Twenty-first, held in Geneva (August 16–23, 1939), the Czechoslovak area occupied at the time by the Nazis was divided into two Territorial Federations, both recognized by the congress, one consisting of Bohemia and Moravia-Silesia and the other Slovakia. (Subcarpathian Ruthenia was by that time part of Hungary.) The former was represented by eight delegates, the latter by six.[63] These did not belong to any political party within the Zionist Organization but appeared at the congress and acted there as purely territorial representatives. They attended the congress to seek assistance in rescuing as many Jews as possible and to help them reach Palestine.

VII. POLITICAL AND IDEOLOGICAL GROUPING IN CZECHOSLOVAK ZIONISM

(A) GENERAL ZIONISTS

The recognition by Zionist leaders of the developments in Czechoslovak Zionism, as described above, led unavoidably to the conclusion that it was futile to try to encompass all Czechoslovak Zionist groupings in a Territorial Federation. When the leaders of the central and most numerous bloc at the time, within the federation, arrived at this recognition, a political and organizational shift of that center bloc became a matter of utmost urgency.

The existence of Zionist organizations outside the jurisdiction of the Territorial Federation and of formations on its borders causing successive partisan fragmentations brought about a decline in the membership of the remaining middle bloc in the federation, and thus in the influence wielded by it. Soon, therefore, it was no longer possible to speak of a Territorial Federation representing the totality of the Zionist movement in Czechoslovakia, as its name had indicated. In consequence of this development, shared by Territorial Federations in other countries as well, some leaders of these federations felt that the time had come to make an effort to save the situation. On October 14, 1928, a conference of the Territorial Federation of Austria, Czechoslovakia, East and West Galicia, Poland, Transylvania, and Yugoslavia was held in Vienna. Dr. Franz Kahn represented Czechos'ovakia. The conference decided to establish a joint Association of all European Territorial Federations (*Arbeitgemeinschaft aller Landesverbände in Europa*) for the purpose of centralizing the propaganda for strengthening these Territorial Federations and for making their importance as a unifying factor in Zionism understood by Zionist groups and individuals.[64] However, within a year it became clear that these efforts were in vain. It was therefore only natural that the Czechoslovak center group, which still constituted the bulk of the federation, was led to aligning itself with central groupings in other countries, all of whom had shared a similar frustrating experience. This alignment resulted in the formation of the General Zionist Organization, which consisted solely of such central blocs within the various Territorial Federations which, *nolens volens*, had gradually developed into political parties in the World Zionist movement. The fragmentation of the Zionist Organization was thus also formally completed. In spite of this development, externally the existing structure in Czechoslovakia was not altered: the leaders of General Zionism and one or two Zionist socialist groups continued to employ the term Territorial Federation.

It was not only the centrifugal forces that motivated the center bloc to establish its own grouping; there was also another, more fundamental, reason for taking this step. This was the general dissatisfaction of the membership with the rapidly waning influence with which it had to be satisfied, not only in Czechoslovakia but also elsewhere. Many members felt that they had borne, and were bearing, the brunt of the practical, daily, routine Zionist work, that they were giving and collecting the funds without having a say in the councils of Zionism or in Eretz Israel with regard to policy, economics, settlement, and so on. They resented the role to which they saw themselves relegated: that of the providers of the means and resources while others had the influence and reaped the fruits.

On the initiative of Dr. Ignacy Schwarzbard, president of the West Galician Zionist Territorial Federation, Czechoslovak Zionists joined members of other Territorial Federations at a conference held during the Sixteenth Zionist Congress in Zurich (1929) in a decision to form a General Zionist Organization.[65] A leadership of the world movement of General Zionists was elected in which Czechoslovakia was represented by Dr. Josef Rufeisen, who was simultaneously president of the Czechoslovak General Zionist Organization and of the Czechoslovak Territorial Federation.

The platform formulated at this conference and the subsequent ones (1931 in Cracow, Poland, and in June of that year in Basel, Switzerland) was vague and amorphous. The main reason for this was that the General Zionists still entertained the hope of remaining a middle-of-the-road movement, the central link in the chain of Zionist party politics, at a time when the various groupings on the Left and on the Right had already achieved dominance on the Zionist scene.

The main principles of the program were the following:[66] General Zionism regarded itself as representing a Zionism that did not announce or formulate any special program or intend to be guided by any specific ideological orientation (socialist, religious, etc.). It saw its primary objective in the unification of the Jewish people, preceded by a unification of Zionists for the upbuilding of Eretz Israel. Therefore, General Zionism did not define *a priori* its views and position on the various problems as they arose in the course of Zionist developments. Rather, it strove to act as a mediating force between the various sectors of the Zionist movement, which became more and more divided by their different ideologies and differing views on politics, on their relationship to Great Britain and the Arabs, on the social and economic structure of the future national home and on all the other issues. It was the aim of the General Zionists to arrive at a solution which would satisfy all trends in Zionism and to function as a mediator on the premise that those divergent forces which it called upon to unite would accept what "neutral" General Zionism regarded as most useful and necessary in the interests of Eretz Israel and the Zionist Organization.

This was far from a positive program. No wonder that its opponents described the General Zionists as a negative grouping, a sort of collective grouping, consisting of all those in the movement who either did not belong to, or did not want to join, any of the other Zionist groups.

It was a Czechoslovak who took the lead in an attempt to turn this vague program into a positive one. Dr. Felix Weltsch soon became aware of the great gap that separated a positive platform consisting of concrete planks from one of waiting for others to develop their disparate ideas and then hastily trying to mediate among them. In addition, Weltsch, being involved in no personal political struggle and seeking no public office, from what could be termed his "semi-detached" distance, had a good insight into the workings of General Zionism, to which he philosophically and temperamentally belonged.

I have tried to avoid concerning myself with personalities in this sketchy survey of Zionism in Czechoslovakia, except for short characterizations necessary for an understanding of the issues involved. If I now make an exception of Felix Weltsch, it is for two reasons: first, no other individual had a greater influence on Zionist thinking in the Republic between 1918 and 1938 than Felix Weltsch; second, the philosophy which he developed for General Zionism was the only Zionist conception during that period which was not imported into Czechoslovakia from abroad. While all other ideological and political concepts came from the ranks of the World Zionist Organization, the one developed by Felix Weltsch was, so to speak, a native Czechoslovak Zionist creation which found its echo among General Zionists in other countries also.

Felix Weltsch's influence resulted from his editorship of *Selbstwehr*, through which his ideas and interpretations of the contemporary Jewish scene, as well as of the ideological currents, were carried every Friday into the homes of Zionists. They, in turn, disseminated his arguments and ideas among the people around them and examined these ideas in debates which arose in connection with various problems and controversies. Weltsch tried to find the common denominator in divergent ideas and influences and often made practical suggestions, always taking a middle position. His was the typical approach of General Zionism as described above. In the course of these attempts, which were overshadowed by the growing European radicalism of the 1930s, Weltsch developed a "philosophy of the middle," to be applied, first, to political thinking *per se*, and second, to General Zionism. He developed his ideas in a courageous book, *Das Wagnis der Mitte* (*The Daring of the Middle*),[67] in which he arrived at the concept of the "creative middle" (*schöpferische Mitte*) whose importance he emphasized, in contrast to the "negative middle," which he described as nothing but a dividing line between two extremes. Weltsch applied this concept of the "creative middle" to General Zionism in a small but illuminating booklet entitled *Allgemeiner Zionismus: Eine ideologische Skizze* (*General Zionism: An Ideological Sketch*).[68] In contrast to the prevailing assumption that a General Zionist was a Zionist who did not decide for the Left or the Right, Weltsch saw in him a Zionist who, confronted with these two extremes, conscientiously decided for the middle.

Referring to Hegel's dialectics, Weltsch maintained that the Zionist reaches his true self only through a juxtaposition of particular Zionist ideologies (i.e., particular party Zionism) and by deciding the issues for himself becomes a General Zionist. This conscientious middle position, he continued, results from the fact that Zionism is permanently in danger of being torn apart by ideological, political, and other contrasts. It is, therefore, an incessant trial of strength for Zionist ideology to manifest its resistance to the impact of these centrifugal forces and its ability to retain its original meaning. Hence, he concluded, Zionism must not permit itself to be fragmented by separatistic forces, for it can only be maintained through unity; and this unifying factor is found in General Zionism. Thus Weltsch elevated the "middle" and the "unity" concept to the position of conscious ideals of General Zionism. He was well aware of the difficulty of this road, but difficulties he considered merely a challenge. For where doubts arise, he maintained, they must be met by new thinking and new methods of the "creative middle," whose primary purpose is the maintenance of the movement's unity.

Weltsch did not succeed in raising General Zionism to his level, but he was able to elevate the issues and problems and to focus serious discussion on them, which in itself was a positive achievement.

But the 1930s were too late for an ideology of this sort. Zionism consisted of parties, General Zionists by then already among them, and in these circumstances unifying factors could not be created.

As Dr. Schwarzbart, the initiator of the General Zionist Organization, stated when he rejected Weltsch's idea: "It is detrimental to General Zionism as a political movement." But even General Zionism itself could not preserve its own unity — it was already pulled apart by centrifugal forces. It could find no common denominator for its own work. In 1931, on the eve of the Seventeenth Zionist Congress (Basel), when the General Zionists met in conference to formulate a program and resolved to create a world organization, at the first clash with reality they split up into two camps. At the congress in Basel Dr. Weizmann failed to be re-elected president of the organization because of his public statement in which he had expressed his disbelief in the necessity of forming a Jewish population majority in Palestine and had thus rejected the creation of a Jewish state in Eretz Israel as the aim of Zionism.

The great majority of General Zionists at the congress (58 out of 84 delegates) voted against Dr. Weizmann, but a minority stood faithfully with him. Among this minority of 26 were the delegates from Czechoslovakia, England, Germany, and a few individuals.[69] They established themselves as General Zionists Group "A," while the majority from then on was described as Group "B" — a division which continues to exist to this day under the names of World Confederation of General Zionists (for "A") and World Union of General Zionists (for "B"), although it has long since lost its original significance. Also, the subsequent efforts to consolidate the "A" and "B" groups into one General Zionist organization succeeded only for a short period (1933–1934) and culminated in the Third World Conference of General Zionists in Cracow (August 26–27, 1934) at which Czechoslovakia was represented by Drs. Angelo Goldstein, Josef Rufeisen, Heinrich Zador, and Leo Zelmanovits. Yet even during the almost two years of peaceful coexistence the two factions retained their specific designations of "A" and "B".

The loose "unity" fell apart again when Dr. Weizmann was returned to the presidency of the World Zionist Organization in 1935. The final breach occurred at the conference of both sections held in Cracow on June 16, 1935, and could not be healed at a "peace conference," held in the shadow of the approaching Nazi menace, on November 17, 1938.

The formal establishment of the General Zionist Organization in Czechoslovakia took some time to materialize. For several years its leaders nourished in vain the hope of finding a *modus vivendi* with other Zionist groups, so that the center bloc would remain and be recognized as identical with the Czechoslovak Territorial Federation. When the futility of this hope became apparent, the General Zionists nominated an Organizations Committee (May 1934) to take steps for the convocation of their first conference.[70] This commission consisted of the following members: Norbert Adler and Dr. Felix Weltsch (Prague), Dr. Walter Kohner (Karlovy Vary), Leo Eisner, Dr. Leon Kornblüth, Dr. Josef Rufeisen, and Dr. Heinrich B. Zador (Moravská Ostrava). The First Conference of General Zionists was held in Brno (June 17, 1934) with the participation of 110 delegates from all parts of the Republic. It elected its leadership (called *Arbeitskomiteé*) and chose Moravská Ostrava as the seat of its headquarters (which was also the headquarters of the Territorial Federation). The following served on the committee: Dr. Josef Rufeisen, chairman; Dr. Heinrich B. Zador, general secretary; and the members were Leo Eisner, Dr. Franz Kahn, Dr. Leon Kornblüth, Ernst Löwenstamm, Dr. Siegfried Schmitz, and Dr. Leo Zelmanovits.[71] (The majority of those elected also served on the Executive Committee of the Territorial Federation.)

At the Second Conference of Czechoslovak General Zionists (Moravská Ostrava, July 28, 1935) the definitive breach with group "B" of the world movement of General Zionists was approved and a new leadership elected, consisting of those chosen at the First Conference, with the addition of Martha Berger and Friedrich Fränkel. The principal decision concerned the urgency of establishing a proper General Zionist organization in the Republic and the necessity of embarking upon a wide propaganda action to enroll members and sympathizers in the new organization.[72] These resolutions were, however, never translated into action. The General Zionists in Czechoslovakia never did have an organization similar to that of the other Zionist groupings; they remained, until their dissolution in 1939, a loose association of Zionists from all walks of life, with no particular party political or ideological program, a loose association which they actually were as the center bloc of the Territorial Federation from its establishment in 1919.

The attempts at organizing General Zionists in a form similar to that of other Zionist parties or groups led to the one and only serious clash with the Zionist socialist groups in Czechoslovakia. At a conference in Moravská Ostrava (August 1934), a youth movement within General Zionism concerning itself primarily with *Hakhshara* and *'Aliya* came into being, under the name of General Zionist HeHalutz (*HeHalutz Haklal Tzioni*).[73] This arose not as a result of the efforts of General Zionists to organize themselves in Czechoslovakia like other Zionist organizations, including a youth movement of their own; rather, it was formed in the first place because of the great dissatisfaction with the monopolistic position and method of *HeHalutz* in the Republic and the system of distribution of immigration certificates for Palestine. These were grievances which for some time past had also been raised by members of the *Halutz* sectors of the *Mizrahi* and the Revisionists (*Brit Trumpeldor*).[74]

The new General Zionist formation assumed significance because it came from this particular quarter. For years past there had existed a close and friendly cooperation between these two camps. Some speakers, in speeches delivered at the Moravská Ostrava conference, voiced their disappointment openly since, as was pointed out in these speeches, it was the General Zionists whose financial and practical support had enabled *HeHalutz* to attain its leading position from 1923, when it was designated by the Fourth Zionist Territorial Conference (Moravská Ostrava, June 29 and 30 and July 1, 1923) as the sole center for *Hakhshara* and *Halutziut* in the Republic. In retrospect, however, it appears that this challenge of a separate General Zionist *HeHalutz* aimed at reaching some working arrangement with *HeHalutz*. This actually came about when, in February 1935, an agreement was concluded between *HeHalutz* and the Czechoslovak Territorial Federation (then dominated by the leaders of General Zionism) whereby the former was again recognized as the sole center for *Hakhshara* and *Halutziut*, but, from then on, had to maintain close advisory contact with the Executive Committee of the Territorial Federation (which was almost identical with the territorial leadership of General Zionists). The Second Territorial Conference of General Zionist HeHalutz (Užhorod, October 26–27, 1935) endorsed this agreement unequivocally.[75]

This otherwise insignificant matter would have deserved no special mention had it not been for the fact that, although *Hitahdut*, *Po'ale Zion*, and *HaShomer Hatza'ir* stood at one time or another in opposition within or toward the Territorial Federation, there was, in fact, throughout the entire period under review, a close collaboration and significant support of these various socialistic groups by the Territorial Federation's center bloc (later called General Zionist Organization). The basis of this collaboration was not only a good relationship between the leaders and financial support rendered by the center bloc, but also common political interests so far as Zionist policy was concerned.

Czechoslovak General Zionists were from 1919 on one of the strongest pillars of Dr. Chaim Weizmann and his policies (Weizmannism). They were ardently devoted to him, both ideologically and personally, and went along with all his political, financial, economic, and internal Zionist pursuits, and with all other areas of Zionist activities. This devotion found striking expression during Dr. Weizmann's visit to Czechoslovakia as guest of the Territorial Federation and of the *Keren Hayesod* in 1925. Max Brod — the onetime leader of *HaPo'el Hatza'ir* — probably spoke for the great majority of General Zionists in Czechoslovakia when he addressed to him a poem, "Verse an Weizmann" (Verses for Weizmann), which gave expression to their blind adherence to Weizmann and Weizmannism (*Selbstwehr*, January 3, 1925):

> "Bedingungslos will ich von Dir geführt sein,
> Will gehorchen und horchen, wenn Du sprichst."
> (Without conditions do I want to be led by you,
> Will obey and listen when you speak.)

This devotion led, in the final analysis, to the surrender of the clear-cut mediating central position which General Zionism had claimed to occupy — or, as Felix Weltsch had wanted it, the clear-cut position of the "creative middle." In the end they became one more among the Zionist political parties, adherents, and defenders of Weizmannism.

This abandonment of the "middle" did not come suddenly. As pointed out, it can be traced back to the beginning of Zionist work in new Czechoslovakia, long before the official establishment of the General Zionist Organization. As unequivocal and, indeed, uncritical adherents of the Weizmann policies, they became their untiring defenders in the fight against the various parties which had gradually arisen in Zionism in opposition to the official leadership and program of Dr. Weizmann. The first such confrontation occurred in 1919/1920 when the first opposition group in Czechoslovak Zionism arose in the newly formed *HaPo'el Hatza'ir* (later *Hitahdut*), which directed its attacks against what it termed the "official business Zionism" nourished by a postwar "enthusiasm of phrases" and refusal "to face the Palestine reality." It was of short existence. When in 1921 the World Organization of *HaPo'el Hatza'ir* joined the Zionist Executive and thus became co-responsible for the Weizmann policy, the way was opened for the Czechoslovak branch to join the Territorial Federation.[76]

A much more challenging and longer-lasting opposition arose as a result of Dr. Weizmann's efforts to establish, in accordance with Article 4 of the Palestine Mandate, a "Jewish Agency," consisting of Zionists and non-Zionists, henceforth to represent Jewry vis-à-vis the Mandatory power in Palestine. A fierce battle against this proposal was initiated in 1923 by Dr. Emil Margulies, head of the Radical Zionists, and lasted until 1929, when the Jewish Agency became a reality and the Radicals joined it.[77] The struggle against the agency was joined in 1925 by the newly formed Zionist-Revisionist organization and continued until the end of the period under review. The fight against the Jewish Agency was only one sector of the Revisionist opposition which, in fact, concerned itself with every aspect of Zionist ideology, financial, social, and economic policy, the Palestine upbuilding program, and all other activities, and thus embarked upon a comprehensive attack against the entire system in the Zionist Organization identified with Dr. Weizmann.[78]

General Zionists in Czechoslovakia carried on a consistent struggle against all this opposition when it arose. The struggle against Revisionism lasted longer than any other, as it encompassed a period of fourteen years; and it was fought with increased vigor, which reached particular vehemence when, in the early thirties, it became clear that Revisionism was abandoning its opposition status and prepared to form the New Zionist Organization as an independent movement challenging the position of the Zionist Organization.

Apart from carrying on the defense of Weizmannism against the opposing groups, General Zionists also endeavored to align themselves with other forces within the Zionist movement providing the same or a similar support of the official system. These "other forces" consisted of those Zionist socialist groups which, originally in strict opposition to Dr. Weizmann's policies, had gradually aligned themselves with him and had become his strong supporters (cf. the abovementioned development of the *HaPo'el Hatza'ir;* the same applies to *Po'ale Zion*). Through joining the World Zionist Executive, headed by Dr. Weizmann, they not only supported his policies but also became co-responsible for them. This was a strong link uniting in many respects Czechoslovak General Zionists and the various Zionist socialist groups in the Republic. The compromise which the former had made for this purpose expressed itself symbolically in the name they chose at elections to the 1927 Zionist Congress — "Left Center" — which indicated a shift from their central position not only politically but also ideologically toward the socialist concept. Thus, instead of clarifying their position, they retained the vagueness which characterized General Zionism from its very outset.

This led to a further crumbling of their bloc. On the one hand, sympathies with socialist concepts led important Zionists, particularly young people, to convert sympathies into full adherence and thus help the combined Zionist socialist groups to become the strongest force among the various party branches of the World Zionist Organization in Czechoslovakia. On the other hand, there were General Zionists who rejected the close ties with Zionist socialists and were opposed to the changing Weizmann policies as they developed in the early thirties. As mentioned before, in the world movement of General Zionists this led to a schism of "A" (Weizmann supporters) and "B" (opponents of the Weizmann policies) groups, a split which could not be healed. While General Zionists "B" were by far the larger group in the world, in Czechoslovakia the attempt to form a group "B" was doomed to failure. A small band of these Zionists, headed by Dr. Alfred Engel, Egon Jokl, Erwin Huller, Marek Schindelmann (Brno), Philip Munk (Bzenec), Yehuda Weiss (Mukačevo), Samuel Rokotnitz (Prague), and Ignaz Schön (Uherský Brod), were unable to organize a group "B" and therefore decided to join forces for the elections to the Nineteenth Zionist Congress (1935) with the Radical Zionists (now called *Gemeinschaft politischer Zionisten* — Association of Political Zionists), headed by Dr. Emil Margulies, and the Jewish State party, led at the time by Dr. Martin Lichtner (Trutnov) and Yizchak Greidinger (Užhorod). However, all of them together were unable to elect even a single delegate.[79]

The loose group of General Zionists "B" joined forces with the Association of Political Zionists (Dr. Emil Margulies) also for the subsequent Twentieth Zionist Congress (1937), but jointly they received only 632 votes and no delegates, and their votes were added, together with similar remaining votes in other countries, to the world list of General Zionists "B".[80]

There were no further developments of that group in Czechoslovakia. It gradually disintegrated.

It was a fateful road, from the days of an almost completely unified Czechoslovak Zionism in the Territorial Federation at the beginning of the period under review to the transformation of the federation's center bulk into a loose General Zionist Organization in the last years. While the World Zionist Organization had grown from 373,217 *Shekel*-payers in 1921 to 1,042,054 in 1938, and while in Czechoslovakia *Shekel* sales had increased from 8,685 in 1921 to 18,887 in 1938,[81] General Zionism did not keep pace with these increases, as the elections to the Zionist Congress indicate.[82] It was the only sector which, in the process of new party formations in the World Zionist Organization, had become the reservoir for others to draw from, and this of course meant the depletion of its own ranks.

In contrast to this picture, there is the impressive record of the General Zionists' untiring and unswerving work which resulted in important achievements in all spheres of Zionist endeavour, particularly in the field of fund raising (*Keren Kayemet*, *Keren Hayesod*, *Shekalim*, emergency collections, support of economic programs, of *Hakhshara* and *'Aliya*, of settlements in Eretz Israel, and so on). And beyond this, they were prominently active in all Jewish national and cultural activities in the Republic and provided both the bulk of their leadership and the finance. They remained to the last day the working center bloc of the World Zionist Organization on Czechoslovak territory.

(B) SOCIALIST ZIONISTS

1. *HaPo'el Hatza'ir* (*Hitahdut*)

Individuals had supported and propagated the program of *HaPo'el Hatza'ir* already before that date; there were, in fact, two active *HaPo'el Hatza'ir* circles in existence in the Republic in 1919. The group in Prague was headed by Dr. Hugo Bergmann, Dr. Max Brod, Dr. Oskar Epstein, and Alex Feig, to mention only its most prominent members,[83] and in December 1919 a group of *HaPo'el Hatza'ir* was formed in Brno, with the participation of Max Brod, and headed by Drs. Gustav Kohn, Josef Lamm, Karl Teller, and Siegfried Spitz.[84] The program of these groups was vague, not yet adapted to the postwar era. Their members were groping for some answers, but meanwhile they concerned themselves with the question of socialist interpretation of Zionism, the fundamentals of which were crystallized in Max Brod's *Sozialismus im Zionismus* (*Socialism in Zionism*), which appeared soon thereafter (1920). This interpretation was, in fact, nothing but a continuation of the prewar debate between *HaPo'-el Hatza'ir* and *Po'ale Zion*[85] and went back to the beginnings of these movements. In the first postwar years these were still hotly discussed issues in the Czechoslovak Jewish press and in public meetings, and it therefore seems appropriate to devote a few paragraphs to the original program of *Ha'Poel Hatza'ir* (and in the chapter dealing with *Po'ale Zion* we will also examine its original program).[86]

HaPo'el Hatza'ir arose in Eretz Israel in 1906 and was the brainchild of Aaron David Gordon (1856–1922). He settled at the age of fifty in Palestine, where he worked on the land. In his writings and through his own example, he emphasized his belief that external factors condemned Jewry in the Diaspora to a parasitic existence which could be overcome only through a return to the soil of Eretz Israel. There, through labor, moral redemption could be attained. He coined the term *Am-Adam* (People-Person), indicating the renewal of peoplehood in the human being and thus stressing the moral and practical importance of the individual in relation to his neighbors and to his people. Gordon's nationalism was based on these premises, and he set it against Marxist socialism,* as represented in the Zionist Organization by *Po'ale Zion*, which he regarded as the product of rationalism and mechanization of society. In contrast to the Marxian mass-concept (collectivism) he thus set the acts of individuals and stressed that "the salvation of the people can arise only through the salvation of the individual." This he termed *Hiddush HaAdam*, or renewal of the individual, whose primary duty was to return to the land. Gordon's *Four Letters from Palestine* had a great impact on the youth not only in Eretz Israel but also in the Diaspora and led directly to the creation of the *Halutz* movement. In his emphasis on the personal realization of the ideal, Gordon approximated Buber's thinking, and this led many a disciple of Buber's to *HaPo'el Hatza'ir*. Members of *Bar Kochba*, a leading association of Jewish university students in Prague, took the lead in the first attempts after World War I to consolidate the forces adhering to this ideology.

One of the first steps of the *HaPo'el Hatza'ir* in Prague was the publication in Czech of Gordon's *Four Letters from Palestine* (a German translation appeared at the same time in Berlin), which conveyed Gordon's ideas in his own simple, yet fascinating, style.

---

* [Marxist socialism at that time was close to the Social Democrat movement (Labour party in England) (Ed.)]

The first propaganda attempts of the new *HaPo'el Hatza'ir* groups in Prague and Brno showed clearly a desire to stem the tide of the then-growing Marxian *Po'ale Zion* in the Republic. But beyond this, the spokesmen of *HaPo'el Hatza'ir* (like those in the world movement) tried to avoid an internal socialist struggle. They attempted to stress their own program rather than embark on controversy and did so in the very first statement issued by the group in Prague.[87] "We are of the opinion that principally it is the working masses that are interested in the final aim of Zionism, i.e., in the renaissance of the Jewish people. Therefore *HaPo'el Hatza'ir* bases itself in its practical work and in its policy on the national-historical demands and daily duties of the Jewish working masses." However, they saw their principal and wider objective in efforts to influence the Zionist Organization at large to come to their way of thinking.

It was, of course, vital for the new movement to win over young people and educate them in the spirit of their ideology. The leaders of *HaPo'el Hatza'ir* in Prague, therefore, sponsored the creation of a youth organization (*Jungzionistische Organisation*), the first tentative group, which consisted of Ervin Arnstein, Dr. Oskar Epstein, Aaron Hirsch and Mosche Ischaiewitsch, Fritz Kohn, and Dr. Josef Wien.[88] (The youth organization was officially launched during the world conference in Prague, in March 1920.)

All these steps were preparatory to the great event which was to follow and which was to influence both the Zionist World Organization and the Czechoslovak Zionists profoundly — the conference which was to unite the two wings of the adherents of Gordon's philosophy: *HaPo'el Hatza'ir* and *Tze'ire Zion*. The former had its stronghold in Eretz Israel and in some Central European countries, while *Tze'ire Zion* had its large organization in Eastern Europe. In the Central European lands the ideology remained more or less a theoretical matter, but in Eastern Europe *Tze'ire Zion* endeavored to adapt Gordon's philosophy to the reality of Jewish life in that area of Jewish mass settlement. Therefore, their methods differed, but their common denominator was, in the first place, the rejection of Marxist Zionism (*Po'ale Zion*), both in Eretz Israel and in the Diaspora. They regarded a Jewish proletariat in a Marxian sense, even in the Jewish mass settlements, as an insignificant factor of Jewry, maintaining that a class distinction, in the absence of a significant proletariat, could never be the sole determinant of a Jewish socialist society in the Diaspora. They stressed further that the majority of Jewry consisted of middle-class people who would first have to be educated to a life of labor and work, both in the Diaspora and in Eretz Israel. The socialism of *HaPo'el Hatza'ir* and *Tze'ire Zion* was termed *Volkssozialismus* (people's socialism), and it aimed at building up in Eretz Israel a Jewish socialist economy through the productivization of the Jewish masses.[89]

These two organizations decided to call a conference to unify forces for the common aim. It was held, as mentioned before, in Prague in March 1920. Dr. Hugo Bergmann became a member of the organizing committee (together with Josef Sprinzak and Elieser Kaplan) of this world conference. Czechoslovak delegates to the conference were, in addition to Dr. Bergmann, Drs. Max Brod, Oskar Epstein, and Hans Kohn. Ervín Arnstein, who acted as secretary of the preparatory committee, attended the conference as delegate of the youth organization. A new unified organization emerged, called in short *Hitahdut* (Unity). Its full name was *Hitahdut 'Olamit shel HaPo'el Hatza'ir uTze'ire Zion* (World Union of H. H. and Tz. Z.),* with headquarters in Berlin. The final name was given to the united organization some two years later, at a conference held in Berlin (1922): "International Zionist Labor Party Hitahdut" (*Allweltlische Zionistische Arbeiterpartei Hitachdut*).[90]

While unity was established at the Prague conference, there was a group of dissidents within *Tze'ire Zion* who rejected unity and decided to carry on under the name of *Tze'ire Zion* (they finally merged with *Po'ale Zion* at a conference held in Vienna in 1925, under the name *Ahdut HaAvoda* [Unity of Labor]). Although there never existed a *Tze'ire Zion* organization in Czechoslovakia prior to 1920, there emerged after the Prague conference a small circle which attempted to organize a *Tze'ire Zion* group in the Republic. For a while, in 1922, it had an office in Prague headed by Dr. M. Helfman. In the first and only year of their existence, they sold 200 *Shekalim*,[91]† but nothing was heard of the group's existence subsequently.

During the Prague world conference, the first Territorial Conference of the Czechoslovak *HaPo'el Hatza'ir* took place.[92] It decided to open a central office in Prague, headed by Dr. Oskar Epstein. Less than a year later (1921) an official branch office was opened in

---

* [HaPo'el Hatza'ir and Tze'ire Zion (Ed.)]

† Plural of *Shekel*, the yearly contribution of members of the Zionist Organization.

Brno with Siegfried Spitz in charge.[93] The new organization quickly embarked upon an extensive propaganda activity. This was greatly enhanced due to the deep impression which the Prague world conference had made on the new Zionist generation. When men like Chaim Arlosoroff, Martin Buber, Aaron David Gordon, Joseph Sprinzak, and Robert Weltsch, whose names were household words among Bohemian and Moravian Zionists, expressed their thoughts on the issues of the new era, the greatest attention focused on them. The fact that a host of other socialist Zionist leaders from all over the world attended the conference, many of whom participated also in public meetings in Brno, Moravská Ostrava, Plzeň, and Prague, enhanced the impact of these events. Czechoslovak members of the new organization endeavored to keep this spirit alive, and meetings as well as discussion in the press helped considerably to keep it in the forefront of Zionist interests.

It made itself manifestly felt at the meeting of the Bohemian Zionist District (May 15, 1920), which was dominated by this vibrant first opposition in Czechoslovak Zionism.[94] This opposition was based on the recognition that new methods were required for cartying out Zionist work after World War I.[95] Political victories, so the argument went, brought fellow travelers into the movement and encouraged speculators in Eretz Israel, so that national salvation was being reduced to a business affair. The opposition further maintained that current Zionist leadership had become stagnant and therefore incapable of remedying the situation. *HaPo'el Hatza'ir*, therefore, demanded: (1) a colonization in Palestine on national territory, solely owned by the Jewish people; (2) exclusive employment of Jewish labor in the upbuilding of Eretz Israel; (3) the maintenance of all establishments in accordance with the spirit of social justice; (4) pursuit of and personal commitment to the third *'Aliya*.[96] In short, Eretz Israel must be built in the spirit and practice of socialism. The program also foresaw the strengthening of Jewish national life in the Diaspora, with particular emphasis on the study of Hebrew, the fostering of relationships between Palestine labor and those sections of Jewry in the Diaspora out of which labor was to be recruited, and participation in all Zionist activities, including Jewish national political work (*Landespolitik*).

Although the bulk of the leadership of the new organization in Czechoslovakia was derived from *Bar Kochba*, there arose from within *Bar Kochba* opposing trends, whose spokesman was Dr.

Richard Karpeles. This opposition centered on the Diaspora aspect of *HaPo'el Hatza'ir*, which it described as a "nationalistic and romantic ideology which should be replaced by the concentration of Zionism on Eretz Israel only."[97] However, this was to remain a theoretical opposition only, aired in the press. It had no practical consequences for the new organization, for the lively debate on these issues actually died down when *HaPo'el Hatza'ir* joined the Zionist Territorial Federation in 1921,[98] and when the Territorial Federation decided not to pursue Diaspora political work on its own and supported the establishment of an independent organization for that purpose.[99]

Thoughts such as those expressed in this debate, which actually were an echo of the discussion already referred to[100] (whether or not Zionism should concern itself with Diaspora politics), ripened at the time when they were hotly debated not merely in *HaPo'el Hatza'ir* but also within Czechoslovak Zionism as a whole. They were the fruits of Dr. Ignatz Zollschan's endeavors to do away with "Galut nationalism" and to bring Zionism back to its "original natural purposes," i.e., concentrating solely on the upbuilding of Eretz Israel. One of the foremost Zionist theoreticians, a profound thinker and originator of new aspects of Diaspora activities, Dr. Zollschan developed his idea in a remarkable study, published in 1921, entitled *Revision des jüdischen Nationalismus* (*Revision of Jewish Nationalism*), which caused a stir in Zionist circles. He was one of the initiators and founders of the *Binyan HaAretz* (Upbuilding of the Land) group, which for a number of years flourished in Germany and fought for the idea of confining Zionist work to Palestine only. However, attempts at setting up a *Binyan HaAretz* organization in Czechoslovakia met with no success. Apart from the establishment of a short-lived preparatory committee (1921–1922), headed by Dr. Alfred Löwenstein (Karlovy Vary), nothing came of these efforts.[101]

The Second Territorial Conference of *HaPo'el Hatza'ir* took place in Brno on the eve of the Zionist Territorial Conference (March 27, 1921) and through their delegates at the latter exercised strong influence on decisions regarding Zionist work and Diaspora activities.[102] At the conference, Dr. Epstein announced the decision of *HaPo'el Hatza'ir*, taken at their conference, to join the Zionist Territorial Federation.[103] Four of their members were elected to the Zionist Central Committee: Dr. Oskar Epstein, Alex Feig (Prague), Dr. Alfred Grünfeld, and Siegfried Spitz (Brno). The last-named became head of the youth department of the Czechoslovakia Zionist Organization.[104]

Strengthened through their successes, *HaPo'el Hatza'ir* prepared for the elections of delegates to the first postwar Zionist Congress (the Twelfth, held in Karlovy Vary in 1921). After heated debates on the issues in press and meetings, their list, headed by Dr. Hugo Bergmann and Dr. Max Brod, obtained 616 votes and 1 delegate out of a total of 5,279 votes and 9 delegates.[105]

Yet, notwithstanding all the efforts in meetings, in the press, in conferences, and in elections, *HaPo'el Hatza'ir* in Czechoslovakia did not become a genuine organization but remained a loose association of similarly thinking individuals. It was expected that this situation would be remedied once the world movement finalized its inner consolidation. As mentioned, this took place at the Berlin conference in 1922, when not only the final, definitive name was given to the united organization but also the program was confirmed which, in outline, had already been discussed at the Prague unity conference in March 1920. This centered, as pointed out before, on two basic aims:(1) creation of a free working society in Eretz Israel on the basis of socialism and Hebrew culture, as A. D. Gordon had formulated; and (2) strengthening Jewish national life in the Diaspora, participation in all Zionist activities, propagating its own concept, especially in the sense of the *Halutz* idea, and establishing its own organizations everywhere.

But the situation in the Czechoslovak movement did not change then either. As a matter of fact, soon thereafter it became obvious that it would not be able to emerge as a serious alternative in Czechoslovak Zionism. By the time preparations were made for a distribution of mandates without election to the Thirteenth Zionist Congress (Karlovy Vary, 1923), the Czechoslovak organization, now called *Hitahdut*, did not qualify for a mandate and therefore joined with other existing *Hitahdut* groups in the Argentine, Belgium, and the U.S.A. to secure for all of them one mandate (which was given to M. Lipton of the U.S.A.).[106]

From this time on, hardly any reference was to be found in the Zionist press about the movement in Czechoslovakia. Only a group of stalwarts in Brno continued to pursue some sort of activity. Thus for 1924 there is to be found only one reference to "organized" *Hitahdut* activity in the Republic in the report on the Sixth Zionist Territorial Conference (Olomouc, September 7 and 8, 1924) when three delegates, Drs. Eduard Drachmann, Adolf Grünfeld, and Karl Teller (all from Brno) were elected as "*Hitahdut* representatives" to the Zionist Central Council.[107] But at the conference itself these representatives played no visible role.

Characteristic of this situation were the preparations which *Hitahdut* members made, on the spur of the moment (with insignificant results),[108] for the elections to the Fourteenth Zionist Congress (Vienna, 1925).[109] It is, however, noteworthy that in its call to the electorate, the group had actually deviated from the congress program of the World Organization *Hitahdut*, inasmuch as it returned to the *Hitahdut* program it had pursued when it originally emerged in Czechoslovakia as an opposition group.[110] With this election campaign, actual *Hitahdut* activities had totally ceased in the Republic and a new group, comprising basically the same leadership, emerged under a new name: Zionist Realists.[111] The next section is devoted to this group.

The reasons for this development of Czechoslovak *Hitahdut* were twofold:

In the first place, it rested on the choice of Dr. Oskar Epstein, a prominent member of *Bar Kochba* (Prague), as head of the organization's central office. He was a theoretician, a prolific writer, and a fighter for his ideas which were, in many respects, original and the result of serious thinking. He was one of the very few Zionists born in Bohemia to acquire a good knowledge of Hebrew. But he was by nature incapable of practical application of his ideas and of organizing people in systematic activities.

There existed also, in the second place, objective reasons for this development. The fortunes of *Hitahdut* in Czechoslovakia were unavoidably tied up with those of the world organization. Thus, as *Hitahdut* played a dominant role in all spheres of the life in Eretz Israel, the Czechoslovak branch, notwithstanding its relatively small numbers, attained importance because it was the only group in the Republic which represented one of the strongest factors in the Palestine reality. This also accounts for the influence which *Hitahdut* had exercised in the first years of *HeHalutz* in Czechoslovakia.[112] But at no time throughout its existence was the Czechoslovak branch capable of living up to its attained position. Therefore its influence stood in sharp contrast to the actual strength of the movement and gave it a sense of importance which proved to be unjustified.

To this must be added the fact that a general feeling of decline had permeated the Zionist Organization in the first years — after the great hopes which had arisen out of the political victorjes at the end of World War I gradually became overshadowed by the reality of day-to-day work. At that time the absence of the two most prominent spiritual guides of *Hitahdut* left the movement orphaned. Martin Buber had withdrawn from political work (1921) and A. D. Gordon had died (1922). This was after *Hitahdut* had become the first socialist sector in the Zionist World Organization to join the Zionist World Executive and thus become co-responsible for its policies and activities. And yet at the Twelfth Zionist Congress (1921), *Hitahdut*, as a constructive opposition, played a dominant role, and the speeches of its delegates (Dr. Max Bienenstock, Elieser Joffe, Dr. Abraham Katzenelson, Kurt Blumenfeld, Martin Buber, Joseph Sprinzak, and Itzhak Wilensky), as well as the practical propositions made in the various congress committees by their representatives, largely influenced decisions in matters of *'Aliya*, the relations to the Arabs, and organizational reforms. But after the delegating of Joseph Sprinzak to the newly elected Executive under Dr. Chaim Weizmann, *Hitahdut* naturally ceased to remain an opposition party. This alignment with the leadership of Dr. Weizmann made the task of *Hitahdut* in Czechoslovakia much more difficult,[113] since the Czechoslovak Zionist Territorial Federation was one of the staunchest supporters of the president of the World Zionist Organization and of Weizmannism, as his political concept had come to be known.

In addition, from the outset the Zionist Territorial Federation was a strong supporter of *HeHelutz* and of all labor efforts in Eretz Israel, and thus shared the most important program of Zionist policies and practical activities with *Hitahdut* and with all other subsequently emerging socialist groups in the Republic. From this purely Zionist viewpoint, their differences were undistinguishable.

On the other hand, the Zionist Territorial Federation had practical reasons for having a socialist group within the federation; otherwise, it would have been a one-party formation and not a "Territorial" Federation comprising other Zionist groups also. The Executive, under Dr. Rufeisen, therefore during all those critical years supported strongly the fiction of an existing *"Hitahdut"* in Czechoslovakia — for instance, by allocating to it in 1924 (as mentioned above) three seats on the Central Committee; this allocation was not based on any elections preceding the Olomouc conference and was out of proportion to the number of members of *Hitahdut*.

It was, to no small degree, in light of these considerations that the Territorial Federation presented a list of candidates for the elections to the Sixteenth Zionist Congress (Basle, 1927) "jointly with *Hitahdut*" under the name "Left Center-Working Eretz Israel," although in 1927 a *Hitahdut* did not exist in the Republic.[114]

But this brings us already ahead of the developments of *Hitahdut* in Czechoslovakia. In our survey, we still find ourselves in the critical years 1923–1925, which saw the conclusive failure of *Hitahdut* to establish a genuine organization in the Republic.

The first group of individuals to attempt to remedy the situation emerged in Brno. It abandoned the names *HaPo'el Hatza'ir* and *Hitahdut* and any designation as socialist Zionists and preferred to call itself Zionist Realists.

(2) *Zionist Realists*

In Czechoslovak Zionist circles it was generally accepted that the term "realists" was appropriated from the Czech Realist party (later called the Progressive party), founded in 1900 and headed by Tomáš G. Masaryk. The similarity was not only in name but also, basically, in their programs. "Realism," said Masaryk,[115] "means to me politically: do not lose yourself in a glorious past but make every effort for a glorious present; do not adhere to phrases and words but to deeds, for only then can you improve matters and put them in order; do not float in clouds but hold on to your earth, it is the most secure and infallible basis. And whatever cause you serve, keep to reality." Czech realism also rejected Marxism. Its socialism, like that of Gordon, was based on what Masaryk termed the "philosophy of humanism."

The program of the Zionist Realists emerged only gradually. A first outline appeared in the proclamation issued by a group of former *Hitahdut* candidates to the elections to the Fourteenth Zionist Congress (1925) referred to above.[116] Therein emphasis was laid on the demand "to recognize the difference between substantial and formal Zionism," or between proclamatory Zionism and a Zionism of deeds. "In its practical aspects the election manifesto and the propaganda preceding the convening of the congress were based on the ideas which *HaPo'el Hatza'ir* had originally pursued before the congress in 1921, i.e., as an opposition party within the Zionist Organization, but now, in 1925, it was entirely out of line with the program of the world movement *Hitahdut*. The election platform centered around two demands: (1) An election reform of the World Zionist Executive. The proposed leadership should be presented to the congress at the beginning of deliberations, elaborate its program (which the congress should fully debate), and elections should then be proceeded with (as against the practice of electing the new Executive at the end of the congress meetings, without an action program being presented or, as happened frequently, its being compiled in haste during the last stages of deliberations). (2) The Fourteenth Congress should discuss and decide upon this reform as the first point on its agenda.

For the purpose of organizing the election campaign, a committee of "national consolidation" was established, with A. S. Bienenfeld České Budějovice) as its secretary.[117]

A list of candidates was speedily put together "without consultation owing to shortage of time."[118] The whole campaign started about two weeks before election date. It is indicative of the complete breakdown of communication within the remnants of *Hitahdut* that, in their proclamation of assistance for the list addressed to *Hitahdut* adherents, each candidate on the list had to be "introduced." The candidates were Robert Anders, Dr. Oskar Epstein (Prague), Dr. Bachrach (Bratislava), and Dr. Kamil Kohn (Volkan near Ústí nad Labem). Conspicuously absent from this list are the names of any from the group in Brno, which formerly was one of the largest *Hitahdut* centers in the Republic.

Two weeks later the elections took place. The Zionist Realists received 360 votes and no delegate out of a total of 5,407 votes and 5 delegates.[119] It is indicative of the chaotic conditions which then prevailed that, although the Zionist Realists went to the elections not on a *Hitahdut* program, their 360 votes were added to the splinter votes received by *Hitahdut* in Belgium and Estonia, so as to enable all of them together to have one delegate at the congress, Menahem Bader (Eretz Israel), a member of *Hitahdut*.

As soon as the congress was over, a complete reorganization of the group took place. It coincided with Dr. Epstein's settlement in Brno where he joined the teaching staff of the *Jüdisches Reform-Real-Gymnasium* (Jewish Secondary School). It so happened that the bulk of its teaching staff consisted of old members of *HaPo'el Hatza'ir* (*Hitahdut*). It was from the midst of this circle that the initiative committee of Zionist Realists in Czechoslovakia was formed and headed by

Dr. Epstein. Its other members were Dr. Eduard Drachmann (the director of the Jewish Secondary School), Dr. Norbert Fein, Dr. Leopold Schnitzler, Alois Zaitschek, and Dr. Samuel Zeisel.[120]

Their first task was to prepare for the elections to the Seventh Zionist Territorial Conference (July 3–6, 1926, Brno). In May they published their *Thesen des zionistischen Realismus* (Theses of Zionist Realism)[121] which comprised a program for every problem, facet, and activity of the Zionist Organization. It was presented as an "alternative program to present-day official Zionism." The authors did not refrain from stating that they were prepared to take over the leadership of Czechoslovak Zionism.

The program was based on the publications of Dr. Epstein,[122] elaborated and expanded by the members of the preliminary committee. They emphasized A. D. Gordon's concept of the duty and responsibility of the individual. They stressed, however, that neither social questions nor religious affairs were matters of separate organizations but integral parts of Zionist work. They also abandoned the socialist basis of the future Jewish national home in Palestine and stressed the humanitarian aspect based on social justice (almost identical with Masaryk's "Realism"). A large part of the theses was devoted to the question of Hebraization and youth leadership, but apart from the emphasis on Jewish schools on a national basis (most members of the initiative committee were teachers), there were no new aspects discernible in these chapters. With regard to finances they suggested the expansion of the selective *Einheitsaktion* (United Appeal) operating in Czechoslovakia since 1924 and comprising regular monthly payments by members for local and territorial affairs, Hebrew schools, *Hakhshara*, cultural activities, *shekel*, political work, Jewish National Fund, and propaganda. They suggested placing all fund-raising activities (including the *Keren Hayesod* in the future) under the supervision of a single controlling body. They continued to accept political activities in the Diaspora as part of Zionist work and laid stronger accent on the necessity of basing all these activities on the Jewish religious congregations. With regard to the upbuilding of the Jewish national home they demanded that the establishment of a Jewish state in Palestine be recognized as the principal aim of Zionism, and elaborated a program by which to convince the Arabs to "accept the Judaization of Palestine." (These were more radical demands than any issued by any other Zionist group up to that time.) Two aims were proposed: (1) to persuade world powers to make it abundantly clear that they supported with all strength the establishment of a full national life of the Jews in Palestine; and (2) to provide the Arabs in Palestine and in all other Arab lands with suitable leadership and experts to assist them in building up their own national cultural sector in Palestine and a life of complete national independence in the various lands which they ruled. Parallel with this, they insisted that the upbuilding of Palestine through Jewish endeavor and work should proceed and that this was primarily a matter for labor. To solve the manpower problems involved, it was necessary to intensify planned training *Hakhshara* in the Diaspora before *'Aliya.*

The rest of the platform was devoted to the necessity of reorganizing Zionist leadership and its structure. The Zionist Realists now repeated what the *Hitahdut* had said prior to the Congress in 1921: that the present Zionist leadership was unsuitable for the task; but they also added that, since the withdrawal of Martin Buber from active political work and since the death of A. D. Gordon,[123] *Hitahdut* was incapable of doing the job. They repeated their demand for election reform of the Zionist Executive[124] and suggested the appointment of departmental heads to be responsible for the work of the organization (political, upbuilding of Palestine, youth, *Hakhshara*, finances, press, and organization of all Jews via the congregations). They further suggested a pension scheme for Zionist officials and insisted that members of the Zionist Organization should become and remain only those who were prepared to sacrifice.

At the Zionist Territorial Conference in July 1926 the Zionist Realists were represented by the following delegates: Robert Anders (Prague), Dr. Oskar Bachrach (Bratislava), Dr. Eduard Drachman, Dr. Oskar Epstein, Ernest Lamberger, Alois Zaitschek, Mrs. Leopold Schnitzler, Dr. Samuel Zeisel (all Brno), and Dr. Hans Zweig (Prostějov).[125] In many respects these delegates dominated the conference. They spoke on various occasions, pressing for the ideas expressed in their platform. Nonetheless, they were unable to persuade the conference to their way of thinking or to the adoption of any of their proposals. Disappointed with the results, the Zionist Realists refused to delegate representatives to the Czechoslovak Zionist Council.[126]

The negative result of the efforts at the Territorial Conference seems to have had a deeper effect on the group than could have been expected. For almost a year external activity was hardly noticeable.

Only with the elections to the Fifteenth Zionist Congress (Basle, August 30 to September 11, 1927) did they come to life again. They started their campaign early (April) and in the main it consisted of articles which members had published in *Selbstwehr* or which were distributed by way of circular letters to various Zionists.[127] Noteworthy in this connection are the few changes which the group had made in its program. The Realists warned the Zionist Organization of becoming simply a pro-Palestine organization without regard to the renaissance of the Jewish people, the majority of which lived in the Diaspora,[128] and demanded, further, the abandonment of the *shekel* as the basis of membership and voting rights in the Zionist Organization; they insisted on the right to a vote "of every Jew and every Jewess willing to participate in the upbuilding of Palestine."[129]

But notwithstanding all these election activities, they remained what they had been from the beginning — a preparatory committee only. The group never was in a position to create an organization. Naturally, on such a basis, there was no question of becoming an alternative to the Czechoslovak Zionist leadership. The reasons were the same as those which led to the failure of *Hitahdut*[130]: Dr. Epstein's incapability of organizing men, aggravated by the fact that none of his colleagues on the preparatory committee had any better qualities for this task. To this must be added the fact that, while the Zionist Realists had issued their program for the congress, the Zionist Territorial Federation forestalled them by selecting former members of *Hitahdut*, which no longer existed, and presented to the electorate of the Fifteenth Zionist Congress a joint list of the Territorial Federation and a random selection of former *Hitahdut* members under the name of *"Linkes Zentrum-Arbeitendes Eretz Israel"* (Left Center-Working Eretz Israel).[131] Under these circumstances, the Zionist Realists did not submit even a list of candidates to the congress. They were sufficiently realistic to know that their appeal to old members of *HaPo'el Hatza'ir* and *Hitahdut* would be in vain.

From the end of 1927 on, there are no signs of any activity of this group.

The significance of this offspring of *Hitahdut* lies in the fact that it was a purely Czechoslovak affair. No similar grouping within the Zionist World Organization or within *Hitahdut* emerged anywhere else. It is to no small degree because of this that space has been given to this group in this survey. It should be added, however, that despite an absence of practical results, this group was able to stimulate debates and to create for almost two years serious and often heated discussions on problems pertaining to all aspects of Zionist life and activities; it did so at a time when Zionism in the world and in Czechoslovakia had become a more or less mechanical machinery. It was only in 1927 and 1928 that new forces were to come to the fore in Zionism in the consolidating efforts of socialists of all shades and in the emergence of the Zionist Revisionist movement.[132]

(3) *Working Association of Socialist Zionists*

While the circle of former *Hitahdut* members under the name of Zionist Realists had created a stir at the Seventh Zionist National Conference in Brno[133] (1926), other former members of *HaPo'el Hatza'ir* and *Hitahdut*, who attended that conference in a personal capacity, met and decided on the formation of a group which was to represent socialist Zionism in the Czechoslovak Territorial Federation. The Realists, they maintained, had diverted from the original *Hitahdut* program, while *Hitahdut* as a world movement continued to play an important role both in Eretz Israel and in the World Zionist Organization; but it had no organized branch on Czechoslovak soil. The initiative for forming a new group was taken by Drs. Adolf Grünfeld and Karl Teller (both of Brno), who had called the meeting and temporarily headed a small preparatory committee.

Unlike the Zionist Realists, they did not commence activities by announcing comprehensive programs or stimulating discussion in the press and in public meetings. They concerned themselves with contacting former members of *Hitahdut* with the object of inviting them to join an organization to be created within the framework of socialist Zionism on Czechoslovak territory.

Progress was very slow. It was not even evidenced a year later when preparations for the elections to the Fifteenth Zionist Congress (Basle, August 30 to September 11, 1927) commenced. At that moment, as already pointed out,[134] help came from Czechoslovak Zionist Territorial Federation, which was most anxious to maintain the status of representing all or most Zionist groupings in the Republic. Since no organized group of socialist Zionists had been represented in the Federation since the disintegration of the Czechoslovak *Hitahdut* (1923/1924), an arrangement was made with the Brno preparatory committee of the contemplated new party to present to the electorate a joint list of candidates for the congress under the name *Linkes Zentrum* (Left Center). For a while it appeared as if a new party with its own ideology would arise in Czechoslovakia, instead of a mere amalgamation of two groups. Its principal theoretician was Dr. Hugo Herrmann, a prominent member of the Prague *Bar Kochba*, chief organizer of the *Keren Hayesod* in Czechoslovakia, and now one of the leading members of the Zionist Territorial Federation (and of the General Zionists who emerged soon hereafter).

The idea of the Left Center was born in Germany,[135] but Dr. Herrmann deepened its "philosophy" and adapted its practical application to Czechoslovak conditions in a preliminary article, "Ein Programmvorschlag" (Proposal for a Program).[136] This was followed by a series of articles under the title "*Was will das Linke Zentrum?*" The aim of the Left Center,[137] Herrmann's principal thesis, focused on two aspects: the support of Dr. Weizmann and his policies (vis-à-vis the Arabs, England, within the Zionist Organization) and the support of all endeavors of labor in Eretz Israel as the principal body in the creation of the Jewish national home. This synthesis of "Weizmannism" and "socialism" (both terms are here employed euphemistically) led to Dr. Herrmann's suggestion of the formation of a strong Zionist front consisting of the two elements: the Territorial Federation and the socialist Zionists.

This joint interest in and support of the Weizmann policies and of labor endeavors in Eretz Israel had actually been prevalent in Czechoslovakia since 1921, when the Territorial Federation developed as the staunch supporter of the president of the Zionist Organization and after Joseph Sprinzak had joined the World Zionist Executive on behalf of *Hitahdut;* that movement thus became co-responsible for policies and activities. Sprinzak was still an Executive member when, in 1927, the parties prepared for the elections to the Fifteenth Congress. As mentioned, there was not at the time a *Hitahdut* organization in existence in Czechoslovakia; nor did the newly emerging group assume that name, although it consisted almost in its entirety of former members of *Hitahdut* in the Republic. The joint list for "Left Center" registered a great election victory. It obtained 4,167 votes and six delegates out of a total of 6,514 votes and nine delegates.[138] All delegates were elected under the name "Left Center" without any possible specific reference to party affiliation. We know, however, that of the six delegates, two were socialists — Erwin

Zipper-Vogel and Eliahu Dobkin (a *Po'ale Zion* leader from Eretz Israel).

But this idyllic state of affairs was not to last long. The Fifteenth Congress assembled in a period of grave economic crisis in Eretz Israel and inner strife within the World Zionist Organization (*Po'ale Zion* was then in opposition; the Radical Zionists fought a bitter struggle against Dr. Weizmann's policies, as did the newly emerging Zionist Revisionists).[139] Labor was the principal victim of the crisis, and it was with great hopes of remedying it that delegates of all socialist trends in Zionism went to Basle. At the congress, however, an unexpected situation developed. Labor was unable to find acceptance by Dr. Weizmann and the congress majority for their proposals to remedy economic condition in Palestine. Not satisfied with Dr. Weizmann's vague promise to support the Histadrut (labor union), it abstained from voting for the election of Dr. Weizmann to the presidency and for the new Executive, which was left without *Hitahdut* representation for the first time since 1921. From the platform, Dr. Chaim Arlosoroff, the *Hitahdut* spokesman, branded the new Executive as "directed against the labor movement," and was prevented by stormy protests from concluding his speech.[140]

The Czechoslovak Zionist Territorial Federation, as mentioned, was closely tied to Dr. Weizmann in the policies he pursued internally and externally, and it happened that four of the six Czechoslovak delegates of the "Left Center" voted in the crucial division at the congress for Dr. Weizmann and for his new Executive. This came as a shock to Czechoslovak socialist Zionists who regarded this as a breach of the "united front," as it constituted a vote against labor. They felt that at that moment they "had been used and let down" by the Zionist Territorial Federation. One of their younger spokesmen concluded that the term and concept of "Left Center" had lost all meaning and that it was not the time to pursue it any further.[141]

The year 1928 opened in Czechoslovakia in an atmosphere of confusion arising from the tactical maneuvering at the congress, but to no small degree also because of the great influence which the situation in Palestine and its disappointed labor element had exercised on all socialist Zionist elements in the Republic. Moreover, the stoppage of immigration into Palestine, proclaimed by the British administration (1926), led to a great decline of Czechoslovak *HeHalutz* (which was also under the influence of socialist elements). Of the 380 members (including 266 in *Hakhshara*) in 1926/1927, the Slovak sector had been almost completely lost, and in the rest of the Republic there only remained 210 members (of whom 160 were in *Hakhsharot*)[142]

On the other hand, Revisionist opposition began to make itself felt and its youth wing, *Brit Trumpeldor* (*Betar*), was to attain a remarkable success in Subcarpathian Ruthenia, at least partly as the result of this development, when the conference of *HaShomer-Kadimah* (Berehovo, April 22, 1928) decided to join *Betar* corporatively.[143]

Socialist Zionists, aware of the urgency to regain their former — or at least a strong — position in Czechoslovak Zionism, initiated a number of organizational steps which were to make them within five years the strongest grouping within the Zionist Organization in the Republic.

To start with, individuals had formed local groups of the "League for the Working Eretz Israel" (*Liga für das arbeitende Eretz Israel*) in various centers of Czechoslovakia. The first such group was established in Prague.[144] Officially, it was not a political party or organization. Its aims were to create a Friends of Labor Movement for Eretz Israel without regard to political affiliation and primarily to raise funds and organize moral support for the workers in Palestine,[145] but there was no doubt as to its socialist leanings. In a short period of time, the "unpolitical" league was able to register successes in all areas of the Republic.

A further considerable strengthening of the socialist trend in Zionism was caused by the decision of a preparatory committee to renew the activities of *Po'ale Zion* in Czechoslovakia.[146] This last event carried with it the possibility of a frontal effort of merging in the Marxist group (*Po'ale Zion*) all elements of the different socialist shades in Zionism, none of which had hitherto had a proper organization in Czechoslovakia. This "danger" reawakened the old antagonism between the two principal socialist concepts in Zionism, *Hitahdut* and *Po'ale Zion*.[147] It added impetus for former members of *Hitahdut* to reshape life in a new movement, now called the Working Association of Socialist Zionists (*Arbeitsgemeinschaft sozialistischer Zionisten*, mostly referred to in its abbreviated form, AGSZ).

They did not elaborate a program. In all their endeavors they were guided by the policies and activities of the world movement *Hitahdut* and simply regarded themselves as representatives of that concept, if not of that party by name,* on Czechoslovak territory. They remained, as they had been individually throughout the years since 1921, members of the Zionist Territorial Federation and continued also to support the Jewish party with regard to political activities in the Diaspora (*Landespolitik*).[148]

The association was fortunate in that a number of younger men had joined its ranks, who in the course of time were, next to some *Po'ale Zion* leaders, to become the architects of the great successes already mentioned.[149] At first the association's main working basis became the "League for a Working Eretz Israel," which in those days, comprised most of the socialist Zionist elements in the Republic and a great number of unaffiliated friends of Palestine labor. When the league met in Prague in June 1928 for the purpose of unifying all leagues in Czechoslovakia, it was discovered that at that meeting the most active elements were adherents of *Po'ale Zion* (although that organization was by then not yet officially re-established) and, as a matter of course, had taken over the leadership of the preparatory committee.[150] But when, some six months later, the league met for its first ordinary Territorial Conference in Brno (December 30, 1928), the Working Association was able to reverse the trend, have two of its members (Dr. Alfred Grünfeld and Samuel Rosenkranz) in the presidium of the conference, and to occupy eight of the seventeen seats of the newly elected Territorial Committee of the league.[151]

As mentioned, the Working Association was an integral part of the Zionist Territorial Federation, and their delegates, therefore, participated for the first time in strong numbers at the Eighth Zionist Territorial Conference (Brno, December 30 and 31, 1928). Its spokesmen (Jakob Edelstein, Dr. Alfred Grünfeld, Dr. Karl Liebstein [later Eliahu K. Livneh], and Dr. Oskar Neumann) participated in the debates but in no sense in a spirit of opposition. The association's numerical strength was also apparent in the elections to the new Czechoslovak Zionist Central Committee of the following seven members (out of a total of 38 members): Leo Bergmann (Prague), Dr. Adolph Grünfeld (Brno), Jecheskel Jaffe (Nitra), Hans Lichtwitz (now Uri Naor), Otto Schleim (Prague), Moritz Löbl (Karlovy Vary), and Dr. Oskar Neumann (Bratislava).[152]

These successes encouraged the leadership to more intensive

---

* See the article by A. M. Rabinowitz, The Jewish Party, pp. 253–346.

organizational activities. It expected substantial gains at the elections to the Sixteenth Zionist Congress which was to assemble in Zurich on July 28 to August 14, 1929. It will be remembered how disappointed Czechoslovak socialist Zionists had been over the voting of the delegates of the "Left Center" at the previous congress.[153] Before the new elections they were warned by Chaim Hoffmann (Yahil), one of the leaders of the newly formed *Po'ale Zion*, not to reiy upon a repetition of the "Left Center" miracle but rather to turn toward other socialist Zionists in the Republic, in order to avoid an internal socialist conflict. He warned that the General Zionists (still identified with the Territorial Federation to which *Po'ale Zion* did not belong) were antilabor and anti-*Halutz*.[154]

Notwithstanding this warning, the Working Association and the Zionist Territorial Federation were to enter another election agreement by the end of June 1929. It is not without interest to note that the announcement of the agreement still maintained that it was made between *Hitahdut* and the Territorial Federation, although the name *Hitahdut* had been changed to *Working Association of Socialist Zionists*.[155] The agreement foresaw for this joint list of candidates not the old name "Left Center" but the new slogan, "For a Strong Zionist Organization — For the Working Eretz Israel."[156] One of the Working Association's members was elected a delegate (Dr. Chaim Kugel). However, it was ironic that on the very same joint list which had been decried by the *Po'ale Zion* leader, Ignatz Rokach (who was to join *Po'ale Zion* at the Zionist Congress [157]), was also elected.

Numerically, however, the result of this joint list must be regarded as a failure. In 1929 it obtained only 61 votes more than in 1927, with the same number of delegates (six), although the total number of votes cast had increased by 530 votes.[158]

A further blow to the combination of the Territorial Federation and the Working Association came at the congress itself, when representatives of the Zionist Territorial Federation joined members of other Territorial Federations in eliminating the proclaimed "neutrality" and forming a new political party — the General Zionist Organization.[159]

All this led to a rethinking and re-evaluation by members of the Working Association. They commenced an overall organizational drive which in less than six months was to produce its first striking success. When the Ninth Zionist Territorial Conference assembled in Brno (December 25 to 29, 1929), the Working Association was already able to send a delegation of fifty-nine members. At the conference, however, its delegates did not exhibit a unified picture, nor had their proposals any specific new aspect different from those of the General Zionists. It was a sort of peaceful coexistence, and the "new ideas" at the conference came mostly from the camps of the Radical Zionists and the Revisionists. The only controversial suggestion by the Working Association was the demand of a censure of the Revisionists; but the chairman of the conference refused a demand for a vote.[160]

While the increase in membership of the Czechoslovak Working Association went on, the tendency grew to turn toward unity with other socialist groups rather than to adhere to the uncertain combination with General Zionists or with a vague Territorial Federation.

The unity of socialist Zionists came strongly to the fore at the Second Territorial Conference of the Working Association, held in Brno (February 2, 1930) at which a new leadership was elected, consisting of the following members: Jakob Edelstein, Prof. Viktor Freud, Dr. Hans Lichtwitz, Hans Thein (all Prague), Dr. Adolf Grünfeld (Brno), Dr. Chaim Kugel (Mukačevo), Moritz Löbl (Karlovy Vary), Ernst Fuchs (Brno), Max Kolisch (Užhorod), and Viktor Kaufman (Prešov). The four Prague members constituted the secretariat of the organization.[161]

The subsequent conference of the Working Association, held in Prague (September 6, 1931), dealt with the question of unity but still could not see how to achieve it. "Nothing should be done that would hinder final achievement of unity," it decided. It further demanded a strengthening of the Zionist Territorial Federation, stressing that at the next Territorial Conference only those who genuinely strove for a strong Territorial Federation should be elected to the leadership.[162]

At the Fourth Territorial Conference of the Working Association (Prague, August 20, 1933) the increase in membership was hailed as a good omen for an eventual amalgamation with *Po'ale Zion*. Seventy-one delegates representing thirty-eight local groups attended, and it was emphasized that eighteen members had been elected to the Zionist Territorial Central Committee; but the most important feature of the conjerence was the report of the great changes in the basic structure of the Working Association. Hitherto a loose association of friends and adherents, it now became, for the first time, a strong, self-contained organization.[163]

The Conference of the Working Association at Moravská Ostrava (December 31, 1934 to January 1, 1935), which was to be the last national conference, did little but concentrate on the final steps for the establishment of a socialist Zionist united front in Czechoslovakia. The new leadership that was to accomplish this unification consisted of Dov Biegun, Fini Brada, Jakob Edelstein, Dr. Karl Grünberger, Oskar Karpe, Dr. Hans Lichtwitz, Ernst Pollak, and Dr. Felix Resek (all Prague). A large council elected at this conference consisted of representatives from all areas of Czechoslovakia.[164]

Parallel with these activities ran continuous efforts at achieving socialist Zionist unity in practice. It was a thorny and most difficult way. The stages leading to it and the final achievement are dealt with in the following section.[165]

(4) *Po'ale Zion*

Unlike *HaPo'el Hatza'ir*, the *Po'ale Zion* movement was born not in Eretz Israel but in the Diaspora. Its spiritual father was Dov-Ber Borochov (1881–1917), who had come from the Russian Social Democratic party and made the first attempt at analyzing and scientifically justifying Jewish national demands on a Marxist basis.[166] While, according to his thesis, no nation in a capitalist society could be said to live a normal life, Jewry's abnormal existence was more acute and more painful than that of many other people. As the main cause of this situation Borochov recognized the economic condition of the Jews in the Diaspora: they were forced out of the primary sectors of production (agriculture and industrial production) and had to concentrate on the secondary sectors of commerce and trade. This led to the theoretical formulation of a law: the more removed an occupation was from nature, the more Jewish labor concentrated on it. The reason for the Jews' drifting farther and farther away from the natural sources of livelihood was their lack of a territory of their own. Therefore, the Jewish working classes required a "strategic basis" to enable them to return to natural and normal conditions. Thus the need for a state in Eretz Israel constituted the link between Borochov's socialism and Zionism.

Borochov, however, did not conclude that this socialist Zionist solution could only be achieved through the "bourgeois" Zionist Organization. On the contrary, he believed in the necessity of a separate effort to be made by all Jewish socialist forces for the colonization of Eretz Israel. He even advocated a complete severance of relations with the Zionist Organization, a step rejected by other *Po'ale Zion* leaders. In fact, Borochov and, following him, Russian *Po'ale Zion* put greater emphasis on socialism, while Austrian and American leaders of the movement stressed Jewish nationalism more emphatically.

In 1907, at the First World Conference of *Po'ale Zion* in The Hague, the local and territorial groups which had come into existence since 1903 (in Austria, America, Great Britain, Eretz Israel, and Russia) united in a world organization. No representative from the territories which subsequently were to become Czechoslovakia attended this world conference, even though an organization of national Jewish trade employees named Emunah had existed in Brno (Moravia) since 1898.[167] Max Hickl, the delegate of this society at the Second Zionist Congress (Basle, 1898) signed a proposal to the effect that the congress recognize organized labor within the Zionist Organization.[168] By 1907, out of the Emunah circle emerged a *Po'ale Zion* group in Brno, headed by Siegfried Kessler (who until 1939 was to play an important role in the Czechoslovak movement and was to head a Czechoslovak section of the *Po'ale Zion* in Great Britain during World War II).

Borochov's concept of noncooperation with the "capitalist" Zionist Organization and nonparticipation in Zionist Congresses was in accordance with the tendency that also prevailed at the time among the social democratic organizations of other peoples. Although Borochov arrived at his views independently, and on the basis of purely ideological considerations, it must not be overlooked that *Po'ale Zion*, as a member of the socialist Internationale, could not but adhere to the latter's proclaimed principles of noncooperation with bourgeois groups. As it developed, though, the elements of *Po'ale Zion* seeking cooperation with the Zionist Organization prevailed. However, up to World War I they refused to participate in the Zionist Actions Committee because they wished to have no part of the responsibility for Zionist policies. Their platform of 1909 formulated the basic clauses of their program as follows:[169] "The International Socialist Jewish Labor Confederation *Po'ale Zion* embraces all those who recognize the principles of socialism and have the following aims: (a) The overthrow of the capitalist order and class rule through the economic and political class struggle of the proletariat, and the socialization of the means of production. (b) The territorial solution of the Jewish question through the establishment of a Jewish commonwealth [*Volksgemeinschaft*] in and around Palestine."

Accordingly, *Po'ale Zion* strove for the upbuilding of Palestine, the socialization of the entire production through the struggle of the workers against the capitalist bourgeoisie in the country. They demanded individual freedom and independence in all cultural questions (including religion) and fought politically against the application of capitalist-imperialistic methods in Zionist policies (i.e., any eventual joint venture of bourgeois Zionism and British imperialism).

In 1918, when the Czechoslovak Republic was established, *Po'ale Zion* had a few local groups functioning in the territory. These groups had been inactive as a result of war conditions. But in 1918/1919, with the great upswing in Zionist and Jewish national activities in the new Czechoslovakia, and as a result of the trend toward the Left among Jews and non-Jews alike,[170] *Po'ale Zion* was brought to new life. In Prague the group headed by Rudolf Kohn joined, as already mentioned, the Jewish National Council, which consisted of six Zionists and five *Po'ale Zion*ists.[171] But they also formed a Jewish Socialist Council, which remained affiliated with *Po'ale Zion* and on whose behalf Rudolf Kohn participated at the Conference of Czech Social Democrats in Prague (December 27, 1918).[172] It thus appears that, at least at the beginning, *Po'ale Zion* participated actively both in the Jewish national political work and in general social democratic political activities. Alas, this situation did not last for long due to the stand of *Po'ale Zion* in matters of Jewish Diaspora politics, as already mentioned.[173]

The Prague *Po'ale Zion* group registered a great inerease in membership in 1919. It felt strong enough to call its members and friends to a march on May 1, 1919, (labor day), and to an open-air demonstration on *Staroměstské náměstí*, at which some 500 persons participated.[174] In June of that year elections to the municipality took place, and *Po'ale Zion* was able to obtain 1,218 votes and one delegate (the Jewish national list received 1,286 votes and one delegate).[175]

The *Po'ale Zion* group in Brno, headed by Siegfried Kessler and his deputy Dr. Felix Brunner, established contact with other individuals and the local groups in Moravská Ostrava and Olomouc at the beginning of 1919, and formed the first Moravian provincial central office headed by the two above-mentioned leaders and by the following: Ing. Gewürz, Dr. Felix Loria, Jitzhak Rosenberg, Ernst Schuschny (sports section), and Dr. Eugen Zeisel (representative of the Academic Society of Jewish Socialists, formed at the beginning of 1919, and affiliated with *Po'ale Zion*).[176]

This central office initiated and formed the first Union of Private and Business Employees in Brno, headed by Dr. Felix Loria (chairman) and Felix Brunner (secretary).[177] This union called the first Czechoslovak conference of Jewish private and business employees, which was held on February 2, 1919, in Brno; Siegfried Kessler was elected chairman of the newly created territorial organization there.

On behalf of this organization, Drs. Loria and Brunner attended the meeting of the Jewish Teachers' Association for Bohemia (Prague, August 25, 1919) and convinced those present to organize a union of all employees of Jewish religious congregations in Bohemia and, following this, in the whole of Czechoslovakia. The following were elected as an interim board: Dr. Samuel Arje, Dr. Aladar Deutsch, Moritz Mandl, Siegmund Springer (all Prague), and Dr. Richard Feder (Kolín) (up to 1969, when he was aged 95, the Chief Rabbi of Czechoslovakia). The secretary was Dr. Zemanek, the treasurers, Otto Beck and Gabriel Leiden (all Prague).[178]

Simultaneously, the central office of *Po'ale Zion* called the first Moravian conference of the movement for March 22, 1919, in Brno, at which the local branches of Boskovice, Břeclav, Hodonín, Jihlava, Moravská Ostrava, Olomouc, and Prostějov were represented. Dr. Loria was elected chairman of the Moravian district.[179]

For the elections to the municipality in Brno (June 1919) the local *Po'ale Zion* submitted its own list and received 1,475 votes and one delegate (the Jewish national list received 6,571 votes and three delegates).[180]

The first Territorial Conference of all groups of *Po'ale Zion* in Czechoslovakia was called for July 17–19, 1919, in Prague, but this was interrupted owing to the world conference of *Po'ale Zion* which took place at the same time in Stockholm (Sweden).[181]

The above short survey of *Po'ale Zion* activities in the first year after the emergence of new Czechoslovakia is quite impressive. Yet, notwithstanding all these successes and widespread penetrations, the impact of *Po'ale Zion* on Czechoslovak Zionism cannot compare with that of the then newly organized non-Marxist socialist *HaPo'el Hatza'ir*, to which reference has already been made.[182] This in spite of the fact that *Po'ale Zion* published its own organ, *Der Jüdische Socialist* (*The Jewish Socialist*) at that time, while *HaPo'el Hatza'ir* had no organ of its own and had to rely on the hospitality of the general Zionist (and Jewish) press; and in spite of the fact that *Po'ale Zion* could count on the enthusiasm of its energetic membership and on some outstanding younger men, among whom Rudolf Kohn (Prague) became its most prominent spokesman.[183]

The principal reason for the insignificant impact on the Zionist movement in Czechoslovakia as a whole, and for its final failure after about a year's activity, lay in the world movement of *Po'ale Zion* itself. At its first postwar world conference in Stockholm (1919),[184] world *Po'ale Zion* could point to a considerable increase in membership all over the world (which had risen from 5,000 in 1914 to 60,000).[185] Yet the problems of the relationship to the Russian Revolution, to the Third Internationale (which had then come into existence), to the Zionist Organization, and to the work in Eretz Israel itself prepared the ground for disunity which was soon to come to a head and cause a serious split in the movement. A Left and Right wing emerged in *Po'ale Zion*, as in most social democratic organizations of the time. The Left (referring repeatedly to Borochov's concept) fought throughout against what it termed the illusion of the Right that a socialist Eretz Israel could be built up in a joint effort with the bourgeois Zionist Organization under the protection of "imperialistic" Britain. The first attempt at persuading *Po'ale Zion* to join the Third Internationale came at a meeting of the *Po'ale Zion* delegates who attended the international socialist conference in Lucerne (Switzerland)[186] in August 1919. There the Vienna delegation suggested joining the Third Internationale, but this was rejected by a large majority.[187]

The final clash came at the Fifth World Conference of *Po'ale Zion* in Vienna (July, 1920) and ended with a definite breach in the party. The point of division was the question whether or not to join the Third Internationale. There were 179 votes for and one vote against, with 179 abstentions. This led to on-the-spot separate conferences of each wing. The Left refused to attend the next Zionist Congress (1921) and refused to participate in the foundation of a World Jewish

Congress, which was then contemplated (but was not realized until 1936). The Right remained in the Zionist Organization as a greatly reduced force.[188]

The repercussions of this split were far reaching. In Czechoslovakia they resulted in an immediate standstill, after the revival of *Po'ale Zion* had begun only a year before. The Left, headed by Rudolf Kohn and Dr. Arthur Polak (both of Prague) and Dr. Felix Loria (Brno), proclaimed its independence in Czechoslovakia, but by May 1921 it dropped the term "Zion" altogether and called itself "The Jewish Communist Party of Czechoslovakia."[189]

The split in the party caused also some peculiar anomalies which occasionally were fought out in the open. Thus, for instance, there appeared in the *Selbstwehr* an announcement signed by the Prague *Po'ale Zion* group, which had remained in the Zionist Organization, that Dr. Arthur Polak, "though now a member of the Communist party still clings to his mandate in the Prague municipality, which he obtained on the list of *Po'ale Zion*."[190] In other cities, and particularly in some Jewish religious congregations, both in Bohemia and Moravia, similar situations had arisen, but there was nothing *Po'ale Zion* could do but await new elections. By then, however, the organization had deteriorated and by the end of 1921 had disappeared altogether.

For the subsequent seven years *Po'ale Zion* did not exist in Czechoslovakia. At a meeting in Olomouc on January 22, 1928, attended by representatives of former *Po'ale Zion* groups in Brno, Olomouc, and Prostějov, it was decided "to found in Czechoslovakia an International Jewish Social Democratic Party '*Po'ale Zion.*'" A temporary secretariat was set up in Olomouc[191]. A similar consolidation process took place also in other countries where the 1920 split had paralyzed *Po'ale Zion* activities. These efforts led to a conference in Olomouc (April 14 and 15, 1928) at which representatives of Austria, Germany, and Czechoslovakia participated. They decided to form a unified but loose association with centralized propaganda in Vienna. The *Po'ale Zion* organ published there, *Der Jüdische Arbeiter*,* was to become the mouthpiece of all three countries.[192] Each constituent was, of course, to remain independent so far as internal political activities was concerned. They also decided at the conference to

* [*The Jewish Worker* (Ed.)]

participate actively in the League for a Working Eretz Israel that was then emerging.[193] It seems, however, that the unified propaganda center of these territorial groups actually never commenced functioning. Differences of a local nature in each land made the arrangement unworkable.

Soon thereafter the First Territorial Conference of Czechoslovak *Po'ale Zion* was called to Olomouc. It was attended in behalf of the world organization by Berl Locker, one of the principal theoreticians of the pro-Zionist Right in the movement. The Czechoslovak *Po'ale Zion* was officially re-established at that conference, with headquarters in Brno. Siegfried Kessler, the untiring leader of the movement since 1907, became chairman, Herrmann Grün and Karl Baum were elected members of the executive committee. Other members of the council were Oskar Huber (Olomouc), Rudolf Jokl (Moravská Ostrava), Arthur Heller, and Jakob Reiss (both Prague).[194]

It was at the Second Territorial Conference, held in Brno (May 19 and 20, 1929), that the first organizational achievements of Czechoslovak *Po'ale Zion* were announced. Ten functioning local groups sent delegates to the conference, as did four Jewish socialist youth groups. The conference adopted resolutions conforming with the demands of the world leadership, decided upon the publication of its own weekly, *Der Jüdische Sozialist* (*The Jewish Socialist*) which was edited by Karl Baum from 1929 to 1932. It was to be followed as the official organ of *Po'ale Zion* in Czechoslovakia by *Der Neue Weg* (*The New Road*), published under the same editor from 1933 to mid-1934. In the early part of 1934 *Der Neue Weg* also published an Austrian edition to fill the gap after the cessation of *Der Jüdische Arbeiter* as a result of political developments in Austria. The conference emphasized, in particular, close cooperation with the League for a Working Eretz Israel. The new *Po'ale Zion* leadership consisted of Siegfried Kessler (chairman), and these members: Karl Baum, Herrmann Grün, Hans Grünberger, Oskar Huber, Jakob Morgenstern, Ernst Neumann, and Ignatz Rokach. Eldad Lindenbaum (now Tirzi) became general secretary.[195]

As soon as their internal consolidation was accomplished, *Po'ale Zion* regarded as its first objective the establishment of relations with the existing Zionist groups and organizations in the Republic. As a matter of principle they did not contemplate any contact whatever with either *Mizrahi* or the Revisionists.[196] In their relationships to the various Zionist groups they were guided by their world organization. As mentioned,[197] a decision of the Twelfth Zionist Congress enabled them, as it did all other Separate Unions, to choose their method of Zionist work in accordance with the conditions assessed by them in their respective countries. In Czechoslovakia *Po'ale Zion* decided not to join the Zionist Territorial Federation. There were, however, areas of Zionist activities in which *Po'ale Zion*, like any other Separate Union, for instance *Mizrahi*,[198] actively participated. These activities included the *Keren Hayesod*, *Keren Kayemet*, Palestine Office, Jewish and Hebrew schools, *Shekel* Commission, and similar general functions. For this purpose they entered into an agreement (as did *Mizrahi*) with the Czechoslovak Zionist Territorial Federation to have representatives in all central and local commissions which were responsible for these activities.

Po'ale Zion retained, however, complete independence as regards Czechoslovak general politics, as well as international Zionist policies and activities toward the upbuilding of the Jewish national home in Eretz Israel. Apart from *Tze'ire Zion*, which had refused to unite with *HaPo'el Hatza'ir* in 1920,[199] *Po'ale Zion* had, since the first post-World War I Zionist Congress (1921), been in strong opposition to the Zionist Executives headed by Dr. Chaim Weizmann. *Po'ale Zion* was guided in this respect by Borochov's thesis that they could not bear responsibility for Zionist work if this was performed in cooperation with the British "imperialistic" administration in Eretz Israel. "The political course of the present government in Eretz Israel is reactionary and anti-Jewish," declared the *Po'ale Zion* spokesman, Yithak Ben-Zvi (subsequently the second president of Israel) at the Twelfth Zionist Congress (1921);[200] therefore Palestine workers had no confidence in the British administration of the time. In 1925 (at the Fourteenth Zionist Congress in Vienna), *Po'ale Zion* spokesman David Ben-Gurion (subsequently first prime minister of Israel) asserted that the Zionist leadership had thus far disregarded the emergence of the Labour party in England as a governing body (it was the dominant member of the coalition government under Ramsay MacDonald) and did not foresee the unavoidable development that Labour, for long an ardent friend of Zionism, would attain a majority in British Parliament. Palestine should be prepared for such a moment.[201] The conclusion of this was apparently to point out that such a constellation would lead to a solidarity among socialist workers (Jewish and British) and thus put an end to the anti-Jewish course then still prevailing in the Palestine administration.

These principles governed the opposition policies of *Po'ale Zion* vis-à-vis the Zionist Executives in the first decade after the Balfour Declaration. By 1927 a change in these views occurred, leading to closer ties with the Weizmann policies. At the time, as already mentioned, there prevailed serious difficulties in a great number of areas of the work in Eretz Israel; above all, the economic conditions in the country adversely affected labor, which to no small degree contributed to this change.[202] All socialist groups in the Zionist Organization by then came to believe that Dr. Weizmann had found a way to financial salvation through the formation of the enlarged Jewish Agency[203] which was to include wealthy non-Zionist individuals and groups and which came officially into existence in the summer of 1929.[204] Together with the representatives of the *Hitahdut* who joined the Zionist leadership from 1921 (with the exception of the years 1927–1929), *Po'ale Zion* strengthened socialist influence in the Executive by now (1929) sending Solomon Kaplansky as a delegate to it. Thus *Po'ale Zion* assumed co-responsibility for international Zionist policies as well as all official Zionist activities in Eretz Israel. It could have been expected that this change in the World *Po'ale Zion* would also influence its branch in Czechoslovakia to join forces with other socialistic groups (remnants of *Hitahdut*) and with the General Zionists who had all along supported the policies of Dr. Weizmann's Executives. However, Czechoslovak *Po'ale Zion* even then retained independence and remained outside the Zionist Territorial Federation.

Objectively, there were no internal Zionist matters in Czechoslovakia which would have rendered *Po'ale Zion* different from the above-mentioned two constituents of the Territorial Federation. Questions of class distinction did not arise so far as Jewry or Zionist activities in the Republic were concerned. The only area where such a difference could, and in fact did, arise was in the field in political activities in the Diaspora (*Landespolitik*), to which reference has already been made.[205] *Po'ale Zion*, as a social democratic party, decided to join other social democratic parties in Czechoslovakia to strive for the fundamental socialist principles — together with working classes of all nations — to overthrow capitalism and to establish a socialist system of society. In internal Czechoslovak affairs *Po'ale Zion* had its ties with socialists, while in the upbuilding of Eretz Israel it retained its link with the Zionist Organization. Indeed, even on this basis there was no factual reason for separation from the Territorial Zionist Federation, since the Second Czechoslovak Zionist Conference (1921) had decided not to conduct Diaspora political work in the Republic but to leave this to a separate National Jewish Council (later the Jewish party).[206] Whatever the reasons of principle and practical application may have been, *Po'ale Zion* remained until 1937 outside the Zionist Territorial Federation.[207]

In that period *Po'ale Zion* was able to establish local groups, a number of them in Slovakia and Subcarpathian Ruthenia of Czechoslovakia. However, it was faced with stiff competition from other Zionist groups, in particular, socialist groups and General Zionists. These groups not only did not differ from *Po'ale Zion* in the support of the Weizmann policies but also aided all labor efforts in Eretz Israel and showed their tendencies in the designation of "Left Center," under which they presented a joint list for the elections to the Fifteenth Zionist Congress (1927).[208] Thus, none of these Zionistically almost indistinguishable parties was able to become predominant by itself.

This reflected a similar situation which prevailed in the world organizations of all these parties. While there were no objective, but probably some subjective, reasons why an alignment or even an amalgamation between these three important sectors should not be feasible, there was, on the other hand, every pressing reason for socialist groups to unite and establish a unified labor front in Zionism. The differences between the Marxist tendencies of *Po'ale Zion* and the "people's socialist" *Hitahdut* had lost their significance with the passage of years. There were many more areas of identity than of divergence. No wonder that the two principal components at that moment came seriously to consider a unification in the world movements.

It was under the growing impact of these tendencies that a similar attempt was made in Czechoslovakia when Dr. Chaim Hoffmann (Yahil) proposed at the Second *Po'ale Zion* Conference to reject the vague and misleading concept of a "Left Center" and instead bring about a unification of socialist forces.[209] While the conference adopted Hoffmann's suggestion, an open fight against "Left Center" actually never developed, and paradoxically it even led to the election of a *Po'ale Zion* delegate on that very same list.[210] *Po'ale*

Zion by itself was still too weak to put up its own list of candidates both for the Fifteenth (1927) and for the Sixteenth Zionist Congress (1929).

Meanwhile, like the Working Association of Socialist Zionists,[211] *Po'ale Zion* carried on their work independently while considering forms and ways for a united front. *Po'ale Zion* in this respect was at a greater disadvantage because of its clear-cut Diaspora political position. It was bound to collaborate with other social democratic forces in Czechoslovakia. At its Third Territorial Conference, held in Brno (June 8 and 9, 1930), the party devoted most of its deliberations to the question of a separate policy with regard to Jewish religious congregations. The principal speaker was the Viennese *Po'ale Zion* leader Mendel Singer, who outlined the policy to be pursued on the basis of the Austrian example.[212] It was decided to embark upon a policy of gaining influence in these congregations. Problems of Diaspora politics were also the main topic of the subsequent extraordinary conference held in Moravská Ostrava (September 6, 1931), at which it was decided to nominate independent *Po'ale Zion* candidates in the oncoming municipal elections in places where *Po'ale Zion* existed. In all others, members of *Po'ale Zion* were to be encouraged to try to have candidates put on the list of that social democratic party that was competing at these elections. The conference further welcomed attempts in the world movement at a unification of socialist Zionists.[213]

At the ordinary Fourth Territorial Conference, held in Bratislava (November 1, 1931), the decisions taken in Moravská Ostrava were repeated, apart from a resolution to establish a political office in Prague for political negotiations with the Prague authorities. That office was headed by Jakob Reiss. The remainder of the leadership remained in the same hands as hitherto, with the addition of Slovak members — which pointed to an increase of the organization in the eastern sector of the Republic. These new members were Dr. A. Bauer (Bratislava) and Max Freilich (Užhorod).[214]

The subsequent Territorial Conference, while dealing with daily matters of the organization's activities, had not shifted principally from its position. It was insistent on conducting separate domestic political activities, while on the Zionist front it intensified the demand for a united front. This remained the position at the Sixth Territorial Conference, held in Prague (July 5 and 6, 1934), at which thirty-six delegates from twelve local groups participated. The basic change which occurred was the strengthening of the executive seat in Prague, consisting then of Jacob Reiss, Dr. Arthur Heller, Dr. Eliezer Schächter (who was to become deputy mayor of Tel Aviv after the establishment of the State of Israel), Lederer, and E. Kaufman, while Siegfried Kessler (Brno), Rudolf Jokl (Moravská Ostrava), and Dr. A. Bauer (Bratislava) remained its provincial members.[215] Finally, at the Seventh Territorial Conference, held in Moravská Ostrava (July 5 to 7, 1935), which was predominantly devoted to the question of unity with the Working Association of Socialist Zionists, the increase of the organization to twenty-seven local groups was welcomed as a sign of growing strength, which was to be of importance at the unification deliberations.[216]

As seen from these short descriptions, unification of socialist forces in Czechoslovakia was in the air. It is remarkable how long is took to attain it. Its story is told in a separate section.[217]

(5) *HaShomer Hatza'ir*

In the strict sense of political parties, with which we deal in these pages, *HaShomer Hatza'ir* does actually not require special mention, since it was created as a youth movement in Danzig in 1925 and recognized as a Separate Union of the World Zionist Organization in 1935 only.[218] It was from the outset, and remained, a strict Palestino-centric organization, not concerned with any aspect of Diaspora activities. It did not pursue any political work and concentrated solely on the education of the young Jew for his final settlement in Eretz Israel, where he would help to build up a purely socialist society. *HaShomer Hatza'ir* geared its activities to age groups: the first up to the age of 14; the second between 14 and 17; and the third 18 and beyond.

Those 18 and older were, of course, *shekel*-payers and thus *eo ipso* members of the Zionist Organization, entitled to a vote and to all other rights of Zionist membership. In this respect, *HaShomer Hatza'ir* members were left a free hand.

This applied to the world organization of *HaShomer Hatza'ir* as well as to that in Czechoslovakia. There it came into existence in 1927; within ten years it was to become the strongest youth movement within the Zionist Organization in the Republic. It had fifty units and 4,000 members, primarily in Slovakia and Subcarpathian Ruthenia.[219] Having had a free choice, its members over 18 mostly supported *HaPo'el Hatza'ir* (*Hitahdut*) in Czechoslovakia and participated as a special youth group at the conferences of the Working Association of Socialist Zionists. All adult members of *HaShomer Hatza'ir* were active in the League for a Working Eretz Israel and in the *HeHalutz* movement.

When in 1935 *HaShomer Hatza'ir* was recognized as a Separate Union of the Zionist Organization, this had no impact whatever on the socialist Zionist movements in Czechoslovakia, since it did not attempt even then to create a political organization in the Republic. As hitherto, members of *HaShomer Hatza'ir* remained free in their choice of support of socialist Zionist groupings. Because of this position, *HaShomer Hatza'ir* could not and did not affiliate with the Zionist Territorial Federation, even when the *IHUD* became its constituent and *Po'ale Zion* had joined it in 1937.[220]

(6) *United Socialist Zionists* (*IHUD*)

As indicated in the preceding sections, a common denominator of the activities of *HaPo'el Hatza'ir* (*Hitahdut*) and *Po'ale Zion* was the continuous desire to unite all socialist Zionist elements in Czechoslovakia. Not a single one of their local or Territorial Conferences passed by without adopting a resolution emphasizing the importance of unity and calling on the leadership to work toward it. But as years passed by it became obvious that from within these Czechoslovak groupings this much-desired unity would never arise. It was not the ideological differences (Marxism and/or people's socialism) that kept them apart but rather the traditional position concerning the Zionist Territorial Federation (*HaPo'el Hatza'ir* inside, *Po'ale Zion* outside), the peculiar "power" struggle for the control of the Palestine Office, *HeHalutz*, and the League for a Working Eretz Israel. Ideological differences had almost disappeared in the middle twenties, and what remained as a reminder of old differences, when *Po'ale Zion* reorganized itself in 1928, was solely the aspect of Diaspora political activities.

Under these circumstances, when unity was unattainable from within, it would have to come from above, i.e., from the world leadership of these parties, and to be, so to say, morally enforced on the Czechoslovak organizations (like on those of other countries where similar conditions prevailed). The great crisis in Palestine in the second half of the 1920s, to which repeated reference has been made, was predominantly instrumental in speeding this development.[221]

It will be recalled that the first great unification conference of socialist Zionists took place in 1920 in Prague when *HaPo'el Hatza'ir* and *Tze'ire Zion* created a united organization — *Hitahdut*.[222] This unity was created out of the ideological identity of both these groupings. Also in the realm of an ideological amalgamation was the unification of *Po'ale Zion* and the section of *Tze'ire Zion* which, since the Prague conference in 1920, had continued to pursue independent activities. The leaderships of these two parties met during the Fourteenth Zionist Congress in Vienna (1925) and decided to unite in one organization under the name of *Ahdut HaAvoda*.[223]

But now, in consequence of the great changes that the economic crisis in Palestine, the Arab attack of 1929, and the creation of the enlarged Jewish Agency had caused in Zionist thinking and life, the Eretz Israel sections of these two major socialist Zionist unions within the Zionist Organization met at a conference in Tel Aviv with the purpose of finding a common platform. This conference took place on January 5–7, 1930, and centered around the two programmatic speeches by Joseph Sprinzak (for *Hitahdut*) and David Ben-Gurion (for *Ahdut HaAvoda*). The unification of both Palestine parties under the new name *Mifleget Po'ale Eretz Israel* (Eretz Israel Labor party), for short called MAPAI,[224] was agreed upon.[225]

While this was a decision of two local parties, nevertheless because it occurred in Eretz Israel it was only a matter of time before the world leadership followed this important initiative, for after a unity of the front there was not much sense in the same parties remaining separated in the hinterland. After all, the Diaspora branches were primarily concerned with the advancement and support of their Eretz Israel sectors. However, it took almost two years before the world organizations of these two socialist Zionist movements in the Zionist Organization were able to unite on a worldwide basis. The *Po'ale Zion* headquarters were at that time in Warsaw and those of *Hitahdut* in Lodz (both in Poland). Both parties called their respective world conferences in 1931, and both conferences endorsed the necessity of unification, based on the Palestine example. Negotiations between the two leaderships commenced soon thereafter but lasted until May 1932, when, at the conference of their representatives in Lwow (Poland), an agreement was initialed to establish one united socialist Zionist organization (*IHUD*). Their agreement was finally endorsed at the joint world conference of both parties in Danzig in August 1932.[226]

The program adopted in Danzig showed elements of an ideological compromise between the two streams in socialist Zionism, but on the whole there cannot be any doubt that the *Po'ale Zion* concept became predominant in a number of important areas. The *IHUD*, as the program stated, as part of the international working class, fought capitalist economic system and of every form of social exploitation, and for the establishment of a socialist economy. To strengthen its endeavor and to express its solidarity, *IHUD* joined the Second Internationale. It fought for these socialist principles in the Eretz Israel reality as well as in the lands of the Diaspora. While *IHUD* thus regarded itself an integral part of the international working class, it was simultaneously an integral part of the Zionist Organization, where it enjoyed the status of a Separate Union.[227] As a Zionist party it endeavored to imbue the Jewish youth with the idea of *Halutziut*, in which it saw the most realistic way to the upbuilding of a socialist Eretz Israel. In countries where Hebrew was the language of the Jewish masses, *IHUD* fought for the recognition of Hebrew as the language of the Jewish minority; where Yiddish was that language, *IHUD* fought for its recognition. The parties of *IHUD* conducted their independent policies in the general Jewish life. Its territorial organizations were entitled to conclude election agreements with other parties or groups, subject to the provision that the principles of *IHUD* and the interests of the Jewish working masses were safeguarded.[228]

As can be seen from the above sketchy outline of the program, it contained a sufficient number of elements which were apt to make the establishment of *IHUD* in Czechoslovakia extremely difficult. Both parties, as we have seen in the sections describing their activities, had set principles as regards class struggle, Hebrew and Yiddish, Diaspora politics, and it was up to them to find ways and means to overcome these difficulties on Czechoslovak territory. They became increasingly aware of the fact that negotiations or dialogues on these issues would not lead to the desired results. The idea then emerged to put aside ideological or political talks and try by way of practical steps to reach unity in specific areas.

The most appropriate first step in this direction appeared to be a united list of candidates for the elections to the next Zionist Congress. This would, so it was hoped, demonstrate the strength of socialist Zionism and thus establish its importance in Czechoslovak Zionism.

We have noticed the general dissatisfaction among socialist Zionists with the election arrangements entered into with the Zionist Territorial Federation for the Fifteenth and Sixteenth Zionist Congresses.[229] Now the Seventeenth Congress was approaching (Basle, June 30 to July 15, 1931), an opportune moment for a first attempt at a joint effort. At this moment a coup occurred which seriously impaired the unification efforts.

In May of that year it was announced[230] that a list of candidates for the congress elections, under the name of "Working Eretz Israel," had been submitted and approved. The candidates were Dr. Adolf Grünfeld, Hans Gross, Dr. Chaim Hoffmann, Ferdinand Kraus, Gora Schliesser, and Viktor Zaitschek. A week later an announcement in *Selbstwehr*,[231] signed by Jakob Edelstein and Oskar Karpe, stated that the list was compiled without the cooperation of the Working Association of Socialist Zionists, but in view of the grave situation in the Zionist Organization and in Eretz Israel there would be no separate list of the Working Association. The members were advised to vote for the only list of socialist Zionism.

At an emergency meeting of the Working Association held in Prague on June 21,[232] it came to light that the list of candidates for the congress was the result of private negotiations between leaders of *Po'ale Zion* and some members of the group of the Working Association in Brno (Moravia). The "independent" coup was condemned by the conference and the resignation of Dr. Grünfeld accepted. It was further decided that the Working Association "is the only association of all socialist Zionist elements in the Czechoslovak Zionist Territorial Federation." A new leadership was elected (without any Brno member) consisting of Jakob Edelstein, E. Fuchs, Dr. Heinz Guttenstein, Oskar Karpe (all Prague), and Max Oliner (Teplice-Šanov).

Dr. Grünfeld, in self-defense, declared that he acted properly as a member of *Hitahdut*. As there was no *Hitahdut* organization in Czechoslovakia, the Brno group was its sole representative.[233]

The results of the elections were rather disappointing to the new bloc. It received 2,243 votes and two delegates out of a total of 9,830 votes and eleven delegates.[234] It was thus clear that, notwithstanding the appeal by Edelstein and Karpe, the socialist electorate did not follow their advice. This was a bad omen for unification in Czechoslovakia.

The year 1932 came with its important decision at the joint conference in Danzig,[235] but in Czechoslovakia there was still no move to implement these decisions. The *Report* of the Zionist Executive to the Eighteenth Zionist Congress (Prague, August 21 to September 4, 1933) stated[236] that there existed a united party in Czechoslovakia[237] but there was also "another group of socialist Zionists, who belong to the general Zionist Territorial Federation.[238] The negotiations with this group for unity have not led to the desired success, because there exist principal and organizational difficulties."

But as the elections to the Prague Congress neared, the two groups were able to forget their differences and disagreements and decide on a joint list of candidates. The Brno group of *Hitahdut*, which played so important a role in the previous elections, was completely disregarded, and the united list recorded a gigantic victory by obtaining 5,476 votes and three delegates out of a total of 16,246 votes and nine delegates.[239]

One would have thought that on the basis of this example of success the door to complete unity was now opened, but this was not yet to be. On the eve of the congress, Jakob Edelstein, the then moving spirit of the Working Association of Socialist Zionists, published an article[240] in which he called for the establishment of a proper and strong organization of the hitherto loose Working Association with the object of remaining in the Zionist Territorial Federation which, in his opinion, should be converted into a proper federation comprising all groupings within the Zionist Organization in the Republic. This was clearly aimed at *Po'ale Zion*, then outside the federation. And he added: "We welcome the unification of the world organizations. The local *Po'ale Zion* was unfortunately not willing to surrender egoistic party advantages. The Working Association of Socialist Zionists has hitherto avoided becoming a really rigid party, in order not to make the attainment of *IHUD* more difficult; but to my regret I must confess that just the fact of the lack of a proper organization is continuously misused by *Po'ale Zion* to boast of their own strength. The last elections have shown clearly that *Po'ale Zion* comprises only a fraction of socialist Zionists in the country, and that the Working Association of Socialist Zionists, together with *Tehelet Lavan* and *HaShomer Hatza'ir*,[241] constitute the actual heart of socialist Zionism in Czechoslovakia."

Positions such as these and their airing in public made the task of unity still more difficult, of course, but the remarkable sense of practical interests seems to have again overcome these deep gaps between the two groups, when the elections to the Nineteenth Zionist Congress (Lucerne, August 20 to September 4, 1935) neared. They again put up a joint list and gained another striking victory by receiving 7,198 votes and five delegates, out of a total of 17,620 votes and eleven delegates.[242] The lead among parties of the Zionist Organization in Czechoslovakia, which they had established in 1933,[243] was not only maintained but strengthened, not to be taken away from them by any other party until the end of the period under review.

It was at Lucerne, during the congress days, that representatives of both Czechoslovak groups met in conference (August 26, 1935) and took the final step toward unity in the Republic.[244] *Po'ale Zion* was represented by Karl Baum (Brno) and Dr. Arthur Heller (Prague), the Working Association of Socialist Zionists by Jakob Edelstein (Prague) and Dr. Chaim Kugel (Mukačevo). They decided to adopt the Danzig basis of *IHUD*[245] and to call a joint conference "as soon as possible," and establish *IHUD* in Czechoslovakia.

But the "as soon as possible" was to be almost another two years. The conference was not yet called when the elections to the Twentieth Zionist Congress (Zurich, August 3 to 21, 1937) induced them to submit another joint list of candidates for the elections, which again confirmed their numerical lead in the Zionist Organization of Czechoslovakia. They obtained 4,331 votes and five delegates out of a total of 12,148 votes and twelve delegates.[246]

Three months later, on November 27 and 28, 1937, the first and founding conference of *IHUD* in Czechoslovakia took place in Prostějov (Moravia). Eighty delegates from all over the Republic attended. Dr. Arye Tartakower, of the World Executive of *IHUD*, delivered the principal address, and the program of the new party was presented by Jakob Edelstein and Dr. Chaim Hoffmann. At the conference there was a dramatic moment when Dov Biegun asked the delegates to omit the word "Labor" from the name of the new organization ("Labor party"), and this was carried by a majority of one. The *Po'ale Zion* stalwarts Siegfried Kessler (Brno), Julius Hut (Olomouc), and Ladislaus Süss (Moravská Ostrava) left the hall[247] in protest, but reconciliation efforts bore fruit and a joint leadership was elected with headquarters in Prague. The central office was headed by Jakob Edelstein, Dr. Chaim Hoffmann, and Jakob Reiss. Members of the Executive were Fini Brada, Dr. Kurt Grünberger, Dr. Wolf Guttmann, Dr. Arthur Heller, Oskar Karpe, Ludwig Kaufmann, Dr. Salamon Sokolovič, Jaromir Winternitz, and Ben Josef. In addition, a council, consisting of twenty-eight members from all parts of Czechoslovakia, was elected.

In accordance with the Danzig program, whereby each territorial group remained free to decide on its political activities in the Diaspora, *Po'ale Zion* in Czechoslovakia, even after the formation of *IHUD*, retained its traditional position in this respect,[248] but by 1938 its representative in the Zionist Territorial Federation, Dr. Chaim Hoffmann, submitted proposals for remolding political Diaspora activities which, if adopted, would have established a fully united front of all groups and members of the Zionist Territorial Federation. This program could not be put into practice however. It was the last year of the First Czechoslovak Republic.

Similarly, there is no possibility of ascertaining and evaluating the impact of *IHUD* on the Zionist Organization in the Republic. In fact, it had no chance of proving itself.

(7) *Mizrahi* *

The formal reason for the establishment of *Mizrahi* within the Zionist Organization was a negative one. When in 1901 the democratic faction at the Fifth Zionist Congress presented its demands, which centered round the expansion of the hitherto political program of Zionism into cultural spheres, Orthodox members of the up to that time unified Zionist World Organization rose in opposition. "What sort of culture," they asked, "is it that Zionism is to pursue?" There was no doubt about its essence — a wide contrast to the traditional beliefs of Orthodox Jewry, for whom "culture" and "religion" were synonymous. The leaders of the democratic faction — Martin Buber, Berthold Feiwel, Leo Motzkin, Dr. Weizmann, and their friends — were men who had abandoned Orthodox beliefs

* [The manuscript designated by the author as "final" did not include the sections on *Mizrahi* and *Zionist-Revisionists*. The following two sections are reproduced verbatim from an earlier version of the manuscript which does not contain any annotations. We decided to publish them "as is" because of their inherent value for the future historian (Ed.)]

and practices; if their cultural program was to become an integral part of Zionism, it could only be one free from traditional religious tenets. To safeguard these tenets Rabbi Reines of Lydda, an old and staunch adherent of Herzl's, assembled his friends in Wilna (1901) and took the first preliminary steps for the organization of the religious counterforce against these attempts.

There was also another "negative" element which probably strengthened the desire to close the ranks in a separate religious organization. Two distinct camps of religious Jews had stood outside the Zionist Organization and, in fact, had fought bitterly against it — in the name of Jewish religion. There were, first, the ultra-Orthodox who, while believing in the ultimate restoration in Eretz Israel, regarded any cooperation with "atheistic" and "unbelieving" elements, even for the sake of the Jewish future, as prohibitive according to Jewish tradition. Some elements among them regarded it as sinful even to commence any practical steps toward that restoration without waiting for the Messiah and relying on God "to bring His people back in His own time and with His own hands."

Besides these religious elements, which were deeply rooted in tradition in its strictest sense, there were Jews who insisted on Jewry's being a religious community only, without any trace of ethnic or national characteristics; and they maintained that because of this identification with a religious community, Jews were neither justified nor right in aiming at restoration of a Jewish nation in their own State.

This, then, was a controversy as to the meaning of Jewish religion and its role, both in Jewish nationalism and in assimilationism; and it was up to those in the Zionist Organization to concentrate on efforts to convince the elements who believed (or very often pretended to believe) in Jewish religion of the correctness of the Zionist concept.

Accordingly, *Mizrahi* had to fight on two principal fronts: internally, within the Zionist Organization, against all attempts at reducing it to a worldly cultural movement; and, externally, by winning over to Zionism as many as possible of those who believed in religion.

These were only the formal and external factors which led to the establishment of *Mizrahi* and to its struggle on the mentioned two fronts. There were, in fact, deeper motives which went to the roots of Jewish history and religious tradition, which to no small degree caused the emergence of a movement such as *Mizrahi* — for individual religious members of the Zionist Organization saw in Zionism the *realistic* practical possibility for the fulfillment of what they, based on the promises of God through His prophets, in their religious creed hoped and prayed for. For them, religion formed the basic ideology, not Zionism; but Zionism was its political instrument for realization. Viewed from this vantage point it is obvious that *Mizrahi* could not be satisfied with remaining a watchman over religious practices or their neglect in the Zionist Organization, or with proving to adversaries in the non-Zionist religious camps that Zionism and religion were compatible and, indeed, complementary. From its Zionist viewpoint *Mizrahi* recognized the destructive tendencies which in the Diaspora, by necessity, must lead to Jewry's internal dissolution, including Orthodoxy. Therefore, the re-establishment of national independence was recognized as an unconditional precondition of a truly living future of Jewry and Judaism.

But "what kind of independence?" *Mizrahi* leaders asked themselves. They recognized one concept only: the Jewish people could be preserved only by an independent state in Eretz Israel based on the understanding that Jewish religious tradition and law are indissolubly inherent in Jewish peoplehood and that, accordingly, the preservation of the Jewish people through independence in Eretz Israel was only possible if the Torah dominated the life of the people there, and through this strong center also helped strengthen Diaspora Jewry. The very name of the organization indicates this aim: MerkaZ RuCHanI (spiritual center). Its program was simply formulated: "*Mizrahi* is an association of Zionists which strives for the realization of the Basle Program on the basis of and in accordance with tradition and Jewish law." *Mizrahi* was the "religious Zionist" group whose motto was *Eretz Yisrael le-am Yisrael al pi Torat Yisrael* (The Land of Israel for the People of Israel in Accordance with the Torah of Israel).

Thus from its inception *Mizrahi* demanded on this basis the application of traditional religious, cultural, and legal concepts in the upbuilding of Eretz Israel as the Jewish land, and the creation of establishments in which these concepts were to be activated.

Mizrahi had no easy way, both in the Zionist Organization and in the Jewish world. Seen retrospectively it did not succeed in either of its original purposes — within and outside the Zionist Organization. Large sectors of the Zionist Organization remained unconcerned about religious matters, and large sectors of Orthodox Jewry were not won over to Zionism. But its impact in cultural and educational fields was strong and, notwithstanding bitterness and resentment in nonreligious circles, *Mizrahi* was able to succeed in many fields, such as the acceptance of the observation of the Shabbath and the adherence to *kashruth* in Zionist official activities and functions, apart from its own practical achievements in Eretz Israel, in a series of settlements and important economic, financial, educational, and other institutions.

Mizrahi in Czechoslovakia dated back to the beginnings of the movement. The very first International and Founding Conference of *Mizrahi* was held in Bratislava (August 21–23, 1904), as mentioned before.* One of its organizers and member of the conference presidium was Samuel Bettelheim (Bratislava), who unswervingly served his party for many years. *Mizrahi* in those areas which were part of Hungary, maintained its independence from 1910, having then left the Hungarian Zionist Territorial Union. There were individual adherents, and some small groups even existed throughout World War I which were "ready" for a renewal of activities when, in 1918, Czechoslovakia was proclaimed. The most active among these groups was that of Bratislava, and it was due to the initiative of its secretary, Moshe Itzhak Müller, that Bratislava assumed the territorial leadership soon after the Czechoslovak Zionists had assembled at their first conference in Prague in 1919.† Chairman of the first and temporary *Mizrahi* leadership in the Republic became Dr. Siegfried Steiner, with Moshe I. Müller as secretary. The other members of that committee were Rabbi Moshe Asher Eckstein (later Chief Rabbi in Sered), Simon Fisch, Wilhelm Fischer, Joseph Grünberg, Salamon Hornig, Menachem Katzburg, Franz Lipkovitz, Rabbi Chajim Rosenzweig, Dr. Baruch Tomaschoff, B. Turk, Rabbi Hillel Unsdorfer (later Chief Rabbi in Lučenec), and Rabbi Schemuel Weinreb.

Their task was a difficult one. Organizationally, the *Mizrahi* World Organization was recognized as a Separate Union within the World Zionist Movement. In accordance with its status, *Mizrahi*, as branch of the world organization, did not join the Czechoslovak Zionist

---

* See p. 25.

† [July 26–27, 1919 (Ed.)]

Territorial Union and therefore attempted to build up its own organization. Its strength lay primarily in the eastern sector of the Republic, and the Zionist leadership which set out in 1919 to organize Zionism in the Republic recognized this fact. This led to some regional and other cooperation which turned out most useful for the cause. Thus, when a new Zionist district was to be established in 1920 in Subcarpathian Ruthenia and the Zionist Organization there was only in an embryonic state, the leadership approached *Mizrahi*, asking them to agree to the establishment of a joint Zionist district under the name "Zionist-*Mizrahi* District." A further agreement was reached for the collaboration in those fields where cooperation was wise and useful, such as *Keren Kayemet*, *Keren Hayesod*, Palestine Offices, and others. *Mizrahi* had representations in each of the commissions heading these institutions. Cooperation went also in another direction. In contrast to the then only other Separate Union in Czechoslovakia, *Po'ale Zion*, *Mizrahi* had no interest in a separate Jewish *Landespolitik*, but supported throughout the Jewish National Council and subsequent Jewish party, in both of which it had its representative members.

Mizrahi did not develop in Czechoslovakia an organization in the sense and in the form of other Zionist organizations, notwithstanding all the attempts made throughout the twenty years — till 1939 — of its existence. It was a closely knit yet organizationally rather loose association of individuals and of a number of local groups.

It was with these individuals and groups that the temporary leadership in Bratislava established contact, and it testifies to the zeal and enthusiasm of these few that resounding successes could be registered. They became apparent at the first regular Territorial Conference which was held in Košice (May 16–20, 1920), attended by 120 delegates from 48 local groups. Dr. Siegfried Steiner was there confirmed as president, and Moshe I. Müller as secretary. Bratislava was also retained as the seat of the Czechoslovak *Mizrahi* leadership. The new Executive Committee regarded as its primary objective the expansion of the movement not only in Slovakia and Subcarpathian Ruthenia but also in the western sector. Success in Bohemia and Moravia-Silesia was, however, limited for reasons which were mentioned above, and remained so. One can, in fact, refer to local *Mizrahi* groups only in Brno, Moravská Ostrava and Opava (Moravia-Silesia), and Prague.

It was also this leadership which prepared and carried out the elections of the first postwar Zionist Congress in Karlovy Vary (1921). At this congress the *Mizrahi* World Organization emerged as the strongest Zionist party. It had ninety-five delegates (22 per cent) out of a total of 440. The Czechoslovak *Mizrahi* considerably outpaced its mother organization. It had at that congress three delegates (34 per cent) out of a total of nine. The picture changed, however, at the subsequent congress. In 1923, World *Mizrahi* had seventy delegates (24 per cent) out of a total of 292, while the Czechoslovak *Mizrahi* declined to one delegate (20 per cent) out of a total of five. Up to the end of its existence Czechoslovak *Mizrahi* never again attained its strength of its proportional representation at the Twelfth Congress (1921). At the last congress (1937) it had three delegates (25 per cent) out of a total of twelve (see Appendix C).

(8) *Zionist-Revisionists*

As the name "Union of Zionist Revisionists" (Hebrew: *Brith HaTziyonim HaRevisionistim*, abbreviated *Brith HaTzohar* or *HaTzohar*) indicates, the basis of this party's formation had no religious, socialistic, or any other external motive, only a purely Zionistic one. The name "revisionism" was intended as a transitory term which was to be abandoned once the "revision" at which it was aiming was accomplished. *HaTzohar* strove for a revision of the overall Zionist policies and their ideological basis, as they had developed after World War I under the guidance of Dr. Chaim Weizmann. It stood for a return to the original Zionist political conception enunciated by Theodor Herzl and the first Zionist Congresses. The spiritual and organizational father of Revisionism was Vladimir (Z'ev) Jabotinsky (1880–1940).

Two factors influenced Jabotinsky in developing the Revisionist program: a negative and a positive one. They were (1) the anti-Zionist tendency which from the beginning characterized the British administration in Eretz Israel; and (2) the conviction that political success was possible even against overwhelming odds, as shown by his own experience in World War I with the creation of the Jewish Legion, which fought alongside the Allies in the conquest of Eretz Israel.

Although during the two years of the military administration in Eretz Israel (1918–1920) it was generally assumed that its anti-

Zionist poicy was based on military and strategic considerations, Jabotinsky had spoken up against both the attitude of this administration and its acceptance by the Zionist leadership as a traditional regime, not representative of official British policy. When, however, the civilian administration under Sir Herbert Samuel was established in 1920, it became evident that Jabotinsky's fears were well founded. The British military administration's anti-Zionist attitude was taken over by the British Mandatory government, and this led Jabotinsky to the conviction that one could not count on the fulfillment of the British promises made to the Zionists. It was characteristic of Jabotinsky that he reached his conclusion on the basis of Sir Herbert Samuel's first official act: the dissolution of the Jewish Legion. Jabotinsky regarded the legion's presence in Eretz Israel as the basis of a secure Jewish colonization of the land and of the *Yishuv's* self-defense. Its removal, he believed, made both the *Yishuv* and the colonization work a prey to a willful British policy and to Arab onslaughts.

In 1920, when Jabotinsky organized Jewish self-defense during an Arab riot, he was imprisoned and only freed in response to a worldwide wave of indignant protests. All this Jabotinsky recognized as the first signals. The others followed in quick succession: the Arab riots (of 1920 and 1921) were not only tolerated but rewarded by a stoppage of Jewish immigration, which had been the original motive of the riot's instigators; one of them, Hajj Amin el-Husseini, was appointed by Sir Herbert Samuel to the post of Grand Mufti of Jerusalem, in which position he was the *de facto* head of the Palestine Muslims (in World War II he directed anti-Jewish propaganda among Arabs from Berlin); Crown land, which according to the Palestine Mandate was to be given to Jews for settlement, was instead given to Arabs; the high commissioner submitted proposals (subsequently incorporated into the British White Paper of 1922) which put limitations of the Jewish national home, on the political status of the Zionists, and on Jewish immigration, and it became the basis in 1923 of the partition of Palestine area into Cis- and Transjordan.

These were, in Jabotinsky's opinion, most alarming danger signals for the future. At first he believed in the possibility of remedy from within. Having reached an agreement with Dr. Weizmann, president of the World Zionist Organization, he joined the Zionist World Executive (1921–1923) but was unable to persuade his colleagues in that body to undertake those bold steps which he regarded as imperative. In 1923 Jabotinsky resigned from the Executive and left the Zionist Organization.

A number of former Russian Zionists gathered around Jabotinsky in Berlin and organized a group of "Zionist Activists" (October 1923). Encouraged by the enthusiasm of this circle and of other young Zionists in many European countries which he had visited on his lecture tours, Jabotinsky reopened the battle for his ideas. Shortly thereafter he rejoined the Zionist Organization (1924) and called a conference to Paris, where he then settled. At that conference (April 25, 1925) the "Union of Zionist Revisionists" was founded. No Czechoslovak delegate participated.

By this time it had become clear to Jabotinsky and to his colleagues that the organization of an opposition against single measures in Eretz Israel would not suffice to effect a change. Their conclusion was that the entire Zionist policy must be geared to the ultimate purpose and aim of Zionism; thus they decided that a full revision of contemporary Zionism was urgently needed, with regard to both ideology and practical work. To this end they devised a comprehensive program which can be summarized as follows:

Zionism aims at the total solution of the Jewish problem in all its aspects: political, economic, and spiritual. It means, therefore, independent statehood as enunciated by Herzl, which will enable Jewry to enact its own legislation so as to achieve this aim. To achieve statehood, as many Jews as are able and wish to must settle in Eretz Israel. To make their settlement possible, the area must be sufficiently large and therefore the whole of Palestine, as provided in the Mandate (i.e., both Cis- and Transjordan), must be available. While immigration, settlement, and colonization are practical and economic matters, they can only be attained through the instrumentality of political power, because they require the active assistance of sovereign power at every phase of development and progress. Accordingly, Zionism is, in the Revisionist concept, a political movement, striving to create and to secure those political conditions without which colonization, leading to independence, is impossible.

All this re-echoed Herzl's Zionist maxim: *"Wir schaffen Bedingungen, nicht Dinge"* (we create conditions, not things). In the Revisionist view, the Mandatory power, which represented the temporary state power, could not remain neutral, but must purpose an active policy as the Mandate foresaw ("to *secure* the establishment of the

Jewish national home," etc.) in order "to facilitate Jewish immigration." The Mandatory power must take legislative and administrative measures calculated to assist in the achievement of the Zionist aims.

What these measures were to be constituted the central part of the Revisionist program. Jabotinsky summarized them by the term "colonization regime" (in contrast to Britain's "colonial regime"), which foresaw:

(1) As a precondition, a friendly Palestine administration to consist of officials who recognized the upbuilding of the Jewish national home as the basis of the administration's policy.
(2) Immigration regulated by the Zionist Organization.
(3) Land reform, based on the transfer to the State of the ownership of all uncultivated or inadequately cultivated land in order to form a "land reserve" for agricultural settlement.
(4) This land reserve to serve as security for an international loan to be raised.
(5) To allow colonization to proceed smoothly, a radical reform of taxation, customs' duties, transportation, and trade policy to be carried out to protect local industries; this reform to be based on the requirements of the developing country.
(6) To maintain order and secure peaceful develooment, the disbanded Jewish Legion to be reorganized. Only individuals whose loyalty to the Mandate was beyond reproach to be allowed to join the Palestine police force. Simultaneously, the Jewish youth both in Eretz Israel and in the Diaspora to receive military training for these tasks.
(7) In the process of development work, the rights of non-Jews in Eretz Israel not to be infringed on; land settlement not to be effected through the replacement of Arabs by Jews, but only through the expansion of arable land.
(8) In the period preceding the establishment of the State only one social law to exist in the land, that of upbuilding.

To this concept, termed "monism" by Jabotinsky, all interests of individuals, groups, and classes were to be subordinated. Differences were to be settled not by strikes, lockouts, boycotts, or other methods which would result in a slowdown of the upbuilding process but by arbitration, both on the state and local levels, through impartial judges (tribunals) selected from all elements of the production branch concerned.

The problem was how to persuade the Mandatory power to introduce the "colonization regime." Jabotinsky and his colleagues believed that this could be attained by what he termed a "political offensive." This was, in fact, an enlarged and intensified version of his political struggle for the creation of the Jewish Legion in World War I, referred to before. Its guideline was: "A minister's 'No' is not a nation's definite and final answer." Britain, the Revisionist leadership emphasized time and again in this new struggle for Jewish rights, would also not be persuaded by threats, "force" or declarations of war, but only by an all-powerful moral pressure. This meant that the aim of Zionism had to be stated uncompromisingly and with untiring regularity; it had to be made clear that no interpretation which implied a whittling down of Jewish needs and Britain's obligations was acceptable; manifestations on an international scale had to be embarked upon so as to show to the world that Jews suffered because of Britain's failure to fulfill her duty, even if this irritated the British authorities; simultaneously, the world had to be shown that the countries were Jews lived also suffered, because their Jewish citizens lived in misery — and for this, too, Britain's retreat from her duty bore full responsibility. The international community and the countries primarily concerned had to be invited to assist in a direct approach to Britain, as well as through the League of Nations, to which Britain was responsible for carrying out the Palestine Mandate; these sentiments had to be impressed upon public opinion in Britain herself, for it was public opinion which ruled the country rather than the government of the day.

To propagate these thoughts, from 1924 on Jabotinsky visited many European lands to win adherents. In the spring of 1924 he also went to Czechoslovakia. A small group in Brno gathered round him (Hans Löw, Leo Pollak, and Oskar Rabinowicz), and they set out, soon after, to organize the Revisionist movement in the Republic. Subsequently, Löw and Rabinowicz attended the Revisionist Conference held during the Fourteenth Zionist Chngress in Vienna (1925), where they reported on the official foundation of the *Union der Zionisten-Revisionisten in der ČSR*, with local groups in Bratislava, Brno, Moravská Ostrava, and Prague. In November 1925, during Jabotinsky's second visit to Brno, the First Territorial Revisionist Conference was held, at which Dr. Rabinowicz was elected chairman and Hans Löw secretary. The Executive Board consisted of Karl Baum, Leo Hickl, and Leo Pollak. Soon thereafter, Leo Baumgarten joined the Executive and represented Czechoslovakia (1926–1928) in the World Council of the Revisionist movement. He was elected to this position at the Second Revisionist World Conference (Paris, December 26–30, 1926), in which Hans Löw participated as the only delegate from Czechoslovakia. The Brno weekly *Jüdische Volksstimme* (published by Hugo Gold) opend its pages to the propagation of the new organization. At the founding conference in Brno (1925) it was resolved to join, not individually but as a group, the Czechoslovak Zionist Territorial Union and to participate in all activities. (This membership was to last until 1932, when the Revisionists seceded from the union.) In July 1926 five Revisionists attended the Czechoslovak Zionist Territorial Conference in Brno, and two members, Löw and Rabinowicz, were elected to the Central Committee.

With the help of guest speakers from abroad, the Revisionists now embarked upon an intensive propaganda of their ideas, touching critically on every aspect of Zionist ideology and practical work in Eretz Israel and in the Diaspora. Heated debates ensued, in whose cause it became evident that all other Zionist parties and groups had, to a large extent, common interests and identical approaches to Zionist issues. They became thus an almost unified force against Revisionism. The intensity and bitterness of this controversy grew as years passed and new developments were used by both sides for "proving" their case. An added reason for the bitterness was the growth of membership in the Revisionist organization. This was the situation not only in Czechoslovakia but in the Zionist world movement as a whole.

On November 13, 1927, the Second Revisionist Conference took place in Brno attended by representatives from local groups in all parts of the Republic. Julius Grosz (Bratislava) announced at the conference the establishment of the youth organization *Brit Trumpeldor* (*Betar*), which was to become the core and soul of Revisionist activities in Czechoslovakia. A complete reorganization of the movement was decided upon at the Third Revisionist Conference, held in Bratislava on December 23, 1928. The secretariat headed by Löw was moved to Prague, while the presidency (Rabinowicz) remained in Brno. A few days later, at the Third Revisionist World Conference (Vienna, December 26–30, 1928), Rabinowicz reported on the progress to date; there were twenty-two groups in Czechoslovakia with a registered membership of 655. In addition, there were twenty separate local *Betar* groups with a membership of 1,500. In the spring of 1929, the presidency (and Dr. Rabinowicz) moved to Bratislava to be closer to the Jewish masses in the eastern sector of Czechoslovakia.

In that same year the Revisionists submitted for the first time a list to the Zionist Congress elections and obtained 571 votes and no delegate (out of a total of 7,044 votes and nine delegates). At the Ninth Zionist Territorial Conference (December 25 and 26, 1929) Revisionists had thirty-nine delegates, elected in a bitterly fought campaign. Eight Revisionists, out of a total of forty members, were elected to the Central Committee. They were Leo Baumgarten, Dr. L. L. Gottesmann, Julius Grosz, Dr. Martin Lichtner, Hans Löw, Dr. Rabinowicz, Dr. Alexander Spiegel, and Béla Szerényi.

At the time, besides the *Jüdische Volkstimme*, a weekly published in Hungarian in Užhorod (ed. Béla Szerényi) the *Zsidó Néplap* also became an organ of the party.

Soon thereafter, at the elections to the Seventeenth Zionist Congress (1931), the Revisionists received 2,056 votes and two delegates (Dr. Rabinowicz and Hans Löw), out of a total of 9,830 votes and eleven delegates.

Simultaneously, the internal upbuilding of the organization from one of opposition to an all-embracing party proceeded apace both in the world movemen and in Czechoslovak organization. *B'rith Hachayal* (headed by Julius Grosz and Berci Bäck, Bratislava) was formed as a "sector of veterans within the movement." *B'rith Yeshurun* (headed by Hochauser (Frank Horny) and E. Weinberger, Košice) was formed as the religious wing in the organization, *B'rith Nashim Leumiyoth* (headed by Mrs. O. Rabinowicz and Mrs. E. Kohn, Prague), the movement's women's organization; but above all, an independent financial instrument was created — this was the *Keren Tel Hai* (headed by A'exander Rabbinowitz, Hranice), which was to be complementary to the existing Zion st funds, the *Keren Hayesod* (for settlement) and *Keren Kayemet* (for acquisition of land). *Keren Tel Hai* served the preparation and education of youth in the Diaspora for self-defense and for the support of the national labor movement in Eretz Israel.

In 1932 the Revisionists World Union was recognized as a Separate Union, and the Czechoslovak organization had the choice of either remaining in a position similar to that of the other two separate

Zionist organizations in Czechoslovakia, *Mizrahi* and *Po'ale Zion* or joining the Territorial Union.

All these efforts at reorganization were paralyzed, however, by the internal controversy that had broken out in the Revisionist world leadership. The controversy revolved around the question of whether or not to remain in the Zionist Organization. The opponents of secession, headed by Meir Grossman, Richard Lichtheim, Robert Stricker, Selig Soskin, and others, argued that there was a possibility of carrying out both the Revisionist program and the struggle for control of the Zionist Organization; they pointed to the fact that at the 1925 Zionist Congress the Revisionists had four delegates, in 1927 six delegates, in 1929 nine delegates, in 1931 forty-seven delegates, and that this indicated the road to victory. They further stressed that after the election of Nahum Sokolow to the presidency of the World Zionist Organization, which took place at the 1931 congress with the help of Revisionist votes, a new era may have commenced, even though no Revisionist had joined the new Executive. Moreover, for both moral sentimental reasons they should remain in the organization founded by Theodor Herzl, the return to whom Revisionism had written on its banner.

The adherents of an independent organization, headed by Jabotinsky and some younger leaders of the movement, contended that it was impossible to carry out the Revisionist program and simultaneously carry out the lengthy and exhausting effort of winning adherents in the Zionist Organization, until they attained a majority. For, in fact, the number of Revisionist delegates to the Zionist Congresses had increased from 1925 to 1933; the numbers of the delegates elected by other Zionist parties had also increased, especially those of the Zionist labor groups (from 35 to 132). Experience had also shown that the struggle for mandates had absorbed almost all Revisionist activities. Therefore, if one was convinced that the Revisionist program was correct and capable of realization one was bound to concentrate on it rather than on a protracted struggle for power within the Zionist Organization. The hour was too late to remedy by the situation, and the time had come to carry out the program, instead of quarreling with others. They thought that much of the bitterness and sharpness that had characterized the fight of other Zionists against the Revisionist movement would abate once the Zionist parties did not feel endangered in their dominant position in the Zionist Organization. This, the secessionists stressed, would finally lead even to some future collaboration in areas where cooperation was possible and desirable.

At a conference in Calais (September 1931) the Revisionist leadership tried to bridge the two opposing views. It decided on an unrealistic compromise to the effect that the movement be constituted as an "Independent Revisionist Union" whose members either belonged or did not belong to the Zionist Organization. It was left to each individual Revisionist and each Revisionist territorial group whether to remain in the Zionist Organization or not. The Czechoslovak Revisionists decided at the meeting of the central committee in Prague (December 1931) to remain in the Zionist Organization, as well as in the Czechoslovak Zionist Territorial Union, and to continue participation in all activities, both Revisionist and Zionist in general.

However, by its very nature this Calais decision was of only a temporary character. The final split was unavoidable. It came after the conference in Kattowice (Poland) in February 1933 (at which Czechoslovakia was represented by Dr. Rabinowicz). An attempt to work out another compromise proved unsuccessful. On March 14, 1933, Jabotinsky dismissed the Revisionist World Executive and simultaneously asked the movement to express its opinion on the issue in a plebiscite. The result in Czechoslovakia showed an overwhelming acceptance of Jabotinsky's decision to secede from the World Zionist Organization.

Some 350 Czechoslovak Revisionists, however, disapproved of the measures, and joining up with the minority in the world movement (which was headed by Meir Grossman), they formed also in Czechoslovakia a Jewish party. This new party was headed by Yitshak Greidinger, principal of the Hebrew high school in Užhorod, who was assisted by a number of individuals in Moravská Ostrava (Marcel Färber), Prostějov (Fritz Sborowitz), Brno (Fritz Stecklmacher), and Prague (Jacob Fränkel). They proclaimed themselves officially as the Czechoslovak organization at their first conference held on August 27, 1933, in Prague (during the Eighteenth Zionist Congress). They already had a list of candidates of their own to the congress and had received 376 votes but no delegate (the Revisionists then received 2,520 votes and one delegate). But they had not functioned as an organization, constituting a loose association only. The Czechoslovak Jewish State party did not join the Territorial Union because as part of the Revisionist movement it had, since

1932, the privileges of a Separate Union and was free to make its own decisions. After 1935, when the Revisionists completely seceded from the World Zionist Organization and established the new Zionist Organization, some members joined the Jewish State party; most prominent among them was Dr. Martin Lichtner (Trutnov), formerly a member of the Revisionist Central Committee.

Finding that politically, ideologically, and in other respects it could identify itself with Dr. Emil Margulies and his group, the Jewish State party and the Radical Zionists joined forces for the congress elections in that year (1935). Their joint list received 1,208 votes but no delegate.

Shortly before the 1937 Zionist Congress, the Jewish State party in Czechoslovakia set out to reorganize itself, and at its Second Territorial Conference, held in Prostějov (May 8, 1937) with the participation of Robert Stricker (Vienna), it transferred its headquarters from its temporary (inactive) seat in Prostějov to Prague. The new leadership consisted of Jacob Fränkel, chairman, and the following members of the central committee: Heinrich Barber, Dr. Erwin Fischel, Otto A. Fischel, Leo Glückseling, Josef Mandl, Fritz Sborowitz, Willy Stricker, and Fritz Stecklmacher. However, with all their efforts, they received only 253 votes and no delegate. Thereafter, they did not develop any further activities, to the end of Czechoslovakia's existence.

The independent Revisionist Union in Czechoslovakia continued its activities as formerly, after the secession of the Jewish party, which event did not affect it numerically. Having accepted Jabotinsky's concept of the necessity of independent political work, the world leadership mapped out the steps to be taken, and the Czechoslovak organization adapted these to their local conditions. In 1934, in the course of its first steps in the "political offensive," the leadership decided on a "petition movement."

NOTES

1. This was formed in 1908 after the abandonment of a unified Zionist organization embracing all areas of the monarchy outside Hungary.
2. For a comparison of the development of Zionism in these two areas — the eastern and western parts of what was to be Czechoslovakia — it may be useful to record the following data. Of all the four territories which later formed Czechoslovakia, the following were represented at the first Zionist Congress in Basle (1897):

   Bohemia, 1 delegate: Dr. David Neumark (Rakonice).
   Moravia-Silesia, 11 delegates: Dr. Berthold Feiwel, Siegmund Kohn, Dr. Siegmund Kornfeld (Brno) — (the only delegate of these territories to be elected to the Zionist Actions Committee at the First Congress), Leopold Huppert, B. Kraus (Frýdek), Dr. Moritz Kornblüh, Dr. Wilhelmine Kornblüh (Frýštát), Dr. J. Gleisner, Dr. Adolf Wertheimer (Jamice), Dr. Siegmund Werner (Jihlava), M. Kramer (Miroslav).
   Slovakia, 2 delegates: Julius Davidovits, Julius Davidsohn (Bardejov).

   At the last prewar Zionist Congress in Vienna (1913), the representation was as follows:

   Bohemia, 9 delegates: Emilie Löwy, Hugo Slonitz (Prague), Dr. Emil Margulies (Litoměřice), Otto Kohn (Most), Elisabeth Perutz, L. Steiner (Teplice-Šanov), Dr. Angelo Goldstein, H. Stern (Trutnov), Louis Schiff (Ústí nad Labem).
   Moravia-Silesia, 10 delegates: Dr. Wilhelm Wanger (Bielsko), Dr. A. Schönhof (Brno), Friedrich Glass (Jihlava), Leo Krieger (Moravská Ostrava), Oskar Huber (Olomouc), Gustav Finzi, Isidor Muller (Opava), Dr. Viktor Altar, J. Neumann (Prostějov), Prof. Oskar Lieben (Uherské Hradiště).
   Slovakia, 2 delegates: Samuel Bettelheim, Emil Felix (Bratislava).

   Up to World War I there were in Bohemia 25 and in Moravia-Silesia 12 local Zionist societies; in Slovakia there were 5 and in Subcarpathian Ruthenia 1 — the latter in two areas as part of the Hungarian organization. (In those years one town could comprise one or more Zionist societies, each of which was counted separately.)
3. Founded in 1892 under the name *Maccabaea*, after the first Zionist Congress it assumed the name *Bar Kochba*. See the literature about *Bar Kochba* in the Bibliography. Also Julius Löwy, "Das Jubiläum des 'Bar Kochba'" (The Jubilee of B.K.), in *Die Welt*, Vienna, April 3, 1908, p. 5; Karl Schwager, "Ein kleines Kapitel zur Ge-

schichte des Bar Kochba" (A Small Chapter in the History of B.K.) in *Zirkular*, (*Circular Letter*), ed. R. G. Pacovský, Tel Aviv, January 1966, pp. 3–8; and "Zur Geschichte des Bar Kochba" (To the History of B.K.) by Dr. Alfred Löwy, Viktor Freud, Dr. Pepa Kohn, and Emmy Herrmann, in *Zirkular*, op. cit. November 1966, and still continuing (1968).

4. "Zionism is the homecoming to Judaism still before the return to the Jew's land" (Herzl in his opening speech of the First Zionist Congress). Cf. *Protocol* of the First Zionist Congress (new ed. German) Prague, 1911, p. 16.
5. Among these were Dr. Oskar Epstein, Dr. Hugo Herrmann, and Dr. Richard Karpeles.
6. To mention just a few outstanding names of this group: Norbert Adler, Ervin Arnstein, Eduard Aschermann, Drs. Viktor Fischel (Avigdor Dagan), František Friedmann, Angelo Goldstein, František Gottlieb, Kamil Kohn, Zdeněk Landes, Otakar Pacovský.
7. See the literature about *Barissia* in the Bibliography.
8. Names such as those of Drs. Herbert Birnbaum, Hugo Brauner, Viktor Bauer, Frederick Eckstein, Alfred Engel, Kurt Grünberger, Walter Kohner, Herbert Pick, and Fritz Tauber became household names in Czechoslovak Zionism.
9. This applies to the publication of Zionist pamphlets as well as to organizational reforms, suggested, in the first place, by Dr. Walter Kohner (see Notes 52 and 53).
10. The first *Halle* was formed in 1894 in Vienna. It was among the first students' societies which enthusiastically welcomed Theodor Herzl. (Cf. Herzl's *Diaries*, German ed., Berlin 1922, vol. I, p. 343.)*
11. To mention just a few names: Henry Gach, Menachem Goldenzahl (Golan), Dr. Ernst Lebenhart, Ernst Taussig, Walter Weber.
12. A study concerning Zionist youth movements (also in Czechoslovakia) was published by Siegfried Bernfeld, *Zionistische Jugendbewegung* (*Zionist Youth Movement*), Leipzig, 1927.†
13. Its founders were Siegmund Bergmann, Dr. Moritz Kohn, Filipp Lebenhart, Moritz Levy, Friedrich Mautner, Karel Resek, Hugo Slonitz, Moritz Weltsch, and Jacob Wertheimer.
14. Apart from the few names already mentioned in Note 2, several others (not all by far) come to mind (I enumerate only the names of those who worked for Zionism in both these periods): Jakub Adler, Dr. Samuel Arje, Emil Arnstein, Eduard Aschermann, Oskar Aschermann, Dr. Arthur Bergmann, Dr. Herbert Birnbaum, Albert Bobasch,

---

* [See also Goshen's article, Zionist Students' Organizations, pp. 173–183 (Ed.)].

† [On Maccabi, see Pick's article on Sports, pp. 185–228 (Ed.)].

Karel Fanta, Dr. Siegfried Federmann, Eduard Fischl, Robert Fuchs-Robětín, Anton Glaser, Dr. Ernst Gütig, Moritz Graf, Arthur Kauders, Dr. Viktor Kellner, Dr. Kamil Kohn, Viktor Kohn, Dr. Walter Kohner, Filipp Lebenhart, Julius Lampl, Julius and Moritz Löwy, Dr. Emil Margulies, Friedrich Mautner, Siegfried Polak, Emil Popper, Erwin Popper, Dr. Julius Reich, Erwin Reiner, Dr. Felix and Karel Resek, Dr. Max Saudek, Dr. Gustav Sicher, Simon Stern, Dr. Friedrich Thieberger, Emil Waldstein, Prof. Wilhelm Weleminsky (member of the Zionist Actions Committee elected at the Seventh Zionist Congress, Basel, 1905), Moritz Weltsch, Jakob Wertheimer, Dr. Ignaz Zollschan, Otto Zucker. Still others will be mentioned in the course of this essay.

15. It appeared uninterruptedly until October 1938.
16. It appeared uninterruptedly until October 1938.
17. See comments above on students' societies in Bohemia. (See also Goshen's article on students' organizations, pp. 173–184 [Ed.].
18. See Goshen on students' organizations, pp. 173–184 [Ed.].
19. Outstanding Zionist work was rendered by *Halle* members such as Henry Beer, Josef Zweigenthal, and Michael Hutter (its last president).

    Veritas, as the first students' society in the area of future Czechoslovakia to become Zionist, had a great number of outstanding workers for the Zionist cause in Czechoslovakia, but in a number of cases its members attained recognition and renown in World Zionism, for instance, apart from the two already mentioned (Feiwel and Stricker), Dr. Otto Abeles, Dr. Desider Friedmann, and Dr. Gustav Zweig.

20. See Meir Färber, "Mittelschülerverbindungen in der Zionistischen Bewegung in der ČSR" (Secondary School Associations in the Zionist Movements in Czechoslovakia), in *Zeitschrift für die Geschichte der Juden* (*Periodical for the History of the Jews*), ed. Hugo Gold, Tel Aviv, Nos. 2/3, 1966, pp. 95–101.

    Bar Kochba, Prague, in its earlier years established a high school society, *Hashachar*, to secure young blood once these young students would enter the university. This society published its own information sheet. But in 1905/06 the Bohemian *Zemský školní úřad* (Provincial School Office) prohibited the participation of students in Zionist activities, as result of a denunciation by an assimilationist functionary in the Prague Jewish religious congregation (information given to me by Dr. Hugo Bergmann). This and other events in the early days of *Bar Kochba* are described in the *Zirkular*, op. cit. (see Note 3) beginning with the November 1966 issue.

21. There existed before World War I a number of other such vacation societies but, to my knowledge, these others existed only temporarily.

22. See Note 12. As in Bohemia there existed also in Moravia groups of *Tehelet Lavan* (Blue-White) and of Maccabi before 1918.
23. The names of all those who had a lion's share in Zionist work in Moravia-Silesia cannot be enumerated in a short survey. Apart from those already mentioned in Note 2, one can point (from memory) to names of persons whose activities continued also in the new Czechoslovakia, such as Dr. Otto Baru, Leo Baumgarten, Dr. Siegmund Birnstein, Dr. Alfred Engel, Dr. Reuben Färber, Dr. Arthur Feldmann, Gustav Finzi, Dr. Max Grünfeld, Dr. Hugo Hermann, Dr. Emil Herzog, Max Hickl, Paul Hornung, Oskar Huber, Siegfried Kessler, Dr. Gustav Kohn, Dr. Leopold Leschner, Dr. Jakob Rabbinowitz, Dr. Josef Rufeisen, Karl Schindler, Dr. Philipp Schreier, Dr. Karl Sonnenfeld, Bertha Schnabel, Dr. Robert Sonnenmark, Hermann Stapler, Arthur and Berthold Tintner, Dr. Rudolf Tramer, Ernst Vogel, Dr. Wilhelm Wagner, Dr. Siegmund Werner (under Herzl, the editor of *Die Welt*), Dr. Felix Winterstein, Heinrich Zaitschek, Dr. Gustav Zweig, and many others.
24. I deal with the aspect of *Landespolitik* in some detail in *Jewish Social Studies*, New York, 1967, No. 4 (October), 250/1 and 252/54.
25. On *Po'ale Zion* see further below, pp. 126–128.
26. It appeared uninterruptedly until 1938.
27. For the foundation conference of the Hungarian Zionist Federation see *Die Welt*, April 3, 1903, pp. 12–13. For the *Mizrahi* foundation conference, see Samuel Bettelheim, "Der I. Weltkongress der Misrachi in Bratislava, 21–23 August 1904" (The First World Conference of *Mizrahi*), in *Judaica* (ed. S. Bettelheim), Bratislava 1934, Nos. 3/4, pp. 15–19.

    A few names of prewar Slovak Zionists whose activities continued also after 1918 come to mind. Samuel Bettelheim (founder of the first Zionist society in Hungary [1897]), Ahavat Zion (Bratislava) (member of the first Hungarian Zionist Territorial Committee) (*Landes Komiteé*, member of the Zionist Actions Committee, elected at the Zionist Congresses 1903, 1907, and 1909), Harry Bleiweiss, Emil Felix (delegate at the Zionist Congress, 1913), Dr. Karl Ferbstein, Dr. Elek Füredi, Isidor Goldberg, Dr. Emil Hertzog, Dr. Samuel Klein, Izidor Knöpfelmacher, Dr. Arpád Kondor, Hermann Kopp (founder in 1900 of the Association Yishuv Eretz Israel in Lipjany near Prešov), Dr. Joseph Lövy, Moses I. Müller, Emil Neumann (member of the first Hungarian Zionist Territorial Committee), Moritz Quastler, Adolf Reichenthal (member of the first Hungarian Zionist Territorial Committee, one of the cofounders of *Mizrahi* in Bratislava in 1904), Dr. Alfred Rosner, Ludwig and Wilhelm Steiner, Dr. Leo Sipos, Dr. Baruch Tomaschoff, Philipp Weinberger, Bernard Weiss, Dr. Moritz Zobel.

To these can be added Mosche Guttmann, Dr. Alexander Spiegel, Béla Szerényi, Dr. Wilhelm Sternbach from Subcarpathian Ruthenia.

28. The organization was established in 1903 and the statutes were approved by the Hungarian government in 1927 only.
29. On the impact of these minority treaties on the relationship between Zionists and assimilationists, see further below; also A. M. Rabinowicz, Jewish Minority, in vol. I, pp. 155 ff.
30. Document No. 100 (102514/801/44), Dispatch No. 220, in *Documents of British Foreign Policy* 1919–1939, vol. IV (1919), London, 1952, pp. 313/14.
31. The Czech-Jewish assimilationist movement was established by students on March 4, 1876.*
32. *Selbstwehr*, February 5, 1929, and *Židovské Zprávy* of the same date.
33. See Note 29.
34. This council consisted of members of the Zionist Territorial Federation (Norbert Adler, Max Brod, Alfred Engel, Ludvík Singer, Hugo Slonitz, and Miss Ida Zapper). For the four *Po'ale Zion* members, see Note 37.
35. *Protocol* of the Twelfth Zionist Congress (German), pp. 770/71 (Resolution 8/VIII).
36. *Mizrahi* is further dealt with below on pp. 94–99; and *Po'ale Zion* on pp. 76–87.
37. Other *Po'ale Zion* members who were on the council in 1918/19: Oskar Altschul, Karel Fischel, Ludwig Schönfeld, and Emil Waldstein (subsequently editor of *Židovské Zprávy*).
38. On this development and the activities of *Hitahdut* see below, pp. 55–64.
39. On the *Zionist-Revisionists* and the New Zionist Organization see pp. 99–108.
40. For the events and resignations, see *Medina Iwrit-Judenstaat*, Prague, April 17, 1935, p. 7; and May 3, 1935, p. 8.
41. There were two such cases, both in Subcarpathian Ruthenia. The Revisionist local group in Mukačevo was dissolved in 1928 and its leading members, Alexander Sauber and Dr. Alexander Spiegel, excluded from the organization because of political alignment with non-Jewish political parties for the elections (*Selbstwehr*, July 1928). In 1935 Dr. Alexander Spiegel left the Revisionist organization, having decided to associate with a Czech political party for the parliamentary elections (*Medina Iwrit-Judenstaat*, April 17, 1935, p. 7).

---

* [See also Czech-Jewish Movement, Hostovsky, pp. 148–154 (Ed.)].

42. On *HaShomer Hatza'ir* see below, pp. 87–88.
43. On the Jewish State party see below, pp. 128–129.
44. See Polak on WIZO, pp. 137–147 (Ed.).
45. See Note 1.
46. For these organizational changes, see *Rechenschaft über die Vergangenheit — Programm für die Zukunft* (*Report on the Past and Program for the Future*), published by the Zionist Territorial Federation, Moravská Ostrava, 1928, German, pp. 5–8; on the Slovak district. *Selbstwehr*, August 22, 1919, and *Jüdische Rundschau* (Berlin), September 19, 1919. For an overall report on the organization to date, see *Selbstwehr*, October 20, 1922 (Report to the Third Zionist Territorial Conference).
47. *Selbstwehr*, November 5, 1920.
48. A new Zionist Executive was elected in 1920 only. Although at the last Zionist Congress (Vienna, 1913) Berlin had been chosen as the official seat of the Executive, headquarters were moved at the beginning of the war (1914) to Copenhagen (Denmark) in order to preserve contact with all sections of the Zionist Organization from a neutral country. Between 1918 and 1920 the actual leadership resided already in London, which, as was mentioned, became the official seat of the world organization.
49. The information on this and all other conferences of Czechoslovak Zionists is derived from the periodicals and literature enumerated in the Bibliography.
50. This aspect is further dealt with below on p. 124.
51. For statistics of *Shekalim* sold in Czechoslovakia see Appendix A.
52. He was, for instance, the "inventor" of IMI pockets. IMI in Hebrew means "with me." IMI was a miniature of a Jewish National Fund box, made of paper, carried all the time "with me" and used on every occasion for the fund's collections. Kohner's ideas on the problems of reorganization were laid down in fundamental articles, as for instance, those which appeared in *Selbstwehr*, December 16, 1921, and September 18, 1925.
53. Walter Kohner initated in 1931 the publication by *Barissia* (Prague), whose distinguished member he was, of the *Schriftenreihe zur Diskussion des Zionismus* (*Series of Writings for the Discussion of Zionism*) which contained contributions by Alexander Adler, Dr. Hugo Bergmann, Dr. Salomon Goldelmann, Dr. Nahum Goldmann, Richard Lichtheim, Dr. Arye Tartakover, and Dr. Robert Weltsch. Other publications were: Viktor Bauer, *Der moderne Zionismus* (*Modern Zionism*) and *Kurze Soziologie des jüdischen Volkes* (*Short Sociology of the Jewish People*); František Friedmann, *Einige Zahlen über die čechoslovakische Judenheit* (*Some Statistics about Czechoslovak Jewry*). Among Kohner's theoretical writings, reference should

be made to his "Allgemeiner Zionismus" (General Zionism) in *Selbstwehr*, December 24, 1930, and his brochure *Einführung in den Zionismus* (*Introduction into Zionism*), twelve letters, Prague 1931.

54. For dates and places of conferences, see Appendix B.
55. This development is dealt with in detail on pp. 55–64.
56. See pp. 64–69.
57. On the *Zionist-Revisionists* and the New Zionist Organization, see pp. 99–108.
58. On the Jewish State party see pp. 76–87.
59. On *Po'ale Zion* see pp. 76–87.
60. On the establishment of the unified Zionist socialist bloc, see pp. 88–94.
61. On *HaShomer Hatza'ir* as a Separate Union, see pp. 87–88.
62. See Polak on WIZO, pp. 137–147 (Ed.).
63. See Appendix C. Cf. also *Protocol* of the Twenty-first Zionist Congress, Geneva, 1939.
64. *Selbstwehr*, October 26, 1928.
65. *Ibid.*, August 9, 1929.
66. The program is outlined in the literature referred to in the Bibliography.
67. Published in Moravská Ostrava in 1937.
68. Published as No. 5 of the *Kleine Zionistische Bücherei* (Small Zionist Library) ed. by Dr. Solomon Goldelmann, Prague, 1936.
69. *Protocol* of the Seventeenth Zionist Congress (1931), pp. 385 ff.
70. *Selbstwehr*, May 25, 1934.
71. *Ibid*, June 22, 1934.
72. *Ibid.*, September 6, 1935.
73. *Ibid.*, September 7, 1934.
74. The controversy and the grievance against *HeHalutz* are referred to in the sources of Notes 73 and 75 and in Dr. Rufeisen's statement in *Selbstwehr*, October 25, 1935.
75. *Selbstwehr*, November 1, 1935.
76. For details on this development, see below, p. 116, n. 90.
77. See below, p. 116, n. 90.
78. See below, p. 116, n. 90.
79. For all this, see *Selbstwehr*, June 21, 1935. See also Appendix C.
80. See Appendix C.
81. See Appendix A.
82. See Appendix C.
83. For the activities of this group, see *Selbstwehr*, February 28, 1919.
84. *Ibid*, December 26, 1919.
85. On *Po'ale Zion* see below, pp. 76–87.

86. For literature, see the Bibliography.
87. *Selbstwehr*, February 28, 1919.
88. *Ibid.*, Jannuary 30, 1920.
89. The development and concept of this trend is dealt with in Chaim Arlosoroff, *Der Jüdische Volkssozialismus* (*Jewish People's Socialism*), Berlin, 1919.
90. For the conference and its decisions, see *Die Arbeit* (*Work*), the organ of *Hapo'el Hatza'ir* in Germany, April and May 1920. And Robert Weltsch, "Die Prager Konferenz" (The Prague Conference) in *Der Jude* (*The Jew*), Berlin, 1920, pp. 37 ff. For the Berlin conference, 1922, see Rudolf Samuel, "Nach der III. Weltkonferenz" (After the Third World Conference), in *Die Arbeit*, September 22, 1922, pp. 4–9.
91. *Report* of the Zionist Executive to the Thirteenth Zionist Congress (1923), p. 48.
92. *Selbstwehr*, April 2, 1920.
93. *Ibid.*, January 9, 1921. Also *Die Arbeit*, September 22, 1922, p. 5.
94. *Ibid.*, May 21, 1920. The last strong stand of the *Hitahdut* delegate took place at the conference of the Bohemian Zionist District in Prague in Dec. 11, 1921 (see *ibid.*, Dec. 16 and 23, 1921).
95. *Ibid.*, May 7, 1920.
96. The first *'Aliya* is usually defined as the immigration into Palestine between 1880–1905, which commenced under the impact of the Russian and Rumanian pogroms and was primarily furthered by Baron Rothschild. The second *'Aliya* covers the period of 1906–1914. It arose after the collapse of the Russian Revolution and was in the main carried on by working (labor) elements. The third *'Aliya* set in after World War I, as a result of Zionist political successes; it consisted in the first place of *Halutzim* and youth elements and lasted from 1919–1924.
97. The controversy was then aired in the *Selbstwehr*, space being given to the views of both the opposition and the defenders of Diaspora political activities. See, in particular, the issues of *Selbstwehr* for March 18 and 25, 1921.
98. See p. 36.
99. See pp. 37–39.
100. See p. 43.
101. *Selbstwehr*, March 25, 1921. The program of the Berlin group of *Binyan HaAretz* was published *ibid.*, March 18, 1921.
102. *Selbstwehr*, April 1, 1921.
103. See p. 37.
104. *Ibid.*, October 22, 1922 (Report to the Third Zionist Territorial Conference). Spitz resigned his office at the end of 1921 (*Selbstwehr*, Dec. 23, 1921).

The world movement *HaPo'el Hatza'ir* constituted a Separate Union within the World Zionist Organization, and each territorial branch was free to decide upon joining or not joining a Territorial Federation on its own. (See p. 37.)

105. See Appendix C.
106. See Appendix C.
107. *Selbstwehr*, September 12, 1924.
108. See Appendix C.
109. *Selbstwehr*, July 24, 1925.
110. See p. 32.
111. See the next section.
112. *Hehalutz* as a unified organization in Czechoslovakia was launched at a meeting in Teplice-Šanov on March 27, 1921, in the presence of twenty-four delegates from Boheuiia. The first leadership consisted of Dr. Karl Alter (Litoměřice), chairman and finance department; Rudi Feigl (Teplice-Šanov) secretary for advising artisans; Marzell Wagner (Děčín), secretary for advising agricultural workers; Fritz Fauska (Děčín), cultural activities; Dr. Franz Kahn (Prague), representative at the Palestine Office; Hans Strasser (Chomutov), controller. (See "Chaluzverband für die Tschechoslovakei" in *Jüdische Jugendblätter*, Prague, March 1921, pp. 9/10.)
113. See p. 42.
114. See below, p. 118 n. 137.
115. Karel Čapek, *Hóvory s T. G. Masarykem* (*Conversations with T. G. Masaryk*), Prague 1935, vol. III, p. 208. For the program of Czech Realists, see *Červená knížka* (*The Red Book*), Prague 1900; T. G. Masaryk, "O realismu u nás "(About Our Realism) in *Čas* (*Time*) II, Prague 1888; and *idem*, *Naše nynější krise* (*Our Present Crisis*), Prague 1895.
116. See p. 62.
117. *Selbstwehr*, July 24, 1925.
118. *Ibid.* for the list of candidates.
119. See Appendix C.
120. *Selbstwehr*, May 7, 1926.
121. *Ibid.*
122. In particular his brochure *Proklamations-oder Tatsachen-Zionismus ?* (*Proclamation Zionism or A Zionism of Deeds ?*), Prague, 1925.
123. See p. 56; also Oskar Epstein, "Zum Zionistischen Realism" (On Zionist Realism) in *Selbstwehr*, September 28, 1926.
124. See p. 60.
125. *Selbstwehr*, July 9, 1926; also see this for report on the Territorial Conference.
126. *Ibid.*, July 16, 1926.

127. April 22 and 29; May 13; June 10, 1927.
128. Dr. Schnitzler, *ibid.*, April 22, 1927.
129. Dr. Epstein in *ibid.*, June 10, 1927. This comes very close to what, years later, the Zionist Revisionists demanded when insisting on the right of every Jew and every Jewess to a vote because they were born as Jews (see pp. 99–108).
130. See pp. 55 ff.
131. See Appendix C, and p. 70.
132. On the socialist consolidation and final unification, see p. 88; for more about the Revisionists, see pp. 99–108.
133. See p. 66.
134. See pp. 67–69.
135. *Selbstwehr*, June 3, 1927.
136. *Ibid.*
137. *Ibid.*, June 10, 17, 24, and July 1, 1927. Strong exception to this program was taken by Dr. Nahum Goldmann, the then leader of Radical Zionism, in his article "Kritik am Programme des linken Zentrums" (A Critique of the Program of the Left Center), *ibid.*, July 22, 1927.
138. See Appendix C.
139. About *Po'ale Zion*, see p. 76; on *Radical Zionists*, see p. 54; on Revisionists, pp. 99 ff.
140. *Protocol* of the Fifteenth Zionist Congress (German), p. 422.
141. Hans Lichtwitz in *Selbstwehr*, October 4, 1927.
142. *Ibid.*, March 9, 1928. The leaders of *HeHalutz* elected at the conference in Vrútky, (Slovakia) held from December 24–26, 1927, were Chaim Hoffmann, Uriel Löwy, Erna Schön, Kurt Thieberger, and Dr. Polda Zwillinger (*ibid.*, January 6, 1928).
143. *Ibid.*, May 4, 1928. See also Jehoshua Halevy, *History of Czechoslovak Betar* (Hebrew), Tel Aviv, 1960, p. 29.
144. *Selbstwehr*, May 27, 1928.
145. The first article on the necessity of forming a league in Czechoslovakia was written by Kurt Jilowsky, "Eine Liga für das arbeitende Palästina" (A League for Working Palestine) in *Selbstwehr*, January 1, 1927. See further below, note 151.
146. See p. 78.
147. See p. 88. At first the movement was Marxist. It later moved closer to a social democrat ideology.
148. See p. 32.
149. See p. 72. Among those worthy of mention are Dov Biegun, Jacob Edelstein, Dr. Heinz Guttenstein, Oskar Karpe, Dr. Chaim Kugel, Dr. Hans Lichtwitz, (all Prague), Samuel Rosenkranz and Viktor Zaitschek (Brno), Dr. Ernst Löbl (Prostějov), Dr. Oskar Neumann (Bratislava).

150. Jacob Reiss became chairman and Dr. Arthur Heller vice-chairman (*Selbstwehr*, June 22, 1928).

151. *Ibid.*, January 11, 1929. This conference of the league took place during the days of the assembly of the Eighth Zionist Territorial Conference (Brno, December 30 and 31, 1928). For the *Po'ale Zion*, Siegfried Kessler and E. Kaufmann were elected to the presidium. The principal speaker was Abraham Herzfeld, the Palestine labor leader, who outlined the scope and plans of the league. He particularly stressed that it was surely the duty of every socialist Zionist to join the league; others, too, should be induced to join because the league was not to be a political grouping or party but was to be solely confined to the support of Jewish work in Palestine, and particularly to the support of the following principles: (1) nationalization of the Palestine land in the hands of the Jewish National Fund; (2) demand for properly organized Jewish work in Palestine; (3) freedom and independence in every respect; and (4) people's mass *'Aliya*. A new central committee was elected consisting of seventeen members, and the presidium was divided between the Working Association of Socialist Zionists (Dr. A. Grünfeld, Brno) and the *Po'ale Zion* representatives (Siegfried Kessler, Brno, and Jakob Reiss, Prague). For the deliberations, see *Selbstwehr*, January 11, 1929.

The league existed until 1939. It received support also from non-socialist individuals, but, in fact, it was at the beginning and remained to the very end a financial instrument of the socialist Zionist groupings, although of some considerable importance with regard to appeals for the support of the upbuilding in Palestine *per se*.

The First World Conference of all leagues took place in Berlin (September 27–29, 1933); it decided to centralize the activities through a European central office, with the seat in Berlin. No Czechoslovak participated in that conference, but Dr. Chaim Hoffmann was elected member of the larger council (*Hauptrat*). See *Selbstwehr*, October 3, 10 and 17, 1930.

By 1933 the Czechoslovak league reported a great increase in its membership. It had thirty local groups with 1,500 paying members. At the Second Territorial Conference, held on August 27 during the Eighteenth Zionist Congress in Prague (1933), it was decided to transfer headquarters from Brno to Prague. Prof. Salomon Goldelmann became chairman, and Jakob Edelstein and Chaim Hoffmann, members (*Selbstwehr*, October 13, 1933).

152. For the report on the conference and elections, see *Selbstwehr*, January 4, 1929.

153. See p. 71.

154. *Selbstwehr*, June 14, 1929. Hoffmann had a particular reason for observing the anti-*Halutz* tendency of the Zionist Territorial Federation. As a representative of *HeHalutz* he reported to the Eighth Territorial Conference on its activities. He was bitterly attacked by Dr. Pavel März (now Merez) because as a *Po'ale Zion* member he not only did not belong to the Territorial Federation but in matters of parliamentary and local general elections his party had stood against the Jewish party. He demanded, therefore, that *HeHalutz* should not be represented by Dr. Hoffmann but by another member of the movement (*Selbstwehr*, January 4, 1929).
155. See p. 69.
156. See Appendix C.
157. *Ibid.;* see also *Protocol* of the Sixteenth Zionist Congress (German), pp. vii and xxxiv.
158. See Appendix C.
159. See p. 44.
160. *Selbstwehr*, January 1, 1930, also for the report on the conference.
161. *Selbstwehr*, February 7, 1930.
162. *Ibid.*, September 11, 1931; this carries a full report on the conference.
163. *Ibid.*, August 25, 1931; here there is a full report on the deliberations.
164. *Ibid.*, January 5, 1935.
165. See p. 88.
166. There exists a vast literature about Borochov and his philosophy. A comprehensive picture can be derived from his selected writings published in German (*Sozialismus und Zionismus, eine Synthese* [*Socialism and Zionism, a Synthesis*], ed. by Mendl Singer, Vienna, 1932); and in English (*Nationalism and the Class Struggle*, New York, 1937; and *Ber Borochov: Selected Essays in Socialist-Zionism*, ed. by Dr. Solomon Levenberg, London, 1948).
167. See p. 24.
168. *Protocol* of the Second Zionist Congress (German), p. 721.
169. For full text, see Fineman, *Po'ale Zion*, New York, 1918, p. 48.
170. See 30 ff.
171. See p. 31.
172. *Selbstwehr*, January 5, 1919.
173. See p. 32.
174. *Selbstwehr*, May 9, 1919.
175. *Ibid.*, June 27, 1919.
176. *Ibid.*, February 5, 1919.
177. *Mitteilungen des Israelitschen Landes-Lehrervereines in Böhmen* (*Bulletin of the Jewish Teacher's Association in Bohemia*) Prague, September 1919, p. 5.
178. *Ibid.*, pp. 5–10, for full report on the conference. The Prague union published its own organ in the form of a supplement in

Mitteilungen, which appeared for the first time in November 1919. It ceased publication in 1923.

179. *Selbstwehr*, March 28, 1919.
180. *Ibid.*, June 27, 1919.
181. The world conference lasted from July to October 1919. It was interrupted after the first meeting of July 27–29 to enable some delegates to participate in the socialist conference which took place in August 1919 in Lucerne (Switzerland). The world conference resumed in Stockholm on August 22–28, was again interrupted, and was reconvened for the third session in Stockholm (September 24–October 4) (*Jüdische Rundschau*, October 17 and 24, 1919). Rudolf Kohn represented the Czechoslovak *Po'ale Zion* at the conference and was for the last meetings joined by Dr. Felix Brunner (*ibid.*, November 14, 1919).
182. See pp. 55–64.
183. Kohn gained the attention of the world movement when he participated in the socialist conference in Berne (Switzerland), on February 3–6, 1919, and submitted there a joint proposal of *Po'ale Zion* and the Armenian socialist delegation (*Jüdische Rundschau*, February 14, 1919).
184. See note 181.
185. *Jüdische Rundschau*, October 24, 1919.
186. See note 181.
187. *Jüdische Rundschau*, August 29, 1919.
188. On the splits in the labor movement, see Aryeh Tartakower, *History of the Jewish Labor Movement* (Hebrew), vol. II, Warsaw, 1930, Section 7. See also Adolf Böhm, *Die Zionistische Bewegung* (*The Zionist Movement*), vol. II, Berlin 1937, pp. 77–79.
189. *Selbstwehr*, May 20, 1921. Both Kohn and Loria played in subsequent years prominent roles in the communist movement — the former in the highest executive offices of the Czechoslovak party, and the latter as one of the defense counsels of Georgi Dimitrov in the Leipzig trial for the burning of the Berlin Reichstag on February 27, 1933, after the advent of the Nazi regime.
190. June 24, 1921.
191. *Selbstwehr*, January 27, 1928.
192. *Ibid.*, February 20, 1928. A similar attempt at unifying a number of Zionist Territorial Federations was made by General Zionists (see p. 44).
193. See p. 42.
194. *Selbstwehr*, June 7, 1928.
195. See *ibid.*, June 14 and 21, 1929, for full report.
196. About *Mizrahi*, see pp. 94–99; about the Revisionists, pp. 99–108.
197. See p. 76.

198. See p. 98.
199. See p. 56.
200. *Protocol* of the Twelfth Zionist Congress (German), 1921, p. 721.
201. *Protocol* of the Fourteenth Zionist Congress (German), 1925, p. 206.
202. See pp. 71 ff.
203. See p. 64.
204. See p. 69.
205. See p. 30.
206. See p. 31.
207. See p. 32.
208. See p. 74 and Appendix C.
209. See p. 74.
210. See p. 74.
211. See p. 81.
212. *Selbstwehr*, June 13, 1930.
213. See *ibid.*, September 4 and 11, 1931, for full a report.
214. *Ibid.*, November 6, 1931.
215. *Ibid.*, July 13, 1934.
216. *Ibid.*, July 16, 1935.
217. See p. 69.
218. *Report* of the Zionist Executive to the Zionist Congress, 1937.
219. *Ibid.*
220. See p. 34 and the following sections.
221. See pp. 31 and 42.
222. See pp. 55 ff.
223. Adolf Böhm, *Die Zionistische Bewegung* (*The Zionist Movement*) vol. II, p. 76, Berlin 1937.
224. The acronym consists of the first letters of each of the four words in the new party's Hebrew name.
225. *Report* on the conference in Moshe Brasklavsky, *The Eretz Israel Labor Movement* (Hebrew), Hakibbutz HaMe'uhad, 1957, vol. II, pp. 134–35. The decision of the January 1930 conference was a foregone conclusion after a plebiscite within the two parties, taken in 1929, had shown that 85 per cent of *HaPo'el Hatza'ir* and 81.6 per cent of *Po'ale Zion* favored such a unification (*ibid.*).
226. For the development of this unification, see *Report* of the Zionist Executive to the Eighteenth Zionist Congress, 1933, pp. 178–184.
227. About the status of a Separate Union, see p. 88.
228. The outline of the program is in *Report* of the Zionist Executive to the Eighteenth Zionist Congress, loc. cit.
229. See p. 68.
230. *Selbstwehr*, May 22, 1931.
231. May 29, 1931.
232. Report on the conference, *ibid.*, June 29, 1931.

233. *Ibid.*, September 4, 1931. This did not stand scrutiny, because Dr. Grünfeld was the initiator of a conference which led to the establishment of the Working Association of Socialist Zionists in 1928 and became one of its leading members.
234. See Appendix C.
235. See p. 90.
236. Page 125.
237. This obviously refers to *Po'ale Zion* and the Brno group of *Hitahdut*, who had represented socialist Zionism in Czechoslovakia at the congress in 1931.
238. That is, the Working Association of Socialist Zionists.
239. See Appendix C.
240. *Selbstwehr*, August 15, 1933. This was written on the eve of the conference of the Working Association of Socialist Zionists in Prague on August 20.
241. *Tehelet Lavan* (*Blau-Weiss* — Blue White) was a youth organization in 1912 in Germany on the pattern of the *Wandervogel* (hikers) and had an organization in Bohemia and Moravia before 1918. After World War I it became a *Halutz* movement proclaiming change of profession adapted to the requirements of Eretz Israel as its educational aim in the Diaspora.
     For *HaShomer Hatza'ir* see p. 87.
242. See Appendix C.
243. See p. 93.
244. *Selbstwehr*, August 30, 1935.
245. See pp. 89 ff.
246. See Appendix C.
247. *Mitteilungen* (*Informations*), a stenciled sheet issued by the *Po'ale Zion*, Brno, No. 1, 1938. (Reprinted in *Medina Iwrit-Judenstaat* Prague, January 28, 1938.)
248. See p. 76.

APPENDIX A

SHEKALIM* PAID BY CZECHOSLOVAK ZIONISTS, 1921–1939

Year	*Number*	*Year*	*Number*
1921	8,685	1931	16,170
1922	10,432	1932	10,599
1923	9,138	1933	23,140
1924	7,608	1934	12,861
1925	13,528	1935	25,616
1926	13,365	1936	17,619
1927	13,433	1937	20,848
1928	12,092	1938	12,677 (Protectorate)
1929	14,970	1938	6,210 (Slovakia)
1930	15,472	1939	9,840 (Protectorate)

APPENDIX B

PLACES AND DATES OF THE ZIONIST TERRITORIAL CONFERENCES

1. July 26 and 27, 1919, Prague
2. March 27 and 28, 1921, Brno
3. November 1 and 2, 1922, Moravská Ostrava
4. June 29, June 30, and July 1, 1923, Moravská Ostrava
5. May 4, 1924, Brno (extraordinary conference)
6. September 7 and 8, 1924, Olomouc
7. July 3–6, 1926, Brno
8. December 30 and 31, 1928, Brno
9. December 25 and 26, 1929, Brno
10. July 5 and 6, 1932, Moravská Ostrava
11. December 30 and 31, 1934, Moravská Ostrava
12. March 6 and 7, 1938, Moravská Ostrava

---

* The *Shekel* was the membership dues to the Zionist Organization. In Czechoslovakia its price was 10 Kč (30c). A *Shekel*-payer had active and passive voting rights. The number of delegates for the Czechoslovak Territorial Conferences was based on the total *shekalim* sold in the year when the conference assembled.

APPENDIX C

ELECTIONS TO ZIONIST CONGRESSES

		List No. 1		*List No. 2*		*List No. 3*		*List No. 4*		*List No. 5*		*List No. 6*		*Totals*	
Congress	*Year*	*Votes*	*Delegates*	*Votes*	*Delegates*	*Votes*	*Delegates*	*Votes*	*Delegates*	*Votes*	*Delegates*	*Votes*	*Delegates*	*Votes*	*Delegates*
XII	1921	(See note)	4	616	1	968	1		3					(See note)	9
XIII	1923	(See note)	3	(See note)		(See note)	1	(See note)	1					(See note)	5
XIV	1925	2,947	4	360		1,073		1,073	1					5,407	5
XV	1927	4,167	6	(See note)		1,329	2	1,018	1					6,514	9
XVI	1929	4,228	6	(See note)		1,018	1	1,227	2	571				7,044	9
XVII	1931	3,078	4	2,243	2	976	1	1,477	2	2,056	2			9,830	11
XVIII	1933	3,436	2	5,476	3	1,381	1	3,057	2	2,520	1	376		16,246	9
XIX	1935	4,479	3	7,198	5	(See note)		4,735	3	(See note)		1,208		17,620	11
XX	1937	4,292	4	4,331	5	632		2,640	3			253		12,148	12
XXI	1939	(See note)		(See note)		(See note)		(See note)				(See note)		(See note)	

The number of delegates to Zionist Congresses was based on the number of *shekalim* sold in the two-year period between Zionist Congresses. If any contending party failed to obtain the necessary votes at elections, or if after the calculation of the required votes per delegate there remained a surplus of votes, these fractional votes were added to fractional votes of the same party in other countries, and a joint delegate was allocated to them on the so-called World Election list (*Weltwahlliste*).

NOTES to Appendix C

1921: Voting took place according to districts and therefore differed from all elections to congresses in subsequent years. This difference does not appear in the above table. The results of the first postwar election were as follows: List Norbert Adler: 158 votes, no delegate. List Dr. Josef Rufeisen: 855 votes, 1 delegate. List Dr. Samuel Klein: 317 votes, 1 delegate. Joint *Mizrahi*-East Slovakia and Subcarpathian Ruthenia districts, headed by Mosche Goldstein: 2,169 votes and 5 delegates. (These were allocated as follows: 3 to *Mizrahi*, 2 to the Territorial Federation.) List *Hitahdut*, headed by Dr. Hugo Bergmann: 616 votes, 1 delegate. List Dr. Emil Margulies: 968 votes, 1 delegate.

The distribution of the mandates appears in the above table. It shows:

1. Territorial Federation: Dr. Karl Ferbstein. Dr. Samuel Klein, Dr. Josef Rufeisen, Dr. Wilhelm Sternbach.
2. *HaPo'el Hatza'ir* (*Hitahdut*): Dr. Hugo Bergmann (who at that time settled in Palestine and was substituted for at the congress by Dr. Max Brod).
3. Dr. Emil Margulies: Dr. Emil Margulies.
4. *Mizrahi:* Chief Rabbi Dr. Heinrich (Chaim) Brody, Mosche Guttmann, Mosche Itzchak Müller.

Gustav Finzi participated as member of the Actions Committee (elected in 1913). Other Czechoslovaks also participated. Thus *Hitahdut* Poland was entitled to a number of delegates who, however, were unable to proceed to the congress, owing to political conditions. The congress decreed that in such cases *Hitahdut* candidates on *Hitahdut* lists in other countries should be permitted to fill in as Polish delegates. Accordingly, Dr. Oskar Epstein, Mosche Ischayewicz, and Alex Feig became *Hitahdut* delegates. The same ruling also applied to the list of *Tze'ire Tzion*, and accordingly Dr. Hans Kohn became their delegate at the congress.

1923: There were no elections. The parties distributed the delegates among themselves and submitted one single list of candidates. The distribution was as follows:

1. Territorial Federation: Norbert Adler, Dr. Josef Rufeisen, Dr. Wilhelm Sternbach.
2. *Hitahdut* did not participate in this distribution of delegates. It associated with *Hitahdut* organizations of America, Argen-

tine, and Belgium for the nomination of one joint delegate: M. Lipson (U.S.A.)

3. Dr. Emil Margulies.
4. Chief Rabbi Dr. Heinrich Brody.

1925: 1. Territorial Federation: Dr. Angelo Goldstein (substituting for Dr. Karl Ferbstein, who resigned), Franz Lederer, Dr. Josef Rufeisen, Herman Stapler.

2. The 360 votes received by *Hitahdut* were combined (in accordance with the rules of the World Zionist Organization pertaining to fractional votes) with fractional votes received by *Hitahdut* in Belgium and Estonia. All three countries qualified together for one delegate: Menahem Bader (Eretz Israel).
3. Dr. Emil Margulies (Radical Zionist): No delegate.

1927: 1 and 2. Joint list of Territorial Federation and *Hitahdut* under the name "*Linkes Zentrum-Arbeitendes Eretz Istael*" (Left Center-Working Eretz Israel): Dr. Fritz Eckstein, Dr. František Friedmann, Dr. Hugo Herrmann, Moritz Singer, Elijahu Dobkin (an Eretz Israeli elected on the joint list who at the congress joined the *Po'ale Zion* faction), Erwin Zippor-Vogel.

3. Radical Zionists, Dr. Emil Margulies, Dr. Miriam Scheuer.
4. *Mizrahi:* Albert Günsberger.

Dr. Josef Rufeisen participated at the congress as member of the Actions Committee.

1929: 1 and 2. Joint list of Territorial Federation and *Hitahdut* under the name "*Für eine starke Zionistische Organisation — Für ein arbeitendes Eretz Israel*" (For a Strong Zionist Organization — For a Working Eretz Israel): Dr. Fritz Eckstein, Dr. František Friedmann, Dr. Chaim Kugel, Dr. Emil Müller, Dr. Oskar Neumann, Ignatz Rokach (who was elected on the list and at the congress joined the *Po'ale Zion* faction).

3. Radical Zionists: Dr. Emil Margulies.
4. *Mizrahi:* Albert Günsberger, Shemuel Hakohen Weingarten.
5. Revisionists: No delegate.

1931: 1. General Zionists: Harry Bleiweiss, Dr. Angelo Goldstein, Dr. Robert Sonnenmark, Dr. Wilhelm Sternbach.

2. *Po'ale Zion* and *Hitahdut*: Dr. Adolf Grünfeld, Eldad Lindenbaum.
3. Radical Zionists: Dr. Emil Margulies.
4. *Mizrahi:* Dr. Bela Beer (substituted for at the congress by Dr. Pinkas Keller), Mosche Arye Kastner.

5. Revisionists: Hans Löw, Dr. Oskar K. Rabinowicz.

Dr. Josef Rufeisen participated as member of the Actions Committee.

1933: 1. General Zionists: Dr. Angelo Goldstein (substituted for later by Dr. Moritz Singer), Dr. Hugo Meissner.
2. *Po'ale Zion-Hitahdut:* Siegfried Kessler (substituted for later by Jakob Reiss), Dr. Chaim Kugel (substituted for later by Jakob Edelstein), Erwin Zippor-Vogel.
3. Radical Zionists: Dr. Emil Margulies.
4. *Mizrahi:* Mosche Goldstein (substituted for later by Moses Glaser), Prof. Eliezer Grünwald (substituted for later by Juda Deutsch, and subsequently by Mosche Arye Kastner).
5. Revisionists: Dr. Alexander Spiegel (substituted for later by Dr. Leopold Ludwig Gottesmann).
6. Jewish State party: No delegate.

Dr. Josef Rufeisen and Dr. Oskar Rabinowicz participated as members of the Actions Committee.

For the Revisionists a Czechoslovak, Oskar Herlinger, became a delegate as substitute for Dr. Max Kiewe (Austria).

1935: 1. General Zionists: Leo Czuczka, Bela Gross, Dr. Oskar Neumann.
2. *Po'ale Zion-Hitahdut:* Jakob Edelstein, Dr. Arthur Heller, Berl Katzenelson (Eretz Israel), Schlomo Lipsky, Yehuda Tubin.
3. Radical Zionists did not submit a list under their own name. They joined List No. 6 under the name of Association of Political Zionists.
4. *Mizrahi:* Max Amber, Mosche Goldstein, Yehuda A. Eliasch.
5. Jewish State party jointly with Association of Political Zionists: no delegate. Dr. Josef Rufeisen participated as chairman of the Zionist Court of Honor, Dr. Angelo Goldstein as a member of the Actions Committee, substituting for Dr. Josef Rufeisen.

The Revisionists, having left the Zionist Organization, did not participate in this or the subsequent congresses.

1937: 1. General Zionists: Ignatz Deutsch, Dr. Angelo Goldstein, Dr. Paul März, Hanna Steiner.
2. *Po'ale Zion-Hitahdut*, under the name "Liga für das arbeitende Eretz Israel" (League for the Working Eretz Israel): Fini Brada, Dr. Arthur Heller, Dr. Heinrich Hoffmann, Dr. Chaim Kugel, Elieser Reich.

3. Federation of General Zionists and Association of Political Zionists, under the name *"Liste der Nein-Sager — Gegen die Teilung Palästinas"* (List of Nay-Sayers — Against the Partition of Palestine): no delegate.
4. *Mizrahi* and *Tora VaAvoda:* Mrs. Hartwig Engel, David Intriliger (this name is incorrectly spelled in the *Protocol;* it was impossible to ascertain the correct one).
5. Jewish State party, under the title *"Auf Herzls Weg zum Judenstaat"* (In Herzl's Way to the Jewish State).

Dr. Josef Rufeisen participated as member of the Actions Committee.

1939: There were no elections, since Czechoslovakia was occupied and broken up. From the Protectorate Bohemia-Moravia eight delegates were approved, but only five attended the congress: Jacob Edelstein, Josef Fränkel, Dr. František Friedmann, Dr. Franz Kahn, Dr. Karl Sonnenfeld.

From Slovakia all six nominated candidates attended: Jakob Berger, Abraham Ben David, Siegmund Klinger, Dr. Oskar Neumann, Dr. Ladislav Rosenzweig, Dr. Berthold Weiss.

Dr. Josef Rufeisen attended as member of the Actions Committee (but from Tel Aviv), and Mosche Goldstein for *Mizrahi* (for Hungary).

APPENDIX D

*Elections at Zionist Congresses**

A number of Czechoslovak delegates to Zionist Congresses were elected by the congress to various functions both of the congress and of the World Zionist Organization. They were:

XII (1921): Dr. Emil Margulies, Reporter on elections to the congress and the distributions of delegates. Elected: Congress Attorney and member of the Committee on Statutes.

* The following abbreviations are employed:
AC. = Actions Committee of the World Zionist Organization
M. = Memb r
DM. = Deputy Member
Terr. Fed. = Territorial Federation
GZ. = General Zionists
Rad. = Radical Zionists
Rev. = Revisionists

XIII (1923): Dr. Josef Rufeisen, Secretary of Congress for duration of deliberations.
Elected M. C. (Terr. Fed.).
Dr. Emil Margulies, elected DM. T.C. (Rad.).

XIV (1925): Elected: Dr. Josef Rufeisen M. AC. (Terr. Fed.); Dr. Emil Margulies DM. AC. (Rad.).

XV (1927): Dr. Hugo Herrmann, Congress Secretary for the duration of Congress, and DM. AC. (Terr. Fed.).
Dr. Josef Rufeisen M.AC. (Terr. Fed.).

XVI (1929): Elected: Dr. Josef Rufeisen M.AC. (GZ): Dr. Hugo Herrman DM.AC. (GZ); Dr. Fritz Eckstein, M. Congress Court.

XVII (1931): Elected: Dr. Josef Rufeisen, M.AC. (GZ); Dr. Angelo Goldstein, IM. AC. (GZ); Dr. Emil Margulies DM.AC. (Rad.); Dr. Oskar Rabinowicz, DM. AC. (Rev.).

XVIII (1933): Dr. Josef Rufeisen, Vice-President of Congress and Chairman of Court of Honor. Elected M.AC. (GZ); Dr. Angelo Goldstein DM.AC. (GZ); Dr. Oskar Rabinowicz, DM. AC. (Rev.); Dr. Fritz Eckstein, Deputy of the Congress Attorney.

XIX (1935): Dr. Josef Rufeisen, M. of Congress Court, and elected M. AC. (GZ), Dr. Angelo Goldstein DM. AC. (GZ); Dr. Fritz Eckstein M. of Congress Court.

XX (1937): Elected: Dr. Josef Rufeisen M. AC. (GZ) and Congress Court; Dr. Angelo Goldstein, DM. AC (GZ); Dr. Fritz Eckstein M. Congress Court.

APPENDIX E

TECHNICAL ORGANIZATION OF ZIONIST CONGRESSES

Many Czechoslovak Zionists were prominently active in the preparations and technical carrying out of the administrative organization of all Zionist Congresses before 1921 and 1938. They were:*

XII (1921): Dr. Hugo Herrmann, Daily Congress Newspaper (German).
Dr. František Friedmann, Daily Bulletin (Czech).
Fritz Ullmann, Hotel and room accommodations.

* There are no records available for the technical and administrative work pertaining to the organization of the congresses in 1921, 1923 and 1925. I am grateful to Dr. Fritz Ullmann for the information given in this survey for that period. The information on the subsequent congresses is recorded in the published *Protocols* of each congress.

Active in various departments: Messrs. Altmann, Isaiah Becker, Viktor Kellner, Dr. Chaim Kugel, Schrecker, Emil Waldstein, Felix and Robert Weltsch, Otto Zucker, and Misses Hedwig Gellner, Fantel, Lise Weltsch-Katzenelson, and Mrs. Gut.

XIII (1923): Dr. Hugo Herrmann, Daily Congress Newspaper (German).
Dr. František Friedmann, Congress Bulletin (Czech).
(No other names were ascertainable.)

XIV (1925): Dr. Franz Kahn, General Secretary and Deputy Chairman of Congress Office. Member of Office: Dr. Fritz Ullmann.
Dr. Hugo Herrmann, Daily Congress Newspaper (German).

XV (1927): Dr. Franz Kahn, Head of Congress Office; Dr. Ernst Mechner and Dr. Fritz Ullmann, Deputies.
Dr. Hugo Herrmann, in charge of the Congress *Protocol.*
Victor Zaitschek, Copying.
Otto Wallisch, Illustrations.
Ernest Goldschmied, Head of the department for the maintenance of order.

XVI (1929): Dr. Hugo Herrmann, Head of Congress Office; Dr. Franz Kahn and Dr. Fritz Ullmann, Deputies. Dr. Hugo Herrmann, Editor of Congress Newspaper (German); Viktor Zaitschek, Copying. Otto Wallisch, Illustrations. Friedrich Fränkel, office of admission tickets.

XVII (1931): Dr. Franz Kahn, Head of Congress Office; Dr. Fritz Ullmann, Deputy.
Dr. Hugo Herrmann, Editor of Congress Newspaper (German) and Congress *Protocol.*
Karl Baum, Editor Congress Bulletin.
Victor Zaitschek, Copying.
Otto Wallisch, Illustrations.

XVIII (1933): Dr. Franz Kahn, Head of Congress Office; Dr. Fritz Ullmann, Deputy.
Dr. Hugo Herrmann: Editor of Congress *Protocol.*
Bedřich Mandelík, Editor special Congress edition of *Židovske Zprávy.*
Eduard Pataky, Editor Congress Bulletin.
Viktor Zaitschek, Copying.
Erwin Elbert, Head of department for the maintenance of order.
Valerie Waldstein, Administration of Congress Newspaper.

XIX (1935): Dr. Franz Kahn, Head of Congress Office; Dr. Fritz Ullmann, Deputy.

Dr. Siegfried Schmitz, Editor Congress Newspaper (German).
Otto Moller, Illustrations.
Otto Feldmann, Copying.
Dr. Paul Koser, Head of the department for the maintenance of order.

XX (1937): Dr. Franz Kahn, Head of Congress Office; Dr. Fritz Ullmann, Deputy.
Dr. Siegfried Schmitz, Editor Congress Newspaper (German).
Otto Feldmann, Copying.
Dr. Paul Koser, Head of the department for the maintenance of order.

BIBLIOGRAPHY

As far as possible I have avoided using reference notes in this collection of impressions and reminiscences about Czechoslovak Zionism. In the first place, this is not a definitive history; the investigation and collection of materials still goes on while this book goes to press. Second, a volume such as the present one, aiming at reaching a wide readership, should by its very nature not be hardened by too many reference notes. What was intended in the above essay was to present an overall picture of Czechoslovak Zionism as it developed and progressed after emerging from the ruins of the former Austrian organization and within a short period of fifteen years grew into one of the model organizations within the world movement.

As sources for this essay I have used, in the first place, my own collection of documents, newspapers, minutes of meetings, and personal notes at the time. To them was added material I collected in the Central Zionist Archives in Jerusalem, and the Zionist Archives in New York. My brother Dr. Aharon Moshe Rabinowicz in Jerusalem looked up additional sources in the archives there and interviewed on my behalf several old stalwarts of Czechoslovak Zionism. I received valuable information from Dr. Chaim Yahil (Hoffmann) on the Zionist socialist movement in the Republic, from Mr. Shemuel Hakohen Weingarten about the *Mizrahi*, and from Dr. Fritz Ullmann about a number of specific organizational aspects. The late Dr. Karel Stein's collection of contemporary notes was also most useful for my article.

The newspapers which I consulted most frequently were *Selbstwehr* (Prague), *Jüdische Volksstimme* (Brno), and *Medina Iwrit* (Prague). The *Jüdischer Almanach* (Prague), *Židovský kalendář* (Prague), and *Jüdischer*

Volkskalender (Brno) were also consulted for particular articles and statistics. For special aspects I consulted various issues of *Listy židovské mládeže* (*Jewish Youth Magazine*), 1922 (Prague), *Jüdische Jugendblätter*, 1922/1923, (Prague), the Zionist Executive's *Zionistisches Bulletin*, London, 1922/1923, and *Judaica*, ed. by Samuel Bettelheim, Bratislava, 1934–1937.

Several volumes of collected essays contained important information. I have used the following:

Neue Wege (*New Ways*). Volume published on the occasion of the tenth year of the existence of *Bar Kochba*. Prague, 1909.

Semestralberichte des Vereins Bar Kochba (*Term Reports of Bar-Kochba*), Prague, 1910–1913.

Zirkulare (Circular letters) issued by Old Bar-Kochba-Theodor Herzl (ed. R.G. Pacovsky) Tel Aviv, since 1951 and still continuing. "Barissia," volume published on the occasion of its 50th semester, Prague 1928. *Mitteilungen* (*Informations*), Tel Aviv 1954. Special issue: *50 Years of Barissia.*

Für den Aufbau der jüdischen Heimstätte in Palästina (*For the Upbuilding of the Jewish National Home in Palestine*). Report on the first *Keren Hayesod* Conference in Czechoslovakia, Prague, 1925.

Rassviet (ed. Vladimir Jabotinsky), Berlin, 1925.

Misrachi Festschrift, (*Mizrahi Festive Volume*) Berlin, 5677/1927.

Rassviet (special edition), Paris, 1931.

Památník hebrejského gymnasia v Mukačevě (*Memorial Volume of the Hebrew Gymnasium in Mukačevo*), Mukačevo, 1932.

Report submitted to the Fifth World Conference of *Po'ale Zion* (Yiddish) for the period 1914–1920.

Prague and Jerusalem (Hebrew), Memorial volume for Leo Hermann, (ed. Felix Weltsch), Jerusalem, (undated).

Zeitschrift für die Geschichte der Juden (*Magazine for the History of the Jews*), (ed. Hugo Gold). Special issue: Czechoslovakia, Tel Aviv, February, 1966.

I extracted information from the following official Zionist publications:

Reports of the Zionist Executive to the XII–XXI Zionist Congresses. Many of these *Reports* (partly in German, English, and Hebrew) contain, in the section on "Organization," reports supplied by the Executive Committee of the Czechoslovak Zionist Territorial Federation, by the Palestine Office, WIZO, *HeHalutz*, and all Separate Unions (*Mizrahi*, *Po'ale Zion*, *Hitahdut*, Revisionists, etc.), for the information of congress delegates.

Protocols of the XI–XXI Zionist Congresses (statistical tables of delegates to the Zionist Congresses and to the Council of the Jewish Agency).

VIII. Zionistentag, Brünn 30–31, XII. 1928 (Eighth Zionist Territorial Conference). A Survey by the Czechoslovak Zionist Executive Committee about the work and development of Czechoslovak Zionism in the preceding decade (1918–1928). An important source of information.

Other books, brochures, and essays consulted were:

Adler, J., and Meyer, Franz, "Die jüdische Arbeiterbewegung in der Galuth" (Jewish Labor Movement in the Galut) in *Zionistisches Handbuch* (*Zionist Manual*), (ed. Gerhard Holdheim), Berlin, 1923, pp. 225–31.

Adler, Norbert, *Nová doba a Židé* (*The New Times and the Jews*), Prague, 1919.

Bauer, Viktor, *Der moderne Zionismus. Ziele und Zahlen* (*Modern Zionism, Aims, Figures*), Barissia Books, Prague, 1934.

———, *Volk unterwegs, Staat unterwegs* (*People on the Way, State on the Way*) Mukačevo (Nekudah), 1936.

Bergmann, Hugo, "The Daring of the Middle" (Hebrew), in *HaAretz*, February 25, 1966, pp. 10, 15 (review of Felix Weltsch's book).

———, "Barissia," in *Mitteilungen*, Tel Aviv, 1954 (Special issue: 50 Years of *Barissia*).

Bettelheim, Samuel, "Der I. Weltkongress des Misrachi in Bratislava" (The First World congress of *Mizrahi* in Bratislava), August 21–23, 1904. In *Judaica*, Bratislava, 1934, Vol. I., pp. 15–19.

Böhm, Adolf, *Die Zionistische Bewegung* (*The New Zionist Movement*), Berlin, vol. I, 1935; vol. II, 1937.

Braslawsky, Moshe, *The Labor Movement* (Hebrew), 3 vols., Tel Aviv, 1955.

Brauner, Hugo, *"Geschichte der Barissia,"* (*History of Barissia*), Prague, 1929 (new ed., Haifa, 1944).

Brod, Max, and Weltsch, Felix, *Zionismus als Weltanschauung* (*Zionism as a Weltanschauung*), Moravská Ostrava, 1925.

Engel, Dr. Alfred, *"Ein Jahrzehnt jüdischer Schulentwicklung"* (A Decade of the Development of Jewish Schools), in Hamoreh: *Zprávy učitelské* (*Teachers' Information Bulletin*), Brno, October 1928, pp. 4–6.

Farber, Meir, *Dr. Emil Margulies*, Tel Aviv, 1949.

Fineman, H., *Po'ale Zion*, New York, 1918.

Goldelmann, Salomon, *Das arbeitende Palästina* (*Labor Palestine*), Prague, 1936.

Hoffmann, Chaim, *Träger der Verwirklichung. Die Zionistische Arbeiterschaft in Aufbau* (*Bearers of Realization. Zionist Workers in the Upbuilding*), Small Zionist Library, Prague, 1937.

Jabotinsky, Vladimir, *State Zionism*, London, 1934.

———, *Was wollen die Zionisten Revisionisten* (*What the Zionist Revisionists Want*), 1926.

Kaufmann, Leo, "Von Anfängen der Hechaluzbewegung" (On Beginnings of the Hehalutz Movement), in *Werk und Werden: Eine Chaluzische Sammelschrift* (*Work and Growth: A Halutzic Anthology*), Berlin, 1934, pp. 35–41.

Kestenberg-Gladstein, Ruth, "The Beginnings of Bar Kochba" (Hebrew) in *Prague and Jerusalem* (see above), pp. 86–110.

Kohner, Dr. Walter, "Barissia," in *Zeitschrift für die Geschichte der Juden* (*Periodical for the History of the Jews*) (ed. Hugo Gold), Tel Aviv, 1966, pp. 125–132

Landau, Saul Raphael, "Die Anfänge der jüdischen Arbeiterbewegung in Österreich" (The Beginning of the Jewish Labor Movement in Austria), in his *Sturm und Drang im Zionismus* (*Storm and Stress in Zionism*), Vienna, 1937, pp, 147–158.

Lauterbach Dr. Leo, *Die Zionistische Organisation* (*Zionist Organization*), Small Zionist Library, Prague, 1936.

Lewinson, Zeew, "Die Hechaluzbewegung" (HeHalutz Movement), in *Zionistisches Handbuch* (ed. Gerhard Holdheim), Berlin, 1923, pp. 250–267.

Lichtheim, Richard, *Revision der zionistischen Politik* (*Revision of Zionist Politics*), Berlin, 1930.

———, *Revisionisten*, Barissia Books, Prague, 1931.

Locker, Berl, *What Is Po'ale Zionism*?, London, 1938.

Lubotsky, Benyamin, *Revisionism and Brith Trumpeldor* (Hebrew), Jerusalem, 1946.

Mandelík, Simcha-Manor, "Naši v Palestýně" (Ours in Palestine), in *Židovský Kalendař*, Prague, 5698 (1937/1938), pp. 80–85.

Pasmanik, Daniel, *Theory and Practice of Po'ale Zion* (Yiddish), Krakow, 1906.

Rabinowicz, Oskar K., "Wir und der Zionistische Landesverband" (We and the Zionist Territorial Federation), in *Selbstwehr*, November 11, 1931.

Rufeisen, Dr. Josef, *National und Soziale Judenfragen* (*National and Social Jewish Questions*), Moravská Ostrava, 1919.

Salomonsohn, H. (pseudonym of Chief Rabbi Dr. Heinrich Chaim Brody, Prague) *Widerspricht der Zionismus unserer Religion?* (*Does Zionism Contradict Our Religion?*), Berlin, 1898 (reprinted Prague, 1921).

Schechtman, Joseph, *Grundsätze des Revisionismus* (*Basic Elements of Revisionism*), Paris, 1929.

———, *The Jabotinsky Story*, two vols., New York, 1956 and 1959.

Schmitz, Siegfried, and Brauner, Hugo, *Die Wahrheit über den Revisionismus* (*The Truth about Revisionism*) Prague, 1934.

Schwarzbart, Dr. Ignacy, *General Zionism*, New York, 1954.

Walk, Joseph, "The Torah va-Avodah Movement," in *Leo Baeck Year Book*, VI, London, 1961, pp. 236–256.

Weltsch, Robert, "Die Prager Konferenz" (The Prague Conference) in *Der Jude*, Berlin, 1920, p. 37.

Wolfsberg, Dr. Oskar (Yeshayahu), *Mizrachi* (German), Small Zionist Library, Prague, 1935.

———, *Mizrachi and HaPo'el HaMizrahi* (Hebrew), Jerusalem, 1946.

World Union of Zionist Revisionists, *The World Jewish Petition*, London, 1934.

Zollschan, Ignaz, *Krise und Sezessionsgefahr* (*Crisis and Danger of Secession*), Karlovy Vary, 1921.

THE ZIONIST WOMEN'S MOVEMENT

by Irma Polak

The women's movement played an important part in the Zionist organization of Czechoslovakia, achieving much in the fields of Zionist education and fund-raising, the care and welfare of *Halutzim*, and the dissemination of the Hebrew language. In many instances, the initiative for important Zionist projects came from the women's movement. At the same time, the movement was active in social work within the Jewish congregations of Czechoslovakia, providing constructive assistance wherever it was most needed.

The Women's Zionist Organization of Czechoslovakia had its beginnings in Prague. Mrs. Olga Bobasch, its last chairman, is now living in Israel. Eighty-five years old and a survivor of four years in Terezín, she recently recalled those early years.

"The first Zionist association," she wrote, "was formed in Prague in the year 1900 under the name of Jüdischer Volksverein (Jewish People's Association). Among the founders, as I remember them, were Moritz Löwy, Professor Jakob Wertheimer, Philip Lebenhart (later the editor of *Jung Juda*, the first Jewish youth periodical published in Prague), Rabbi Aladar Deutsch and Anton Glaser.* Their wives participated in the meetings and activities of the People's Association, but in 1901 the women organized a group of their own — Der Jüdische Frauenverein (Jewish Women's Association). The first chairman of this group was Mrs. Sofie Roubitschek, an educator, the principal of a Jewish boarding school for girls in Prague. In July 1904, Roubitschek and Professor Jakob Wertheimer attended

* [Cf. vol. I, Dagan, p. 525; and O. Rabinowicz, pp. 19–136 (Ed)].

Theodor Herzl's funeral in Vienna as delegates of the Zionist organization of Prague. The Women's Association included in its program the dissemination of the Zionist ideal, the revival of the observance of Jewish holidays, the organization of classes in the Hebrew language, and the raising of monies for the Jewish National Fund."

The first years were difficult ones, since most Jews considered the Zionist ideal to be a Utopian dream; but thanks to tireless educational work, Zionism gradually gained ground. Many children and adolescents were attracted to the movement by Purim and Hanukka celebrations. Prominent lecturers were engaged, and the Zionists went forth to seek the support of Jewish women's organizations which until that time had confined their activities to social-welfare work. In this manner, the Jewish Women's Association gained a growing number of adherents and promoted increasing interest in its activities and aims.

World War I temporarily interrupted Zionist activity in the country. Now the Association had another emergency to contend with. The first refugees were arriving from Galicia in numerous transports, and the members of the Women's Association worked day and night at suburban railroad stations, serving warm meals and beverages to the arrivals. That was the beginning of organized refugee aid during World War I.

During that war, the Jewish Women's Association set up a thirty-five-bed hospital under the supervision of the Karlín Army Hospital. This hospital, supported entirely by Association funds, received the Jewish wounded. Miss Leipen and Dr. Abeles, two Jewish volunteer nurses, worked tirelessly. After the war, Mrs. Else Deutsch and Mrs. Olga Bobasch received the Cross of Honor award from the Czechoslovak Red Cross.

Changing circumstances opened a new field of activity, that of social work, to the members of the Jewish Women's Association as well as to the Girls' Club. Thousands of Jewish refugees from Galicia had to be cared for, and a special school system was organized for the refugee children. While the members of the Women's Association attended to the sick, the Girls' Club, led by Grete Obernik, volunteered to supervise the educational work.

After the end of World War I, the Jewish Women's Association in the new Czechoslovak State found still another field of endeavor beyond its Zionist activities. The incorporation of Subcarpathian Ruthenia, with its large Jewish population, most of whom were very poor, posed new and difficult problems for Prague. All the sick from that eastern region who, in the past, would have been sent to Vienna or Budapest for treatment, now came to Prague. Dr. Salomon Lieben, a charitable and self-sacrificing physician who was a daily witness to this misery, turned to the Jewish Women's Association for help. This was the beginning of the Association welfare work for the sick which accomplished a great deal of good under the leadership of Mrs. Auguste Rosenbach.

Also pouring into Prague from Subcarpathian Ruthenia were groups of young men and women who wanted to prepare for emigration to and settlement in Eretz Israel. A special *Hakhshara* Committee was set up to find housing and employment for these young people, most of whom were uneducated, and to supervise their training. The advisor of this Committee was Dr. Michael Rosenbaum, who died in Haifa.

Another important endeavor of the Women's Association was the organization of the Prague Jewish kindergarten which, within a relatively short period, developed from a small class into an important educational institution. This kindergarten subsequently evolved into the Jewish Parochial School, with a large enrollment, which continued to draw students until the time of the Nazi invasion. Many of its graduates have achieved outstanding records in their entrance examinations for institutions of higher learning. Dr. Max Brod lent valuable assistance in the organization of the kindergarten.

At the request of Dr. Ernst Lebenhart, who was particularly interested in the project, the members of the Jewish Women's Association opened a dining hall for Jewish students. They supervised the kitchen, the food service, and the purchases and menu planning.

However, all these projects did not divert them from Zionist activities; indeed, the Jewish Women's Association of Prague was the nucleus of many other groups which led to the rise of an effective women's movement within the Zionist Organization. One of these groups was the Zionist Women's Girls' Club which was formed in Prague in 1912. In order to gain a better understanding of the rise of this organization and the subsequent growth of the Zionist women's movement, we shall briefly consider the setting in which it had its beginnings and in which it developed.

As has been discussed in other articles in this volume, assimilationist tendencies led some Jews to ally themselves with the German minority group, while others joined the Czech nationalist elements. Prior to World War I, opposition to Zionism in Czechoslovakia came mainly from the German-oriented assimilationists, but after 1918 and the formation of the Republic, the Czech assimilationists, most of them organized in the Svaz Čechů-židů (Association of Czech Jews), came to the fore.*

However, the political struggle between the Zionists and the assimilationists did not interfere with the activities of the Jewish Women's Association. As a matter of fact, some aspects of the Zionist program actually found their way into the camp of the Czech assimilationists. Many of the assimilationists were in accord with the movement to preserve traditional Jewish religious observances and were willing to emulate the (Zionist) revival of Jewish holiday and ritual observances.†

But even these activities of the two Zionist groups, the People's Association and the Women's Association, could not in the long run meet the needs of the young who sought new paths to fulfillment. Therefore the young men and women living in Prague struck out on their own. The organization of the Bar Kochba Students' Association (founded in 1885) by such Zionist students as Ernst Gütig, and Hugo and Arthur Bergmann, marked the beginning of a new era in the history of Zionism in Prague.**

The wives, sisters and girl friends of the Bar Kochba members joined together to form the nucleus of the Zionist Women's and Girls' Clubs in Prague. Their intensive cultural and educational work had the active support of men like Max Brod, Robert Weltsch, and Hugo Bergmann. The Girls' Club embarked on a propaganda campaign, and the groups were visited by many prominent Zionist women from abroad, including Bertha Pappenheim from Frankfort and Nancy Auerbach-Margulies from Berlin. As a rule, the early meetings sponsored by the Zionist women were held in the Jewish Town Hall. The programs were on a high cultural level and did much to further the cause of the women's movement.

It is not surprising, therefore, that the first Jew from Bohemia to settle in Palestine should have been a member of the Girls' Club. Today it is hard for us to conceive what a revolutionary step this was

* [Cf. Hostovsky, pp. 148–154. (Ed.)]

† [Cf. vol. I, Stransky, pp. 330–357 (Ed.)]

** [Cf. Kestenberg, vol. I, p. 60; and O. Rabinowicz, pp. 19–136. (Ed.)]

for that young lady, whose name was Martha Schick. By her *aliya*, in 1913, Martha Schick created a stir not only in her own family, but in all of the Jewish society in Prague. Soon after the end of World War I — from 1918 to 1920 — most of the members of the Girls' Club followed in Miss Schick's footsteps and left for Eretz Israel. Members of the Girls' Club were among the first Jews from Czechoslovakia to settle in Israel. Fifteen of these original members are still living in Israel. Milka Saphier taught home economics and nutrition; Frieda Löwy was one of the founders of Hefziba, a settlement at the foot of Mount Gilboa. Erna Feig was an employee of the National Library. Hedwig Gellner was a social worker employed by the City of Tel Aviv, while her sister Tony taught languages. Irma Singer-Berkowitz, who wrote children's books, settled in Degania; Olga Kulka settled in Ra'anana. The late Grete Obernik achieved prominence as a kindergarten teacher and educator. Also in this group was Elsa Bergmann, the wife of Professor Hugo Bergmann.*

For all practical purposes, however, this wholesale emigration put an end to the Girls' Club. Those members who still remained in Prague joined the Women's Association.

In 1919, the organized Jewish community of Czechoslovakia held its first elections. The list of candidates presented by the Jewish community of Prague included the name of Mrs. Leopoldine Klein, the vice-president of the Jewish Women's Association. This fact alone demonstrates the recognition which women were able to attain even then in Zionist public life.

The board meetings of the Jewish Women's Association were held each Wednesday afternoon in the smoke-filled back room of the Café Central on the Příkopy. Over coffee, the women discussed fund-raising campaigns, entries into the Jewish National Fund (JNF) Golden Book, contributions to the JNF on joyous occasions, children's parties, and more elaborate festivities for adults. On June 15, 1919, the group in the Café's back room celebrated the election of Prague's first Jewish City Council member, Dr. Ludvík Singer.

Some of the women who have made valuable contributions to the work of the Association (of which this author was an active member for many years), and the affiliated WIZO (Women's International Zionist Organization) Federation, should be mentioned here. The work of these women was inextricably tied to the

* Cf. Brada, pp. 589–598. (Ed.)

growth of the Zionist movement in Czechoslovakia. In 1919, the Association was joined by the wife of the editor and secretary general of the Jewish National Council, Emil Waldstein. Wally Waldstein had excellent connections in non-Jewish circles. When the Association learned that a world-wide organization of Zionist women had been established, and after the visit in Prague of Miriam Mechner, the secretary of WIZO in London, it was decided to organize a WIZO Federation in Czechoslovakia. Under the dynamic leadership of Hanna Steiner,* the younger women left the Women's Association and founded the Czechoslovak WIZO in 1925. Hanna Steiner had joined the Association in 1919, when her husband, a high school teacher, was transferred to Prague from Česká Lípa. She attended a meeting of the World WIZO Executive in Vienna in 1927, and gave a comprehensive report of the session to a small but active group of interested women in Prague. She delivered the same report in Brno, where she gained the cooperation of Bertha Schnabel and Gisella Feldmann, who were active in Jewish institutions and were now ready to form a WIZO group.

The newly formed WIZO Executive in Prague was one of the first Jewish organizations to make contact with the large Jewish population of Slovakia and Subcarpathian Ruthenia. Before that time, as has been noted earlier, there had been no contact between the Jewish communities in the western part of the country and those of the new eastern territories. In Bratislava, WIZO enlisted the aid of Gisi Fleischmann, a young woman of many talents; in Košice, WIZO found Tony Winkelsberg. When Emil Waldstein was transferred to Subcarpathian Ruthenia, his wife Wally began an educational campaign there in behalf of WIZO. Thanks to the assistance she received from the late Dr. Chaim Kugel, a pioneer in Hebrew cultural activities and founder and principal of the Hebrew high school in Mukačevo, WIZO gained a foothold even in these incredibly poverty-stricken and backward Jewish communities, and managed to form a number of groups there.

The Prague Executive was soon joined by Anny Parkus, Olga Winternitz, Minna Arje (a rabbi's wife), Martha Tauber, Thekla Freud (who became WIZO's most efficient treasurer), Fini Brada (who had led a WIZO group in the town of Podmokly), and Lene Hofmann.

---

* [Cf. Yahil, pp. 393–400; Grossmann, pp. 565–581; Brada, pp. 589–598. (Ed.)]

Acting as advisor to the Executive was Dr. Miriam Scheuer, a dentist and a close friend of Hanna Steiner. Although Dr. Scheuer did not live in Prague and therefore could not attend the meetings, she exerted considerable influence in the organization. Indeed, it may be said that while Hanna Steiner gave the group an organizational cohesiveness unparalleled by any other WIZO branch in the world, Dr. Scheuer was its spiritual molder. The Executive established contacts wherever Jews resided in larger numbers, sending out WIZO members as speakers, until, eventually, there was hardly a large Jewish community in Czechoslovakia that did not have a WIZO group. By 1938, Czechoslovakia had a total of 104 WIZO groups with a membership of about 12,000.

WIZO sponsored its own publication, *Blätter für die Jüdische Frau* (The Jewish Women's Pages), a section of the Zionist weekly *Selbstwehr* (Self-Defense). This paper was read not only in Czechoslovakia, but also by German-speaking Jewish women abroad, particularly in Austria and Germany, and, together with the publication *Pioneers and Helpers* (published in London), it became WIZO's German-language medium of information dissemination, and education.*

As WIZO grew in importance within Czechoslovakia's Zionist organization, its representatives were invited to join the movement's other organs — the Zionist Central Committee in Czechoslovakia, the Jewish Party, the territorial governing bodies of the JNF and Keren HaYesod, the HeHalutz, and the Tarbut organization. Many WIZO Executive members also served outside the Women's movement. Olga Winternitz was "Mother to the *Halutzim*," Fini Brada was politically active in the Socialist Zionist organization, and I myself worked for Tarbut.

HeHalutz, and also the Tarbut organization which worked for the promotion of Hebrew schools in Subcarpathian Ruthenia, and for the dissemination of the Hebrew language in the provinces of Czechoslovakia, were subsidized by WIZO, though much of WIZO's budget went to institutions in Eretz Israel.

The WIZO Executive gained a most valuable addition to its ranks in the person of Marie Schmolka. She came from a Czech assimilationist background. On a world tour she had taken after the death of her husband, Mrs. Schmolka visited Eretz Israel. Deeply impressed by what she saw there, she resolved to work for the Zionist cause.

---

* [Cf. vol. I, Dagan, p. 530. (Ed.)]

She was endowed with many outstanding qualities, including a fine intellect, breadth of vision, determination, and the ability to carry out her ideas. I received invaluable support from her in a matter I considered to be highly important, but for which until that time the Czechoslovak WIZO had shown little understanding: the establishment of closer contacts with Czechoslovak women's organizations.

The women of Czechoslovakia were national in orientation, exceptionally progressive, and they enjoyed the respect of women's organizations elsewhere. They were organized in a National Council of Czechoslovak Women. Marie Schmolka was the link between this organization and WIZO. WIZO became part of the National Council as the official spokesman of national Jewish groups, with Marie Schmolka and this writer serving as WIZO's delegates to the Council. Our work was supported by a Czech-language women's journal which appeared as a supplement to the Zionist weekly *Židovské Zprávy* (Jewish News), and of which this writer was the editor. Within the framework of the National Council of Czechoslovak Women, we created a Jewish group of the Women's League for Peace and Freedom.

When Dr. Emil Margulies, the chairman of the Jewish Party of Czechoslovakia, called for a campaign to aid the Jews in Subcarpathian Ruthenia, it was WIZO that took charge and responded most generously. An appeal from the Committee to Aid the Jews of Subcarpathian Ruthenia resulted in contributions such as had never before been collected in all the history of Czechoslovak Jewry. This highly successful campaign made possible a program of constructive assistance, which included the distribution of milk and clothing. All members of WIZO took an active part in the project, some making tours of the tiny, neglected hamlets of Subcarpathian Ruthenia, to ascertain the needs of the inhabitants and to make sure that the work was done well. The greater part of the work was done by Marie Schmolka, who, in close cooperation with the representatives of the American Jewish Joint Distribution Committee there, set up an impressive program of relief work for the Jews in Subcarpathian Ruthenia.*

By that time WIZO was a well-established organization, greatly respected in Czechoslovakia as well as abroad. Its district and provincial conventions were always arranged in exemplary fashion, and the work done by its local groups within the Jewish congregations

* [Cf. vol. I, Sole, pp. 125–154. (Ed.)]

enjoyed high regard. It should be remembered that this large organization had neither an office nor a paid secretary of its own. All the clerical work was done by volunteers, and the correspondence was supervised by Mrs. Jappke, the secretary of *Selbstwehr*, whose services were available to WIZO three days a week. Administrative costs were kept at a minimum, and even traveling expenses were defrayed by the Executive members making trips.

The terrible blow sustained by the Jews of Germany in 1933 also had a profound effect on the Jews of the neighboring Republic of Czechoslovakia. WIZO undertook to adapt its program to the challenges presented by the changed circumstances. The masses of Jewish refugees streaming into Prague from Germany found Hanna Steiner and Marie Schmolka ready to give them aid and protection. The program of refugee aid which these women started and conducted together with the international Jewish organizations took on huge dimensions and absorbed all their energies. The work done by Hanna Steiner and Marie Schmolka during the years from 1933 to 1939 in behalf of the refugees exceeds the scope of this article. It is part of the history of the Jewish people of that tragic era. So is the work of Gisi Fleischmann, who, bravely and in utter disdain of danger, worked tirelessly in behalf of her people during the Nazi occupation. Suffice it to say here that these three members of the Czechoslovak WIZO helped thousands of Jews and saved countless Jewish lives, and that, in the end, Mrs. Fleischmann made the supreme sacrifice.*

After the occupation of the Sudeten territory in 1938, hundreds of WIZO women and their families went from there to Prague preparatory to emigration to Palestine or other overseas countries. Most of these women had had no occupational training whatever. They were upper-middle-class housewives who had been accustomed to doing only light housework and supervising paid help who did the heavier chores. Others had worked in their husbands' business enterprises. Of those few who had been trained in some occupation, most had done office or sales work, skills that would do them little good in a new country whose language they would not know. All of these women were eager to use the interim period before their emigration for training in some practical occupation. But at that time there still was no agency whose function it was to provide the vocational training they needed.

---

* [Cf. Yahil, pp. 393–400, and Grossmann, pp. 565–581. (Ed.)]

The Prague WIZO promptly and energetically took the initiative. First, it opened its clubhouses to members from Nazi-occupied areas to give these homeless women a pleasant and friendly atmosphere in which to meet their friends in Prague, who did their best to ease their plight. The WIZO women assisted them in finding apartments, and collected clothing, linens, and household furnishings for them. They arranged for lunches and temporary shelters, visited the sick, and settled official business of women who could not speak the Czech language. WIZO also organized an employment agency, day centers, and a home for children. In addition, WIZO created vocational reorientation courses, taught by expert instructors. There, for a small tuition fee which could be reduced and was sometimes waived altogether, depending on the circumstances, the refugee women could obtain training in dressmaking, millinery, sewing, cutting, baking, hairdressing, manicuring, massaging, beauty culture, dry cleaning, ironing, photography, child care, invalid nursing, and in simpler handicrafts such as making belts, bags and artificial flowers. There were also language courses in Hebrew, English, and Spanish. Special attention was given to courses in cooking and homemaking.

At that time, a project was started in London to place women and girls from Nazi-occupied areas in British homes as cooks and maids, and WIZO was requested to provide training in this work. With monies supplied by the Lord Mayor's Fund from London, WIZO rented classrooms, engaged two home economics instructors, and set up an excellent cooking school in which more than six hundred women and girls received instruction. Only those who had received a diploma from the WIZO school were considered as candidates for a "permit" to enter England as "domestics." Prospective emigrants to Palestine received special instruction in Palestinian foods and cooking.

While WIZO supervised the training of women for urban occupations, HeHalutz saw to the agricultural training of prospective *halutzot*. The annexation of the Sudeten territory and the subsequent occupation of all of Czechoslovakia posed a grave challenge to HeHalutz. Masses of young men and women streamed to Prague and Brno for training for resettlement in Eretz Israel. The girls were placed in homes especially set up for this purpose, and subsequently assigned to various *p'lugot*, (groups). A number of them were placed in *hakhsharot* abroad.

The selection of girls to be given the limited number of Palestinian immigration certificates available to WIZO was made by a committee consisting of an equal number of representatives from WIZO and HeHalutz. The girls selected were given examinations in the Hebrew language, Zionist history, and Palestinography.

During the Munich crisis, the Czechoslovak WIZO participated in all the protests sent abroad by the National Council of Czechoslovak Women, before and after the Munich Agreement. In addition, WIZO independently sent cables to London, the United States, and the Union of South Africa, desperately urging that everything possible be done to persuade the governments of those countries to raise their voices in protest against the annihilation of Czechoslovakia, a truly democratic country.

On March 16, 1939, the day after the Nazi occupation of Prague, Hanna Steiner was arrested by the Gestapo at the Refugee Aid Office and taken to the police lockup. Mrs. Jappke, who was present at the scene, remained in the office to warn Marie Schmolka. But instead of heeding the advice to get away as quickly as possible, Marie Schmolka went to the police station and gave herself up in hopes of effecting Hanna Steiner's release. Hanna Steiner was indeed released three weeks later, but Marie Schmolka was questioned repeatedly by the Gestapo in the Petschek Building and finally transferred to Pankrác Prison.

During those trying days, the Czechoslovak women proved their solidarity. Senator Plamínková used her influence with the highest authorities and finally effected Marie Schmolka's release after three months' imprisonment.

The spirit which pervaded the Zionist women of Czechoslovakia gave them strength to do their work in peacetime and to bear the sorrow and suffering that came to them with the Nazi occupation of their country. Proof of this may be found not only in this article, but also, and particularly, in the reports of their conduct and their activities during the Nazi era and in the concentration camps, as well as in the records of their contribution to the rebuilding of the land of Israel.

THE CZECH-JEWISH MOVEMENT

by Egon Hostovsky

The Assimilationists and the Zionists

In studying the literature on the activities of the Czech-Jewish movement in the period between the two world wars, one is under the strong impression that the organized Jewish assimilationist endeavor in Czechoslovakia was directed in the main toward the ideological struggle against the political and ethical principles of the Zionist movement. Actually, this was not the case. The debates carried on at meetings or in the press between the Czechoslovak Zionists and the assimilationists were for the most part related to secondary issues and did not revolve around the intellectual essence of assimilationism as expressed in the philosophies of its foremost exponents.

The Jewish assimilationists of Czechoslovakia as a political group were unique in that, unlike similar groups in other countries, they tried to achieve a Jewish transformation by means of a transformation of the host nation. On the other hand, the Zionist movement in Czechoslovakia, too, was different from that in most other countries in that it constituted a political party in the State, representing the national Jewish movement of the Jewish minority group in the Czechoslovak National Assembly.*

Thus the unusual status of the Jews of Czechoslovakia and the unusual political atmosphere combined to give rise to an unparalleled political and ethical struggle within the ranks of Czechoslovak Jewry.

The Zionists, for their part, asserted that the assimilationist move-

* [See A. M. Rabinowicz, The Jewish Party, pp. 243–346 (Ed.)]

ment comprised simply a group of opportunists, while the assimilationists claimed that Zionism in Czechoslovakia was just a cloak which concealed the Germanizing movement. Neither of these allegations was justified. It would be difficult to demonstrate that the theorists of assimilationism, from the philosopher Jindřich Kohn down to the younger generation of Czech-Jewish poets, journalists and sociologists nurtured by the academic "Kapper Club"* were opportunists or Jewish apostates. By the same token, it was grossly unfair to equate Zionism with the "Germanizing" element in Czech Jewry because the die-hard group of German Jews was altogether indifferent not only to the religious tradition of Judaism, but also to every form of Jewish nationalism, so that the Zionists had nothing whatever in common with them.

The fact was that the outstanding thinkers of the Czech-Jewish movement were not greatly at odds with the chief exponents of Zionism in Czechoslovakia, and certainly not in the final years of the Republic. Zionists could hardly have found anything objectionable in the slogan of the Czech-Jewish movement which was carved on the headstone over the grave of the physician and philanthropist Dr. Viktor Vohryzek, a Czech thinker and pious Jew who had been one of the founders of the movement: "Of Jewish descent, with the Czech nation above all [other] nations."

The history of Czech Jewry in the nineteenth century, which gave rise to the Czech-Jewish movement, closely resembles the history of Jews in other European countries of that period. Emancipation led to a widespread desire, particularly among the young, to speed up the process of Europeanization. However, the situation in the Czech provinces was unique in that these provinces were not autonomous, but subordinate to a foreign power — Austria — and that the relationship between the Czech lands and their German-speaking overlords at that time was one of constant conflict. The fact that the Jews found themselves as a rule compelled to use the German language in their dealings with the Austrians earned them the hostility of their Czech neighbors. Only a few Jewish intellectuals of that era, like Moritz Hartmann and Siegfried Kapper, summoned up the courage

* The "Kapper Club" — in Czech, *Spolek akademiků Čechů-židů Kapper* — underscored the affiliations of Czech Jews to the Czech people. It subsidized poor Czech-Jewish students in its own branch organization ("Opora") and published a monthly bulletin.

to resist this "Germanizing" trend. But these initial attempts were curtly rejected by Karel Havlíček-Borovský,* the well-known author who was then the leader of the Czech national movement. This rejection was not motivated by anti-Semitic feelings on Havlíček's part, but simply by his conviction that the Jews of Bohemia would always side with the Germans. Though Havlíček's rebuff came as a shock to the Czech Jewry, it did not deter individual Jews from continuing to strive for what they believed would be a cementing of close ties between Jews and Czechs who, as they pointed out, shared the same fate. The zealous efforts of Jews like Bohumil Bondy, Professor Alois Zucker, and Mořic Baštýř in behalf of assimilation and their open expression of solidarity with the oppressed Czech people did much to dispel the notion of Havlíček, prevalent in many circles, that the Jews always sided with the dominant element.

The Czech-Jewish Movement from 1919 to 1939

This was the beginning of the era of Jewish assimilation in the Czech lands. The history of Jewish assimilationism in what later became Czechoslovakia may be divided into two distinct phases: (1) the eighteenth and early nineteenth centuries, and (2) the late nineteenth and early twentieth centuries down to the Nazi era. In the earlier phase, the ideal of assimilation centered around religious liberty and human freedom in general, while in the later phase the stress was on the desire of the Jews to live side by side with the Czechs, sharing the Czech national ideals.

It may be thought that the Czech-Jewish generation of this second phase, absorbed in nationalist goals as it was, did not pay much attention to the religion and ethics of Judaism; but this assumption is not borne out by the facts. As an illustration we may take the activities of Augustín Stein (1854-1935), who was a leading official of the municipal council of Prague, and later head of Prague's Jewish Religious Council and finally of the Supreme Council of Jewish Religious Congregations of Bohemia, Moravia, and Silesia. Stein made several outstanding contributions to Jewish thought and literature. His interpretation of Jewish ethics, based on the original biblical texts, and his commentary of the Five Books of Moses have yet to be evaluated. Both show great originality of thought and a

* In the literary magazine *Česká Včela*, Prague, 1846 — a critical essay.

brilliant style. Stein's desire to bring about a better mutual understanding between the Czech and Jewish peoples in their ethical values may be regarded as no less significant in the history of Czech Jewry than the efforts of Moses Mendelssohn in the history of the Jews of Germany.

Other leading personalities of this era were Karel Fischer (1859–1906),* Dr. Edvard Lederer-Leda (1859–1941), Dr. Viktor Vohryzek (1868–1918),† Dr. Bohdan Kleinberger (1859–1934),** and Dr. Jindřich Kohn (1874–1935). The ideas of these five men represented the foundation on which the philosophy of the Czech-Jewish movement was based until the Nazi occupation. Vohryzek and Kleinberger were thinkers in the field of Jewish ethics; Lederer-Leda was the political theorist of the Czech-Jewish movement, and Jindřich Kohn was the interpreter of universal assimilationism.††

The end of World War I seemed to bring fulfillment to the dreams of the thinkers who had stood at the cradle of the Czech-Jewish movement. Not only were the Jews in the new Czechoslovak Republic adopting those elements of the Czech nation that were healthy, ethical and creative, but the Czech nation, too, was beginning to accept many of the contributions of the spirit of Judaism.

In 1919, the *Tribuna*, a political and cultural daily newspaper whose owners belonged to the Czech-Jewish movement, made its first appearance. This paper carried excellent commentaries on political, economic, and cultural life by Jewish journalists of note (including the drama critic Josef Kodíček, author Karel Poláček, Jan Münzer, and experts on national economy like Bedřich Weiner and Gustav Stern), as well as by well-known non-Jewish writers, including the great Czech critic František Xaver Šalda.***

---

* The editor of twenty-two volumes of the annual *Česko-Židovský Kalendár* (Czech-Jewish Almanac), Fischer inspired Jaroslav Vrchlický, one of the foremost Czech poets, to write his famous epic "Bar Kochba."

† A physician and founder of *Rozvoj* (Evolution), the organ of the Czech-Jewish movement, Vohryzek was the author of a philosophical work *The Book of Life's Wisdom — A Philosophy for the Average Man* in which he sought to demonstrate elements of Jewish ethics in the relationship between philosophy and religion. [Cf. vol. I, Stransky, p. 351, n. 7 (Ed.)].

** A lawyer and member of Masaryk's Sociological Society, Kleinberger wrote essays dealing with what he regarded as the constantly recurring Jewish dualism in history as an index of national conservatism and progressivism.

†† On the literary activities of all these men, see vol. I, Hostovsky, pp. 439–453. (Ed.)

*** Cf. vol. I, Dagan, p. 530. Ed.)]

Edvard Lederer-Leda and Jindřich Kohn, too, were among the contributors to the *Tribuna*. Leda's articles, which dealt with Jewish problems in Czechoslovakia and which later were published in book form, included such topics as "German and Czech Anti-Semitism," "The Jew in Contemporary Society," and "The Crisis in Judaism and Jewishness." Kohn's views of Judaism, as expressed in his essays, may be summarized as follows. Like all other ancient traditions, the tradition of Judaism, too, is the product of a long process of evolution reaching back into antiquity. In this process, Judaism absorbed various elements of other cultures which influenced its development. The Bible, Kohn asserted, was also the result of an evolutionary process. It did not come into being all at one time. Eventually, the evolution of Judaism branched off into two different directions — Christianity on the one hand, and the phenomenon of the Jewish diaspora on the other. In the course of time, these two elements grew so far apart from each other that their original relationship was all but forgotten, all the more so since the Christian element viewed the Jewish diaspora in the Christian world with hatred and rejection. According to Kohn, only historic efforts by great minds on behalf of all mankind could alleviate at least the worst of the prejudices that divided the two. It was in this task, Kohn felt, that the special mission of the Jews among the nations rested. This was a "chosen-people" concept, refined and reinterpreted to suit the modern age. Because of their acute sensitivity to threats of prejudice and persecution, the Jews were ordained by destiny to be the guardians of all past achievements of human civilization, and the protectors and defenders of all the cultural developments that would lead to a better tomorrow not only for the Jews, but for all peoples of the world. To Kohn, the ideological content of assimilation represented one of those great ideas which Masaryk had said were needed to keep mankind's growth from being stunted, and Kohn attempted to demonstrate how all of humanity, and indeed the whole world, had originated and evolved only by virtue of its physical and mental adaptability to change.

However, the tragedy of the Czech-Jewish movement was that long before its official liquidation under the boot of Nazidom, it had begun to disintegrate from within. Moving farther and farther away from the ideals of mutual understanding evolved by its theorists, the Czech-Jewish movement gradually came to regard assimilation as an end in itself, with its political representatives striving, directly or indirectly, for a complete amalgamation of the Jewish element into the Czech people.

It is interesting to note that when a reaction set in against this distortion of the original aims and purposes of the movement, it came from young people who had been raised in Czechoslovakia and educated in Czech schools. This younger generation, which included writers like Hanuš Bonn, Jiří Orten, Egon Hostovský, Zdeněk Tohn, and Ervín Neumann, declared its stand in lectures and essays read at the Kapper Club. The members of this student organization were concerned with the study of Judaism and not with its liquidation. Their monthly magazine, which first appeared in 1934, engaged in more debates with *Rozvoj*, the official organ of the Czech-Jewish movement, than with the Zionists. In their attempt to gain a better understanding of Jewish problems, these young people developed an interest in Orthodoxy and in the Hasidic movement, enlisting as their advisor in this field Jiří Langer, the well-known expert on Eastern European Jewry. The members of the Kapper Club invited Augustín Ṣtein to write for their monthly on the foundations of the Jewish religion, brought out a Czech edition of an anthology of the works of Yiddish writers, published the monumental work of Professor Čeněk Zíbrt on the origin and influence of the Passover Haggada, and produced a posthumous edition of the works of Jindřich Kohn in a two-volume set entitled *Assimilation and the Ages*.

As the specter of Nazism came closer to the borders of Czechoslovakia, dissension sprang up within the Czech-Jewish movement. The dispute was brought to a head during the period of the Nazi rump state by an unfortunate statement in *Rozvoj* about the necessity in times of danger of drawing a sharp line of distinction between the Jews of Czechoslovakia and other Jews.

The Nazi occupation dealt the final blow to the Czech-Jewish movement. As we have said at the outset of this article, the Czech-Jewish movement was unique and unparallelled in its day. In our own day, there is no need for organized political assimilation on the part of the Jews. But even now, when the Jews have a state of their own in Israel, the ideals advanced by the early great thinkers of the Czech-Jewish movement still have not lost all their validity. For today, just as they did in the past and as they probably always will in the future, most of the Jews still live in the midst of non-Jewish nations. And as in the past, so, too, in the present and for many years to come, books will be published with titles and subject matter similar to that of Joachim Prinz's *Dilemma of the Modern Jew*. Prinz finds no satisfactory solution for the dilemma of modern Jewry, which neither desires to merge with the world that surrounds it, nor is willing to live in the land of its fathers. Perhaps Prinz's particular difficulty in finding a way out of this problem is due to his belief that there is little metaphysical content in Judaism. The thinkers of the Czech-Jewish movement, on the other hand, never claimed anything of the sort. Indeed, they acknowledged that it was Jewish metaphysics, such as the mystery of the law of the eternal alternation in Jewish history between dispersal and ingathering, that gave comfort to the Jews throughout the ages. It was comfort derived from philosophy or, if you will, from the knowledge that, according to all past experience, there was a wisdom greater than the human mind, watching over the lives of men, of peoples, and of nations. To realize this means to reach some understanding of the metaphysics that inheres in the destiny of Judaism. To fail to realize it means confrontation with an endless search for a way out of the so-called Jewish dilemma.

THE HISTORY OF AGUDATH ISRAEL IN SLOVAKIA (1918–1939)

by Gertrude Hirschler

Agudath Israel[1] *is a worldwide organization of strictly Orthodox Jews, known for its uncompromising stand on the absolute authority of Jewish religious law in all aspects of Jewish personal and communal life the world over.*

Agudath Israel was founded shortly before the outbreak of World War I by eminent Orthodox rabbinical scholars and lay communal leaders of Germany, the Austro-Hungarian monarchy, Poland, and Lithuania as an instrument for concerted, effective action to check the drifting away from tradition due to the growing influence of secular culture and of secularist ideologies in the Jewish world.

The platform adopted by the founding conference, which was held in Kattowitz (now Poland) in 1912, states that

the aim of the Agudath Israel is to solve, in the spirit of the Torah, all problems arising in the life of the Jewish people. Hence, the Agudah desires... to organize in a union and to bring about a close rapprochement of the scattered portions of Orthodox Jewry, especially of Eastern and Western European Jewry... to foster... the study of the Torah and to promote Jewish education... to improve the economic conditions of the Jewish masses in poverty-stricken countries and in Palestine... to promote Jewish literature and a Jewish press which will be in accord with the Jewish spirit... to represent Orthodox Jewry in its totality before the outside world and to defend the Torah and its adherents against attack.[2]

The Agudah, as it soon became popularly known in the Jewish community, established groups for adults and young people which engaged in educational and propaganda work and raised funds to support the great yeshivot of Eastern and Central Europe and a number of social service projects in the Holy Land and in the Diaspora. At times Agudath Israel has appeared as the spokesman of Orthodox Jewry before governments and international bodies. Its supreme authority in all matters of policy has been the Mo'etzet Gedole HaTorah (*Council of Torah Sages*), *an informal group of rabbinical leaders noted for their talmudic scholarship and unbending Orthodoxy.*

During the years between the two world wars the most important branches of Agudath Israel were in Germany (its first world headquarters were located in Frankfurt am Main), Poland, Lithuania, Palestine, Austria, Hungary, and Slovakia. Since World War II Agudath Israel has developed considerable activity in the Western Hemisphere, and today a major part of Agudah's work is carried on in and through the United States.

Opposed to the secular concepts of Zionism, Agudath Israel originally took an anti-Zionist position. However, it consistently aided the settlement of religious Jews in pre-Israel Palestine, and today its Israeli section is represented in the Knesset, the parliament of the State of Israel. At various times the Agudah was even represented in the Israeli cabinet.

This study deals with the history and activities of Agudath Israel in Slovakia during the era of the Czechoslovak Republic (1918-1939), which coincides with the interwar period. It deals almost exclusively with Slovakia, for while there were also scattered Agudah groups in the other provinces of the Czechoslovak Republic, most of the branches by far were in Slovakia, where two-thirds of the Jewish population were officially affiliated with Orthodox congregations and communities. Agudah's national headquarters in Czechoslovakia were not in Prague but in Bratislava, the capital of Slovakia. For all practical purposes, therefore, the story of Agudism in the Czechoslovak Republic is synonymous with that of the Agudah of Slovakia.

* * *

In reviewing the beginnings of Agudath Israel in Slovakia and its subsequent development it must be borne in mind that when Agudath Israel was first founded — six years before the establishment of the Czechoslovak Republic — Slovakia had been a province of Hungary for over a thousand years and that the basic attitudes of Orthodox

Jewry in Slovakia were, in most respects, identical with those of its counterpart in Hungary.

In view of the fact that Agudath Israel sought a "close rapprochement... especially of Eastern and Western European Jewry" it must be pointed out, too, that Jewish Orthodoxy in Hungary—and Slovakia—was different from the Orthodoxies of Eastern Europe, on the one hand, and of Western Europe (notably Germany), on the other — not in its basic attitudes toward Judaism, to be sure, but in the external manifestations of its "Jewishness." Unlike the strictly Orthodox Jews of Russia, Poland, and Lithuania, most of pre-1914 Orthodox western Hungarian and Slovak Jews had adopted modified forms of modern dress, did not speak Yiddish, and were generally able to read and write in the vernacular.[3] On the other hand, the rabbinical leaders to whom the strictly Orthodox of Hungary and Slovakia looked for spiritual guidance had little formal secular education. As a consequence, the average Orthodox Jew in that region did not quite know how to assess those rabbis in Germany who enjoyed positions of leadership in western Orthodoxy but were familiar with studies and ideas that had nothing to do with the yeshiva world.

Unlike their brethren in the East — who had been subject to violent persecution for centuries and who, in the final decades of the nineteenth century, had endured a number of bloody pogroms and thought in terms of emigration, partly to Palestine — the Jews of pre-1914 Hungary and Slovakia, Orthodox and non-Orthodox alike, who had been spared such excesses of Jew-hatred, did not view mass Jewish settlement in Palestine as practical. As for the Hungarian Orthodox, the support they gave to the small Jewish community in the Holy Land was confined for the most part to yeshivot and to the "Hungarian Houses" in Jerusalem, where Jews from what was then the Hapsburg monarchy spent full time on sacred studies. They certainly had no common ground with western-style political Zionism, because they considered the establishment of a Jewish state in the Holy Land to be the task of the Messiah and not of mere mortals, especially not of the nonobservant Jews who were then the spokesmen of the World Zionist Organization.

Like their counterparts in Germany, but unlike those in Eastern Europe, where each congregation was largely on its own, the Orthodox communities of Hungary proper and Slovakia were organized into a countrywide union, separate from the other Jewish congregations which belonged to the *Kultusgemeinden* or "official" Jewish communities. The "autonomous" Orthodox communities of Hungary and Slovakia were subject to the authority of the Orthodox Israelite Bureau (*Landeskanzlei*) in Budapest, organized in 1871, which had obtained separate government recognition similar to that extended to the *Kultusgemeinden*. They were opposed to cooperating with the *Kultusgemeinden* or with other non-Orthodox Jewish organizations even in matters of common interest to all Jews in the country.

In view of these differences, it was not surprising that those Hungarian and Slovak Orthodox communities which shared the basic views represented by Agudath Israel should nevertheless have been somewhat reserved in their response to the new organization, which was to include Orthodox Jews from many different countries, East and West alike.

Doubts were entertained by these communities also on ideological and political grounds. To begin with, they relied for spiritual guidance almost exclusively on their own rabbinical leaders, most of whom had graduated from indigenous yeshivot conducted in the tradition established by such Orthodox authorities as Rabbi Moses Schreiber (1763–1839), the *Hatam Sofer*, spiritual leader of the renowned yeshiva of Pressburg (as Bratis ava was then known). To be sure, the Orthodox of Hungary and Slovakia, and especially their rabbinical leaders, had a profound respect for the yeshivot of Eastern Eurppe and for their mentors who were taking a prominent role in the organization of the Agudah, but the masses of Hungarian and Slovak Orthodoxy had had little contact with those strongholds of Jewish tradition in the East. It is equally true that they greatly admired the unswerving devoutness of the rabbis and laymen in Germany who were taking over the practical administration of the Agudah, but they considered them too much under the influence of "German" ways and methods, which seemed to carry a threat of assimilation.

Second, some of the East European and German founders of the Agudah had attended early Zionist congresses and in several instances had been members of the Mizrahi movement. While these leaders had quit Zionism because of its attempts to foster a secularist Jewish culture and had been disillusioned even by the Orthodox Mizrahi, many of them still had a positive interest in the settlement of religious Jews in the Holy Land beyond the confines of the yeshivot. The Orthodox of Hungary and Slovakia feared that to join an organization with leaders holding such views might in time bring them into a position where they might have to cooperate with the Zionists whom they had consistently mistrusted and attacked.

Finally, while East European Orthodoxy — which had no all-embracing, articulate organization — welcomed the advent of the Agudah, which it felt would provide a platform for Orthodox unity the world over, the Orthodox of Hungary and Slovakia felt that the Orthodox Israelite Bureau (*Landeskanzlei*), which had effectively promoted Orthodoxy and represented its interests in the Jewish and non-Jewish world for over four decades, was organization enough for them. Besides, at the time the Agudah seemed willing to accept members of Orthodox congregations in Germany and elsewhere which had not made themselves autonomous, but were part of larger Jewish communities embracing Orthodox and non-Orthodox elements alike. The communities represented in the Budapest *Landeskanzlei* feared that by identifying with what they considered a "mixed" organization they might strengthen the hands of those Orthodox Jews in Hungary and Slovakia who had elected to remain part of the Jewish community at large as "status quo congregations," and who were therefore no longer considered impeccable in their Orthodoxy. Having succeeded in building up a staunch, self-sufficient fortress of Torah in the face of a powerful, government-supported *neolog* (Liberal) wing of Judaism, the *Landeskanzlei* communities were understandably reluctant to make common cause with any force that might so much as threaten to infringe upon their independence.

It took World War I and the upheavals that followed throughout Europe to bring about a change in this attitude. As the war went on, the leaders of Central Bureau (*Landeskanzlei*) Orthodoxy in Hungary — and Slovakia — realized that the help of a worldwide body more powerful and articulate than any local organization would be needed to fight the forces of irreligion that seemed to be gaining the upper hand on the Jewish scene, particularly among the youth, and to counteract secular Zionism, which had acquired international recognition as result of Britain's promise (the Balfour Declaration) to aid in the establishment of a Jewish national home in Palestine.

Accordingly, Slovak Orthodoxy sent delegates to the international conference called by the Agudah in Zurich in the spring of 1919 for the purpose of reorganizing, electing a temporary executive, and making plans for the movement's first world congress (*Kenessiah Gedolah*). Among the delegates from Slovakia — which by then, of course, was no longer part of Hungary but a province of the newly created Czechoslovak Republic — was Jacob Joel Braun of Bratislava, who later was to become director of the Central Office of Agudah for Czechoslovakia and then national president during the final years of the organization. In the fall of that year, when the Organization of Autonomous Orthodox Congregations of Slovakia met in Bratislava to found a Central Bureau (*Landeskanzlei*) of its own, Rabbi Abraham Aaron Katz of Nitra spoke at length about the importance of Agudath Israel.[4]

At a meeting of autonomous orthodox congregations held in Bratislava on December 3, 1919,[5] it was decided to establish in Slovakia a countrywide organization which would become a constituent of the Agudath Israel world movement, "with certain reservations necessitated by the special requirements of Orthodoxy in Slovakia." A committee was appointed to enter into negotiations with the world Agudah. However, due to transportation difficulties, the representative of the world organization, Rabbi Pinchas Kohn, of Ansbach, Germany,[6] was not able to get to Bratislava until May 1920. At the meeting with Kohn, Rabbi Koloman Weber of Piešťany,[7] the newly elected cochairman of the Central Bureau (*Landeskanzlei*) of the Organization of Autonomous Orthodox Congregations in Slovakia, explained the objections of "old" Hungarian Orthodoxy to the Agudah. But now, he said, when world organizations "posing a threat to the most vital interests of Torah-true Judaism require [a response of] more positive action for the preservation of the Torah-true spirit, Orthodoxy in this country considered that the time had come to join the Agudah,"[8] albeit under certain explicit conditions. These conditions were then read to the meeting by Rabbi Simon Hirschler of Bratislava:[9]

1. The Slovak Agudah is to be a separate group within the world organization; it will manage its internal affairs independently and will have sole jurisdiction over the acceptance of members for the Agudah of Slovakia.

2. It goes without saying that the Agudah of Slovakia will be firmly rooted in the *Shulhan Arukh* and *minhage Yisrael.*[10] The guidelines for each district group shall be set by the local district rabbi, whose rulings shall be binding in every respect.

3. In all questions concerning Eretz Yisrael, be it in matters of education or any change whatever in existing institutions or in the creation of new Jewish political institutions, approval must first be sought from the authorities of the *Va'ad HaIr Ashkenazi.*[11]

4. One of the tasks of Agudah shall be to support and promote the *Kupat Eretz Yisrael*[12] in the form in which it has existed heretofore.

The leaders who attended the Bratislava meeting — among them Rabbi Akiba Schreiber (the chief rabbi of Bratislava and dean of the Pressburg yeshiva linked with the name of his ancestor, the *Hatam Sofer*), and the chief rabbis of such communities as Dunajská Streda and Pezinok — heard a report from a visitor from Jerusalem, Rabbi Löbl, who urged the Agudists of Slovakia to give spiritual-moral, and financial support to the old established Orthodox com, munity of Palestine.

Throughout the twenty years of its existence, Agudath Israel of Slovakia was to identify with the right wing of Agudah, consistently opposing cooperation with any other Jewish organization even in areas not related to religious life as such, and also rejecting the view held by the left wing of the Agudah that it would be permissible for Agudath Israel to work with Zionist groups in economic and political matters whenever that would serve the best interests of religious Jews in Palestine. This attitude, of course, was motivated by still-fresh memories of years of struggle against well-organized non-Orthodox and secular Zionist groups, which had been competing for influence in the Jewish community, and which the *Landeskanzlei* type of Orthodoxy considered threats to the survival of historic Judaism.

Agudath Israel in Slovakia was not particularly active in promoting new organizational methods on the world Agudah scene or as an instrument of overt political action in world Orthodoxy. It was primarily known and respected for the saintly scholars (such as Rabbis Hirschler, Moshe and Abraham Aaron Katz,[13] Schreiber,[14] and Weber) who stood at its helm, and as a mass movement commanding the unquestioning loyalty of its active members, which by the 1930s numbered tens of thousands.

Before long, Agudath Israel groups for adults (men only, in keeping with the separation of the sexes favored by strict Orthodox tradition) had been founded in Bratislava and in dozens of cities and towns all over Slovakia. In time scattered local groups also emerged in Moravia and Bohemia, the strongholds of assimilationism, and in Subcarpathian Ruthenia, the outpost of fiery East European Hasidism. But unlike their counterparts in Slovakia, which grew apace in numbers and influence, these branches made little progress. In Moravia and Bohemia, Orthodoxy of the Agudah type represented a dwindling minority, while at the other extreme, some Hasidic rabbis of Subcarpathian Ruthenia, led by Rabbi Eleazar Spira of Mukačevo, prevented the growth of Agudah by refusing to give their approval to the organization, which they considered too modern.

In March 1921 the Agudath Israel of Slovakia held its first national convention in Trenčianske Teplice under the chairmanship of Rabbi Lemel Spitzer of Spišské Podhradie, with at least a dozen rabbis and nearly two hundred delegates present. It was this convention that elected Rabbi Abraham Aaron Katz as president of the Agudath Israel of Czechoslovakia. Also elected was a national executive board consisting of such men as Rabbi Samuel David Ungar (then rabbi in Trnava), Eliezer Fonfeder of Prešov, and Isidor Pappenheim of Bratislava.[15]

By that time Slovakia already boasted of a very active and vociferous Agudist young men's organization (*Jugendgruppe*), which aided the parent body in its work. On June 6, 1920,[16] young men from Bratislava, Topolčany, Nitra, Stupava, Trnava, Pieštany, and Komárno met in Bratislava to form a countrywide youth organization which would "attract the youth to work for Palestine in the genuine Jewish spirit"[17] and conduct educational, social, and propaganda activities. The *Jugendgruppe* proved to be a potent force in keeping young men in the Orthodox camp. Faced by the challenges and persuasive arguments of new trends in the Jewish world, these young people needed the support of a mass movement of like-minded contemporaries which would strengthen them in their own uncompromising (and in some areas unpopular) religious convictions and teach them how to put up an effective fight against the attacks of opposing ideologies.

Fathers and sons, in their own groups and jointly, found much work to do. Both endeavored to strengthen religious observance and the Orthodox communities in their localities,[18] and organized Talmud study groups and lectures on the "Torah attitude" toward current events and issues.[19]

In 1920 the Organization of Autonomous Orthodox Congregations and Agudah in Slovakia founded a German-language weekly, *Die Jüdische Presse*, which had its headquarters in Bratislava. A short time later this journal merged with another Orthodox periodical, the *Jüdische Korrespondenz*, and moved to Vienna, where it appeared until 1938 with a regular supplement dedicated to Agudist and autonomous Orthodox life and activities in Czechoslovakia, provided by the office which the paper continued to maintain in Bratislava. Other weekly publications sponsored by Agudah Orthodoxy were the *Jüdische Nachrichten* in Prešov, *Jüdischer Herold* in Dunajská Streda, and *Jüdische Tradition* in Košice. In 1924 the Slovak Agudah collaborated with the Hermon Verlag of Frankfurt am Main in the publication of a new edition of the *Sefer Hafetz Hayim*, the works of Rabbi Israel Meir Kagan, the noted and universally respected Polish sage and Agudah leader.

During the 1920s the Agudah youth movement of Bratislava[20] set up a *Shomre Shabbos* employment agency which found positions — mostly as clerks, domestics, artisans, and apprentices — for Sabbath-observing men and women. It published "Help Wanted" and "Situations Wanted" advertisements in the *Jüdische Presse*. In addition, the Bratislava youth group provided moral and financial support for the students of the Bratislava (Pressburg) yeshiva.

Agudah's social work started soon after World War I. In 1920 Agudah groups in Gúta, Topolčany, Vrbové, and Nitra sponsored vacation trips for undernourished refugee children who had found shelter in Vienna. That same year, the Agudah of Bratislava supplied food for three hundred refugees housed in barracks set up by the American Jewish Joint Distribution Committee in that city. As winter drew near the Bratislava group found itself faced with the task of providing fuel and winter clothing for the refugees as well. In response to visits from two Austrian Agudah leaders, a number of Orthodox landowners gave temporary employment to Sabbath-observing young men who wanted to obtain training in agriculture before moving on to Palestine to establish farm villages run along strictly Orthodox lines.[21]

Like other Jewish organizations, the Agudah groups sponsored social functions and banquets to raise funds and to celebrate *siyumim*.[22] Each of these affairs, of course, included what might best be described as "pep talks" on Agudist thought and conduct by local and international Agudah leaders.[23]

In its eagerness to recruit the support of the masses of loyal Agudists in Slovakia, and perhaps also owing to the central location of the country, the World Agudah for a time considered holding its first world congress (*Kenessiah Gedolah*) in Bratislava. This possibility was apparently explored as early as the summer of 1920 at a meeting of Agudah leaders in Bratislava, which was attended by representatives from over a dozen countries (including the United States) and by such world Agudah leaders as Nathan Birnbaum, Rabbi Pinchas Kohn, and Jacob Rosenheim. One of the prominent visitors to address that meeting was Rabbi Kahanemann of the famous yeshiva of Poneviezh, who urged the Agudah to promote and support the large-scale settlement of middle-class religious Jews in Palestine.[24]

When the first *Kenessiah Gedolah* was finally held late in August 1923, it did not meet in Bratislava but in Vienna. However, Slovakia (along with other provinces of the Czechoslovak Republic) was duly represented there. About fifty of Czechoslovakia's most prominent Orthodox rabbis, constituting a good geographical cross-section of the country, had signed an appeal calling on all Orthodox Jews to join and support the Agudah. Of the nine hundred delegates who converged on Vienna from all parts of the world, some forty came from Czechoslovakia. Jacob Joel Braun, Berthold Donnenbaum, and Karl Rosenbaum (all of Bratislava) represented the leadership of the Slovak organization. Bohemia was represented by Dr. Josef Flesch and an alternate, Jacob Schwartz (both of Prague) and Moravia by Gustav Springer of Boskovice. Others came from Galanta, Trnava, Topolčany, Dolný Jatov, Bratislava (Rabbi Simon Hirschler and Lazar Adler, delegates, with Lajos Kastner and Isidor Pappenheim as alternates), Dunajská Streda, Myjava, Nitra, Nové Zámky (Rabbi Josef Tiegermann), Pieštany, Prešov, Stupava, and Zlaté Moravce. Rabbis Abraham Aaron Katz of Nitra, Akiba Schreiber of Bratislava, and Koloman Weber of Piešťany were elected to the Kenessiah presidium and took part in the deliberations of the *Mo'etzet Gedole HaTorah*, the supreme rabbinic body of the world organization.

The 1923 *Kenessiah Gedolah* established two worldwide funds, *Keren HaTorah* and *Keren HaYishuv*, both of which gained generous contributions in Slovakia. *Keren HaTorah* was intended for the support of yeshivot, particularly those of Eastern Europe which had suffered during World War I. *Keren HaYishuv* was to aid Agudah's practical and religious settlement work in Palestine. Now that the *Mo'etzet Gedole HaTorah* had given its official sanction to efforts at settling Orthodox farmers and workers in Palestine, Agudah in

Slovakia — particularly the youth groups — displayed an ever-increasing interest in Eretz Yisrael work. At a joint meeting of the Agudah adult and youth groups in Trnava on May 17, 1925, Alexander Beck, on behalf of the young men, enumerated the spiritual, intellectual, and emotional qualifications required of Agudists desiring to settle in Palestine to help keep it a "holy land, the original place of Torah cultivation."[25] These included "a boundless love for Torah, unshakable *yirat shamayim*,[26] belief in the holiness of the land," and practical virtues such as "proficiency in one's chosen occupation and understanding for the importance of having all Torah-true Jews organize into one body." Youth groups began fund-raising campaigns to purchase land in Palestine. Thus, by January 1925,[27] the youth group in Topolčany was able to announce that it had bought a total of 20 dunams (five acres) of land in Eretz Yisrael.

When the world movement held its second *Kenessiah Gedolah* in Vienna in the late summer of 1929, Czechoslovakia was represented by some 150 delegates from such stalwart Agudah communities as Bratislava, Nitra, Trnava, Šurany, Nové Zámky, Topolčany, Galanta, Piešťany, Kežmarok, Dunajská Streda, and Prešov and also from smaller enclaves outside Slovakia such as Prague, Mukačevo, Karlovy Vary (Carlsbad), Marianské Lázně (Marienbad), and Těšín. Once again the Czechoslovak delegation was led by Rabbis Katz, Schreiber, and Weber; it was the last *Kenessiah Gedolah* to be attended by Katz, who died the following year, and Weber, who was to lose his life in a tragic accident in 1931.

A novel feature at this worldwide convention was a conference of women (*N'she Agudath Israel*), held separately from that of the men, under the chairmanship of Mrs. Sarah Schenierer of Cracow, who shortly after World War I had founded the Beth Jacob School movement. (This movement — as we shall see — was soon to establish branch institutions also in Czechoslovakia.) It may be assumed that this conference was attended also by women and girls from Slovakia, for such groups had been in existence in Czechoslovakia since 1924, when Mrs. Jacob Joel Braun and the wife of Chief Rabbi Akiba Schreiber had founded an Agudah organization for women and girls in Bratislava. This group arranged Sabbath afternoon walks and lectures and engaged in such good works as procuring winter clothing for needy schoolchildren, sponsoring vacations for undernourished youngsters, bringing food to poor families, and paying Sabbath and holiday visits to patients at various local hospitals. Before long groups of this type had emerged also in such towns as Nitra and Dunajská Streda. In Dunajská Streda[28] alone about 120 girls and young women attended a founding conference at which the widow of the town's chief rabbi, Samuel Levi Weinberger, led a discussion on modesty in dress and behavior. The Sabbath lectures sponsored by the Dunajská Streda group were so successful that, as the *Jüdische Presse* reported:[29] "Last Sabbath no truly Jewish girl was seen walking on the promenade (*Korso*); they all were attending the lecture sponsored by the girls' group."

For some time Orthodox circles in Slovakia had been agitating for the establishment of schools where girls would receive formal, systematic training in the tenets of Judaism as interpreted by strict Orthodoxy. A situation had evolved where Orthodox boys received an extensive Jewish education through the yeshivot, home tutors, and informal study groups such as those sponsored by the Agudah, while girls knew little more than how to read the Hebrew prayers. As to practical religious observance, the girls as a rule followed the lead of their parents without understanding the reasons for these customs. In "A Letter to a Friend" an anonymous writer, identified only as "Mordechai," called on Agudists to see that girls received formal Jewish education sufficient to counteract the secular influences by which they were surrounded in public school and in daily life outside the home:

> Unfortunately the days are gone when the blessed ways of the Jewish home were enough to educate our daughters to become Jewish women. Today, when the influence of modern literature (if, indeed, we may refer to the products of today's press and pen as such) and the unfortunate stratification of society [*sic*] are not without effect on the tender emotions of our daughters.... We must open up to them the deeper meaning of Judaism.[30]

More specifically, "Mordechai" urged that girls be given formal instruction in Jewish ethics, worship, and literature.

In an essay reprinted in the *Jüdische Presse* of March 2, 1928, Chief Rabbi S. Reich of Vrbové called upon the local Agudah to join the world Agudah movement in supporting the Beth Jacob schools and to help set up such institutions in Czechoslovakia also.[31]

Many Slovak Agudah girls were already familiar with the work of the Beth Jacob schools. In the 1920s some of them had attended summer courses at camps sponsored by the Austrian Beth Jacob movement. In the summer of 1931 several Agudah women's and girls' groups arranged a camping session in Zobor near Nitra where, under the guidance of Beth Jacob teachers from Vienna, young girls spent a summer of recreation coupled with intensive Jewish religious training.

The early 1930s at last saw the establishement of Beth Jacob schools in over twenty localities in Czechoslovakia, such as Bratislava, Galanta, Šala n/Váhom, Nové Zámky, Komárno, Dunajskà Streda, Vel'ký Meder, Sered, Prešov, Košice, Michalovce, Humenné, Hust, Piešťany, etc.[32] Smaller communities would be visited by teachers from the Beth Jacob Seminary in Vienna.

In 1936 the Agudah founded a Beth Jacob Teachers' Seminary in Bratislava. The first principal of this institution was Miss Eva Landsberg, who had worked with Mrs. Schenierer in Cracow and in Vienna.[33] As it happened, Miss Landsberg left Bratislava that same year and was succeeded by Miss Netti Michaels of Berlin, who was assisted by Miss Lea Petényi of Bratislava. Many of the graduates of this seminary (a large proportion of whom had come from Slovakia and Subcarpathian Ruthenia) later taught at Beth Jacob schools in Bratislava and Vienna. The Beth Jacob movement remained active in Slovakia until 1942.

However, reports in contemporaneous sources indicate that, for the Slovak Agudah organization as such, the early 1930s were years of comparative stagnation. The August-September 1934 issue of *Judaica*[34] announced that plans were under way for the first national conference of Agudath Israel in Slovakia to be held after a lapse of over a decade. An editorial in the *Jüdische Presse* of October 5, 1934, attributed this inactivity to the fact that, in Slovakia, an active program of religious work was being carried on by the Orthodox communities of Slovakia, most of whose members were, in fact, affiliated with Agudath Israel:

> The... Czechoslovak Agudah Israel as an organization has rested much too long. However, it is equally true that Czechoslovak Orthodoxy has stolen a march on much of this work in the little, everyday activities it carries on in the communities. All those... who have worked among their families, friends, and communities for the strengthening of Orthodox ideas and for the upbuilding of traditional institutions... all these, knowingly or unknowingly... have been doing Agudist work and preparing the ground for our ideal.

With the growing menace of Hitler in neighboring Germany, Agudath Israel in Czechoslovakia began to stir its members to renewed effort. A letter from Nitra to the editor of *Judaica*[35] deplored the fact that, with the Agudah quiescent, the Hasidic *rebbes* of Subcarpathian Ruthenia were becoming increasingly vociferous in their opposition to the organization they still considered little better than Zionism, while the young people were bceoming confused and weakened in their convictions for lack of strong leadership from an overall organization of like-minded Jews.

The fact that the Holy Land was becoming a haven for ever-growing numbers of refugees from the Nazi threat gave new impetus to the Agudah of Slovakia in its work for Palestine. At a February 1936 meeting, the Agudah youth of Bratislava, under the chairmanship of Max Weiss, expressed concern over the lack of religious observance among the Jews of Palestine but at the same time took pride in the success of Po'ale Agudath Israel, the Agudah's labor wing, which planned to establish kibbutzim and other settlements there. On February 21, 1937, an audience of over six hundred gathered in Bratislava to hear Rabbi Moshe Blau, leader and spokesman of Agudath Israel in Palestine, and Dr. Isaac Breuer, one of the leading ideologists of the movement, who by then had settled in Eretz Yisrael.

In August 1937 Agudath Israel of Czechoslovakia received a signal honor; the third *Kenessiah Gedolah*, the last to be held before the outbreak of World War II, met in the Czech resort of Marianské Lázně (Marienbad). Hundreds of delegates, representing twenty-eight countries, and an equal number of interested visitors from all over Czechoslovakia arrived at the famous spa, where some of the greatest Orthodox rabbinical authorities of the day had assembled. The delegation from Palestine was led by Rabbi Joseph Zvi Duschinsky, rabbi of the "independent" Orthodox community of Jerusalem, and longtime spiritual leader of Agudath Israel in the Holy Land, who originally had lived in the town of Hust in Subcarpathian Ruthenia. The Slovak and Hungarian delegations were headed by Chief Rabbi Akiba Schreiber who, along with Chief Rabbi Samuel David Ungar of Nitra, was elected to the *Mo'etzet Gedole HaTorah*, which at the time had a total of eighteen members.

The final chapter in the history of Agudath Israel of Slovakia was, perhaps, the one for which it most deserves to be remembered by Jews the world over, no matter what their religious ideology. Following the Nazi occupation of Austria in March 1938, Agudists bent all their energies toward a mass effort of rescuing and aiding their fellow Jews across the border. Agudath Israel brought many Austrian Jews to Czechoslovakia; it procured permanent residence permits for some of the refugees and helped others obtain visas for more remote countries. The women and girls of the movement sent food packages to Jewish families in Austria; after *shehita*[36] had been banned in Austria and Germany, they sent thousands of cans of kosher meat to the Jews in those countries. Even more important, they opened their homes to refugees who had no other means of securing shelter.

Agudath Israel of Slovakia, under the chairmanship of Dr. Karol Rosenbaum,[37] continued its rescue and relief activities even after Bohemia, Moravia, and Silesia had been annexed by Nazi Germany and Slovakia had become a puppet state under the protectorate of the Third Reich; they even continued these activities following the Nazi occupation of Poland in the fall of 1939, when thousands of Jewish refugees poured into Slovakia.

During those final years before the total Holocaust, the outstanding single individual engaged in Agudah's rescue efforts in Czechoslovakia was Rabbi Michael Ber Weissmandl, the son-in-law and successor to Chief Rabbi Ungar of Nitra. A brilliant young talmudic scholar, Rabbi Weissmandl proved no less adept in the practical work of helping organize an incredible "underground railroad" by way of which Polish Jews were brought first to Slovakia and from there to Hungary, which was still considered comparatively "safe" at the time. When the Germans embarked on their systematic program to effect a "final solution" of the "Jewish problem," Weissmandl, putting aside the separatist scruples of the type of Orthodoxy in which he had been reared, joined with Mrs. Gisi Fleischmann, the Czechoslovak WIZO (Women's International Zionist Organization) leader, in an organized effort to rescue Jews no matter what their ideological affiliation. The committee led by Weissmandl and Mrs. Fleischmann, known as the "Working Group",[38] managed to transmit messages to Jews in the democratic states, informing them of what was about to happen and appealing to them to take action to avert the catastrophe. Thanks to the efforts of the "Working Group," deportations of Jews from Slovakia were actually stopped for a time in 1942, during which a considerable number of Jews succeeded in escaping and finding shelter in places where they survived the war. Miraculously, Weissmandl himself managed to survive the Holocaust; however, his wife and children were murdered. After the war Weissmandl remarried and with his new family settled in the United States. There, with help from American Jews, some of whom had been students or friends of the yeshiva led by his late father in-law in Nitra, he built up a new yeshiva of Nitra at Mount Kisco, in New York's Westchester County. He envisioned the new yeshiva as an institution where, in addition to their talmudic training, the students would acquire skills in farming and trades such as printing. Unfortunately, it was not given to him to see his vision come to full fruition. His health broken by the horrors he had seen during the years of war and persecution, Michael Ber Weissmandl died in 1958.

NOTES

1. Hebrew for "Union of Israel."
2. *Universal Jewish Encyclopedia*, vol. I, entry on "Agudath Israel."
3. The exception, of course, was Subcarpathian Ruthenia in the east, where the Orthodox Jews did speak Yiddish and in general followed most of the ways of East European Jewry.
4. Katz was to become the first national president of Agudath Israel in Czechoslovakia.
5. *Jüdische Presse*, June 18, 1920.
6. Kohn, for many years chairman of the World Executive of Agudath Israel, had helped organize the Agudah in Poland during World War I.
7. Weber was to hold this office until his death in 1931 at the age of sixty-one.
8. *Jüdische Presse*, June 18, 1920.
9. Hirschler was Weber's cochairman of the Slovak *Landeskanzlei* and remained in office until 1932.
10. *Minhage Yisrael*: time-honored Jewish custom, especially local usage, which was considered as binding in many respects as actual Jewish law.
11. The independent Orthodox community of Jerusalem, which did not accept the authority of the chief rabbinate of Palestine and supported the world Agudah movement.
12. Fund for the support of the old Orthodox community in Palestine.
13. Moshe Katz, who died in 1926 at the age of eighty-five, was the father of Abraham Aaron Katz, who survived him by only four years. Both father and son had served as chief rabbis of Nitra and had been

founders of Agudah in Slovakia. The younger Katz was succeeded as chief rabbi of Nitra by another leader, Rabbi Samuel David Ungar of Trnava.

14. After the Nazi invasion of Czechoslovakia, Rabbi Schreiber was to move to Israel, where he reestabished the Pressburg yeshiva which is still in existence today under the leadership of his grandson.
15. Pappenheim, who became president of the Slovak Central Bureau (*Landeskanzlei*) in 1932 (he was to die in Bratislava during World War II), belonged to an old Austro-Hungarian Orthodox family. His father, Wolf Pappenheim (1848–1938), who lived in Vienna, was a leader of the world Agudah movement.
16. *Jüdische Presse*, June 18, 1920.
17. Presumably as a counterfoil to the secular Zionists and the religious Mizrahi and HaPo'el Hamizrahi, who were becoming increasingly active in the Holy Land.
18. In most instances Agudah worked with and through the autonomous Orthodox communities, so that the activities of the two units in Czechoslovakia were practically synonymous.
19. The *Jüdische Presse* (September 11, 1925) reports one lecture on a subject that is of interest to this day; delivered by Ignaz Gips at an Agudah meeting in Piešťany, it dealt with the attitude of Jewish tradition toward Darwin's theory of evolution, as argued in the "Monkey Trial" which was being held in the United States at the time.
20. Which had been founded in 1920 by Rabbi Samuel Schreiber, son of Rabbi Akiba Schreiber.
21. Again, to act as a countering influence in the face of the growing Zionist presence in Palestine.
22. Conclusion of the study of a Talmudic tractate. Regular classes in Talmud were an integral part of the Agudah cultural program.
23. Such as the venerable Wolf Pappenheim of Vienna, Dr. Isaac Breuer of Germany (the eminent theorist of the movement), Dr. Leo Deutschländer (educator and Agudah worker), and of course the world Agudah leader Jacob Rosenheim, of Frankfurt.
24. The Poneviezh yeshiva now has an impressive campus in B'nei Brak, Israel.
25. *Jüdische Presse*, May 22, 1925.
26. "Fear of heaven", i.e., unquestioning piety and obedience to Jewish law.
27. *Jüdische Presse*, May 22, 1925.
28. Dunajská Streda was a small town whose Jewish community during the period under consideration centered around a well-known yeshiva and a landed estate owned by a Jewish family.
29. *Jüdische Presse*, February 24, 1928.
30. Ibid., September 18, 1925.

31. Aided and encouraged by the Agudah (notably Dr. Leo Deutschländer, director of *Keren HaTorah*) Sarah Schenierer had started out with a nucleus of young girl students in Cracow, which eventally was to grow into a worldwide network of religious schools (and later Jewish day schools) for girls, and seminaries at which young women teachers for these institutions were trained. The Beth Jacob movement has raised generations of Jewish women with a thorough Jewish education and genuine pride in the strictly Orthodox tradition they observe.
32. Information on Beth Jacob activity in Slovakia is taken from reminiscences of a Beth Jacob graduate, obtained through the courtesy of Mrs. Elizabeth Müller of New York City.
33. According to Mrs. Judith Grünfeld of London, an early student of Sarah Schenierer, Miss Landsberg later moved to Israel, where she continued to be active in the Beth Jacob movement until her death in 1947.
34. German-language periodical published in Bratislava.
35. January-February 1935 issue.
36. Ritual slaughtering of animals.
37. Židovská Ročenka pre Slovensko 5700 (1940), Bratislava, David Gross.
38. Nora Levin, *The Holocaust*, p. 535.

3. Organizational Life

ZIONIST STUDENTS' ORGANIZATIONS

by S. Goshen

The young people who flocked to the Zionist students' organizations of Czechoslovakia during the two decades between 1918 and 1938 were of varied backgrounds and beliefs. The students in the Historic Lands of the west who joined the Zionist movement were mostly middle class in background, the majority of whom had found their way to Zionism through a process of ideological evolution. On the other hand, those in the eastern part of the country had backgrounds of greater variety; unlike their western colleagues, they had come to the movement as a result of the natural trend toward Zionism that prevailed in the eastern regions of Europe.

Following the establishment of the Republic of Czechoslovakia, these young people, through their Zionist youth movements, became the spearhead of the Jewish national minority group recognized by the new state.*

The Jewish students' organizations in pre-1938 Czechoslovakia could be classified in two main categories: regular Zionist students' associations and those of the *couleur* students (named after the "colors" worn by its members).

* [See also J. C. Pick, pp. 185–228 (Ed.)]

Juedische Akademische Verbindung Barissia — Barissia Jewish Students' Association

Founded in Prague in 1903 to "combat Czech and German assimilationism among Jews," this organization was the most important and influential of the *couleur* students' associations.

Although World War I had made deep inroads into Barissia's membership, it held a convention in Teplice-Šanov on November 2, 1917. In December of that year Dr. Walter Kohner founded the news bulletin *Barissenblaetter*, and preparations were made for the formation of an alumni association.

The official reactivation of Barissia took place in January 1919. But as Dr. Brauner, the historian of the association, put it, "although the association had been reactivated, it was not active." This lack of enthusiasm was due in part to increasing doubts as to whether the new era ushered in by the end of the war justified the continuation of the activities for which the *couleur* groups were known. The government of the new Czechoslovak Republic had officially prohibited the wearing of the "colors" as well as dueling; besides, times were not appropriate for *Kneipen*, the drinking bouts customary among *couleur* associations.

However, due to a new influx of students — a number of whom had come to Barissia from the Czech University of Prague — the worst of the crisis seemed to have been over by the academic term 1922/1923. The extramural activities of Barissia were not so prominent as those engaged in by other students' associations, but in 1924 it had a major share in the reorganization of the "Rede-und Lesehalle" in Prague, of which a Barissia member named Knoepfelmacher became the head.

In 1923, when the German University of Prague was the scene of anti-Semitic demonstrations aimed at the removal of Professor Samuel Steinherz from the chancellorship of the institution, it was Barissia that organized the Jewish students of the university for self-defense. In 1928 Barissia played a prominent part in the revival of the *Verband Zionistischer Akademiker* (Association of Zionist Students). The sole students' group to take an active part in the work of the Prague Zionist District Committee, Barissia, beginning in 1930, was also the only Jewish students' organization which consistently fulfilled — and mostly exceeded — the quota set for it by the Zionist organization for Jewish National Fund collections and the sale of *shekalim*.

These accomplishments were the result of the discipline that prevailed within Barissia, partly because of the powerful influence of the alumni association, whose leaders included such prominent Zionists as Ing. Fraenkl, Dr. Friedrich Eckstein, Dr. R. Birnbaum, Dr. Walter Kohner, Prof. Alfred Engel, Richard Steiner, Dr. H. Pick, K. Bauer, Dr. O. Neumann, Dr. Hugo Brauner, Dr. K. Gruenberger, and others. Between 1929 and 1937 the Alumni Association published a series of brochures under the title of *Schriften zur Diskussion des Zionismus* ("Discussions on Zionism"). Among the authors participating in the project were Walter Kohner, Yitzhak Gruenbaum, Felix Weltsch, Hugo Herrmann, Victor Bauer, František Friedmann, Jacob Lestschinsky, and Max Brod.

Juedische Akademische Verbindung Veritas — Veritas Jewish Students' Association

This organization was founded in Brno in 1894, several years before the inception of the world Zionist movement. Unlike the overwhelming majority of Barissia's members, most of the leaders of Veritas did not remain in Czechoslovakia but became active in Zionist groups abroad. Thus, Dr. Otto Abeles and Robert Stricker became prominent in Zionist circles in Vienna; Emil Deutsch settled in Belgrade and Dr. E. Rosenberg in Berlin; and Berthold Feiwel moved to Berlin, then subsequently to London. As a result of this geographic dispersion, the alumni association of Veritas, unlike that of Barissia, was unable to keep close contact with the membership of the group.

As opposed to Barissia, which still cherished some of the principles held dear by the *couleur* organization prior to the founding of the Czechoslovak Republic, Veritas concentrated on Zionist and nationalist Jewish activities. When it was expected, after October 28, 1918, that the proclamation of the State of Czechoslovakia might be followed by anti-Semitic riots, Veritas established a *Juedischer Soldatenrat* (Jewish militia) which later became the nucleus of the *Juedischer Volksrat* (Jewish People's Council) in Brno. Veritas members played a prominent part also in the "Zionization" of the local *Kultusgemeinde* (the official Jewish religious communal organization) and in the establishment of the nationalist Jewish school system in their city.

Veritas also helped establish the *Makkabi* sports organization,* the Bar Kochba swimming club, a Home for Jewish Students and a Jewish students' dining hall (*Mensa Academica*).

In 1924, the year of its sixtieth semester, Veritas was at the zenith of its activities. Gradually, however, the number of members decreased, and by 1934 Veritas had ceased to be an active group. Its alumni association did remain intact and still exists in Israel under the chairmanship of Willy Wagner (now Zeev Ben-Ari).

Interestingly, the *couleur* spirit attracted not only those students who came from areas where they could have been influenced in that direction by German-speaking students' associations, but also those who stemmed from a background entirely foreign to it. Thus, some organizations of students from Eastern Europe established *couleur* associations of their own in Prague, such as "Bargiora," "Hazmonea," and "Hatchiya Libanonia," to mention a few. Increasing the contrast between these new groups and their older counterparts and lending added spirit to their activities was the fact that many of their members were strictly Orthodox in their religious outlook and practice.

Ben Guria

Formed in February 1931 by three students from Poland who were enrolled at Komenský University of Bratislava, this group, while adhering to the principles of the pre–1918 *couleur* groups, insisted on strict Zionist discipline among its members. Ben Guria grew rapidly, and by 1933 it carried on its rolls a number of out-of-town students, including one from Petah Tiqva in Palestine. Ben Guria engaged in serious Zionist activity and as a unit joined a local Zionist group called Ahavat Zion.

In 1931 Ben Guria founded the El Al Zionist High School Society. In 1934 it joined the *Juedische Partei* (Jewish party), a Czechoslovakian political party championing the ideals of nationalist Judaism. Ben Guria did not devote much time to *couleur* activities, and gradually its Zionist endeavors took first place on its program. It therefore did not find it difficult, in the winter of 1935/1936, to establish close ties with Arlosorovia, a society of socialist academicians.

---

* [See also Pick, pp. 185–228 (Ed.)]

Ben Guria continued to be active until the Nazi occupation of Czechoslovakia.

Verein der Juedischen Hochschueler in Prag Bar Kochba — Bar Kochba Jewish Students' Federation in Prague

Originally founded in 1892 as a nationalist Jewish students' society under the name of "Makkabaea," this organization changed its name in 1896 to *Verein der Juedischen Hochschueler in Prag*, adding *Bar Kochba* when it officially adopted the Zionist cause in 1899. The influence of Bar Kochba, which was the precursor of the Zionist students' movement in Czechoslovakia, was felt far beyond the borders of the old Austro-Hungarian monarchy. Its membership included personalities whose names have become household words in the Zionist movement, such as Hugo Bergmann, Artur Bergmann, Martin Buber, Leo Hermann, Hugo Hermann, Viktor Kellner, Emil Margulies, Oskar Epstein, and Robert Weltsch, to name a few.

The activities of Bar Kochba prior to 1918 are described in great detail in the literature cited in the bibliography at the end of this article.

The years following the end of World War I saw a decline in the group, but it was clear that its teachings had borne fruit, for in 1926, with the emigration of Leo Hermann, the number of Bar Kochba members to settle in Palestine reached thirty-six.

The promotion of *'aliya* found expression in the *Juedische Jugendblaetter** ("Jewish Youth Journal") published by Bar Kochba independently and sometimes in conjunction with "Blau-Weiss" between 1921 and 1923. This paper was definitely *Halutzic* in spirit, form, and content, with very little space devoted to academic or student activities.

During the late 1920s, however, the activities of Bar Kochba centered mainly on Jewish National Fund campaigns and occasional lectures.

In the years that followed there were only a few times in which Bar Kochba seemed to take on a new lease on life — as, for instance, in the period from 1926 to 1929, when its alumni association merged with its counterpart in the Theodor Herzl Group.

Between 1926 and 1930, Bar Kochba was under the chairmanship

* [See vol. I, article on the Jewish press, pp. 523–531 (Ed.)]

of Artur Bergmann, who was succeeded by Emerich Hoffmann. Its program during that time concentrated on Jewish National Fund work and occasional lectures. Its most memorable postwar festivity was held in November 1932 to mark its eightieth semester anniversary. On that occasion the alumni association bestowed honorary membership on Max Brod and Felix Weltsch, who, though associated with Bar Kochba for decades, had not originally been members of the organization. By 1935, the name Bar Kochba no longer appeared on the list of Zionist students' groups active in Zionist fund raising.

The alumni association is still in existence in Israel, where surviving members occasionally gather for reunions.

Theodor Herzl Group

The Theodor Herzl Group was founded in 1909 at the Czech University of Prague by some members of the Bar Kochba organization. Owing to the small number of Jewish students then enrolled at the Czech University,* it was difficult for the new group to gain members. However, its initiators and charter members played a role of no small significance in Zionist life, both prior to 1918 and thereafter in independent Czechoslovakia. Among those leaders who left their mark on the development of Zionism in the Czech-speaking areas of Bohemia were Norbert Adler, Eduard Aschermann, Franta Friedmann, Angelo Goldstein, Camil Kohn, Felix Kornfeld, and Arnošt Kollman.

The decline of Bar Kochba during the years immediately following World War I went hand in hand with a period of ascendancy for the Theodor Herzl Group, in which young men such as Arnold and Erwin Arnstein, Karel Fleischmann, Otokar Pacovský, and Emil Waldstein had a prominent part. Some of the Bar Kochba members transferred to it, and the Alumni Society, too, gave its main support to the new organization.

---

* Enrollment of Jews at the Czech University of Prague from 1909 to 1917: 1909–67; 1910–86; 1911–101; 1912–100; 1913–106; 1914–67; 1915–49; 1916–49; 1917–0. From 1918 to 1935, the figures were: 1918–257; 1919–270; 1920–444; 1921–469; 1922–369; 1923–616; 1924–663; 1925–800; 1926–746; 1927–805; 1928–960; 1929–1,146; 1930–1,421; 1931–1,613; 1932–1,318; 1933–1,031. Enrollment of Jews at the German University from 1921 to 1935 was: 1921–1,400; 1922–1,321; 1923–1,020; 1924–1,140; 1925–1,390; 1926–1,379; 1927–1,380; 1928–1,431; 1929–1,281; 1930–1,069. (See *Židovský kalendár*, 1937, also *Selbstwehr*, 1929, No. 53).

There was a basic difference between the Bar Kochba organization and the Theodor Herzl Group with regard to the scope of their activities. While the former concentrated on the formulation of Zionist ideology, the latter considered its main task to be the struggle against Czech assimilationism, particularly the Kapper Club,* the students' organization of the assimilationists. Many of the Herzl Group's members, including Otto Arie, Viktor Fischl, František Gottlieb, Jiří Kraus, Erich Kresta, Walter Kauders, Zdeňek Landes, Karel Stein, and Leo Zelmanovits, gained prominence as Zionist leaders. The Herzl Group took an active interest in the Jewish school system of Prague, published *Listy židovské mládeže* ("Newsletter of Jewish Youth") and two important brochures, *Sionism, idea a skutečnost* ("Zionism, Ideal and Reality") and *Opportunita či mravnost* ("Opportunism or Morality"). The group also supplied editors and contributors for the newspapers *Židovské zprávy* and *Židovský kalendář*.†

The Theodor Herzl Group did not represent a specific Zionist ideology, and its ranks included exponents of every shade of Zionist thought. This ideological independence can best be seen in the outside activities of some of the group's outstanding members, as for example writings in literary publications and in the press.** While these differences frequently led to internal clashes they could not destroy the sense of fellowship which united the members of the organization. In the late 1930s, under the chairmanship of Pavel Kohn, efforts were made to channel the Theodor Herzl Group into *Halutzic* lines, confronting the membership with a dilemma formulated by E. Tochten in the Jubilee volume issued on the occasion of the group's fiftieth semestral anniversary in 1934: "We have the right to demand a decision whether Eretz Yisrael is to become a homeland or a land of dreams. We have the right to demand that everyone among us should make a serious decision on this problem."

Lese-und Redehalle Juedischer Hochschueler in Prag — Reading Room and Lecture Hall for Jewish Students in Prague

This students' society, which was founded in Prague during the winter term 1908/1909 along the lines of similar organizations in

---

* [See Hostovsky's article, pp. 148–154 (Ed.)]

† [See vol. I, article on the Jewish press, pp. 523–531 (Ed.)]

** [See vol. I, article on Jews in Czech literature, pp. 439–453 (Ed.)]

Vienna and Brno, was not officially Zionist but was Jewish nationalist in character.

The *Lese-und Redehalle* inaugurated its activities early in 1919 with a memorial meeting for fifteen members who had lost their lives in World War I. On November 2 of that year, on the second anniversary of the Balfour Declaration, the group sponsored a concert of the Prague Philharmonic Orchestra at the Rudolfinum Hall which was attended by President Tomáš G. Masaryk and the British ambassador, Sir Cecil Gosling. Speakers on that occasion were Max Brod, Dr. Ludwig Singer, Dr. Lebenhart (the president of the organization), Dr. L. Lieben, and Dr. R. Raudnitzky.

Soon thereafter, the *Lese-und Redehalle* also felt the effects of the general crisis through which Prague's Zionist students' organizations were then passing. However, by 1925, thanks to the reorganization work done under the chairmanship of Walter Weber, assisted by Taussing and Gach, the group had forty-five new members.

The average membership of the *Halle* was between seventy and a hundred. Its primary object was to provide the Jewish student with a social forum, a place where he could spend his leisure hours and browse in a well-stocked library. Lectures on Jewish and general subjects were organized. While the *Halle* was officially a Jewish nationalist and not a Zionist group, it took an active part in Zionist activities — as did all the Zionist student groups in Prague. In 1926 the Prague *Halle* joined the *Halle Kartell*, an association of similar groups in Prague, Brno, and Vienna.

The *Halle* conducted its activities through public functions to a greater extent than did the Zionist students' groups. One of the outstanding functions sponsored by the *Halle* was its fiftieth semestral anniversary in 1933 at which Arnold Zweig and Otakar Fischer* were guest speakers.

The *Halle* remained active until the end of Czechoslovakia's independence. In 1937, Menachem Goldenzeil (Golan), its chairman, together with Michael Hutter (of the *Halle* in Brno) and Jakov Berger (of the Arlosorovia of Bratislava), became heads of the Association of Jewish University Students in Czechoslovakia. This association, which included all Zionist and Jewish students' organizations in Czechoslovakia except the assimilationist Kapper Club, became a constituent group of the "International Student Service," which had

* [See vol. I, article on Jews in Czech literature, pp. 439–453 (Ed.)]

its headquarters in Geneva and was to be of great assistance in the emigration and relocation of Czechoslovakian students.

Juedisch-Akademische Lese-und Redehalle in Brno — Jewish Students' Reading Room and Lecture Hall in Brno

Founded in 1901 and reorganized during the academic term of 1902/1903, this organization began as a *couleur* association but dropped the *couleur* formalities after World War I. Unlike the *Halle* in Prague, the Brno group soon changed its bylaws to make it a Zionist students' organization. Led by Zweigenthal and Beer, the Brno *Halle* became a center of activity for the Jewish National Fund in Moravia. Its members traveled around the country making Zionist speeches and starting fund-raising campaigns, and visited provincial towns to organize Zionist seminars. The group insisted on strong internal discipline to the extent that all applicants for membership had to pass an examination on Zionist history and ideology before being accepted.

Like all the other Zionist students' organizations, the Brno *Halle* also went through a severe crisis in the early 1930s when young people were faced with the decision whether to remain in Czechoslovakia or to leave for Palestine. In 1934 ten members of the *Halle* resigned in protest when certain candidates for membership were not admitted because their views on Zionism were considered unacceptable.

By 1937, however, when the Brno *Halle* held a reunion to mark its seventieth semestral anniversary, the crisis seems to have been at an end. The celebration featured a paper "The Jewish Center" by Josef Kastein, and a keynote address, "Aims and Duties of Jewish Students' Societies Today" by Prof. Teller.

By 1938, ten percent of the membership had settled in Palestine. Unlike that of other Jewish students' associations, the membership of the Brno *Halle* consisted chiefly of students of the Technical College of Brno. Accordingly, these highly skilled *'olim* proved a valuable addition to the *Yishuv*.

Just before the Nazis entered Brno, Michael Hutter, the last chairman of the *Halle*, burned all the papers as well as the nameplates of the members. Some members were able to escape but many remained, including Erwin Elbert, an engineer, who was later to become the head of the Jewish Religious Community of Brno.

Spolek Sionistických akademiků v Brně — Society of Zionist University Students in Brno

Brno, which was primarily a German-speaking city, had a number of Jews who were German assimilationists. Unlike Prague, however, Brno did not have a militant group of Czech-Jewish assimilationists. Nevertheless, after World War I it seemed a natural development that the students who came to the Czech Technical College and the Masaryk University, both Czech-speaking institutions, should organize on a Zionist basis.

The *Spolek Sionististických akademiků v Brně* was founded during the winter term of 1925/1926 under the auspices of Prague's Theodor Herzl Group. Among its charter members were Bedřich Beneš, Otto Heilig, Erich Munk, Otto Pollak, E. Reichenbaum (Rosh), Oskar Smetana, and Schlesinger.

Beginning in 1933 the *Spolek*, which had an average enrollment of only fifteen to twenty, also accepted women students for membership.

Like the *Halle*, the *Spolek* was organized along lines of strict discipline. Applicants for membership had to pass an examination on Zionism and wait one year before being accepted. A closely knit group, the *Spolek* held regular meetings, with emphasis on discussion. It hardly ever sponsored public functions, but when a branch of the Czech assimilationist Kapper Club attempted to gain a foothold in Brno, the *Spolek* prevented it from becoming a force of significance in the community.

The *Spolek* set up an office which maintained contact among the members during the long summer vacation periods and kept files of information on their activities in their hometowns.

When the Nazis occupied Brno a number of *Spolek* members were able to flee the country. Many, however, were deported, including Dr. Willy Schwarz and Dr. Erich Munk, the latter becoming a highly respected leader in the Terezín (Theresienstadt) ghetto.

Slovakia and Subcarpathian Ruthenia

During the period immediately following World War I, most of the Jewish students from Slovakia and Subcarpathian Ruthenia would go to either of the two Universities of Prague or to the Technical College in Brno. The Slovak University had been founded in Bratislava in 1919.

Bratislava for years had only one Zionist students' organization — the Ben Guria group, described at the beginning of this article.

The academic term 1933/1934 saw the formation of the Arlosorovia, a Socialist-Zionist students' group, which had an enrollment of sixty but only a very small active nucleus. Unlike other Zionist students' organizations, this group was able to win new friends for the cause of Zionism and Judaism from nonacademic and even non-Jewish circles by establishing close contacts with Slovak socialist groups. Arlosorovia sponsored courses and seminars and in 1938 ran a summer camp with an enrollment of one hundred members. One of the prominent speakers to address the group was Dr. Emil Margulies. After Arlosorovia's founder, Jaacov Berger, and others left for Palestine, the group was dissolved.

Slovak students attending schools in Bohemia or Moravia at first joined students' organizations in Prague or Brno. But as their numbers increased, they formed a group of their own in Prague. This society, known as "Judaea," had a large membership and was quite active from 1931 to 1934. Their principal activity was sponsoring of lectures on Zionism.

Other Student Organizations

Three rather short-lived Jewish students' organizations in Czechoslovakia were *Hatikvah* in Brno and Prague and the *Kartell Sozialistischer Akademiker* (Socialist Students' Corps). The Brno *Hatikvah*, a student society formed at the Business College of that city, was active from 1925 to 1926 and published its own journal, *Hatikvah*. The Prague *Hatikvah* lasted from 1923 until 1925. Most of its activities were centered around lectures for members, but during the academic term 1924/1925 it held a number of public meetings, addressed by such personalities as Max Brod, Paul Kraus, Professor Friedrich Thieberger, and others. *Hatikvah* helped set up a Bar Kochba society in Bratislava — for high school rather than university students — and a "Blau-Weiss" group in the provincial towns of Smíchov and Mukačevo. In 1925 the society gave up its purely academic character and no longer maintained contact with other students' organizations. The *Kartell Sozialistischer Akademiker*, which first appeared in Prague in 1934, was one of the capital's most active students' societies between 1935 and 1938, concentrating on political and propaganda work.

Based on the conditions as they prevailed in the period 1918–1938, one must conclude that students have endeavored to do their best under the prevailing conditions.

BIBLIOGRAPHY

Selbstwehr and *Židovské Zprávy* for the years 1920–1928 for all societies mentioned.

Barissia, published on the occasion of the 50th semestral festivities in 1928.

"The History of the Association from the 50th to the 80th semester," ibid., by Hugo Brauner.

J.A.V. "Veritas" in *Herzl Year*, Tel Aviv, 1954.

Ben Guria, published on the occasion of the 10th semestral anniversary, Bratislava, 1936.

Prague and Jerusalem. Volume in Memory of Leo Hermann (Hebrew), edited by Felix Weltsch, Jerusalem (undated).

Juedische Jugendblaetter, 1921–1923.

Various circulars of the Old Boys' Society Theodor Herzl–Bar Kochba (Tel Aviv), especially No. 6, 1959, on the occasion of the 100th anniversary of "Theodor Herzl."

Halle Blaetter, reports of the Jewish academic Lese-and Redehalle Brno, No. 2–10 (1924–1934).

Semestralberichte des Vereines Bar Kochba in Prague 1910–1913 (semestral reports of the Society Bar Kochba in Prague).

Vom Judentum — ein Sammelbuch (About Judaism — A Collection of Essays), edited by Bar Kochba, Leipzig, 1913 (preface), Hans Kohn.

Hans Kohn, *Martin Buber*, Hellerau, 1930, pp. 90, 314.

Letters, questionnaires supplied by members of almost every one of the societies mentioned.

SPORTS

by Joseph C. Pick

Introductory Remarks

Sports and gymnastics did not play as important a role in the lives of the old Hebrews as they did among Romans and Greeks, although a physically strong and well-trained youth was the *sine qua non* of the security of the state and of the preservation of the nation. This sense of physical preservation has not lessened in the centuries following the loss of Jewish independence in Palestine.[1] The greater part of the Diaspora history is one of physical survival. However, actual sports activities were carried on with only occasional marked success by individuals.

With the spread of sports and gymnastics as integral parts of national culture among the peoples of the world, Jews did not remain unaffected. Since the emancipation period — particularly since the second half of the nineteenth century — Jews have taken part in sports and gymnastics, but on the whole in service of other peoples. Following the emancipation, Jews in sports, as in other fields of human endeavor, achieved some remarkable successes. They even became pioneers in this field during that early period — a remarkable achievement and one which Bohemian Jewry can record with pride. Two Jews of the land, Dr. Arnold Hirsch[2] and Dr. David Seegen, became the "fathers" of a completely new school of gymnastics, which was soon adopted generally and from which the famous Czech "Sokol" derived some of its founders and leaders.

On the whole, one can say that as the understanding and practice of sports among the nations progressed, Jews were gradually more and more drawn into a similar development.

The turning point came with the ascendancy of Zionism. Hitherto sports were, as mentioned, more or less a personal interest of the individual Jew. However, after Professor Max Mandelstamm's analysis, at the Second Zionist Congress in Basle in 1898, of the necessity of physical training for the Jew as an integral part of national regeneration,[3] and after Max Nordau made his great appeal, at the Fifth Zionist Congress in Basle in 1901, for the physical strengthening of Jewish men and women and for the transformation of the people into a *Muskeljudentum* (muscular Judaism),[4] sports and gymnastics became a national issue and part of the Zionist program. A new basis was created. The individual Jew no longer had to seek physical amelioration in other nationalities' clubs and societies (where he was "admitted" or, more often, "not admitted"). From that time on, Jewish sports clubs and societies were formed by Jews and joined by Jews as Jews for a collective attempt at physical national regeneration.

The first Jewish national sports club was formed in Berlin on October 22, 1898.[5] It assumed the name "Bar Kochba," after the great Jewish warrior. From then on most Jewish national sports clubs adopted either this name or chose that of another great warrior Juda Maccabi; occasionally they adopted other symbolical Hebrew names.

The first club in the territory of Czechoslovakia was created in Moravská Ostrava (1899),[6] although students from Bohemia and Moravia who had studied in Vienna (Emil Fried, Dr. Max Jerusalem, Dr. Ludwig Werner, and Dr. Egon Zweig) had already created in that city the First Jewish Gymnastic Society on January 28, 1899. In 1901 sports clubs were established in Olomouc and Uherské Hradiště (both in Moravia); in 1902 in Kolín (Bohemia) and Opava (Silesia); and in 1903 in Prostějov (Moravia).

In that year, on the occasion of the assembly of the Sixth Zionist Congress in Basle (August 23–28, 1903), the first international gymnastic exhibition exercises took place in the local *Burgvogtei* (August 25) in the presence of Theodor Herzl, Max Nordau, and the other Zionist leaders. Members of the clubs of Moravská Ostrava and Uherské Hradiště participated and earned general praise.[7] From then on it became general practice for sports functions to be organized at the p ace and time of Zionist Congresses.

In Basle (1903) the assembled delegates of the ten represented sports clubs created the first organizational unit, the Jewish Gymnastic Organization (Die Jüdische Turnerschaft, Verband der Jüdischen Turnvereine), based on the following program:

The Jewish Gymnastic Organization regards gymnastics as the best meants to improve the physical fitness of the Jewish people in line with the Jewish national idea.

The movement rapidly grew — nowhere else, however, as fast as in the Historic Lands where, in addition to the above-mentioned clubs, the following were formed (year of formation in parentheses): Přívoz (1905), Znojmo (1906), Brno (1907), Prague (1908), Boskovice (1909), Mikulov and Jihlava (1910), Prague-Hagibor and Bratislava-Maccabäa (1912), Břeclav, Mislice, Miroslav and Olomouc-Hakoah (1913), Chomutov, Hodonín and Kroměříž (1914).

These clubs in the Historic Lands were divided into two groups: Bohemia and Moravia-Silesia. All the clubs of both these groups were incorporated in the larger organizational unit, the West Austrian Region.[8] The delegates of that region met the first time in December 1912 in Vienna, concentrating in their deliberations on ideological questions, but primarily on the preparation of a grand sports exhibition of clubs from all over the world during the Eleventh Zionist Congress, to be held in Vienna in 1913. The festivities started as planned in September of that year and were crowned with great sports successes.[9]

The second general assembly of the West Austrian Region (the last prior to World War I) was held from December 6 to 8, 1913, in Vienna. Delegates from the Historic Lands represented the following clubs: Boskovice, Brno, Břeclav, Miroslav, Moravská Ostrava, Olomouc, Prague, and Uherské Hradiště. At that time this region already comprised 23 clubs with 2,500 registered gymnasts and athletes. This conference adopted some important decisions which were to shape the gymnastic and sports movement after the end of the war for years to come. Every member club had to adopt the name "Maccabi," Hebrew commands were made compulsory, and sports activities were put on an equal footing with gymnastics.[10]

The activities of these clubs were mostly interrupted by World War I, but they resumed independently after demobilization in each of the succession states.

The Revival after 1918

Sports activities, even if only on a very limited scale, were carried on even during the war years in a number of clubs. It was out of these remnants that the new Maccabi organization arose in Czechoslovakia. This was to become one of the stalwarts of World Maccabi and one of the major groupings of Czechoslovak Jewry.

The first steps toward gathering the remnants and creating a representative body of all existing Jewish sports clubs were made early in 1919 by Maccabi Prague.[11] Their leaders contacted individual members of the fourteen still-registered and existing clubs in Bohemia and Moravia-Silesia. By March 29 and 30, 1919, forty-four delegates of these gymnastics and sports clubs had already assembled for a first conference in Brno.[12] An ideological program was presented to the conference by the moving spirit of Prague Maccabi, Richard Pacovský, who also suggested the creation of a unified organization subdivided into districts (*župy*) covering the various areas of the Republic; but the conference cou'd not arrive at a unanimous decision with regard to this. The postponed decision was raised and finally adopted at the subsequent conference in Brno (June 1919). This conference accompanied the first public gymnastic and sports exhibitions in Czechoslovakia. Delegates from 21 clubs participated and decided to establish a temporary Czechoslovak Territorial Maccabi Association. The new leadership, unanimously elected, consisted of chairman Richard Pacovský and members Artur Herzog, Klára Mauthnerová, Viktor Mauthner, and Elsa Singerová; its headquarters were in Prague. At that conference the Czechoslovak Jewish Soccer Association was also officially established.

Thanks to the activities of the new leadership, the organization had grown from 21 clubs in 1919 to 31 clubs (and 2,000 members) in 1921. This became an important year in the history of the Czechoslovak and World Maccabi movement. In the first place, in July of that year the First Czechoslovak Territorial sports meeting took place in Brno with the participation of 650 active sports members from 27 communities. Two months later, during the assembly of the Twelfth Zionist Congress held in Karlovy Vary (September 1–14), the usual sports exhibition took place, at which Czechoslovakia was strongly represented. At that time, the first international conference of Maccabi societies to be assembled after World War I (representing ten countries, including Palestine) met and decided to renew the association of gymnastics and sports societies under the newly adopted name "Maccabi World Association" (Makkabi-Weltverband), headed by Heinrich Kuhn (Berlin).[13]

All the mentioned attempts at unification of the clubs in Czechoslovakia encountered what then seemed to be insurmountable obstacles in the first years. It was only in May 1922 that the first breakthrough occurred. Moravia took the lead. All its Maccabi societies decided to subdivide their organization into northern and southeastern districts. Each district was autonomous but no unified leadership of both districts could be established. It took two more years before this was achieved.

Meanwhile, Maccabi had grown also in other areas. In 1923 the Prague leadership established contact for the first time with Maccabea Bratislava (which had been in existence — then under Hungary — since 1912) and with the newly created Jewish sports club in Banská Bystrica, with the view to forming a Slovak Maccabi district. It was at the Bratislava conference of March 7, 1924, that the Slovak Territorial Maccabi Association was formed.

Great impact on the Maccabi development was exercised by the Maccabi World Conference held during the assembly of the Thirteenth Zionist Congress, in Karlovy Vary (August 6–18, 1923). Apart from being accompanied by the usual public sports exhibition, the conference was now able to survey a consolidated world movement stretching over eighteen countries.

The Official Maccabi Association

This process of consolidation came to the fore also in Czechoslovakia. A new leadership was elected in March 1924, headed by Dr. Robert Heller (Chomutov), chairman, and Viktor Mauthner (Prague), commander. Richard Pacovský retained the department of the technical commission. The new leadership embarked on an all-out effort to establish the unified Maccabi movement. Two important developments contributed considerably to the success of these endeavors.

On September 7, 1924, the two Maccabi districts in Moravia-Silesia met in Brno and established the unified Moravian Maccabi Association. It was to become the nucleus of the Czechoslovak unified movement.

The other great leap forward was attained in 1924 when the statutes of the Maccabi Association were officially ratified, and thus the temporary status of the organization converted into a permanent one. The official name of the movement from then on was Maccabi Association in the Czechoslovak Republic (Svaz Makabi v Československé Republice).

By the year 1924 the movement had grown considerably in Czechoslovakia. It comprised 32 clubs and 2,500 members (those numbers were still increasing from year to year). On the basis of the Moravian example, the organization was divided into districts (as first suggested by Pacovský in 1919, see above, p. 188). This division remained in its original form until the end of the first Republic. At that time it consisted of the following local organizations:

District Bohemia: Prague (Maccabi and Hagibor), Chomutov, Karlovy Vary, Liberec, Most, Pardubice, Plzeň, Teplice-Šanov, Ústí nad Labem.

District Brno: Brno (Maccabi and Bar Kochba), Boskovice, Břeclav, Jihlava, Mikulov, Podivín, Pohořelice, Znojmo.

District Moravská Ostrava: Moravská Ostrava, Bohumín, Hrušov, Nový Jičín, Olomouc, Vítkovice.

District Uherské Hradiště: Uherské Hradiště, Hodonín, Kroměříž, Kyjov, Prostějov, Strážnice, Uherský Brod.

District Slovakia: Bratislava (Maccabi, Maccabea, and Bar Kochba), Banská Bystrica, Hlohovec, Košice, Nitra, Nové Mesto nad Váhom, Pezinok, Piešt'any, Šaštin, Sered, Trnava, Velké Šurany.

The activities were not confined to gymnastics. They had spread out, over the years, into all strata of sports and comprised athletics, hockey, winter sports, soccer, and swimming, for each branch of which there was a special referent at the seat of the organization's headquarters.

At the territorial conference in Brno (1926) a new leadership was established, headed by Artur Herzog (Prague). He remained at the helm of the movement to the end of the first Republic, having achieved during his time of office remarkable progress in all fields of Maccabi endeavors. The commander (*náčelnik*) of the association became Max Gelbkopf (Brno) and in 1927 Dr. Otto Hirsch (Brno).

With the growing movement the financial burden had grown also, and in line with the established policy of the Czechoslovak government to support physical training of youth, a delegation — consisting of Dr. Angelo Goldstein, Dr. Evžen Justic, and Dr. Egon Štern — called, on February 10, 1926, on the then minister of public health and physical education, Dr. Ludwig Czech (a Jew himself), to demand financial support. The government consented, and increased its subsidy from year to year, thus enabling Maccabi to create new facilities and improve existing ones.

The consolidation of Czechoslovak Maccabi made it sufficiently strong that after the failure of the Vienna world conference of Maccabi (1927) to elect a leadership, Czechoslovak Maccabi took over the temporary leadership of the world movement. At its helm stood the vice-president of the world organization, Dr. Karel Sonnenfeld (Brno).

This temporary situation lasted until the subsequent conference, held in Brno on May 27 and 28, 1928: Dr. Hermann Lelewer (Berlin) was then elected chairman and Dr. Karel Sonnenfeld (Brno) vice-chairman.

A few months later (August 5 and 6) a public exhibition day was organized in Brno, and the participants then had occasion to visit, for the first time, the newly founded Maccabi Youth Camp in Blansko (about ten miles to the north of Brno). Later in 1928 (October) a sizable delegation of the Czechoslovak Maccabi participated at the thirtieth anniversary of the Berlin Bar Kochba.

The Second Czechoslovak Territorial gymnastics and athletic show was held in Moravská Ostrava in 1929. The Czechoslovak sportsmen were joined by guests representing the Maccabi Unions of Austria, Belgium, France, Germany, Latvia, Palestine, Poland, Romania, and Yugoslavia. Some 2,000 performers, among them 350 gymnasts, showed remarkable skill before an audience of 6,000. At that same time a conference of World Maccabi took place in Moravská Ostrava which became of significance for the further organizational development of the movement. Maccabi had made great inroads in the ranks of Jewish youth all over the world, and some remarkable sports achievements were attained by Jewish sportsmen in Austria, Czechoslovakia, Germany, Poland, and other countries. For the purpose of consolidating this work, both organizationally and financially, the entire leadership of the World Union was moved to Berlin and was headed by Dr. Hermann Lelewer. Apart from this organizational unification, the conference of 1929 reaffirmed an original decision made at Karlovy Vary in 1921 — but not carried out thus far — to intensify the educational aspect and in particular to emphasize the

Palestino-centric tendency of the movement. A far-reaching decision was also taken at Moravská Ostrava on the suggestion of Josef Yekutich, the delegate from Palestine: to organize the first Maccabia, the first Jewish Olympiad, in Eretz Israel.

This dream was realized in the spring of 1932. Sixteen countries sent 500 active sportsmen to this first Maccabia, to which should be added the 2,000 active sportsmen from Palestine — which testified to the strength which Maccabi in Palestine had meanwhile attained. More than 25,000 Jews from all over the world participated in this historic event. Czechoslovakia was represented by 120 athletes and gymnasts.

With this success in mind the Maccabi leadership organized a winter Maccabia in February 1933 in Zakopané (Poland), which occurred during Hitler's ascendancy to power in Germany. Soon thereafter the world headquarters was transferred to London, where it was headed by Dr. Lelewer, who had moved there from Berlin.

The second Maccabia took place in Palestine from April 2 to 7, 1935. Although it already stood under the shadow of Nazism, which had badly affected the Jewish community in Germany and thus also the sports movement, it was an outstanding success. All 27 countries sent active sportsmen to this event and, in addition to the 2,100 athletes and gymnasts from abroad, 2,400 Palestinians participated in the various competitions. For the first time also, 200 members of the Maccabi Hatza'ir from abroad and 2,600 from Palestine marched in the big parade.

The height of this Olympiad was reached when Menahem Ussishkin, the president of the Jewish National Fund, handed over the land on which the first Maccabi village — K'far Maccabi — was to be erected. In part this was made possible by money collected in Germany but primarily from contributions by the Czechoslovak Maccabi members.

In August 1935 the World Congress of the Maccabi Union assembled in Brno, and the events that had overtaken Germany showed their results. The world leadership was now put into the hands of Professor Selig Brodetsky (London), who became chairman of World Maccabi, and Lord Melchett, the honorary president. By that time the world Maccabi numbered over 200,000 members; Czechoslovakia had 82 societies and 10,300 members.

The second winter Maccabia was held in Banská Bystrica (Slovakia) in February 1936. Its preparation and organization were carried out by the Czechoslovak leadership. Its sports results brought attention and recognition in wide Jewish and non-Jewish circles.

This was the last international meet to be held on Czechoslovak soil. In the following year, the third and last territorial conference of the Czechoslovak Maccabi Association took place in Žilina (July 4–6, 1937) which was, as usual, accompanied by a public exhibition and various sports competitions. Two thousand members of the Czechoslovak Maccabi participated. The leadership had remained in the hands of Artur Herzog from the time he had been elected in 1926, and his commanders (apart from those mentioned before) were Leo Bleyer (Moravská Ostrava, 1928–1931); Richard Pacovský (1931–1934); Viktor Mauthner (1934–1936); and from then to the end of the period under review, Dr. Otto Hirsch (Brno).

The Maccabi Ideology

In the first place, it was under the impact of emerging Zionism (see above, p. 186) that the necessity of the physical regeneration of the Jewish people gave rise to the forming of special gymnastic and athletic clubs. In addition to physical amelioration, sports as an educator of men played an equally important part in the development of the Maccabi idea. Gymnastics taught the young man to synchronize physical and spiritual elements, to develop a sense for aesthetics and strong moral character, to learn to be part of a larger unit and to remain in it with discipline and conscious integration, so that there arose no distinction between man and man. To these physical and moral aspects there has to be added one more which characterizes Maccabi and makes it the national movement into which it had developed. As Beda Brüll, its excellent Czechoslovak secretary, stated in a historical survey:[14]

> Maccabi undertook to educate the Jewish youth systematically and in an all-embracing way. This undertaking derives from the recognition of the fact that it does not suffice to encourage young people to become enthusiastic and attain highest expansion of strength which very often results from a gymnastic exhibit, but that it is necessary also to understand deeply the urgency of knowledge and independent expression of thoughts. The answer of Maccabi to an education which very often is very close, if not identical, with propaganda, is hard educational work, in Hebraic and general culture. Therefore do leaders and teachers attain in our annual schools education in the history of Zionism, and of our movement,

and therefore at exams for the gymnastic and sportive symbol knowledge of Jewish and Zionist history by the candidate is very carefully considered.

Maccabi was, throughout the period under review, supported by the Zionist press appearing in Czechoslovakia, and many a fundamental ideological article can be found either in *Selbstwehr* or in *Židovské Zprávy*. Both papers published in the thirties special weekly editions of *Hamakabi*, the official organ of the movement. They contain, in great detail, all the events of these years as well as the names of the successful sportsmen and the nature of their achievements.

Maccabi actively participated in Czechoslovakia in all activities connected with the Zionist movement and the upbuilding of Palestine. They had their delegates in the highest and local societies, particularly the popular Jewish National Fund. While from 1933 it had become obligatory for Maccabi members to acquire the *Shekel*, the membership card of the Zionist Organization, it was made quite clear that this obligation arose only once a gymnast or athlete had definitely become a member of Maccabi.

The height of this ideological development within Maccabi was reached in 1926, when an independent youth organization, Maccabi Hatza'ir, was formed as a result of an internal spiritual development, whereby youth demanded personal participation in the upbuilding of Palestine. It became one of the idealistic Halutz groups in Czechoslovakia, with a membership of some 2,500.* Even before the abovementioned K'far Maccabi was near reality, the first Czechoslovak Maccabi Halutzim had already settled in Kibbutz Ra'anana and thus established a living link between Palestine and Czechoslovakia.

The end was, alas, by then already in sight. In 1938 Czechoslovakia was dismembered, and 1939 saw the end of the Maccabi Association in the Czechoslovak Republic.

Sports results

What now follows is a chronological survey of Maccabi sports activities, arranged in groups according to the branch of sports with which they deal. It was, of course, impossible to incorporate every exhibit and every sports event, but the selected cross-section provides

* [Cf. Brada, pp. 589–598 (Ed.)]

a glimpse of a highly active, enthusiastic, and very often quite successful Jewish national sports community.

Gymnastics

As pointed out in the preceding pages, the Jewish national sports movement and, accordingly, Maccabi started out as primarily concerned with gymnastic exercises. This aspect of sports action has remained basic throughout the period under review. In all public meets the largest part was always devoted to gymnastic exercises. There was not a single group in a single city that at one time or another did not organize public exhibits on some festive occasion. In the short survey which now follows only a few important — and, alas, not even all important — meets will be listed. They had some significance either for the Maccabi movement *per se* or for the district and area in which they took place.

1919:

In June, on the occasion of the conference of Czechoslovak Maccabi, the first public gymnastic and sports exhibition in new Czechoslovakia took place in Brno, with the participation of 650 active sports members from 27 communities.

1921:

In July, the first official territorial sports meeting took place in Brno with the participation of 650 active sports members from 27 communities.

A World Maccabi sports exhibition took place on the occasion of the Twelfth Zionist Congress in Karlovy Vary (September 1–14), and Czechoslovak Maccabi societies were strong y represented.

1923:

Another strong representation of Maccabi members attended the sports exhibit in Karlovy Vary on the occasion of the Thirteenth Zionist Congress held there (August 6–18).

In December, Maccabi Teplice-Šanov organized a sports meet of the Northern Bohemian clubs.[15]

1924:

In February, Maccabi Plzeň had a successful regional gymnastic exhibition.[16]

1925:

During the Fourteenth Zionist Congress held in Vienna (August 18–31) Czechoslovak Maccabi was strongly represented in all sports exhibits.

1926:

An exhibit of the Czechoslovak Maccabi, attended by hundreds of participants, took place in Brno on the occasion of the Territorial Conference of the movement in the Republic.

1927:

Czechoslovak Maccabi again participated with a large representation at the sports exhibits during the Fifteenth Zionist Congress in Basel (August 30 to September 11).

1928:

On August 5 and 6, public exhibition days were organized in Brno. The participants had occasion to visit, for the first time, the newly founded Maccabi Youth Camp in Blansko (about 10 miles north of Brno).

On September 2 and 3, a large number of Czechoslovak Maccabim participated in competitive meets in Breslau (Germany).

In October, a sizable delegation of Czechoslovak Maccabi participated in the public exhibits of the Berlin Bar Kochba on the occasion of its thirtieth anniversary.

1929:

The Second Czechoslovak Territorial gymnastic and athletic show was held in Moravská Ostrava. The Czechoslovak sportsmen were joined by guests representing the Maccabi Unions of Austria, Belgium, France, Germany, Latvia, Palestine, Poland, Romania, and Yugoslavia. Some 2,000 performers, among them 350 gymnasts, showed remarkable skill before an audience of 6,000.

Another strong representation of Czechoslovak Maccabim participated in the sports exhibits organized during the Sixteenth Zionist Congress in Zurich (July 28 to 10).

1930:

The participation of the Czechoslovak Maccabi Union at the World Maccabi Games in Antwerp in July 1930 was one of the outstanding events of that year.

1931:

Prague Maccabi opened its new gymnasium in the modern Bet HaAm with an exhibit.[17]

Again, a large group of Maccabim attended the sports exhibit at the Seventeenth Zionist Congress, Basel (June 30 to July 15).

1932:

The main event of that year was the First Maccabia in Tel Aviv to which reference was made already (p. 192). Czechoslovak sportsmen took third place among all the districts of the World Maccabi.

1933:

In February the Winter Maccabia took place in Zakopané (Poland) see p. 192).

Maccabi Uherské Hradiště presented its Juniors in an exhibit of the district.[18]

This exhibition was duplicated by Maccabi Mikulov with a fine performance.[19]

On the occasion of the Eighteenth Zionist Congress, held in Prague (August 21 to September 3), a sports exhibition took place. It fell to the Czechoslovak organization to prepare this event, and it was one of the greatest shows in the Maccabi history. Alas, it turned out to be the last Maccabi show at a Zionist Congress. Thousands of spectators crammed the Belvedere Stadium every day and Czechoslovak athletes and gymnasts won a number of prizes. The festivities concluded on August 27 with a grand march by all the competing countries.

1934:

In December, Maccabi Brno presented its Juniors to the public.[20]

1935:

Two hundred and seventy gymnasts from Czechoslovakia participated in April at the Second Maccabia in Tel Aviv, mentioned above (p. 192). Czechoslovak gymnasts again took third place among all the districts of the World Maccabi, as they had at the First Maccabia.

In August, during the height of the season, Maccabi Piešt'any organized a sports exhibit of the West Slovakian district.

1936:

The second Winter Maccabia took place in February in Banská Bystrica (Slovakia). Its preparation and organization were carried out by Czechoslovak Maccabi. It gained attention and recognition in wide Jewish and non-Jewish circles with its sport results.

1937:

The last Czechoslovak Territorial Maccabi sports event took place in Žilina (Slovakia) on the occasion of the Third Maccabi Conference held there (July 4–6). Two thousand members of the Czechoslovak Maccabi participated in all branches of sports activities.

Soccer

When soccer was introduced in the Historic Lands in the last century from England, Jews, too, took an early interest in this sport.[21] Like gymnastics, mentioned above, soccer had also drawn the attention and interest of individual Jews in various clubs before Zionism had encouraged the formation of Jewish national sports clubs.[22] In those early years Jews helped to establish unified soccer organizations[23] and even formed clubs under entirely non-Jewish names, although Jews constituted the majority of their founders and supporters.[24] Active Jewish soccer players found general recognition for their achievements. Four among them, Dr. Samuel Schillinger (Shilling), Pavel Mahrer, František Kummerman, and Bedřich Taussig, deserve special mention in this connection.[25]

There were a number of Jewish soccer clubs in existence prior to 1918, and among them the most active were in Bratislava, Brno, Prostějov, and Prague (Hagibor). The founders of the latter came from the ranks of Poale Zion.[26]

As previously mentioned, the Czechoslovak Jewish Soccer Association was established at the conference in Brno in June 1919. In it, as well as in the Jewish League of Soccer Referees and other such organizations, the use of the Hebrew language (besides the Czech language) was permitted by the authorities, in accordance with the Czechoslovak minorities law.* The statutes of the Jewish Soccer Union were filed by Dr. Egon Štern under the name K'vutzat Mosahake Kadur Regel Yehudit (KMKRY), and those of the Jewish League of

* [Cf. A. M. Rabinowicz, vol. I, pp. 193–200 (Ed.)]

Soccer Referees under the name Agudat Shofte HaHakhra'a HaYehudit (ASHY). The chairman of KMKRY was Oskar Kaminský (Prague) and the chairman of ASHY Dr. Otto Baru (Brno). Both statutes were approved by the authorities in 1920.

The year 1922 saw the formation of the countrywide Československá Associace Footbalová (ČSAF) — the Czechoslovak Football (Soccer) Association. Both of the above-mentioned Jewish organizations were charter members of ČSAF, which comprised, in addition, Czech, German, and Magyar Soccer Unions.[27] Within the framework of the ČSAF there was a Health Council headed by district physician Dr. Jakub Stránský (Hlubočepy), who was assisted by other Jewish physicians such as Dr. Arnold Brandeis, Dr. Leopold Fürst and, in special medical sports counseling and preventive sports medicine, by Dr. Jiří Král. Of great importance was the creation of a special Heart Department at the Czech Polyclinic of Professor Dr. Václav Libeňský, to serve as a medical sports research center.

Many of the Jewish soccer clubs in the Republic were amateur societies, as only the larger Jewish communities of cities like Bratislava, Brno, Prostějov, and Olomouc could afford professional soccer teams, and even these for a few years only. However, while in existence, these professional clubs were able to achieve great victories in the Republic as well as abroad, and at one time Maccabi Brno ranked among the prominent soccer clubs in Central Europe.

In Prague, the professional players were dismissed because the club had lost its lease on the Sparta Sport Club, and this created the opportunity to renew soccer activities from scratch with a team of youngsters on a purely amateur basis. Dr. František Lagus and the present writer were able to organize the finance committee for a new stadium, which soon became a reality.[28] It became an important center for Prague's Jewish youth and was inaugurated with a competitive meet of Jewish youth on *Yom Hano'ar* (Day of Youth) specially prepared for that occasion.

With the elimination of most professional soccer players from the Jewish Soccer Union, which had commenced in 1922, a parallel decline both in the number of registered players and clubs was noticeable. Thus in 1922 there were still 1,654 players active in 44 clubs; by 1926, only 194 registered players remained in 8 clubs. However, a sudden increase became conspicuous in 1933 when the number of players increased to 550 and that of clubs to 15.[29]

Track and Field Athletics

Track and field athletics first developed as a sideline of gymnastic activities. Cross-çountry runs were soon included when they became an organized division of sports clubs.

The 10-kilometer run Běchovice-Praha made history as the most cherished national cross-country competition in the annual championships. Jakub Wolf (AC Sparta) became famous with his record time of 39:03.0 minutes in the first year of this race in 1897. He repeated his victory in 1898 and improved his record in 1899 to 38:54.0 minutes.

Later, in 1921, other members of the track team of AC Sparta, Dr. Josef Alcantara Wiener (Winn — called Strach) and Karel Frankenstein (called Frank) with their clubmates Josef Skokan and Václav Vohralík, established in the 4 x 400-meter relay a new Czechoslovak record of 3:40.8 minutes; Frankenstein became holder of the national record of 800 meters in 1:58.0 minutes.

In 1923 only three Jewish sports clubs in Czechoslovakia had track and field divisions: Hagibor (Prague), Hakoah (Olomouc), and Maccabi (Prostějov). All three were members of the Československá amatérská atletická unie (ČAAU) (Czechoslovak Amateur Athletic Union), the countrywide athletic organization comprising all ethnic groups.

The Maccabea (Bratislava), was the only unit which cultivated boxing, wrestling, and weightlifting in an organized manner, achieving remarkable results in regional, national, and international competitions.[30]

There is very little literature available on the activities of these Jewish clubs. Thus there was only one Jewish club, Hagibor, which published annually its track and field records from 1923.[31] From personal experience and knowledge this author can, therefore, more aptly concentrate on the club of his own association — Hagibor. This club was, throughout its existence, concerned to attract the greatest possible numbers of youth and to branch out in all strata of sports activities. Teamwork was its guiding principle (*Leitmotiv*) and when Max Löwy (called McLoy by his friends) set out to form the athletic league of Hagibor he was already able by 1923 to present a team competing in all events at interclub and international meets. The fine sportsmanship shown by these athletes won praise from the authorities and the sports world. The chairman of ČAAU, Consul Vincenc Macháček, volunteered to become gentleman coach and gave his best to Hagibor until his premature death in 1929. He had already in 1923 eighty-three athletes in custody. That year alone brought fifty-six trophies to Hagibor, of which twenty-six were first prizes. Thanks to his training, captain Egon Simeles, registrar Miloš Ginz, secretary Ervín Mautner, timekeeper Valter Kesler, and Ota and Pavel Wittler were able to carry on magnificently.

To show the many successes of Hagibor in this fiəld it will suffice to survey some of the most outstanding events in a chronological survey:

1923:

Hagibor won the first prize in the "Cross-Prague" relay run, in which it competed against the high-class old-timers of the Czech Clubs, Slavia and Sparta, and the German Eis Hockey Gesellschaft (Ice Hockey Society).[32]

At the cross-country run "Across Stromovka," park in Prague, six clubs participated. Hagibor's Junior team took third place.[33]

1926:

Hagibor athletes participated in the Hvězdicový závod napříč Prahou (Star Run across Prague), organized by the daily *České Slovo* on October 28, the anniversary of Czechoslovakia's founding. Sixty club teams started on a 4-kilometer run to the Tomb of the Unknown Soldier in the center of Prague.[34]

1927:

On June 12, the new Hagibor stadium was opened in Prague-Strašnice with a sports festival, under the auspices of the Ministry of Public Health and Physical Education. Hagibor earmarked the net proceeds of this festival for the Jewish Association for Students' Care and the Mensa Academica Judaica.[35]

On October 28, Hagibor again participated in the "Star Run across Prague." Four of its teams of eighteen athletes each constituted the strongest club participation in the history of this competition.

1928:

On the tenth anniversary of the founding of Czechoslovakia a relay run organized by the Czechoslovak Amateur Athletic Union saw twenty Hagibor athletes competing on the long route from the White Mountain to Prague.

Two important sportsmen strengthened the club in November: Walter Frankel (formerly of Hakoah, Vienna), an excellent athlete and new editor of the club magazine *Hagibor-Hamakabi*, and Dr. H. A. Zander (Zador), a former champion jumper from Hungary. He immediately won the championship of the Central Bohemiao District of ČAAU with a broad jump of 6.6 meters.

1929:

On March 1, Hagibor was entrusted with the preparation of the first Macháček Memorial, in memory of Consul Macháček, the first honorary coach of the club.

At the sports festival in Moravská Ostrava (June 27–30), mentioned above (p. 191), 1,658 athletes took part in the track and field activities, 127 of them from abroad.[36]

Andrej (Bandi) Engel (Žilina) joined the Hagibor team and won the 100-meter Czechoslovak championship (11.45 seconds) as a member of the athletic club of the Prague Universities.[37]

Oskar Hekš (Hostomice) joined Hagibor and became the most famous Jewish long-distance runner of Czechoslovakia.

The records in track and field activities as of December show some remarkable achievements.[38]

1930:

Engel represented Czechoslovakia in Antwerp and came in third in the 100-meter and second in the 200-meter dashes.

Walter Frankel, Erich Reichmann, and Dr. H. A. Zander participated in the championship of the German Maccabi held in Hamburg and won five first prizes. They, together with others, also participated in the World Maccabi games in June, in Antwerp.[39]

In September the Memorial Championship for the late Consul Macháček, organized for the ČAAU by Hagibor (see reference for 1929), became the ČSR Track and Field Championship and Marathon run. Bedřich Allina, Oskar Hekš, and Emil Klein became a three-man team at the Marathon. Hekš finished first.

In October the 4-kilometer annual forest run in Mladá Boleslav saw Walter Frankel finishing third, Emil Klein ninth, and Bedřich Allina twelfth.

In November, in the "Across Stromovka" run, these three athletes repeated their great performances.

1931:

Andrej Engel won the Czechoslovak record for 200 meters at 22.4 seconds. He also won the 100-meter dash at the international meet in Pardubice, at 10.7 seconds.

On July 7 Engel, in a Copenhagen meet, reached 100 meters in 10.5 seconds; in August he reached, in Budapest, 200 meters in 21.6 seconds and retained the Czechoslovak championship for 200 meters. Oskar Hekš again finished first in the Czechoslovak Marathon of 1931.

1932:

The Olympic Committee nominated Andrej Engel and Oskar Hekš for the Czechoslovak representative team for the Olympic Games in Los Angeles. Hagibor raised the funds to enable its members to participate. Engel did not qualify for the semifinals. Hekš came in eighth in the Olympic Marathon, in 2 hours 41 minutes 35 seconds. Of the 28 who started, only 20 finished this race, which took place on August 7.[40]

1933:

Andrej Engel participated in the Students' World Games at Torino, Italy, and won the 200-meter dash.

From August 23 to 29, during the assembly of the Eighteenth Zionist Congress in Prague, World Maccabi Games were held at which 1,000 sportsmen and 1,000 gymnasts from eighteen Maccabi districts participated. Hagibor Prague, like the other Maccabi clubs in the Republic, took a very active part in the preparation of the events and in sports activities.

In the Macháček Memorial Meet Oskar Schnabel won a surprise victory in the Junior class of 1,000 meters, and Oskar Hekš finished the 15-kilometer cross-country run in 54 minutes.

In the Marathon, Emil Klein finished sixth (2.56 hours), Bedřich Allina was ninth, and a newcomer, František Polák, finished in the middle group of 24 runners.

Oskar Hekš held the record for the one-hour race with 17,501.5 meters, and also won the Běchovice-Prague, Dobříš-Příbram, and Prague-Beroun races.

1934:

In May Engel retained his titles for 100 and 200 meters at a meet of the Prague University versus the Technical College, and Hekš again took first place in the Czechoslovak Marathon in 2 hours 46 minutes 38 seconds.

At an international meet of the Slavia club Jiří Freund threw the discus 38.7 meters. Later in that year (July) he improved it to 42 meters.

In the Army championship in October, Dr. Hugo Schuller, Bar Kochba (Brno), placed second in the 100 meters.

1935:

At the second Maccabia in Tel Aviv a complete Czechoslovak track and field team participated. First prizes were won by Bedřich Wasser (Warren) in broad jump, with 6.44 meters, and high jump, with 1.70 meters. Vilda Petschau won the first prize in decathlon with 4,666 points.

Jiří Freund won the first prize with a discus throw of 44.94 meters at the international meet held at the Hagibor stadium in Prague in July.

In August Engel and Jiří Freund represented Czechoslovakia against Japan.

In October Hagibor athletes competed in Frankfurt am Main, where Engel won the first prize on an inside track.

Hekš retained his champion title in the Fourth Masaryk Marathon run.

1937:

In the Břenev circle run of the Army, Jakub Birnholz-Kubík of Hagibor won the first prize.

Árpád Blödy, champion athlete of Hakoah (Vienna), joined Hagibor and strengthened the team considerably.

On May 28, Hagibor's *Yom Hano'ar* (Day of Youth) took place. Its principal event was the competition for the Dr. František Friedmann Cup, a grant from the chairman, and for the Czechoslovak Maccabi Trophy. Over 200 youngsters competed in this youth meet. Brit Trumpeldor won both these cups.

On May 30, Maccabea Bratislava celebrated the 25th anniversary of its foundation with the opening of its new sports stadium and a well-organized sports event.

In November, the ČAAU commemorated the 15th anniversary of the founding of the track and field division of Hagibor (Prague) with a meet in which Jiří Freund won the Czechoslovak discus-throwing record with a throw of 46 meters. Ludvik Schipper made 3.30 meters with the pole vault, and Árpád Blödy ran three kilometers in 9:07 minutes.

1938:

On September 1 Hagibor, for the last time, organized the Macháček Memorial Meet combined with the Czechoslovak Junior Championship. Hagibor's girls' team took second prize, the boys' team third.

September 24–25 Hagibor held the last athletic event at the Strašnice stadium, on its last *Yom Hano'ar* (Day of Youth). The results of this event were published in the Prague Jewish weeklies *Selbstwehr* and *Židovské Zprávy*, after the resignation of President Beneš on September 30; and in the last issues of these papers before their cessation, thus marking the end of a memorable era in Jewish athletics in Czechoslovakia.

Field Hockey and Ice Hockey

Field hockey was a favorite sport in Czechoslovakia. The Jewish sports clubs in Prague — Moravská Ostrava, Brno, and Bratislava — had their hocky divisions. There was a steady interchange between Hagibor Prague and Hagibor Moravská Ostrava. Most of the players were university students who, upon graduation, continued to practice their favorite sport.

In December 1923 the Hagibor team took second place in the tournament of the Czechoslovak champion club S. Karlín.[41]

The organizer of the field hockey division in Brno was Walter Wolf. Training started in February 1924. Dr. Eric Kresta, Pavel Corwin, Kurt and Hanuš Lehrfeld, and Armin Herz were the most prominent hockey players of Moravská Ostrava; they competed with Zdeněk Fantl, Max Posin, and others already named for the Theodor Herzl Cup at the opening of the new Hagibor stadium (1927). Dr. Arnošt Katz took care of the administration of the hockey division, and Arnošt Fuchs — with Hella Hahn — organized the women's hockey team. In the playoff of the Czechoslovak Field Hockey Championships, Hagibor women competed with the Deutsche Eis Hockey

Gesellschaft. All Jewish hockey teams of Czechoslovakia kept close contact with the teams of Hakoah, Vienna, and with the Maccabi clubs of Germany. Bar Kochba, Berlin, was the winner of the Theodor Herzl Cup, played in Prague at the Congress of World Maccabi Union in September 1931. The Theodor Herzl Cup was awarded every year until 1938.

The only Jewish player of the Czechoslovak national ice-hockey team was Dr. Karel Hartmann, a Prague attorney, who for many years was on the Board of A. C. Sparta. He was a member of the Czechoslovak ice-hockey team at the 1920 Olympic Games in Antwerp, the 1924 games in Chamonix, and the 1928 games in St. Moritz. Another Jewish member of the Sparta hockey team was George Taussig. In 1926 Josef Laufer, the prominent sports journalist and official radio broadcaster of domestic and international sporting events, started the domestic broadcasting of soccer matches, and in 1929 made his first international radio broadcast from Vienna. Laufer was also the international secretary of the Slavia club in Prague and sports editor of the semigovernmental daily *Prager Presse.*[42]

In the early days of hockey a great promoter of this sport in Prague was J. V. Kaufmann, editor and publisher of the magazine *Sport a Hry* (*Sport and Games*).

Skiing and Skating

Maccabi Most was the first Jewish club to found, in October 1923, a winter sports division.[43]

Maccabi Teplice-Šanov followed with its ski division in February 1924; and Hagibor Prague in October 1924.[44]

In the 1924 Czechoslovak Skating Championships, Ota Margolius (Hagibor) won the first prize in the 500-meter speed run and second prize in the Junior class in figure skating.

Winter sports soon became very popular among the Jewish sportsmen of Czechoslovakia. A regulatory institution for organizing, coordinating, and supervising competitive meets became necessary. Thus, in January 1933 the Jewish Winter Sports Association was founded in Bratislava, with Dr. Pavel März (Nový Bohumín) as chairman and a membership which exceeded 3,000. It was decided to participate in the World Maccabi Ski Championships in Zakopané, in the Tatra Mountains on Polish territory.[45]

The trials were held January 21–23, 1933, by the Bohemian clubs in the Krkonoše Mountains, by the Moravian and Silesian clubs in the Beskydy Mountains, and by the Slovak clubs in Lubochňa. From February 2 to 5, 1933, in the World Maccabi Winter Games themselves, Austria, Czechoslovakia, Germany, Hungary, Italy, Latvia, Norway, Poland, and Romania participated.[46]

This first great showing of the World Maccabi Union in winter sports attracted 350 active participants, more than 10,000 spectators, and 46 press reporters, among them Arnošt F. Taussig, sports editor of the daily *Prager Tagblatt*. He was the main speaker at the closing ceremony.

The increasing number of Jewish skiers made the building of mountain lodges possible. The first to open (in January 1933) was Maccabi Teplice-Šanov lodge in Cinvald (Zinnwald). A group of Zionists from Jablonec, headed by Dr. K. Liebstein, František Synek, and Felix Rafael, together with friends from Liberec and Trutnov, opened their winter sports home in Kořenov (Wurzelsdorf) in December 1934. The Maccabi lodge on the Klínovec (Keilberg), in the Krušné Hory, was opened in February 1935 with a comprehensive sports program available to all members of the Jewish Winter Sports Association of the Republic. To qualify for the long-distance races, certificates of the medical council of the association were required. Artur Herzog, chairman of Czechoslovak Maccabi, Dr. Angelo Goldstein, and Dr. Fritz Ullmann conducted the opening ceremony. The trophy was the Karel Koretz Cup.

In September 1935, the Chata Maccabi nad Králíkami, a Maccabi winter home accessible from both Banská Bystrica and Kremnica (Slovakia), was opened. The Ski Championships of the Second Maccabiah were held there in February 1936. The last important event in the history of winter sports in the first Republic was the Ski Championship, on the occasion of the 30th anniversary of Maccabi Prague, in February 1938, under the auspices of the World Maccabi Union of London.

Swimming

The Czechoslovak Amateur Swimming Association (Československý Amatérský Plavební Svaz) was founded in January 1919; the Jewish and Magyar clubs joined in 1922, the German group in 1925. The Svaz was the sole representative of Czechslovakia in the Fédération

Internationale de Natation (FINA), whose congress was held in Prague on May 25, 1925. As of March 1, 1925, seventy-two clubs were registered in the Svaz.

The leading Jewish clubs were Bar Kochba (Brno) and Hagibor (Prague). The Magyar group PTE (Bratislava) had outstanding Jewish swimmers who later formed the Bar Kochba of the city. A great number of Jews actively remained swimmers in other clubs. In 1924, at the Olympic Games in Paris, five Jews out of fourteen were on the Czechoslovak team.[47] The highest credit for promoting swimming among the Jewish population was due to Bar Kochba Brno, which produced two Olympic champions, Rudolf Piowati and Julius Balázs (Baláš). Balázs started his swimming and diving career in his native Žilina (Slovakia), developed a unique spring-board and high-diving skill, and became Czechoslovak champion of Olympic caliber. Later on he moved to Prague and joined Hagibor.

In Prague and Bratislava, swimming developed at a slower rate. Owing to intensive work, however, Prague took the leadership from Brno in Jewish swimming, only to pass it on to the Bar Kochba champion teams of Bratislava. Hagibor was fortunate to have in Hugo Steiner a leader of the swimming division, which was reinforced by such members as Franz Stern and Pepi Sticker of Hakoah Vienna.

The first swimming show was presented to the public at the Institute for the Blind, where Hagibor used the pool for training. This marked the beginning of the career of František Getreuer, holder of twenty-five Czechoslovak swimming records and inspiring star of the water polo team which four times (in 1928, 1935, 1936 and 1937) held the Czechoslovak championship. Helli Bester, who at 14 showed high class in free-style swimming and with her sisters Tilli and Bessie won several relays for Hagibor, was also discovered on that occasion. Helli Bester and Anka Klempfner later were nominated to the Women's Representative Team of Czechoslovakia. Hugo Steiner reported to the general assembly of Hagibor that in 1923 the swimming division participated in thirteen national and three international swimming meets and won 79 awards, of which 27 were first prizes.

On April 6, 1924, Maccabea Bratislava organized an international swimming festival in the Grössling pool under the lead of Dr. Vilém Lénart and Dr. Jiří (Juraj) Barta, with Julius Balázs responsible for the technical program. Many young talents — such as Kurt

Rado, Fred Fuchs (Fox), Arnošt Spitz, and Hanuš Sicher — were discovered at this meet which, according to the press reports, greatly advanced the cause of swimming in all Slovakia. The 10-year-old Kurt Rado swam the 35-meter free-style in 30 seconds.

From June 20 to 25, 1925, Hagibor commemorated the 30th anniversary of the first swimming contests which were held in Prague under the lead of Ignát Hermann in 1895. For the first time since World War I, Hungarian swimmers were invited, with the consent of the Czechoslovak government. Vajda and Teddy Glück of VAC, Budapest, faced Piowati and Getreuer in the Arnošt Friedmann Cup in swimming and in the Pepi Sticker Cup in water polo. These two cups were established in memory of two deserving athletes who had died prematurely.

In 1926 two new Jewish records were achieved in the ČSR championships by Jiří (Juraj) Messinger (Košice) in the 100-meter back stroke and Elsa Messingerová (Košice) in the women's 100-meter free-style. Balázs was again first, and qualified for the European High Diving Championship in Budapest, where he reached third place. In the club classification of the Svaz in 1926, Hagibor's women's team was second, the men's team third.

At the national swimming meet held in Terezín/Bohušovice on August 20, 1926, twenty-five boys and girls of Hagibor and many other Jewish swimmers participated.

The year 1927 had special significance for Jewish swimmers. It was the first time that PTE Bratislava, with Dr. Pavel (Pali) Steiner, made headlines in the press by winning the Czechoslovak water polo championship. Steiner was nominated to represent ČSR in the European swimming competition in Bologna (Italy), and at the Slavic championships in Beograd (Yugoslavia). He won first prize in Beograd. The government health insurance organization built a modern swimming pool in its new office building in the Klimentská street in Prague, and opened it with an international swimming festival. Arne Borg competed with František Getreuer and Steiner in a diversified exhibition program.

In the 1928 club classification of Czechoslovak championships was the water polo final between ČPK and Hagibor, with the latter winning 6 : 1. At the 1928 Olympic Games in Amsterdam Kurt Epstein, František Getreuer, František Schulz, and Dr. Pavel Steiner were members of the Czechoslovak Representative Water Polo Team and Julius Balázs a member of the high-diving team.

The year 1929 was another step forward in the Jewish swimming sector: 14 records were achieved in the Czechoslovak championships.[48]

In 1930 Dr. Steiner improved his 100-meter free-style record to 1:02.9 Getreuer his 200-meter to 2:26.8 and his 400-meter to 5:26.6. As swimming competitions became more inspiring for the Jewish youngsters, the membership in Hagibor grew and exceeded 1,000; the number of sports enthusiasts in other centers of Jewish sports activities rose in the same proportion.[49]

At the Maccabi Festival in Antwerp, Czechoslovakia was well represented.[50]

On May 8, 1931, the French swimming champion Taris participated in a swimming meet in Prague and won all events. But in July 1932 Dr. Steiner won the Grand Prix of Paris by swimming 100 meters free-style in 1:03.2.[51]

In June 1931 the new Bar Kochba Bratislava, formed by Jewish swimmers of the PTE, had an interclub match with Bar Kochba Brno.[52] In 1931 Czechoslovakia also participated in the European water polo championship meet in Paris. On the team of seven, two were Jewish: Pavel Steiner and Kurt Epstein.

In October 1932 the Hagibor swimming division became the "Jewish Swimming Club Hagibor in Prague," led by Samuel Beinhacker. In March 1933 three special events took place: Dr. Steiner temporarily moved to Prague to swim for Hagibor at the ČSR championships; Hagibor won a final match in water polo against APK; and the tenth anniversary meet of Bar Kochba Brno was held with an exhibition arranged by its long-time president, Bohdan Huber.[53]

In 1933 a memorable event took place in Warsaw: the swimming, diving, and water polo matches of Poland versus Czechoslovakia. On the Czechoslovak team, five were Jewish: František Schultz, Arnošt Reiner, Hanuš Abeles, Kurt Epstein, and Dr. Pavel Steiner.

In 1934 Hagibor swimmers went on a tour of France and England with Dr. Steiner, and in 1935 they were guests of Bar Kochba Berlin at a swimming meet in which VAC of Budapest participated. At the Second Maccabiah in Tel Aviv, 1935, Balázs was first in diving. In the ČSR championship of 1935 in the Barrandov pool in Prague, several teams participated.[54]

In February 1937 Hagibor invited the originator of modern water polo, Béla Komjády, to a swimming meet in Prague with his Budapest club. Hanuš (Heini) Baderle (Bar Kochba, Bratislava) swam the 100-meter back stroke in 1:10.6 minutes, a new Czechoslovak and Maccabi world record. The ČSR championship of 1937 were held in the Lido establishment in Bratislava. The star performer was 14-year-old Erica Singer, who swam the 200-meter breast stroke in a record time of 3:16 minutes. This was the last participation of Jews in swimming and water games before the Nazi invasion.

Rowing and Canoeing

Though Jews of Czechoslovakia did not compete under their own flag in rowing and canoeing, the achievements of a few Jews were recorded in the international annals.

In 1923, Emil Ascher, honorary international secretary of the Svaz Veslařů ČSR (Rowers Union of Czechoslovakia), participated in the Congress of the International Rowing Federation (FISA) in Como, Italy; this group entrusted Czechoslovakia with the organization of the next European Rowing Championships, held in Prague September 5 and 6, 1925. Ascher earned credit for his contribution to the faultless organization of this championship.

In 1929 Viktor Langer, member of the Eight Oars crew of the ČAC Roudnice, was one of the Eight who broke the Czechoslovak record for 2,000 meters in 6 minutes 21 seconds in the Primatorská Osma, the mayor's race for the trophy of the City of Prague for Eights with coxswain.

In 1930 the pair Steinerová-Kende, members of the Touring Club, Praha, placed first in canoe doubles for 1,000 meters in 5 minutes 31.6 seconds, in competition with 18 countries participating in the Third Women's World Games of the Fédération Sportive Féminine Internationale (FSFI), held in Prague.

Lawn Tennis

Jews began to compete in tennis in the early 1900s. Prior to 1918 Ernst Deutsch, the well-known actor, achieved top performance, as did Herbert and Karel Fuchs, Stědrý, and Schidloff.

After 1918 Arnošt Gottlieb (Brno) was the first Jewish member of the Czechoslovak Olympic tennis team. In 1924 he reached, with Rohrer, the semifinals of the men's doubles, defeating the British team of Godfree and Woosnam 6–3, 6–4, 6–2 in Paris. František

Soyka of Prague-Smíchov fought his way to the men's finals of the 1925 Czechoslovak championships against the unbeaten Jan Koželuh and won second place. Ota Herrmann (Mladá Boleslav) won in the 1925 match of Czechoslovakia versus Italy. By that time, all ethnic tennis groups, with over 17,000 registered players, were united in the Czechoslovak Lawn Tennis Association (ČLTA), whose recognized leader and organizer was Karel Fuchs Robětín, one of the leading paper manufacturers of Czechoslovakia.[55]

In 1927, the ČSR Davis Cup team who played against Greece included two Jewish players, František Soyka (Prague) and Arnošt Gottlieb (Brno).

From 1931 to 1938 Ladislav Hecht, a native of Žilina (Slovakia) was a permanent member of the Czechoslovak Davis Cup team. During this time Czechoslovakia reached the finals in the European zone three times. Hecht also played as Czechoslovak representative in championships in Wimbledon, Paris, Rome, and overseas in the United States, Canada, Japan, China, and India. He won the championships of Hungary and Poland, and the Czechoslovak Robětin Cup six times. Twice he ranked among the first ten tennis players in the world, three times among the first five in Europe. In 1936 and 1938 he was number one in Czechoslovakia.

In 1938, the ČSR Davis Cup team went to Zagreb, Yugoslavia, for the play-off of April 29 and 30 and May 1. On the Yugoslav frontier, the Yugoslav passport controller denied entry to Hecht because he was a Jew, but the team captain insisted that either the whole team would go to Zagreb or no one would. After an hour's delay, passage was granted to the whole team. The atmosphere in Zagreb had already been poisoned by the Nazis, and the ČSR team lost under protest to London.[56]

Table Tennis

Until 1924 table tennis in Czechoslovakia was played as an unorganized leisure-time activity in some lawn tennis clubs and student's dormitories. A group of enthusiasts under the leadership of the sports editor of the *Prager Tagblatt*, Arnošt F. Taussig, together with Miloš Bondy, an aircraft manufacturer, took the first steps to play the game in an organized manner. The first tournament was held in the Albertov Students' Home in Prague.

In 1925 the Czechoslovak Table Tennis Association (ČSTTA) was founded. A year later, it became a member of the International Table Tennis Federation. In 1928 the ČSTTA was authorized by the government to function as a countrywide organization and to include all ethnic groups. The ČSTTA had at the time sixty-two clubs with 1,046 registered players. Miloš Bondy served as honorary chairman.

Czechoslovakia was brilliantly represented at the world championship matches in Olomouc by the 15-year-old Truda Klein (Maccabi, Brno), who defeated, early in 1935, the Czech women's world champion Marie Kettner and was thereupon nominated for the Czechoslovak team for the world championship of 1935, held in London. At those matches the ČSR women's team won the first prize. Among the group of individuals in London, Truda Klein placed third in the women's singles. In 1936, in Prague, the Czechoslovak women's team repeated the victory, and in 1937 it again placed third in Baden, near Vienna. Truda Klein with Ervín Kohn [Korda], the champion of World Maccabi Union, won the mixed doubles world championship. In 1937 she won first prize in the Moravian-Silesian championship.

Among other outstanding Jewish players was Albert Bergman (Košice), the winner of the men's singles of the World Maccabi Games, held in Prague, August 23–29, 1933, in the presence of the chairman of World Maccabi Union, Lord Melchett, and the patroness of the games, Lady Erleigh, the sister of Lord Melchett. Albert Bergman also won the Slovak Table Tennis Championships held in Žilina in 1935 and 1936, and kept this title for the East Slovakian District as well as for the local matches of Košice, Mukačevo Užhorod, and Prešov. Imre Salzer (Bratislava), Jindřich Heitler, and Pavel Löwy (Prague) successfully represented their clubs in regional matches.

Fencing

The popularity of fencing as a sport in Czechoslovakia was different in the Historic Lands and in Slovakia. In the Historic Lands it was the sport of a few in upper-class clubs and among students. In Slovakia fencing was taken up by the middle class on a broad basis and was influenced by the more emotional Hungarian tradition: duels, often much publicized, of the aristocracy and Army personnel. The Jewish sector of the middle class is credited by Ivan Tänzer and Slavo Kalný, in their book *Prvý Gol* (First Goal) (Východoslovenské vydavatelstvo 1964), with the promotion of fencing in Eastern Slovakia. Alexander Šalamon founded the first fencing school in Levoča prior to World War I; in 1919, upon his transfer to Košice, he promoted fencing there with great success. The first championship of Košice was held in 1922 — Edmund Szenes took the first prize in sabers. The Košice school, which was later headed by Docent Samo Pačenovský, is credited from 1927 to 1938 with a number of international and national champions, such as Dr. Tibor Klein, Alcxander Barta, Dr. Herbert Gádor, Dr. Gejza Neményi, and Oto Lewith. In 1927 Lewith was victor over the Olympic champion, the Hungarian Dr. Posta, in Košice.

Bureš and Plichta (see note 2) mention, in the records of the Czechoslovak Fencing Championships: in 1922, Alexander Barta (Kassai AC), Košice, third in sabers, improving in 1923 to second place; Miss Fuchs, who placed third in foils; in 1928, Dr. A. Edvard (Tibor) Klein, Košice, who was first in sabers; in 1929, Captain Benedikt, Levoča, in first place in sabers, repeating his victory in 1930, Klein taking second place and followed by Dr. Géjza Neményi.

The same year, 1930, A. C. Slavia organized an international fencing tournament, where Emil Ascher (Prague) took third place in sabers. Dr. František Vohryzek [Vernon] achieved championships of all Czechoslovak Universities in all three weapons (saber, épée, and foil) while he was at the law school of the Charles University in Prague and Junior championships of Czechoslovakia in épée and foil throughout the years until 1934, when he became a member of the Czechoslovak Representative team participating in the Berlin Olympic Games in 1936. At the last Fencing Championship of the Czechoslovak Republic, held in Piešt'any, April 3, 1938, Miss Kohn is listed second in foils.

Horsemanship

Organized horsemanship started in the territory of Czechoslovakia in 1838 when Prince Franz Liechtenstein, the commander of the Hussar Cavalry Regiment in Pardubice, founded the Parforce Hunting Society. The hunts were organized in the English style. The horses came from state-owned and private stud farms on the estates of the nobility, many of them leased to Jewish farmers who became experts in horse breeding. Baron Moritz Bethman was the founder of the

Spolek českých pěstitelů koní (Association of Bohemian Horse Breeders) in Poděbrady; it later changed its name to Český dostihový spolek (Bohemian Racing Association), which in 1874 organized the Great Pardubice Steeple Chase. This race made history. Captain Arnošt Eisner, riding Dunka, was the only Czechoslovak Jew who successfully traversed the difficult 6,400-meter track. In 1927 he placed third against heavy international competition.

Only the Pražský jezdecký klub (Prague Riding Club), founded in 1923, had a Jewish membership of any significance.[57] There were many other Jews, especially those engaged in agriculture, who rode on their farms or estates. Others, such as Hugo and Artur Perutz, Pavel and František Kominík, and František Klinger, were interested in the Jockey Club.

The central organization of the equestrian sport was the Československý jezdecký svaz ČJS (Czechoslovak Riding Association), founded in December 1929. It consisted of twenty-two clubs with 1,874 members, and organized twenty-four local races, one countrywide race, and one international race. The countrywide race was the annual Concours Hippique, founded in 1921 by the state-operated Equestrian Institute in Hodonín (Moravia).

Harness racing was under the supervision of the Klusácký závodní a všesportovní spolek (Harness Racing and All-Round Sports Association), founded in 1921 in Prague. Two Jewish members were on the board: Karel Friedman, a farmer in Prague-Nusle, chairman, and Josef Mändl, leather goods manufacturer of Prague-Vysočany. They worked hard to build a modern race track on the Letná plateau in Prague.

Aviation

There is some sort of scientific connection between Jews from Bohemia and aviation. There is, in the first place, the famous utopian Josef Popper-Lynkeus (from Kolín), who made vast experiments in matters of aviation technique and in 1911 published the results of his continued experiments.[58]

Another outstanding aeronautical scientist was Karl Arnstein, a native of Prague, chief designer and constructor of the Luftschiffahrts Gesellschaft Zeppelin in Friedrichshafen. He built forty airships, among them the famous dirigible "Graf Zeppelin," which opened new vistas for transoceanic tourism in flights between Europe and

America. In 1924 Dr. Arnstein went with his crew of engineers to Akron, Ohio, as Director of Research and Development of airship construction at the Goodyear Zeppelin Company, to continue building blimps and rigid airships for the United States Navy, which used them later in àntisubmarine warfare and air-sea rescue operations. Arnstein switched his production in 1939 from lighter-than-air ships to heavier-than-air planes, and was responsible for the design and construction of fighter planes for the U.S. Navy as vice-president of the Goodyear Aircraft Corporation, until his retirement in 1959, after which he continued to serve as consultant.

Among the aircraft produced by the factory Letov in Letňany was the Š–139, which was purchased by Mrs. Margaretta Ferrari-Kohn, wife of a brick manufacturer in Maloměřice near Brno. She was the only Jewish woman pilot in Czechoslovakia who distinguished herself in a number of aviation events, such as the International Challenge in June 1933, organized by the Aero Club of Poland. She won four first prizes, the trophies offered by the Polish prime minister, the Polish Foreign Affairs Ministry, the Polish Ladies Club, and the Aero Club of Warsaw. The leading Czechoslovak aviation magazine *Letectví* (*Aviation*) stressed the fact that Mrs. Ferrari-Kohn reached the highest points in the classification of the entire contest. Mrs. Kohn flew a modified Š–139 airplane and established a number of Czechoslovak records in women's categories.[59] In 1934 during the Slavic National Aircraft Closed Aircircuit, organized by the Moravian Aero Club in Brno, Mrs. Kohn won third prize against heavy competition by professional and military pilots. She was the only woman pilot in this contest. The Letov type Š–139 airplane was the newest Czechoslovak sports craft in the lowest-priced category. Many were sold abroad after the excellent performance by Mrs. Kohn.

Zdĕnek Mayer's hobby* was gliding, and he popularized this sport among Jewish youngsters. He participated in many cross-country glider contests, organized by the Masarykova letecká liga (MLL) (Masaryk Flight League), founded March 6, 1926.

On July 12, 1938, at the last prewar countrywide gliding meet held at Raná near Louny, 103 pilots participated with forty-four gliders.[60]

The Jewish public patronized flying within the ARČS and MLL. An active member of the ARČS board was František Stein, manufacturer of aeronautical instruments ("Toka"), who was also on the

---

* [See Pick, vol. I, p. 408 (Ed.)]

editorial board of the official publication *Letectví*. He worked hard to raise funds for equipment for local MLL chapters, assisted by Karel Bondy, Otakar Berka, and Otto Wurm, all of Prague. There were several Jews working actively in MLL chapters all over the country. In July 1935, Mrs. Gisela Schlesinger and Mrs. Erža Reichel (Trenčin, Slovakia) sponsored two new gliders at the opening of the new hangar at Malej Sihoti. On July 6, 1936, Mrs. Reich (Žilina, Slovakia) sponsored a new glider, which was the product of a local amateur effort of young MLL members. On May 15, 1938, Mrs. Vlasta Eisner (Ústí nad Orlici, Bohemia) was the patroness of a new glider built by the boy members of the chapter. In the České Budějovice chapter of MLL, Ota Teller, a bank clerk, served as treasurer. He was an enthusiastic aircraft pilot, and took part in the 1931 First-of-May Flight of his town. After a perfect flight, his Be–50 lost speed and crashed on descent. Teller, 26 years old, was killed. He was buried in the Jewish cemetery of České Budějovice with all official honors.

The fliers of the Czechoslovak Air Force were excellently trained. In 1931 one of the first to be trained in the use of the new PAK parachute, a Czechoslovak product, was private first class pilot Bohumil Stein, a native of Vlaším, who successfully jumped from a burning light bomber of the Š–16 type from an altitude of 2,000 meters. As reward for his bravery he was made a sergeant-field pilot and commented publicly by the commander of his flight regiment.

The conscientious training of Czechoslovak pilots, not only in military aircraft but also in the premilitary use of gliders in the Masaryk Flight League, was recognized in World War II by the Allied forces on all fronts in the West, Middle East, and Eastern Europe.

NOTES

1. A comprehensive survey of physical training and sports in Jewish history, from the earliest times until the first years after World War I is to be found in Dr. Süssmann Muntner, "Leibesübungen bei den Juden" ("Physical Exercises among Jews"), in *Menorah*, Vienna, June/July 1926, no. 6/7, pp. 378–393. Valuable surveys may also be consulted in Felix Aaron Teilhaber, "Sport und Körperkultur bei den Juden" ("Sport and Physical Culture among Jews"), in *Jüdisches Lexikon*, Vol. V, Berlin, 1930, col. 560–567; and an unsigned article on the same subject in *Encyclopaedia Judaica*, Vol. X, Berlin, 1934, col. 740–754.

2. Having observed during his studies in Dessau the mechanical drill practiced by the "founder" of gymnastics in Germany, Ludwig Jahn, Hirsch returned to Prague and in 1840 opened an orthopedic institute. He maintained that the mechanical discipline does not suffice; gymnastics must also improve health. He envisaged homeopathic methods as guiding principles of gymnastic exercises. Dr. Seegen, his cousin, confirmed these ideas through independent research carried out in his own institute. They thus are the fathers of the modern-style gymnastics accepted by the entire world. Students from their institutes were among the founders of the famous Czech (and indeed Slav) gymnastic organization "Sokol."

   The importance of these two Jewish physicians of Bohemia for the sports movement *per se* has been described in Dr. Prokop Bureš, *Sport a tělesná kultura v Československé republice a v cizině* (*Sport and Physical Culture in Czechoslovakia and Abroad*), co-authored with the Czechoslovak Army Captain Jan Plichta, Prague, 1931. For their role in respect to the "Sokol," see Dr. Josef Scheiner, *Dějiny sokolstva v prvním pětadvacetiletí* (*The History of the Sokol in Its First Twenty-five Years*, Prague, 1877).
3. *Protocol* of the Second Zionist Congress, Vienna, 1899, p. 90.
4. *Protocol* of the Fifth Zionist Congress, Vienna, 1902, pp. 11 ff.
5. Eli Samgar, "Jüdische Turnvereine," in *Die Welt*, Vienna, no. 49, December 9, 1898, pp. 8–10.
6. For the formation of this club and of all other clubs mentioned, and for all sporting activities until 1922, see *Jüdische Turnzeitung* (*Jewish Gymnastics Magazine*), Berlin 1900–1922.

   Reports on the foundation and activities of most of these clubs were also published in *Die Welt*, op. cit., for the respective dates.
7. *Die Welt*, Separat-Ausgabe no. 6 (Special Congress Edition no. 6), Basle, August 29, 1903, and the article *ibid.:* Heinrich Löwe, "Judenmuskeln" ("Jews' Muscles"), pp. 15–17.
8. This coincided geographically with the incorporation of the Zionist districts of Bohemia and Moravia-Silesia in to the West Austrian Zionist Region.
9. It was up to that time the largest and most impressive event organized by any Jewish gymnastic organization, with 1,100 active participants (this writer was one of them). See *Die Welt*, September 9, 1913, and the article by Otto Abeles, "Zehn Jahre Muskeljudentum" (Ten Years of Muscular Judaism), *ibid.*, p. 85.
10. Report on the conference in *Die Welt*, December 12, 1913, p. 1704.
11. See *Makkabiblätter* (*Maccabi Magazine*), published by Maccabi, Prague, January 1919.

12. For this and for all subsequent references to the development of Maccabi in Czechoslovakia, see Beda Brüll, "Československý Makkabi" ("Czechoslovak Maccabi") in *Židovský Kalendář* 5698 (1937–1938), Prague, 1937, pp. 97–107.
13. For this and for all subsequent developments in World Maccabi, see *Das jüdische Sportbuch* (*The Jewish Sports Book*), compiled by Dr. Martha Wertheimer, Siddy Goldschmidt, and Paul Yogi Mayer, Berlin, 1937.
14. See note 12.
15. The first three prizes in gymnastics went to Leo Grünbaum (Teplice), Hanuš Pick (Chomutov), and Herman Semmel (Teplice) for men; Grete Fleischman (Chomutov), Tiny Ungar (Teplice), and Vally Heller (Teplice) for women. This sports show was prepared by the Maccabi board: Miss Bobek, Dr. Herbert Birnbaum, Erich Kusiner, Jakub Oliner, and Rabbi Dr. Friedrich Weihs.
16. The board of the Plzeň Maccabi in 1924 comprised Bernhard Kohn, Josef Klein, Helly Liebstein, Dr. Arnošt Münz, Arnošt Saxl, and Dr. Alfred Weisl.
17. On that occasion a new flag was presented by Olga Auerbach (wife of the president of Hagibor, Josef Auerbach) to Dr. Josef Fleischner, at that time head of Maccabi, Prague.
18. The organization was headed by Walter Eisinger. The entire meet was carried out by the club's Juniors.
19. The Mikulov arrangement was, as in Uherské Hradiště, entirely carried out by the Juniors, with a fine performance led by Oskar Adler and Vally Teltscher. The board of the local Maccabi was at the time headed by Hanuš Bauer, Manfred Fischer, Robert Fuchs, Josef Grossman, Cantor Adolf Hellmann, Salo Kaufmann, Hanuš Österreicher, and Robert Toch.
20. The Juniors were led by coach Bruckner. Erica Fischbach, Stella Liebmann, and Hermann Liebschütz excelled with their groups in allegoric dances and rhythmic calisthenics for women.
21. For the early period and later development of soccer, see Karel Petrů, *Dějiny české kopané* (*History of Czech Soccer*), Prague, 1946.
22. Petrů (see note 21) mentions the names of Jewish leading organizers in various soccer clubs (Prof. Jakub Wolf, the Lažanský family (Prague), Julius Kann (Plzeň), the Abeles family (Horšův Týn), and banker Artur Kraus (Pardubice). Petrů also mentions active Jewish sportsmen — for instance, the brothers Baroch (Pyšely) and the Brandeis family (Suchdol, near Prague), relatives of the late United States Supreme Court Justice Louis D. Brandeis.
23. Petrů (note 21) mentions Jewish executives in Czech soccer clubs. On the board of AC Sparta: Julius Saxl, chairman; Dr. Karel Hart-

mann, vice-chairman; Dr. Jiří Glücklich, international secretary; and Jiří Traub, treasurer. In SK Náchod those who were active were Pavel and Karel Strass, Ota and Honza Stein, Egon and Honza Pick. In other clubs they were František Glück (Benešov), Zdeněk Metzl (Heřmanův Městec), Lev Kosiner (Dobříš), V. Schleissner (Klatovy), Artur Fischer (Mladá Boleslav) and Rudolf Singer (Stará Paka). Three Bohemian sports districts were the result of the efforts of Dr. Karel Meissner (Mladá Boleslav) for the North Bohemian district, Viktor Popper (Pardubice) for the Eastern Bohemian district, and Joseph Neuman (Zdice) for the Podbrdský district.

24. Thus they formed the Deutscher Ballspiel Klub Sturm (German Ball Club Sturm) where, according to Sigmund Knina, more than 80 per cent of the members were Jews. Egon Ervin Kisch, the well-known writer, was chairman for many years. The club was liquidated by the Nazis.

Jews also actively participated in the organizing of the Deutscher Fussballklub in Prague (German Soccer Club, known under the initials DFC).

25. Dr. Samuel Schillinger (Shilling) played seventeen times on the representative soccer team of Czechoslovakia (1922–1938), and once played for Maccabi Tel Aviv when the team was on a visit in the USA (1939). Pavel Mahrer played eighteen times in international matches for Czechoslovakia, and for a time, during his stay in the USA, played for Hakoah, New York (1929–1932). František Kummerman and Bedřich Taussig played many times for the international competition in Czech soccer. Dr. Karel Bondy, Emil Karst, and Dr. Paul Schneider were among the leaders of the DFC.

26. I was unable to obtain the names of those organizers and prominent sportsmen in the various Jewish clubs mentioned. The information with regard to Hagibor, Prague, reveals that the initiative for forming the club was taken by Josef Flusser and Dr. Julius Eisner; and among the "old guard" of the soccer division prior to 1918 were Ota Brückner, Alex Dubský, Ada Edelstein, Oskar Fanta, Valtr Frankl, Rudolf Fuchs, Emil Gruschka, Josef Karpeles, Pavel Kersten, Karel Knöpfmacher, Viktor Kohn, Pavel Lederer, Oskar Pick, Pepa Pollak, Ota Stein, Ota Vohryzek, Emil Winter, Rudolf and Hynek Wodička, and Rudolf Zentner.

The administration comprised Dr. Rudolf Beck, Dr. Karel Friedmann, Dr. Otakar Löw, Dr. Josef Parkus, Dr. Arnošt Desensy, and Hynek Mahler.

27. Serving on the boards of the Jewish soccer organizations were Dr. Eugene Justic (Justic-Dajan), chairman of the World Maccabi Union in 1947, Pavel Black, Max Bäumel, Dr. Pavel Farkas, Rudolf Fischl, Leo and Pavel Freund, Ervín Fischer, Viktor (Gyuszy) Czeisler,

Capt. Oskar Fischer, Rudolf Grünhut, Otto Geduldig, Ludvík Glückman, Bedřich Janowitz, Josef Jarolim, Eric Juhn, Dr. Pavel Hirsch, Hugo Kahn, Zikmund Klinger, Dr. Josef Lasus, František Löwy, Mořic Mandl, Arnošt Pretzelmayer, Richard Repper, Jizchak Rosenberg, Pavel Roth, Ota Rosenzweig, Leo Saphier, Hanuš Sborovitz, Albert Schleissner, Pavel Schliesser, Julius Schuller, Dr. Arnošt Spitz, Pavel Steiner (Eng.), Jacques Sternfeld, Kurt Strach, Zikmund Sametz, Dr. Bedřich Tauber, Prof. Arnošt Vogel, Karel Vinařský, and Dr. Karel Weil.

28. Dr. Jaroslav Hovorka, personal secretary of the minister of public health and physical education, served on the Board of Sponsors, which included a great number of leading Jewish personalities. The funds were collected in a short period of time, and land-lease was secured from the Dr. David Seegen Foundation (see note 2) thanks to the efforts of Dr. Ludvík Singer, Dr. Angelo Goldstein, and Dr. František Friedmann (councilman of the City of Prague). The latter became a most successful chairman of Hagibor. Architects Ota and Karel Kohn contributed the design and specifications of the stadium, which was built by the construction firm of Rudolf Winternitz under the technical supervision of Heřman Abeles.

29. Arnošt Roubík in *Selbstwehr*, March 24, 1933.

30. The leader of the wrestling team was Pharmacist Pal, whose members were David Unreich, Sandor Rosenberger, Imre Lichtenfeld, Arpad Frommer, Karel Löwinger, Goldberger, and Schwartz.

31. Results for 1923 in track and field records of Hagibor, Prague, *Selbstwehr*, December 21, 1923:

100 yards	10.6 s.	Miloš Ginz	YMCA Kladno (July 22)
100 m.	11.5 s.	Bedřich Abeles	Bar Kochba, München (Sept. 3)
200 m	25.2 s.	Walter Abeles	A. C. Příbram (Oct. 7)
400 m.	53.3 s.	Miloš Ginz	A. C. Kolín (Sept. 23)
1,500 m.	4:35.4 m	František Lagus	Bar Kochba, Frankfurt a/M (Aug. 26)
4×100 relay	46.2 s.		Bar Kochba (Bedřich Abeles, Walter Abeles, Miloš Ginz, Ota Margolius), Frankfurt a/M. (Aug. 26)
4×200 relay	1:20.8 m.	Same team	Junior ČSR Championships, Nymburk n/L. (Sept. 17)
Broad jump	6.26 m	Ota Margolius	Bar Kochba, Frankfurt a/M. (Aug. 26)

High jump	1.58 m.	Rudolf Bondy	Bar Kochba, München (Sept. 3)
Shot-put	9.72 m.	Jindra Klempfner	ŽSK Hagibor (Sept. 30)
Discus	27.26 m	Robert Bix	S. K. Lysá (Sept. 19)
Javelin	36.15 m.	Jindra Klempfner	ŽSK Hagibor (Sept. 30)

32. The team, wearing the blue Magen David on white shirts when it ran through the streets of Prague, consisted of Walter Abeles, Gustav Bišický, Ferdinand Goldhammer, Jindra Klempfner, Dr. František Lagus, Viktor Lederer, Ota Margolius, Ferdinand Perlitz, Josef Reach, Jindřich Rimpl, and Arnošt Vinařský. Viktor Lederer (called Hašík), one of the sportsmen, had joined Hagibor in his early teens, later became one of the best swimmers and polo players.
33. The team consisted of Ota Adler, Harry Freund, František Gütig, Hanuš Janowitz, Julius Hartstein, Emil Klein, and Jaroslav Svoboda. Emil Klein in 1924 was the first Jewish athlete to start and finish the 42.2 kilometer Marathon of Czechoslovakia. He was eighteenth out of thirty runners.
34. In the "Star Run across Prague," October 28, 1926, Hagibor's two teams took third and fourth places. The Senior team, consisting of Zdeněk Fantl, Miloš Ginz, Hugo Jellinek, Emil Klein, Dr. Franišek Lagus, František Petschau, Ota Margolius, František Polák, Josef Reach, Max Reiniš, Gustav Strašic, and Oskar Weleminský, started from Libeň, and the Junior team — Vilda Beckmann, Bedřich Berger, Hanuš Bergmann, Otto Fischer, Gory Freund, František Hermann, Lev Komarin, Hugo Lengsfeld, Heřman Steiner, Oskar Rothbaum, and Jiří Waldstein — started from Vinohrady. The Seniors were guided by Egon Simeles, Hanuš Waldstein, and Pavel Wittler, and the Juniors by Ota Wittler, Bedřich Borges, Gustav Waldstein, and Villi Roth.
35. Karel Schablin and the organizer of this meet, Albert Heller, represented the Students' Care Association on the organizing committee, and Dr. Arnošt Lebenhart represented the Mensa Academica. The main events of the program were the track and field competitions, the soccer and hockey matches. One hundred and seventy-nine athletes from the following clubs participated: Bar Kochba (Berlin), Bar Kochba (Frankfurt a/Main), Bar Kochba (Breslau), Bar Kochba (Leipzig), Hakoah (Vienna), Makkabi and Jutrzenka (Cracow), and Maccabi (Cernauti).
36. Among first-prize winners were Andrej Engel in the 100- and 200-meter runs, Hanuš Buchsbaum in the 400-meter, Walter Frankel in the 800- and 1,500-meter, Feri Fehér in the javelin, and Dr. H. A. Zander in the broad hop, step, and jump.

37. See Alfred Janecký, *Československá lehká atletika* (*Czechoslovak Light Athletics*), Prague, 1954.
38. See *Selbswehr*, December 6, 1929, article by sports editor Walter Frankel. The records in track and field activities as of December 31, 1929, were listed also on p. 377 by Dr. Bureš and Captain Plichta in their book (see note 2):

100 m.	František Polák	Hagibor 11.1 s.	Vratislav 1928
200 m.	František Polák	Hagibor 23.2 s.	Vratislav 1928
400 m.	Ota Margolius	Hagibor 53.5 s	Prague 1927
800 m.	Walter Frankel	Hagibor 2:6.4 m.	Nymburk 1929
1,500 m.	Walter Frankel	Hagibor 4:24.6 m.	M. Ostrava 1929
3,000 m.	Adolf Weiss	Hagibor 9.26.4 m.	Berlin 1929
5,000 m.	Walter Frankel	Hagibor 15:53.3 m	Prague 1929
10,000 m.	Walter Frankel	Hagibor 34:0.3 m.	Vienna 1929
4 × 100 relay	Hagibor, Prague	45.7 s.	Prague 1929
3 × 1,000 relay	Hagibor, Prague	9:00.4 m.	Prague 1929
Shot-put	Jindra Klempfner	Hagibor 12.33 m.	Prague 1928
Discus	Dr. Vilmos Görög	Maccabi, Bratislava 41.85 m.	Bratislava 1925
Javelin	Feri Feher	Maccabea, Bratislava 44.70 m.	M. Ostrava 1929
High jump	Josef Reach	Hagibor, Prague 1.70 m	Vienna 1928
Broad jump	Dr. H. A. Zander	Hagibor, Prague 6.72 m.	Berlin 1929
Hop, step, and jump	Dr. H. A. Zander	Hagibor, Prague 12.90 m	Brno 1929

39. The results at the World Maccabi Games in Antwerp: František Polák was second in the 100-meter dash; Walter Frankel second in the 300-meter dash; and Dr. Zander first in broad and high jump in the Senior class. In the Junior class, Karel Hahn was second in broad jump, Josef Friedmann second in shot-put, and in the medley relay Valter Kessler, Arnošt Freudenhein, and Willi Freund were second among nine teams.
40. Having known Hekš thoroughly and having appreciated his ability and also his need for encouragement, this writer communicated with Alfred M. Cohen, president of B'nai B'rith, Cincinnati, to urge sports-loving members of B'nai B'rith to attend Los Angeles Olympic Games and place themselves at the seven control stations of the 26-mile-385-yard-long Marathon route and shout Hekš's name as an encouragement. This was done, and it proved of great moral help to Hekš. All reports evaluated highly the unusual brisk finish of Oskar

Hekš when he returned to the stadium, in his circuit of the track to the finish line; he cut the tape only 117 seconds after the first representative of the United Sates, Albert R. Michelson, followed 77 seconds later by the Japanese Taika Gon, who dragged himself, exhausted, the last five meters to the finish line.

41. The team consisted of Gustav Bišický, Ota Justic, Dr. Vilém Leckner, Jula Mahler, Ota Margolius, and Ota Vohryzek, and in reserve Ferdinand Goldhammer, František Schrecker, Rudolf Bondy, and Bruno Haftel. Its captain was Dr. František Lagus, who represented the Jewish teams in the Czechoslovak Field Hockey Association.
42. Laufer survived the Nazi persecution and wrote a book, *Hokej můj osud* (*Hockey My Destiny*), Prague, 1960, a documentary of half a century of hockey.
43. It was headed by Vítěslav Kohn, Wilhelm Lederer, and Josef Mühlstein; Karel Fanta was in charge of the technical instruction and schooling of the youngsters.
44. Karel Eisler, Karel Kraus, František Margolius, and Pavel Weigl headed the administration, and Jula Mahler was coach of the dry ski course and youth training at Špindlerův Mlýn in the Krkonoše Mountains.
45. Those nominated for the 18-kilometer run were Ludvík Salomon (Brno), E. Apfel (Banská Bystrica), Diamant and Egon Hahn (Olomouc), Spitzer and Weider (Žilina), Leo Wolf (Prostějov), Mikuláš (Mikloš) Rosenbaum (Ružomberk), Burstin, Leopold Nacher, and Pavel Wurzel (Moravská Ostrava).
46. Some of the results were: In the 18-kilometer ski race, Senior Class A, Wurzel (Moravská Ostrava) took second place; in the Senior Class B, Arnošt F. Taussig (Prague) won first place. The time for Class A was 2.08.49; for Class B 3.15.08 h. On the 4-kilometer run, the time of the winner, Emerich Freimann (Košice), was 45.34 minutes. In the 5×10 kilometer relay, Poland was first in the men's class and Czechoslovakia second with Pavel Wurzel, Leo Wolf, Egon Hahn, Ludvík Salomon, and Emerich Freimann. On the 3×4 kilometer relay for women, Poland took first prize and Czechoslovakia second with Lilla Löwy, Ditta Berger (16 years old) (Uherské Hradiště), and Ella Blau.
47. Swimmers in the 1924 Olympic Games in Paris were Rudolf Piowati (Bar Kochba, Brno), who swam the 200-meter breast stroke in 3:02 minutes. Julius Balázs (Baláš) (Bar Kochba, Brno) competed in high diving. Hugo Klempfner (Sparta, Prague), Béla Neményi of the Amateur Swimming Club (APK), and Jiří Reitman of the Czech Swimming Club (ČPK), were members of the water polo team. Besides Reitman the outstanding polo players and swimmers were Kurt Epstein, Jiří Fischer, and Eric Weiss. Kurt Epstein represented Czechoslovakia

fifty-four times, participated in two Olympic Games and two European Swimming Championships. He also served many years as the treasurer of the Svaz and the ČPK. Leopold Hájek (Hagibor) was 1937 vice-president of the Svaz.

48. Record list of the ČSR championships of 1929 showing results achieved by Jewish swimmers:

Men's 100 m. free-style	Pavel Steiner	1:03.9 mins.
200 m. free-style	František Getreuer	2:29.2 mins.
400 m. free-style	František Getreuer	5:30.6 mins.
4×200 relay	Hagibor	10:34.6 mins.
4×100 relay breast stroke	PTE	5:46.2 mins.
3×100 relay medley relay	PTE	3:53.4 mins.
Women's 100 m. breast stroke	Olga Hansel (Lederer)	1:34.9 mins.
200 m. breast stroke	Olga Hansel (Lederer)	3:27.2 mins.
100 m. back stroke	Eva Doppler (Verebes)	1:34.2 mins.
3×100 relay	PTE	3:53.4 mins.
High diving	Julius Balázs Fist	143.40 points
Water polo	PTE	
Men's team	PTE	

49. The Hagibor swimming division was taken over from Hugo Steiner by Bertl Black, followed by Samuel Beinhacker, with Jaroslav Svoboda as secretary.

50. The first water polo team in Antwerp World Maccabi Games included Josef Fischer, František Getreuer, Adolf and Samuel Pollakoff, František Schulz, Hanuš Wollner, and Fritz Kantor-Torberg (the well-known author); the second, Egon Simeles, Pavel Pick, Rudolf Sabudko, Arnošt Wilheim, Kurt Rado, and Hanuš Abeles. Julius Balázs won the first prize in the diving contest. Other firsts were made by Getreuer, Abeles, Mrs. Hansel-Lederer, and the 3×100 relay team.

51. Dr. Steiner, a physician in Slovakia, wrote in the November 1960 issue of *Vodní sporty* (*Water Sports*) an article on the 50th anniversary of the Czechoslovak Swimming Association. Fritz Kantor, mentioned in the preceding note, became deeply involved in studies of the ethical value of sports for Judaism. His thesis, *Jugend-Sport-Judentum* (*Youth-Sport-Judaism*), was published under the pen name "Friedrich Torberg" in the *Selbstwehr* on April 7, 1931.

52. In this interclub match Mrs. Hansel-Lederer improved her own record on the 200-meter breast stroke. Dr. Pavel Steiner and Arnošt Reiner took first and second places in free-style 100 meters, and all

relays were won by Bedřich Eisler, Jindřich Lustig, Arnošt Reiner, and Pavel Steiner (Bratislava) against Weiss, Rudolf and Otto Piowati, and Landau. In water polo, Brno won 4–3. The children's class, trained by Pavel Steiner, was the highlight of the match.

53. The Board of Bar Kochba Brno consisted of Dr. Arnošt Spitz, Arnošt Wilheim, Mrs. Hansel-Lederer, Grete Huber, Liselott Spitz, the Piowatis, and the technical head of the meet, Kurt Rado.

54. Bar Kochba Brno was represented by Irene Karpeles and Bar Kochba Bratislava by Dr. Pavel Steiner, Martin Frucht, Bedřich Baderle, Jindřich Lustig, and the Misses Klari Magyar and Edith Keppich. Hagibor won the final match in water polo against ČPK 2–1, with both goals shot by Franzi Beck (formerly with Hakoah, Vienna).

55. His father, Robert Fuchs Robětín, was a great benefactor of the Jewish sports movement and served until his death as chairman of the greatest social event of the Prague Jewish community, the annual Hagibor Ball. After him, his son Herbert Fuchs Robětín, the brother of Karel, took over this honorary function.

56. Lawn tennis was a very popular sport in Jewish circles. Among the outstanding Jewish club teams were Maccabi Košice, with the brothers Drs. Alex and Leopold L. Gottesmann, the latter the winner of the Slovak tennis championship in 1932. (Their brother Emil, an engineer, was the founder of Maccabi Košice in 1923.)

In the First Maccabiah Ladislav Hecht, Laci Klein, and Dr. L. L. Gottesmann played. Hecht won the men's singles and, with Laci Klein, the men's doubles. This Czechoslovak team also participated in the Second Maccabiah, where Czechoslovakia, as a team, was third. In other competitions, Maccabi Prostějov was represented by Kurt and Bedřich Zwillinger and the Keményi sisters, Brno by Alfred Ripper and Leo Drucker, Chlumec by Miss Stutz, Pardubice by Miss Edith Schütz, SK Náchod by Jindřich Löwenbach, Honza Goldschmidt, and Mrs. Klára Weisskopf, Hagibor Prague by Franta Kohn, Egon and Edgar Lebenhart, Simon Golodetz, Ota Löwy, Pavel Koretz, Bedřich Laufer, Ervín Sobotka, Misses Hammerschlag and Lamberg, and Mrs. Alfred Merory, to mention only these few clubs and names through lack of published records.

57. The first board consisted of Josef Pick, manager of the Bohemian Union Bank, chairman; Richard Jerie, shirt manufacturer, vice-chairman, and Dr. Pavel Eisner (Edwards), attorney-at-law, secretary.

Among the Jewish members of the Prague Riding Club were Arnošt Barth, Dr. František Diamant (Demant), Robert Eisner, Oswald Gellert, Dr. Richard Kleiner, Dr. František Schmolka, Hynek Weinmann, and Artur Wengraf; among the ladies, Eva Barth, Nina Bina-Brunner, Ilse Hoffman-Kraus, Marta Steiner-Barth, and Gerti Turnovský.

58. In his book *Die Maschinen und der Vogel-Flug* (*Engine Flight and Bird Flight*). As far back as 1888 he published his first book on the subject: *Flug Technik* (*Flight Technique*).
59. Aviation records established by Mrs. M. Ferrari-Kohn:

   Class C aircraft, with 80 HP Pobjoy engine, on November 21, 1933, altitude 5, 249 meters.
   Class C light aircraft, 1st category, multi-seater, November 21, 1933, altitude 4,169 meters.
   Class C light aircraft, 2nd category, single-seater, November 21, 1933, altitude 5,249 meters.
   Class C aircraft, speed, 100 kilometers, November 22, 1933, 161.002 km/hour.
   Class C light aircraft, 1st category, multi-seater, 153.433 km/hour.
   Class C light aircraft, 2nd category, single-seater, 161.002 km/hour.
60. The following Jewish participants are recorded: Bator Klein (Velká Bytča, Slovakia) won first prize, improving the Czechoslovak record of Karel Prachář. The second prize was won by Pavel Pick, and the third by Zděnek Mayer, both of the Aero Club Škoda in Prague. Other Jewish participants were Josef Sachs (Brno), Zděnek Pražák (Bratislava), Ferdinand Fanta and Adolf Kešner (České Budějovice), Bedřich Taschner (Humpolec), Josef Pollak (Náchod), Otakar Kafka (Semily), František Kantor and Evžen Weil (Prague), Samuel Rychnovský (Zlín), Jiří Hostovský (Žamberk), Hanuš Löwy (Žatec), Otto Schiller (Brno), and Jiří Fürchgolt (Trenčín).

BIBLIOGRAPHY

Apart from the literature quoted in the notes, the following sources were consulted:

Allen, Hugh: *The Story of Airships* (Akron, Ohio, 1943).
———: *The Story of Goodyear* (Akron, Ohio, 1945).
American Men of Science, The Physical and Biological Sciences, 10th ed., "Dr. Karl Arnstein" (Temple, Arizona, 1960).
Čechoslovák (*The Czechoslovak*, a Czech weekly, London), 1940.
Doherty, J. K.: *History of Modern Track and Field* (New York, 1953).
Goldschmidt, S.: *Makkabi* (*History of the Maccabi*) (Berlin, 1938).
Grix, Arthur E.: *Olympische Tage in Los Angeles 1932* (*Olympic Days in Los Angeles 1932*) (Berlin, 1935).
Hagibor-Hamakabi (magazine of the Jewish Sports Club Hagibor, Prague), 1926–1936.

Henry, William: *Approved History of the Olympic Games in Antwerp, 1920* (New York, 1937).

Janecký, A.: *Slavné postavy naši atletiky* (*Famous Personalities of Our Athletics*) (Prague, 1954).

Janes All World Aircraft, annual almanacs 1924–1938.

Jüdische Monatshefte für Turnen und Sport (*Jewish Monthly for Gymnastics and Sport*), special issue on the occasion of the tenth anniversary of the Jewish National Gymnastics movement, Vienna, 1913 (with articles by Arnold Katzinsky, Max Nordau, Henry Unna, and Robert Weltsch).

Květon, Vladislav: *Letecká kniha československé mládeže* (*Book of Aviatics for the Czechoslovak Youth*) (Prague, 1937).

Laufer, Josef: *50 let v našem sportu* (*50 Years in Our Sports*) (Prague, 1955).

———: *Hokej můj osud* (*Hockey My Destiny*) (Prague, 1960).

Letectví (*Aviation*, monthly official publication of the Aero Club of Czechoslovakia [Aeroklub Republiky Československé], Prague), 1923–1939.

Naše osvobození (*Czechoslovak News Service in the Middle East*) vol. 3, no. 5 (Jerusalem, 1943).

Náučný Slovník Aktualit (*Educational Dictionary of Current Events*), L. Mazáč, Prague, 1937/1938).

Němeček, Václav: Československá létadla (*Czechoslovak Aircraft*) (Prague, 1958).

Philipp, Rudolf: *Wir Juden und der Sport* (*We Jews and the Sport*) (Vienna, no date).

Pick, Joseph C.: *Jewish Sport in Czechoslovakia*, Bulletin of Czechoslovak Jewish Representative Committee, affiliated to the World Jewish Congress (New York, 1943).

Shafte, Dene: *Trail Blazing in the Skies*, (Goodyear Aircraft Corporation Akron, Ohio, 1943).

United States Olympic Committee, Report on 9th Olympic Games, Amsterdam, 1923.

United States Olympic Committee, Report on Los Angeles, July 30 to August 14, 1932.

United States Committee for Sports in Israel, New York, World Maccabi Union records of the six Maccabiahs, Tel Aviv (New York, 1961).

Unna, Henry: "Die jüdische Turnerschaft 1903–1913" ("The Jewish Gymnastic Movement, 1903–1913"), in *Die Welt*, Berlin, 1913, no. 34. p. 1,094.

Vodní Sporty (*Water Sports*, official monthly publication of the Czechoslovak Amateur Swimming Association (Československý Amatérský Plavební Svaz]), 50th anniversary issue, vol. 16, no. 9 (Prague, 1964).

JEWISH LODGES AND FRATERNAL ORDERS PRIOR TO WORLD WAR II

by Meir Färber

Like their coreligionists in other countries, the Jews of Czechoslovakia organized Jewish lodges and fraternal orders which served to foster friendship among Jews linked by certain views held in common, to meet their cultural needs, to render mutual assistance, and to support Jewish and general communal welfare institutions.

In view of the fact that the Czechoslovak government recognized the Jews of Czechoslovakia as a nationality group in its own right,* and on occasion officially expressed sympathy for Zionism, it was relatively easy for the Jewish lodges in the Czechoslovak Republic to come around to a pro-Zionist viewpoint. Even the non-Zionist members of so influential an organization as the Czechoslovak District of B'nai B'rith raised no objections to the support the lodges and the Grand Lodge were giving to Zionist funds in general and to the Keren Hayesod in particular. Thus Dr. Armin Weiner, a vice-president of the Grand Lodge of B'nai B'rith in Czechoslovakia, though himself a non-Zionist, accepted the chairmanship of the Czechoslovak Keren Hayesod Committee, and in a resolution adopted on March 19, 1921, the Grand Lodge officially recognized support of Keren Hayesod and of the work of rebuilding Palestine as tasks entirely in keeping with, and worthy of, the aims of B'nai B'rith.

B'nai B'rith

The most important Jewish fraternal order in Czechoslovakia was the Independent Order of B'nai B'rith. The first B'nai B'rith lodge

* [See A. M. Rabinowicz, The Jewish Minority, in vol. I (Ed.)]

in the territory now part of Czechoslovakia was the "Union" Lodge of Plzeň (Pilsen), which was founded on December 25, 1892, and was the second B'nai B'rith lodge to be established in the Austro-Hungarian monarchy. By the outbreak of World War I, there were lodges also in Prague, Karlovy Vary (Karlsbad), Liberec (Reichenberg), Brno (Brünn), Opava (Troppau), České Budějovice (Budweis), and Teplice-Šanov (Teplitz-Schoenau).

As of October 28, 1918, the date of the establishment of the Czechoslovak Republic, these lodges — all located in Bohemia, Moravia, and Silesia — had a total membership of about 1,400. There were then no lodges in the eastern sector of the country since that area, including Slovakia, had belonged to Hungary, which did not permit the establishment of lodges of this type. In 1924 three more lodges were organized, one of them in Bratislava, the capital of Slovakia, and by 1936 the Czechoslovak District of B'nai B'rith, known as District No. 10, had a total of sixteen lodges (three of which were in Prague) with a total membership of nearly 2,000.

In line with the principles laid down by the first B'nai B'rith lodge, which had been founded in New York on October 13, 1843, the official statement of aims of B'nai B'rith declared the objectives of the organization to be "to strengthen the spiritual and moral character of our coreligionists, to impress upon them the pure principles of love of mankind, to support the arts and sciences, to bring relief to the poor, to visit and care for the sick, and to render assistance to victims of persecution." Members of the order in German-speaking areas would mark their letters with the initials *W*, *B*, and *E*, which stood for *Wohltaetigkeit*, *Bruderliebe*, and *Eintracht* (Benevolence, Brotherly Love and Harmony).

In order to avoid discord and conflict within the membership, great care was taken at meetings and cultural affairs to avoid discussions and programs involving controversial themes such as party politics or religious differences. The founders of B'nai B'rith in Czechoslovakia were not out to create a substitute for the Masonic lodges — to which Jews were not admitted — but to set up a specifically Jewish fraternal order, as distinct from the international brotherhood represented by the Masons. Their main concern was to form a congenial Jewish organization, to cultivate a specifically Jewish spirit and consciousness, and also to assist the Jewish needy. Subsequently, B'nai B'rith was to add to its program the support of

Zionism and Jewish settlements in Palestine. After the founding of the Czechoslovak Republic, the lodges also extended aid to Jews who had moved into the various cities and towns from the remote regions in the east to the western part of the country.

The leadership of B'nai B'rith in Czechoslovakia included several outstanding personalities in Jewish and public life. One of the early presidents of the Grand Lodge was Dr. Salomon Ehrmann, a noted dermatologist and physiologist who had also made a name for himself as a painter and historian. Another physician, Dr. Joseph Popper of Prague, was president of the Grand Lodge for twenty-nine years until the collapse of the Republic. Popper, who also served for a time as president of the Supreme Council of the Federations of the Jewish Congregations of Bohemia, emigrated to Palestine, where he died several years prior to the establishment of the Jewish state. Among his close collaborators in the B'nai B'rith for a span of over two decades were Dr. Armin Weiner, a former president of the Moravia Lodge in Brno, Dr. Emil Wiesenmeyer, Adolf Lilling, and Dr. Bohumil Stein, who was treasurer of the Grand Lodge. Another prominent figure in Czechoslovakia's B'nai B'rith was Dr. Friedrich Thieberger, ex-president and cultural chairman of Bohemia Lodge in Prague, who edited the monthly bulletin put out by the B'nai B'rith in that city.

The B'nai B'rith lodges in Czechoslovakia, unlike those in the United States, were very exclusive. Applicants for membership had to meet rigid social and cultural qualifications and had to be approved by secret ballot.

B'nai B'rith service projects included aid to homes for the aged, a school for the mentally retarded, public soup kitchens for the indigent, an employment agency, residence and club centers for students and young people, homes for apprentices, and orphanages. All these institutions were constituted as official organizations in their own right, and each member of the sponsoring B'nai B'rith lodge or lodges had to hold membership in them as well, his dues being assessed as part of the membership dues he paid to his lodge. In addition, B'nai B'rith made regular contributions to the cultural department of Prague's Jewish community and to such institutions as the Jewish Orphanage of Prague and the Jewish Convalescent Home in Karlovy Vary (Karlsbad).

The outstanding cultural accomplishment of Prague's B'nai B'rith lodges was the Society for the Study of the History of the Jews of

Bohemia, Moravia and Silesia.* This enterprise owed its existence primarily to the work of Dr. Samuel Steinherz, a professor of German history who belonged to the Praga Lodge, and who was the subject of lively controversy in 1922 when German students at the German-language Charles University in Prague staged an anti-Semitic demonstration to protest against his reelection to the chancellorship of the university. The society published a yearbook and supervised the collection and cataloguing of documents in private and public archives pertaining to Jewish life in Czechoslovakia.

The Praga Lodge itself published an anthology entitled *The Jews of Prague* in commemoration of its twenty-fifth anniversary.

The B'nai B'rith of Czechoslovakia contributed also to the Central Library, which had been founded by the Jerusalem Lodge in Palestine in 1892 and which was to become the nucleus of Israel's Hebrew University and National Library. The Czechoslovak Friends of the Hebrew University in Jerusalem was presided over by Josef Langer, a non-Zionist businessman, who was a former president of the Bohemia Lodge in Prague.

B'nai B'rith in Slovakia and Subcarpathian Ruthenia

The relationship existing between the Jews of the Historic Lands and those of the "new" provinces in the east somewhat resembled that between a wealthy big brother and a younger brother in need of financial assistance. The affluent lodges in Bohemia, Moravia, and Silesia participated willingly and generously in relief work in behalf of the Jews of Subcarpathian Ruthenia, with special emphasis on aid to Jewish education in the eastern provinces of Subcarpathian Ruthenia and Slovakia where, as distinct from the western regions, there were Jewish masses living in indescribable poverty. Unfortunately, however, this relief program was not set up until a relatively late date.

The first B'nai B'rith lodge to be founded in the eastern sector of the Czechoslovak Republic was Fides Lodge in Bratislava (on November 16, 1924). The second — and the last to be founded in the Republic — was Concordia, which was organized in Košice on December 6, 1931. Each of these two lodges met twice a month, with

* [See also Guido Kisch, Jewish Historiography, in vol. I (Ed.)]

Fides eventually attaining a membership of eighty-two, and Concordia reaching an enrollment of seventy-four.

Important liaison work in behalf of B'nai B'rith's activities in the eastern provinces was done by Dr. Chaim Kugel, a member of Concordia Lodge and principal of the Hebrew high school in Mukačevo. Kugel was also a member of the Czechoslovak Parliament, where he collaborated closely with Dr. Angelo Goldstein, a representative of the Národní Shromázdění faction, who belonged to Bohemia Lodge in Prague. It was at Kugel's suggestion that the Grand Lodge appointed a committee for the vocational training of Jewish youth and the organization of social assistance. However, the committee encountered some resistance to its work on the part of old-fashioned Orthodox parents, who were reluctant to send their children to schools where secular subjects were taught alongside Jewish lore.* Also at Kugel's suggestion, the Grand Lodge met with a group of B'nai B'rith members from Subcarpathian Ruthenia in the summer of 1938 for the purpose of working out a social service program. Due to the Munich agreement that fall, however, by which part of Czechoslovakia was ceded to Nazi Germany, these plans came to nothing.

Fides Lodge (which had a number of wealthy members) and Concordia both concerned themselves extensively with social work projects, for which they received assistance from the lodges in the western part of the country, Fides cofounded a Jewish hospital in Bratislava and, together with Concordia, helped support the Jewish school system in the east. While most of the members of these two lodges were non-Zionist, they participated in the work of rebuilding Palestine; and two members of Fides Lodge, Dr. Viktor Stein and Dr. Aladar Porzsolt, joined the Jewish Agency when it was enlarged to include non-Zionist representatives.[1]

The Johann Gottfried Herder Union

The Johann Gottfried Herder Union, a B'nai B'rith youth organization founded by the Bohemia Lodge in Prague, at first represented a viewpoint of positive Jewish consciouness without commitment to the concept of Jewish nationalism.

---

* [See also Sole, Hebrew Education, pp. 401–439 (Ed.)]

Soon after the founding of the Czechoslovak Republic, the union published a statement of aims entitled "Jewish Action," which Max Brod, in his book *Im Kampf fuer das Judentum* (Vienna, 1920; R. Loewit-Verlag), characterized as "one of the most interesting recent publications on the subject of the Jewish problem." Despite the union's reserved attitude toward Jewish nationalism — based on the fear that its negative aspects, such as chauvinism and insistence on special privileges, might outweigh its positive features — the organization fully appreciated the spiritual heritage of the Jewish people and the necessity for its survival and cultivation. Brod and other members of the enlightened Zionist intelligentsia acknowledged the basic attitude of Herder Union as a valid "declaration of faith in the spirit of Judaism," and Brod went so far as to say: "This point in the [Herder Union's] statement of aims shows that the difference between this new group and ourselves is practically nil, or at any rate not as great as that between any two factions within national-oriented Jewry. For it is *only* in that same sense that my friends and I, too, are nationalists."

By the end of the 1920s however, the Herder Union had abandoned its reservations and had committed itself fully to the cause of Jewish nationalism.

The ideological pattern of the Herder Union played a significant role in the subsequent ideological development of the parent order in Czechoslovakia, for this youth group represented the growing new generation of B'nai B'rith. While Herder members had to go through the regular procedure for acceptance into a lodge of the parent order like all other applicants, it was no more than a mere formality in the case of veteran members of the Herder group. It is hardly likely that a lodge ever refused the application of a candidate recommended by the Herder Union as a member in good standing.

World War II and the Postwar Era

In an effort to save at least their considerable financial assets from confiscation by the Nazis, the B'nai B'rith lodges in Czechoslovakia changed their names, dropped their elaborate ritual, and adopted amendments to their bylaws specifying that in case the group was liquidated its assets were to go to the local Jewish religious community. Unfortunately, these precautions proved to be of little avail. All the newly elected members of the executive board, except one, were killed in concentration camps. Dr. Angelo Goldstein and Chaim Kugel succeeded in emigrating to Palestine, where Goldstein, who died in 1948, became a founder and the second president of the Jakob Ehrlich Lodge in Tel Aviv, and Kugel a founder and the first mayor of Holon, a town south of Tel Aviv-Jaffa.

Early in 1946, the small remnant of B'nai B'rith members who had returned to Prague and various other cities of Czechoslovakia in the middle of 1945 secured permission from the police authorities to revive the Bohemia and Praga Lodges of Prague, but they did not succeed in getting back the order's assets, which had first been confiscated by the Nazis and then by the Communist régime. Between 1945 and 1948 they managed to arrange a few social gatherings and to give some modest assistance to the members and to the widows of members who had survived the concentration camps. In the end, most of the B'nai B'rith returnees left for Israel and other countries.

Today all that is left of the Tenth District of the Independent Order of B'nai B'rith is the Joseph Popper Lodge of New York, which was founded by B'nai B'rith members from Czechoslovakia.*

Société

The fraternal order known as Société, which also had a lodge in Vienna, aimed to promote solidarity among its members, engaging in social service, assisting widows and dependents, and providing guardians for orphans.

Most of the members of the Société, which was founded in 1910, were businessmen, physicians, and lawyers of more modest economic strata than the members of B'nai B'rith. The order had been founded by Siegfried Sternschuss, Max Růžička, and Eduard Kraus, three Jewish members of the Guild of Commercial Travelers who had resigned from the guild due to certain differences of opinion.

At the organization meeting, attended by sixty-four charter members, Dr. Erwin Roubitschek, an attorney whom the three founders had consulted for legal advice, was unanimously elected president. The first general meeting of the Société was held in January 1911, with 108 men attending, of whom however only 42 took membership vows. The local branches founded in Plzeň (Pilsen) and Vienna by

* [See also H. Kohn in vol. I. (Ed.)]

Josef Beck and Josef Frankenstein, respectively, set the pattern for the organizational structure and ritual of the Société, which was modeled on that of Masonic and B'nai B'rith lodges of Austria and Czechoslovakia. The Société's first "Brotherhood Banquet," which closely resembled similar events sponsored by the Masons and the B'nai B'rith, was held in April 1911 in Plzeň (Pilsen) in the dining hall of a local hotel. A similar function took place that year in Vienna with Josef Frankenstein in the chair and thirty "brothers" in attendance. The first permanent clubhouse in Prague was dedicated on April 28, 1911.

As new lodges and chapters were formed and enrollment grew, the Société adopted exclusive policies of membership selection much like those of the B'nai B'rith lodges. Eventually, the mother lodge in Prague assumed a position of considerable influence as the highest authority in the organization; as the organization gained in prestige, care was taken to ensure a high standard of programming for meetings and cultural events.

During World War I the social service activities of the Société consisted primarily of assistance to the families of members who had been drafted into the army. The years immediately following the war were devoted chiefly to the economic reestablishment of returning veterans.

After the founding of the Czechoslovak Republic, the Société was completely reorganized. Ignaz Pick, the former treasurer of the Prague Lodge, was elected president, while his predecessor, Dr. Roubitschek, joined Josef Beck, Eduard Kraus, Siegfried Sternschuss, and Max Růžička in the ranks of the honorary presidents. With Czechoslovakia now independent of Austria, the Vienna Lodge formally severed its ties with the mother lodge in Prague, although it continued to maintain contact with the Czech groups. After 1918, the Vienna Lodge was a stagnant, dying organization.

In 1926 the Grand Lodge of the Fraternal Order Société was founded, with Ignaz Pick as president, assisted by Brothers Ehrmann, M. Koerper, Kafka, and Raudnitzky. The Grand Lodge proceeded to draft bylaws and ritual regulations for itself and for the lodges in Vienna, Plzeň (Pilsen), Karlovy Vary (Karlsbad), Teplice Šanov (Teplitz), Moravská-Ostrava (Mähr. Ostrau), Budějovice (Budweis), Liberec (Reichenberg), and Brno. Each of the lodges was required to make a contribution of 150 Czech korunas per member to provide the Grand Lodge with initial capital.

After Pick's death in 1933, the order set up a "Brother Ignaz Pick Fund for the Support of Widows and Orphans" with a principal of over 300,000 Czech korunas, the income from which was used to assist the needy widows and children of deceased members.

Pick was succeeded in the presidency of the Grand Lodge by Miroslav Koerper, who served for a year. Koerper was followed by Dr. Rudolf Raudnitzky, president of the Prague Lodge, who held the office until the order disbanded in 1938.

In 1929 the order first published a bulletin which was converted into a periodical in 1932. The Société's pro-Palestine activities during that period included assistance to orphans of the Petljura pogroms in the Ukraine in emigrating to Palestine, participation in the "Help through Reconstruction" campaign to aid victims of the 1929 Arab riots, contributions to the founding of the colony K'far Masaryk in honor of the eightieth birthday of the president of Czechoslovakia, and later on Youth Aliya aid. In addition, the Société engaged in such Jewish social projects as aid to Jewish orphanages and homes for apprentices, free lunches and clothing for school children, organized visits to the sick, and general relief work for the starving Jewish masses in Subcarpathian Ruthenia. The Société contributed also to social services not limited to Jews, such as free public soup kitchens for the unemployed.

When Dr. Raudnitzky assumed the presidency of the Grand Lodge, he was succeeded in office in the Prague Lodge by Wellemin, who was particularly concerned with the cultural program of the organization and expanded its library.

The Plzeň (Pilsen) Lodge, which had been started in 1910 under the leadership of Josef Beck and officially organized in 1914, moved into its own clubhouse in 1923. Beck's successors in the presidency of the lodge were Dr. Friedrich Taussig, Karl Beck, and lastly Hugo Feigl.

The Karlovy Vary (Karlsbad) Lodge, which had been founded in 1922, evolved the ritual which was eventually accepted as the pattern for ritual regulations of all the other Société lodges. In 1932 it celebrated its tenth anniversary in the building of the local B'nai B'rith lodge, a fact which indicated the existence of friendly relations between the two groups. Among the presidents of the Karlovy Vary (Karlsbad) Lodge were Alfred Kohn, S. Goldberger, and — during the final years of the Czechoslovak Republic — Josef Lederer.

The Karlové Vary (Karlsbad) Lodge organized a small branch also in nearby Marianské Lázne (Marienbad), which was headed by Dr. Egon Steiner.

The Teplice-Šanov (Teplitz) Lodge, which was founded in 1923 under the leadership of Max Mueller, grew rapidly, and by the time Dr. Hugo Dux took over as president in 1931, it had over a hundred members. Dux died that same year and was succeeded by Rudolf Bauer, who remained in office until 1934. In the mid–1930s this lodge was the second largest in the Société and had assets in the amount of half a million Czech korunas when Max Baier assumed the presidency, an office he held until the breakup of the order.

The Moravská-Ostrava Lodge was founded in 1922 and officially organized on March 24, 1923, with twenty-six charter members. In 1932 this lodge, which was headed by Dr. Sandor Teichner from 1927 until 1938, founded a group of thirteen members in Olomouc, which was under the jurisdiction of the Moravská-Ostrava branch.

The České Budějovice (Budweis) Lodge, which was founded in 1924 under the leadership of Theodor Fried and a Mr. Fantl, was the first in the Société to introduce the intimate *du* as an obligatory form of address between members.

Under the leadership of Fritz Loewy, the Liberec (Reichenberg) Lodge, which was founded in May 1926, took a prominent part in Jewish social service activities. Eleven members of the lodge were elected to membership in the executive boards of the Jewish community and its institutions.

The Brno Lodge, which was founded in September 1925, with Julius Schuller as president — he was succeeded by Dr. Otto Sonnenfeld and Hugo Koenigstein — was generally regarded as the cultural and humanitarian elite group of the Société.

Almost all the lodges, with the exception of Prague, were predominantly Zionist in orientation.

In 1938 the Société, faced with insuperable problems and demands arising from the Nazi annexation of part of Czechoslovakia, disbanded.

Those members who managed to escape to Palestine, including Dr. Sonnenfeld, joined together in Tel Aviv to form Yedidut Lodge, which remained an independent group until 1964, when it joined the B'nai B'rith.

The "Hort" Mutual Assistance Association

"Hort" (Tower of Strength), was a fraternal order smaller than B'nai B'rith and Société but similar to them in ritual and organizational pattern. The membership of the two lodges and chapters of Hort — one in Prague, the other in Brno — consisted preponderantly of businessmen and white-collar employees.

The objectives of this mutual assistance organization were the fostering of brotherly love among the members, the cultivation of ethical and cultural values, and moral and practical aid to the needy, to widows, and to orphans.

During World War I, Hort contributed generously to war relief work and sent gift packages to soldiers at the front. According to *Das Juedische Prag*, an anthology published by *Selbstwehr* in 1917, Hort as an organization participated prominently in the war loan campaign and made considerable funds available for refugee relief.

The Prague Lodge, which was founded in 1909, was presided over by Dr. Rudolf Bloch, an attorney, who became grand president when the Brno Lodge became an autonomous group. The last president of the Prague Lodge was Dr. Emil Feuerstein, who died in Terezín (Theresienstadt). Hugo Freund, a wholesale textile dealer, who was the last president of the Brno Lodge, was deported to Lodz. Dr. Bloch was deported to Mauthausen. Six weeks after his arrest, his ashes were sent to his relatives.

Originally the Hort was not Zionist-oriented. After the founding of the Czechoslovak Republic, however, the leaders of the Zionist movement in the country urged active Zionists to join the lodges in order to make the Zionist influence felt there.

The prominent Zionists who entered the Brno Lodge at the time were Dr. Otto Ticho, Nathan Ticho, Paul Ticho, Dr. Egon Nath, Max Tintner, Julius Gottlieb, Leo Drucker, and Rudolf Kraus.

Among the active members of the Prague Lodge were Dr. Paul Loewy, who was president of the Jewish religious congregation of Prague until the Nazi invasion, and Rudolf Pollak, the father of Frank Pelleg, the Israeli musician.

The two lodges, each of which had permanent club headquarters, published a bulletin and had an emblem, an enamel pin consisting of a golden "H" against a blue background, with the numerals 1909 and four hands joined in a circle.

During the peak period of Hort, the Prague Lodge had 150 members and the Brno Lodge about 80.

Confraternitaet and *Opora*

Two smaller independent Jewish lodges in Czechoslovakia were Confraternitaet and Opora. Confraternitaet, whose aims approximated those of the Société and many of whose members belonged to the latter lodge as well, had a permanent meeting hall in the building which also housed the Prague Lodge of the Société.

Membership in Opora Lodge was not officially limited to Jews, but 90 percent of its members were Jewish or at least of Jewish descent. The orientation of the group was assimilationist, along the lines of the Czech-Jewish movement.* Opora's philanthropic program consisted of contributions to local Jewish institutions. The performances by musicians and other artists which Opora sponsored were not specifically Jewish in character.

NOTES

1. B'nai B'rith Lodges in Czechoslovakia, as of 1936, the last year concerning which reliable records are available, had 1,911 members, of whom the numbers enrolled in the sixteen individual lodges can be seen from the table below.

   B'nai B'rith life in Czechoslovakia started in the last quarter of the nineteenth century when the Historic Lands of Czechoslovakia, Bohemia, Moravia, and Silesia, were still provinces of Austria and when Slovakia was a part of Hungary, the other half of the Austro-Hungarian monarchy. Names of locations at that time were mainly known by their German-language version. Our table shows them in Czech and German languages:

* [See also Hostovsky, The Czech-Jewish Movement, pp. 148–154 (Ed.)]

Name of Lodge	*Location*	*Year of foundation*	*Members*
Union	Plzeň (Pilsen)	1892	139
Bohemia	Praha (Prague, Prag)	1893	293
Karlsbad	Karlové Vary (Karlsbad)	1894	139
Philantropia	Liberec (Reichenberg)	1894	115
Moravia	Brno (Brünn)	1896	197
Silesia	Opava (Troppau)	1898	78
Praga	Praha (Prague, Prag)	1902	189
Alliance	České Budějovice (Böhmisch Budweis)	1906	103
Freundschaft	Teplice-Šanov (Teplitz-Schönau)	1912	132
Veritas	Žatec (Saaz)	1924	65
Fides	Bratislava (Pressburg)	1924	82
Ostravia	Moravská Ostrava (Mährisch-Ostrau)	1924	71
Humanitas	Praha (Prague, Prag)	1925	114
Menorah	Trutnov (Trautenau)	1930	49
Adolf Kraus	Olomouc (Olmütz) Prostějov (Prossnitz)	1931	71
Concordia	Košice (Kaschau)	1931	74
			1,911

In 1945, members from Czechoslovakia B'nai B'rith lodges who had escaped the Holocaust in their homeland received a charter from the Supreme Lodge of B'nai B'rith to establish Joseph Popper Lodge, B'nai B'rith No. 1525, in New York. It was named in honor of the late Grand Lodge president of District No. 10, Czechoslovakia, Dr. Joseph Popper. The 37 charter members came from these lodges: Bohemia (6), Concordia (1), Fides (1), Freundschaft (1), Humanitas (7), Karlsbad (3), Menorah (1), Moravia (4), Philanthropia (6), Praga (6), and Veritas (1). Most of them were members of long standing who had proven their dedication and efficiency as leaders and officers. The names of Harry Basch (Philanthropia), Emil Benedict (Bohemia), Frederick B. Berger (Praga), Frederick Fried (Bohemia), Alfred Gessler (Humanitas), Richard Glauber (Philanthropia), Emil Karst (Praga), Paul Korda (Humanitas), Arthur and Hugo Perutz (Humanitas), Joseph C. Pick (Bohemia), Felix Rafael (Philanthropia), Willy Reiner (Praga), Felix Resek (Humanitas), Leo Schick (Praga),

Paul Ullman (Humanitas), Charles Wachtel (Bohemia), and Armin Weiner (Moravia) are closely linked with the history and the development of Joseph Popper Lodge which, over the years, grew to more than four times its original number, despite a death toll of more than 75 members by the time of its 25th anniversary in 1970.

Joseph Popper Lodge, the only existing organized group of Jews from Czechoslovakia in the United States, has worked in various areas in the interest of Czechoslovak Jewry and World Jewry. It has devoted much of its activity to the preservation of the memory of Czechoslovak Jewry. As early as 1945 its *Czechoslovak Auxiliary Group*, in cooperation with the *European Advisory and Consultation Group* and the *American Jewish Joint and Distribution Committee*, worked on the problems of emergency relief for the surviving Jews in Czechoslovakia and those displaced; later, for their restitution out of seized, frozen, and hidden war spoils. It established, together with other *Landsmannschaft* groups, the *Leo Baeck Lodge* and *Liberty Lodge*, the *Special Relief Committee of B'nai B'rith*, which cares for the needy Jews behind the "Iron Curtain"; and in 1961, upon Kurt Wehle's initiative and under Paul Schlesinger's presidency, it founded the *Society for the History of Czechoslovak Jews*, successor to the *Society for the History of Jews in the Czechoslovak Republic*, initiated by *Lodge Praga* in Prague in 1928. Predecessor of Czechoslovakia's B'nai B'rith District No. 10 was B'nai B'rith District No. 9 of Austria, whose Grand Lodge vice president, Dr. Joseph Schanzer, joined District No. 10 in the same capacity after the emergence of the Republic of Czechoslovakia. [Ed.]

JEWS IN POLITICAL LIFE

by J. W. Brügel

When the first anti-Jewish measures of the Hitler régime shocked the world in April 1933, the German Foreign Ministry tried to counter this reaction by pointing out that legal or factual discrimination against the Jewish part of the population was not an isolated German phenomenon. The German diplomats abroad were instructed to collect and present relevant material concerning the countries to which they were accredited. The answer received from the German minister in Prague, Dr. Walter Koch (1870–1947), was not very encouraging and must have been felt as deeply disappointing in Berlin. In his report, dated May 3, 1933, Koch said:

> There is no discrimination against Jews in Czechoslovakia, either in civil service careers or in the sphere of society, economy, or anywhere else, not even in sports. Such steps would be in contradiction to the tendencies of President Masaryk, who has always acted as an outspoken friend of Jewry . . . who counted and still counts . . . Jews . . . among his best friends. Jews in Czechoslovakia are not only professors at Czech and German universities, but in many cases high officials of the state . . . headmasters or teachers at grammar schools, etc. The most important Czech club, the *Společenský Klub*, accepts Jewish members without any hesitation; Jews are likewise recognized as equals in sport clubs. In view of these facts it does not seem possible to me, when refuting attacks on measures taken in Germany, to point to similar occurrences in the field of racial policy in Czechoslovakia.[1]

One month later, Dr. Eduard Beneš, the then Czechoslovak foreign minister, answered questions put to him by a writer in connection with Hitler's anti-Jewish policy and its repercussions on

Czechoslovakia. Beneš's answers were very definite and unambiguous:

> There is no Jewish question in Czechoslovakia. I would not like to be a member of a government which recognizes the existence of such a question. We in Czechoslovakia will direct our state in future as in the past in accordance with the principles of liberalism and humanism. During the last weeks there were quite a few people who came to see me and regarded it as necessary to persuade me that the moment had come for a more outspoken or most outspoken nationalistic régime in our country. My attitude to their ideas is absolutely negative. *I do not intend to betray the basis of my whole thinking and convictions to a transitional constellation.*[2] It is my belief that in Czechoslovakia all nationalities must be fully recognized and protected. No one, and naturally no Jew, declaring himself a member of the German nation — and I underline that — could in our country be persecuted because of this, as long as his allegiance to our state remains beyond doubt.[3]

Even if these lofty principles were conveniently forgotten after the Second World War, the fact remains that they were the guiding light during the existence of a free and democratic Czechoslovakia from 1918 to 1938.

Jewish participation in public life was nevertheless confined almost completely to the parties of the Left. The reasons were manifold. Unlike the proportionally much more numerous Jewish population in Slovakia and Subcarpathian Ruthenia, where many Jews were leanin toward religious Orthodoxy, the emancipated Jews in the western provinces — Bohemia, Moravia, and Silesia — to a high degree identified their status and its security with the striving for more social and economic progress for everybody. Though at least on the Czech side there were no political parties banning Jewish membership — the parties based on allegiance to the Catholic Church may be disregarded in this respect — most of them did not encourage Jews to join them, being afraid that their competitors would denounce them as being "under Jewish influence." This was the particular form of Czech anti-Semitism which equated the Jews (many — although not all — of whom spoke German, and in many cases only German) with the Germans, whom every patriotic Czech distrusted. In Slovakia and Subcarpathian Ruthenia the same applied to Hungarian-speaking Jews.

Politicians of Jewish origin active in Czech bourgeois parties, or in the one German bourgeois party open to them, had almost all converted to Christianity in the old days of the Austro-Hungarian monarchy, when the Jewish faith, though not a particular hindrance in economic life, had been a great handicap to any participation in civil service, the judiciary, teaching, etc. Jews active in Socialist parties had, with insignificant exceptions, abandoned their faith for quite different reasons, underlining, in common with their non-Jewish comrades, that the only spiritual home to which they owed allegiance was the Socialist movement. By and large, only the representatives of the Jewish party were fully committed to Jewish traditions and values.

The most prominent politician of Jewish origin in the camp of Czech nationalists was Dr. Adolf Stránský (1860–1932) who, after long years of struggle with the German majority in his native town Brno (Bruenn), became one of the members of the Moravian *Národní Výbor* (National Committee). It was this committee, which, on October 28, 1918, following the Prague example of the day before, took over the administration of the province of Moravia from the last Hapsburg *Statthalter*. Stránský, who had been a member of the Austrian Parliament for many years, became Czechoslovakia's first minister of commerce in November 1918, and was from 1920 until his death a member of the Senate, the country's second chamber, in which he represented the National Democrats, the party of Dr. Kramář. Known as an ardent Czech nationalist and at the same time famous for his mordant wit and sarcasm, he exerted great influence as the founder and proprietor of the Brno paper *Lidové Noviny*.

The paper was taken over in 1922 by his son Dr. Jaroslav Stránský (born 1884, living now in London), who gradually transformed it from a mouthpiece of Czech nationalism to a journal with a more cosmopolitan outlook, until it achieved the position of being considered Czechoslovakia's *Manchester Guardian*. Jaroslav Stránský, professor of penal law at the Masaryk University in Brno and one of the country's best known parliamentary and journalistic followers of Dr. Beneš, during the war joined the government-in-exile in London as minister of justice; as representative of the Czechoslovak National Socialists (not to be confused with their German namesakes), he served in 1945–48 as deputy-premier, minister of justice, and minister of education.

The best known and the most respected among the men of Jewish origin who were active in the Czechoslovak Social Democratic party were two lawyers, Alfred Meissner and Lev Winter. Dr. Alfred Meissner (1871–1952) was a prominent member of the Revolutionary National Assembly (1918–20) and one of the main authors of the country's democratic constitution of 1920. He was elected and regularly reelected to Parliament until the sad end in 1939. He became minister of justice for some months in 1920 and later for a longer period (1929–34), and was instrumental in modernizing and humanizing many aspects of the existing law. In 1934 he took over the Ministry of Social Welfare, which he held until the elections of 1935, thereafter devoting his activities to the chairmanship of his party's parliamentary group.

In 1942 he was deported with his wife to Terezín (Theresienstadt) but withstood the strain remarkably well until liberation. The pro-Communist Fierlinger wing, which had taken over the leadership of the reborn party in 1945, tried to prevent Meissner's return to active politics. Meissner was known as an uncompromising defender of democratic principles, and when the democratic forces regained strength and, at the Brno Conference in November 1947, ousted the leadership imposed by Moscow, he, in his last public speech, energetically defended "old-fashioned" democracy. His speech deeply impressed the delegates and influenced their final decision.

The three brothers Winter, hailing from a little village near the southern Bohemian town of Tábor, left their mark on Czechoslovak politics. Dr. Lev Winter (1876–1935) became the country's first minister of social welfare in 1918 and thus the "founding father" of Czechoslovak policy. Though he remained in office only until 1920 (he returned to the ministry for a few months in 1925–26), his personal contribution to social progress and to the shaping of the country's social policy was considerable. He was a member of Parliament from the beginning until his death, and his country's representative at many international gatherings (e.g., the International Labor Conference, the Interparliamentary Union, etc.), devoted his attention in later years mainly to international affairs, and was the Czechoslovak Social Democrat's main spokesman on this subject in Parliament.

His younger brother, Dr. Gustav Winter (1889–1943), lived from 1919 as a newspaper correspondent in Paris, was considered Czechoslovakia's unofficial ambassador in the French capital, and represented the Czechoslovak Social Democratic party in the Executive Committee of the Labor and Socialist International. He was the author of many books, dealing mostly with French problems. His last book, on the French collapse of 1940, was translated into English. He died as a refugee in London.

The youngest of the three, Arnost Winter, a high railway official by profession, was a member of the Czechoslovak Senate (1935–39), where he specialized in questions of foreign policy. He most probably perished in Hitler's great extermination drive.

A member of the Senate for the whole time (i.e., from 1920 to 1938) was Dr. Zikmund Witt, a highly respected attorney from Mor. Ostrava. There is no trace of him, and unfortunately there can be no doubt that he perished in his seventies in one of Hitler's extermination camps.

A towering figure in the Czechoslovak trade union movement and in the International Federation of Private Employees was Robert Klein, the leading representative of the country's white-collar workers. The powerful union of which he was secretary comprised Czech, Slovak, German, and Hungarian members — rather an exception in a country where every language group had its own trade unions. A member of Parliament from 1920 to 1939, Klein was able to exert considerable influence in matters of labor legislation, mainly insofar as the legal position of private employees was concerned. He died a martyr's death in the notorious Buchenwald camp in 1941.

The Hungarian Social Democrats in Czechoslovakia, who maintained an independent political existence in the 1920s, later merged with the Czechoslovak Social Democratic party, which at the time presented Slovak and Hungarian candidates to the electorate in Slovakia. (Among the five Hungarian Socialist members of the first Parliament, 1920–25, one was of Jewish origin: Samu Mayer.) In this manner the trade unionist Ignaz Schultz (1894–1954) became a member of Parliament in 1935, in which capacity he tried hard to win over the Hungarian population to the ideals of Czechoslovak democracy. In 1939 he fled to Norway and then to the United States, where he organized the World Federation of the Hungarian Jews, with headquarters in New York. He died in March 1954 while on an official visit to Israel. Dr. Zoltan Farkas (1880–1940), another Hungarian Social Democrat of Jewish extraction, who was an attorney at Košice, likewise was elected to the Senate in 1935 as representative of the Czechoslovak Social Democratic party. He was deported to the east and died at Auschwitz.

On the German side, only the small Democratic party (*Deutsch-*

demokratische Freiheitspartei), the remnant of the once-important Liberal party of old Austria, opened its doors to Jewish members. Their undisputed leader was Dr. Bruno Kafka (1881–1931), professor of civil law at Prague German University, and a cousin of Franz Kafka. A forceful personality, he was one of the most respected members of Parliament, where he sat from 1920–25 and from 1929 to his premature death. His criticism of Czechoslovak foreign policy in the first years of the Republic was occasionally resented by his Czech colleagues, who saw in it an attack on the foundations of the state.

Like many others in both camps, Bruno Kafka might not have fully grasped in the early 1920s the natural community of interests between Czech and German democracy, clearly visible only after the establishment of the Third Reich. But what he criticized was the apparent lack of Czechoslovak support for the democratic forces inside Germany, and this criticism was entirely vindicated when Dr. Beneš, as Czechoslovak foreign minister, signed the Locarno Treaties guaranteeing a democratic Germany her rightful place in the world and assumed a leading role in guiding her into the League of Nations.

Another prominent member of the party was Dr. Ludwig Spiegel (1864–1926), professor of constitutional law at the Prague German University and member of the Czechoslovak Senate from 1920 to 1925. It is a sad irony that both Spiegel and Kafka died shortly after having been elected rector of their university for one year. The German University in Prague was the first of all German universities to witness a strike by nationalistic students; the occasion was the election of the Jewish historian Professor Samuel Steinherz (1857–1942; died at Terezín) to the rectorship in 1922. The students' intentions, however, were frustrated by the firmness of the Czechoslovak minister of education, Rudolf Bechyně (1881–1948), a Czech Social Democrat. It would have been interesting to see whether the German nationalists at the university would have dared to apply the same tactics had Spiegel or Kafka assumed the function of rector: both men had been known as staunch defenders of the rights of Czechoslovakia's German minority, though not for nationalistic reasons.[4]

After Kafka's death, his parliamentary seat was taken over until the elections of 1935 by Dr. Franz Bacher (born 1884), a Prague political journalist who, from 1935 to 1938, was a member of the Bohemian Diet. His non-Jewish wife saved him from deportation;

he was allowed to remain in Prague until his death in January 1945.

Many progressively minded German Jews from all walks of life found it possible to promote their ideals of human brotherhood, social justice, and international understanding in the German Social Democratic party of Czechoslovakia, the country's largest German party and, after Henlein's election victory in 1935, the largest German democratic party. Dr. Ludwig Czech (1870–1942), a Brno attorney, had been the leading representative of the German Socialist movement in Moravia since the beginning of the century. After 1918 the German Social Democrats in Bohemia, Moravia, and Silesia, who had been the strongest component in the former all-Austrian party. had to build up their own political existence in the new Republic, Dr. Ludwig Czech was elected vice-chairman in 1919 and took over the leadership of the party in 1920 following the premature death of the first chairman, Josef Seliger (1870–1920). Dr. Ludwig Czech held this important office for the record time of eighteen years, during which the masses of the German workers gradually found their way to an ever-closer collaboration with the Czechoslovak Social Democrats and with all democratic forces on the Czech side.

After an election victory in 1929, the German Social Democrats joined the government coalition and Dr. Ludwig Czech took over the Ministry of Social Welfare, exchanging it later for the Ministry of Public Works and the Ministry of Health.[5] In the years of the world economic crisis, which hit especially hard those industrial regions of Czechoslovakia inhabited mainly by Germans, Dr. Ludwig Czech's policy of improving the lot of the unemployed, carried out with strict adherence to absolute national justice, was Czechoslovak democracy's main weapon in the fight against the rising attractiveness of German National Socialism. To a large extent it was due to Dr. Ludwig Czech and his followers' striving for a democratic understanding between Czechs and Germans that up to the last moment great masses of German democrats were ready to defend freedom and democracy together with the Czech people against the onslaught of Hitlerism. As an old and sick man, Dr. Ludwig Czech was mercilessly deported by the Nazis to Terezín, where he died several months later.

One of Dr. Ludwig Czech's closest collaborators, and like him a member of Parliament from 1920 to 1939, was Siegfried Taub (1876–1946), the first managing director of the Brno Workers' Health

Insurance Fund, the party's general secretary after 1924, and deputy speaker of Parliament from 1929. He is mainly remembered for his tireless work in organizing help for refugees from Germany and Austria who streamed into Czechoslovakia, then the last political democracy east of the Rhine. After the occupation of Prague, Taub escaped to Sweden and from 1941 until his death lived in the United States.

Among the intellectuals representing the German Socialist movement in the Czechoslovak Parliament, two lawyers must be mentioned: Dr. Carl Heller (1872–1942) and Dr. Victor Haas (1882–1964). Heller, an attorney in the northern Bohemian town of Teplitz, member of the Senate from 1920 and its vice-chairman from 1929 on, died in exile in Sweden, where he escaped after the German occupation of Denmark, his first refuge. Dr. Haas, an authority on labor law, left Parliament in 1925 to take over the country's largest miners' insurance institution in his native Moravská Ostrava (Mährisch Ostrau). Dr. Arnold Holitscher (1869–1943), a medical officer by profession and president of the German Socialist Medical Association, member of Parliament from 1920 to 1925 and member of the Senate from 1925 to 1929, won fame as the only Czechoslovak parliamentarian who managed to steer a private members' bill through the house: the law forbidding the sale of alcoholic drinks to young persons. As in many other cases, the fact that Holitscher had a non-Jewish wife saved him from deportation; he died during the war in Prague. Johann Polach (1874–1942), a teacher of classical languages at a Brno high school and member of the Senate from 1920 to 1935, was the party's leading theoretician and interpreter of Marxism. He died in the Terezín camp.

Two women of members Parliament, who were of Jewish origin, belonged to the German Social Democratic Parliamentary Group. Fanni Blatny (1873–1949), president of the party's Women's Organization up to 1938 and well known in the international Socialist women's movement, was during her days in Parliament (1920–35) a frequent speaker on matters of social and health policy. She died in her London exile. Irene Kirpaı (born 1886) was a member of Parliament from 1920 to 1938 and devoted her activities mostly to questions of education. During the war she lived in exile in London; in 1946 she returned to her native country.

Among the politically active German trade unionists we find Ernst

Hirsch, secretary of the Union of Commercial Employees, who entered Parliament in 1920, but died young in 1924. Dr. Otto Hahn (1885–1946), secretary of the Union of Public Employees, entered Parliament in 1920 but joined the Communists when the break came in 1921. Quickly disillusioned, he resigned his parliamentary seat a few months later and returned to the Social Democratic party, which sent him to the Bohemian Diet from 1935 to 1938. During the World War II, he organized the German workers among the Czechoslovak refugees in Great Britain on a trade union basis. He died in his London exile.

Last but not least, Dr. Emil Strauss (1889–1942) must be included in this list of honor. Strauss was an economist and a historian of his party and the state, in addition to being his party's leading journalistic spokesman for years in his capacity as editor of the Prague daily *Sozialdemocrat* since 1935. His books on the history of the German labor movement in Bohemia and the birth of the Czechoslovak Republic are standard works, still frequently quoted. From 1929 to 1939 he represented the German Social Democratic party in the Bohemian Diet. Arrested a few days after March 15, 1939, in his hiding place near his native town of Prague, he was dragged from one prison to another and had to pass the hell of Buchenwald before he met his final doom in one of the extermination camps in the east.

Quite a few of Czechoslovakia's leading Communists were of Jewish origin, though this fact was hardly ever stressed before anti-Semitism was utilized by the Communists in their frantic search for scapegoats to blame for the failure of their policy. The most vocal of the prewar Communist members of Parliament (1925–34), and for this reason the best known, was Dr. Viktor Stern (1885–1958). The most notorious Communist of Jewish extraction was Rudolf Slánský (1901–52). Though he entered Parliament as early as 1935, he did not attract much attention outside party circles until his return from exile in Moscow in 1945 as newly installed secretary general of the Communist party. One of the main points in the indictment in the show trial of fourteen leading Communists (eleven of them of Jewish origin) which amazed the world at the end of 1952 was the allegation that Slánský and the others had been guilty of "Jewish-Zionist" activities. Slánský and ten other defendants (eight of them of Jewish origin) were hanged. Subsequently it was admitted that none of them had been guilty of the alleged "crimes." Anti-Semitism as practiced in the early fifties has been quietly dropped as a weapon in the Communist armory, but so far it has not been plainly stated that neither Slánský nor any other of the defendants had anything to do with Zionist or other specific Jewish activities.

NOTES

1. Koch to Auswärtiges Amt, May 3, 1933, *German Foreign Ministry* files (photostat copies), Serial 9470, Frame E 667960. The drafting officer of Koch's communication was the then press attaché of the German Legation, Johannes Urzidil, who died in Rome, 1971.
2. Italics in the original.
3. Fritz Jellinek, *Die Krise des Bürgers*, Zurich, 1936, p. 25–28.
4. Spiegel's daughter, Dr. Käthe Spiegel, a librarian and a gifted writer, met her death in the Auschwitz extermination camp in 1943.
5. For details see J. W. Brügel, *Ludwig Czech, Arbeierftührer und Staatsmann*, Vienna, 1960.

THE JEWISH PARTY

A STRUGGLE FOR NATIONAL RECOGNITION, REPRESENTATION AND AUTONOMY

by Aharon Moshe K. Rabinowicz

The period from 1918 to 1939 represented an important phase in the development of Czechoslovak Jewry. Now that they had been granted official recognition as a national minority, the Jews sought participation in every phase of the upbuilding of the new Czechoslovak state through representatives of their own. They underlined their new independent-nationality status by putting up their own lists of candidates for local and parliamentary elections. There was hardly a city or village in Czechoslovakia with Jewish inhabitants whose governing bodies did not include Jewish representatives who spoke for national Jewry. Frequently these delegates sat side by side with other representatives of the Jewish faith who had not, or not yet, declared themselves members of the Jewish nationality.

Having fought for the concept of Jewish nationhood, the Jewish National Council proceeded to translate the idea into reality. After several setbacks, the council paved the way for a unified political representation of the Jewish minority by joining with other Jewish political factions to form the Jewish party.

The creation of the Jewish party of Czechoslovakia marked a turning point in the Jewish struggle for political rights and recognition. Here for the first time was a central Jewish political party which conducted Diaspora-oriented political activities in Czechoslovakia and operated separately from, and independently of, the Zionist Organization.*

---

* See my article, vol. I, *The Jews of Czechoslovakia*, p. 160: "To this end, a conference of National Jewry was called in Prague in January 1919, at which the 'Jewish Party of Czechoslovakia' was created."

In his famous Fourteen Points message to the United States Congress on January 9, 1918, President Woodrow Wilson cited as one of the war aims of the Allied Powers the free right of self-determination for all nations.* Point 10 stated that "the peoples of Austria-Hungary should be accorded the freest opportunity of autonomous development."[1]

His address had immediate repercussions in Austria, with all the constituent nationalities of the Hapsburg monarchy[2] preparing to draft declarations of independence. The Jews were in a difficult position. They did not come within the scope of the Imperial Manifesto because they did not form a separate nationality unit within any of the states of the monarchy. On the other hand, they refused to be treated as mere pawns in the partition of Austria, subject to the whims of whatever nation they happened to live in. At this juncture the Zionists of Austria took the initiative and called a conference in Vienna on October 14, 1918. In an appeal addressed to "The Jewish People in Austria," the Zionist Executive Committee of Austria declared:

> We demand the same freedom and right to self-determination which is to be granted to all nations, for our own development as a nation.
>
> We must assert our will so that our voice may be heard also in the reorganization of the state and national structure of Austria. We demand recognition as a nation and the guarantee that we will be able to live a national life of our own as a national minority among the peoples of Austria. To secure these rights, we demand political rights and political representation. We further demand a radical internal reform of the organizational structure of Jewry in character with the principles of democracy.[3]

The Vienna conference voted to create a Jewish National Council at once to present the claims of the Jewish people, consisting of five main points as follows:[4]

1. The Jews were to be accorded recognition as a nationality.
2. The Jews were to be represented at the peace conference.
3. A Jewish national home was to be created in Palestine.
4. The Jews were to be accorded nationality rights in any country where they resided in large numbers.

* Cf. my article, The Jewish Minority, in vol. I, *The Jews of Czechoslovakia*, p. 155 ff.

5. The Jews were to be given recognition, at once, as a nationality in Austria and accorded the right to participate in deliberations on any and all issues affecting Austria.

These claims were presented on the floor of Parliament in Vienna[5] by Dr. Benno Straucher, a deputy representing national Jewry. He added the following four points to the list:

6. The Jews had the right to raise their children in the spirit and tradition of Judaism.
7. A union of all Jews residing in the country was to be organized.
8. A "Jewish Chamber" was to be set up which would exercise authority within the framework of cultural and national autonomy for the Jews.
9. The Jews were to be represented in the legislative and governing bodies of the State.[6]

These demands could not be fulfilled in all of Austria, as originally intended, because the monarchy collapsed. But in the reorganization of Europe that followed, the Jewish problem aroused interest the world over. President Wilson hailed the Jewish Congress movement (American Jewish Congress), led by Supreme Court Justice Louis Dembitz Brandeis and Stephen S. Wise, and its demand for equal nationality rights and self-determination for Jews in all the Diaspora countries. Dr. Von Lodgmann, the German-Bohemian deputy representing the constituency of Ústí nad Labem (Aussig), came out in support of national autonomy for all peoples and particularly advocated the just recognition of the national claims of the Jews.[7] It is significant that these claims should have been put forward by a German parliamentarian. The Jewish problem also engaged Czech politicians of the day. Thus, Václav Klofač, a member of the Czech Parliament, addressed a meeting in Prague on the subject of "The Attitude of the Czech People toward the Jews."[8] He was interrupted by a remark from a heckler in the audience that most of the so-called German manufacturers in Bohemia were Jewish. Klofač thereupon stated that while it was true that the Jews had committed many wrongs during the war, not all the Jews could be judged by the same standards. There were, he explained, individual Jewish groups with special viewpoints of their own. What was more, the Jewish people carried considerable weight with the Entente Powers and particularly with President Wilson. Therefore, any rash action on the part of the Czech people against the Jews in Bohemia might have dangerous repercussions. Coming from the respected leader of the radical Czech National Socialist party, these remarks were significant; they constituted a clear warning against anti-Semitic excesses.

Such was the political background of the creation of the Jewish National Council in the Czechoslovak state. The council was formed from middle-class and socialist elements within national Jewry. On October 28, 1918, the presidium of the council — Dr. Ludvik Singer, Dr. Max Brod, and Karel Fischel — called on the Národní Výbor (National Committee) of the Czechoslovak State. The three men were received by the chairman of the Národní Výbor, to whom they presented a lengthy memorandum[9] summarizing the situation of the Jews and their claims in the new state.

At that time the Jewish National Council consisted of Dr. Ludvik Singer, Inspector Hugo Slonitz, Norbert Adler, Dr. Max Brod, Professor Alfred Engel, and Miss Zapper, who represented the Zionists, and Karel Fischel, Emil Waldstein, Mr. Schönfeld, and Oskar Altschul, who represented the Socialist Workers' party, Po'ale Zion.

In addition to these men, the following delegates were coopted from Moravia: Dr. Josef Rufeisen, Dr. Altbach of Moravská Ostrava, Mayor Dr. Gustav Zweig of Prostějov (Prossnitz), and Mr. Schuller, president of the Commercial Employees' Union of Brno.

The creation of the Jewish National Council in Czechoslovakia and the presentation of the council's memorandum to the Národní Výbor[10] were events of great significance. It must be remembered that Jews figured prominently in the economy and culture of the new Czechoslovak Republic. In many places they had acted for decades as influential factors in the relations between the German and Czech population elements.* As a result they frequently allowed assimilationists in their midst to inveigle them into misusing their position and becoming pro-German chauvinists.

On the other hand, Czech socialist circles and the Czech Social Democrats showed understanding for the national aspirations of the Jewish people.

---

* [See Ruth Kestenberg-Gladstein, The Jews between Czech and Germans in the Historic Lands, vol. I, *The Jews of Czechoslovakia*, pp. 21–71 (Ed.)]

The Národní Výbor of the Czechoslovak state gave a sympathetic reception to the spokesmen of the Jewish National Council. Offering his felicitations to the Národní Výbor upon having attained the Czech people's objective of statehood, Dr. Singer pointed out that, as individuals and through the four deputies of the former Jewish National Club in Parliament, the Jews who were conscious of their identity had aided the oppressed peoples of Austria in their struggle for their rights. During the interview Dr. Singer also described the situation of the Jews, presented their claims, and then proceeded to elaborate on the program outlined in the memorandum:

(a) Recognition of Jewish nationality, and freedom of individuals to profess it. On the other hand, Jewish nationality was not to be imposed upon those Jews who considered themselves to be of Czech or German nationality.
(b) Full civic equality for Jews.
(c) Cultural autonomy for Jews.

The members of the Národní Výbor present at the meeting with the deputation from the Jewish National Council were Messrs, Antonín Švehla, Dr. František Soukup, Jiří Střibrný, and Prof. Otakar Srdínko. In reply to Dr. Singer's address, Švehla, the vice president of the Národní Výbor, emphasized that the representatives of the Czech people had profound sympathy and understanding for the claims of the Jews.

Shortly after this meeting, the Národní Výbor officially assumed the government of Czechoslovakia. The Jewish National Council received a cable from the Zionist Central Office in Berlin. Sent via the Jewish Press Bureau in Stockholm and addressed to Dr. Max Brod, this cable reported that Professor Tomáš G. Masaryk, the president of the Czechoslovak National Council, had informed the Zionist Organization of America that the Jews in Czechoslovakia would be given full civic equality. Masaryk had expressed his sympathy with Zionism, stating his conviction that it was not a movement of political chauvinism but one striving for the moral rebirth of the Jewish people.

The reorganization of the state proceeded in an orderly and peaceful manner. Abuses by subordinate agencies were stopped with the cooperation of the leading members of the new government.

Among the early problems facing the new state was that of the refugees from Galicia, who were in a difficult situation because they were stranded in the country due to lack of transportation facilities.

Meanwhile, the Jewish national movement won increasing influence in Czechoslovak Jewry. The large majority of the Jewish religious congregations (*Kultusgemeinden*) of Moravia had accepted the Jewish National program.

In every major Jewish community Jewish-National Soldiers' Councils had been set up, which in many instances were recognized by the authorities as the representatives of the Jewish soldiers.

But the efforts to contain anti-Semitic manifestations were not always successful. Pogroms frequently occurred. These outbreaks of anti-Semitism are discussed in detail in my article in *The Jews of Czechoslovakia*, Volume I.[11]

The Jewish National Council soon started out on its practical work. The first Congress of Czechoslovak Jews was held in Prague from January 5–6, 1919, with 340 delegates from Bohemia, Moravia, Silesia, and Slovakia in attendance.[12] The opening ceremonies were attended by representatives of the government and of the Czech political parties and by prominent figures in Czech and Jewish life. President Masaryk, unable to attend, sent his regrets.

Greetings were received from Jewish National Councils and Zionist Federations of other countries and from the leaders of the World Zionist Organization — Nahum Sokolow, Chaim Weizmann, and Lord Rothschild. Jaroslav Kvapil appeared at the congress as the representative of the Czech Writers' Association. A newspaper editor named Kouša, speaking on behalf of the Czech Social Democratic Deputies' Club, emphasized the close relations that linked the Czech and Jewish proletariats. Hugo Bergmann delivered his opening address in Hebrew, something not often done in those days. The demands of the socialists were presented by Rudolf Kohn; those of Orthodoxy, by Dr. Eugen Lieben. The Inner Actions Committee of the World Zionist Organization was represented by Leo Herrmann; the Vienna National Council by Robert Weltsch; the National Council in Lvov by Mr. Herz. The leaders of the Czech Jewish National Council gave detailed reports on the situation of the Jews. Dr. Singer discussed the ethical significance of the national movement in general, while Dr. Max Brod dealt with the role of Jewish nationalism as a humanitarian movement in promoting peace among the nations. Dr. Alois Hilf, president of the Regional Federation of Jewish Congregations in Moravia, was elected president of the congress. The agenda consisted of reports and organizational business presented by Dr. Ludvik Singer, Dr. Angelo Goldstein, and Dr. Josef Rufeisen. Max Fischl gave a financial report. Mayor Gustav Zweig of Prostějov (Prossnitz) reported on the Jewish communities in Moravia; Dr. Theodor Haas, of Brno, on the Jews in Slovakia, and Emil Waldstein on the press. The delegates of the congress split up into several committees.

The Slovak Committee elected a board of directiors in Piešťany.

Prof. Alfred Engel of Brno reviewed the Jewish educational system, Hugo Bergmann spoke on the problem of the Jewish religious congregations, and Mr. Engländer submitted a report on social welfare. On the strength of Leo Herrmann's report on arrangements for the peace conference, the congress adopted a resolution to send a delegation to the conference and allocated the funds needed for that purpose.

The congress met under the influence of the interview which President Masaryk had granted to Dr. Singer, Mr. Kohn, and Dr. Brod on December 31, 1918. During that interview Singer had expressed to Masaryk, on behalf of the Jewish nation, his appreciation for the message which the president had sent to the Zionist Organization of America stating that he recognized the Jews as a national minority with legal and political rights. President Masaryk had confirmed the authenticity of the English text of the message, which had been shown to him, and stressed that he would continue to abide by the principles set forth in it. The president's specific questions had indicated his great interest in Jewish affairs. He had discussed cultural and educational problems with Brod. The delegation had taken the opportunity to mention the epidemic of anti-Semitism that was sweeping the country and had made reference to the anti-Jewish riots that had already taken place.

The Jewish national movement made notable strides forward also in Moravia. A People's Council was elected in Brno as the local organ of the Jewish National Council; it was received by the Národní Výbor, which promised to comply with the national demands of the Jews. The Národní Výbor recognized only the following national Jewish organizations as representative bodies of the Jewish minority: the People's Council (in local matters), the Union for Religious Affairs (for the entire region of Moravia), and the Jewish Soldiers' Council (for military matters). Jewish National Councils had been formed in most of the cities in Moravia. The officers of the Regional

Federation of Jewish Congregations in Moravia were Dr. Alois Hilf, of Moravská Ostrava, president; Rabbi Dr. L. Lewy, of Brno, vice president; Dr. Fuchs, of Moravská Ostrava, secretary; Mayor Gustav Zweig and Rabbi Dr. Goldschmidt, of Prostějov (Prossnitz); Dr. Haas, Dr. Schreier, and Dr. Sonnenfeld, all of Brno.

Jewish national representatives joined local administrative bodies, in which they took action to protect the Jews from the ever-growing incidence of anti-Semitic outrages.

The Jewish national movement became active in Slovakia as well.[13] Dr. Vavro Šrobár, the minister for Slovak affairs, made the following declaration to a visiting deputation of Jews from Nitra, Hlohovec, and Piešt'any:

> The Jews living on Slovak territory would do well to form Jewish National Councils in the various towns of Slovakia and to join them. Having been the exponents of Magyarization, the Jews would forfeit their reputation for political reliability if they were now to declare themselves as Slovaks. On the other hand, I cannot accept them as Magyars. However, if they were to adopt Jewish nationality, as [their coreligionists] have done in Bohemia and Moravia, we would be ready to grant them full cultural and lingual minority rights.

The Jewish National Council gained increasing influence and sympathy in public life and was generally recognized as the legal representative body of the Jews. The Jewish national movement won electoral victories in most of the religious congregations. These developments were duly noted by Czech public opinion. Thus, a magazine edited by Jaroslav Krejčí, a well-known professor of philosophy in Prague and friend and associate of President Masaryk, carried an article entitled "On the Jewish Problem," which seems to have been written by Krejčí himself.[14] It closes with a reference to an official resolution that had been adopted by the Czech Socialist party, popularly known as the "Klofáč party":

> The formation of the Jewish National Council is hereby noted with approval; we are prepared in principle to support the claims deriving from the concept of self-determination, insofar as these are not incompatible with the unity of the political and cultural organization of the Czechoslovak State. Specific details would be subject to special discussion; an opportunity for such a discussion will be provided when appropriate educational legislation will be framed.

The first event of significance for the recognition of the national rights of Diaspora Jewry was the meeting of the Conference of Jewish National Councils in Paris, at which Czechoslovak Jewry was represented by Hugo Bergmann and Norbert Adler. Attended by forty-four delegates from all over the world, the conference met on April 5 and 6, 1919, at the headquarters of the Paris Jewish Consistory, in the Rue de la Victoire, beneath a painting of the Synhedrion which in 1807 had declared that the Jews were not a nation but only a religious community. Now, delegates of Jewish National Congresses from the constituent nations of the former Hapsburg monarchy, from Russia and Rumania, from the American Jewish Congress, from the Union of Jewish Communities of Italy, and from B'nai B'rith had assembled in Paris to take joint action to secure national rights for the Jews. The opposition was represented by delegates of the Alliance Israélite Universelle and the Conjoint Foreign Relations Committee of the Board of Deputies of British Jews and the Anglo-Jewish Association. Also participating in the sessions was a committee of Paris Jews of Russian origin, which worked to help bring about a compromise between the two opposing factions. Sir Herbert Samuel, speaking on behalf of the Conjoint Foreign Relations Committee of the Board of Deputies of British Jews and the Anglo-Jewish Association, said that he did not understand why the Jews should demand national rights; however, he stated that if these demands came from the Jewish National Councils, his organization would support them.

The Conference of Jewish National Councils was only a prelude to the great World Jewish Congress, which brought into being the Comité des Délégations Juives auprés de la Conférence de la Paix (Committee of Jewish Delegations at the Peace Conference) in Paris. On June 12, 1919, the *comité* formally presented to the secretariat of the peace conference a memorandum in English and French, setting forth the claims of the Jewish people with regard to the following points:

1. Citizenship and freedom of choice of nationality.
2. Equal rights for all citizens and the outlawing of discrimination.
3. Language and education.
4. Autonomy (minorities to be organized on autonomous lines).
5. Participation in the government of the State.

6. Sabbath observance.
7. Provisions [for the protection of minorities] as integral and irrevocable components of the constitution.
8. The right of petition for minorities in cases of violation or failure to enforce the provisions.[15]

In the meantime, the Jewish National Council in Czechoslovakia continued its activities. At the very first local elections the National Jews won sweeping victories. Thus, the National Jewish list obtained three seats in the Prague City Council; Po'ale Zion obtained one. In the suburbs the Jews won no less than five seats. Altogether, 8,046 Jewish votes (representing 60 per cent of the Jewish electorate) were cast in Greater Prague. One Jewish delegate each was elected in Plzeň, Litoměřice, Chomutov, Most (Bruex), Náchod, Dobříš, Klatovy, Mios, Postelberg, and Kasejovice; three each were elected in Mariánské Lázně (Marienbad), Teplice-Šanov, and Wottritz. Election results in Moravian cities showed a similar trend. In Brno, one National Jew and one member of Po'ale Zion were elected: two were elected in Olomouc; four in Lipník, n.B.; three each in Holešov, Uherské Hradiště (Ungarisch-Hradisch, Třebič, Vyškov, Hodonín, and Gaya; and one each in Přerov, Prostějov, Kremenice, and Uherský Ostroh. The Jewish community elected eight Jews and the community of Boskovice, one Jewish delegate. All told, the Jews won a total of seventy local council seats.

On May 25, 1919, the National Federation of Slovak Jews held a conference in Liptovský Sv. Mikuláš, at which Leo Šipoš, chairman, and Emil Waldstein, secretary, reported on the activities of the organization. On the basis of information received, the federation, which cooperated closely with the Jewish National Council in Prague, had been requested to intervene with the competent authorities of the Republic to demand fair treatment for Jewish citizens. It had also been asked to create a Jewish press in Slovakia. Much of the conference was devoted to a discussion of the problems of Slovakia's Jewish schools. At the time there were in Slovakia more than one hundred Jewish elementary schools, several higher-grade elementary schools, and one nonclassical high school. Adolf Reichenthal of Trnava found fault with the background of the teachers employed at the Jewish schools. He claimed that many of them had been educated at non-Jewish institutions and had not received adequate Jewish religious training. As for those teachers who had been trained at Jewish institutions in Budapest, they, too, had not been educated in the spirit of National Judaism. Most of the teachers, Reichenthal stated, were assimilationists. In view of this deplorable state of affairs, he concluded that the most important task of the federation in the field of Jewish culture was to train properly qualified teachers. Moreover, he felt that the federation should establish schools for girls, give aid to youth projects, set up libraries, promote the study of Hebrew, and support agricultural and trade schools.

On June 21, 1919, the Literary and Lecturing Society (*Lese-und Redehalle*) of Jewish students in Prague held a Jewish National Celebration to mark the recognition of the national rights of the Jewish people by the peace conference. Dr. Ludvik Singer, chairman of the Jewish National Council, conducted the proceedings. Also in attendance were two distinguished guests: Cecil Gosling, the British chargé d'affaires in Czechoslovakia, and Tomáš G. Masaryk, the president of the Czechoslovak Republic. In his response to the addresses of welcome, President Masaryk said:[15a]

Both the speakers have mentioned my relationship with the Zionist and Jewish National movements. You know that I attach very great importance to the moral aspect of this movement. Today I can only repeat that my attitude toward the National Jews has not changed. I do not see why in our state, where a number of nationalities have been dwelling together side by side, the Jewish nation alone should be regarded as an undesirable factor. I can assure you that, consistent with my constitutional powers, I shall put my views into action, also in the field of politics. You may always count on me.

The Jewish National Council was active in three distinct areas: (1) the fight against assimilation within; (2) combatting anti-Semitism and anti-Semitic riots which frequently occurred; and (3) efforts to obtain official recognition for the cultural and political rights of the Jews. A report of the National Federation of Slovak Jews issued by the Jewish Press Bureau in Bratislava on August 1, 1919,[16] reveals the close ties that existed between the federation and the Jewish National Council. Thus, on June 24 Dr. Singer, speaking on behalf of the Jewish National Council, intervened with President Masaryk for the protection of the rights of the Jews in Slovakia. The president promised to support the demand of Slovak Jewry for special representation in Parliament and "to see to it that the Jews of Slovakia will always be treated as fully equal citizens."

Yet on many occasions the Jewish National Council and the Jewish National Committee in Slovakia encountered opposition from the authorities. Thus despite the efforts of the committee, Jews were not permitted to list their nationality as "Jewish" in the population census held in Slovakia. The Czech policy toward the Jews, or at least toward the Jews of Slovakia, was definitely anti-Semitic. The conduct of the authorities toward the Jews of Slovakia and especially the violently anti-Semitic diatribes of Dr. Vavro Šrobár, the minister for Slovak affairs, gave rise to grave concern; moreover, an economic campaign in the form of licensing restrictions was launched against the Jews. The prohibition against listing Jewish nationality in the census was only another link in the concatenation of anti-Jewish manifestations. The National Fedeertion of Slovak Jews spared no effort to inform the public that the Jews had been accepted as a national entity by the peace conference, by President Masaryk, and by other members of the Czechoslovak government. Nevertheless, the Jews were branded in high places — officially, as it were — as criminals and enemies of the Slovak people. No matter what the authorities said whenever the Jewish National Council or the National Federation of Slovak Jews drew their attention to recurring incidents of physical, civil, economic, and political persecution, it was clear to the Jews that the anti-Semitism which was rife in Slovakia (and in neighboring areas) was more than just a matter of isolated abuses by subordinate agencies.

This climate of anti-Semitism prevailed even while the peace conference in Paris was formulating legal provisions for the protection of minority rights. On his return from Paris in mid-September 1919, Dr. Singer, reporting on the activities of the Comité des Délégations Juives, said that the peace treaty between the Allied Powers and Czechoslovakia did not contain specific clauses regarding the protection of Jewish rights such as had been incorporated into the treaties signed by the Allies with Poland and Rumania.[17] The rights of the Jews were merely implied in the general provisions concerning the rights of linguistic and religious minorities.

However, the Zionist press in Bohemia and Moravia accepted the treaty as it was because it felt that the Czechoslovak government could be trusted to respect the rights of the Jews.

The Jews in the autonomous territory of Subcarpathian Ruthenia organized a National Federation of their own. At the request of the National Federation of Slovak Jews, they addressed a memorandum to the governor of Subcarpathian Ruthenia, which was to be submitted to Prime Minister Vlastimil Tusar. In this memorandum the Subcarpathian Ruthenian federation demanded the right to form an autonomous religious organization and the freedom to profess Jewish nationality. It was further pointed out that the representatives of the Jewish population — which constituted 15 per cent and in urban areas as much as 40 per cent, of the total population — had not been given a voice in the upbuilding of the state. Now the federation demanded that in the future these representatives should be consulted by the government.

Putting their faith in President Masaryk and in the government, the Jews hoped that before long they would be freed from anti-Semitism and discrimination. However, anti-Semitism showed no sign of abating in the eastern sector of the Republic (Slovakia and Snbcarpathian Ruthenia). This may have been due in part to the increasingly acrimonious debate conducted in the Czech press on the Slovak problem; the Jews were caught between the two nationalities.

The major activity of the Jewish National Council at the time was in the field of politics; more specifically, the council was engaged in preparations for the national elections of 1920. Under the Czechoslovak National Assembly Elections Law, which had been proposed by the government and partially amended by the Constitution Committee of the Assembly, the decision whether or not the Jews of Czechoslovakia would be represented in this, the first elected Parliament of the new Republic, would hinge on their ability to present a unified list of candidates for the entire country.

Another function of the council was the protection of Jewish rights. The work load in this field had become so heavy that, in order to ease the pressure on its own staff, the council opened an Office for the Defense of Jewish Rights. This office did not cater to any one trend in Czechoslovak Jewry but was intended to protect the rights of all Jews, irrespective of political or religious persuasion. It was aided in its efforts by a legal advisory council, in which the various Jewish parties were represented.

The Jewish National Council also sought to aid Jewish prisoners of war in Siberia and Jewish war refugees. Dr. Alfred Engel of Brno was placed in charge of a special Office for Refugee Aid. By personal intervention with provincial authorities and with the Ministry of the Interior, Engel worked to secure permanent residence permits for those refugees who had attained positions of trust in their new homes as workmen, artisans, commercial employees, teachers, and bank clerks.

Special mention should be made of the council's Education and Organization Committees. The Education Committee set out to organize a school system extending over the entire country. By intervening in Prague, the National Council helped build up the Jewish trade school which had been founded by the Jewish religious congregation of Moravská Ostrava. The National Council did important work also in the fields of press and publications.

The Jewish National Council was frequently called upon to take action in cases where Jewish civil rights were violated by anti-Semitic discrimination. In an advertisement for a law student to do clerical work, the Moravian Revenue Office in Brno stated that applicants would be required to present certificates of baptism. The National Council made representations to the Ministry of Finance, which promptly eliminated the discriminatory requirement. In another instance, the council's intervention with the director of the Ministry of the Interior and with the Office of the President of the Republic brought about the revocation of an order from General Hennacque under which Jewish storekeepers in Subcarpathian Ruthenia had been compelled to keep their businesses open on the Sabbath.

The officers of the National Council worked closely with public officials in Slovakia and with the World Zionist Organization.

As already mentioned earlier, the Jewish National Council decided to take an active part in parliamentary elections. Among those participating in the discussions on this subject was a delegate of the National Federation of Slovak Jews. An executive committee was chosen to direct the work and to represent the Jews, and to effect cooperation with other political parties.

Speaking in Parliament on February 19, 1920, Dr. František Krejči, a member of the assembly's Committee on Worship, eloquently hailed the recognition of Jewish nationhood in Czech circles in general and in Parliament in particular — a testimonial to the efficacy of the Jewish National Council.[18]

In the midst of the council's intensive preparations for the parliamentary elections, a number of developments occurred which disrupted the unity of the Czechoslovak National Jews and prevented them from securing seats in that election. At the meeting of the Jewish National Council held on January 20, 1920, Po'ale Zion, the Jewish Social Democratic party, quit the council. Among those present at that meeting was Theodor Wister, the president of the National Federation of Slovak Jews, who reported on the situation in Slovakia. A communication from the Po'ale Zion saying that it withdrew its delegate from the Jewish National Council was read. From the debate which followed, it was clear that the Po'ale Zion wanted to give its support to the Social Democratic party and not to the Jewish National list.

Further difficulties were created by the Czech-Jewish assimilationist party. Still another factor in the failure of the Jews to produce a unified electoral list was the opposition of the Autonomous Orthodox Regional Bureau in Bratislava to the political aims of the Jewish National Council.*

With all these internal conflicts it was clear that the National Jews would not be represented in the first Parliament to be elected by the Czechoslovak Republic.

The Second Congress of Czechoslovak Jews met in Brno on June 14 and 15, 1920. By that time the Czechoslovak Republic had already adopted its constitution, in which the Jewish nationality group had been given official recognition. Accordingly, the congress set about to organize the Jewish minority and to deal with issues pertaining to the Treaty for the Protection of Minorities. The congress further adopted an "Organizational Statute for the Representation of the Jewish Ethnic Minority."

This period saw the beginnings of clarification in the relationship between the political organization of Czechoslovak Jewry and the Zionist Organization. In 1921 the Jewish party and the Zionist Organization parted company. Adolf Pollak, who visited a number of countries, including Czechoslovakia, on behalf of the World Zionist Organization, sent an informative report (February 19, 1920)[18a] on these developments to Arthur Hantke, who was then a member of the London Zionist Executive. Pollak urged action to bolster the qualitative leadership of the Zionist Organization in Czechoslovakia because "all the capable individuals" were active in the Jewish National Council, while the leadership of the Zionist Organization was, at best, "of second quality only." The Zionists were eager to perform their work effectively through their own organization.

Following the emergence of the Czechoslovak Republic, Zionist organizational centers were set up in the various provinces of the

* Cf. vol. I., *The Jews of Czechoslovakia*, pp. 274, 275.

country. At the time, the Prague office acted as central headquarters, taking charge of Jewish National Fund campaigns, supervising Hakhshara and Aliya (Palestine Office) and maintaining contact with World Zionist Organization headquarters, first in Copenhagen and then in London. Following the Second Zionist Territorial Conference in Brno (1921), the seat of the Czechoslovak Zionist Executive was transferred from Prague to Moravská Ostrava. Moravská Ostrava was closer than Prague to the centers of Jewish population in Slovakia and Subcarpathian Ruthenia, where the Zionist movement spread apace. Dr. Josef Rufeisen served as chairman of the executive until 1938, when he was succeeded by Dr. Paul März. Dr. Franz Kahn was secretary of the executive throughout this period.* Despite the organizational and functional separation between the Zionist Organization and the Jewish National Council, the two bodies remained closely linked.

The second local elections were called for September 16, 1923.† The Jewish party set about to convince the public that the nomination of candidates by the Jews as a distinct political party did not mean that the Jews wanted to "separate" themselves from the rest of the population. Such a separation, the Jewish National Council emphasized, was out of the question; on the contrary, the Jewish representatives would be ready to cooperate with all the other parties in every area of local politics. Such cooperation had already earned the respect and understanding of the non-Jewish authorities for the good will and the abilities of the Jewish representatives and for the minority which had elected them. This could be clearly seen, for example, in the Prague City Council, where anti-Semitic attacks were frequent and had to be effectively countered. In time these incidents decreased, yielding place to friendly cooperation. The Jewish voters were informed of the benefits of having Jewish City Council members serve on the Housing Committee and support applications for naturalization. In many cases even gentile citizens turned for help to the Jewish delegates, who took up their cause with the same devotion that they showed in pleading the cause of their fellow Jews. During its first term the Prague City ouncil Chad ninety members, chosen by an electorate of nearly 120,000 voters. The District Council of

* [See study by O. K. Rabinowicz, Czechoslovak Zionism, pp. 19–136 (Ed.)]

† The first local elections after the founding of the Czechoslovak Republic had been held in 1919.

Greater Prague had one hundred members, chosen by an electorate of 400,000. A total of 3,800 Jewish votes were needed to elect the Jewish representatives to the City Council. (Note the appeal by Arthur Kauders, member of the Central Administrative Commission for Greater Prague: "Jews, vote Jewish!")[19]

Parliamentary elections in Subcarpathian Ruthenia were called for March 16, 1924, with nine deputies and four senators to be elected. This province had ninety thousand Jewish inhabitants. Of these, some were Zionists; the majority were Orthodox. However, nearly all of them were National Jews.

The elections in Subcarpathian Ruthenia set off a counterblast from tne Czechoslovak Agrarian party, which wanted to capture the votes of the Jews. Led by Prime Minister Švehla and Jan Malypetr, minister of internal affairs, the Agrarians had other plans for the Jews. "Virulent agrarian propaganda" had been rife among the Jews of Subcarpathian Ruthenia for a long time. Švehla and Malypetr invited leading Jewish personalities for an audience. The following report was given in *Českéslovo* (Feb. 16, 1924) on the meeting with Malypetr:

> The Agrarian party is getting up "Magyar elections" [rigged elections] in Subcarpathian Ruthenia. We have incredible but well-founded reports that the representatives of the Jewish parties of Subcarpathian Ruthenia were called to Prague, where Malypetr, the minister of internal affairs, sought to persuade them to dissolve their elections committees and to give their votes (more than 30,000) to the Agrarian party. The minister tried friendly persuasion as well as threats (hints at the possibility of anti-Semitic incidents occurring in Subcarpathian Ruthenia); he applied unfair pressures exploiting his position in the government to secure Jewish votes for his party. When he saw that the representatives were not about to accede to his request, he changed his tactics and attempted to point out how little weight the one representative whom the Jews would be able to elect would actually carry in Parliament. However, he could not prevail against them....

Prime Minister Švehla was willing to let the Jewish representatives keep their organization but advised them against putting up a list of candidates.

Thus, the election campaign continued. Subcarpathian Ruthenia (Twenty-third District) had not participated in the preceding parliamentary elections, in which the Jews had failed to secure mandates.

The three Jewish groups — the National Jews, the Conservatives, and the Bourgeois party — joined forces in the local elections as the Jewish party. Of the leadership of these three groups, the only one to insist on the constitutional rights of the Jewish minority was the chairman of the National Jews.

Upon their return from the interviews in Prague, the representatives of the Conservative and Bourgeois parties realized that the Jews of Subcarpathian Ruthenia were set on having a candidate of their own; however, Ruthenian Jewry did not get its list.

The tragedy of the split which had occurred in the Bohemian lands in 1920 recurred in 1924. As a result, the Jewish party received 18,032 votes for the Chamber of Deputies and 15,924 for the Senate. The Jewish Democratic party (the Conservatives) won 9,909 votes for the Chamber and 5,980 for the Senate. Since neither of the parties was able to muster the required number of votes (not even the required minimum of 20,000) the Jewish parties did not obtain any seats in the Chamber of Deputies.[20]

Meanwhile, the Jewish National Council continued active also in day-to-day matters. In local governments the National Councils concerned themselves with local affairs. The council saw to it that kosher food was provided for army reservists. To this end Dr. Ludvik Singer, the president of the Jewish National Council, and Arthur Kauders, its vice president, intervened with the Ministry of National Defense; the request was approved and the local Jewish religious congregation saw to it that the soldiers received their kosher rations.

Menwhile, the third convention of the National Federation of Slovak Jews was held on June 18 and 19, 1924, in Poprad, Slovakia. The convention, which was attended by more than one hundred delegates from forty-four communities, heard reports of what the federation had achieved in the five years of its existence in its endeavors to safeguard the social, political, and economic interests of the Jews. One of the resolutions adopted by the convention deplored the fact that "to this day Jewish affairs in the Ministry of Education are still being entrusted to an individual who is an outspoken opponent of the Jewish ethnic minority and of its cultural program." The convention took up the cause of those Jews who had been denied citizenship due to a misinterpretation of the law. The delegates vigorously protested against the distorted view of the law which had led the authorities to deny citizenship to those Jews who had legally acquired it even prior to October 28, 1918, simply because they had not been taxpayers as of January 1, 1906. (This despite the fact that they had lost their former citizenship.) The convention drew up an educational program and voted to form a central executive committee jointly with the Jewish National Council in Prague and the Jewish party in Subcarpathian Ruthenia to deal with election and party matters of mutual concern.

The Jewish students also made their views known to the public,[21] refuting the claim advanced by the Academic Senate of Prague's German University that "the German University was created, first and foremost, for those students who profess German nationality."[22]

When a proposal was introduced in the municipality of Plzeň to prohibit *shehita* (ritual slaughter), the Jewish National Council made representations to the Ministry of the Interior. An official *Shehita* Commission, headed by Dr. Eugen Lieben of Prague, was set up.

The struggle for the Hebrew high school, too, was difficult, especially after the minister of education had "not granted the application for permission to open a *Reformrealgymnasium* [reform-type modern secondary school] in Mukačevo with Hebrew as the language of instruction...."[22a]

Abetted by anti-Jewish publications in the Czech language, anti-Semitism in the country continued to be virulent. One need only mention the famous debate that took place in the Prague City Council between Dr. Singer and Professor Juethner of the German National party.[23] On that occasion Juethner declared: "I am an anti-Semite and I won't deny it."

To this Dr. Singer replied:

> Ho canw you compare Czech anti-Semitism . . . with that dirty business which got imported into this country from Germany? One would be hard put to find anything equaling the attacks the Swastika people have had the effrontery to make on the Jews in literature and in private and public life.

Meanwhile, elections for both houses of the Czechoslovak Parliament had been called for Sunday, November 12, 1925. The platform of the Jewish party consisted of three principal planks:

1. Complete and genuine equality for the Jews.
2. The healthy social and cultural development of the Jews and particularly economic protection of the Jews.
3. Peace and progress in Czechoslovakia.

Heeding the lesson of previous elections, the National Council warned the Jews not to become involved in the election campaigns of other political parties. Negotiations were initiated for the formation of a unified Jewish list. Meanwhile, in Bratislava, a separate party, the Jewish Economic party, had been organized on the initiative of the Autonomous Orthodox Regional Bureau under the leadership of Rabbi Koloman Weber. The candidate of this party for Subcarpathian Ruthenia was Markus Ungar, who had played the role of mediator between the Agrarian party and the Jewish party. Actually, Ungar had been the prime figure in the attempt to hand Subcarpathian Ruthenia's Jewish votes over to the Agrarian party. According to reliable sources (Dr. Paul Meretz), it seems that Ungar received from Governor Rozsypal of Subcarpathian Ruthenia the munificent sum of 300,000 korunas "for election purposes."

Negotiations were begun to prevent a split in the Jewish vote. The National Council made every effort to bring these talks to a successful conclusion. In the meantime, however, the Hungarians in Slovakia and in Subcarpathian Ruthenia were publishing appeals in their organ, *Prágai Magyar Hirlap*, urging the Jews to remain true to Magyarism.

In the end, all the Jewish parties joined forces, retaining the designation "Jewish party." The names of the principal candidates of the Jewish Economic party, Dr. Markus Ungar and Dr. Julius Reisz, appeared on the electoral list of the Jewish party, leaving Rabbi Weber as the sole candidate on the list of the party he had set up.

The Czech National Democrats, the Czechoslovak Agrarian party' and the Czechoslovak Social Democrats carried on an unscrupulous election campaign, using every conceivable type of propaganda technique — good will and hostility, blandishments and threats — to win Jewish votes. Meanwhile, of course, the Jewish party was conducting a vigorous campaign for its own electoral list.

Although the overall voting strength of the Jews had increased, the Czechoslovak Agrarian party (which was then in power) and its exponents in Subcarpathian Ruthenia, on the one hand, and Autonomous Orthodoxy, on the other, combined to bring about the defeat of the Jewish party. Dr. Singer made a detailed public report of the reasons why, once again, the Jewish party had failed to enter Parliament.[24]

A plenary session of the Jewish National Council was held on

December 8, 1925, to reexamine past policy. Dr. Singer resigned from the chairmanship of the council but subsequently withdrew his resignation. The Jewish party submitted a complaint to the Elections Tribunal, alleging that the Jewish voters had been subjected to illicit pressures from official circles.[25] However, this complaint was dismissed. Emil Hácha, the chairman of the fourteen-man tribunal, was also the presiding judge of the Czechoslovak Administrative Court. The Jewish party was represented at the hearing by Dr. Ernst Lebenhart.

At its session of April 27, 1926, the Jewish National Council found that

> neither the written refutation from the Ministry, nor the hearing before the Elections Tribunal, nor the verdict handed down by the latter, has served to contest, much less to refute, the substance of the charges made in the complaint, especially with regard to the formation of the opposition list of the Jewish Economic party and the influence exerted by official organs on behalf of that party. . . .[26]

At the plenary session the chairman submitted a detailed report on the elections. Numerous members, including Rufeisen, Dr. František Friedmann, Ernst Frischer, Herman Lichtig (of Prešov), and Dr. Emil Margulies (of Litoměřice) participated in the debate that ensued. The resolutions introduced by Dr. Margulies were unanimously adopted.

The fourth convention of the National Federation of Slovak Jews was held on February 20, 1926, in Žilina, with sixty delegates from communities throughout Slovakia in attendance. The report submitted to the convention pointed up the importance of the federation for the Jews of Slovakia. The need of the hour, it was emphasized, was to translate the ideal of Jewish unity into reality as quickly as possible. At the request of the Press Committee of the *Jüdische Volkszeitung*, Dr. Oskar Neumann, in his report, enumerated guidelines for the molding of Jewish public opinion. Dr. Karl Ferbstein proposed that the Jewish party, rather than the National Federation, should be developed as the overall representative body of organized Slovak Jewry.

On March 5, 1926, while he was in Vienna for the signing of the Austro-Czechoslovak Arbitration Agreement, Foreign Minister Dr. Beneš was questioned by the press about the elections. In the course of the interview, Dr. Beneš said:[27]

> We do not meddle in the quarrels between the Zionists and the non-Zionists; nevertheless, this matter must be of some concern to us. A question has been put to me here regarding the attitude of the government toward the Jewish minority in the last parliamentary elections. The question was phrased as if the government's attitude toward this minority group had not been favorable. I do not think this is correct. We have permitted maximum freedom for all. The troubles were strictly within this minority group itself.

In reply to a question regarding the elections in Subcarpathian Ruthenia, Dr. Beneš said:

> It is true that in some localities local forces tried to secure additional mandates for the coalition parties by meddling in the election campaign among the Jewish parties. The government has had no part in these incidents and the Council of Ministers is unanimous in its view that such things must not be allowed to happen again.

The above statement speaks for itself; it clearly indicates that government circles had known of these illegal activities.

The seventh Zionist Convention, which met in Brno from July 3 to 6, 1926, heard a detailed political report from Dr. Singer. The work of the Jewish National Council, Dr. Singer explained, comprised several distinct areas: the defense of the rights of individual Jews; general Jewish affairs, particularly the rebuttal of anti-Semitic attacks; political action; culture; and religious affairs. The council was an arm of the Jewish party, which sent its representatives to government agencies. Discussing the question whether "we should go in for politics," Dr. Singer explained that all the Jews within the Jewish party were united by virtue of having declared themselves members of the Jewish nationality, and since Jewish nationhood had been recognized in the Czechoslovak Constitution, it was clear that the Jewish party should act as an independent body and should pursue a policy of its own.

On October 3, 1926, a countrywide conference of Federations of Jewish Religious Congregations met in Prague. The five constituent federations — the Provincial Federations of Jewish Religious Congregations of Moravia and Silesia, the Federation of Bohemian Religious Congregations (Svaz českých náb. obcí.), the Prague Federation and the Federation of German-Speaking Religious Congregations in Bohemia — voted to put an end to the disunity within Czech Jewry by creating an overall organization for the protection of the interests of all the Jews in Czechoslovakia. This union was brought about by a development outside the Jewish community; namely, the impending enforcement of the so-called *Kongruagesetz* (Conformist Church Law). Under Article 5 of this law religious communities were given subsidies from public funds to supplement the salaries of their clergy, the amounts in each case being computed on the basis of congregational membership. Now the question of what constituted a "religious community" arose. The Ministry of Education and Schools held that this term should be taken to refer to the Jewish religious congregations, which represented the sole form of Jewish organization to be recognized under the law. However, under this arrangement those congregations which had no rabbis of their own would have received nothing. The situation was even less favorable in Bohemia. The overall Jewish representative body envisioned by the federation was intended to avert this threatened loss of financial benefits. The Supreme Council of the Federations of Jewish Congregations which emerged from the deliberations in Prague worked out an arrangement whereby the subsidy was to be paid out not to the congregations but to the federations of congregations, which were able to effect a more equitable distribution of funds to the congregations.*

At a meeting of the Jewish National Council on November 7, 1926, Dr. Ludvik Singer tendered his resignation, giving practical and personal reasons for his decision.[28] However, he was to retract his resignation at a plenary session of the Zionist Central Committee (March 6, 1927), which was devoted to problems of Diaspora politics.[29]

In the field of Diaspora politics the Jewish National Council at the time concerned itself with the local elections which the government had set for October 16, 1927. It was clear to the leaders of the Council that the Jews were not present anywhere in the Historic Lands in concentrations sufficient to give them a decisive voice in the local council chambers. Nevertheless, it was considered imperative that even in localities where they only formed small minorities, the Jews should put up electoral lists of their own in order to stress the unity of the Jewish nationality not only to themselves but also to their fellow citizens of other nationalities.

---

* [See Gustav Fleischmann, The Religious Congregation, 1918–1938, vol. I, *The Jews of Czechoslovakia*, pp. 267–357 (Ed.)]

In Greater Prague numerous election rallies were held at which Jewish leaders appealed to the Jews to vote for the Jewish party. The rally which took place in Prague on October 16, 1927, under the chairmanship of Dr. Angelo Goldstein, was attended also by members of the assimilationist Czech-Jewish faction. Dr. Ludvik Singer engaged the assimilationists in a debate, particularly with regard to the appeal they had published in their organ, *Rozvoj*, calling on Jewish citizens not to "vote Jewish." In Czechoslovakia, Dr. Singer pointed out, there were tasks of a specifically Jewish character for politicians to perform, tasks which had nothing to do with Zionism or Zionist views. In their appeal the assimilationists had openly called on the Zionists to "go to Palestine." In reply, Dr. Singer declared that "without Palestine, there can be no Jewish dignity. The fate of Palestine is the fate of the entire Jewish people."

The eighth Czechoslovak Zionist Convention represented a new phase in the discussion of future Jewish national policies on the one hand, and in the relationship between the World Zionist Organization and Jewish National Diaspora politics, on the other. Dr. Selig Brodetsky,[30] the representative of the World Zionist Executive, said to the delegates:

> If we engage in Diaspora politics, we must always remember that these are only a means to an end and that, for the Zionist Organization, there is only one ultimate goal; namely, Palestine.

During those years the Jewish National Council carried on its day-to-day activities without interruption. It protested against the groundless deportation of a Jewish teacher from Sevljuš to Rumania; it helped set up a Federation of Jewish Religious Congregations in Greater Prague, and promoted Jewish religious instruction and the publication of Jewish religious textbooks.

Meanwhile, the debate on Diaspora politics continued. Dr. Walter Kohner, a staff member of *Selbstwehr*, wrote:

> The weighty argument against Diaspora politics within the Czechoslovak Republic is based on the fact that at present we do not have one united Jewry but at least four separate Jewries. As things stand now, it would be impossible to formulate a program which would reconcile the cultural, economic, and linguistic demands of the Jews in the East and in the West.

Should the Jewish people in the Czechoslovak Republic join forces with the government, or should it act as an opposition party? Diaspora politics cannot provide solutions for such problems as the separation of Church and State, agrarian and customs questions, and so forth. Even if, in the final analysis, the autonomy sought by the National Council has become confined to school problems, recent developments in particular have shown us quite clearly that in this area, too, no solution can be found.[31]

Another argument against Diaspora politics was based on the view that parliamentary representation for a minority was effective only if it was an instrument for organic development. Nothing had been done to mold a unified Jewish public opinion. Those Jews who were interested in political action had not been brought together into one party. No Jewish people's party had been formed, nor was there any organization linking Jewish communal representatives. There was no political guidance and no central clearinghouse of political information. Not one political brochure discussing the problems of Jewish Diaspora politics had been published. National politics only served to perpetuate disunity among the Jews of Slovakia and Subcarpathian Ruthenia.

There was an ever-growing demand for the creation of a modern Jewish political party, whose functions would include educational work.

Concern was felt about the situation of the Jews in Subcarpathian Ruthenia, who comprised 16 per cent of the total population of the province. There, the modern Hebrew schools had been neglected by the government, while Czech schools had been opened throughout the region. The enrollment at the Czech institutions consisted almost entirely of pupils of Jewish nationality. Thus the Jews were forced to assert their identity even while they were demonstrating their loyalty to their country. "Jewish communal autonomy," *Selbstwehr* complained, "has been the political football of the authorities for a long time now."[32]

Podkarpatské Hlasy (*Subcarpathian Voices*), the newspaper published in Užhorod by the government of Subcarpathian Ruthenia, asserted that

there is just one thing left for the Jews of Subcarpathian Ruthenia to do in the field of politics; namely, to destroy Zionism root and branch. This end can best be attained by taking the most severe measures possible against the Joint. . . .* [33]

Things looked better in Moravia. The Provincial Federation of Jewish Religious Congregations of Moravia held a convention in Brno on May 5 and 6, 1929. The assembly was opened by the chairman, Dr. Alois Hilf, of Moravská Ostrava. The report of activities submitted to the delegates stated that "a significant amount of work has been done in various social, religious, and cultural areas." [34]

The report stressed the close cooperation the federation had been able to maintain with the authorities, on the one hand, and with its constituent congregations, on the other. The convention also "took vigorous steps to counter the increase in civil marriages." A resolution was adopted with regard to "the question of naturalization in Czechoslovakia," requesting the Supreme Council of Jewish Religious Congregations to "enter a protest against the naturalization practices of the government authorities and of the Ministry of the Interior and to adopt an activist policy in this respect."

In Slovakia a convention of the Jewish party took place in Žilina on May 19, 1929, with Dr. Paul März of Moravská Ostrava in attendance as the representative of the national Political Commission. Dr. Julius Reisz of Bratislava, who opened the proceedings, reported on the electoral successes of the Jewish party of Slovakia. By polling the required forty-five thousand votes, the party had obtained representation in the Provincial Diet. The Jews had won additional seats also in local and district councils. The purpose of the convention, Dr. Reisz declared, was to further consolidate organized Jewry.

A number of delegates, including Harry Bleiweiss, called for a platform resolution to the effect that the conduct of Jewish politics in Czechoslovakia should be left exclusively to one party under one unified leadership. The appropriate resolutions, of which excerpts are quoted below, were to be formulated in consultation with the Jewish National Council in Prague: [34a]

* * *

2. The politics of the Jewish people in Czechoslovakia may be conducted... only by one united party for all of Czecho-

* ["Joint" is the name by which the American Jewish Joint Distribution Committee (JDC) is commonly known in Europe. The JDC was founded by American Jews in New York as a strictly nonpolitical philanthropic organization (Ed.)]

slovakia under one unified leadership in which all the lands of Czechoslovakia shall be represented....

4. The Jewish party is eager to participate actively in the upbuilding of the Czechoslovak state, and to cooperate in a positive manner to the best of its abilities in the legislation and in the administration of the country. It expects that it will be enabled to carry out this resolve in Parliament through representation in proportion to its numerical strength....
6. The Jewish party will cooperate with the Jewish parties in the Historic Lands in matters of concern to all of Czechoslovak Jewry....

These resolutions clearly show the policies which the Jewish party intended to follow.

Elections to the National Assembly and to the Senate were called for October 27, 1929. Jewish participation in these elections was the subject of widespread concern. Twice, the Jewish party had failed to attain its objective, i.e., representation in the Czechoslovak Parliament. Now the time had come to test whether this objective was attainable at all in Czechoslovakia. In 1920 the number of Jewish voters in the individual constituencies had not yet been known. In that election, in which Subcarpathian Ruthenia had not participated, the Jewish list had obtained a total of seventy-nine thousand votes. In 1925 the Jewish party had again failed to enter Parliament. That year, Subcarpathian Ruthenia figured in the elections; thirty thousand votes were needed in that province for one seat in Parliament. The Jews were unable to poll the required number of votes. On the other hand, the Jewish list received a countrywide total of ninety-eight thousand votes — an impressive achievement, considering political conditions in Czechoslovakia at the time.

By 1929 it was generally agreed that the Jewish party would not be able to "go it alone" and that as a consequence it would have to join forces with another group. After mature deliberation, the choice of the Jewish party fell upon the Polish Middle-Class (Bourgeois) and the Polish Social Democratic Workers' parties. The three parties put up a joint list of candidates (List No. 5) under the name of "Electoral Union of the Polish and Jewish Parties."

This was not the first time that a Jewish party in the Czechoslovak Republic had made an electoral pact with another political faction.

In 1928 the Jewish party had conducted a joint campaign with the Polish Middle-Class party for elections to the Provincial Diets of Moravia and Silesia. The combined list had obtained twenty thousand votes in the constituency of Moravská Ostrava. The Polish Social Democrats had put up a list of their own and polled a total of ninety-five hundred votes. In 1929 the Jewish-Polish coalition was widened in order to assure the Jews a seat from the Moravská Ostrava constituency — it being understood, of course, that after the elections the Jewish party would be completely independent of its Polish campaign partners.

The Jewish party and Po'ale Zion each conducted its own campaign. In the parliamentary elections, the "Jewish Social Democratic Workers' Party Po'ale Zion" appealed to the voters to elect the Social Democratic list.[35] Once again, the political parties used a combination of terror, intimidation, and blandishment to obtain votes. Not only in Slovakia and Subcarpathian Ruthenia but even in northwestern Bohemia the German Workers' and Economic Union published a broadsheet, signed by a "Committee of Jewish Voters" with the slogan: "Not one vote for the Polish-Jewish list!"

This time, however, the Jewish party achieved its aim; it obtained two seats in Parliament. A total of 104,464 votes went to the combined Polish and Jewish list, and Dr. Ludvik Singer and Dr. Julius Reisz were seated in Parliament as the representatives of the Jewish party. In an interview, Dr. Singer stated:

> It is obvious that we must join forces with one of the larger parties. It is necessary for us to do this if for no other reason than that we may be able to serve on parliamentary committees and to exercise the right of interpellation. . . . On no account do we want to be cast in the role of tie breakers. . . .
>
> We shall attempt to join forces with the government majority since we attach great importance to cooperating [with the government] and since this is also the best way of promoting our own basic claims.[36]

Concomitantly with the parliamentary elections, the Prague Jewish religious congregation was in the midst of its own campaign; elections to its representative body were held on November 10, 1929.

These elections yielded approximately the same results as those of 1921 as regards party representation.

The anti-Semitic tide that had inundated Vienna, Berlin, and

Cracow spread not only to the German University and to the German Technical University (Deutsche-Technische Hochschule) in Prague, but also to the Czech faculties, particularly the medical school of Charles University. A riot broke out on November 18, 1929, in which nineteen Jewish students were injured. Dr. Ludvik Singer, the Jewish National member of Parliament, intervened at police headquarters. Accompanied by a delegation of Jewish students, consisting of Dr. Eugen Justic and Dr. Zděnek Landes, Deputy Dr. Singer paid a personal call on Dr. Anton Štefánek, the minister of education. Dr. Štefánek promised to take vigorous action to deal with the situation and in parting said to his visitors: "Let the Jewish students keep calm, as they have in the past, and continue their studies." The Zionist Students' Association presented a memorandum to the rectors of Prague's two German universities.[37]

On November 8, 1929, immediately following the publication of parliamentary election results, Deputy Dr. Singer had stated that it would be necessary for the Jewish party and its representatives to join forces with one of the larger political parties, primarily in order to be able to exercise the right of interpellation and to obtain representation in those parliamentary committees which dealt with matters of direct concern to the party. However, it was to be a union for purely parliamentary and technical purposes only. The Jewish and Polish deputies decided to join the club of Czechoslovak Social Democrats as "guests."

In the midst of the turmoil accompanying the establishment of a countrywide Jewish political organization, attention was focused on new problems posed by the population census which had been set for December 2, 1930. Census data for each individual had to include nationality. Preparatory to the 1930 census, the Government Bureau of Statistics recommended a change in the census regulations, suggesting that the nationality of each inhabitant should be listed in accordance with his "mother tongue," i.e., the language with which he was most familiar and which he spoke best. In addition to Hebrew, Yiddish was also accepted as a "Jewish" language. This could have been construed to mean that Jews who did not use one of these two "Jewish" languages could not belong to the Jewish nationality group. The National Jews regarded this proposed change in regulations as a violation of the constitution, which had specified that in the case of the Jews the mother tongue was not to be regarded as a criterion of nationality except among those Jews whose mother tongue was

Yiddish or Hebrew. The constitution had explained its stand in the Meissner-Bouček motion of February 29, 1920:

> The charter of the constitution does not explicitly enumerate the national minorities because that would have involved finding the answer to problems that are still debated by scholars. After all, the very concept of nationality has yet to be defined in precise terms. Thus, for instance, the question whether the Jews are a nation is still a matter of debate. The charter of the constitution uses the phrase "irrespective of race, language, or religion." This means that the constitution has left it to the individual to interpret what traits constitute the criteria of his nationality. . . . Thus, anyone who regards the Jews as members of a separate nation has the privilege to declare himself a Jew by nationality even if, say, he has no religious affiliation and would be a Czech, a German, or a member of some other nationality by mother tongue. In other words, Jews are not compelled to declare themselves members of any other ethnic-national group than the Jewish nationality at censuses, elections, etc. [Commentary to the Charter of the Constitution of the Czechoslovak Republic, 31, § 128].

It was on the basis of this statement that the political leaders of Czechoslovak Jewry argued their case against the change in census regulations proposed by the Bureau of Statistics. The proposal, they asserted, had been deliberately aimed at the Jewish nationality.[38]

Non-Jewish circles, too, were drawn into the dispute. Ministerial counselor Dr. Boháč suggested that "mother tongue as well as nationality should be determined by declarations freely made." The Jews, it was felt, should be allowed to declare themselves as Jews by nationality in an additional column to be provided in the questionnaires for that purpose; however, they would have to opt for a specific mother tongue in the first column.

The dispute ended in a major political and moral victory for National Jewry. On June 26, 1930, due in large measure to the efforts of the Jewish National members of the Chamber of Deputies, and particularly of Dr. Ludvik Singer, the government passed the following ordinance:

> As a rule, nationality shall be listed in accordance with the individual's mother tongue. An individual can list a nationality other than that indicated by his mother tongue only when he does not use said mother tongue in everyday conversation with his family and at home and he is thoroughly familiar with the language of the nationality he desires to

list. However, Jews may list their nationality as Jewish (without regard to mother tongue).

Shortly before the census, the Jewish party issued a final appeal to the Jews of the country: "Declare yourselves members of the Jewish people!... We have lost our land and our language; nevertheless, we are a people."

On August 17, 1930, the officers of the Jewish party of Slovakia met in Bratislava, with eighty delegates from all over Slovakia in attendance. Deputy Dr. Julius Reisz, the chairman, reported on the party's political and parliamentary activities, and Dr. Leo Šipoš dealt with local and communal politics. Dr. Baruch Tomaschoff described the dismal state of Jewish education and culture in Slovakia. More than half the Jewish schools of Slovakia had been taken over by the state and had been stripped of their Jewish character. Dr. Oskar Neumann discussed the tasks and objectives of the Jewish press; Harry Bleiweiss, the economic situation.

On September 26, 1930, the front of the Bet Ha'Am (Cafe Aschermann), Prague's Jewish social center, was wrecked in an anti-Semitic outbreak. Deputy Dr. Singer made a protest to Dr. Sobotka, director of the Ministry of the Interior. Dr. Sobotka declared that the government was determined to restore order and not to permit further disturbances of the peace.

At the Zionist convention held in the fall of 1930 it was decided to establish one overall Jewish party organization for all of Czechoslovakia. To this end, several important meetings were held in Moravská Ostrava on January 4, 5, and 6, 1931. The result of these deliberations was the official establishment of the Jewish party on January 6, 1931, at a founding convention attended by over one hundred delegates and guests from all over Czechoslovakia.

The convention opened with a large political rally at which Dr. Ludvik Singer and Dr. Emil Margulies discussed the problems of Jewish Diaspora politics and Dr. Singer traced the history of Jewish politics in Czechoslovakia.

We saw anti-Semitism on the rise everywhere [Dr. Singer recalled]. We saw Jews ousted from public office, and it became clear to us that no outside group would come to our aid. We participated in the elections. We were defeated four times; we were double-crossed four times to make sure that no Jew would be able to enter the legislative chamber as a representative of the Jewish people. Our political activity had its beginnings even before October 29, 1929, the day when, thanks to this electoral district, we were able to send two Jewish deputies to Parliament. You know that prior to the last parliamentary elections we joined forces with the Polish minority and emerged victorious in the voting. But be it said to the credit of the Poles that they were the only ones who were not afraid to link their name with ours.

The delegates to the founding convention of the Jewish party represented electoral districts from all over the country. Dr. Angelo Goldstein was chairman of the convention. Dr. Emil Margulies reported the bylaws of the party, which provided for an Executive Board of nine members, a Central Committee of forty-two, district boards, and local groups. Delegates to the conventions were to represent the parliamentary constituencies.

In the bylaws, which were the legal basis of the party, it was further stated:

> The party bases its program on the principle that the Jews in the Czechoslovak Republic constitute a national minority fighting for equal rights among the other nationalities in the Republic and for the preservation and development of its national and cultural individuality, as well as for freedom of religious practice and the equal rights of all religions in the state. The Jewish party in the Czechoslovak Republic is the political organization of national Judaism in this country. It is the legitimate representative of the Jewish people in its fight for nationality rights, for national and cultural development, and for civic and political equality based on the laws of this Republic and within the framework of its constitution.

A budget in the amount of 230,000,00 korunas was proposed and accepted.

The following officers were unanimously elected: *Executive Board:* Norbert Adler (Prague); Dr. Arthur Czeczowiczka (Nový Jičin); Dr. Artur Feldmann (Brno); Dr. Angelo Goldstein (Prague); Arthur Kauders (Prague); Dr. Chaim Kugel (Mukačevo); Dr. Emil Margulies (Litoměřice); Dr. Paul März (Moravská Ostrava); Dr. Leo Šipoš (Bratislava). Ex officio: Deputies Dr. Ludvik Singer (Prague) and Dr. Julius Reisz (Bratislava). *Central Committee:* Ernst Frischer, Dr. Othmar Huss, and Dr. Hermann Fuchs (Moravská Ostrava); Dr. Alfred Grünfeld, Theodor Huber, Dr. Karl Sonnenfeld, and Dr. Siegmund Bernstein (Brno); Max Munk (Uh. Hradište); Fritz Sborowitz (Prostějov); Dr. Eugen Justic (Prague); Dr. Oskar Zweigenthal (Olomouc); Leopoldine Klein (Prague); Dr. Fritz Eidlitz

(Plzeň); Wilhelm Heller and Dr. Fritzi Margulies (Litomeřice); Dr. Herbert Birnbaum (Teplice); Emanuel Kraus (Liberec); Dr. Alfred Löwenstein (Karlovy Vary); Dr. Milan Kollman (Hradec Králove); Isidor Knöpfelmacher (Bratislava); Dr. Michael Eisler, and Jozef Müller (Hlohovec); Alois Jellinek (Štubn. Teplice); Dr. Matej Weiner (Turč. Sv. Martin); M. Salzer (Sered); Dr. Tyroler (Žilina); Dr. Bedrich Beer (Bratislava); Dr. Sigmund Neuwirth (Prešov); Goldberger (Košice); Dr. Wilhelm Görög, Sigmund Brand, and Dr. Sigmund Fürst (Bratislava); Wilhelm Sternbach, M. Goldstein, Jehuda Weiss, and Deutsch (Mukačevo); Messrs. Falkowitz, Wolf, and Hartmann (Užhorod).

At the first meeting of the board, which was held following the adjournment of the party convention, Emil Margulies was elected chairman.

Deputy Dr. Ludvik Singer emphasized that the two Jewish deputies should join one of the "clubs" in Parliament. The Jewish party chose the club of the Czechoslovak Social Democrats.

The National Jews appeared to be making considerable headway among the Jewish masses. Of the 101,000 Jews living in Subcarpathian Ruthenia in 1930, 94,000, or 93 per cent, declared themselves to be of Jewish nationality. In 1921, when the Jewish population of the province had been 93,000, only 80,000 (or 87 per cent) had made such a declaration.

Meanwhile, the revision of the citizenship code had changed the citizenship status of a large segment of Czechoslovakia's Jewish population. This important legal problem was a subject of major concern to the Jewish party and its representatives in Parliament. Many families who had lived for decades in the territory of what was now Czechoslovakia had been denied Czechoslovak citizenship after the founding of the Republic in 1918. In many cases this came about because the forebears of the individuals concerned had happened to have established residence in a community which was a few miles beyond the borders drawn for the new Czechoslovak Republic. Under the Czechoslovak Constitution all those who, as of January 1, 1910, had been officially domiciled in a locality that had become part of Czechoslovakia, automatically became Czechoslovak citizens. But there were many who had lost their former right of domicile subsequent to that date and had not acquired a new one in its place. These individuals were declared stateless and left to the mercies of the various authorities, which as a rule kept the applicants waiting for years, only to reject their petitions for citizenship in the end. The authorities were under no obligation to give reasons for their rulings. Among the applicants thus rejected were men who had served their two years in the Czechoslovak Army and had taken part in the mandatory military exercises. Now they found that they were considered unworthy of receiving Czechoslovak citizenship. Minister of the Interior Juraj Slávik and Foreign Minister Beneš promised to see that something was done for such individuals. The Lex Dérer, which had been enacted for Slovakia and Subcarpathian Ruthenia in 1926, brought only partial relief. The old Austrian laws were still in force in the Historic Lands.

The club of the Czechoslovak Social Democratic deputies, which the two Jewish National deputies had joined as guests, introduced a new bill for the adjustment of citizenship status, with the following main provisions:

(a) Citizenship (or naturalization) shall no longer be an act of grace conferred at the discretion of the State but, under conditions to be duly specified, a right which the petitioner can legitimately claim, particularly if he has resided in the Republic for a longer period of time and has not been guilty of any offenses punishable under the law.

(b) Regulations applicable to married women and to aliens.

(c) Renunciation of citizenship shall be a right freely exercised by the individual concerned.

(d) Naturalization procedures shall be simplified. Petitions submitted to a political authority of first instance (particularly issues involving individuals who are already citizens) must be acted upon within three months. In cases where the petitioner has a legal claim to naturalization or to renunciation of citizenship, the political authority of second instance must hand down its ruling within six months. If such a ruling is not handed down within this period, the petition shall automatically be considered as approved.

(e) Another change in the code concerns the status of former citizens of Austria, Hungary, and Germany. The new code shall include a stipulation to the effect that the following shall be considered Czechoslovak citizens: all those who have acquired citizenship under the laws hitherto in force, and all

> those who have no other citizenship and have established residence in the territory of the Czechoslovak Republic no later than October 28, 1918, and have resided there continuously from that time on.

In short, decisions regarding citizenship status were no longer to be left to the discretion of government officials but were to be based on unambiguous legislation.

Since the settlement of the citizenship question affected many Jewish families, the Jewish party and its deputies in Parliament actively participated in the drafting of the proposed new law.

At the same time, the Jewish party developed intensive activity in the fields of organization and propaganda. Electoral districts were organized, a membership enrollment campaign was launched, and numerous district conventions were held. A pamphlet by Dr. František Friedmann describing the Jewish party and the political activity of the Jews of Czechoslovakia since 1918 was published in the Czech language.

The Jewish party protested against a government decree introducing compulsory Sunday rest in Slovakia, which posed a serious economic problem for Sabbath-observing Jewish shopkeepers in Slovakia and Subcarpathian Ruthenia. The matter was discussed in detail at a district convention (Nové Zámky District) held on May 10, 1931, which requested the Executive Board to secure an exemption whereby Sabbath-observing Jewish shopkeepers would be permitted to keep their stores open on Sundays between 8 and 10 A.M. Deputies Dr. Reisz and Dr. Singer were instructed to state the party's views in Parliament and to intervene with the appropriate government authorities. Dr. Reisz, Dr. Singer, and Dr. Béla Beer, an attorney and Mizrahi leader, thereupon submitted a memorandum to the government, citing the precedent of England, where Jews were permitted to make up for their Sabbath rest by doing business on Sundays.

Another district convention of Jewish party delegates, this one for Subcarpathian Ruthenia, was held in Mukačevo on June 21, 1931. Among the leaders present were Dr. Singer and Dr. Leo Zelmanovits, the party's parliamentary secretary. Dr. Reisz was absent, due to illness. In the debate the Jewish party was taken to task for having "so little to show" for its activities. The Jewish masses, the delegates pointed out, were primarily interested in seeing successes in matters relative to "daily bread." The Jewish population of Subcarpathian Ruthenia had been pauperized and was exposed to harassment from the authorities in the assessment and collection of taxes. The urgent need for action in the citizenship problem was also stressed. As to the Hebrew school system, it was held that despite the efforts made in this respect the competent government agencies still did not show sufficient interest in this important field of cultural activity.[39]

On July 23, 1931, Dr. Ludvik Singer died at the age of fifty-six in the midst of his many labors.[40] Even before the birth of the Czechoslovak State Dr. Singer had followed a consistent policy in his political work. His attitude toward the Czechoslovak government had been one of "prudent trust."

In his eulogy of Dr. Singer, Max Brod wrote:

> Jewish political life in our country has brought forth many valiant fighters and enlisted the services of many co-workers. Some of them were imbued with the spirit of brotherliness; many others, less so. But it has produced only one father. To all those of us who have waged the good fight and will continue to do so under the Jewish banner, Dr. Ludvik Singer represented a sort of stern, calm father image. . . .[41]

On September 6, 1931, the Executive Board and the Central Committee of the Jewish party met in Brno under the chairmanship of Dr. Emil Margulies, chiefly for the purpose of naming Singer's successor in Parliament. Dr. Angelo Goldstein was chosen for the post by unanimous vote. Dr. Eugen Justic was named general secretary of the party and Dr. František Friedmann, member of the Executive Board. The other items on the agenda were local elections, the Jewish school system, and the Jewish press.

In an interview following his election, Deputy Dr. Goldstein stated that he would carry on in the spirit of the principles established by Dr. Singer, based on the agreement with the Social Democrats and on a continued electoral partnership with the Poles. He said:

> I consider Jewish politics as a means of achieving the aim of Zionism. I view it as an educational instrument, which is conducive to the proud avowal of Judaism and as a practical instrument in that it builds a mighty dam against the corrosive elements that nibble at the body of Diaspora Judaism. Jewish politics has made us eligible political partners and has enabled us to take up mutual relationships with people and parties, with both rights and duties of our own. Such a policy of partnership

contains an important spiritual element: we are enabling the Jews to live and to think as equals among equals.[42]

Meanwhile, the Jewish party continued its manifold activities. New electoral districts were set up (e.g., in Trnava). On August 23, 1931, Deputy Dr. Reisz met with the minister for trade, Dr. Matoušek, to discuss the question of compulsory Sunday rest. Matoušek stated that while he himself would be willing to make compromises in the matter, he felt that the other ministers would also have to be won over.

The local elections in Prague, which were held on October 4, 1931, yielded very satisfactory results for the Jewish party, which received a total of 9,937 votes in Greater Prague.

On November 26, 1931, Deputy Dr. Goldstein delivered his maiden speech in Parliament. Among the issues he discussed on that occasion were citizenship, excesses perpetrated by administrative officials in the eastern sector of the Republic, and the numerous complaints about government officials who misused their authority for partisan purposes. Dr. Goldstein called for the democratization of the electoral law, impartiality in law enforcement,* and more generous attention to the religious needs of the Jews in the Historic Lands. He also made reference to the regulations of compulsory Sunday rest. Dr. Reisz then took the floor, calling upon the minister of finance to make allowances in tax collection procedures for the deteriorating economic situation of the Jews in Slovakia and Subcarpathian Ruthenia. Dr. Reisz further demanded indemnification for those Jews who had lost their means of livelihood as a result of the looting they had suffered.

At the first district convention of the Jewish party in Subcarpathian Ruthenia (January 3, 1932), Dr. Goldstein discussed the party's program. At this convention the party district of Subcarpathian Ruthenia was officially constituted, and a twelve-member Executive Board and forty-two-member District Central Committee were elected.

Meanwhile, anti-Semitism in the eastern sector of the Republic continued unabated. Public opinion in Subcarpathian Ruthenia was shocked by a ritual murder trial which took place at Starý Simeri.

---

* Goldstein was referring to the Horák case. (See Livia Rothkirchen, Slovakia: II, 1918–1938 in vol. I, *The Jews of Czechoslovakia*, pp. 118–19.)

Slovakia, too, was the scene of anti-Semitic trials (e.g., the Weissberger case), which were abetted by a press campaign. Mass arrests of Jews were made in Slovakia on the "grounds" that Slovak Jews serving as officers of the Revolutionary National Council had ordered looters to be shot during the riots in the fall of 1918. These arrests were carried out by the country police "in the best interests of the state."

The Jewish party took action at once. Deputy Dr. Angelo Goldstein and Dr. Emil Margulies, the party's chairman, met with the minister of justice in a lengthy conference. On February 23 Goldstein was received by Dr. Juraj Slávik, minister of the interior. Slávik promised that no further arrests "of that sort" would be made; he gave his solemn word that all the cases would be dismissed as quickly as possible and that no one would be wronged in the process.

The secretary-general of the party met with General Weinerek, the director of the Ministry for National Defense, to discuss the religious needs of Jewish personnel in the armed forces. Specifically, the party asked that Passover furloughs be granted to all Jewish soldiers requesting them and that Jewish members of the armed forces be given opportunities to attend religious services during the High Holidays. General Weinerek replied that he would instruct the military authorities accordingly.

As the sole legitimate mouthpiece of *Landespolitik* in Czechoslovakia, the Jewish party was also faced with "ideological" problems. Thus, it had to announce its stand on the worldwide effort to convene a World Jewish Congress. In this connection, the chairman of the Jewish party said:[43]

> *Galut* [Diaspora] work is part of the Zionist program, of the program of the World Zionist Organization, and of the work of the Zionist Territorial Federations. At present, the international organization [for dealing with] Diaspora problems in a World Jewish Congress is *de facto* a wide-open field. These problems are urgent, especially now. They call for a unified organization and leadership. For this reason we support the idea of a democratically organized congress of the Jewish people [to deal with] Diaspora problems. . . .

Dr. Emil Margulies was elected to the eighteen-member presidium chosen by the World Jewish Conference which met in Geneva to discuss the tasks of the projected congress.[44]

The Jewish deputies in the Czechoslovak Parliament took a keen interest also in issues other than those of strictly Jewish concern. Thus, Deputy Dr. Goldstein took part in the debate on the question of the right of distraint, which was held in the Parliament's Constitution Committee, with Dr. Alfred Meissner, the minister of justice (who happened to be Jewish),* in attendance. Dr. Goldstein pointed out the necessity of reforms not only in the laws of distraint but also in the legislation regulating civil law suits, He demanded relief in cases of distraint resulting from tax arrears and called attention to the inequities in administrative distraint procedures in the eastern sector of the Republic. Dr. Goldstein was appointed reporter for a bill dealing with the protection of the Czechoslovak currency.[45]

When Foreign Minister Dr. Eduard Beneš visited Subcarpathian Ruthenia in 1932,[46] a delegation from the Jewish party, consisting of Dr. Chaim Kugel, Dr. Wilhelm Sternbach, Dr. Saphir, and Josef Deutsch took the opportunity to meet with him and present to him the cultural demands of the Jewish minority. Dr. Beneš replied as follows:

> You yourselves have pointed out my attitude toward your endeavors. My line [in this respect] has not changed since 1920. This is my policy and also the policy of the president. I understand your aspirations and want to help you. You are right in not wanting to be an instrument of Czechization; that would not be good for you — nor for us. We would not want that, either. I will study with interest the problems of the Hebrew school system and of the high school, which you mention in your memorandum, and I promise you my support.

The leaders of the party continued to travel all over the country, maintaining close contact with local party groups and keeping them informed on current affairs.

With the mounting threat of Nazi anti-Semitism in Germany, Czechoslovak Jewry became active in refugee relief work. Many transports of German Jewish emigrants on their way to Palestine passed through Czechoslovakia; there, Jewish communities gave them whatever aid they needed and helped them move on.†

Deputy Goldstein found it necessary to turn his attention to the fight against Nazi propaganda in Czechoslovakia.[47] He intervened

---

* [See Brügel, Jews in Political Life, pp. 243–252 (Ed.)]

† [See K. R. Grossmann, Refugees to and from Czechoslovakia, pp. 565–581, and M. George: Refugees in Prague, pp. 582–588 (Ed.)]

with the ministers of the interior and of justice regarding anti-Semitic publications which had been appearing in Czech and in German all over the country.

Meanwhile, Dr. Margulies and Dr. Reisz participated in demonstrations organized by the Jewish party in Slovakia. At district conventions held in Pieštany and Trnava (December 1934) Margulies attacked gentile attempts to buy Jewish votes for the impending parliamentary elections in Subcarpathian Ruthenia (1935). The central Jewish figure in this election was Rabbi Chaim Eleazar Spira of Mukačevo, who supported the party in power. While Rabbi Spira had only a small fanatical following, his political activities posed a threat to the prestige and the good name of the Jewish people. Dr. Margulies declared that Czechoslovak Jewry had to fight for the practical enforcement of the constitutional principles of equal rights in order to show that the Jews were indeed worthy of complete emancipation.

In the parliamentary debate on the budget (November 29, 1934), Dr. Reisz declared that "in these difficult times" the Jews were ready to assume all the burdens imposed by the budget and to make even greater sacrifices, if necessary, for the Jews wanted to continue to fulfill their patriotic obligations toward Czechoslovakia as they had done in the past.

At a mass rally of the Jewish party in Prague (December 19, 1934) Deputy Goldstein, referring to the situation of the Jews in Subcarpathian Ruthenia, declared that it was necessary to continue "the fighr against Rabbi Spira and his followers" because he felt that they constituted "one of the biggest obstacles to the future development of Jewry in Subcarpathian Ruthenia." Goldstein then pointed out the necessity for the democratization of the Jewish communities in Subcarpathian Ruthenia, and stressed the fact that Minister Dr. Beneš had shown genuine understanding for the demands of the Jewish party. Another speaker, the Czechoslovak Social Democratic deputy Jaromír Nečas, reported that shortly before the rally he had received a telegram from Mukačevo's Orthodox Jewish congregation urging him not to attend the Jewish party function. Nečas personally felt that as a non-Jew it was not his place to meddle in the internal affairs of the Jews.

> However [he said], Rabbi Spira's antics have taken on such dimensions that an honest and progressive-minded Gentile cannot ignore them.

The progressive-minded Czech public sides with the Zionists in their fight for the democratization of the Jewish communities in Subcarpathian Ruthenia. We respect and esteem the loyalty of the Jewish minority in this state because it is being offered in good faith and with no strings attached. . . .

On December 30 and 31 the Zionist Organization of Czechoslovakia held its eleventh national convention under the chairmanship of Dr. Paul März and with ninety-six delegates representing forty local groups in attendance. This convention elected a political *Reichskommission* (National Commission), which was independent of the Jewish party but whose decisions in any eventualities arising from the following year's parliamentary elections were to be binding on all the Zionist members of the party.

At the same time the convention of the Jewish party took place. Here, too, much of the agenda dealt with the approaching parliamentary elections. A new law on parliamentary parties had been enacted, and no one knew whether this law would cause difficulties for the Jewish party in the voting. The convention was the arena for an old battle, fought all over again, between ideology and political expediency, a struggle between radical policies and *Realpolitik*.

The convention proceeded to the task of electing a party chairman, who was to be chosen from the plenum so that he might enjoy a maximum of authority. The choice fell on Dr. Emil Margulies. At the same time a special council, consisting of the chairman, his three deputies, and the two deputies in Parliament, was named to decide on important issues in cases where there would not be enough time to convene the Executive Board.

It was also decided to expand the Counseling Office for Vocational Reorientation, which had been set up in Moravská Ostrava by Dr. Othmar Huss and had been operating very effectively. Plans called for the extension of its activities to all the areas in which the Jewish party was functioning. The work of this office did not entail the psychological or technical counseling of individuals but the organization of an employment service, which, in view of the economic situation, was to be of great importance for the Jews in Czechoslovakia.

In addition, the convention had to deal with questions of party personnel, such as the case of Dr. František Friedmann, who had joined the opposition.

The convention drew up guidelines[48] for the approaching parliamentary elections and succeeded in creating a synthesis between realistic flexibility and adherence to the political party line.

On March 13, 1935, Deputy Dr. Goldstein delivered an important speech in the debate conducted by the Parliament's Constitution Committee on the "Law Regarding the Residence of Aliens." The legislative report on this law notably revealed a tendency to protect the domestic labor market from competition by foreigners.

Only those [Dr. Goldstein said] who were fortunate enough to be domiciled as early as January 1, 1910, in one of the localities located within the present borders of the new state automatically acquired citizenship under the law. But all those unfortunate individuals whose status was changed after that fateful January 1, 1910, suddenly became people without a country. . . .

To these thousands of pitiable folk we must now add the emigrés — all those who were forced by sudden political changes to leave their country. It started with the emigration from Russia and it has ended, for the time being, with the exodus from Germany. These emigrants number into the hundreds of thousands. . . . These victims of our times have been joined by the many who have been deprived of their citizenship by a legal contrivance which had never been known before and which was only devised by the Third Reich. . . . Their uncertain legal status and their resulting material insecurity has reduced them to despair, and recent events have only served to deepen their desperation. We have learned from newspaper reports that those Jews who [are forced to] return to Germany are immediately taken to concentration camps by the Third Reich. The change in the law under consideration here poses the threat that, within two months, these people may even lose their tenuous right of asylum. . . .

In the name of all these people I herewith request the Czechoslovak government and the minister of the interior that those aliens who, through no fault of their own, are compelled to live within the borders of our state, and who have never violated, and never will violate, our laws and statutes, should be permitted to petition the authorities for residence permits without being subjected to trouble and difficulties and that they may obtain the right to reside here in accordance with the new law. . . .

Goldstein's remarks were seconded by the German Social Democrat deputy Schweichhart and received the unanimous approval of the Constitution Committee.

The Jewish party was occupied with preparations for the parliamentary elections. The Central Committee of the Jewish party, meeting in Moravská Ostrava on April 14, 1935, passed a decisive resolution; it approved the party's electoral alliance with the Czechoslovak Social Democratic party. This arrangement assured the Jewish party's parliamentary *status quo*; two seats in the Chamber of Deputies and — depending on the results of the election — a chance for one seat in the Senate. The committee nominated Deputy Dr. Angelo Goldstein and Dr. Chaim Kugel, the principal of the Hebrew high school in Mukačevo, for the seats in the Chamber. Ernst Frischer, of Moravská Ostrava, was designated as the candidate for the Senate seat.

Under this bipartisan scheme the Jewish voters could not cast their votes directly for the Jewish party, but could do so only in a roundabout way by voting for the Czechoslovak Social Democratic ticket. However, this agreement was a purely technical arrangement for election purposes only. It did not imply Jewish adherence to the Czechoslovak Social Democratic party. But under the election law, a political party could pass to second *scrutinium* (second count) only if it had received at least 20,000 votes in one constituency or a total of at least 120,000 votes throughout the country, and the leaders of the Jewish party thought it highly improbable that the Jewish party would be able to meet these two requirements if it were to "go it alone."

A total of fifty-two delegates cooperated in the decision to join forces with the Czechoslovak Social Democrats. However, the decision, though supported by a large majority, was not unanimous. Among those who opposed the agreement for ideological reasons was the chairman of the party, Dr. Emil Margulies, who insisted that the Jewish party should stand for election alone and under its own name. When he was outvoted, he resigned from the chairmanship of the party. His resignation was accepted and Ernst Frischer was elected temporary chairman in his place.

Before Parliament adjourned, Dr. Goldstein, in a speech on electoral reforms, stated the position of the Jewish party as follows:

> I have not asked for the floor in order to make a public indictment; on the contrary, I want to give praise where praise is due. I gladly admit that, despite this and other faults, Czechoslovakia is an island of democracy in Europe, and I do not hesitate to say this even now, when I am of the opinion that we are being wronged.[49]

As the electoral campaign got under way, the Central Committee of the Jewish party received word from the executive of the Mizrahi Organization of Czechoslovakia that the Mizrahi membership would give the Jewish party its active support. The territorial conference of the Czechoslovak *HeHalutz* movement, which was held in Mukačevo, also advised its members to vote for the Jewish party through the Czechoslovak Social Democratic ticket.

In the provincial and district elections of Slovakia and Subcarpathian Ruthenia (May 26, 1935), however, the Jewish party ran for election under its own name. The election campaign set off renewed anti-Semitic agitation in the press. The anti-Jewish Stříbný papers published sensational reports of a "secret" agreement between the Jewish party and the Social Democrats, and *Polední Listy* agitated against the Jewish politicians.

The election of May 19, 1935, yielded the expected results. Dr. Angelo Goldstein and Dr. Chaim Kugel were sent to Parliament as the representatives of the Jewish party. The party received a substantially greater number of votes than it had polled in previous local and district elections (in Brno, the increase amounted to one thousand).

On June 25, 1935, Deputy Dr. Goldstein, in his first speech before the new Parliament, criticized the election law because it "deprived" the small national minorities of "the opportunity to stand for election as independent entities." Setting forth the program of the Jewish party, he said: "You'll find us wherever democracy and the interests of this state will be in need of defense." He urged tax reforms, pointing out that the tax burden had become intolerable for small and middle-class entrepreneurs. He further advocated a change of government for Subcarpathian Ruthenia.

On July 6 and 7, 1935, the Jewish party held its third Extraordinary Conference in Trenčianské-Teplice. Eighty-four delegates representing all the electoral districts of the Republic were present. The agenda included the adoption of a party program and a party budget, and the election of a permanent chairman to succeed Margulies, who had resigned. The permanent chairmanship of the party went to Ernst Frischer, who had served as temporary chairman since April of that year. The other officers elected were Otto Zucker (Prague), Dr. Mathias Weiner (Lipt. Sv. Mikuláš), and Dr. Wilhelm Sternbach (Mukačevo), vice presidents, and Dr. Leo Zelmanovits (Moravská Ostrava), secretary-general.[50]

The appointment of the representatives to the Provincial Assembly of Slovakia set off renewed anti-Semitic agitation. In his party organ, *Slovák*, Andrej Hlinka, the leader of the Slovak People's party (Slovenská L'udová Strana), published an article sharply attacking the government. He claimed that his party had been short-changed when the delegates to the Provincial Assembly had been appointed. "It is a flagrant injustice," he wrote, "that the government should have appointed one delegate for 36,000 Jewish votes, while we Slovaks received [only] one delegate for 107,000 voters."

It must be pointed out that under the law for the appointment of Provincial Assembly delegates, the number of representatives named was not dependent on election results, i.e., on the strength of the parties to be represented. On the contrary, the filling of one-third of the assembly seats by appointment rather than by election was intended to enable the government to benefit from the cooperation of those population elements which had been passed over in the elections, particularly experts in economics and autonomous administration. The government's intention in also naming a Jewish delegate to the Provincial Assembly of Slovakia (he was Dr. Julius Reisz, who had represented the Jewish party in Parliament) was to give Slovakia's Jewish minority of over one hundred thousand an opportunity to make its voice heard in the affairs of the province. Moreover, the figures cited by Hlinka were not correct because the Republican party had received one Provincial Assembly representative for only forty-eight thousand Slovak voters.

Hate was rife also within the Jewish community. Rabbi Chaim Eleazar Spira of Mukačevo agitated against the Jewish party and the Hebrew school system in Subcarpathian Ruthenia. In a sermon on June 21, 1935, he anathematized the Hebrew high school in his city:[51]

> Whosoever sends his children to the accursed Hebrew school shall be wiped out and shall not be permitted to live to raise his children. The children will not live to see the next year. A Zionist must not be called to the holy ark, and no one may partake of his wine. For the past ten years I have spat whenever I pass the godless Hebrew high school.

The Hebrew high school instituted legal proceedings against Spira. Although the District Court of Užhorod dismissed the case, the Court of Appeals found that Rabbi Spira had been guilty of a misdemeanor and sentenced him to a fine of one thousand korunas or twenty days in prison.

The year 1935 saw the promulgation of the infamous Nuremberg Laws in neighboring Germany. In September 1935 the Jewish party issued the following proclamation:[52]

PROCLAMATION BY THE JEWISH PARTY

Shocked by the reports of the monstrous moral and physical indignities to which the Jewish population in Germany has been subjected for manifest reasons, we note that our brethren, deprived of all elementary human rights, have been virtually outlawed.

We are aware of the true reason for these acts of inhumanity; it is not at all the alleged inferiority of the Jewish race but simply an attempt to divert the attention of world opinion from the true intentions of the present regime and from the domestic troubles with which it is beset.

Let the fate of the Jews in Germany be a warning to all the others. The present trend of events shows that after their destruction, the others will be next in line.

At a time when the forces of barbarity are threatening to overwhelm the seemingly defenseless values of the human spirit, we, the Jews of the Czechoslovak Republic, as free citizens of a free and democratic state, herewith call upon the groups which have earned our trust and upon the leading individuals of all the civilized nations to become aware of the responsibility that has fallen to the present generation and to take up the struggle for the defense of the basic rights of man.

The provocation of anti-Semitic tendencies threatens to undermine the power of resistance of the countries that are within the reach of this expansionist thirst for power.

To the Jewish public we herewith turn with this solemn plea: let every one of you for himself and all of you together remain true to your faith and to your convictions. In whatever you say and do, consider the honor of Jewry and the fate of the Jewish community.

The Jews must become aware of the great constructive tasks which the needs of the hour impose upon them. Morality and self-preservation dictate that we perform them with selfless devotion.

The more we are degraded and humiliated, the more we must rally around the timeless moral values of Judaism and make every sacrifice needed for the fulfillment of the tasks which have been thrust upon us.

The Executive Board of the Jewish Party

The Jewish party also protested to the Assembly of the League of Nations and submitted the following letter of protest to Foreign Minister Dr. Beneš:[53]

The Jewish party in Czechoslovakia turns to you, as the chairman of the Sixteenth Assembly of the League of Nations and as the authorized defender of human rights and of the principle of the equality of all mankind, with the request that you communicate to the League of Nations our protest against the disfranchisement and defamation of the Jews in the German Reich which have culminated in the anti-Jewish laws recently enacted there.

(signed) Frischer,
Chairman of the Jewish party

On October 3, 1935, Deputy Dr. Goldstein and Mrs. Marie Schmolka,* the head of the Jewish Refugee Relief Committee, were received by the minister of the interior, Dr. Josef Černý. They discussed with Dr. Černý the problems of refugees, aliens, and "stateless" individuals, and specific complaints relating to actions taken by several district authorities in Bohemia and Moravia. Dr. Černý promised to investigate the complaints and to provide relief. He also assured his visitors that no injustice would be done in cases involving the deportation of aliens and that no one would suffer discrimination because of his Jewish nationality.

In December 1935 Tomáš G. Masaryk resigned from the presidency of Czechoslovakia due to his advanced age. His favorite disciple and co-worker, Dr. Eduard Beneš, was elected to succeed him. The Jewish party sent the following telegrams to the two Czechoslovak leaders:

To T. G. Masaryk, Liberator-President, Prague-Lány.
It is with great regret that the Jewish party in the Czechoslovak Republic has learned the news of your resignation from your high office and shares in the general sadness occasioned by [your decision]. We thank you for the exceptional understanding which you have always shown for us and for our aims....

For the Jewish party in the Czechoslovak Republic: Ernst Frischer

---

* Mrs. Schmolka was also the chairman of the *Comité National Tchecho-Slovaque pour les Réfugiés provenant d'Allemagne* (Czechoslovak National Committee for Refugees from Germany) to which all the refugee aid committees belonged and of which Kurt R. Grossmann was executive secretary (see pp. 565–581).

To Dr. Eduard Beneš, President of the Czechoslovak Republic, Prague

We herewith wish to express to you, dear Mr. President, our most heartfelt congratulations on your election to the presidency of the Republic and at the same time recall with sincere gratitude your work as a statesman in the past and its beneficial import to the Jewish Renaissance movement....

For the Jewish party in the Czechoslovak Republic: Ernst Frischer

That same month (December 30, 1935), the twelfth convention of the Zionist Organization of Czechoslovakia took place in Moravská Ostrava. Once again, the relationship of the national organization to the Zionist Territorial Federations and to Diaspora politics was discussed. The following two definitions of these relationships emerged from the convention: "The Zionist Territorial Federations are the guardians of *Landespolitik*" and "Every Zionist will always be responsible to his Zionist Territorial Federation for any and all of his activities in *Landespolitik*."[54]

Meanwhile, the Secretariat of the Jewish party in Subcarpathian Ruthenia provided assistance to Jews in tax questions and in problems involving citizenship, residence permits, public assistance, health insurance, and other matters.

From its inception the Jewish party considered it one of its principal tasks to conduct a purposeful social policy for the Jewish minority group.

At its convention in 1935 the party had adopted the following resolution on the social problems of Czechoslovak Jewry:

> The economic situation of the Jewish population of Czechoslovakia is steadily deteriorating. The main cause [of this state of affairs] is that the Jewish population is concentrated in only a few occupations. It is therefore imperative that Jewish vocational guidance offices be set up in every city or town with a relatively high percentage of Jews in order to influence the youth in their choice of vocation so as to promote the normalization of the economic structure of Czechoslovakia's Jewish population.

With the economic improvement of the Jews in mind, Deputy Dr. Goldstein, in a speech in Parliament in 1935, criticized the Elections Bill, demanded tax reforms, and expressed the hope that the regime which had been holding power in Subcarpathian Ruthenia would be replaced by a just government which would seek to raise the impoverished and socially and culturally underprivileged population of that country to a level that would assure its normal and healthy development.

A deputation from the Jewish party called on the minister of social welfare to acquaint him with the problems of Jewish welfare work for the young. The party requested government support for those institutions which trained the Jewish population for productive employment.

In March 1935 Deputy Dr. Goldstein addressed the Parliament's Constitution Committee on the legal protection needed by Jewish refugees from Hitler's Germany who were entering Czechoslovakia in ever-increasing numbers. He was received by the minister of the interior, who promised that the authorities would be duly considerate of those aliens whose "political conduct" was "irreproachable."*

On February 22, 1936, the Jewish party held a convention in Banská Bystrica, Slovakia. Ernst Frischer, the chairman, and Deputy Dr. Goldstein discussed the problems of Jewish politics and party organization. Frischer also reported on the creation of an independent Jewish social welfare agency and of vocational guidance bureaus, and dealt with problems relating to vocational reorientation which had become an inescapable necessity. The party's Executive Board was soon to set up an economic advisory council.

On the following day (February 23) Paul März, on behalf of the party's Executive Board, addressed a meeting of delegates of the Western Slovak District. He reported on the situation of the Jews and called for a systematic reorganization of the party.

The problems of the Jews in Subcarpathian Ruthenia were of constant concern to the parliamentary representatives of the Jewish party. On March 5, 1936, a delegation from the permanent committee of deputies and senators representing the coalition parties for Subcarpathian Ruthenia submitted to President Beneš a detailed memorandum setting forth the demands of the population of Subcarpathian Ruthenia. One of the delegates was Deputy Dr. Chaim Kugel, who represented the interests of Subcarpathian Ruthenia's Jewish population on the committee.

The memorandum stated that all the deputies and senators of the coalition parties for Subcarpathian Ruthenia had joined in supporting the basic claims of the Jewish party and recommended that

* See Grossmann, pp. 525–581.

government-supported public schools with Hebrew as the language of instruction should be set up wherever parents of school-age children requested it.

President Beneš replied that he approved of the idea in principle. Prime Minister Dr. Milan Hodža, whom the delegation also visited, likewise took a positive view of Kugel's request.

On April 6, 1936, a joint conference of the Jewish party districts of Olomouc and Uh. Hradiště took place in Olomouc. In his report Dr. Goldstein stressed the great extent to which the principle of an independent and positive Jewish policy was still being justified by the political situation. It was the supreme task of the party and its members "to defend democracy without reservations," and Dr. Goldstein added that the parliamentary representatives of the party had done valuable work in that area.

On April 22, 1936, President Beneš received the Jewish National deputies (Dr. Goldstein and Dr. Kugel), the chairman of the Jewish party (Ernst Frischer) and the chairman of the Central Zionist Federation (Dr. Josef Rufeisen).

Congratulating the new president on his election, the spokesmen of the Jewish party stated that they considered his accession to the presidency a victory for the ideals of democracy.

In his reply, Dr. Beneš said:

> You know what my policy was toward the Jewish Renaissance movement while I was minister for foreign affairs. I want to assure you that I will continue to pursue the same policy also in my new position. The creation of a Jewish national home will have a salutary effect on the position of the Jews all over the world and will serve to end, or at least to mitigate, the hardships which the Jews are suffering in many countries.

The delegates handed to the president a memorandum requesting his support for their efforts to nationalize and develop the Hebrew school system in Subcarpathian Ruthenia, improvement of social welfare work for Jewish youth linked with vocational reorientation and other social action, the democratization of the election bylaws of the Jewish religious congregations and their leading constituent organizations, especially in the eastern part of the Republic, sympathetic consideration on the part of the authorities in questions of citizenship, and the elimination of abuses in cases of deportation.

President Beneš promised to support these demands within the framework of his constitutional powers.

The Jewish party continued active also in the internal affairs of the Jewish community. Thus, it issued an appeal to all Jewish landowners, farmers and tenant farmers in Czechoslovakia to take in *halutzim* who wanted to train for work as pioneers in Palestine.

On May 2, 1936, the founding conference of the Central Federation of Jewish District Youth Organizations was held in Moravská Ostrava, under the chairmanship of Dr. Othmar Huss. Dr. Kugel stated the purpose of the new organization; namely, to see to it that welfare work for Jewish youth should be conducted in a unified, systematic, and rational manner, and should be subsidized by funds from the government and other autonomous governmental agencies rather than depend on charitable contributions. Such centers for youth work, Dr. Kugel declared, should be set up in all the major cities of the Republic.

Early in the summer of 1936 the Jewish party issued a call to all Jews to subscribe to the Defense Loan and to participate in the Defense Training Program:[55]

> The Executive Board of the Jewish party has noted with great satisfaction that the Jewish population of the Czechoslovak Republic has shown a complete understanding of the importance of the Defense Loan which has been issued recently, and that Jewish public bodies and Jewish individuals alike have done their civic duty . . . and subscribed to the loan. The Jews have thus demonstrated that they fully understand the ideals for which the Republic stands and that they are willing to participate in the defense of [our] free, democratic state toeether with their other fellow citizens, at all times and in every way.
>
> The Executive Board of the Jewish party hereby calls on those members who are still in arrears with their subscriptions to subscribe to the loan at the earliest possible moment.
>
> We are taking this opportunity to inform the Jewish population that civil defense courses [*kursy brannosti*], air raid defense courses and nurses' training courses have been set up in most of the cities of the Republic. . . . [The board called on the Jews to enroll in these defense training programs.]

Meanwhile, Slovakia was the scene of vicious anti-Semitic agitation, with the newspapers close to the Slovak People's party taking the lead in attacking the Jews. Dr. Matej Weiner, the deputy chairman of the Jewish party in Czechoslovakia, requested an interview with the chairman of the Slovak People's party, the prelate

Andrej Hlinka. During the conference with Weiner, Hlinka said, among other things:[56]

I am not an enemy of the Jews, nor is the political party of which I am the leader anti-Semitic. Anti-Semitism is not part of our program. As a Catholic clergyman I am fully aware of the great moral, religious, and historical significance of Judaism for all of civilized mankind, especially for Christianity. As long as they will be guided by the spirit of their religion as handed down by their prophets, adhere to their faith, and refuse to be diverted from the ethical principles of that faith, the Jews in Slovakia will have nothing to fear from the Slovak people whose leadership [*sic*] has been entrusted to me. . . .

I am sincerely happy that the Jews in Slovakia and in the rest of the Republic have organized themselves in their own Jewish party and do not want to be the hirelings of other parties. This is the only true guarantee for a relationship of fruitful coexistence with us. Please assure your party that it can always count on my sympathetic support in its endeavors. All I ask of the Slovak Jews is that they will show understanding for our own cultural endeavors, for Slovak art and literature, and that they will also support them. If they will do so, I can assure you that nothing will happen, and nothing will be permitted to happen, that would in any manner obstruct our peaceful, common efforts for the preservation of the moral, social, and administrative order of this state. My personal background rules out any anti-Semitic agitation. You know that at the time of the collapse [of the monarchy] it was I who used my influence and my personal popularity — at the risk of both — to protect the Jews whenever their lives and property were threatened. . . .

At the end of the conversation, Hlinka declared that he would have his party press stop printing attacks on the Jews.

On August 23 and 24, 1936, the Central Committee of the Jewish party in Czechoslovakia met in Štub. Teplice. Deputy Dr. Goldstein and Dr. Weiner, the party's deputy chairman, reported on the first World Jewish Congress, which they had attended. Deputy Dr. Kugel reviewed the political situation and the activities of the party's representatives in Parliament, and Dr. Reisz reported on his activities as a member of the Slovak Provincial Assembly. Dr. Leo Zelmanovits, the party's secretary-general, dealt with the organizational work of the party, while Ernst Frischer, the party's chairman, surveyed the overall situation and activities of the party and its Executive Board. The meeting dealt in detail with the relationship between the Jewish party and the other political parties in the country.

The two representatives of the Jewish party in parliament maintained close contact with their constituents. Their day-to-day schedule included numerous and varied interventions with the authorities. Deputy Dr. Kugel succeeded in bringing relief to the Jewish inhabitants of Dusina, Subcarpathian Ruthenia, who had been passed over in the reallotment of farm land by the Agricultural Bureau some time before. While seventy gentile peasants had received one to three *joch** of land each, the Jews had received nothing. Twenty-three Jews turned to Dr. Kugel and to the Secretariat of the Jewish party in Mukačevo, stating that they had to have pastureland in order to be able to get sufficient milk from their cattle for their personal needs. Thanks to Dr. Kugel's intervention with the Agricultural Bureau, nineteen Jewish families were given two *joch* of land each.

There were many complaints that Jews in student military training units and Jewish military personnel were not being permitted to declare themselves members of the Jewish nationality. As a consequence, Deputy Dr. Goldstein put the following questions to the minister of education and the minister of national defense:

1. It has repeatedly come to my attention that teachers at Czech and Slovak schools are putting some pressure on Jewish students not to list their nationality as "Jewish" when filling in their personal records. I am herewith asking the minister for schools and education whether he has knowledge of this and what steps the minister intends to take to remedy the situation and to prevent the recurrence of such incidents.

2. The forms that are given to military personnel to fill in for registration provide space only for entering Czechoslovak, German, Polish, or Hungarian nationality; there is no space for entering Jewish nationality. As a consequence, Jewish soldiers have no way of declaring Jewish nationality. I am herewith asking the minister whether he has knowledge of this and what steps the minister intends to take to remedy the situation and to prevent the recurrence of such incidents.

In a debate on the budget, Dr. Kugel brought additional complaints before the Chamber of Deputies:

Save for a few exceptions, the Czechoslovak Republic is the only state in Europe that has not violated the equality of its Jewish citizens. . . .

* European land-measuring unit (1 joch = $2\frac{1}{2}$ acres).

This imposes on us obligations which, I sincerely declare, we want to discharge with loyalty and dedication. . . . It is in this spirit, too, that we raise our youth to be fit for military service. . . . [Nevertheless] anti-Semitic pamphlets and broadsides have been appearing with growing frequency, and we must note to our regret that these publications, whose contents in many instances clearly run counter to the law for the protection of minorities, have not been confiscated by the Public Prosecutor's Office or by the agencies under the direction of the minister of the interior. In many instances the effects of this [anti-Semitic] propaganda can be seen in the action taken by the authorities in filling vacancies in the civil service, in decisions regarding naturalization, and in the harsh procedures followed by the internal revenue agencies [when dealing with Jews]. . . . Its effects can be seen also in the deportation of many individuals who were born in this country and have been living here for many years. Thus, only a short time ago, thirty-five Jewish families from Michalovce have been arbitrarily deported by the authorities.

The fact is that the economic and social situation of 90 per cent of the Jews in Subcarpathian Ruthenia is distressing in the extreme. . . .

The Jewish minority has been treated unfairly in matters of education. The Jews are the only minority that must support its schools alone (i.e., without government aid).

On December 6, 1936, the Eastern and Western Slovak Districts of the Jewish party met in Žilina to discuss ways of extending the organizational activity of the party's Provincial Secretariat in Bratislava to the region of eastern Slovakia. Dr. Oskar Neumann, who submitted an organization report, made the following motion:

The Bratislava district office of the Jewish party shall open up the region of eastern Slovakia by stages; the first stage shall be the area extending as far east as Košice. Membership dues received from that area shall be turned over to the Bratislava District with the consent of the party leadership.

Dr. Paul März, of Moravská Ostrava, representing the party presidium, expressed his views in the name of the party executive and seconded Neumann's motion. It was agreed that the Provincial Secretariat in Bratislava should establish contacts at once with the individual local groups and delegates in eastern Slovakia.

The Žilina conference also discussed the problem of compulsory Sunday rest, which had aroused considerable controversy even within the Jewish community. The following motion was adopted by the conference:

The conference of the Jewish party held in Žilina on December 6 considers the introduction of general compulsory Sunday rest a serious economic threat to the Jews in Slovakia and Subcarpathian Ruthenia. The Jewish party has been opposed, and is still opposed, to the introduction of compulsory Sunday rest and hereby instructs its representatives in Parliament to continue opposing [the measure].

On November 2, 1936, a draft law designed to weld the Jews in the Historic Lands into a more closely knit unit was debated in the Chamber of Deputies. The bill, which had already been passed by the Senate, provided for a coordinating organization of Jewish religious congregations in Bohemia and Moravia-Silesia. The law in force at the time dated back to 1890. Dr. Goldstein, who presented the proposed new law in the Chamber, said:[57]

As a result of Jewish population mobility many provincial congregations have suffered great losses in their membership so that many of them are no longer in a financial position to discharge their tasks. Relief must be provided. It is imperative that those congregations, which are now barely subsisting, be merged, but this can be done only if there will be in existence higher [Jewish] public bodies with the legal authority to effect such mergers despite possible resistance from separatist and particularistic elements.

The overall organizations existing at present, namely, the Federations of Jewish Religious Congregations and the Supreme Council, do not now possess such authority. The purpose of the new law will be to invest these public bodies, which were originally created on a more or less voluntary basis, with the necessary powers to carry out these important functions.[58]

The debate which ensued produced opposition, which was colored by anti-Semitism. Deputy Jan Ivak, a member of the Slovak Fascist party, attacked the ethics of the Talmud:

The Fascists [he said] do not want to build up barricades against the Jews nor do they want to persecute the Jews. All they ask of the Jews is that they adapt to present-day conditions. The law is inadequate because it does not include a provision compelling the Israelite religious congregations to accommodate the religious sentiments of the Jews to present-day conditions. There is [an element of] danger in the fact that the Jews still believe in the Talmud as they have done for centuries, because the Talmud teaches that Jews need consider only other Jews as their fellow men. For this reason the Fascist party will vote against the law.

On January 15, 1937, a delegation of the Jewish party and the Zionist Organization called on the governor of Subcarpathian Ruthenia. Touching on current Jewish problems, also in connection with the planned gradual establishment of autonomy for Subcarpathian Ruthenia, Dr. Kugel requested the governor to support the endeavors of the Jewish people to develop its national and cultural individuality. The governor replied that

> the population of Subcarpathian Ruthenia is averse to anti-Semitism in every form. There is no fertile ground for Jew-hatred in Subcarpathian Ruthenia, and the fascist elements who want to transplant this bad seed here will fail. . . . The autonomy [of Subcarpathian Ruthenia] will not be to the detriment of any minority. As long as the governor continues in office — and there is no reason for a change in this respect — he will, by virtue of his authority, put a stop to any excesses of hostility. He will also see to it that the Jewish school system will be placed under the care of the state and will be developed as are the Ruthenian schools. . . .

The Jewish party held firm to its demands with regard to Jewish schools. Time after time, delegations were dispatched to the competent authorities. On January 29, 1937, a delegation consisting of Ernst Frischer (the chairman of the Jewish party), Deputies Dr. Goldstein and Dr. Kugel, and Mrs. Irma Polak (who represented the Czechoslovak Tarbut Hebrew Culture Society) was received by Dr. Emil Franke, the minister of education.

The Jewish delegation presented to Franke a detailed oral report and a memorandum setting forth the main problems of Czechoslovak Jewry that were in the province of the ministry of education, particularly problems relating to the Hebrew school system in Subcarpathian Ruthenia. The minister promised to make a serious study of these matters and to do his "utmost" to meet the just claims of the Jewish minority.

Subcarpathian Jewry became a subject of prime concern for the Jewish party. Whatever the Jews in the western part of the Republic knew about Subcarpathian Ruthenia and about their brethren there had been gleaned from lectures and news items. The Jewish party considered it imperative to supplement this lack of knowledge by creating direct personal contacts between these two elements of Czechoslovakia's Jewish population. For this purpose, the Jewish party decided to organize guided tours of Subcarpathian Ruthenia.

The manifold activities of the Jewish party yielded gratifying results. On March 12, 1937, Prime Minister Dr. Milan Hodža received Deputies Dr. Goldstein and Dr. Kugel, and Otto Zucker, the deputy chairman of the Jewish party. The three Jewish spokesmen once again set forth to Hodža the cultural, economic, and social claims of the Jewish minority. Prime Minister Dr. Hodža stated that all the regulations enacted by the government under the declaration on minority questions of February 18, 1937, automatically applied to the Jewish minority as well. Accordingly, the Hebrew elementary schools in Subcarpathian Ruthenia — there were seven such schools at the time — would come under the care of the state.* Likewise, the government accepted the obligation to make proportional allocations from state and other public welfare funds to the newly established Jewish agencies engaged in work for the welfare of the young. Furthermore the bill regarding the introduction of compulsory Sunday rest throughout the Republic would give due consideration to the religious feelings of the Orthodox Jewish population.

The prime minister promised that the other wishes of the party also would be handled favorably and satisfactorily through administrative channels.

It was further agreed that a representative of the Jewish party would be named to the Governor's Council for Subcarpathian Ruthenia, which was about to be established. The function of this body, which consisted of twenty-four members (six members of the Provincial Executive, nine members of the Provincial Assembly, and nine delegates-at-large who were appointed by the government), was to advise the governor of the province on all matters of importance. Dr. Leopold Palkovits was chosen to represent the Jewish minority on the council. This was a great achievement in which the Jewish party could justly take pride.[59]

The Jewish party had planned to hold its national convention in Brno from October 30 to November 1, 1937. However, due to the tense political situation, the party was forced to cancel the convention at the last minute (October 26, 1937):[60]

* [See also Aryeh Sole, Modern Hebrew Education, pp. 401–439 (Ed.)]

JEWISH PARTY CONVENTION POSTPONED

To our Members:

The government's ban on political assemblies also affects our party convention which was called for October 30 to November 1, 1937, in Brno.

We greatly regret that the convention cannot now take place. Our agenda would have included many important items; namely:

1. An analysis of the political situation of the Jewish minority in Czechoslovakia and a solemn demonstration to show that the Jews of the Czechoslovak Republic in these difficult days are giving their loyal political support to democracy and to the leadership of the state.

2. A detailed report to the party delegates setting forth what the party has done for Czechoslovak Jewry within the past two years. The party leaders expected in good conscience that the report would meet with the approval of the convention.

3. We planned to acquaint all the members of our party, and through them the entire Jewish public, with the importance of the work of the Jewish party in view of present political conditions. We had hoped that our urgent appeal and the effect of the grand scale of the convention — we already had received reservations from 240 delegates — would further inspire the Jewish populations of Czechoslovakia to take an active part in the political struggle for Jewish rights. We also planned to discuss the extent to which Jewry should take action against anti-Semitism, which is on the rise also in Czechoslovakia.

4. The convention was to have elected a new slate of officers and new members for the party's various governing bodies (Executive Board, Central Committee, et al.) in accordance with democratic principles and with the provisions of the party bylaws. In this election of officers we had planned to see to it that . . . only such individuals would be chosen of whom we could have expected a maximum of achievement for the party.

Since we no longer have a suitable date available in 1937 for a two-day party convention, we have had to postpone the convention indefinitely.

Of course, our party will not stop its work at this time. We shall endeavor to find other means of propaganda in place of political assemblies. Within the next few days we intend to send to all our party members a brief report accompanied by some material which we had planned to present to the convention. Our officials will travel to maintain personal contacts with the local groups.

We expect all our party members and party branches to intensify their efforts to solicit new members and, wherever circumstances will permit it, to organize local groups in cities where such groups do not yet exist.

We trust that our members are aware of the seriousness of the political situation and of the fact that if the question of a law on political parties should arise again we will need a well-organized and strong Jewish party to make sure that the Jews will not be eliminated from the political scene. We trust, therefore, that everyone will do his duty.

Within the last two years the Jewish party has grown into an organization numbering thousands of members. Still, this is not in proportion to the total number of Jews in this country and to the magnitude of the tasks which the party will have to accomplish.

The enforced postponement of the convention will give those who have not yet met their election quotas an opportunity to do so.

We call on all our party officers, officials, and members, from now until the next convention, to do their job to the best of their ability so that the achievements of the period to come will be equal to those of the period just past.

For the Executive Board of the Jewish Party in Czechoslovakia

(Ernst) Frischer
Chairman

Dr. Leo Zelmanovits
Secretary-General

Moravská Ostrava, October 26, 1937

On December 3, 1937, the press carried the following release from the Jewish party with regard to the conference of Dr. Goldstein, Dr. Kugel, and Zucker with Prime Minister Hodža:

GOVERNMENT'S PLEDGE TO JEWISH MINORITY TO BE CARRIED OUT

Meeting of Deputies Dr. Goldstein and Dr. Kugel with Prime Minister Dr. Hodža and Minister [of Social Welfare] Nečas.

In connection with the parliamentary debate on the state budget for the coming year, Deputies Dr. Goldstein and Dr. Kugel had a conversation with Prime Minister Dr. Milan Hodža, who announced to them that the promises which had been made to the Jewish minority this past year would be fulfilled in the very near future.

In view of the revived rumors regarding the introduction of compulsory Sunday rest throughout the state, the deputies had a conference with Minister of Social Welfare Nečas, which yielded satisfactory results.

During a heated debate on the budget in the Slovak Provincial Assembly (November 25, 1937) the Lutheran elder Ludevit Šenšel claimed that the Jews in Slovakia, particularly the young people, were ostentatiously avoiding the use of the language of the state and were conversing loudly in Hungarian in the streets, in the cafes, on trains, and so forth, thereby angering the Slovak public and perhaps provoking the latter into adopting coercive measures. To this Dr. Reisz replied:

> The Jewish youth enjoys speaking the Slovak language and speaks it well. Jewish enrollment at the Slovak schools is relatively large; in the cities of Bratislava and Košice, where there are German and Hungarian as well as Slovak high schools, the Jewish students are mostly to be found in the Slovak high schools. You will find that Jewish university students use Slovak as the official language even in their clubs, and the Makkabi Sports Club has joined the Czechoslovak Athletic Organization rather than its Hungarian counterpart. The Jewish youth in Slovakia vies with Slovak youth in cultivating the Slovak language and literature, and so I submit that the accusations from the Elder might only be true in the case of a very few isolated and regrettable exceptions. . . .

The new year brought grave anxiety to Czechoslovak Jewry. It was becoming clear that Europe was headed for a new and terrible crisis. Within a few short years Hitler had occupied the Rhineland, introduced universal conscription in his country, and incorporated Austria into "Greater Germany." The democracies had not even attempted to stop him. With neighboring Austria occupied by Hitler's armies, the future of Czechoslovakia and her 325,000 Jews — not counting the many Jewish refugees who had found a haven there — was increasingly in doubt.

On May 15 and 16 — a little over two months after Hitler's annexation of Austria — the Jewish party held the national convention which originally had been scheduled for the preceding fall. Special attention was given to current events within the country and the imminent local elections. The chairman of the party reported on "The Basic Principles of Jewish National Politics in the Czechoslovak Republic":

> The Jews have fully identified themselves with the Republic. They know very well that they will have to share its fate for better or for worse. Without exception and without reservations, they stand behind the Czechoslovak people and the Czechoslovak State. They have placed all their moral and economic resources at its disposal and are ready to give their lives and their possessions if need be.

The Jewish party called for an amendment of the electoral law for small nationality groups to enable these groups — including the Jews — to put up their own candidates for Parliament without having to enter into complicated election agreements with other parties. The party further demanded that the Hebrew school system should come under the care of the state, and that the state should subsidize the Jewish school system in the Historic Lands and accord official status to Jewish welfare agencies.

Deputy Dr. Goldstein addressed the convention on "The Political Situation in Czechoslovakia and the Jewish Minority" and on the Statute of Nationalities which was then being prepared by the government.

Chairman Frischer called on the delegates "to weld the party into an instrument which, by virtue of its unity . . . will be able to make the vital self-defense of Czechoslovak Jewish rights even more effective than it was in the past."

During the general discussion it was suggested that the next party convention take place in Košice to enable a larger number of Jews to attend.

Deputies Dr. Goldstein and Dr. Kugel came under criticism from Moshe Goldstein of Mukačevo for their handling of the problems of compulsory Sunday rest and ritual slaughter.

Frischer was reelected chairman of the party; Otto Zucker and Schwarzbarth were elected vice presidents. Moshe Goldstein of Mukačevo was elected third vice president. No changes were made in the Central Committee.*

Bratislava's local elections were called for June 12, 1938.

The slogan of the Jews was: "Not one Jewish vote must be lost!" This time the Jewish National party, the Orthodox party, and the Po'ale Zion stood for election together. The unified party list constituted a significant political and moral achievement. However, the atmosphere of Jewish unity was spoiled two days before the election when leaflets were distributed in the Jewish neighborhoods calling on the Jewish voters to support the list of the government coalition. In addition, Hasidic circles launched a whispering campaign

---

* Paul März noted that this party convention foreshadowed the "disintegration of the Jewish party and the passing of Jewish leadership to the Zionist Organization of Czechoslovakia. Yet, as late as in the later summer of 1938 [i. e., subsequent to the partial mobilization of the country declared on May 21 (Ed.)], while the Zionist Organization was addressing itself to *Aliya*, *Halutziyut*, and basic vocational reorientation, the Jewish party launched a propaganda campaign for the purpose of rescuing the Jews in the Sudetenland." See Grossmann, pp. 571 ff.

to spread the word that "a Jew must vote for the government." As a result, the Jewish list was deprived of a substantial number of Jewish votes.

Despite the increasing Nazi threat to Czechoslovakia, the Jewish party continued to concern itself with the plight of the Jews in other countries. Thus, it carefully studied the questions raised at the Evian Conference on Refugees (July 6, 1938) and adopted a special resolution on the subject.[61]

Echoing the declaration made at the party's Brno Convention that the Jews were ready to sacrifice their lives and possessions for Czechoslovakia, the Organization Committee of Jewish War Veterans and Ex-Servicemen issued the following proclamation:

> The anxieties with which our community is beset demands complete devotion from each and every one of us. Each and every one of us is duty-bound to support Jewry in its struggle. . . . We therefore call upon the Jewish war veterans and ex-servicemen to join in one union, not only in order to guard our interests, but also in order to demonstrate in a manifest and vigorous manner that we are one with our native soil and with the ideals of our republic in devotion and in sincerity. An organization of Jewish war veterans and ex-servicemen will be best suited to give the lie to the myth that the Jews are "slackers."

Meanwhile, the debate on Jewish minority rights set off by the proposed Statute of Nationalities triggered a bitter press campaign against the Jews. An editorial in the *Nedělní Listy* (*Sunday News*) of July 31, 1938, warned that the ratio of Jewish employees in the civil service was too high and would work to the detriment of the Czechs and Slovaks who sought employment there. In reply it was argued that the local German nationals would not consider Jewish officials as Germans — even though they spoke German — but would count them as Czechs.

> In the case of the railroads, for instance, only 0.54 per cent of the employees are Jewish, or 73.8 per cent less than would be commensurate with the proportion of Jews in the total population. Only 1.02 per cent of the civilian employees of the army in Slovakia are Jewish, or 77 per cent less than would be the Jewish share according to the total population. Of the postal, telegraph, and telephone employees, only 1.46 per cent are Jews, or 67 per cent less than would correspond to their quota. Of the state and public administrative employees, 3.2 per cent are Jews, or 29 per cent less than would correspond to their quota. The percentage

of Jews in the total population of Slovakia is 4.35, and by rights this should also be the approximate proportion in which the Jews should be represented in the civil service. The ratio in the Historic Lands is much the same. Hence, if we really were to accept the demands of the *Nedělní Listy*, the civil service actually would have to accept an even greater number of Jewish employees.*

Noted liberal Czech journalists took up the problems of anti-Semitism, refugees, and Jewish assimilation to the Czech people. In the popular periodical *Přítomnost* (*The Present*), of which he was the editor, Ferdinand Peroutka published (January 19, 1938) an editorial entitled "Comments on the Czech People and the Jews." Since Peroutka was not an anti-Semite but a liberal journalist and a disciple of both Masaryk and Beneš, his editorial evoked wide discussion in the Jewish press and elsewhere.[62]

Notwithstanding the developments in the Sudetenland, anti-Semitism and anti-Semitic press agitation showed no sign of abating. A Sunday edition of *Národní Politika* (*National Policy*), the newspaper with the largest circulation in Czechoslovakia, carried an article entitled "Židé mezi námi" (The Jews in Our Midst). Among other things, the author of the article wrote:[63]

The Jews are always concerned only with their own, and never with national or human interests. The Jews have acquired the habit of exploiting other races for their own benefit. Generous funds were raised here for the Jewish immigrants while our own citizens could have starved [for all the Jews cared]. These immigrants have found employment and protection at the expense of our citizens. They earn money but evade the tax laws. In return for the support they enjoy here, they behave in a most reprehensible manner. They are spies. . . . As far as the Jews in general are concerned, authors of world renown have taught us and demonstrated that the Jews suffer from an inferiority complex which they convert into a lust for power. The Jews — and the writer wishes to emphasize that this does not only apply to Jewish refugees — spread unrest and revolt wherever they may be. They are making money here and they think that we, the Czechs, should make it possible for them to return to Germany, at the cost of our own possessions and our own lives. The Jews are incapable of making sacrifices or of taking chances on their own. Note also that the Jews who are vacationing at Czech and Slovak

* It should be noted that this debate took place only eight weeks prior to the Munich Agreement, which in effect delivered Czechoslovakia into the hands of Nazi Germany.

spas are talking in German. Now that they have been thrown out of the spas in Germany, they display their lust for power here in our midst. They demand the best rooms, the best seats in the dining rooms; they act as if they alone were entitled to special privileges. . . . Naturally, we shall close with a warning. Let the Jews be less pretentious and show more gratitude to Czechoslovakia in the way they act. They ought not pto rovoke our people by talking German and by their lack of consideration for others. Their conduct could easily produce an anti-Semitic movement even here with all the consequences which the Jews would not find to their liking at all. . . .*

It was hoped that in those days of crisis the nationwide local elections would provide a link of moral unity for Czechoslovak Jewry. The Jewish party spared no effort to this end, and issued a special appeal to the Jews of the country.[64] The difference between these elections and those of the past was only too clearly apparent. The Jewish party had to contend with a "liquidation psychosis" that had gripped the Jews of Czechoslovakia. At the same time, the Jews considered themselves inextricably bound up with the Republic, which was fast approaching its hour of decision. It was the hope of the Jewish party that the election campaign would be characterized by calm and moderation throughout the state. In those days anti-Semitic agitation was a matter of concern not merely to the Jews; it constituted a serious disturbance of the peace and of amicable relations among the nationalities within the Republic. The Jews were faced with the challenge of mustering their forces under completely new conditions. The position of the Jews in the border areas of Czechoslovakia was particularly precarious; they suffered from economic and political terror and from the fanatical elements who clamored for total Germanization.

The local elections were conducted with exemplary discipline and with democratic freedom and fairness. The Jewish party was successful wherever it put up candidates, even in communities where it had not won representation before. The number of votes polled by the Jewish party in Greater Prague showed a slight increase as compared to previous elections, although the number of mandates obtained by the Jews remained the same as in the past.

---

* These accusations of course, were not founded on fact. Most of the refugees in Czechoslovakia — both Jews and Gentiles — were subsisting on relief. Cf. Grossmann, pp. 567 ff.

The Jewish party succeeded in obtaining most of the Jewish votes cast. Those Jews who in the past had voted for German parties now gave their votes to Czech parties.

For the first time, a major Czechoslovak political party had run on a clear-cut anti-Semitic platform — Stříbrný's National League, which also dominated much of the tabloid press. Every day the public was bombarded with vitriolic anti-Semitic newspaper articles, especially in the *Express* and in the *Pražský List* (*Prague News*). Yet, surprisingly, this party went down in utter defeat, losing 50 per cent of its former strength — a development which spoke well for the good common sense of the Czech people.

The third phase of the local elections yielded the good results which the Jewish lists had expected. Altogether, the Jews received more than eleven thousand votes and gained over sixty seats in local governing bodies throughout the nation. The total number of votes received by the Jews in all three phases of the elections was thirty-five thousand; they obtained a total of 130 seats in local governing bodies.

The increasingly critical political situation gave rise to a new phenomenon in Czechoslovak Jewish communal life; namely, a rise in the number of official resignations from membership in the Jewish community. During the first half of the year 1938, 31 individuals took this step in Moravská Ostrava (as compared to 29 during the entire year of 1937). In Brno, 38 individuals did so. In Prague (District I–VII), as many as 154 individuals left the Jewish community during that period as compared to 65 during the entire preceding year; in Prague's Twelfth District, the number of resignations for that time span was 73, as compared to 57 during all of 1937. Within a few weeks, 11 persons had resigned from the Jewish community in the small Slovak town of Banská Bystrica.

On September 30, 1938, immediately after Czechoslovakia had been forced to cede the Sudetenland to Nazi Germany, the Jewish party issued the following proclamation:[65]

Our Republic has been dealt a severe blow. An undeserved grievous wrong has been done to the Czechoslovak people. At this moment we gratefully recall the twenty years of the history of this young state which, in the midst of a world infested with anti-Semitism, invited its Jewish citizens to participate in its peaceful upbuilding and granted them full civil and national rights.

We solemnly reiterate our vow of unchanging love and loyalty to this state to whose service the Jews will continue to devote the best of their energies. We have faith and confidence in the state and in its duly constituted leaders. We have faith in the genius of the Czechoslovak people and believe that it will continue unswervingly upon the path of justice and humanity marked out for it by destiny and by its leaders.

At the same time, we are mindful of the bitter fate of our Jewish brethren who are directly and personally affected by this tragic change in our borders and who now must find new places in which to live and work in this state. Bound up with them, as we are, by destiny, we are ready to assist them, and together with them we shall continue to work for our Republic, for the Jewish people, and for our Zionist ideals.

The Executive Committee of the Central Zionist Federation for the Czechoslovak Republic

The Jewish Party

The watchword of the hour was "An Appeal to Ourselves."[66]

In these days we Jews sympathize with this people from the depths of our hearts; we share with them this crisis which, in fact, is our own crisis too. . . . At this time the Czech people has the right to expect us to show consideration for all its sensitivities. This applies to every aspect of public life and also to the matter of language. This must become second nature also with all those of our brethren from the Sudetenland who have moved into Czech areas. . . . We are not asking you to lead lives of unworldly asceticism, but we are asking that you give up, for good and all, the luxuries, the finery and those shallow ways of life. . . which seem out of place and downright lurid in these times. Whatever any one of us may do is subject to more stringent scrutiny than ever before and carries more weight on the scales upon which all the various aspects of the "Jewish problem" are being piled. Today, Jewry must accept collective responsibility for the conduct of each and every Jew no matter how far away he may have been from us only yesterday. . . . The momentous decision that has been made now, and the political changes that are in store for us, will present us with new, and in many instances, very difficult problems. . . . We sense that we have come to a crucial turn in our history. This realization must be reflected also in our own lives, and within the Jewish community for which there is but one common destiny. . . . Our generation is facing a life that is difficult and without mercy, but then who can count the generations before us that found themselves face to face with similar crises? No matter what befell, through centuries of darkness, insecurity and danger, they continued on their way. Almost without cease they were forced to run the gantlet of the ages. And even then they trod their path with dignity and inner strength, with yearning and with greatness. Now the chain has passed into our hands and we shall pass it on.[67]

September 30, 1938, the day of the Munich Agreement, marked the end of an era in the history of the world. After the signing of this treaty, which was meant to buy peace at the expense of Czechoslovakia, that Republic could no longer be considered as a state composed of many nationalities but had to be viewed as one single national entity. However, the Jews wanted to remain loyal to the Czechoslovak State as a nationality group in their own right. They took an active part in the mobilization of the country. They resolved to keep calm, to do their duty, and to carry on their Zionist work in all its aspects.[68]

The resignation of Eduard Beneš from the presidency of the Czechoslovak Republic marked the end of the Jewish party as an active entity in the country.[69] Jewish leaders who had been entrusted with the task of protecting the rights of Jewish citizens in a democratic state still stood waiting in the wings. However, they were forced to watch helplessly while the Jews were being stripped of their rights — a process which the great powers of the world were unable or unwilling to arrest.

Thus, a great and honorable chapter in the history of Jewish epresentation in the Diaspora was forcibly brought to an end.

* * *

APPENDIX A

BRATISLAVA, AUGUST 1, 1919
THE NATIONAL FEDERATION OF SLOVAK JEWS
REPORT FROM THE JEWISH PRESS BUREAU, BRATISLAVA

As is well known, the Paris Peace Conference, in June, drew up the permanent frontiers between the Czechoslovak Republic and Hungary. Under this agreement, the entire northern part of the former kingdom of Hungary, which is chiefly inhabited by Slovaks, and where Czechoslovak military and civilian authorities have been in control since the beginning of this year, goes to the new Czechoslovak State.

This development has brought an important change in the citizenship status of several hundred thousand Jews. Thanks to the efforts of the Prague Jewish National Council, the representatives of the most influential Jewish communities in Slovakia met as early as March 25 last in Piešťány to discuss steps to be taken for the protection of the political, economic, and social interests of Slovak Jewry within the framework of the new state. At this conference it was decided that a National Federation of Slovak Jews should be created, with headquarters in Bratislava.

The federation will endeavor to bring all the Jews of Slovakia into its organization in order to develop it into an influential, legitimate representative body of the Jewish people. It may be said that, by virtue of the recognition it immediately received from the state, the federation has attained a public and legal status which augurs well for its effective performance.

The aims of the Federation are as follows:

Political: The assertion of the civic and communal rights of the Jews in the measure as such rights have been guaranteed by the Constitution of the Republic to all other citizens, religious communities, and races.

Economic: Free and unhampered activity for Jews in commerce, industry, the trades, and agriculture; the unrestricted practice of all the professions; the preservation of all the rights to which the Jewish population is entitled under the law in this area, within the framework and in the spirit of the present constitution.

Social: The furtherance of all endeavors to promote harmony, peace, and unity within Jewish society; the awakening and strengthening of Jewish public-spiritedness and solidarity; the enlistment of the broadest possible strata of the Jewish population for full-fledged cooperation in the affairs of the communities and of Jewish public institutions in the spirit of our times.

In its brief existence the federation has already achieved notable successes. Mention should be made, first and foremost, of the change for the better in the treatment accorded to Jewish refugees; this change is due to the efforts of the federation in cooperation with the Jewish National Council for Bohemia. The Social Commission of the federation is working to the best of its ability to prevent the pauperization of the Jewish masses. For the time being, the commission has received a subsidy in the amount of 100,000 korunas from the American Jewish Joint Distribution Committee (JDC), through the good offices of Mr. H. Alsberg, the JDC representative. On the basis of data gathered on past anti-Semitic lootings in Slovakia, the commission is to work toward the economic rehabilitation of the Jews who have lost their livelihoods [as a result of these outrages].

By intervening with the competent authorities, the Bratislava office of the federation in innumerable cases was able to help individual Jewish victims of persecution obtain their rightful due. Particularly, the office has successfully pleaded the cause of Jews held as hostages and of a large number of Jewish citizens who had been placed under arrest on unfounded charges. In most instances the office was able to secure the release of such individuals.

On June 24 a large deputation from the federation was received by President Masaryk at Hradčany Castle. Acting as spokesman of the deputation, Dr. Ludvik Singer, a member of the Prague Jewish National Council, described the frequent harassments to which the Jewish population of Slovakia has been subjected and asked the president for protection. A memorandum from the federation was handed to the president. Theodor Wister, of Nové Mesto nad Váhom, the president of the federation, pointed out that the Jews in Slovakia sought no special privileges of any sort; they only wanted to register their claim to equal rights under the law and before the government. It was for this reason, too, that they attached great importance to obtaining representation in the legislative branch of the government.

In his response, President Masaryk said that he was aware of the precarious situation of the Jews in Slovakia, which was due primarily to political circumstances. He promised to make a careful study of the complaints and the wishes of the Jews. In conclusion, he assured his visitors that he would give his active support, within the scope of his constitutional powers, to the demand of the Jews for the seating of Jewish representatives in Parliament. The president noted down the individual cases, reported to him by the deputation, of illegal acts perpetrated against Jewish citizens and showed special interest in the problems of Jewish schools, the [unlawful] internment of Jews, and the distribution of anti-Semitic broadsides. The president parted from the deputation on the friendliest terms and with the assurance that he would see to it that the Jews in Slovakia would be treated as equal citizens at all times.

One of the main tasks of the federation will be to support the Jewish school system in Slovakia, the survival of which has been gravely endangered by the shortage of Slovak teachers. The federation has already taken steps to ensure the continued survival of Jewish schools as far as possible.

Within the next few days a new Jewish newspaper, edited by Moritz Zobel, will make its debut in Bratislava under the aegis of the federation. For the present it will appear weekly, but it is hoped that it will eventually beome a daily. Entitled *Jüdische Volkszeitung* (*The Jewish People's Paper*), it will primarily serve the political, economic, and social interests of Slovak Jewry and maintain contacts with the Jewish world abroad. The publisher is the Jewish Publishing Company of Prague, which already has sizable capital reserves and is planning to publish also other Jewish publicistic, scholarly, and belletristic writings.

The address of the federation and of the *Jüdische Volkszeitung* is 14 Turnergasse, Bratislava, Czechoslovakia.

APPENDIX B

MEMORANDUM FROM THE JEWISH STUDENT BODY TO THE ACADEMIC SENATE

Following an announcement from the Academic Senate of the 16th of this month to the effect that a Students' Council is to be created for which only students who profess German nationality will have the right to vote and to be elected to membership, the representatives of the Central Federation of Jewish University Students and its affiliated fraternities have presented the following memorandum to the rector:

The Central Federation of Jewish University Students in Prague and its affiliated fraternities most sharply protest against the announcement posted on the notice board by the honored Academic Senate regarding the creation of a Students' Council at the German University in Prague, for which only students who profess German nationality will have the right to vote and to be elected to membership. The Central Federation of Jewish University Students and its affiliated fraternities wish to point out that the demands submitted in its memorandum late in June of this year have been quietly ignored by the honored Academic Senate. Therefore, in order to assert its rights in the face of this practice, which constitutes a gross violation of all academic and civil rights, the Jewish student body finds itself compelled to turn to the competent authorities for redress.

(signed) Central Federation of Jewish University Students in Prague; Union of Jewish Medical Students at the German University in Prague; Jewish Academic and Technical Clubs "Barissia"-"Jordania"; Literary and Lecturing Society of Jewish University Students in Prague; Bar Kokhba Association of Jewish University Students; Makkabi Association of Jewish University Students

At the same time the Central Federation of Jewish University Students has issued the following appeal:

AN APPEAL TO JEWISH STUDENTS

Jewish Fellow Students:

Not long ago the entire intellectual public which still possesses a sane sense of justice was shocked by the notorious Steinherz affair. More recently, we have learned of another *coup de main*, this one aimed at the Jewish students of the German University. This blow constitutes a gross violation of all academic law and dignity. What is more, it appears that the members of the committee in charge of arrangements for the Students' Council, who seem to be endowed either with great optimism or with abysmal naiveté, have given no thought to the serious consequences of such action. For we read in the announcement from the Academic Senate, dated June 23, 1924, and posted on the notice board of the German University, that only those students who profess German nationality will have the right to vote in elections to the Students' Council or to be elected to the council. The Jewish student body, which, as is well known, constitutes a minority at the German University, was quietly ignored; thus its future was left to the mercies of a "German-Aryan collective," from which we have cause to expect only the final [indignity]; namely, the establishment of a *numerus clausus* [Jewish quota].

Therefore, as the principal and central corporation of all the Jewish university students in Prague, the Central Federation of Jewish University Students in Prague appeals to you, Jewish follow students, to stand behind us in our common struggle against this outrage, unless each and every one of us is willing to accept responsibility for the complete disfranchisement of the Jewish students. In a day and age and in a state in which the equality of all citizens has been recognized as an immutable principle before the law, not to speak of the clause in the peace treaties guaranteeing complete equality for all citizens with respect to education, we Jews, who have liberally given of our talents and industry to all branches of modern culture, the sons of a people of learning and of zest for study, have the right to be accepted as equal academic citizens also at the German University in Prague. It seems to us that, in view of the principles of autonomy which it has consistently stressed, this university in particular should be practicing to a greater extent the lessons learned from the struggle which its own representatives waged for minority rights in our own state.

How can the parliameutary representatives of the Germans demand equal rights for themselves in Czechoslovakia if, once they themselves have autonomous powers, they will act every day and at every hour in violation of their own principles and demands?

Jewish fellow students, your attitude alone will determine your future position at the German University.

(signed) Central Federation of Jewish University Students in Prague; Union of Jewish Medical Students at the German University of Prague; Jewish Academic and Technical Clubs "Barissia"-"Jordania"; Literary and Lecturing Society of Jewish University Students in Prague; Bar Kokhba Association of Jewish University Students, Prague; Makkabi

Association of Jewish University Students, Prague; Theodor Herzl Association of Jewish University Students

— *Selbstwehr*, September 26, 1924

APPENDIX C

MEMORANDUM FROM THE ZIONIST STUDENT BODY TO THE TWO RECTORS

The Conference of Zionist Students has voted to send delegations to the rectors of the German University in Prague to explain the viewpoint of the Zionist students and to present to the rectors the following memorandum:

Your Magnificence:

The undersigned representatives of the Jewish National Student Body, delegated by the conference which was held on Tuesday, the nineteenth of this month, in the auditorium of the Jewish Town Hall, herewith rake the liberty of submitting to you the following statement:

On the eighteenth of this month Jewish students who, in fulfillment of their academic duty, had reported for lectures and classes at a number of institutions of the German University and Technical College, were attacked by organized groups of anti-Semitic demonstrators, physically assaulted and injured, and forcibly removed from the premises. The demonstrators went so far as to physically attack our female fellow students.

The Jewish National Student Body is deeply shocked at these incidents.

The Jewish academic corporations are doing all they can to calm down the Jewish students and to combat these attacks in a completely legal and academic fashion.

In view of this loyal attitude on their part, the Jewish students are taking the liberty of informing Your Magnificence of these incidents and, at the same time, of protesting to the honored Academic Senate against any and all abuses of academic freedom.

At the same time the representatives of the Jewish students respectfully request Your Magnificence to make every effort to ensure freedom of teaching and study and the security of the Jewish students.

— *Selbstwehr*, November 22, 1929

Resolution Adopted by Conference

The Jewish student body, which met on November 19, 1929, in the auditorium of the Jewish Town Hall in Prague, has noted recent events at the German Universities with profound regret. The Jewish students are deeply shocked at the barbaric but obviously organized attacks by rowdyish anti-Semitic students on Jewish students of both sexes who had come to the lectures with the intention of quietly pursuing their work and their duties.

The Jewish student body sharply condemns the acts of the anti-Semitic demonstrators and is determined to employ every legal means to counter the attacks made on the personal safety of peaceable Jewish students of both sexes and on the academic freedom of Jewish students. The Jewish students of both sexes expect the academic authorities to take all the necessary steps to ensure the undisturbed continuation of academic activities. They further expect the academic authorities to conduct a thorough investigation of the incidents and to call the instigators and all the guilty parties to account.

The Jewish student body, which has united to form a defense organization, has approved the steps which its leaders have taken to date; it has complete confidence in them and has called upon them to take effective action against this terror with all the means at their disposal. The Jewish student body is firmly determined not to allow itself to be provoked by the acts of the anti-Semitic rowdies but to maintain discipline and to follow the instructions of its leaders. It expresses its appreciation to its leaders for their effort in preserving order and moderation among the Jewish students. The Jewish student body has complete confidence in the government and in the authorities of the Czechoslovak Republic and is certain that the competent agencies will exert every effort to guarantee the personal safety and the academic freedom of all the students at the universities in Prague.

— *Selbstwehr*, November 22, 1929

The Views of the Press

On the whole, the Czech press has shown considerable understanding and sympathy for the claims of the Czech medical students, although it has treated the problem of foreign students with great reserve. On the other hand, it has been most outspoken in its opposition to the acts of terror perpetrated by the Deutsch-Völkische [German nationals] at the German University and Technical College and has demanded that the most stringent measures possible be taken to stop these disturbers of the peace.

The nationalist *Národní Listy* alone was unable to refrain from also taking this opportunity to agitate against the Jews in the basest fashion. It has hurled sensational accusations at the Jewish students for supposedly having arranged demonstrations together with the Communists against the state and the Czech people. Of course, not one syllable of these charges is based on fact. The Jewish students have never had a part in such demonstrations; on the contrary, the Communists had actually attempted to break up the Zionist mass protest rally held at the Jewish Town Hall.

As regards the problem of aliens, the *České Slovo*, the newspaper of Foreign Minister Beneš, states:

The reputation and renown of any university is measured primarily in terms of its enrollment of foreign students, and if anything were to change in this respect, institutions like Oxford University in England and the Sorbonne in Paris would have had to close down long ago. The Charles University of Prague has enjoyed an excellent reputation ever since the Middle Ages. Today, primarily in the eyes of the Balkan States, Prague represents a mecca of learning with the school of medicine in particular enjoying universal esteem. It goes without saying that foreign students will continue to study in Prague and that they will always be welcome here.

— *Selbstwehr*, December 13, 1929

APPENDIX D

A conference of delegates from the Subcarpathian Ruthenian District of the Czechoslovak Jewish party took place on June 21, 1931, in Mukačevo. It acknowledged with thanks a report made by Deputy Dr. Singer, and after giving him an unqualified vote of confidence, pledged its most vigorous support for his future efforts.

The conference then welcomed the newly organized branch of the Jewish party in the Subcarpathian Ruthenia District and appealed to all Jews to work for it with dedicated vigor. The party's representatives in Parliament were urged to pay frequent visits to the district to keep in close touch with the Jewish masses there.

The conference noted with regret that, throughout the prevailing economic crisis, the Provincial Authority for Subcarpathian Ruthenia had done nothing to alleviate the particular hardships of the pauperized Jews in the province.

On the other hand, we noted with satisfaction Dr. Singer's report that naturalization matters have been handled with more consideration. Furthermore, the conference urged all Jewish deputies in Parliament to make a concerted effort to see that the naturalization law is enforced in such a manner as to ensure that the thousands of homeless individuals concerned will receive their rightful due.

The conference noted with regret that the two Jewish members of Subcarpathian Ruthenia's Provincial Assembly, who owed their election to Jewish votes, had seen fit to support every measure of the assembly designed to bring about the economic ruin of Jews in small businesses and trade, especially those living in rural areas. A blatant example was the vote taken to guarantee ten million korunas which the Provincial Assembly appropriated for the support of the National Association of Cooperative Stores.

"We wholeheartedly approve of Dr. Singer's standpoint," the conference declared, "as repeatedly expressed by him in his parliamentary statements, thereby demonstrating our wholehearted sympathy for the emancipation of the Ruthenian people. We protest against, and resolutely denounce, any attempt to exploit certain Jewish elements for the purpose of stunting the development of the Ruthenian people by means truly unworthy of the cultural tradition of the Czech nation. At the same time, we request justice for the Jewish minority. We are determined to stand up for our rights."

— *Selbstwehr*, June 29, 1931

APPENDIX E

RESOLUTIONS OF THE PARTY CONVENTION POLICY

The convention noted the reports of the party officials and gave its approval to the political activities of the party's leadership and of its deputies in Parliament. In view of the approaching new elections, it proposed that the Jewish National minority continue its present policy. The convention then authorized all the competent party authorities to institute steps necessary to assure the continuation of this political activity.

JEWISH VOCATIONAL COUNSELING

The economic situation of the Jewish population in the Czechoslovak Republic is deteriorating by the day. One of the causes of the rise in poverty is the fact that the Jewish population is concentrated in only a few occupations. It therefore seems imperative that Jewish vocational guidance offices should be set up in every locality with a large Jewish population in order to influence the Jewish youth in their choice of vocation so as to promote the normalization of the economic structure of Czechoslovak Jewry. The convention called upon its delegates to use their influence to help set up Jewish guidance offices in localities with a substantial Jewish population without delay, i.e., before the end of the current academic year. The proposed guidance offices are to be patterned on those already existing in Moravská Ostrava.

The Elections

Chairman of the party: Dr. Emil Margulies, Litoměřice.

Executive Board: Vice-chairmen: Ernst Frischer (Moravská Ostrava); Dr. Chaim Kugel, (Mukačevo); Dr. Matej Weiner (Liptovský Sväty Mikuláš).

Other members of the Executive Board: Norbert Adler, Ernst Freud, Dr. František Gottlieb, Dr. Zděnek Landes, Marie Schmolka, and Paul Zucker (Prague); Dr. Paul März (Moravská Ostrava); Dr. Karl Sonnenfeld (Brno); Dr. Josef Michael Eisler (Hlohovec); Dr. Alexander Márton (Žilina); Dr. Leo Sipos (Parkaň); Dr. Adalbert Winterstein (Bánovce n/Bebr); Dr. Wilhelm Sternbach (Mukačevo).

Central Committee: Dr. H. Birnbaum (Teplice-Šanov); Dr. E. Justic (Plzeň); Paul Kauders, and Leopoldine Klein (Prague); Dr. Milan Kollman (Hradec Králové); Dr. Fritzi Margulies (Litoměřice); Irma Polak, and Hanna Steiner (Prague); Dr. Hugo Stránský (Náchod); Rudolf Vodička and A. Kubiček (Prague); Dr. S. Bernstein, Dr. A. Feldmann, and Theodor Huber (Brno); Dr. Ottmar Huss (Mor. Ostrava); Dr. Robert Lichtwitz (Opava); Dr. Marek Lasus (Prostějov); Julius Pick (Znojmo); Fritz Sborowitz (Prostějov); Dr. Leo Zelmanovits (Mor. Ostrava); Dr. Oskar Zweigenthal (Olomouc); I. Sommer and D. Schüller (Brno); Dr. Ernst Bermann (Nový Jičín); F. N. Reisner (Bratislava); Isidor Rosenfeld (Trnava); B. Jellinek (Štub. Teplice); Director Isidor Knöpfelmacher (Bratislava); E. Magram (Trnava); H. Slattner (Košice); Dr. Fischer (Ružomberok); Dr. Tiroler (Banská Bystrica); Dr. Erdös (Dunajská Streda); A. Wohlstein (Nové Mesto n. Váhom); Dr. Gartner (Prešov); Dr. Otto Löbl, S. Schwarzbart, and J. M. Schwarz (Bratislava); I. Winkelberg (Košice); Dr. Süss (Trenčín); Dr. L. Nagy (Lučenec); Josef Müller (Hlohovec); I. Goldberger (Košice); Siegmund Franz (Bratislava); Dr. Pollak (Nové Mesto); Moshe Goldstein (Mukačevo); Dr. Breslauer (Užhorod); O. Goldberger (Užhorod); Dr. Leopold Palkovits (Užhorod); B. Koreny (Užhorod); Dr. Lesmann (Sevluš); Dr. Bolgar (Hust).

Alternates: Dr. Skutetzky (Trutnov); Dr. M. Goldes (Teplice-Šanov); Olga Bobasch (Prague); E. Kohner (Podhořany); Dr. Königstein (Litoměřice); B. Kier (Mor. Ostrava); Karl Finzi (Opava); Dr. Silbiger (Bohumin); Dr. Richard Teltscher (Mikulov); Dr. Willi Samstag (Znojmo); Dr. O. Mayer (Olomouc); Edmund Gold (Břeclava); Adler

(Trnava); Fried (Žilina); Auriel Altmann (Rajec); N. Reiss (Vel'ká Bytča); Dr. Erwin Müller (Bratislava); Dr. Oskar Neumann (Bratislava); Dr. E. Reitler (Bardejov); Dr. D. Kronovits (Košice); Dr. Bernard Fürst (Bratislava); Rudolf Braun (Žilina); Sigmund Berger (Mukačevo); David Steiger (Velké Berezné); J. Rosenberg (Mukačevo); J. Rosenberg (Bratislava); K. Ornstein (Košice); Dr. Max Roth (Nitra).

Court of Arbitration: Dr. Ottmar Huss (Mor. Ostrava), chairman; Dr. Emil Müller (Mor. Ostrava); Dr. Auerbach (Český Těšín); Dr. Füredy (Bratislava); Dr. E. Roth (Žilina); Dr. J. Goldes (Teplice-Šanov); Dr. W. Spitz (Karlovy Vary).

Auditors: Paul Vodička (Prague); Rudolf Eisenstein (Prague).

— *Selbstwehr*, January 4, 1935

APPENDIX F

RESOLUTIONS ADOPTED BY THE CONVENTION

POLITICAL RESOLUTIONS

1. The convention notes with satisfaction and gratitude the reports submitted by the temporary chairman, the Executive Board, and the secretary-general concerning past activities and action in connection with the parliamentary, provincial, and local elections. At the same time the convention herewith approves the resolutions adopted by the Central Committee, which alone, under the present circumstances, has enabled the Jewish minority to obtain representation in Parliament.

The convention especially desires to express its gratification that the electoral agreement and the orderly conduct of the Jewish electorate clearly demonstrated the democratic principles of the Jewish party, and that, thanks to the Jewish electorate, the democratic front of the state was strengthened and thus achieved success in the election.

The convention offers its felicitations to the newly elected deputies, Dr. Angelo Goldstein and Dr. Chaim Kugel, and anticipates their parliamentary activity with trust and confidence.

The convention expresses its appreciation to the Jewish electorate for its loyal adherence to the party platform, and hereby pledges that the party will continue to act purposefully and with vigor to protect the interests of the Jewish people, as it has in the past.

2. Convinced that unity and harmony in the ranks of Jewry are the only effective means of coping with the menace of anti-Semitism, the

convention hereby instructs the executive vigorously to defend the unity and harmony of the party against all who would destroy it.

Accordingly, the convention hails the harmonious cooperation of Czechoslovak Jewry with world Jewry and notes that the Jewish party has named the following gentlemen as its delegates to the *Délégation des Juives** and the organs of this cooperation: Ernst Frischer and Deputy Dr. Angelo Goldstein. Dr. Michael Eisler and Deputy Dr. Chaim Kugel have been named alternates.

3. In view of the important political and economic role of the Jewish nation in Czechoslovakia, the convention hereby expresses the hope that the government will appoint Jewish representatives to the Provincial Assemblies and to the various bodies of local government.

Economic Resolutions

The convention hereby resolves to create an Economic Advisory Council, to consist of experts in the field of economics, whose function it will be to submit to the Jewish party suggestions, recommendations, and plans relating to the economic problems of the Jewish minority. In addition, the Jewish party shall support all endeavors aimed at the improvement of Jewish economic life in this state.

Resolutions on Social Issues

The convention requests the executive to give vigorous support to all Jewish welfare work in Czechoslovakia.

It hereby expresses its appreciation to the Jewish Ladies' Aid Committee for Subcarpathian Ruthenia for its achievements. It also hails the creation of the agency for welfare work with Jewish youth and of the vocational counseling service for the vocational reorientation of Jewish youth in the Diaspora and for emigration to Palestine.

The convention regards the creation of Jewish legal aid bureaus, particularly in the eastern part of the Republic, as an important instrument for legal assistance to indigent Jews, and advises the Executive Board to cooperate with institutions working in this field.

Resolutions on Cultural Affairs

The convention demands electoral reforms in all the religious congregations and in their central bodies throughout Czechoslovakia so as to conform to the democratic principles of the state and to the pertinent declaration issued by the minister of education.

* [I. e., the Comité des Délégations Juives (Ed.)]

The convention invites the Executive Board to work toward the expansion of the Hebrew school system under the auspices of the Czechoslovak State and to see to it that the Jewish school system in Czechoslovakia will be assured financial support within the budget of the state.

The convention hereby instructs the executive to intensify its activities in behalf of the recruitment and political education of Jewish women and of youthful voters [for the party].

The convention calls upon the representatives of the Jewish party in municipal governments to induce these municipalities to allocate funds for the establishment and maintenance of Jewish libraries in conformity with the provisions of the law and with their [municipal] budgets

Religious Institutions

The endeavor to bring about economic conditions permitting the observance of the Sabbath, and to obtain adequate state subsidies for [Jewish] religious institutions is one of the foremost duties of the Jewish party. . . .

The complete text of amendments to the party bylaws approved and of the financial resolutions adopted by the convention will be published in a bulletin to be sent out to all the branch offices of the party.

Elections:
Presidium: Chairman, Ernst Frischer (Mor. Ostrava); vice-chairmen: (1) Otto Zucker (Prague); (2) Dr. Mathias Weiner (Liptovský Sv. Mikuláš); (3) Dr. Wilhelm Sternbach (Mukačevo).

Executive: (members) Dr. Othmar Huss, Dr. Paul März, Leo Frank, and Dr. Hugo Brauner (Mor. Ostrava); Irma Polak, Dr. František Gottlieb, and Dr. Zděnek Landes (Prague); Dr. Michael J. Eisler (Hlohovec); Dr. Alexander Márton (Žilina); Dr. Adalbert Winterstein (Bánovce n/Bebr); Dr. Julius Reisz, (Bratislava); Herman Lichtig (Prešov); M. Goldstein (Mukačevo); Emil Schwartzbart (Bratislava); Superior Provincial Court Councilor Dr. Bernstein (Brno); Dr. Leopold Palkovits (Užhorod).

Secretary-General: Dr. Leo Zelmanovits (Mor. Ostrava).

Replacements for the Central Committee: Fini Brada (Prague); Dr. K. Sonnenfeld (Brno); Bakon (Mor. Ostrava); Bertl Zaitschek (Mor. Ostrava); Dr. Rudolf Braun (Prague); Ludwig Berger (Uherské Hradiště); Ester Fischer (Trenčanske Teplice); Hugo Kohn (Diviaky); Elsa Rosenthal (Jasina).

New Alternates: Dr. Otto Arie (Prague); Dr. Adolf Teitelbaum (Freistadt); Dr. Forgač (Sabinov).

— *Selbstwehr*, July 12, 1935

APPENDIX G

THE LAW OF THE ORGANIZATION OF THE JEWISH RELIGIOUS COMMUNITY

On the twenty-first of this month the Supplement to the Law of the Organization of the Jewish Religious Community in the Historic Lands will come up for final debate in Parliament. The leading article in this issue [of *Selbstwehr*] features comments on this law by Deputy Dr. Angelo Goldstein, who originally presented the bill in Parliament. At the same time, the text of this law, together with the legislative report, has been published in the Reports of the Chamber of Deputies under NR 676. Signed jointly by Dr. Patejdl, the chairman of the Committee on Constitutional Questions, and Dr. Goldstein, the legislative report presents an interesting treatise on the situation of our Jewry and its organizational structure. It deals comprehensively with the intolerable conditions prevailing in the religious congregations of Slovakia and Subcarpathian Ruthenia and presents a brief monograph on the Orthodox, *neolog*,* and *status quo*† congregations. The report also analyzes Jewish population mobility over the past half century; that is, since the enactment of the last law [on Jewish communal organization].

The legislative report contains the following data:

In 1890, i.e., in the year the original law regulating the internal affairs of the Jewish religious community was enacted, there were in Bohemia 94,479 Jews, representing 1.62 per cent of Bohemia's total population.

In 1900 there were in Bohemia 92,745 Jews, or 1.47 per cent of Bohemia's total population.

In 1919 there were in Bohemia 85,827 Jews, or 1.27 per cent of Bohemia's total population.

In 1921 there were in Bohemia 79,675 Jews, or 1.19 per cent of Bohemia's total population.

In 1930 there were in Bohemia 76,301 Jews, or 1.07 per cent of Bohemia's total population.

The Jewish population of Greater Prague was as follows:

In 1890: 23,473 (24.85 per cent of Bohemia's Jewish population, and 5.91 per cent of the total population of Prague).

In 1900: 27,289 (29.43 per cent of Bohemia's Jewish population, and 5.31 per cent of the total population of Prague).

In 1910: 29,107 (33.91 per cent of Bohemia's Jewish population, and 4.72 per cent of the total population of Prague).

---

* Equivalent to Conservative or moderate Reform congregations in the U.S.

† Moderate Orthodox.

In 1921: 31,751 (39.95 per cent of Bohemia's Jewish population, and 4.69 per cent of the total population of Prague).

In 1930: 35,463 (46.45 per cent of Bohemia's Jewish population, and 4.18 per cent of the total population of Prague).

This table shows a steady and rapid decrease in Bohemia's Jewish population (by almost 40 per cent within the past forty years). Since the total population is increasing, the proportion of Jews in the total population diminishes even more rapidly (from $1\frac{2}{3}$ to 1 per cent).

These changes, which have depleted the small communities to a point where they can no longer exist independently, are the main reason for the enactment of this [new] legislation. This is explained in greater detail in our lead article. The legislative report clearly spells out the advantages of the legal mergers of communities and underlines the significance of the two resolutions calling upon the government to effect the democratization of the religious congregations throughout the Czechoslovak Republic and the merger of Prague's Jewish community into one single entity; [namely,] the Jewish Religious Congregation of Greater Prague.

The Cultural Committee of the Chamber of Deputies has also discussed this law and, in a report composed by its chairman, Dr. Jaša, and Deputy Dr. Kugel, the reporter, has recommended the adoption of the law by the Chamber.

— *Selbstwehr*, January 22, 1937

APPENDIX H

JEWISH PARTY AND WORLD CONGRESS COMMITTEE ADDRESS EVIAN CONFERENCE

The Jewish party of Czechoslovakia, representing the Jewish minority in Czechoslovakia, and the Czechoslovak Committee for the World Jewish Congress have studied the issues raised at the Evian Conference, called at the initiative of President Roosevelt, and have adopted the following resolutions:

We hereby express our profound appreciation to President Roosevelt for his generous initiative in calling a conference for the purpose of aiding refugees. The convocation of this conference of international magnitude represents a protest by the civilized world against the barbaric abuses which the present rulers of certain Central European countries are perpetrating against half a million of their Jewish fellow citizens, who have resided in those countries for hundreds of years.

We demand that the Evian Conference register a powerful protest against the persecution of national minorities in Eastern and Central

Europe and that it wield its great authority to condemn the shocking acts of cruelty with which the German rulers torment and humiliate their Jewish fellow citizens.

It is to the vital interest of the countries of immigration, whose representatives have assembled at Evian, that immigration should proceed in a well-organized manner, so that these countries should not come into a position where they will be forced to accept masses of desperate and pauperized [refugees].

It is the paramount and urgent task of the conference to save the Jews of Austria and Germany from pogroms and torture. In order to find a radical solution for this problem, the conference must broaden its program and deal with the problem of Jewish emigration in its entirety.

Jewish emigration is a problem of international character which can be resolved only through cooperation among the powers and with the participation of Jewish organizations and Jewish social agencies, all based on international financial support.

For various reasons, the political and economic factors which prompted Jewish mass emigration from Eastern Europe even prior to the [First] World War have assumed even larger dimensions since the war, necessitating emigration on an unprecedented scale. However, there has been a commensurate narrowing of possibilities for entry into countries of immigration. Between 1900 and 1914 alone, a total of 1,700,000 Jews emigrated from Eastern Europe. By contrast, only 650,000 Jews have been able to emigrate from Central and Eastern Europe during the twenty years that have passed since the war.

National and economic developments in the countries of emigration have kept down emigration in general to a minimum, consisting of individuals in certain specific occupational groups, mainly in agriculture.

The only way of creating constructive conditions for the mass immigration of the persecuted Jews is to make possible the agricultural colonization of vast, uninhabited areas. The productive efforts of the first 50,000–100,000 immigrants would establish a basis for normal development, permitting an influx of Jewish masses from the countries of emigration.

A concentrated resettlement of Jews in vast, unpopulated areas would require [vast] resources. This huge and difficult but promising task can be carried out only with the concerted aid of international resources.

The Jewish national home in Palestine assumes a place of special significance in the overall solution of the problem of Jewish emigration.

The conference, which has been called by the president of the greatest and most powerful democracy in the world, should set up a commission for the purpose of studying the problem of Jewish emigration not only from the viewpoint of immediate rescue but also from the point of view of effecting a long-range, global solution.

We are hereby instructing the World Jewish Congress to represent us at the Evian Conference with these demands in mind.

The Jewish party in the Czechoslovak Republic:

(signed) E. Fischer, Chairman
(signed) Deputy Dr. A. Goldstein
(signed) Deputy Dr. Ch. Kugel
(signed) Dr. L. Zelmanovits, Secretary-General

The Czechoslovak Committee for the World Jewish Congress:

(signed) Dr. Emil Müller
(signed) Fritz Jellinek

— *Selbstwehr*, July 5, 1938

APPENDIX I

THE COMING ELECTIONS

The daily press has reported that local elections may be called at a very early date.

Political developments of recent months have shown irrefutably that, in a democratic state, it is of the utmost importance for the Jewish population to share in the work of the public authorities.

Particularly at this time it is imperative that the Jewish population stand firmly united in the ranks of the democratic camp and assume a share in the rights and the duties entailed in [the work of] those public bodies where electoral regulations permit it to do so. Only those who stand for election on a Jewish list will be able to represent the Jews and to intercede in their behalf.

Jewry would be guilty of a fatal political misstep if, particularly at this time, it were to exclude itself by its own choice from participation in local self-government. On the other hand, it would be an equally serious error if Jewish individuals in localities where Jews have no opportunity to put up a list of their own were to inject themselves into the political campaigns of non-Jewish parties. Such action would only serve to introduce the element of anti-Semitism into the campaign.

Without the sympathetic understanding and support of the public institutions we will be unable to effect a solution of the enormous social problems which confront Prague Jewry and which recent developments have aggravated.

Only individuals who will be directly responsible to us [because they] have been elected by our votes and on our platform will be likely to inform the bodies of local self-government with regard to the attitude and the requirements of the Jewish population and will stand up for these demands without reservation.

As a consequence, the Jewish party has decided that, in case local elections are held in Prague, it will run for election and will make all the necessary arrangements for that eventuality.

We appeal to the sense of solidarity of the entire Jewish population [in the hope that they will] give us their most effective support in our preparations for these elections.

It is the democratic duty of Jewry as a body to make it clear to the general public that the Jews want to cooperate with all the other citizens for the welfare of the metropolis of Prague.

The Jewish Party
District of Prague

— *Selbstwehr*, April 21, 1938

APPENDIX J

THE JEWS IN THE BORDER AREAS OF CZECHOSLOVAKIA

The territorial changes which have already occurred as a result of the redrawing of the borders [of Czechoslovakia] and the border alterations which probably will be made following the plebiscite and the negotiations with Hungary will affect a considerable segment of Czechoslovakia's Jewish population.

In studying the pertinent population statistics we must give separate consideration to each of the three foreign-language areas (German, Polish, and Hungarian) that will be affected by the changes. While all these three areas will fall to countries practicing anti-Semitic policies, the hardships that await the Jews will not be the same in each case. Accordingly, the Jews in these three territories will not show identical patterns in preparing for the future that is in store for them and in their decision whether to stay on in their old places of residence or to move [further inland, into the territory left to the Republic].

The most catastrophic problem in this respect will be posed by the Jews living in the German-language areas of Bohemia and Moravia. True, there are fewer Jews living in the German-language area of the Historic Lands than in the Hungarian-language area of Slovakia. However, in the case of the Jews in the German-language area, the future holds such a swift and complete loss of economic opportunities that we can hardly expect the Jews — who have been living in these areas for many centuries — to remain [there] in significant numbers.

In fifty political districts [in the Republic] altogether — forty in Bohemia and ten in Moravia — the population census of 1930 recorded an overwhelming majority of Germans (ranging from 98.8 per cent in Graslitz to 57.9 per cent in Bruex). Eight years ago, these fifty districts had nearly 2,500,000 Germans (by today this figure has grown by 150,000). Living alongside this German majority were a substantial Czech minority of about half a million and a very small Jewish minority, numbering about 24,000, or 23,925 if foreigners are not counted. Of these Jews, 6,345 professed Jewish nationality; of the remaining 17,580, about 15,000 had declared themselves as German nationals. The rest had professed Czech nationality.

The above figures show that there are a sizable number of Germans living outside the German area of settlement who will be able to get there only by opting for it or through an exchange of populations. In 1930 there were about 600,000 such Germans in Bohemia and Moravia, and another 160,000 in Slovakia and in Subcarpathian Ruthenia. Aside from these last-mentioned Germans, who are very unlikely to want to leave their present places of residence, we must figure on a population exchange involving the Czech minority of half a million and most of the Germans who today form minorities outside the fifty German political districts.

On the other hand, we must definitely think in terms of a resettlement of most of the 24,000 Jews now living in the area ceded to Germany.

The loss of the area which already has been ceded to Poland is a serious one from the economic point of view. As regards size and geopolitical position, on the other hand, it is rather insignificant when compared to the Sudetenland. Actually, there was in the Republic only one political district with a Polish majority. This is Český Těšín, where the Poles make up 51.8 per cent of the total population. Within that district, this percentage is exceeded only in Jablunkov, where 67.1 per cent of the total population is Polish. The district of Fryštat also has a sizable Polish population, but the majority of the inhabitants (63.7 per cent) is Czech. Only in the town of Karvinná do the Poles constitute a relative majority (47.8 per cent) over against the Czechs, who comprise 44.6 per cent of the total population. Here we have the classic picture of a polyglot area where, in fact, a border readjustment along ethnic lines simply means that part of the ethnic groups involved have formally ceased to be a minority, while other groups are formally reduced to minority status.

In 1930 there were only 2,500 Jews in these two districts. Although compared to Czechoslovakia, Poland presents a much less favorable picture as regards its official attitude toward the Jews and its general economic conditions, it is not very likely that Jews in the area ceded to Poland will leave in large numbers to search for new homes and economic opportunities in Czechoslovakia or abroad.

At present the question of the settlement with Hungary is still undecided. At this writing it is not certain whether or not there will be a border adjustment and, if so, what the extent of the change will be. According to the population census of 1930, there were in this area fourteen districts (thirteen in Slovakia and one — Berehovo — in Subcarpathian Ruthenia) with Hungarian majorities ranging from 87.8 to 55.6 per cent of the total population (in 1930). The total population of these fourteen districts was 640,000 (today, it is about 700,000). In 1930, there were in these districts 445,000 Hungarians and 31,000 Jews. Of the latter, only 22,500 professed Jewish nationality. In other words, one-third of the Jews in the area had already been assimilated and largely Magyarized. Even though Hungary has recently adopted a sharply anti-Semitic policy, especially in economic matters, there is little likelihood that, in case of a border adjustment [with Hungary], Jews will move away from this area in large numbers.

On the basis of the above statistical and other considerations, we arrive at the conclusion that when the new boundaries of the Republic are drawn, we need expect only part of the Jewish population of the foreign-language border areas to emigrate. Altogether, there are now between 56,000 and 57,000 Jews in those foreign-language sectors. Of these, about 25,000 may be expected to remain in their present places of residence. Thus, the problem facing us will be the resettlement and integration of some 30,000 individuals; i.e., between 7,000 and 8,000 families or households.

In this process, the present social and occupational structure of the Jewish population that may have to be resettled will be a factor of major — indeed, crucial — significance.

Up to now, most of the 24,000 Jews living in the Sudetenland resided in the larger urban communities of the region. Only the twenty-two cities with total populations of more than 100,000 also had more than 10,000 Jews. In other words, the Jews here, as everywhere else in the Historic Lands, represent an urban and even a metropolitan element. The social and occupational structure of these 24,000 Jews probably will also differ little from that of Western Jewry in general. Unfortunately, no exact data are available because official statistics class only the National Jews by vocational and social structure; they do not furnish this information about Jews as a group other than those professing Jewish nationality. Assuming that the vocational and social structure of all the Jews in the area corresponds to that of the National Jews, a random sample of ten larger cities with a total of 3,283 National Jewish inhabitants (i.e., over $\frac{3}{5}$ of the National Jews in the entire area) will yield the following significant statistics. Of a total of 1,754 individuals engaged in gainful employment, as many as 1,000 were self-employed (employers), 311 were officials and clerks, 320 were white-collar employees, and 123 held jobs as laborers, hired men, and apprentices. From the viewpoint of social potential, therefore, it may be expected that those Jews from the Sudetenland who will leave their homes will represent a more or less affluent element with some resources that will help them resettle in their new places of residence.

The occupational patterns of these Jews, classed in terms of fields of employment, presents a less favorable picture, as shown by the following sample. Of the 1,000 self-employed individuals, only 89 were engaged in industry; 77 were in the professions, and as many as 414 were merchants or storekeepers. Of all those gainfully employed, 228 were engaged in industry, 601 in [retail or wholesale] trade, and 124 in the professions.

It is clear, therefore, that the Jewish community [of Czechoslovakia] will be faced with a major problem affecting the occupational reorientation [of the emigrés]; namely, from business to industry. Only by introducing new industries in the areas of the Republic to which they will move will the Jews from the Sudetenland be able to make their way and to find ready acceptance in the places where they will make new homes for themselves.

— *Selbstwehr*, October 8, 1938

NOTES

1. *Congressional Record*, 65th Congress, 2nd Session, LVI (Part I), pp. 681–91.
2. The official *Wiener Zeitung*, October 17, 1918. See vol. I, *The Jews of Czechoslovakia*, pp. 155 ff.
3. *Jüdische Rundschau*, October 18, 1918, p. 327.
4. For details, see *American Jewish Year Book*, vol. 21 (1919–1920), Philadelphia, 1919, pp. 209–10. See also vol. II, p. 156–57.
5. Address delivered on October 15, 1918, in *Stenographische Protokolle ueber die Sitzung des Hauses der Abgeordneten* (Stenographic Records of the Austrian House of Deputies), Vienna, October, 1918.
6. See also A. M. K. Rabinowicz, "The Jewish Minority," vol. I, *The Jews of Czechoslovakia*, p. 156.
7. *Jüdische Rundschau*, October 25, 1918, p. 335.
8. Ibid.
9. See A. M. K. Rabinowicz, "The Jewish Minority," vol. I, *The Jews of Czechoslovakia*, pp. 157 ff.
10. For complete text, see vol. I, *The Jews of Czechoslovakia*, pp. 218 ff.
11. Ibid., I, pp. 167, 222 ff., (note 42).
12. *Jüdische Rundschau*, January 10, 1919.

13. Vol. I, *The Jews of Czechoslovakia*, pp. 167 ff.; Appendixes C and D, pp. 222–27.
14. Ibid., pp. 169 ff.
15. See Julius Berger, "Die Nationale Autonomie auf dem Marsche" (Jewish Autonomy on the March), *Jüdische Rundschau*, June 20, 1919.
15a. *Jüdische Rundschau*, July 1, 1919.
16. Zionist Archives, File Z 4/1787. See Appendix A.
17. See vol. I, *The Jews of Czechoslovakia*, pp. 172–73.
18. *Těsnopisecké zprávy o schůzích Národního shromaždění Republiky Československé* (Stenographic Record of the Sessions of the National Assembly of the Czechoslovak Republic), Prague, February, 1920.
18a. Zionist Archives, File Z 4/1886.
19. See *Selbstwehr*, August 31, 1923, p. 2.
20. See Emil Waldstein, "Die Karpathorussischen Wahlen" (Elections in Subcarpathian Ruthenia), and Philip Weinberger, "Die verletzte Parteidisziplin und die Wahlen in Podkarpatská Rus," (Breaches of Party Discipline and the Elections in Subcarpathian Ruthenia), *Selbstwehr*, April 4, 1924.
21. *Selbstwehr*, September 26, 1924. See Appendix B.
22. See *Selbstwehr*, October 3, 1924.
22a. *Selbstwehr*, December 5, 1924.
23. Ibid., December 12, 1924.
24. L. Singer, "Über die Gründe des Misserfolges der Jüdischen Partei" (Reasons for the Defeat of the Jewish Party), *Selbstwehr*, November 20, 1925. See also "Weber und Hirschler vor Gericht, Ein Nachspiel zu den letzten Parlamentswahlen" (Weber and Hirschler on Trial: A Sequel to the Last Parliamentary Elections), *Selbstwehr*, May 6, 1927, p. 3.
25. *Selbstwehr*, December 11, 1925.
26. Ibid., p. 2.
27. Ibid., March 12, 1926.
28. Ibid., November 19, 1926.
29. See Josef Rufeisen, "Zur Frage der Landespolitik" (On the Question of Diaspora Politics), *Selbstwehr*, March 11, 1927.
30. Ibid., January 4, 1929, p. 1.
31. "Zur Diskussion über Landespolitik" (On the Discussion of Diaspora Politics), February 22, 1929.
32. "Der Fluch der inneren Unfreiheit" (The Curse of Inner Constraint), ibid., April 23, 1929.
33. Ibid.
34. Ibid., May 17, 1929, p. 10.
34a. *Selbstwehr*, May 24, 1929.
35. Ibid., October 25, 1929, p. 3.
36. Ibid., November 8, 1929, p. 2.

37. Ibid., November 22, 1929, p. 3. See also Dr. František Friedmann, "Das Ausländer-und Judenproblem an unseren Hochschulen" (The Problem of Aliens and Jews at Our Universities), *Selbstwehr*, December 13, 1929. See Appendix C.
38. "Zur Volkszählungsfrage" (The Census Problem), *Selbstwehr*, February 14, 1930, p. 3. Dr. František Friedmann, "Wessen Schuld?" (Who Is to Blame?), ibid., February 21, 1930, pp. 1–2; "Unsere Grundrechte" (Our Basic Rights), ibid., February 28, 1930, p. 1.
39. *Selbstwehr*, June 29, 1931, p. 11. See Appendix D.
40. Dr. Leo Zelmanovits, "Dr. Singer's letzte politische Reise," *Selbstwehr*, July 31, 1931.
41. Max Brod, "In Memoriam Dr. Ludwig Singer," *Selbstwehr*, July 24, 1931.
42. "Politik als Erziehung zu Freiheit" (Politics as Education for Freedom), *Selbstwehr*, September 11, 1931.
43. Dr. František Friedmann, "Um den Territorialverband und die Landespolitik" (On the Territorial Federation and *Landespolitik*), *Selbstwehr*, June 17, 1932. See Dr. Leo Zelmanovits, "Der Kampf um die Landespolitik" (The Struggle for *Landespolitik*), *Selbstwehr*, July 1, 1932.
44. Dr. Emil Margulies, "Der Jüdische Weltkongress" (The World Jewish Congress), *Selbstwehr*, December 16, 1932.
45. *Selbstwehr*, August 19, 1932.
46. Ibid., July 8, 1932.
47. Ibid., May 11, 1934.
48. *Selbstwehr*, January 4, 1935. See Appendix E.
49. Dr. Fritz Tauber (Olomouc), "Der einzige Weg zu einer jüdischen Vertretung" (The Only Way to Jewish Representation), *Selbstwehr*, May 3, 1935.
50. *Selbstwehr*, July 12, 1935. See Appendix F.
51. *Selbstwehr*, September 6, 1935, p. 3.
52. Ibid., August 23, 1935.
53. Ibid., October 4, 1935.
54. "Zionistische Organisation und Landespolitik" (Zionist Organization and *Landespolitik*), prior to the Moravská Ostrava conventions. *Selbstwehr*, December 28, 1935.
55. Ibid., June 26, 1936.
56. Ibid., August 7, 1936.
57. *Selbstwehr*, January 22, 1937.
58. Ibid. See Appendix G.
59. Angelo Goldstein, "Frucht zielbewusster Arbeit" (The Fruits of Purposeful Toil); Chaim Kugel, "Rückblick auf einen Dornenweg" (Looking Back upon a Path of Thorns), *Selbstwehr*, March 15, 1937.

60. Ibid., October 29, 1937.
61. Ibid., July 5, 1938. See Appendix H.
62. Cf. Dr. Chaim Hoffmann (Yahil), "Bemerkungen zu einem Artikel von Ferdinand Peroutka" (Comments on an Article by Ferdinand Peroutka), *Selbstwehr*, January 28, 1938, p. 3; "Peroutka nochmals zur Judenfrage," (More From Peroutka on the Jewish Problem), ibid., February 25, 1938, p. 2.
63. "Ein antisemitischer Ausbruch der "Národní Politika," (An Anti-Semitic Outburst in the *Národní Politika*), *Selbstwehr*, August 5, 1938.
64. *Selbstwehr*, April 21, 1938. See Appendix I.
65. *Selbstwehr*, September 23, 1938.
66. Ibid.
67. Ibid., October 8, 1938.
68. Ibid., September 30, 1938.
69. Ibid., October 8, 1938. See Appendix J.

BIBLIOGRAPHY

Reference Books and Encyclopedias

Jüdisches Lexikon, 5 vols., Berlin, 1927–1930.

Periodicals

Der Jude, Vienna-Berlin, 1919–1921.
Der Judenstaat-Medina Ivrit, Prague, 1934–1938.
Jüdische Volksstimme, Brno, 1901–1938.
Jüdische Volkszeitung, Bratislava, 1919–1938.
Jüdischer Almanach, Prague, 1924–1931.
Minutes of the Congress of the Organized National Groups in the States of Europe, Geneva, Vienna-Leipzig, 1925–1933.
Selbstwehr, Prague, 1907–1939.
Židovské Zprávy, Prague, 1918–1939.

Articles, Pamphlets, and Books

Baum, Karl, "Das jüdische Prag der Gegenwart" (Present-day Jewish Prague), in *Monatsschrift für die Geschichte und Wissenschaft des Judentums* (*Monthly for the History and Science of Judaism*), Vol. 73, pp. 349–65.

B.D. (pseudonym for Jakob Leszinsky), "Jüdische Universitäts-Studenten in der Tschechoslowakei" (Jewish University Students in Czechoslovakia), in Yiddish, in *Yidishe Ekonomik* (*Jewish Economics*) Vol. 2 (1938).

Bilfinger, Carl, "Das Gutachten des Generalsekretärs der Vereinigten Nationen über die Fortgeltung der nach dem ersten Weltkrieg eingagangenen Minderheitenschutzverpflichtungen" (Opinion of the Secretary-General of the United Nations Regarding the Continued Validity of the Obligations Assumed after World War I for the Protection of Minorities) in *Zeitschrift für ausländisches öffentliches Recht und Völkerrecht*, (*Journal for Foreign Public Law and International Law*), Vol. 15, No. 3 (Heidelberg, 1954), pp. 521–32.

Blau, Bruno, "Bevölkerungsbewegung unter den tschechoslowakischen Juden," (Population Mobility among the Czechoslovak Jews), in Yiddish, in *Yidishe Ekonomik* (*Jewish Economics*) Vol. 3, Nos. 1–3 (Jan.–Mar. 1939), pp. 175–93.

———, "Juden in der Tschechoslowakei" (Jews in Czechoslovakia), in Yiddish, ibid., Vol. 3, Nos. 1–3 (Jan.–Mar. 1939), pp. 27–54.

———, "Nationality in Czechoslovak Jewry," in *Historia Judaica*, Vol. 10, New York: 1948, pp. 147–54.

Böhm, Adolf, *Die Zionistische Bewegung* (*The Zionist Movement*), Vol. 1, Berlin: 1935; Vol. 2 (1918–1925), Berlin: 1937.

Brod, Max and Weltsch, Felix, *Zionismus als Weltanschauung* (*Zionism as an Ideology*), Mor. Ostrava: 1925.

Cohen, J., "Dissolving Jewries, IV — The Jews of Czechoslovakia," in *Congress Weekly*, Vol. 17 (New York, May 14, 1951), pp. 11–13.

Epstein, Leo, *Studienausgabe der Verfassungs-Gesetze der Tschechoslowakischen Republik* (*Students' Edition of the Constitutional Laws of the Czechoslovak Republic*), Liberec: 1923.

———, *Das Sprachenrecht der Tschechoslowakischen Republik*, (*The Language Laws of the Czechoslovak Republic*), Liberec: 1927.

Färber, M., *Dr. Emil Margulies, Ein Lebenskampf für Wahrheit und Recht* (*Dr. Emil Margulies, A Lifelong Fight for Truth and Right*), Tel Aviv: 1949.

Freistadt, Benno, *Im Lande der fluchenden Rabbis und der hungernden Bauern: Karpathorussland* (*Subcarpathian Ruthenia: Land of the Thundering Rabbis and the Starving Peasants*), Leipzig; 1927.

Freund, Karl and Král, Václav, *Lesson from History*, Prague: 1961.

Friedmann, František, "Einige Zahlen, die Juden in unserem Staate betreffen" (Some Statistics Relating to the Jews in Our State) in *Jüdischer Almanach* (*Jewish Almanac*), 5694 (Prague), pp. 72–77.

———, "Einige Zahlen über die tschechoslowakischen Juden. Ein Beitrag zur Soziologie der Judenheit" (Some Statistics Relating to the Czechoslovak Jews. Contribution to Jewish Sociology) in *Barissia* (Schriften zur Diskussion des Zionisms) (Essays for the Discussion of Zionism), No. 9. (Prague, 1933).

———, "Rechtsstellung der Juden im Protektorat Böhmen und Mähren für internen Gebrauch der Kultusgemeinde Prag," (The Legal Position of the Jews in the Protectorate of Bohemia and Moravia — for the private use of the religious community of Prague), Prague: 1942.

Fuchs, Alfred, "Židé a ochrana menšin" (The Jews and the Protection of Minorities), in *Česko-židovský kalendář* (*Czech-Jewish Almanac*) Vol. 42 (1922/1923).

Goldelmann, Salomon, "Die sozial-ökonomische Struktur der Juden Karpathorusslands" (The Socioeconomic Structure of the Jews in Subcarpathian Ruthenia), in *Jüdischer Almanach*, 5694 (Prague), pp. 78–86.

———, "The Jews in Czechoslovakia," in *Contemporary Jewish Record*, Vol. 2, No. 1 (New York, January 1939), pp. 7–16.

———, "The Jews in Czechoslovakia before the Crisis," ibid., Vol. 1, No. 2 (New York, November 1938), pp. 32–37.

Gorin, Menahem, "Jüdische Auswanderung aus der Tschechoslowakei, 1922–1937" (Jewish Emigration from Czechoslovakia, 1922–1937), in Yiddish, in *Yidishe Ekonomik*, Vol. 3, Nos. 1–3 (Jan.–March 1939), pp. 94–101.

Hartmann, Georg, "Die Judenfrage in der Tschechoslowakei" (The Jewish Problem in Czechoslovakia), in *Volk und Reich*, Vol. 14, No. 3 (March 1938).

Hejda, Jiří, "Židé v Československém průmyslu" (The Jews in Czechoslovak Industry), in *Česko-židovský kalendář*; (Czech-Jewish Almanac), Vol. 48 (Prague, 1928/1929).

Hellman, Albrecht, "Die Geschichte der österreichisch-jüdischen Kongressbewegung" (The History of the Austrian-Jewish Congress Movement), in *Der Jude*, Vol. 5 (Vienna-Berlin, 1920), pp. 204–14.

———, "Die Juden in der Weltpolitik" (The Jews in World Politics), ibid., Vol. 3 (Vienna-Berlin, 1918), pp. 7–15.

Hlošek, Jan, *Židé na Moravě*, (*The Jews in Moravia*), Brno: 1925.

Hoch, Charles, *Les Partis Politiques en Tchecoslovaquie* (*The Political Parties in Czechoslovakia*), Prague: 1936.

Holly, Eugen, *Im Lande der Kabbalisten, der Religionskämpfer und des Hungers: Karpathorussland* (*The Land of Cabbalists, Religious Fighters and Hunger: Subcarpathian Ruthenia*), Bratislava: 1927.

Kapras, J., Malypetr, J., and Soukup, F. *Die Tschechoslowakische Republik, ihre Staatsidee in der Vergangenheit und Gegenwart*, (*The Czechoslovak Republic, Its Political Ideology Past and Present*), Prague: 1937, Vols. 1 and 2.

Koberg, Gustav, "Die Juden in Prag" (The Jews in Prague), in *Deutschlands Erneuerung*, (*Germany's Rebirth*), Vol. 23, No.7 (July 1939), pp. 364–69.

Krausz, A., "Dr. Edvard Beneš and die Juden" (Dr. Edvard Beneš and the Jews), in Yiddish, in *Otzar ha-Chaim* (Humene, 1938), 40 pp.

Lehmann, Fritz Karl, "Die Juden in der Karpathen-Ukraine", (The Jews in Subcarpathian Ruthenia), in *Weltkampf*, Vol. 16, No. 183 (March 1939), pp. 117–22.

———, "Die Lösung der Judenfrage in der Slovakei" (The Solution of the Jewish Problem in Slovakia), ibid., Vol. 16, No. 185 (May 1939), pp. 203–11.

Lepar, Zdĕnek, "Národnost židovská a její pomĕr k Israelitům v ČSR" (Jewish Nationality and Its Relationship to the Israelites in Czechoslovakia), in *Národopisný vĕstník Československý* (*Czechoslovak Journal*), Vol. 21 (Prague, 1928), pp. 159–78.

Margulies, E., *Zionismus und Deutsche Fortschrittspartei — Offener Brief*, (Zionism and the German Progressive Party — An Open Letter), Teplice–Šanov: 1904.

Masaryk, Tomáš G., *Der Problem der kleiner Völker in der Europäischen Krisis* (*The Problem of the Small Nations in the European Crisis*), Prague: 1922.

Peška, Zdĕnek, *Kulturní samospráva národnich menšín*, (*Cultural Autonomy of the National Minorities*), Prague: 1938.

Philipsthal, Herbert, "Die Juden in der Tschechoslowakei" (The Jews in Czechoslovakia), in *Zeitschrift für Demographie und Statistik der Juden* (*Journal for Jewish Demography and Statistics*), Vol. 3 (Berlin, 1926), pp. 11–15.

Polaček, Václav, *Die Israelitische Religionsgesellschaft* (*The Israelite Religious Society*), Brno: 1932.

Politis, N., "Le problème des minorités," (The Problem of Minorities), in *Esprit International*, Vol. 9 (Paris 1935), pp. 3–21.

Pražský, V., "Čeští židé s hlediska hospodářsko-sociálního" (The Czech Jews from the Socioeconomic Point of View), *Česko-židovský kalendář*, (*Czech-Jewish Almanac*) Vol. 47 (1928/1929).

Rufeisen, Josef, *Nationale und Soziale Judenfragen* (*Jewish National and Social Problems*), Mor. Ostrava: 1919.

Rychnowský, Ernst, *T. G. Masaryk and the Jews*, New York: 1941.

Spizman, L., "The Hebrew School Movement, No. 5c: Czechoslovakia," in *The Jewish People, Past and Present*, Vol. 2, New York: 1955, pp. 127–28.

Stillschweig, Kurt, "Die nationalitätenrechtliche Stellung der Juden in der Tschechoslowakei" (The Position of the Jews in Czechoslovakia with Respect to Nationality Rights), in *Historia Judaica*, Vol. 1, New York: 1938, pp. 39–49.

Urban, Rudolf, "Judentum und Bolschewismus in der Tschechoslowakei" (Jewry and Bolshevism in Czechoslovakia), in *Weltkampf*, Vol. 15, No. 147 (June 1938).

Weltsch, F., *Prag vi jerushalajim*, Memorial for Leo Hermann, in Hebrew, Jerusalem.

Weltsch, Robert, "Die nationale Revolution im Österreichischen Judentum und die jüdischen Nationalräte" (The National Revolution in Austrian Jewry and the Jewish National Councils), in Otto Abeles and Ludwig Baton, *Jüdischer National-Kalender, 1919–1920* (*Jewish National Almanac, 1919–1920*), Vienna: 1919.

Young, Edgar Philip, *Czechoslovakia*, London: 1938.

4. Religion, Welfare, Education

THE RELIGIOUS LIFE IN SLOVAKIA AND SUBCARPATHIAN RUTHENIA

by Hugo Stransky

INTRODUCTION

As we began to write this essay, complementary to the same theme in the *Historic Lands,** we became more aware of the impossibility of doing justice to the task. Closeness of time is a grave obstacle to objective historical assessment. Personal sentimental involvement, though very helpful in recalling events and experiences as well as their interrelations, constitutes another obstacle. The eminent historian E. G. Boring asserted in 1929 that "the beginning of the 20th century is too close for a just historical evaluation" and "the last two decades are not yet history at all."[1] However, the holocaust of European Jewry under the Nazi régime has relegated to history the once flourishing and religiously vivid Jewish communities in Slovakia and Subcarpathian Ruthenia, then the easternmost part of Czechoslovakia. At present, they are no more than dying embers. Hence, despite the lack of perspective, the recording of an account is needed.

By nature and character, religion as an element in daily life and a spiritual discipline evolves from sources in times far behind us, in a direct stream and by transmission through a chain of generations.

---

* See The Religious Life in the Historic Lands by the author, in *The Jews of Czechoslovakia*, vol. I, pp. 330–357.

In consequence, it was easier than in other disciplines and departments of life to detect and assess developments. Nonetheless, we are able to present only a brief sketch of the principal strides in the religious life of these two separate geographic entities and will concentrate on some case studies of congregations and religious personalities, on religious services and education as well as on religious literature and art.

The reader would do well to acquaint himself also with the historic summaries that appeared in the first volume relating to these two countries.*

TIES AND DIFFERENCES

(A) THE OVERALL ASPECT

Until far into the 19th century, and even longer in many places, faith and religious conduct were the only criterion for defining Jews and Jewish life. Also, those were the ties between Jewries the world over. Thus matters of faith and religious conduct used to govern the legal arrangements imposed upon the Jews and their relations to the non-Jewish environment by State, county and city authorities. In the same way, this applied to the lands of which the Czechoslovak Republic was composed from 1918 to 1939. Faith and religious practice identified the Jew[2] when Ibrahim ibn Jakob[3] observed Jewish merchants in Bohemia who arrived from the Byzantine Empire in 962, when the first Jew in Moravia left a record in 1057,[4] when King Ladislaus in Bratislava in 1092 enacted laws regarding Jews.[4a] In Subcarpathian Ruthenia, Jewish life did not begin until the invasion of Hungary by the Turks in 1526.[5] Faith and religious practice remained the very core of Judaism. They were instrumental in the establishment of Jewish communities around the world, and equally in the areas with which we are dealing.

Constant internal migration between the lands in that part of Europe forged another link between the various Jewish communities. Jews from Germany, driven to flight by onmarching crusaders in the 11th and 12th centuries, settled in the West as well as in the East (Slovakia). Jews from Moravia moved in great numbers to Slovakia,[6] for instance, on account of legislation which permitted only the

* [Slovakia: I & II by Livia Rothkirchen, pp. 72–124, and Subcarpathian Ruthenia by Aryeh Sole, pp. 125–154, *The Jews of Czechoslovakia*, vol. I. (Ed.)]

eldest son of the family to marry. The Chmielnicki revolt of 1648, on the other hand, brought masses of Jews to Hungary (Subcarpathian Ruthenia was settled by Polish Jews). Many of them wandered farther on, to Moravia. Jews expelled in 1670 from Vienna settled in Slovakia, and some wealthy individuals of strong secular Western leanings even penetrated into rural communities of Moravia and Bohemia.

These movements of trading Jews and groups of expelled Jews were the instruments of communication in religious life, the sole basis for social conduct, for moral and spiritual uplift. The legal patterns of the *Shulḥan Arukh* served as a binding element and household code. One group influenced the other, often creating a blend of customs that could be classified neither as strictly Eastern nor as Western. This led to internal dissension, of course; but it was religion that nurtured and maintained the Jewish communities. The religious element was especially the distinguishing mark between Jew and non-Jew. In all encounters with the authorities and the outside world, it was the decisive element.

A third and perhaps the strongest instrument that gradually molded the Jewish communities in various areas into permanent and cohesive parts of Jewry was the rabbinic scholars.[7] These spiritual heads of the *kehilla* (Jewish congregation encompassing all local Jews) created standards and gave status to the community through piety and scholarship.

That ties did exist is evidenced by the responsa between rabbinic men of renown in all three areas of the Czechoslovak Republic, responsa that contain rulings on legal matters concerning Jewish life in all its departments.[8] These legal communications promoted mutual understanding, but also created varying patterns of local or country-wide religious performance and ritual practice.

These, in turn, led in modern times to the division of Jewish religious life of Central Europe into a Western and an Eastern orientation. Within the Austro-Hungarian Empire there developed a Bohemian, a Moravian and a Silesian Jewry under Austrian sway, and a Hungarian Jewry to which Jews in the provinces of Slovakia and Subcarpathian Ruthenia belonged.

Abruptly and without preparation, contrasting religious words. met each other when the Czechoslovak Republic was formed in 1918. Their communities had developed under different historical influences and in specific ethnical and cultural environments, with the

East linked to Hungary and the West to Austria. Their orientations, views and practices set them apart. Not only was the language of daily conversation different, but the acculturated Jews in the "Historic Lands" (Bohemia, Moravia and Silesia) were secularized in their outlook on life. The chasm was even wider in Subcarpathian Ruthenia than in Slovakia, where a segment of the Jewish population was secular in its attitudes and oriented toward the West. Subcarpathian Ruthenia was populated by a Hasidic element, in many respects untouched by Western civilization. Presumably in recognition of this difference in religious outlook and behavior, the new Czechoslovak authorities "made no significant changes in the religious laws" governing the legal structure of the Jewish communities: "The Jewish religious community of Bohemia, Moravia and Silesia had taken over the old Austrian code, while Slovakia and Subcarpthian Ruthenia carried on their books the pertinent legislation enacted by Hungary."[9]

The continuity of the former legal arrangements served, to an extent, to perpetuate existing differences with respect to the religious and congregational character of the various Czechoslovak lands. The congregations in the West as well as in the East of the Republic formed regional federations, based on prevailing conditions.* The prime movers in the "Historic Lands," even in religious communal affairs, were laymen. In Slovakia and Subcarpathian Ruthenia the initiative emanated from the rabbinic authorities and they assumed the leadership. Furthermore, though some of the five congregational federations in the "Historic Lands" granted representation to the rabbinate, they were principally organized on linguistic grounds. In 1926, the Supreme Council of the Federations of the Jewish Congregations of Bohemia, Moravia and Silesia[10] was established for mutual benefit, and in order to enhance the prestige of the Jewish religious communities.

The congregations in Slovakia and Subcarpathian Ruthenia formed completely separate federations. These were either Orthodox or moderately traditional or reform-minded.[11] In 1928, the two non-Orthodox federations set up a loose association called *Jeshurun.*†

---

* For a detailed description of structure and function see G. Fleischmann, The Religious Congregation, 1918–1938, in *The Jews of Czechoslovakia*, vol. I, pp. 267–329.

† Chief Rabbi Armin Frieder succeeded after World War II in uniting the Jewish community of Slovakia.

Due to the wide divergence of the religious elements in the West and the East of the Republic, the federations in the two camps always remained apart and did not even consult with each other. No common religious platform existed, at least not in the two decades which are the subject of this study. Yet a desire for cooperation in the interest of the overall Jewish population was latent.* To a significant degree, the gap was filled by Zionism and by the Jewish party. The religious Zionists of Slovakia, organized in *Mizraḥi*,† played a prominent role in the Zionist movement.[12] The Jewish party was a political group seeking to represent the Jewish national minority which was recognized by the Czechoslovak State, and eventually won two seats in the national Parliament. Naturally, the Jewish party had to lean heavily on the Jewish vote in the Eastern regions of the Republic. Considerable segments of orthodox Jews were thus enlisted in the political and social activities of the total Jewish community.[13] The resulting cooperation with their fellow Jews in Bohemia, Moravia and Silesia angered the uncompromising Orthodox and generated bitter conflict in the East of Czechoslovakia.[14]

(B) THE SPECIFIC ASPECTS OF SLOVAKIA

The norm of Jewish life was basically Orthodox in Slovakia and Subcarpathian Ruthenia. So-called "Progressives" did exist, and were in some ways like the American Reform and Conservative movements, but the role they played in these two regions was far more marginal than their role in what remained of Hungary after the First World War.

Slovakia had inherited three separate congregational federations from Hungarian days. In a nomenclature dating back to the organizational split that took shape after the Congress of Hungarian Jews in Budapest in 1868,** they were known as "Orthodox," "Status Quo Ante" and "Neolog." The 167 Orthodox congregations, formerly part of an association headquartered in Budapest, were the first group to

---

* Karl Kálal, Die boehmischen Juden den slowakischen Juden (The Jews of Bohemia to the Jews of Slovakia), Česko-židovský kalendář (Czecho-Jewish calendar), vol. 39, Praha 1919/20.

† See Oskar K. Rabinowitz, pp. 94–99.

** For proceedings of Congress, see Gruenwald, *Korot Torah VeEmunah* chapter V, pp. 70–79.

receive the Czechoslovak Government's nod of recognition. In April 1920 they were authorized to constitute an Organization of Autonomous Orthodox Congregations in Slovakia. In November 1926 similar Government approval to set up their own Slovakia-wide federations[15] was given to 31 Status Quo Ante congregations and to 29 Neolog congregations. Altogether, these three federations accounted for more than half the 446 Jewish congregations registered in the census of 1926. The Status Quo Ante group, perhaps best described as right-wing Conservative by American standards, in the end joined the Neolog reformers in creating a unified Jeshurun Federation of Jewish Congregations in Slovakia.* These divisions reflected the divided religious self of Slovakian Jewry.

In past centuries, the community had been dedicated solely to the traditional concept of religious Judaism and its manifestations. From the beginning of the emancipation of Central European Jews in the mid-19th century, however, Slovak Jewry was buffeted by the winds of secular civilization. They blew principally from Vienna and Budapest, where Jews had left an autonomous ghetto life for an emancipated and free society.[16]

Slovakia, a province formerly Germanized and Magyarized, became part of the Czechoslovak State in 1918. By its history and spirit, and not least through the personality of its great founder Masaryk, Czechoslovakia was infused with American concepts, among them democratic freedom and what later became known as a "pluralistic society." By and large, this satisfied the diverse religious demands of the Jewish groups that found themselves in the Czechoslovak Republic. State authorities were rarely asked to intervene officially in disputes of a purely religious nature, disputes of the kind experienced prior to the Congress of 1868[17] and lingering on during the Hungarian era of "enlightened absolutism." Every religious and ethnic segment of the population was granted self-expression and the right to govern its own affairs. The State considered Jewish religious matters an affair of the "House of Israel" and, with rare exceptions, they were thrashed out internally.

All the more fierce became the dramatic and often abusive confrontations between ultra-Orthodox elements and the Zionists. The ultra-Orthodox were represented by the Autonomous Bureau in

---

* For structure and function, see Fleischmann, The Religious Congregaion 1918–1938, *The Jews of Czechoslovakia*, vol. I.

Bratislava and by the *Agudath Israel.** The Zionists, allied with the Jewish party, were also joined by a strong *Mizraḥi* movement (the majority of whose members belonged to the Orthodox congregations)[18] during election campaigns[19] for city, provincial and state representation,† elections where Jewish tickets were presented. At times, religious issues of major and minor significance were involved in these political struggles, and this tended to revive old Orthodox-Progressive feuds dating from the Hungarian era.

The Jewish community did not deviate from its reverence for the rabbinate and from respect for the leadership of the elected rabbinic spiritual heads. Their authority was upheld in all three branches. Even when their leadership ran counter to the desires and tastes of lay leaders and members in Orthodox or Status Quo congregations, they were recognized as guides for the mode of Jewish life in the congregation. Their authority as judges in religious matters, and their opinions on educational and social views, were not put into question.

Religious authority vouchsafed a degree of discipline. It manifested itself prominently in Bratislava, generally known as Pressburg at the time. Reaffirming their enlightened views, members of this old community of great fame formed only a Liberal Commission for Supervision and Regulation of the Business Affairs of the Congregation (*Liberale Kommission fuer die Ueberwachung und Regulierung der Angelegenheiten der Kultusgemeinde*) in 1861. This was done upon the initiative of Leopold Schick,[20] in opposition to the orthodox Pappenheim régime. Numerous attempts were made for a reconciliation. After the split at the Congress in 1868, Schick became leader of the Neolog District Committee but, having failed to establish a separate cemetery, eventually returned to the Orthodox fold of the mother congregation. The formation of a Neolog congregation took place only in 1871,** after the death of Bratislava Jewry's spiritual leader Rabbi Samuel Schreiber (*K'tav Sofer*), the son of the world-renowned Gaon Rabbi Moses Schreiber (*Ḥatam Sofer*). The

* Branch of World Organization of Orthodox Jews for solving problems of Jewry according to religious law. [See: Hirschler: *Agudath Israel* in Slovakia, pp. 155–172 (Ed.)]

† See A. M. Rabinowicz, The Jewish Minority, *The Jews of Czechoslovakia*, vol. I, especially "Jewish National Policy," pp. 200–204.

** Its first rabbi was Dr. Ignatz Wilhelm Back from Nové Mesto n. V., a pupil of *the Ḥatam Sofer*, Rabbi Moses Schreiber of Bratislava.

sentiments of loyalty and respect that played a role in this chronology are characteristic of the spiritual climate in this most powerful and influential Jewish community in Slovakia, and for that reason in Jewry of former Hungary. Despite the exodus of the 150 families whose heads joined the Neolog congregation when it was established, social relations were not fractured. Communications remained open between members of the different types of congregations in the same locality. By statute, only one of each type was permitted in one place. A memory of common roots persisted, and different groups worked together, especially in philanthropic causes.

Another case in point, which illustrates the vigor of religious tradition in the period of Czechoslovak rule, was the city of Košice in the East of Slovakia. Košice had a young Jewish community, which traced its beginnings only to the middle of the 19th century.[21] The synagogue, erected in 1867 — its membership was at the time 263 — had no *bima* (*almemor*) in the middle of the sanctuary, as Orthodox rules prescribe, and two church-like turrets adorned the building. Dissatisfied, conservative members demanded the old synagogue in the Zvonárska ulica for their services, but did not leave the congregation. No organ had been installed in the new synagogue at the time, probably in recognition of the sensitivity with which this musical instrument was regarded and because of the desire to maintain unity. An organ was installed in 1911, however, at the initiative of the liberal rabbi and preacher Dr. Josef Klein.* Traditionalist opposition to the move was rejected by the board of the congregation. Both parties turned to the Ministry of Religions in Budapest. Its head, Baron Josef Eötvös, appointed Chief Rabbi Markus Hirsch of Óbuda (Altofen) as commissioner of the government to settle the strife.[22] He did not succeed. After the Budapest Congress of Hungarian Jews in 1868 the traditionalists were granted a separate small prayer house as a Status Quo Prayer Community. Its members reaffiliated with the mother congregation before 1914, however; the two institutions merged by retaining separate services.

The small prayer house was razed to the ground in 1926 and a new synagogue erected in its place. The very first small prayer house in

* He succeeded the renowned Chief Rabbi Dr. S. Hevesi (1894–97 in Košice) of the Neolog congregation in Budapest, Temple in Dohany utca (Tobacco Street). President of the National Rabbinical Association in Hungary, and was followed in 1917 by the scholarly Dr. Emanuel Enten.

the Glockenstrasse, originally a granary, remained in use by the local Orthodox congregation,* which also gained the possession of the 1867 synagogue. To comply with Orthodox strictures, the interior was remodeled and the two turrets removed. Both synagogues, the new Neolog one and the reconstructed large old synagogue of the Orthodox congregants, were solemnly consecrated in 1927. The Orthodox congregation was headed by Rabbi Shaul Brach, an outstanding Talmudic scholar and expert in *Halakha*. The Czechoslovak period brought tranquility and harmonious social life to this community, as to many others, and also spiritual renown.

A trend away from an extreme Neolog position and toward the center could be observed in the vigorous community of Žilina (Sillein) in Central Slovakia. This prominent congregation had a core of members who were secularist intellectuals and a strong Zionist movement. In 1936, they did not hesitate to support the appointment of the writer of this essay to the local rabbinate, although he adhered to traditional Judaism and had been ordained at the Orthodox rabbinical seminary in Berlin. The original idea of installing an organ in the magnificent local synagogue, built during the Czechoslovak era, was abandoned, and services were conducted in the traditional manner.

Zionist education fostered a rejection of assimilation and deeper awareness of the Jewish heritage. This prompted many a congregation within the Jeshurun Federat on to move toward a historically truer Jewish observance. In Bratislava, the oratory efforts of Dr. Samuel Funk, rabbi of the local Neolog congregation, succeeded in 1927 in having the organ removed from his synagogue. On the other hand, a degree of flexibility was introduced into the rigid rules that formerly governed the conduct of students in the *yeshivot*, the main centers of learning in the Orthodox congregations.

A rather paradoxical development in Subcarpathian Ruthenia bears out the fact that organizational affiliation and nomenclature did not imply doubts about the authenticity of any group's Jewish commitment. After the departure of their rebbe for Poland in 1923, the Belzer *Ḥasidim* in Mukačevo wished to sever their ties to the official Orthodox community in their city. They appointed their own rabbi and *shoḥet* and, to give themselves legal standing, formed a Status Quo congregation in 1923. Their by-laws were not approved

* Founded by a small group in 1871.

by the government, however. Thereupon, they proclaimed themselves a Neolog congregation.[23]

(C) THE SPECIFIC ASPECT OF SUBCARPATHIAN RUTHENIA

As this case attests, religious life in Subcarpathian Ruthenia (Karpatorus) had its bizarre aspects. Historically, the Jewish community was a young one. Jews had taken refuge there in the wake of Bogdan Chmielnicki's Podolian pogroms in 1648. The evolution of Jewish life was erratic. Thete were heights of piety and learning,[24] but also depths of faithlessness and moral license[25] until the middle of the 19th century. On the eve of World War I, the Jews numbered 100,000 and were 10 per cent of the total population.

The Hungarian administration neglected the mountainous forest-clad ranges of this region. Little was done for the economic needs and educational or cultural aspiration of a people with its own Ruthenian language and folklore. Indeed, the new Jewish element among the Slavs was for that reason welcomed by the Hungarian government.[26] For Gentile and Jew alike, dire poverty was the rule and few amenities of civilization had penetrated this far. Deprivation and hunger were especially widespread in the rural areas, where two thirds of the Jewish community made their homes.[27] Corn bread was the staple food, white bread a special treat for Sabbaths and Holy Days. Families of eight or twelve were common and, often enough, children grew up undernourished.

Until the Ruthenians decided after 1918 that they wanted their province to be ceded to Czechoslovakia from Hungary, the Jewish community was an isolated one, set apart from the mainstream of life in Central Europe. Save for some scholarly rabbis and writers, it had sparse contact with Jews beyond the borders of Hungary. Marginal and almost forgotten in the Hungarian era, the community of Subcarpathian Ruthenia (Karpatorus) assumed greater significance within the Jewish framework of the Czechoslovak Republic due to its great learning, its dedicated adherence to the laws of the Torah and its strong Hasidic climate.

The founders of the famous community of Mukačevo in 1748 — about 25 families in 5 houses and a *shoḥet* as religious guide and teacher[28] — came from Galicia, and the same may well have been true of the first settlers in Sevljuš. The messianic yearnings aroused by the Frankist movement in Podolia* surely left traces in these groups. They were also moved to mystical exaltation by the influence of the Baal Shem Tov (1700–1760), the foundes of Hasidism, an influence that penetrated to the Carpathian Mountains.

This historical background needs to be taken into account, it seems to us, in assessing the later development and mood of the Jewish religious community in Subcarpathian Ruthenia. In 1918 Subcarpathian Ruthenia, with its self-contained *sui generis* Hasidic world, was included in the Czechoslovak State and entered an era that opened the door to the secularized West, to another world. The basic attitudes of these two worlds were irreconcilable. The various sectors of community life, often interwoven by religious mysticism and by beliefs that bordered on superstition, at times inflamed by warring Hasidic dynasties, made it difficult in their interaction to delineate religious, economic-social and political issues.[29]

From a moral and social point of view, the scholarly rabbis and serious rebbes† launched a series of constructive and pioneering efforts that took prevailing conditions into account. In line with their individual convictions and outlook, they strove to guide their flocks both in cities and villages, into cohesive congregations and into a good society.

The turn from a society in danger of spiritual decline and a disintegration of its religious ties had occurred by the end of the 18th and beginning of the 19th century. Its rabbis, were able, by means of the Hasidic instrumentality, to lead their congregants to a serious and conscientious mode of religious conduct. They brought teachers and *shoḥtim* from beyond the borders, built *mikvaot* (ritual baths) and synagogues in the villages and brought the young people together for traditional songs on Sabbath and Holy Day afternoons, as well as on other occasions. The rabbinic leaders were rewarded with fanatic loyalty. Not only did the rabbis take the children's education in hand but they also provided for adult needs. Their followers accepted willingly the stern demand for a change of their clothing from peasant-like garb to the Polish Hasidic mode: the "Kapote" (a kind of frock coat) with a sash around the body, dividing its upper parts from the lower ones, the "Shtreimel" (cap edged with small

* Jacob Frank, the pseudo-Messiah, lived from 1728 to 1791.

† [Hasidic rabbis and preachers (Ed.)]

pieces of fur), the "Bekishe" (an overcoat lined with fur), white socks and leather slippers. And yet, the learning and mystical erudition of Polish *Ḥasidim* were absent,[30] at least in the beginning. The community as a whole was young and, by comparison with Polish and Hungarian Orthodoxy, small in numbers. It did not offer enough spiritual scope for developing the kind of systematic Hasidic concept represented by *Ḥabad* with its philosophy, and by the Lubavitcher who pioneer in education and social humanity with a sense of a mission to the world. Instead, rivalries arose between the many types of small Hasidic schools. Subcarpathian Ruthenia, and thus the Jews of Czechoslovakia, inherited the Galician type of *batey tzadikim* (Homes of the Pietists), as the centers were called. The homes of *Ḥasidut* founded by Hungarian rabbis were of a different character.

Mukačevo was the main battleground in a struggle of two titans, the powerful City Rav Ḥaim Eleazar Spira and the Rebbe from Belz, Rabbi Yissakhar Dov Rokeaḥ, who had fled from Galicia during World War I and taken up residence in Mukačevo with a large following. The feud raged over a long period and passions ran high. They reached a peak when the Rav of Mukačevo disgraced the entire Czechoslovak Jewish community by intervening with governmental authorities to force the Belzer Rebbe out of the country.*

The Sapinker *Ḥasidim* formed another "Home" in Mukačevo. Their founder, Rabbi Josef Meir Weiss, a great Hebrew scholar and author of significant books, exercised considerable influence on the people in small villages. Rav Joel Teitlebaum, who then resided in Szatmar at the Rumanian border and now lives in Williamsburg, Brooklyn, also had a great following in the land. Social relations were strained between the followers of the different dynasties that included among others the Wishnitzer, Kosover and Sanzer. The Rav of Mukačevo resorted to the proclamation of a ban (*ḥerem*) on every family who would not follow his rulings. Friction and unrest resulted. Smaller Hasidic centers existed in Užhorod and Hust. In the latter resided followers of the "Home of Kaluph." Its founder, Rabbi Yitzḥak Isaac Taub, was well known as a great singer. He transplanted melodies allegedly learned from shepherds into the social life of his own community. The song *Szól a kakas már* ("The Rooster

---

* See the special chapter "Polmos Munkacs-Belz" (Polemic Mukačevo-Belz) by S. Weingarten in *Encyclopedia of the Jewish Diaspora*, vol. VII, pp. 225–232.

Calls by Now") spread throughout the area and its melody was used even for *zemirot* at the Sabbath table.

When the *shoḥet* from Polina suddenly appeared on the Subcarpathian Ruthenia (Karpatorus) scene before World War II as a rebbe pietist foretelling future happenings, and was reported to have performed miraculous deeds, it stirred the community. Because of his saintly and ascetic behavior, this lean and trembling figure even caught the attention of the European and American press. "He presented an unusual apparition,"[31] indced. Masses of people felt drawn to him and followed his wanderings. He distributed among the needy and poor everything he received as gifts or in compensation for his counsel. He rose like a comet, and disappeared again without having established a Hasidic center.

Prior to Czechoslovak rule the organizational pattern that followed the Budapest Congress of 1868 held sway in Subcarpathian Ruthenia. Out of a rabbinical conference in Michalovce, attended by 71 Orthodox rabbis from the whole of Hungary in 1865,[32] emerged the Union of Orthodox Rabbis in Subcarpathian Ruthenia (Karpatorus) five years later. Its president was Rabbi Moshe Schick, the enlightened and moderate spiritual leader of Hust. Some viable Status Quo Ante congregations were formed. Only two small groups joined the Reform movement of the Neolog congregations. One was in Mukačevo and one in Užhorod, where Dr. Mór Klein was installed as its rabbi in 1869. The authority of "the preacher Dr. Klein" was challenged from the outset, and his congregation could not maintain itself beyond 1906. It switched from the Union of Neolog Congregations to that of Status Quo Ante Congregations.[33] The new affiliation was not of long duration either. Its members gradually left the institution.[34]

The formation of an Orthodox central body for Subcarpathian Ruthenia, similar to the existing one in Slovakia and the one in the Historic Lands of Bohemia, Moravia and Silesia, was attempted in the Czechoslovak era, but it was thwarted by the strong opposition of progressive elements and of the Zionists.[35] By state decree in 1923, the Orthodox congregations were, therefore, attached to the "Autonomous Orthodox Congregations in Slovakia," with a separate Orthodox Regional Bureau in Užhorod. That Bureau, however, was closed by the authorities in 1926 because of improper operation.[36]

The years of the Czechoslovak era found the Jewish community of Subcarpathian Ruthenia at the threshold of transition to the Western world. This singular community, perhaps more integrally Jewish than any other of its size in the years between the two world wars, could have contributed a great deal to spiritual uplift and Jewish authenticity.

RELIGION IN OPERATION

One may well choose this title because, as indicated elsewhere, religion per se tended to involve the whole man and served as the integral framework of his existence. Among the *Ḥasidim* of Subcarpathian Ruthenia the gestures of daily life were not empty ones. Every prayer, every move and act was destined to demonstrate the splendor of the Lord or to commemorate an event in Jewish history. From the opening of one's eyes in the morning to the moment of falling asleep at night, directives in Jewish law were taken seriously and obeyed conscientiously, as guides for every move and action.

We shall now proceed to summarize the salient elements that were common to the Jewish religious orbit in both provinces. No effort will be made to examine special characteristics of religious observance in individual localities or in well-defined strata of the population. The encyclopedic work "Past and Present of the Jews and the Jewish Community of Bratislava"* is a good guide to local aspects in the capital of Slovakia. The illustrious history of this city exemplifies the mainstream of experience in all the communities of Slovakia. As to Subcarpathian Ruthenia, information is available in the Hebrew works "Encyclopedia of the Jewish Diaspora"† and "Cities and Mothers in Israel."**

SYNAGOGUE AND ḤAZANUT††

In most congregations, the synagogue was the communal center. Adjoining premises had usually been acquired or constructed for educational, social and cultural purposes and for the poultry slaughterhouse. The *mikva* (ritual bathhouse) was as a rule situated

---

* Hugo Gold: *Die Juden und die Judengemeinde Bratislava in Vergangenheit und Gegenwart*, Juedischer Buchverlag, Brno, 1932.

† *Enciclopedia Shel Galuyot*, vol. VII, Yehuda Erez, *Karpatorus*, Jerusalem–Tel Aviv, 1959.

** *Arim VeImahot Be Yisrael*, vols. I, IV and VII.

†† Liturgical music.

in the same neighborhood and so was the *hekdesh* (a kind of inn for wayfarers). Except in the case of the larger cities, the congregational school (*Talmud Torah*) and the house of learning for adults (*beth hamidrash*), which in many instances served as lecture hall for *yeshiva* students, were also in the immediate proximity of the synagogue. Further, the congregation usually provided homes for the rabbis and other officials in its employ (cantor, *shoḥet*, teacher, sexton) not far distant from the center.

The interior of Orthodox synagogues was in accordance with strict Jewish law. The *bima* (*almemor*, also called "*lemor*"),* adorned by two candlesticks, occupied the middle of the sanctuary as a rostrum, and the *amud* (reader's desk) was placed next to the Ark; in some synagogues the *amud* was below floor level, to demonstrate visually Psalm 130:1, "Out of the depth have I called Thee, O Lord."

Synagogues of Neolog congregations dispensed with the *bima* and placed the Reader's desk before the Ark, introduced choirs and installed organs. Though female worshipers were assigned seats in a gallery, Neolog congregations did away with the *gitter*, the physical screen of separation demanded by Orthodox rule. Their officiants conducted services in black robes and, in most instances, with folded prayer shawls (*tallit*), while in Orthodox synagogues not only the rabbis but also most male worshipers prayed in long woolen shawls that were often pulled over their heads (single men did not wear a *tallit* at all). Of course, all synagogues and places of worship faced east toward Jerusalem.

With rare exceptions, Slovak congregations conducted the prayer services according to the *nusakh Ashkenaz* (the version prevalent in Western and Central Europe), but the pronunciation of certain vowels was identical with that of East European congregations. Worshipers in Orthodox synagogues prayed loudly and emotionally,[37] while the other congregations had adjusted themselves to a service that maintained a Western decorum. There were additional semi-official services and daily private *minyanim* (a quorum of ten males above the age of 13), especially in larger communities.[38] Particularly on the Sabbaths, these services away from the main synagogue made it possible to gain time for studies and courses in the Talmud as well as rabbinic literature, provided by scholarly teachers and learned laymen. In non-Orthodox congregations, sermons were

---

* From the Arabic *al mimbar*.

delivered regularly on Sabbaths and Holy Days in the German or Hungarian vernacular, and in the Slovak language by the younger rabbinic generation that was in command of it by now. In the main synagogues, the rabbi of the Orthodox community delivered serious exhortations twice a year, and preferably in Yiddish.[39] These two occasions were *Shabbath Shuva*, the intermediate Sabbath of the penitential season, and *Shabbath Hagadol*, the Sabbath prior to the Festival of Passover. These arrangements predominated throughout Slovakia and gave the Jewish community a pattern of uniformity.

A variety of prayer orders could be observed in the congregations of Subcarpathian Ruthenia. The principal distinguishing mark was the *nusakh Sepharad.* This denotes the order according to Hasidic ritual and tradition, and should not be confused with the ritual followed by the descendants of the Spanish and Portuguese Jews who are called "Sephardim." Some minor cells of such Sephardim, with their own prayer order, may well have survived in this remote area, however, from the days of the Turkish occupation (1526–1699). This may be gathered from the fact that a small community of Sephardim of the Spanish ritual, with their own Sephardi rabbi,[40] is recorded as having established the first community in Užhorod. Yet the *nusakh Ashkenaz*, the West European prayer rites, were the original version in the principal communities. Berehovo resisted Hasidic rules, and in Mukačevo, for instance, this Ashkenazi order remained in use till 1832, because of the leadership of the famous *halakhist*, Rabbi Zevi Elimeleh Spira, who became known after his work as the *Ba'al Darkhey Teshuva.* In Hust, the *Ashkenazi* version prevailed till the end of the community in 1939; but a sizable number of *Ḥasidim* separated from the mother congregation for that reason. From among the many nuances in the rites of prayers of the "Homes of the Pietists" we like to mention the *nusakh Ari*,[41] a philosopher of the Kabbala, whose mystic teaching exerted great influence on Jewish thinking. Some Hasidic schools put on *Rabbenu Tam tephillin*, in addition to those worn in accordance with the general norm.[42]

In the "Homes of the Pietists," no cantors were employed for the prayer assemblies. Often, the rebbe himself led his followers in prayer. Moral exhortations were delivered at the Sabbath meals when the followers came to partake in the *suda* (festival meal) of their leader. Many traveled from far-distant places, even from beyond the borders of the country, to spend the "solemn" or "joyous" days of the Jewish year with their Teacher, Adviser and Master, while sharing in prayer, study and sense of communion.

The functioning of a *ḥazan** or cantor in the Divine Services, accompanied at times by a boys' choir or an organ in Neolog congregations, was already an established fact — to a lesser extent in Subcarpathian Ruthenia also — prior to World War I. When the doors to the West were opened wide during the Czechoslovak period many fine cantorial singers found new opportunities in Western European communities and America,[43] where some of them embarked upon notable careers. It is significant, however, that magazines of the 19th century[44] voiced dissatisfaction with the misuse of opera melodies in the religious services of some Orthodox Hungarian congregations, and took a stand against showing off and prolonging services. Some writers also opposed the efforts to make a distinction between the pronunciation of two mute consonants in the Hebrew alphabet, the א (aleph) and the ע (ayin), thought lost "for European Jewry."[45] That distinction was still attempted by some Hasidic as well as Dutch Ashkenazi singers, so as to liken their renditions to those heard in Spanish and Portuguese synagogues. In certain houses of worship, like the *Brill-Schul* in Bratislava,[46] services were conducted by laymen in command of the local melodies preserved over generations. They were preferred to singers in possession of a fine voice.

In the congregations of Subcarpathian Ruthenia, former strong and continued opposition to *ḥazanim* or even cantors was overcome, provided they were strictly observant and occupied themselves during the day with the study of Talmudic and rabbinic literature; there was as well an obstinate refusal to form boys' choirs. In addition to those heads of Hasidic establishments who guided their followers in services, there were always traveling *ḥazanim* (religious troubadours) who brought melodies and customs from one community to another. These men contributed greatly to the unification of musical tradition, and were greeted warmly as an instrument of uplift for yearning souls.

---

* *Ḥazan* denotes the singer of Jewish melodies in the traditional mode. *Cantor* denotes a liturgical singer with a technical musical training conforming to the style of composed music.

RITUAL OBSERVANCE AND MINHAGIM*

The scrupulously upheld regulations governing *kashrut,*† and the elaborate ways in which *Shabbath* and *Yomtov*** were observed in the vast numbers of households, created a special problem of refinements in family tradition. To describe it would go far beyond the space of this study. Its folkloristic value would require a composition of book length.

We shall rather stress the economic aspect of the commodities required for the upkeep of a life in strict Jewish law. In most congregations, the right to sell kosher meat,†† *matzot* (unleavened Passover bread), wine and some other provisions, was a community monopoly, with revenues accruing to the congregation and keeping it financially sound. Purveyors of meat and poultry, *matzo* bakeries and sellers of wine paid lump sums to the administration of the community, or each month delivered the sales tax set by the communal administration. The sellers of kosher food, on the other hand, were protected from competition by outsiders, because the rabbi of the community barred from the local market kosher provisions, especially meat, coming from a region not under his juisdiction (*basar ḥutz*). These arrangements, mostly limited to the three aforementioned commodities, represented a continuity of past practice. Centuries ago, Jews were allowed permanent residence only if they did not become a burden, and this presupposed a financially viable Jewish congregation.[47] Therefore, the Christian authorities of those days saw to it that the economic interests of the non-Jewish community were safeguarded.[48] In addition, the levies on kosher food served as security for the tax levy which Jewish residents had to pay through their elders.

The arrangements varied in Subcarpathian Ruthenia, especially in localities where Hasidic rebbes made their residence. Many of their followers preferred to buy only meat and poultry slaughtered by the *shoḥet* whom his rebbe had selected for himself. On occasion, the rebbe channeled the profits realized from the sale of certain commodities to charitable causes under his sole control. At times, he

* Religious customs.

† Dietary laws.

** Holy days.

†† The meat tax was called *gabella* (*Fleischkreutzer*).

also instructed wealthy followers to assume the cost of an expenditure, so that the less fortunate could meet the ritual demands.

Specific local customs handed down over the generations also were a factor in the life of each congregation. In the memory of our contemporaries, the sexton in some small Slovakian communities awakened the members for morning services by knocking on their doors (*Schul-Klofen*). On Sabbaths and holidays, of course, he would only call out with a loud voice that it was time to assemble in the synagogue. Most Orthodox congregations auctioned off the honor of being called up to the Torah, or the performance of some sacred duty within the service. This system was once introduced as one of the main sources of income. It lost its importance in modern times because of general communal taxation, but was nonetheless preserved.

From the numerous special local prayer insertions that have been maintained in Slovakia down to the recent present, we quote two *Seliḥot* (penitential compositions). One is the "Elegy of Jona," bewailing in a poetical style of high quality the martyred deaths of Rabbi Jona and his fellow Jews in Bratislava. That they were killed by crusaders* proves the existence of a Jewish community there in the 13th century.[49] The other, "Elegy of Lament" (*kinah*), included in the services in Trnava (Tyrnau) on the 3rd of Elul, is a moving text about the torture and death of twelve male and two female Jews accused of ritual murder. They were burned to death at the stake on August 22, 1494, when they refused to desert their faith by accepting baptism.[50]

Many a congregation maintained a *sepher minhagim* (*Book of Customs*) for the observance of local ritual and historic dates. These records served as a guide to the rabbi and the lay leaders of the community. One of the old and well-arranged *Book of Customs*, containing references to localities in the area of our essay, was composed in the 15th century by Rabbi Isaac Tyrnau (from Trnava ?), a specialist in collecting local traditions.[51]

One of the most recent is a collection of customs in the community of Komárno. Its author[52] refers to the fact that he used the local Sabbath Prayerbook, which contained notes on the special centuries-old customs in the rite of Komárno.[53] From its contents, we cite a few samples[54] of specific arrangements in that pious community. The rabbi prayed from a prayerbook handwritten on parchment. It

* Probably during the occupation of Bratislava in 1291.

contained a section of prayers which he recited, as local tradition prescribed, before the regular service commenced. He always put on a clean pair of shoes, ready for him in an adjoining room, before entering the *beth ha-midrash* for prayers, study or lecturing. Most unusual was the custom in this community not to recite the mourners' *Kaddish** after the *Aleynu* prayer in the morning service. An extended reference to the rebuilding of Jerusalem was recited in the Grace after Meals, preceding the words *uvney Yerushalayim* (O, rebuild Jerusalem): "May the kingdom of David, Your anointed, return to its place in our days."†

The customs in the communities of Subcarpathian Ruthenia were mainly those of the individual Hasidic centers and "Homes of the Pietists," which we have discussed before. Apart from ritualistic manifestations in Jewish law and practice, they demonstrated beliefs in mystic teachings and messianic traditions that often bordered on superstition.[55] These customs and ceremonies were numerous and differed from each other.

YESHIVA, BETH HAMIDRASH AND SCHOOL

The spiritual powerhouse in both provinces in the east of the Republic were the *yeshiva*, the Talmudic high school or academy, and the *beth ha-midrash*, the house of study for adults. In the latter, studies in rabbinic literature, mainly in the Talmud, were conducted in daily courses by the rabbi with laymen of the community. They assembled as a rule on weekdays, late afternoon or after the evening service.

Occasionally, the building or space assigned for adult studies was called *"klaus"* (also *"shtibel"* — little room), a name derived from this institution in Germany (*Klause*). Members of the courses conducted services there, and the institution thus developed into a second local synagogue with public worship. The *Ḥasidim* named it *"kloiz."* Noted in Subcarpathian Ruthenia was the *kloiz* of the Belzer rebbe in Mukačevo.

In most places, the students for higher rabbinic learning gathered

---

* Prayer of glorification of God. It is assigned to mourners for recitation after the *Aleynu*, a prayer concluding the daily services.

† Presumably to resemble the combination of "Jerusalem" and "David" in the two blessings following each other in the *shemone esre*, the prayer of Eighteen Benedictions.

in the building of the *beth ha-midrash* for the lectures announced by their rabbi or *rosh yeshiva*, the dean of the Talmudic academy. The rabbis of some communities preferred to worship with their students, especially in smaller towns and villages. A number of laymen liked to join them in worship, too.

The greatest fame, spreading far beyond Bratislava and Slovakia, was achieved by the *yeshiva* of the *Ḥatam Sofer* (Rabbi Moses Schreiber, 1762–1839)*, who made it the *"Pressburger Jeschiwa,"* which still continues under that name in Jerusalem. As he began to develop the *yeshiva* in 1806 upon taking office in Bratislava, power in the community was in the hands of lay leaders who advocated enlightenment and sought to introduce secular education. They felt strongly backed in their reform ideas by the aims of the statute which Emperor Josef II promulgated for the Jewish communities[56] in 1782. President Breisach of the Bratislava Community attempted to have the *yeshiva* removed from Bratislava. He and his supporters claimed that "the *yeshiva* students by studying nothing but the Talmud until they reach the age of 20 are without a livelihood and become a burden to the community." Through the counterintervention of the influential Moses Bettelheim the removal was not carried out. The *Ḥatam Sofer* so as to obviate further attacks on these grounds established a trade school for underprivileged children; the school was maintained from the tax on kosher meat (*gabella*).[57] Those were the beginnings of the *Pressburger Yeshiva* an institution of great renown which has given prominent rabbis, teachers and rabbinic scholars to Jewish communities the world over. A noted rabbi and scholar in Czechoslovakia, himself a former student there, describes the spiritual climate that emanated from Bratislava, through the gates of the *yeshiva* the heart of the community. For many a former student of the *yeshiva* made contributions to the Jewish religious aspirations in congregational life of Western Europe principally, and others as scholars, scientists and artists to the community at large. "It is almost impossible to enumerate all the spiritual leaders," he asserts, "who hailed from Bratislava or studied or lived in that city and were active in it."[58]

---

* Born Frankfurt a.M., 1785–1794, dean of *yeshiva* in Prosnice and then for five years rabbi in Strážnice, both in Moravia. Prior to his call to Bratislava, he was Rav in Mattersdorf, one of the famous *sheva kehilot* (seven communities) of the Burgenland which belonged first to Hungary and after World War I to Austria.

The school was guided in an uninterrupted line by the successors of the *Ḥatam Sofer* as heads of the Orthodox community. Chief Rabbi Akiba Schreiber, the last rector of the *yeshiva* and leader of the Orthodox rabbinate in Slovakia, introduced certain reforms. The system was improved and a preparatory school preceding the rabbinic school proper was developed. Also, the by-laws for a rabbinic school with right of ordination were approved by the Czechoslovak authorities. He established a "mensa" (student dining room) and thus eliminated the degrading system of "Taegessen," by which students of moderate means, or none whatsoever, were placed into another family for guest meals every day of the week. In 1931 he took steps that were to lead to the establishment of a dormitory.[59]

The students had their own platform for rabbinical training in homiletics and Talmudic as well as *halakhic* discussions. In two institutions, *Megidet-Ḥevra* and *Ḥarifet Ḥevra*, they could choose their own topics for deliberation. Both of these societies were under the supervision of Rabbi Simche Bunem Schreiber, the second son of the Chief Rabbi.

"In the old ghetto, the rabbi was the sun and the *yeshiva* [was] the radiant light that surrounded him; the key to the importance of a community was not the number of students or the wealth of its members, but the spiritual greatness of the rabbi and of his school (*yeshiva*). It was these factors which enhanced the fame of a community," asserts Samuel Bettelheim.[60] This, indeed, was still the case in the *yeshivot* of the eastern part of Czechoslovakia. Each *yeshiva* had its specific character but varied slightly in its program.* Students tried to spend their years of study in several *yeshivot* and sought to gain from the way of learning and depth of knowledge, and no less from the conduct and piety of the heads of these Talmudic institutions.

The Slovak *yeshivot* of Bratislava, Galanta and Trnava had the largest number of students (150–300), followed by Huncovce. Šurany, Dunajská Streda and Košice. All of them were sought out by students from such neighboring countries as Austria, Germany, Hungary, Rumania and Yugoslavia, and even Switzerland and England. Yet, it was the many youngsters from Subcarpathian

* The arrangement of program of studies, the social life of the students and the spirit that left indelible marks in their character, would require a separate monograph.

Ruthenia who brought the spirit of *Ḥasidut* into the life of the student body. The *yeshiva* heads, in consequence, had to cope with groups from many countries. Small concessions as to the conduct of their daily lives were made to students from the West, but the students from the Hasidic communities were also accommodated through infusions of their spirit and practices.

One of the finest and most successful blendings was accomplished in the *yeshiva* of Trnava by the great teacher and moralist Rabbi Samuel David (Halevi) Ungar. He met the students from the far West of Europe, and equally the ones from the Hasidic East, with deep insight into the soul of men. When elected in 1932 as Rav of Nitra, his *yeshiva* moved with him. His institution continues as the Neutra (Nitra) *yeshiva* in the Yeshiva Farm Settlement of Mount Kisco, New York, headed by his son Rabbi Salomon Ungar.[61]

The most famous *yeshiva* of Subcarpathian Ruthenia, in Hust, was guided by Rabbi Josef Duschinsky, formerly of Galanta in Slovakia. An uncompromising man of deep conviction and a strong adherent to the *nusakh Ashkenaz*, he was elected principal rabbi of separate Ashkenazi Community of Jerusalem in 1932.* Also well known were the *yeshivot* of Mukačevo and Užhorod.

School attendance in the Austro-Hungarian Empire became compulsory through the royal decree of Emperor Josef II in 1783. In Slovakia, a former province of Hungary, with which we are here concerned, the development of different types of schools and educational schemes was set in motion. The primary concern of the rabbinic and lay leaders was preservation of the children's integral religious education which seemed threatened by the mandate of the State. The first document about the setting up of a contractual agreement between the Bratislava Jewish community and the royal inspector of the national schools[62] thus goes back to June 23, 1783. With the passage of time, all secular schools were attended by an increasing number of Jewish children. Bitter conflicts were voiced about the dangerous decline of their Jewish knowledge and religious practice[63] despite religious instruction in the public schools that was, in many cases, supplemented by attendance in Talmud Torah schools and sometimes by private instruction as well. Therefore, better-

---

* *Rav HaRishon Shel Eda HaḤaredit HaNiphredet.* He succeeded Chief Rabbi Ḥaim Sonnenfeld (also from Slovakia) who had joined the *B'rith Shalom* of J. L. Magnes, president of the Hebrew University, and Prof. Hugo Bergmann.

staffed Talmud Torah schools were established by almost every congregation. Most important were the Jewish day schools which received government subsidy. The vast network of day schools, with secular programs taught by licensed Jewish teachers under the supervision of the official school authorities, were a credit to the entire Jewish community. They evoked keen communal interest and loyalty. Thus was secured the religious aspect in the educational sphere of all three types of Jewish congregations.

The Czechoslovak authorities confirmed the general arrangements, previously recognized by the Hungarian government. Some adjustments to suit the changed conditions had, of course, to be made. Above all, the new languages of Czechoslovakia had to be adopted in the curriculum.[64] Religious instruction in the state schools was conducted for two hours a week in the primary and junior high schools. It was continued in the high schools if a sufficient number of pupils enrolled.[65]

The religious education of the girls in Slovakia was not neglected. With the approbation of the *Ḥatam Sofer*, the first Jewish school for girls was formed by Lazar Horowitz and Raphael Basch and may be considered a forerunner of the *Beth Jacob* school movement for girls, founded in 1917 by Sara Schenierer in Cracow, Poland, and subsequently introduced into the countries of the West including Slovakia by the educator Dr. Leo Deutschländer of Vienna, an outstanding leader in the World *Agudath Israel* movement.* The movement in Slovakia also arranged summer resort schools in the Tatra.The school for girls of the Orthodox Bratislava congregation, the only one in the whole of the Republic, was under the honorary presidency of Chief Rabbi Akiba Schreiber. The *Handbook for the Instruction in Religion and Ethics for Jewish Girls' Schools* (*Bnot Zion: Ein Handbuch zum Unterricht in der Religion und Sittenlehre fuer israelitische Maedchenschulen*, Bratislava) deserves mention in this connection.

A different picture presents itself in the Hasidic area of Subcarpathian Ruthenia. The majority of children received basic religious instruction from religious tutors or rabbinic instructors in the *ḥeder*. There they were also taught mandatory general subjects. It took some time before Jewish children attended approved state schools with the new educational program of the Czechoslovak government. The

* [See Hirschler: The History of *Agudath Israel* in Slovakia, pp. 155–172 (Ed.)]

authorities also gave approval for the opening of Hebrew elementary schools. The first was organized in Turan by Rabbi Samuel Freilich.*[66] Strangely enough, this school was the last one to be dissolved when the Jews of Turan were deported by the Nazis in 1941/42. An impressive educational achievement was the Hebrew High Schools in Mukačevo and Užhorod.†[67] They provoked the wrath of the Rav of Mukačevo in particular, but their accomplishments cannot be gainsaid.

In concluding this chapter, one may give expression to the hope that any comprehensive study of Jewish education in the eastern part of Czechoslovakia will include a description of the detailed programs for religious instruction and of the different types of educational facilities.

RABBIS, LAY LEADERS, TEACHERS

Until the 19th century, the principal role of the rabbis was solely that of teachers of Jewish studies as well as judges of Jewish law. But above all they were the moral guides of the community. In exceptional cases they became engaged with the authorities in the arrangements of important tasks and duties of the community toward governmental authorities. Furthermore, they intervened at times with the authorities or even with royal dignitaries for the protection and rescue of individuals and groups of their flock. However, they rarely acted as synagogue functionaries until the time of the legalized emancipation.

The leader of the religious community, called *parnas* or *gabbay*, had earlier been the *rosh kneset* as well, the leader of the synagogue community, ever since the Middle Ages. Often he was a learned layman and lectured in the *beth ha-midrash*. The *parnas*, meaning "provider," was as a rule a financially well-situated personality who took pride in the welfare of the community and the promotion of its spiritual standards. Thus many a *beth ha-midrash* was erected from his own financial resources.[68] In modern times the *beth ha-midrash* remained an institute of study and a center for social activities,

* At present rabbi of Congregation "Ohave Sholom" in Gardner, Massachusetts.

† [See: Sole: Modern Hebrew Education in Subcarpathian Ruthenia, pp. 401–439 (Ed.)].

especially in the provincial communities that loomed larger on the scene than the synagogue proper.

The regulations promulgated by Emperor Josef II in 1783 laid down the status and responsibilities of the rabbi and *parnas* respectively.[69] They also explained the rights and the authority inherent in these two positions. Those allotted to the rabbis at the time were retained by them down to our day, in the eastern communities of the Republic. This contrasted with the position of the rabbis in the Historic Lands[70] (Bohemia, Moravia and Silesia), which evolved in a different direction altogether.

There were no theological or rabbinic seminaries in Slovakia and Subcarpathian Ruthenia.[71] *Yeshiva* graduates who had the minimum secular education in a higher grade elementary school and passed their examinations in the rabbinic subjects prescribed by Jewish law before a council of three recognized rabbis or three individual *halakhic* authorities, could be elected by the congregation. The rabbi was authorized by state law to perform marriages and to keep the official records (*matriky*) of birth, marriage and death. The *yeshiva* in Bratislava and the one in Mukačevo, in addition to a few other prominent Talmudic academies, were granted recognition as institutes for the ordination of rabbis.

The majority of the Status Quo Ante congregations and all Neolog congregations limited their choice of candidates to rabbis ordained by a recognized seminary* who had also obtained an academic degree, preferably a Ph. D. The younger rabbinic generation preached in the Slovak language, in addition to German. Hungarian was rarely used in the pulpit. The Subcarpathian Hasidic rabbis preached in Yiddish exclusively.

In sizable communities, the official title of the principal rabbi was Chief Rabbi because another rabbi known as *dayan* (assessor or judge) assisted him, acting mainly as jurist in ritual practice and commercial litigation. In major congregations with a heavy agenda, more *dayanim* were appointed. The rabbinical court of at least three, formed the *bet din*, with the Chief Rabbi presiding as *av bet din* (head of the court). In smaller congregations, the title *more tzedek* (a righteous teacher) was accorded to non-ordained clergymen who served the community as readers from the scrolls of the law and *ḥazzanim*, as ritual slaughterers or teachers.[72]

* Berlin, Breslau, Budapest, or Vienna.

In congregations which could not afford a larger staff, some of the ritual functions and duties were assigned to one and the same employee. It also happened that Jewish day school teachers performed ritual duties. If qualified, they might also be assigned, with the approval of the authorities, to take the place of the rabbi in maintaining the department that recorded matters of personal status (*matriky*). Occasionally, qualified laymen were also of assistance to the rabbi in his official duties, and even sat as advisers in the rabbinical council. Often, the communal rabbi bestowed the honorary title of *ḥover* upon such laymen or upon others who merited official recognition for philanthropic work, contributions in education and learning or Jewish representation in public affairs.

One of the last leaders of the community who headed the Congress (Neolog) Congregation of Bratislava from 1923 till the outbreak of World War II was Dr. Viktor Stein. He combined a modern approach with an admirable blend of the qualities that befitted a *parnas* and *rosh kneset*. A dignified representative of Judaism, to whom the French phrase *"le style c'est l'homme"* was frequently applied, he also served at the helm of the Jeshurun Federation and of the B'nai Brith Lodge. He had received a strict religious upbringing in his home-town Námestovo, where his father was a physician, and drew his strength from sound Jewish knowledge. Many a philanthropic and cultural institution owed its inception or enlargement to him. When he accepted the presidency of the Congress Congregation, he summed up his philosophy of Jewish public life in these words: "We, members of this congregation, are progressive Jews, but not Jewish progressives. We want to continue toward progress *in* Judaism and not *away from* it."[73]

RELIGIOUS LITERATURE AND PRESS

The former Hungarian community, predominantly Orthodox and moderate traditional and, therefore, guided by the principles of the *Shulḥan Arukh*, produced a uniform extensive rabbinical literature in classical Hebrew. Of the 130 rabbis from Slovakia and Subcarpathian Ruthenia listed as having written books in the years 1420–1840, scholars from Bratislava (Pressburg) were the most numerous. Within the past century alone, sixteen of that renowned group have come from Bratislava.[74]

Responsa occupy the first place in the literature here alluded to. Such works are "usually confined to written replies (*teshuvot*) given to questions (*she'elot*) on all aspects of Jewish law by qualified authorities."[75] At the same time, this genre of literature is a historic treasure chest. Queries as well as answers offer, by their very nature, an insight into Jewish contemporary life — and not in respect to religion alone.[76] Many volumes have become classics that were published by spiritual leaders in the area under our study, for instance those by the *Ḥatam Sofer;* their author, Rabbi Moses Schreiber of Bratislava, is known the world over by the name of his work. To this day they remain pivotal reference literature for rabbinic decisions on religious issues. Frequently, they served as guides for rabbinic leadership elsewhere, notably in western Europe. There is no doubt that the spread of *responsa* literature originating in the area was aided by the fact that many noted rabbis and scholars of pre-Hitler Germany hailed from regions within the orbit of Hungary, and often from our two provinces. There leading rabbis continued to hand down their decisions, a great number of which were published. Considerations of space preclude the attempt to compile a bibliography[77] of this literature and of that referred to in the next section.

Rabbis and scholars in the last years of organized communal life were no less prolific in writing and printing their sermons, homilies and commentaries on biblical themes and their interpretation of Talmudic texts. Their printed exhortations to ethical conduct and their efforts to expand the frontiers of their listeners' and readers' Jewish knowledge, arranged as a rule according to the sequence of the weekly Sabbath portions from the Torah (*sidrot*) and those for the Holy Days, were paraphrased by expositions of verses in the ancient sermonic literature (*midrash*). The rabbis searched for new meanings that would take the needs of the local community into account and shed light on contemporary problems. That this literature was printed, that it was studied by *yeshiva* students and perceptively discussed by adult readers, reflects the religious fervor that permeated those two lands of Czechoslovakia and is evidence that their Jewish society was very much alive.

Yeshivot and *batey midrash* maintained libraries of the basic volumes of Jewish literature — scriptures, Talmud and *halakha* (legal codes), including commentary and interpretations. Of course, there was no lack of midrashic and homiletic literature for the leisure hours of the students and for their own training as preachers. The library in the *beth midrash* in Mukačevo, for instance, consisted of 6,000 volumes. Some city communities, and also the non-Orthodox congregations, maintained libraries of religious and secular Jewish literature for young people* and adults. Furthermore, a library of religious literature was the pride of many a private home that could afford it. It was customary to present a groom, especially one who had studied in a *yeshiva*, at least one complete set of the Talmud and of the legal code (*Shass veShulḥan Arukh*) in the same way "in which it was customary to give to the daughter a dowry."[78]

Almost every Orthodox household, however, was in the possession of the *Kitzur Shulḥan Arukh*, a handbook of the "Code of Law," for daily use and guidance in religious practice and conduct, arranged by Rabbi Salomon Ganzfried†, born 1804 in Užhorod and *Dayan* there until his death in 1886. He was a prolific writer, especially in the *halakhic* field, but offered the greatest service to the religious layman, down to this very day, with his abridged edition of the *Shulḥan Arukh* which went through, since its first appearance (Warsaw 1864), many reprints, editions, translations and paraphrases.

As we have seen, an appreciable number of scholarly rabbis and men of letters hailed from Slovakia and Subcarpathian Ruthenia, but the number who remained in those two provinces was limited. Except for the cities of Bratislava and Košice, the climate for scientific Jewish work was not too propitious. All the same, the erudite spiritual head of the Status Quo Congregation in Trnava, Chief Rabbi Mair Stein, conducted research into the history of the Jewish communities in Slovakia.[79] He was the editor of the *Jahrbuch des traditionstreuen Rabbinerverbandes in der Slowakei* (Yearbook of the Association of the Traditional Rabbis in Slovakia), which appeared from 1923 to 1935. In Košice, the learned Neolog Rabbi Dr. Emanuel Enten engaged in historical studies. Both these scholars wrote in German as well as Hungarian. A prolific learned author was Rabbi Chaim Yuda Ehrenreich, since 1930 spiritual leader of the community

* The higher grade elementary school in Bratislava, founded in 1826, had a youth library of 400 volumes (*Ben Chananja*, vol. II, p. 423).

† His scholarly grandson Dr. Ḥayim (Heinrich) Brody — also a native of Užhorod — author and expert in medieval Hebrew poetry, was first rabbi in Náchod (Bohemia) and from 1912 to 1932 chief rabbi of the Prague Community. Afterwards he headed the Schocken Institute for Hebrew Poetry in Berlin and, from 1934, in Palestine.

in Huncovce (Hunsdorf). He published an erudite periodical, *Otzar haḤaim*, which contained studies in the humanities, in philosophy and philology. It reviewed important Jewish theological books published the world over and maintained correspondence with outstanding Jewish scholars, some of them in the United States. He was the indefatigable author and publisher of a collection of *responsa* to the Jerusalem Talmud called *Mekor Ḥaim* (The Well of Life), a standard work compiled during thirty years of dedicated labor. All maxims of Talmudic teachers mentioned in the Jerusalem Talmud are listed, together with notes on text variants: "This spiritual work of Herculean dimensions, composed in a corner of Slovak Jewry by a single man, illuminates the ways in which great scholars were laboring in small communities, away from the noise of big cities..."[80] He had to defend himself against attacks by some Orthodox and rabbinic authorities on his scientific and secular contributions in his periodical.[81] Another well-known contributor of research to scholarly periodicals in the West was Dr. Samuel Klein, Chief Rabbi in Nové Zámky, who in 1928 was appointed professor of historical geography at the Hebrew University in Jerusalem.* Well known in cultural circles east as well as west of the Czechoslovak Republic was Samuel Bettelheim's periodical *Judaica*, first printed in Budapest and later in Bratislava, in the German language (1934 till 1937). This publication devoted much attention to the study of the religious and historic life in the two lands.

Religious literature in the Slovak language was scarce. A translation of the prayerbook for weekdays and Sabbath did exist, and so did a *Haggada* for Passover with illustrations by the non-Jewish artist Cyril Kutlik.[82] A Slovak translation of the first and second book of the Pentateuch by Rabbi Josef Weiss[83] appeared in 1932. Designed for Jewish schools, it followed the arrangement of the German edition by Rudolf Fuchs, which was used in schools west of Czechoslovakia. A prolific Slovak writer was Rabbi Armin Frieder, the best rabbinical speaker and orator in the Slovak language. He translated portions of the Bible and published chapters from Jewish history as well as essays on Rashi and the Rambam. In 1935, he was preparing to publish a biography of the *Ḥatam Sofer* (Rabbi Moses Schreiber).

---

* Co-editor of "Zion," Hebrew Yearbook of the history and archeology of Palestine. Died 1940 in Jerusalem.

Some non-Jewish scholars were also concerned with Jewish theological literature. One part in the Jubilee Volume for Dr. Ján Kvačal[84] is devoted to the Old Testament (*Starý Zákon*); in 1903, Professor Alexander Hornyánszky issued a Hebrew grammar in Bratislava, and translated the *Mishna* of the Talmud tractate *Yoma* (Day of Atonement). "Yiddish in Czechoslovakia," an essay presented by Dr. Franz Beranek, at the World Congress of Yivo (*Yiddisher Visenshaftlikher Institut* — Yiddish Institute for Jewish Research)[85] in 1935, should, in our view, also be mentioned in this section of our essay.

Three Hebrew theological papers were published in Bratislava. *Yeshiva* students in the principal congregations had, in addition, their own periodicals of good quality, as for instance in Bratislava *Ha'Mayan* (The Fountain), a Hebrew magazine for theology, homiletics and history.[86]

A note may be in order about the press. Neither the Organization of Autonomous Orthodox Congregations in Slovakia, nor the Jeshurun Federation of the Status Quo Ante and Neolog Congregations had papers of their own. The Jewish press in both provinces — it appeared in Slovak, Yiddish, German, Hungarian and Hebrew — also covered religious affairs.*

CEMETERIES AND ḤEVRA KADISHA

The acquisition of burial grounds and the formation of a burial brotherhood (*ḥevra kadisha*) were, in the past, the first acts that led to the establishment of a Jewish community. As in the Historic Lands and in other countries of Europe, cemeteries and burial brotherhoods in Slovakia and Subcarpathian Ruthenia generally antedated the founding of congregations.† Daniel, for instance, the first Jew in Trenčin, was granted the right in 1300 to purchase a piece of land from a non-Jew.[87] The number of Jews in Trenčin substantially increased in the course of time with the arrival of refugees from Hungary and from Uherský Brod. Yet they paid their communal taxes to Uherský Brod and, presumably, buried their dead there.

* See Avigdor Dagan, The Jewish Press in Slovakia and Subcarpathian Ruthenia, *The Jews of Czechoslovakia*, vol. I, pp. 527–529.

† See H. Stransky, Religious Life in Historic Lands, *The Jews of Czechoslovakia*, vol. I, pp. 349–350.

Only in 1736 was a *ḥevra kadisha* founded, which suggests that they must have bought ground for burials not long before. Some time afterward they erected a wooden house of prayer. After suffering damage from fire it was remodeled into a proper synagogue in 1790.[88]

The three branches of congregations had their separate cemetery grounds. For rabbis and scholars, honorary rows of graves were reserved. As a sign of distinction, their tombstones differed in shape and color from the others.* However, the historic significance of these and other tombstones was their poetical inscriptions, which through their contents and the choice of words revealed a high standard of Hebrew knowledge. In these two lands, as elsəwhere, the burial brotherhoods and the men in charge of them were held in high esteem. These sentiments also found their symbolic expression in the great variety of local customs that governed the performance of the last rites.

In contrast to the communities in the Historic Lands, no flowers were permitted to be placed on the graves. Women joined neither the funeral procession nor the last rites at the graveside. In some cemeteries, it was even customary to bury the men and women in separate sections. By design, grass grew over the graves.

In most congregations, *ḥevra* day was a high point of the social season in the community. It was usually scheduled for the 32nd day in the counting of the *omer* (the period of forty-nine days between the festivals of *Pesaḥ* and *Shavuot*). The by-laws of the Society provided among others that the rabbi be called up to the Torah especially on the preceding Sabbath. Members of the *ḥevra kadisha* fasted on *ḥevra* day and visited the graves to recite penitential prayers. The day concluded with a festive meal (*suda*), which featured an address by the communal rabbi and the initiation of new members.

The burial brotherhoods also extended their charitable functions and deeds of loving kindness to the living. It is recorded, for instance that complaints about the neglect of the sick were voiced in Bratislava during the 18th century. The local *ḥevra kadisha* therefore arranged a rotating voluntary nursing service in 1791,[89] a task that gave rise to the additional title *gomley ḥasodim* (performers of loving

* See Eugen Bárkány, Jewish Cemeteries in Slovakia, pp. 558–564.

kindness) in their shield. The burial brotherhoods were acknowledged as the principal charitable institution of the community. On their part, a favorite activity of their members was financial assistance to the upkeep of the Talmud Torah and the *yeshiva*, or other educational institutions.

Most revered in these provinces was the institution of the *ḥalukka* (division) in support of poor scholars in Palestine who were devoted to studying alone or in established academies of learning. These rabbinic scholars came from all parts of the world to complete their lives in the Holy Land and to be buried there. This type of charity from abroad goes back to ancient times and had its national groups, called *kolel*, all over the world from the 13th century. The European division was headed by Chief Rabbi Akiba Schreiber of Bratislava.

Based on messianic yearnings for the rebuilding of the Temple, Subcarpathian Jews supported particularly those of their scholars who retired to Palestine. Zevi Elimelech Spira, the Rav of Mukačevo, intended in 1906 to settle with his family in the Holy Land, to welcome there the Messiah. A row of "Mukačevo Houses" was erected in Jerusalem for those who desired to spend the remaining years of their lives there, moved by religious motives.

A cherished institution in traditional homes for the support of poor Jews in Palestine has been the charity boxes of Rabbi Meir Ba'al HaNes so named after Rabbi Meir of the Talmudic period to whom aggadic literature ascribes the performance of miracles. Before lighting the Sabbath candles, the women were wont to drop a coin into the collection box.

RELIGIOUS ART AND MUSEUMS

Religious expression in art is included in the essays of this volume dealing with the appropriate subjects. Nonetheless, references under the historical aspect are called for in this essay.

It goes without saying that Jewish art was mainly expressed in the synagogues and in articles for the home that were associated with ritual performance. So many of these artworks were destroyed during the Nazi holocaust that it may be appropriate to recall the oldest Torah curtain (*parokhet*) of the Brill Synagogue (*Brill'sche Schul*) in Bratislava. In this house of private worship, erected in 1700 by Heinrich Heine's great-grandfather Simon Michel-Pressburger,[90] hung the oldest Torah curtain in Bratislava. Samuel Bettelheim depicts it in print and gives a full description of its beauty and history.[91] The *Brill'sche Schul*, incidentally, was a repository of local Bratislava religious customs (*minhagim shel Pressburg*).

As to the locations of synagogues which have been the source for certain types of architecture, it is interesting to note that synagogues of old were, until the emancipation period, generally situated outside the town. Within the walls "the practice of an alien cult was usually prohibited."[92] From the Middle Ages onward, as Jews were allowed to settle in a specific district inside the town boundaries, the synagogue found its place and its appropriate architecture.

Many of the more ancient synagogues were wooden structures. In Subcarpathian Ruthenia, where sizable Jewish settlements were of fairly recent date, communities continued to build wooden synagogues, largely because of their desperate economic straits and the ready availability at cheaper prices of wood for construction purposes. In the villages, expressions of folk art could often be observed inside the wooden houses of worship.

Once Austria-Hungary had granted its Jews equal rights, synagogue design was among the spheres of life where gradual adjustment to the non-Jewish environment set in, both in the exterior and in the interior of the buildings. Reform spokesmen contended, and sometimes conservative congregations as well, that the removal of the *bima*, the Torah reader's platform in the center of Orthodox sanctuaries, tended to enhance the importance of the Ark with the Torah scrolls. Organs in Neolog synagogues added a pleasurable element of esthetic beauty, it was stressed.[93] These architectural adaptations were frowned upon by the Orthodox, who considered them of Christian derivation and hence an expression of religious assimilation. Synagogue architecture, as a highly visible outward symbol, became a bone of contention in the bitter controversies that shook the communities in the areas here under review.

The first home of the Jewish Museum in the Slovak town of Prešov (Eperjes) was a house in the former town moat. During renovations in 1928, Hebrew prayer texts and ornamental paintings of Jewish significance were found on its walls.[94] This indicated that Jews had used the building for services at a time when they were barred from residing in the town, which they could only enter on three weekly market days to transact business.[95] Not until 1848 was permission to live in Prešov granted to thirteen families.[96]

It is an interesting sidelight, in this connection, that the Neptune fountain in the main square of Prešov was donated to the town as a token of thankfulness by the first Jew who had been permitted to enter Prešov in 1794, in order to display his wares in the market.[97]

NOTSE AND COMMENTS

1. Edwin G. Boring, *A History of Experimental Psychology*, (New York, 1929) p. 645.
2. V. A. Kaufman, *The Earliest Jews in the Hungarian Danube Basin*, B'nai B'rith Bulletin, Melbourne, Australia, April 1965: "The present capital of Hungary, Budapest, formerly called Aquincum . . . advanced in 194 to the rank of a Roman colonial town . . . of experienced craftsmen, actors and doctors — in those times mostly Greeks and Jews. Jews must have been attracted to fortified Aquincum not only for the protection and occupations it afforded but also for its warm flowing spring, ideally convenient for the ritual bath taken by every Jew on Friday afternoon."
3. Traveler, served as interpreter in a delegation from the Calif of Cordova to Emperor Otto I of Germany. "His descriptions have only survived in quotations," Cecil Roth, *Standard Jewish Encyclopedia*, p. 950.
4. His name was *Podiva*, Oskar K. Rabinowicz in *Notes on 1,000 Years of Czechoslovak Jewry*, 1968, Library Hebrew University, Jerusalem.

4a. *Monumenta Hungariae Judaica*, vol. I, pp. 1 and 52, legal regulations in reference to Jews who married Christians and to Christians employed by Jews.

5. S. H. Weingarten, *LeKorot HaYehudim BeKarpatorus* (Historic Notes on the Jews in Subcarpathian Ruthenia), Encyclopedia of the Jewish Diaspora, vol. VII, Karpatorus, pp. 17 and 18.
6. A census taken by Hungary in 1735 established that, out of the 12,000 Jews living in Slovakia, two thirds hailed from Moravia. *Monumenta Hungariae Judaica*, vol. IV, p. 148: in 1437, the Jew Isserl from Budějovice in Bohemia had a court case in Bratislava (Slovakia).
7. For a selection see Ch. Y. Ehrenreich, *Otzar Haḥaim*, vol. VIII, pp. 16 and 25.
8. *Mazkeres Paksh* (Memorial Book of Paksh), vol. I., p. 28. Rabbi Mordekhai Baneth in Mikulov (Nikolsburg), Chief Rabbi of Moravia,

assisted the stand of the rabbi of Paksh in a controversial ritual issue. The Chief Judge of Bratislava (*Av Beth Din*) and the rabbinate of Prague (*ibid.*, pp. 67–69) were involved in correspondence on this *responsum.* The geographic distribution of the scholars who communicated with each other on this case is further indicated in p. 120, note 11, and in vol. II, p. 195. O. K. Rabinowicz notes in *"1,000 Years of Czechoslovak Jewry"* (see n. 4 above): "While, in fact these three areas appear as separate geographical units, from a Jewish viewpoint the affinity of their Jewish inhabitants is much more realistic than might be assumed."

9. G. Fleischmann, "The Congregation in Law," in *The Jews of Czechoslovakia*, vol. I, pp. 276 ff.
10. *Ibid.*, pp. 270 and 308.
11. *Ibid.*, p. 306.
12. A small group of Mizrahi members existed in Bohemia and Moravia with Chief Rabbi Dr. Ḥaim Brody of Prague as their prominent spokesman until his departure from office in 1931. Rabbi Dr. Aladar Deutsch in Prague followed then as senior and writer of this essay, rabbi in Náchod (Bohemia) as junior spokesman, elected to the executive of the countrywide Mizrahi Organization 1936, then Chief Rabbi of Žilina (Slovakia). Their efforts in some crucial phases of Czechoslovak Jewish history to reconcile divergencies should be put on the record.
13. It may serve as further proof that, out of eight Czechoslovak delegates to the first World Jewish Congress, August 8–15, 1936, in Geneva, three came from Slovakia and none from Subcarpathian Ruthenia. The three were Dr. Ladislav Rosenzweig, Rabbi Dr. Hugo Stransky and Dr. Matej Weiner. Dr. Angelo Goldstein, Deputy of the Jewish Party in the Prague Parliament and head of the Czechoslovak Delegation, selected Rabbi Stransky (then Chief Rabbi-Elect of Žilina, Slovakia), for political reasons and on grounds of religious unity, to deliver the overall review of Czechoslovak Jewish affairs from the rostrum. Fritz Jellinek from Brno (Bruenn) gave the economic report (Protocols du Premier Congres Juif, 1936).
14. G. Fleischmann, "Religious Congregation," vol. I, p. 273.
15. Livia Rothkirchen, "Slovakia II," vol. I, p. 103.
16. *Ben Chananja*, vol. VI, pp. 340 ff., Dr. Adolf Jellinek, famous preacher of Vienna, *Die Autonomie der juedischen Gemeinde* (The Autonomy of the Jewish Community): "The communal freedom and independence was prevalent in the ghetto among those Jews excluded from society." In reference to *Takanot* (regulations for the conduct of the Jewish community), he maintains: "The autonomy of the Jewish communities was a contribution to the consciousness of the time

that human dignity was not completely denied to the Jew" (p. 343). "The Jews were therefore prepared for liberty earlier than those who denied them the same and would like to continue in this denial" (p. 344).

17. An expert opinion was requested of Chief Rabbi Leopold Loew of Szegedin by the authorities in Buda whether the wearing of special robes by rabbis during religious services was obligatory in Jewish law and, if so, he was asked to supply a description (*Ben Chananja*, vol. II, pp. 97, 99 ff.); whether the Jewish oath can only be sworn in a synagogue or if it suffices to do so before the rabbinical court (*Ben Chananja*, vol. VI, pp. 214 and 270, supplement No. 13; also *Wochenblatt fuer juedische Theologie*, Leopold Loew, Szegedin, 1863, study by L. Schwab); whether sucking out the blood by the *mohel* who performs a circumcision is mandatory. On the intervention by authorities to remove the *yeshiva* from Bratislava and the counteractions, see Yehuda L. Gruenwald, *Otzor Neḥmad* pp. 72 and 73, ref. 1. Other objects of constant bickering were the *bima* (reader's desk); *meḥiza* (separating screen between male and female worshippers); organ music during religious services; weddings in synagogues or under open sky, etc. For a detailed account, consult Y.L. Gruenwald, *Korot HaṬora VeEmunah BeHungaria* (The History of Torah and Faith in Hungary), Budapest 1921.
18. Rothkirchen, *Slovakia II*, vol. I, p. 89. Tomaschoff was Orthodox and an ardent Zionist (Mizrahi), in whose home the conversational language was Hebrew; *ibid.*, pp. 93–94.
19. *Ibid.*, p. 91.
20. Schick was at first rabbi of Sered and wrote several volumes on theological themes, but later engaged in business in Bratislava. He was also treasurer in the short-lived *Pressburger Israelitische Auswanderergesellschaft* (Association of Jewish Emigrants in Bratislava); see his call for emigration to America in *Judaica*, vol. II, No. 11–12, 1935.
21. There are different historic versions regarding the exact year of the first Jew. See Emanuel Enten, *Zur Geschichte der Juden in Košice* (About the History of the Jews in Košice) in Gold, *Zeitschrift*, vol. II, pp. 279 ff.; Samuel Kohn, *Geschichte der Juden in Ungarn* (History of the Jews in Hungary) Budapest 1884, p. 240, asserts that Jews lived in Košice prior to the battle at Mohacs in 1526.
22. His "Expert report from the Religious View, presented to the Royal Hungarian Ministry No. 10689/1867," 86 pages, in German and Hungarian, bore the title *"Worte des Friedens und der Wahrheit"* (Words of Peace and Truth). Hirsch was Chief Rabbi of Prague, 1883–1909, before his election as Chief Rabbi of Hamburg. His son, Dr. Isidor Hirsch, was rabbi in the Synagogue Karlín-Praha, lecturer

in Hebrew in the Charles University of Praha, and co-editor with rabbi Dr. Gustav Sicher of the first Czech translation of the Five Books of Moses. (See Stransky, *The Religious Life in the Historic Lands*, vol. I, p. 144).

23. S. Weingarten, "The Polemic Mukačevo-Belz," *Encyclopedia of the Jewish Diaspora*, vol. VII, p. 232 (cites from "calumnious writings," *Magid Mereshit*, Memorial Book, vol. I, p. 23, Lvow 1927, and *Kitve Kodesh*, also titled *Milḥemet Mitzva Heḥadasha*, p. 3, Mukačevo 1928).
24. Alfred Cantarini, *Juden und Judenthuemer in den beiden Donaufuerstenthuemern Moldau und Walachei. Ein Beitrag zur orientalisch-juedischen Geschichte* (Jews and Jewries in the two Danubian Principalities Moldavia and Walachia. A contribution to Oriental-Jewish history), in *Ben Chananja*, vol. II, pp. 12 ff., *ibid.*, pp. 25 and 41.
25. S. Weingarten, "History of Jews Karpatorus," *Encyclopedia of the Jewish Diaspora*, vol. VII, pp. 22 and 23. — L. Gruenwald, *Korot Torah VeEmunah*, chapter II, pp. 25–27.
26. Yehuda Erez, *Encyclopedia of the Jewish Diaspora*, vol. VII, p. 231.
27. A. Sole, "Subcarpathian Ruthenia," *The Jews of Czechoslovakia*, vol. I, p. 126.
28. Andreas Saus, *Juedisches Archiv*, vol. II, Wien 1929. See also S. Weinberg, *Munkacs* (Hebrew), in *Arim VeImahot BeYisrael* vol. I, Mosad HaRav Kook, Jerusalem.
29. A. Sole, *Subcarpathian Ruthenia*, vol. I, pp. 125 and 126.
30. A. Cantarini, *Ben Chananja*, vol. II, pp. 58 and 59.
31. S. Reinherz, "Pirkey Historya" (Historic Chapters), *Encyclopedia of the Jewish Diaspora*, vol. VII, p. 129.
32. Rothkirchen, "Slovakia I," vol. I, p. 74.
33. S. Weinberg, "History Karpatorus," *Encyclopedia of the Jewish Diaspora*, vol. VII, pp. 46 and 47.
34. Yehuda Spiegel, *Arim VeImahot BeYisrael*, vol. IV, pp. 14–15.
35. A. Sole, "Subcarpathian Ruthenia," *The Jews of Czechoslovakia*, vol. I, pp. 135 and 136.
36. G. Fleischmann, "The Religious Congregations," in *The Jews of Czechoslovakia*, vol. I, p. 307.
37. The alleged noise was a cause for a complaint in 1335 by the monks of the Ursulian Order in Bratislava, adjoining the new synagogue. Pope Benedict XII ordered its demolition. Braham and Farkas in *Synagogues in Hungary* by Heller-Vajda, p. 11, quote this as evidence for their thesis of synagogues existing prior to this time in Bratislava. Oskar K. Rabinowicz claims ("Notes on 1,000 Years of Czechoslovak Jewry," 1968, see n. 4 above) that the synagogue in Bratislava

dates from 1368 and is only 100 years younger than the Altneuschul in Prague.

38. In Bratislava there were twenty-four public and private places of worship, among them one for the Polish *Ḥasidim* with the *nusakh Sepharad* in Zsigray House. (Samuel Krauss, *Pressburger Synagogen*, in Gold, *Die Judengemeinde Bratislava*, p. 96).
39. Rabbi Moses Schreiber (*Ḥatam Sofer*) thwarted the first attempts at preaching in German by the Reform Rabbi Aron Choriner from Arad (L. Gruenwald, *Otzar Neḥmad*, p. 72). The rabbinical contference in Michalovce arrived at a decision (*psak din*) in 1866 that opposed preaching in a secular language. It is, however, worthy to note the progress of the enlightenment among the officers of the board of the local community of Bratislava. They offered Dr. Esriel Hildesheimer, the Chief Rabbi of Eisenstadt, the position of Associate Rabbi to the ailing *Ktav Sofer*, Samuel Benjamin Schreiber (1815–1872), the Chief Rabbi of Bratislava (*Hildesheimer Briefe*, p. 68, no. 7, ref. 50), because of his "cultured Orthodox" outlook and in spite of his effort "to keep in touch with the spirit of progress" (*HaMagid*, Berlin 1869, vol. XIII, No. 26). Hildesheimer was the first to introduce secular subjects into the program of his *yeshiva* in Eisenstadt (*ibid.*, p. 41, ref. 69, p. 71). He declined the offer becasne freedom of action in the field of education was not guaranteed to him (*ibid.*, 53 ff. and ref. 142, p. 81). He founded in 1869 the *Rabbinerseminar zu Berlin*, an Orthodox institute for training rabbis on a strict Torah basis combined with modern research.
40. S. Weingarten, *Encyclopedia of the Jewish Diaspora*, pp. 18 and 19.
41. Isaac Ben Solomon Luria (1534–1572), Jerusalem and Safed, renowned for his ascetic life and saintly character.
42. Jakob ben Meir Tam (1100–1171), French scholar. He disagreed with his grandfather Rashi on the order of the verses inscribed in the *tephillin* (phylacteries).
43. Cantor Josef Rosenblatt (1880–1933), one of the finest examples, was first choirboy in Mukačevo, then cantor in Bratislava before he went to America, where he died in 1933. His masterly compositions, apart from his ringing voice, are preserved on records and greatly valued.
44. *Ben Chananja*, voi. VI, pp. 455 ff.
45. *Ibid.*, p. 471, the pronunciation of the Hebrew consonant *ḥet* is found to be easier "by Germans and Slavs."
46. "Brill'sche Shul" in Bratislava (Judengasse 28, formerly Altstadt 258) was known for its preservation of *Pressburg Minhagim* (customs) and melodies. This private synagogue was founded by Ezriel Brill, 1699.

47. In 1376 a regulation was issued for the whole of Hungary, permitting the Jews to buy cattle and slaughter it ritually for their kosher purposes. They were, however, not permitted to sell the non-kosher parts of the cattle, or the unconsumed meat, to the butchers of the city, but had to offer them to non-Jews for purchase by displaying them before their homes or in the market. See *Monumenta Hungariae Judaica*, vol. I, p. 60.
48. See also, for a perfect sample case, "*Geschichte der Juden in Stupava*" (History of the Jews in Stupava) in Gold, *Zeitschrift Geschichte Verlauf der Juden der Tschechoslowakei*, pp. 53–56, and 139 and 204, vol. II, 1931. Further reference, *Monumenta Hungariae Judaica*, vol. V2, p. 168.
49. D. Gross, "*Äusserer Verlauf der Geschichte des Juden* (External Course of the History of the Jews), p. 3 in Gold, *Judengemeinde Bratislava*, *ibid.*, pp. 61–63, Hebrew with German translation. Reference to this elegy Sigmund Salfeld, *Das Martyrologium des Nuernberger Memorbuches* (Martyrology of the Nuremberg Memorialbook), Berlin 1898. Otto Komlos, *Traece documentarie di antiche*, vol. 22, 1956, assumes, in connection with a ritual murder charge, a synagogue in Esztergom in the 11th century.
50. The elegy was written down in a Synagogue codex in Cracow (Poland) by a beadle and is ascribed to the poet Jehoshua ben Ḥami. S. Bettelheim, *Judaica*, vol. IV, Nos. 23–24, p. 9.
51. First edition, Venice, 1616. German translation by Simon L. Ginzberg. The edition of Linevil, 1743, is comprehensive. *Minhagim Shel Kol HaMedinot HaElu Polin UPihem UMeherin VeAshkenaz* (The Customs of all these areas, Poland, Bohemia, Moravia and Germany). About *Gaon* (Supreme Rabbinic Authority) Tyrnau, see L. Gruenwald, *Korot LaTorah VeEmunah BeHungaria* (History of Torah and Faith in Hungary), Budapest, 1921, p. 6.
52. Sis Abraham Aba, *Mínhagey Komárno*, Tel Aviv, 5725.
53. *Ibid.*, p. 2.
54. *Ibid.*, pp. 6 par. 9; 11, par. 27; 21, par. 72; 24, par. 93.
55. S. Reinherz, "Historic Chapters," *Encyclopedia of the Jewish Diaspora*, vol. VII, pp. 125 ff. about the influence of the healing power with amulets by Rabbi Moshe Teitelbaum. Other sources record that mothers had a coin blessed for their babies by the rebbe and worn by them as amulets.
56. For comprehensive description and details consult *Ben Chananja*, vol. VI, pp. 388 ff., M. Zipser, *Josefinische Statuten für sämtliche in Ungarn befindliche Judengemeinden* (Statutes by Josef II, for all Jewish Congregations in Hungary).
57. L. Gruenwald, *Otzar Neḥmad*, pp. 72–73.

58. H. Flesch, *"Das geistige Leben in Pressburg"* (The Spiritual Life in Bratislava), in Gold, *Jews of Bratislava*, p. 57 ff. We quote further: Adolf Altmann, Chief Rabbi in Trier, great orator, historian; Adolf Buechler, Principal of Jews' College London; Charles Duschinsky, private historian and writer, Fellow of Royal Historical Society of England; Benjamin Fischer, Chief Rabbi of orthodox congregation Budapest, formerly Rabbi in Trenčín; David Herzog, Rabbi in Graz and Professor at Graz University; David Hoffmann, Rector "Rabbinerseminar zu Berlin," renowned halakhist and biblical critic; Tobias Jakobovits, librarian in Prague Jewish community and historian; halakhist. Koppel Reich, Chief Rabbi of Autonomous Orthodox Community in Budapest, Member of Hungarian Upper House, whom Emperor Franz Josef I made a Royal Councillor; Arthur (Abraham) Marmorstein, lecturer in Bible and Talmud at Jews' College London, prolific writer in History, *halakha* and folklore; Adolph Neubauer, Professor of oriental languages and literature at Oxford University and librarian of the Bodleian collection of manuscripts; Adolf Salvendy, Rabbi in Karlsruhe, founder of the Zionist Youth group "B'nai Zion" in Bratislava (1883–4), cofounder of the Society for the Colonization of Palestine, Lema'an Zion, and coworker of the Alliance Israelite Universelle, promoter of the Sha'are Zedek Hospital in Jerusalem. On his death, a picture card to his tribute was issued with a biographical sketch in Slovak, German and Hungarian (*Judaica*, vol. IV, nos. 21–22, 1937); Max Schay, rabbi and writer in New York; Salomon Aron Wertheimer, rabbi and bibliographer, researcher in valuable Palestinian and Egyptian manuscripts (Geniza). He has thirty-one works to his name and was eulogized thus: "What he meant to scientific scholarship cannot be estimated, but in the field of talmudic science he belongs to the greatest Gaonim of our time." He died 1935 in Jerusalem (*Judaica*, vol. II, nos. 13–14, vol. III, nos. 17–18).

59. Josef Gruensfeld, *"Neue Geschichte der Jeschiwa"* (New History of the Yeshiva), Gold, *Jews of Bratislava*, p. 67.

60. Gold, *Jews of Bratislava*, p. 61.

61. The "Neutraer Raw" (S. D. Ungar) did not leave the country at the outbreak of the war. Just prior to the liberation he died from starvation and exhaustion in a forest where he was hidden. He is buried in Piešt'any next to his father, a former rabbi there.

62. Complete text in S. Bettelheim, *Judaica*, vol. II, nos. 11–12, pp. 13–14.

63. *Ben Chananja*, vol. II, p. 25, reports that the decline in the knowledge of the sacred teachings in Užhorod was caused by great prosperity and attendance in non-Jewish schools by Jewish children.

64. For a case in point see Gold, *Judengemeinde Bratislava*, "The Schools

of the Orthodox Israelite Community," and in the essay about the Neolog congregation.

65. See G. Fleischmann, "The Religious Congregation," *The Jews of Czechoslovakia*, vol. I, pp. 303 ff. and ref. 24, p. 328 in reference to Jewish schools.
66. M. Freilich, *"Bet Sepher Ivri Rishon"* (The First Hebrew Elementary School), *Encyclopedia of the Jewish Diaspora*, pp. 291–295.
67. A. Rubin, *"Batey hasepher halvri'im"* (The Hebrew schools), *Encyclopedia of the Jewish Diaspora*, pp. 211–320; *ibid.*, pp. 549–550, Dr. Chaim Kugel.
68. The founder of Bratislava's *Beth Hamidrash Synagogue* in 1700 was Simon Michel-Pressburger, a descendant of Samuel Oppenheimer who had been royal commercial agent and overseer in Vienna (Hoffaktor). Pressburger, the greatgrandfather of Heinrich Heine, was accorded the title "Royal Agent for the Mint and Army" by Emperor Josef I (*Judaica*, vol. III, nos. 17–18, pp. 4 and 5).
69. M. Zipser, *Josefinische Statuen für sämtliche in Ungarn befindliche Judengemeinden* (Statutes by Emperor Josef II, for all Jewish Congregations in Hungary), *Ben Chananja*, vol. VI, pp. 388 ff.; A. Kohn, *Josefinische Verordnungen, Kulturverhaeltnisse* (Regulations by Emperor Josef II, Conditions of Culture), *ibid.*, pp. 451–452.
70. For details see G. Fleischmann, "Religious Congregation," *The Jews of Czechoslovakia*, vol. I, pp. 287–288.
71. Already in 1839, a strong article that supported the establishment of a modern theological school for training rabbis and teachers in the Hungarian lands appeared in *Israelitische Annalen* (Jewish Chronicles), J. M. Jost, Frankfurt a.M. 1839. Rabbi David ben Meir Hakohen Friesenhausen, an antagonist of the *Ḥasidim* and Cabbalists and an erudite mathematician, applied to Archduke Josef for permission to set up a theological school for Rabbis. The Ministry of Education and Culture, in a decree of April 7, 1854, No. 5114/53, gave the plan favorable consideration. The rabbinic seminary in Budapest was established 1878.
72. L. Loew, *"Amtswahl der Rabbinen"* (Election of Rabbis), *Ben Chananja*, vol. II, pp. 115 ff.
73. S. Bettelheim, *Judaica*, vol. I, Nos. 3–4, p. 28, 1934.
74. L. Gruenwald, *HaYehudim BeHungaria* (History of the Jews in Hungary), vol. I. p. 5.
75. Cecil Roth, *Standard Jewish Encyclopedia*, p. 1595.
76. B. Suler, *"Rabbinische Geschichtsquellen"* (Rabbinic Sources of History), *Jahrbuch*. vol. VIII, pp. 27–54.
67. In 1930 the late Rabbi Boaz Cohen, then lecturer in The Jewish Theological Seminary of America, compiled a list of volumes of *responsa* up to the end of the 18th century.

78. Ch. Y. Ehrenreich, *Otzar Hahajim*, vol. II, p. 79, 1926; *ibid.*, pp. 79 ff., complains that many books, fine libraries and collections are going astray, changing hands, because they are being sold out of material needs. He commends the example set by Rabbi Eckstein of Sziget (Romania) who started to collect books as a student in Hust. He did not sell his collection of 40,000 books, valued at $25,000, when he moved to America. Instead, he established in New York a center of learning with this library, so as to aid students from Transylvania, Hungary and Slovakia in their studies.
79. *Judaica*, vol. IV, No. 23–24.
80. *Ibid.*, vol. III, nos. 19–20, pp. 32–33.
81. Ch. Y. Ehrenreich, *Ben Chananja*, introduction, vol. VI.
82. Guido Kisch, "*Ein slowakischer Haggada-Illustrator*" (A Slovak Haggada Illustrator), *Judaica*, vol. III, Nos. 19–20 p. 9; Kutlik was a pioneer who departed from the old-fashioned design of *Haggada* pictures and created a new cycle of illustrations that appeared for the first time in the *Haggada*, edited by Prof. Dr. Alexander Kisch, rabbi of the Meisel Synagogue in Prag, 1885–1917.
83. Review in "Selbstwehr," Prag, March 13, 1932, p. 4.
84. Dr. Michael Sučansky, editor of *Sbornik*, *venovaný Dr. Janovi Kvačalovi, profesorovi teologie k sedemdesiatym narodeniniam* (Jubilee volume, dedicated to Dr. Ján Kvačal, professor of theology, on his 70th birthday), Bratislava, 1933.
85. *Iwo Blaetter* (Records of the Yiddish Institute for Jewish Research), vol. IX, nos. 1–2, Wilna, 1936.
86 S. Bettelheim, *Judaica*, vol. I, nos. 1–4, pp. 31–34.
87. *Monumenta Hungariae Judaica*, vol. I, p. 60.
88. M. Stein, "*Aus der Vergangenheit der Trenčíner Judengemeinde*" (From the past of the Jewish Community in Trenčín), *Judaica*, IV, nos. 23–24.; M. S. Herzog, "History of the Jews in Stupava," in H. Gold, *Geschichte der Juden in der Tschechoslowakei*, vol. II, p. 53, 1931.
89. David Gross in H. Gold, *Judengemeinde Bratislava*, p. 120.
90. S. Bettelheim, *Judaica*, vol. III, Nos. 17–18, pp. 4–5.
91. *Ibid.*, vol. I. Nos. 1–2, vol. II, Nos. 15–16.
92. Braham-Farkas, in *Synagogues in Hungary* by Heller-Vajda, p. 6.
93. Ibid., p. 9.
94. Theodor Austerlitz, "*Das Juedische Museum in Prešov*" (The Jewish Museum in Prešov), in Gold, *Geschichte der Juden in der Tschechoslowakei*, vol. I, Brno, 1930.
95. *Ibid.*
96. *Ben Chananja*, vol. II, p. 423.
97. Th. Austerlitz, "*Juedische Museum Prešov*," in Gold, *Geschichte der Juden in der Tschechoslowakei*, vol. I, p. 226.

BIBLIOGRAPHY

Bettelheim, Samuel, *"Judaica," Zeitschrift fuer Geschichte, Literatur und Bibliographie* (Journal for History, Literature and Bibliography). Bratislava, 1934–37.

Blau, Ludwig, *"Hatzophe MeEretz Gor"* (The watchmen from the land of Hungary), *Journal of Jewish Wisdom and Literature*, Budapest, 1911–1932.

Deutschinger, *Fuehrer durch Pressburg und seine Umgebung* (Guide through Pressburg and its environment), S. Steiner, Pressburg, 1873.

Dorfson, S. J., *"50 Yar Idishe Presse In Di Karpaten Berge"* (50 Years of Jewish Press in the Carpathian Mountains), *Literarische Bletter*, vol. 7, Warsaw, 1931.

Ehrenreich, Ch. Y., *"Otzar Ḥaim," Zeitschrift fuer die Wissenschaft des Judendums* (Journal for the Science of Judaism), Humenné 1925–1939.

Eliav, Mordechai, *Rabbiner Esriel Hildesheimer Briefe* (Letters by Rabbi Esriel Hildesheimer), Jerusalem, 1965.

Enciclopedia Shel Galuyot (Encyclopedia of the Jewish Diaspora), col. 7, *Karpatorus* (Yehuda Erez), Jerusalem–Tel Aviv, 1959.

Enten, Emanuel, *"Zur Geschichte der Juden in Košice"* (On the History of the Jews in Košice) in *Zeitschrift fuer die Geschichte der Juden in der Tschechoslowakei* (Hugo Gold), vol. II, Brno, 1931.

George, Manfred, *Juedische Revue* (Jewish Review), Nekudah Publishing House, Mukačevo, 1936–38.

Gold, Hugo, *Zeitschrift fuer die Geschichte der Juden in der Tschechoslowakei* (Journal for the History of the Jews in Czechoslovakia). Brno, Prague, 1930–1938.

———, *Die Juden und Judengemeinde Bratislava in Vergangenheit und Gegenwart* (Past and Present of the Jews and of the Jewish Community of Bratislava), Brno, 1932.

Gruenwald, Jehuda Leopold, *Korot HaTorah VeEmunah BeHungaria* (History of Torah and Belief in Hungary), Brothers Herzberg Printing House, Budapest, 1921.

———, *"HaYehudim BeHungaria," Geschichte der Juden in Ungarn* (History of the Jews in Hungary), vol. I, Biographies of Rabbis and Scholars in Hungary, Kohn Mór, Vácz, 1912.

———, *Otzar Neḥmad* (A Collection of Essays on Law [*halakha*] and Wisdom in Israel) New York, 1942.

———, *LeKorot Haḥasidut BeHungaria* (On Hasidism in Hungary), Vacz, 1912.

——, *Korot Ir Pressburg Ugdoleyha* (History of Pressburg and its great men), Sziget, 1912.

Heller, I. and Vajda Z., *The Synagogues in Hungary*, New York, 1968.

Jahrbuch der Gesellschaft fuer Geschichte der Juden in der Čechoslovakischen Republik (Yearbook of the Society for the History of the Jews in the Czechoslovak Republic), vol. II, Praha, 1930, vol. V, Praha, 1933.

The Jews of Czechoslovakia, vol. I, Philadelphia, 1968.

Jost, J. M., *Israelitische Annalen* (Israelite Chronicles), vol. I, Frankfurt/M., 1839.

Jung, Leo, "Jewish Leaders," *The Jewish Library*, vol. VI, New York, 1945.

——, "Guardians of our Heritage" *The Jewish Library*, vol. VII, New York, 1958.

Kohn, S., *Geschichte der Juden in Ungarn* (History of the Jews in Hungary), Budapest, 1884.

Loew, Leopold, *Ben Chananja, Monatsschrift fuer juedische Theologie* (Monthly, Journal of Jewish Theology), vol. I–X, Szegedin & Budapest, 1858–1867.

Loewinger, Herman, *"Pressburger Ghettobilder"* (Ghetto Scenes of Pressburg), *Wirt'sche Hofbuchdruekerei*, A. G. Mainz, Pressburg, 1900.

Menyhert, Lanyi and Popper, Hermin (Bekefi), *Szlovenszkoi Zsido hitközse gek története* (History of the Jewish Communities in Slovakia) Kassa [Košice], 1933.

Monumenta Hungariae Judaica, vol. I–X, Budapest, 1903–1968.

Olbracht Ivan: *Golet v údolí* (Exil in the Valley) Praha, 1937,

Orgán Československé Památkové Péče (Journal of the Czechoslovak Care of Memoria), vol. 24, no. 7, Praha, 1964.

Pick, J., *Juedische Geschichtliche Staetten* (Jewish Historic Sites), Vienna' 1935.

Rabinowicz, Oskar K., *Notes on 1,000 Years of Czechoslovak Jewry*, Library Hebrew University, Jerusalem.

Roth, Cecil, *The Standard Jewish Encyclopedia*, New York, 1962.

Schwartz, S., *Shem Hagedolim MeEretz Hagor* (History and Biography of Hungarian Rabbis and Authors of Talmudic Works), vol. I and II, Paks and Mukačevo, 1914.

Segert, St., "Hebrew Studies in Czechoslovakia," *Studia semitica, philologica et philosophica*, Slovenskej akademie, Bratislava, 1965.

Sis, Abraham Aba, *Minhagim Komarno* (The Religious Customs of Komarno), Tel Aviv, 5725.

Sofer (Schreiber) David, *Mazkeres Paksh* (Memorial Book of Paks) 2 vols., Jerusalem, 1962.

Stein, Mair *Jahrbuch des traditionstreuen Rabbinerverbandes in der Slovakei* (Yearbook of the Association of Traditional Rabbis in Slovakia), Trnava, 1923–1935.

Weingarten, S., *Arim VeImahot Be Yisrael* (Cities and Mothers in Israel), vol. I–VII, Mosad HaRav Kook, Jerusalem, 1945–66.

Wischnitzer, Rahel, *European Synagogues*, Philadelphia, 1965.

Wohlgemuth, Josef, *Jeschurun*, Ortodox Scientific Journal, vol. 1–18, Berlin, 1914–1930.

SOCIAL WORK IN THE HISTORIC LANDS

by Chaim Yahil

A systematic program of Jewish social work began relatively late in the Historic Lands. At the end of the nineteenth and the beginning of the twentieth century, the Jews of these three provinces were similar sociologically to the Jews of the West. The overwhelming majority belonged to the middle and upper socioeconomic classes. However, at the time, the Jews of the Historic Lands were well outside the mainstream of Jewish migration from Eastern to Western Europe and to the overseas countries, and thus the Jewish communities of Bohemia, Moravia, and Silesia took no part in philanthropic activities carried on by wealthy Jews in the Western countries for the relief of their suffering brethren in the East. At the turn of the present century, the Historic Lands had no organization corresponding to the Jewish Colonization Association, the Alliance Israélite, or the Hilfsverein der Deutschen Juden.

Naturally, there were needy persons even in the prosperous Jewish communities of Bohemia and Moravia. But these — the orphans, the aged, the sick, the deserted wives, the disabled, and those intellectually or morally isolated from society — were cared for by private charity.

From the very beginning, every Jewish congregation had voluntary philanthropic institutions, such as burial societies, Bikkur Holim societies for the care of the sick, women's charitable organizations, and Hakhnasat Kalla organizations which provided dowries for brides without financial means. Thus the Jews of Prague had a Hevra Kadisha for the burial of the dead, a Bikkur Holim society, a Charity Association (Lidumilný spolek, Naechstenliebe-Verein), and an organization known as Mehalke Tarn'golim which served chicken soup every Sabbath to the sick and the poor.

The large influx of penniless students into Prague and Brno at the beginning of the twentieth century led to the formation of such organizations as the Freitischverein, a free-meal kitchen (Židovská stravovna) and Mensa Academica, which served free or low-cost meals to Jewish university students.

In the early twentieth century, several Jewish orphanages were established in Prague, and the inauguration of philanthropic foundations by the Laemel, Seger, and Jeiteles families, and other well-known Jewish families in the city took place.

The heavy migration of Jews from the villages and small towns into the larger towns and cities in the years immediately preceding World War I in the Historic Lands* posed a serious welfare problem. Most of those making the move were able to improve their social and economic status, but there were many who did not succeed in making a living in the big cities and who became a burden to the private Jewish welfare organizations. In addition, there was the problem of the itinerant beggars.

These new social-welfare needs led to the establishment of the Commission for the Poor (Komise pro chudé — Armenkommission), at the headquarters of the Jewish Congregation in Prague just before the outbreak of World War I. Also established in Prague during that period were a Jewish home for the chronically ill, and a Jewish Vacation Association which provided free vacations for the needy.

The war, the subsequent disintegration of the Austro-Hungarian Monarchy, and the establishment of the Czechoslovak Republic brought additional problems. As a result of the war, nearly half a million Jews had fled from Poland and the Bukovina territory to the Western part of the Monarchy, including the Historic Lands. The Jewish congregations of Bohemia and Moravia strained their resources to the utmost, particularly in the area of education and care for refugee children who had to be placed in schools, hostels, and vacation colonies. While the majority of the refugees returned to their former homes at the end of the war, several thousand remained in Czechoslovakia after the breakup of the Monarchy, and these constituted a diverse group of foreign and "stateless" Jews. In the early 1920's, there were in Czechoslovakia over 15,000 "stateless" Jews, and also a large number of war widows and orphans who were

* [Cf. vol. I, Kestenberg, pp. 21–1. (Ed.)]

given support by local Jewish welfare organizations to supplement the public assistance they received fron the State.

The immediate post-war period also brought a heavy influx of refugees from Russia and the Ukraine, victims of pogroms and of political persecutions. Many of these immigrants wanted to continue to Palestine or the United States, but had neither the required documents nor the necessary funds to do so. In addition, Czechoslovakia received large numbers of Jewish students from Poland, Hungary, and elsewhere in Central and Southern Europe who had been refused admission to universities in their native countries owing to religious discrimination in the form of a direct or indirect *numerus clausus*, and who now sought entry into Czechoslovak universities.

Thus cities like Prague, Brno, Moravská Ostrava, and Bratislava became receiving centers for indigent Jewish students from Central and Eastern Europe and for stranded transients. All this, in addition to the pauperization of the Jews of Germany and Austria as a result of the post-war inflation and economic breakdown, confronted the Jews of the western part of the new Czechoslovak Republic with problems and responsibilities for which they lacked financial, organizational, and emotional preparation. The thinking of the leaders of these well-established Jewish communities was still mainly along lines of Jewish solidarity and individual or small-group philanthropy. They were, to an overwhelming degree, ignorant of the concepts of modern social welfare.

The initiative for reform in Jewish philanthropy to meet the needs of the times came from two organizations: the Jewish National Council (Židovská Národní Rada), founded in 1918* which, under the leadership of Dr. Ludvík Singer and Max Brod, played a role of crucial significance among Czechoslovak Jewry in the early years of the Republic; and the B'nai B'rith Lodges, led by Dr. Joseph Popper, which dominated the social and intellectual life of the Jewish community.†

It was on the initiative of the B'nai B'rith Lodges and the Jewish National Council that a Jewish Welfare Center was established in Prague in 1920. This Center was a corporate entity whose membership consisted of Jewish congregations, lodges, and organizations, as well as of private individuals such as the Petschek families in

* [Cf. A. M. Rabinowicz, Vol. I, pp. 156ff. (Ed.)]

† [Cf. vol. I, Fleischmann, p. 312. (Ed.)]

Bohemia,* a well-known Jewish banking family that provided generous financial support. The first president of the Center was Dr. Heinrich (Chaim)Brody, who was then the Chief Rabbi of Prague. Other important participants were Hugo Slonitz, Dr. Wilhelm Wiesmeyer, Dr. Salomon Lieben, and Mrs. Caecilie Ehrenfeld. Originally, the organization had been intended as a central body which was to attend to all Jewish welfare needs throughout the Republic, or at least in the Historic Lands, but because of insufficient funds, the Jewish Welfare Center confined its activities to the care of impecunious students, transient refugees, and children in the city of Prague.

The economic crisis of the 1930's brought home to the Jews of the Historic Lands the realization that problems of Jewish social welfare did not involve only refugees or "foreign" Jews. Many small businessmen in Bohemia and Moravia went bankrupt; employees of commercial enterprises remained without jobs; commission agents lost their sources of income; and university graduates were unable to find positions.

The Jewish Welfare Center in Prague set up a department for emergency relief to assist families made destitute by the economic depression. Funds for this purpose were collected by the Jewish congregations; but it soon became clear that the means at the disposal of the Center were not sufficient to meet the desperate need. The Center then began a program of assistance involving goods and services, the organizing of a clothing depot, and a coal drive for the winter. However, it was now obvious that the times demanded a large-scale and long-range social welfare program sponsored by the Jewish congregations.

The situation was further aggravated by the rise to power of the Nazis in 1933, as a result of which large numbers of German Jews streamed into Czechoslovakia, seeking refuge. In November 1933, Foreign Minister Beneš declared that his government was proud to offer asylum to the victims of Nazism. However, in view of the widespread unemployment then prevailing in the country, only 3,000 of the refugees, "repatriates" of Czechoslovak nationality, were given permission to work; and until they found jobs, most of these 3,000 — like many of the other immigrants — were in need of financial support.

---

* [Cf. Pick, p. 366 in Vol. I (Ed.)]

A Jewish Committee for Refugees from Germany was established and it initiated a major fund-raising drive in the Jewish communities of the Historic Lands. Dr. Joseph Popper, chairman of the Supreme Council of the Jewish Congregations and President of the Tenth District of B'nai B'rith, acted as chairman of the Committee. The bulk of the practical work was done by the two vice-chairmen, Marie Schmolka and Hanna Steiner, who, from 1933 until the end of the Czechoslovak Republic, were the leaders in Jewish social work in the country. The Emergency Committee's funds were derived from allocations from the Jewish communities and from the American Jewish Joint Distribution Committee (JDC).

The Committee set up a special department of occupational retraining which provided agricultural training for young refugees from Germany who intended to emigrate to Palestine. Since the Czechoslovak authorities viewed this constructive program with favor, the future *Halutzim* easily obtained work permits or, in many instances, were permitted to work without papers. At one time, as many as 300 *Halutzim* from Germany were taking the agricultural course in Czechoslovakia. In the summer of 1934, this program was taken over by a special department organized for that purpose by HeHalutz in Germany.

In 1935, the task of coordinating Jewish social work activities was taken over by the Social Institute of the Jewish Congregation of Greater Prague, a branch office of HICEM in Czechoslovakia. HICEM (the acronym representep the names of the cooperating organizations: HIAS, ICA, and EMigration-Direction), with headquarters in Paris and working closely with the JDC, was in charge of the registration of Jewish refugees and of their relief once they settled in their new homes. In the case of emigrants to Palestine, HICEM confined its assistance to the securing of passports and financial help with transportation. Most important among the innovations introduced by the Social Institute was the establishment of departments for economic and vocational counseling. The Institute secured teaching positions for qualified candidates, worked very closely with the three homes for Jewish apprentices, and took over an employment office which, until that time, had been operated under private auspices. The Institute also attempted to set up a *Družstevní záložna* (Free Loan Fund), but did not succeed in doing so. The Jewish congregations in Brno and Moravská Ostrava were more successful along these lines. In the field of youth welfare, the Social Institute opened a registration and classification center, placing young refugees into institutions or as boarders with Jewish families, and working jointly with orphanages, hostels for abandoned children, institutions for mentally retarded children, homes for young girls, and with organizations such as the Židovská stravovna (Jewish free-meal kitchen) and the Jewish Vacation Association.

In time, social-welfare activities other than those connected with refugee relief continued in the hands of the social-welfare institutions of the individual Jewish communities and voluntary organizations. In this connection, mention should be made of the Židovská péče o nemocné, the Jewish Sick Relief Organization, whose chairman, Dr. Salomon Lieben, was immortalized by the famous actor Hugo Haas in the motion-picture version of Karel Čapek's drama *Bílá némoc* (The White Plague).

Soon the Social Institute of the Jewish Congregation of Greater Prague also established a central clearing house for the welfare activities conducted by the congregations and the voluntary organizations. Gradually, the Institute took over the functions of the Jewish Welfare Center, and by 1937 it had absorbed the Center's one remaining independent tacivity, namely, its program for the welfare of transient refugees.

As the old practices followed by the Commission for the Relief of the Poor and other private philanthropic organizations gave way to organized programs of social welfare, it became clear that philanthropic acivity alone was not the answer to the many social problems besetting the Jewish community of the Historic Lands. What was sorely needed was a program of preventive social action, not confined to individual communities but embracing the Jews of the entire Republic. Ways had to be found not only to relieve the misery of the Jewish masses in Subcarpathian Ruthenia, but also to give help and guidance to the Jews in the Historic Lands who were bewildered and shaken by the economic crisis at home and the persecution of their brethren abroad. It became clear that the lack of an all-embracing community organization covering the entire Republic made it difficult to plan social and political action on behalf of Czechoslovak Jewry.

The initiative for these new concepts came from the Zionist camp. Not doubting for one moment that Diaspora Judaism was headed for disaster, the Zionists were not satisfied merely to act in behalf of their followers, but were anxious to have the Jewish community as a whole benefit from their program. In addition to organizing 'Aliya and preparing young people and adults for settlement in Palestine by vocational counseling and retraining, the Zionists devised systematic plans for dealing with social-welfare problems in Czechoslovakia. A program with this aim in mind was outlined by this writer at the last Territorial Zionist Conference held in Moravská Ostrava before the demise of the Republic in 1938. The new Executive Board of the Central Zionist Organization began negotiations for the implementation of the proposals. However, the top leadership of Czechoslovak Jewry, including the chairman of the Supreme Council of Jewish Congregations, the president of the Jewish Congregation in Prague, and particularly Jewish welfare organizations like JDC and HICEM, found the program too radical and Zionist-centered and endorsed a course of action that was more moderate, but also focused upon vocational retraining.

Following negotiations conducted at the close of 1938 by Marie Schmolka with the representatives of JDC and the Supreme Council, a central welfare organization for the Jews of the Historic Lands was set up, headed by Professor Theodor Grushka.

Unfortunately, the plans laid by this organization never came to fruition, for the end of the Jewish community of Czechoslovakia was nearer than even the most outspoken Zionists had predicted. The Nazi annexation of Austria in 1938 resulted in an additional avalanche of Jewish refugees, a large part of whom settled in Brno. In the fall of 1938, following the Munich Agreement, 17,000 Jews from the Sudeten territory streamed into the interior of Czechoslovakia, particularly to Prague.* That November, Czechoslovakia lost additional territory to Hungary and Poland. The rump state which remained after the Munich and Vienna agreements was unequivocally anti-Semitic, making it impossible to carry out a systematic program of Jewish social welfare. Now all that the Jewish organizations and the Zionist movement in Czechoslovakia could do was to provide emergency assistance to the victims of persecution and to expedite their emigration to countries where they would find shelter and freedom.

---

* [Cf. Grossmann, p. 571 (Ed.)]

BIBLIOGRAPHY

František Friedmann, *Einige Zahlen über die Tschechoslowakischen Juden*, Prague, 1933.

P. Garin, *Jüdische Emigracie fun Tschechoslowakei* (Yiddish), *Jüdische Ekonomik*, vol. III, 1939.

E. Hoffmann, *Zum sozialen Problem der Tschechoslowakischen Juden*, *Jüdische Wohlfahrtspflege und Sozialpolitik*, Berlin, 1936.

J. Hoffmann, *K otázce židovskć socialní pćče v Praze*, Věstník, Prague, 1934.

J. Hoffmann, "Židovská sociální prace," in *Židovský kalendář*, Prague, 1938.

Otto Dov Kullka, *The Munich Pact and Czechoslovak Jewry in 1938* (Hebrew), Moreshet, Tel-Aviv, 1965.

Marie Schmolková, "O sociální práci" (On Social Work), in *Židovský kalendář*, Prague, 1937–1938, pp. 114–119.

MODERN HEBREW EDUCATION IN SUBCARPATHIAN RUTHENIA *

by Aryeh Sole

I. INTRODUCTION

On the European map, and certainly on the world map, Subcarpathian Ruthenia occupies only a very small strip of land. From the geophysical aspect, the brown color of the area testifies to its mountainous character, and indeed the land bears the name of those mountain chains that stretch through the length of its northern border. As to "Subcarpathian Ruthenia," that term refers to the population, which consists mostly of Ruthenians and other ethnic groups. For hundreds of years a quiet, laboring population dwelled here and subsisted upon the forests and rivers, mountains and valleys, fields and meadows, vineyards and quarries. Due to its location as a connecting link between East and West, there developed in the course of time a lively trade, especially after the coming of the Jews — who received residence permits from the Austro-Hungarian monarchy, by whom this territory was governed. This political affiliation decided the backward fate of the country economically and forced upon it Hungarization, culturally and socially. Among the numerous ethnic groups — Ruthenians, Slovaks, Germans, Romanians, Jews, and Gypsies — the Hungarian population constituted only a minority; it was, however, a ruling minority. Therefore, the Hungarization process was particularly strong in the cities only, whereas in the villages the Ruthenians preserved their own language;

---

* This study was published by Ogen Publishing House of Histadrut Ivrith, New York, in Hebrew, 1957. Translated into English by Joseph Berger.

in the cities the Hungarization was evident mostly among the Jews, and even there Yiddish continued to exist as a mother tongue and the language of trade in most families.

From the capital cities — Budapest and Vienna — only weak echoes broke through, and only a very few indeed had any business or social contact with the Jews. True, there were some rare cases of individuals who managed to free themselves from the bonds of conservatism and broke through to gain more spacious settlements. But again, this happened in most cases among the Jewish population, whose absolute and relative numbers continued to grow from generation to generation.

World War I constituted, in this context, an important chapter and brought about a complete revolution in all aspects of life. This does not necessarily mean that a radical change took place in one wave of the hand — not at all. Many years of struggle passed until these changes were clearly evident. However, the foundations were laid, the new seeds were planted in the ground, and their robust sproutings came out in full bloom in the course of time.

War captives who had spent some time in Russia brought with them, upon returning home, various rumors about pogroms of Jews, on the one hand, and the movement for national revival, on the other. The slogans of "Nationalism" and "Zionism" became more and more frequent. Those lonely few who expressed an interest in Zionism before World War I now renewed their contacts, spread their information about the movement, and mobilized adherents. The villages bordering Poland and Subcarpathian Ruthenia, which were annexed at the end of the war to the Czechoslovakian Republic, served now as transit centers for the refugees from Ukrainian pogroms whose destination was Palestine. This movement, which was continuing underground, stopped only with the coming of order after the chaotic days of the termination of the war. Another factor for change, for example, was the yeshiva students who returned from Bratislava* or from more distant places bringing with them tidings of a new life. And so the army of converts continued to increase until the representatives of this new heretical "sect" reached the most distant parts of the country, openly or secretly. If this happened in the villages, it certainly developed in such towns as Mukačevo.

* [From the world-renown Pressburger yeshiva of Bratislava. (Ed.)]

The circle became gradually wider and wider; the cloudy concepts cleared up.

In the meantime, the Hebrew-Speaking Union was organized (Agudath Dovrei Ivrith). Soon this movement was to assume a political status, when the Republic proclaimed the rights of minorities, among whom the Jews were also included (even though the gap between proclamation and implementation was still wide, especially with regard to the Jews).

Indeed, national rights were given fully to all minorities. This made possible the erection of public elementary and high schools, where the minority languages received the status of an official language wherever the minority reached 20 percent of the total population, developing thereby a national culture for establishing libraries, newspaper publishing, institutions, etc.

And what was the fate of the Jews? The truth of the matter is that the government encouraged the social consolidation of nationalist Jewry not so much because of "the love of Mordecai," i.e., for its own sake, but rather because "of the hatred of Haman." The government was mainly interested in weakening the influence of the Hungarians, among whom were numbered many Hungarian-speaking Jews. With the strengthening of the national Jewish camp, the percentage of the Hungarians was diminished, and they could not demand too many rights. However, when the issue was actually enabling the development of national Jewish life, the government bureaucracy closed its ears to Jewish demands. We cannot enter here into a detailed account of the Jewish struggle in various spheres of life to bring to reality what they were justly enittled to. Our aim is only the sphere of education, even though we cannot avoid touching upon other spheres directly tied up with education.

National Jewry was not yet properly organized. It was lacking leaders, and those that were on hand were either too young or overly temperamental or more mature but lacking in organizational experience. In any case, the voice of the Zionists became more and more audible. Such organizations as Hatechiyah, Kadimah, and Dovrei Ivrith grew like mushrooms after the rain. Gradually a group was organized whose aim was giving the Jewish child a Hebrew education from the very start; and a Hebrew education meant to them familiarizing the children with spoken Hebrew language from a tender age. This aspiration was also much attended to by the Zionist women, who from the beginning took part in cultural activities and social aid. But as the Zionist camp grew, so did the opposition to it. The communities, their rabbis, and their followers were in the forefront of the opponents. They saw in the projected Hebrew school a menace to their very existence and rule; and particularly did the sight of the yeshiva youths who became "heretics" cause them to shudder.

While the adults were weaving secretly or openly the youthful dreams of a new life, the children continued to breathe in the twilight of a world that was decaying from age — they still ran about in alleys and lots a little while longer, their childhood years passed, and still they did not shake off their frightful war experiences. A rumor passed around in the camp that the schools would be opened and life would go back to its usual course. What should be done? Some children had already grown up and had already started school before the war — these had to continue in the Hungarian schools. But what would the officials say? They established Ruthenian and Czech schools not only for the Ruthenian and Czechs alone but for the whole population. What should the Jew choose then? By rights he should choose a Ruthenian school because he lived among them. But the question arose of whether it was the practical thing to do, when the country was Czech-oriented.

In his great confusion in the meantime, the Jew kept his son back from school and continued to keep him in the Heder. That institution continued its existence as if nothing had happened, and the children went there, some by force and some willingly. At the age of three and four, in some cases, the children wound their way in one of the alleys of the Jewish quarter to the Melamdim, some accompanied by an assistent ("behelfer") or by parents and some by themselves. The Hadarim were spread out in all the towns and villages; there was almost no street that was without this type of "spiritual center." Most of them were operating either in a private dwelling or in a "kloiz" (a small place of worship and learning for adults).

What was the nature of the teachers (the Melamdim) themselves? Of course we should beware of generalizations here. There were among them men who were driven to this profession only because of their economic plight. The seeking of a livelihood forced them to grasp the "Melamed's stick," or more correctly the "Rebbe's strap." These were poor Jews, bitter and nervous, in most cases boorish and ignorant. Woe to the child who fell into their hands. However, there were Melamdim of a different type, Jews with a pedagogical sense, with an understanding and love for children, endowed with a sense of humor, and needless to say learned in the Torah and gifted with the refinement of good manners. Among them were some who had a progressive outlook on life and did not shun innovations, such as teaching Hebrew grammar, the Bible sections of the Prophets and the Writings, and arithmetic and even arranging walks and bathing in the river. It is clear that these were exceptional individuals whose pupils were mostly the children of the rich, or at least respectable members of the community. Between these two extremes there were many categories, some good, some bad; each "rebbe" had his own system. One thing they shared in common: none of them fitted into the contemporary scene and its needs. The first type was obnoxious to the child and even to the parents, whereas the latter type, despite its goodness and nobility, soon became superfluous, since the pupils that usually supplied it turned gradually to the general schools or, after awhile, to the schools which taught Hebrew. There were left, therefore, only those hundreds of Melamdim who were "neither here nor there." And it was indeed from them that the great educational threat was emanating. It was from them that the child learned all too soon ways of trickery and falsehood, how to outsmart the teacher and make fun of him. Such years of study in the Heder served only to gather "life experiences" from impure sources. It was here that a generation of multitudes of children grew up without Torah and without manners, with no morals and no readiness for work. Formal learning won its battle here, but behind it all physical and spiritual decay set in.

We should point out that there was another method of inculcating a Jewish child with a knowledge of "Ivri" (Hebrew reading) and other such "Jewish studies," and that was the house teacher. But this method was favored by only a few, who were already on the verge of assimilation. In the capacity of this sort of private teacher we very often find the "religious teacher" of the public school, or a young adult who acquired a reputation in his circles as a Maskil (enlightened person).

To the childhood environment of Jewish children in Subcarpathian Ruthenia — at least to the children of the wealthy — belonged the gentile maid. This Shikse* had complete sway over the mind of the

* [Gentile maid: female help (Ed.)]

child. She even taught him the "Modeh Ani" and other prayers and blessings. They acquired very quickly a knowledge of the Yiddish language and were well versed in all Jewish modes of life. Needless to say, this did not affect their own way of life, and this "culture" that was brought in from the outside was also "superimposed" on the soul of the child. This consisted largely in terror stories, songs of soldiers, expressions of vulgarity, and indecent mannerisms.

But finally that small Zionist group that still held on to the idea of a school for Hebrews was impelled to take action, for compulsory education for every child from the age of six to fourteen was proclaimed. The debates that were raging regarding this matter were abandoned on many fronts: inwardly and outwardly. Outwardly there existed that formal right to establish such a school, but in practice no recognized pedagogical program was present to the government. All the conditions that were necessary for the establishment of such a normal school were lacking. A building, teachers, textbooks, and finally even pupils were very scarce. And who could bear all the expenses necessary for such a project? The Jewish National Committee in Prague and Užhorod made many efforts to obtain a permit to open Hebrew school but without any practical results. Besides, the Hungarians inaugurated an intensive propaganda campaign against those "Sons of the Religion of Moses," whose mother tongue had been Hungarian for hundreds of years but who suddenly wanted to educate their children in a forgotten Asiatic language — they could not point to a single corner in any part of the world where it was used as a living language. But the difficulties of the inward struggle were sevenfold: assimilators, Hasidim, and the indifferent. The first two were open enemies, and the movement knew to plan its tactics against them. But the main problem was how to break the ice of indifference. To this camp belonged the majority of the people. The ordinary Jew who saw nothing in life outside the actual struggle for existence, whose sole meaning was a livelihood, had no understanding of and was not interested in such concepts as national feeling, national consciousness, or the Jewish problem. It was therefore necessary to develop an apparatus for propaganda, information, and adult education. But within the social economic framework of that time this seemed impossible.

II. MODEST BEGINNINGS (1920–1924)

Nothing stands in the way of will and determination. A handful of Jewish families decided to put a stop to arguments and debates and to get to work. In several places the foundations were laid for a Hebrew kindergarten, in order that they might be able to build the Hebrew elementary school of the institution in a gradual, organized manner. There was also another way: to open immediately a school for Jewish children with all classes. But an institution of that type would turn into a Jewish school rather than a Hebrew one.

The Zionist vision was altogether different. It meant starting everything anew. Also, from a practical aspect it would enable them to put every subject of study in a Hebrew form and prepare teachers for the new classes that would follow gradually. The public at large as well as the parents could in this way be convinced more easily, for they would clearly see the positive results.

This also slowly convinced the government itself that the new Hebrew school did not serve merely as an aid in keeping up sentimental contacts with the age that passed, and that it was also not a transition for adapting themselves to the new environment of the democratic republic, but that it was an indication of the genuine will of that part of Judaism that strives to live according to its national forms just like the other minorities — but with the additional ingredient of a vision of a homeland. Also from the aspect of the material resources this seemed to be the only way, since little by little it would be possible also to draw the attention of the Jews in other parts of the country to this new project that was being built up.

Thus the Organization for Hebrew Schools in Subcarpathian Ruthenia was established, whose function it was to provide for all matters of the Hebrew school, materially as well as pedagogically. But the organization was not in a position to maintain the schools that were being established in some settlements in Subcarpathian Ruthenia. They were forced to collect tuition from the parents. This immediately estranged a large part of the public, who could not meet such an obligation. In order to have a better understanding of the difficult struggle of the organization in its material aspects for the upkeep of the Hebrew schools, it is necessary to know something of the economic condition of the Jewish masses in Subcarpathian Ruthenia at that time.

After World War I, the Jews, with their usual good sense, started to look for the new opportunities that were inherent in the change of environment at the transition to a democratization and capitalization of life. Some succeeded and became rich. These were big merchants, agents, and manufacturers. Most of them lived in the city. But also in the villages there appeared owners of large estates, forests, and industrial and agricultural projects. At the beginning of the organization of the country, it seemed that the middle class also — the small businessman, the storekeeper, the artisan, the official, and the professionals — would fit into the general economic framework. Their hopes, however, were soon smashed. The Czech industrial companies began to flood the market with cheap goods, and the workers could not stand up against this sort of competition.

We should also remember that the distribution of the Jews according to their points of concentration in Subcarpathian Ruthenia was at that time still entirely different from any other country. Two-thirds lived in villages and only one-third in the cities. In the villages, their economic condition was no different from the Ruthenian peasants', especially in the mountainous villages. According to the occupational subdivision of the Jews of Subcarpathian Ruthenia on the basis of the statistics of the year 1920, it is characteristic that 40 percent of the population were registered as lacking any specific form of livelihood — in other words, paupers, supported people, clerics, or others just "roaming about in the air."

No wonder then that such a public could not maintain a network of independent schools with its own resources. Because of that, the very idea of a Zionist youth penetrated at a very slow pace into the ranks of Jewish youth. In the school year of 1920/21, Jewish pupils in the various general schools were found to be 72 percent of total pupil enrollment in the whole of Subcarpathian Ruthenia, and of these only a small number were registered as being of Jewish nationality. The following picture will illustrate more clearly the lot of Jewish nationalism among the youth. In the school year 1920/21 there were 23 Jewish public schools functioning in Subcarpathian Ruthenia and in Slovakia, which had an enrollment of 2,507 pupils. In 16 of these schools the language of instruction was Slovak, in 4 Hungarian, in 2 German, and only in one school (in the town of Mukačevo) the language of instruction was Hebrew; it had an enrollment of 45 pupils. Aside from that, the general census of the population in Subcarpathian Ruthenia in the year 1921 proved that Jews who gave their nationality as Jewish formed 14 percent of the whole population and six-sevenths of the Jewish population as a whole. Nevertheless, no special sum, not even the slightest, appeared in the state and national budget. President T.G. Masaryk made an attempt to soften a little the heavy impression — he made a personal contribution of 10,000 Czech crowns for the benefit of the Hebrew school in Mukačevo. And we should dwell more upon this phenomenon. The government still considered the Hebrew school an institution worthy of philanthropic aid, but not one entitled to an official allotment from the government.

How great was the need for Hebrew schools for Jewish children in Subcarpathian Ruthenia was proven by the political confusion in this field in which, in the final analysis, the Jews suffered from very much more, for in the years 1921/24 the number of Jewish children in the public schools of Subcarpathian Ruthenia in general was about 13,000 annually; from these several hundred went to the Hebrew schools (the high in the year 1923/24 was 950 pupils). So it still does not make any difference if the other thousands of pupils were defined as being of Jewish nationality, since they were spread in Hungarian, Czech, and Ruthenian schools. What an opportunity for anti-Semites to incite all the nationalities about the Jew! The Ruthenians said that the Jews were causing Czechization and Hungarization; the Hungarians accused them of being traitors to their mother tongue. The Czechs claimed that they were not "loyal" to the state. As to the government policy, we may add that for the insignificant German segment in Subcarpathian Ruthenia the government set up seven public schools, and in small places, where there was not even one Czech child, the government set up Czech schools — for the Jews.

But Hebrew schools numbered nine altogether, and all run at the expense of the parents and the Organization for Hebrew Schools. After a hard and continued struggle, the ruling powers agreed to participate in the upkeep of the Hebrew schools with the sum of 50,000 crowns — when the total budget was ten times as much! The problem of maintaining the Hebrew schools engaged wider and wider Jewish circles, and began to awaken the interest of Jewry in the western part of the Republic. As a result, there was established in the year 1923 the organization Tarbut, which in the years to come carried the major brunt of the upkeep of the Hebrew schools. Also the organization (Histadrut) broadened its activities and in the year

1924 had active branches in fifteen districts. The reputation of its schools was widely known. The visits of distinguished people from abroad and the local officials became more and more frequent.

In the cities of Mukačevo, Sevluš, Berehovo, Hust and in towns such as Svaljava, Butčkov, and Turon there were tens and hundreds of pupils who were young missionaries for a new idea and pioneers of a new form of life. For indeed, as far as the first parents who enrolled their children in a Hebrew school were concerned, this was a thrust toward something new, unknown, and fateful. True, the children felt this mission of theirs through spiritual and bodily suffering, but they carried the brunt with pride and with conviction. In Mukačevo, for instance, before the Hebrew school had any permanent place, a building of its own, they were forced to wander from one school to another good enough to make room for them for a specified time. Sometimes they would be lodged in private dwellings, where the disadvantages for teaching were obvious to all.

As detrimental as this wandering was to the pupils and teachers, there was something positive about it. During their peregrinations — especially in the various schools — they brought over something of the new spirit from that wonderful new circle, and more than one Jewish boy who was not privileged to be a pupil in a Hebrew school was at least privileged to be in the *company* of these "new ones," and looked at them with envy and with longing, and later influenced his parents to transfer him. Wherever the Zionist children appeared, they brought with them happiness and the joy of life, that expression of happiness that radiated from their eyes when they opened their mouths to sing a Hebrew song or picked up their feet to dance. From that first moment, they entered into a new environment in regard to their relationship with the teachers and with their friends. And it was not possible anymore not to notice this attitude of theirs at every step in their behavior and appearance. At the very beginning of this new way of life they were already a uniform society, a consolidated group that was inspired by the same spirit.

Not so in the school of the Gentiles, where the Jewish child felt as if he was part of a riff-raff mixture of Gentiles from the city and village and of fanatic as well as liberal Jews; these contrasts were very often the cause of quarrels and fights. Also, not all the teachers, who were all non-Jews, endeavored to bridge the gap of these contrasts with love and patience. At times they even betrayed anti-Semitic attitudes toward the Jewish children, The main sufferers were the ultra-Orthodox children with the long clothes and the curly sideburns that served as a target of derision for teachers as well as hostile children. But all this did not prevent the Jews from being the most distinguished in their studies, to the dismay of the Gentiles.

The comical as well as the tragic side of this matter came to light when for instance such a child brought home a gift at the end of the school year with the inscription: "Because of his progress and excellent behavior." And this gift was a picture of Alexander Dochanovič, a Ruthenian poet and priest, the author of the national Carpatho-Ruthenian hymn. The child was anticipating a warm and festive reception at home for this gift, but instead his angry orthodox father took hold of him and his picture and threw them both out, saying: "What else... a priest he will hang up for us on the wall..." Or here is another example: a Jewish child who had to memorize a famous Ruthenian song, the content of which in English is: "I was a Ruthenian, I am and I shall be, I was born to a Ruthenian, father and mother were Ruthenians." Naturally, the parents that understood Ruthenian could not swallow these words calmly, and they did not let the child continue his memorizing.

No wonder, then, that every Jewish holiday such as Hanukah, Purin, Lag Bəoymer — which had been celebrated until then by the children in various forms — were now, under the influence of the children of the Hebrew schools, turned into profound experiences, not only for those children alone but also for the Jewish public in general. These holidays became big public functions. Long lines of children went through the streets of the city singing en masse, as the Jewish National Fund box and the waving blue and white flag headed the parade. But it was not all idyllic — it could happen in such cases that a fanatic Hasid from among the followers of the rabbi of Mukačevo or Belz would pass by, and he would then close his eyes and spit out three times, saying: "Thou shalt utterly detest it and thou shall utterly abhor it; for it is accursed."

The Zionist atmosphere spread throughout the length and breadth of the land through the various youth movements. At first it was the scout movement, Kadimah, in whose ranks were enrolled adult youths whose spoken language was still Hungarian or Yiddish. Aside from hikes, games, and setting up camp together, these youths were not yet capable of creating an actual Hebrew atmosphere. But, on the other hand, the youth that could have created that sort of atmosphere was not yet in the category of youths — it was still an army of children, aged ten to eleven. It follows, therefore, that rather than being teachers, the mature youths were learning from the younger ones. Through mutual influence upon one another and by the addition of new forces from Slovakia, there already were in existence more developed Zionist youth movements. There were also created in Subcarpathian Ruthenia such movements as the Hashomer and afterwards Shomer Kadimah, which finally became the Hashomer Hatzair movement. After a few years it developed into one of the most blessed pioneer educational movements in that country. Other youth movements also developed, such as Hanoar Hatzioni, Betar, and Bnai Akiva. All of them were more or less affiliated with the Zionist parties of the adults and were under their supervision or inspiration.

An important part in shaping the image of the Hebrew youth was played by the Zionist press, which began in those days to appear in Subcarpathian Ruthenia. Of course these magazines were in various languages: Hungarian, German, and Yiddish. There was not yet sufficient background for a Hebrew press, but Hebrew periodicals were received from abroad (Poland and Eretz Israel). This served as important spiritual food for the adults, and partly also for youth, which was more fluent in reading Hebrew than in speaking it.

In the meantime, the Zionist camp continued to grow. With every new school year an additional class was opened, and at the beginning of 1924 consultations were already started concerning the lot of the children who, in a little while, would be finishing their studies in public school and looking forward to a high school education in Hebrew.

III. PROGRESS AND ACCOMPLISHMENT (1924–1932)

The question of the establishment of a high school was not simple. First of all there was a long drawn-out debate about the character of such a school. The models of the general high schools in the city, and in the country in general, were not in keeping with the needs of the particular aims of that handful of devoted workers for a refined Hebrew education. The difficulties revolved particularly around the problem of the type of high school needed: whether practical, i.e., professional, commercial; or for general educational purposes, i.e., humanistic and social. Those who visualized the graduates of the gymnasium* as pioneers contributing to the upbuilding of the Land of Israel argued for some sort of synthesis, or at least for an emphasis on the practical aspect and perhaps also the agricultural side. And those who assumed that first of all there was a need for modern Hebrew intellectuals, for a new type of person of wider horizons, argued for the second sort of school, and not necessarily in contradiction to the vision of the first group.

It was also clear to all that one cannot leave out the general educational element of every high school, the preparation at one and the same time for the possibility of continued studies on a higher level, in a university or institute of technology, at home or abroad. Many of the parents indeed made no secret of being intreested in such an education. By looking toward the future and considering also the present, a new type of practical reformed Hebrew gymnasium, which fit all needs, accordingly came in to existence. Consequently, for practical purposes a program of studies was formed that suited the practical as well as the humanistic aims at the expense of the classical studies, Greek and Latin, the first of which was eliminated altogether and the second limited. From the point of view of the general spirit, it was clear that the aim was a national education that injected into the heart of the students a pioneering ideal, together with the demands of materialization. But on the other hand one also should not forsake the universal values — Jewish and humanitarian — that build character and endow the student with the means for the life struggle or existence.

A stormy debate was aroused also in connection with the method of teaching the Bible. It is interesting that in this matter even the anti-Zionist and the ultra-Orthodox of all kinds were aroused, and protested violently that such a "house of impurity" was liable to bring a catastrophe upon the Children of Israel because of the desecration of the holy teachings of their Torah.

After these internal obstacles were finally cleared, the main obstacles came into prominence. Who would head the institution? Who would organize it, administer it, care for its existence spiritually and materially? Who would go to the officials and explain the "special" problems that such an institution had to deal with, and find solutions? A man such as that should possess many qualities! First, he should be a teacher with a diploma from the local univer-

* European secondary school.

sity; second, he should be possessed of an exceptional talent for organization, since outside of the pupils with their enthusiasm and their parents with their good will and a few people with an "obsession," this man was not supplied with concrete tools for the creation of such an institution.

After a search throughout the country, the proper man was found, Dr. Chaim Kugel of blessed memory, chosen for this task through the recommendations of the Zionist leaders in Prague, where Dr. Kugel was already known as a young active Zionist who had just finished his course of studies in the University of Prague. Indeed, from the first moment, and particularly in years to come, they were convinced how successful this choice was. According to his background, Dr. Kugel was Russian — that meant that he was in a position to understand Subcarpathian Jewry, which was, after all, much given to the influence of Eastern Europe. His past was a long chain of activity in the life of the Zionist movement and Hebrew culture from his early youth. His education, outside of the Herzliah gymnasium in Eretz Israel, included universities in Russia and finally a doctorate from the University of Prague. His personality was sympathetic and sociable; he was eager to help and had a talent for organization and a desire for activity. When he came to the city of Mukačevo to take upon himself this task there were some who grumbled "what good is this fellow to us?" and the truth is that his youth caused many to hesitate about this man. Could he stand up against this wave of conflict and intrigue, lacking the means and experience, in a hostile and quarrelsome environment? But it did not take long before he proved that his candidacy would not be a passing episode but something more basic, the work of a foundation-builder.

He immediately went to work with much energy. He knew that only deeds would decide the struggle, and following the deeds could also come controversy. In his first steps he found, to his amazement, that in essence there was nothing to "administrate." For there was no school, no building and no accessories, no teachers and no study curriculum, etc. True, good and reliable people were standing at his side, but outside of good advice they could not help him in any way. With so much desolation there was no choice but to make contact with officials, in order to get a permit for opening of the gymnasium, and with individuals and institutions who were in a position to offer some help, material or spiritual. He learned very soon that this matter of the gymnasium would not make any progress if looked upon as a goal for itself — it would instead have to be one link in the chain of *modern* Judaism, where all the cords are inextricably bound and interwoven.

In his first steps he stumbled against all those problems that in the course of time developed: the community, language disputes, the national minorities, the economic and social condition of the Jews of Subcarpathian Ruthenia, the Zionist parties, the Jewish political party, and personal contacts with the officials. In the meantime, he also had to attend to his own private existence; after all, he was in a strange environment — some of the customs and viewpoints were alien to him and completely antagonistic to his spirit. The youth and the younger members of the intelligentsia were also not formed of the same material that he was used to in Ruthenia, in the West, or in Eretz Israel. Finally, the intrigues, the trickery, the contrivances, the jealousy, the fanaticism, the ignorance and pseudo-intelligence, the provincialism — all these did not constitute an attractive state of affairs.

To sum up: this was a lowly Jewish community; while no doubt it had slumbering resources, it lacked the spark that would activate them. It had no leaders to materialize them, no one to bring out that hidden glow in the soul. It would be wrong to let all this go to waste, it should be turned into action — to bring them up to the path of life, to open their eyes and enable them to see what was going on in the world, to awaken them from their slumber and to convince them that they were no more in that prewar world. They should see and understand.

And indeed he was soon enough rewarded for his labor. Not only was the day of the laying of the foundation of the Hebrew gymnasium in Mukačevo worth all his endeavors, but he was also privileged to see with his own eyes how a new generation grew up, fashioned according to his vision and ideals.

Should we wish to enumerate all the obstacles that he had to overcome on the road to the establishment of the institution we would be unable to. Suffice it to mention just a few of the more prominent and characteristic examples. On the doors of the Klausen and Batei-Midrach (Hasidic prayer and study houses) was displayed for a long time a placard: APPEAL TO OUR BRETHREN, THE CHILDREN OF ISRAEL, with the full excommunication text of the Middle Ages. At the very opening of classes in the year 1924 a letter from the ministry specifically prohibited the opening of the gymnasium. The reason given revealed the source of this decree. The letter referred to an ancient Hungarian law, according to which only the religious community was allowed to open religious schools. The government, however ,did not take into consideration the fact that in the meantime the fate of the Jewish community in Mukačevo was sealed; due to some perfidious acts it was dissolved and a commissioner was appointed over it. And this community had to care for the Hebrew education!

Naturally, this government decree aroused waves of protest throughout the land, and the government relented. Things had reached such a state that even Dr. Chaim Weizmann of the blessed memory, during his visit in Czechoslovakia in those days, brought the matter of the Hebrew gymnasium to the attention of President Masaryk and Foreign Minister Beneš.

An obstacle of a different kind was the material existence of the institution. Superhuman efforts were made here by means of public information, debates, journeys, lectures, and campaigns, most of which were carried out by Dr. Kugel himself, and in spite of all difficulties one fine day the miracle was accomplished! One wing of the two-story building was prominently entrenched on one of the beautiful streets of the city of Mukačevo, and great numbers of people from near and far came to feast their eyes upon this splendid sight.

Indeed, not only outwardly did this institution represent something special but particularly from within. From the superintendent, who was one of the first Zionists in the city and a man of letters, to the "omnipotent director" — all carried conscientiously this heavy task that was put upon them, and prevailed.

The teachers? This also is a chapter in itself. Hebrew teachers who were both citizens of the country and in possession of a local diploma did not yet exist. Most teachers were from abroad, immigrants from Poland and Lithuania. How did they reach Mukačevo? On their way to Eretz Israel they made a short stop in order to rest from their tiresome journey, to enjoy a little of the Czechoslovak democracy, to impart something of their spirit to the Jewish children, and to gather a little money for the continuation of their travels in order to reach their destination; but if they succeeded after all, they were certainly disappointed in the latter, for there is no greater pauper than a rich pauper. The institution also had part-time teachers, not necessarily Jews — Czechs who were on loan from the government institutions. They endeavored to adapt themselves to the special environment and would occasionally speak favorably of Jews before their pupils there.

To the regular set-up of the school belonged all sorts of supervisors who came to see the marvel of how the laws of Newton or Pythagoras were being taught in the language of Isaiah or Jesus. Visiting guests who chanced to be in the city, intentionally or not, would not fail to make use of the opportunity to be registered in the visitors' book and take in a conversation — or more correctly, to listen in on a conversation — with the young students.

All this was directed outwardly; from within, the students themselves were perhaps the only ones who really knew the sort of life and social environment that the institution provided. This was felt when the students reached the fourth or fifth school year and were already considered as adult youths — then the walls of the institution were reverberating with activities and discussion. It is noteworthy that also the number of pupils rose from year to year. In the school year 1927/28 the number of pupils in the gymnasium was 120; in 1928/29–124; in 1929/30 — 143; in 1930/31 — 199; in 1931/32 — 232.

Just as the director was not a director only, but also had in his hand all the cords tied into Subcarpatho-Ruthenian Jewry in general, so the students were not occupied with their studies only but, together with their teachers, participated actively in all matters of Jewish communal affairs in accordance with their abilities. The work for the Jewish National Fund, for instance, was central in the institution. It provided the contributors, the collectors, the organizers. When a campaign for a building project in Eretz Israel was undertaken, the students of the gymnasium were immediately at its service. When elections for the Zionist Congress were about to begin, they sold most of the *shekalim*. When a Zionist meeting or celebration took place in the city, again they were the arrangers, the organizers, and most of the time also the exhibitors — and all this in addition to their activity in their youth movement.

The gymnasium itself turned into a cultural center for the Jewish youth in general. The library and, a little later, the spacious hall for physical exercise (incidentally, the only one in the whole country intended for Jewish youth) served many youths outside the walls of the gymnasium. Especially benefiting from the library were young men that "emancipated" themselves, and through all sorts of concealed channels these books reached into the pockets of their kapotes.

From year to year new pupils increased not only in numbers but also in the places and circles from which they originated before joining the movement. Students came to the gymnasium from the most outlying villages and the distant cities of Slovakia. But, as already stated, the growth of the cultural and social influence of the institution was not matched by its income. On the contrary, as the institution grew, it was in need of more and more funds. The voice of Histadrut and Tarbut reached to remote places but, to use a Talmudic saying, "a handful does not satiate the lion."

A turning point for the better occurred after the year 1929, when the Jewish party rose to representation in the Parliament. The topic of the Hebrew schools, especially the gymnasium, was never off the agenda of the party, and every opportunity was exploited to bring it to the attention of the officials. It was discussed in Parliament, in interviews with ministers of state, and in debates on the budget and in various committees. Step by step the gymnasium acquired more *Lebensraum*, living space, sometimes by fighting methods and other times by defensive measures, until the coming of the glorious day of victory: the first graduating exercises, on June 12, 1932, the first ripe fruit after overcoming thousands of obstacles during a period of twelve years. This fact in itself aroused respect and admiration in all segments of the population in the country. The event was celebrated with much festivity and with the participation not only of important Jewish personalities but also non-Jews from among the higher echelons of the government. All expressed unanimously their excitement over this positive undertaking. One of the prominent government educators referred to the institution as a "light illuminating the darkness."

This spiritual inventory should not be limited to summarizing the past only. We should also appraise it in the light of the present — what role this event played as an ethical and social factor in the social life of Jewish youth outside of the gymnasium, how the graduates themselves stood up to the test of values that served as a guiding light in their education; and finally we should turn our gaze to the future — what would the coming commencement exercises look like, what tasks necessitated by the conditions of the new era would this youth be called upon to undertake? Heavy black clouds were accumulating in the skies of Europe, and the youth, as usual, were more sensitive to what was about to happen. Let us see how the sixty-one graduates of the first three commencement exercises reacted.

The roads taken by the first graduates give us reason to think in several directions. Twenty-six of the graduates chose their way of life as follows: teaching in Hebrew public schools — 9; preparing for teaching in the Hebrew gymnasium — 5; scattered about in the whole breadth of the republic for the dissemination of the Hebrew language — 12; in Eretz Israel — 2; in pioneer training (as Halutzim) — 8; in university studies: law — 6; medicine — 15; techology — 2. If we take into account that outside of law and medicine they all chose more or less the pioneering road, either in the Diaspora or in Eretz Israel, we can safely say that a profound revolution occurred in the choice of professions.

The main concern was how to broaden this narrow circle, how to enable wider groups of youths from among the poor masses to learn to write within the walls of the institution, since there were already many who knocked on the doors of the institution but for lack of means were turned away. The institution was already in a position to grant stipends to many poor students, but there was not enough to cover all the needs. Even those that did not succeed in entering the institution for various reasons were already in constant contact with the students of the gymnasium. Moreover, many of them, particularly from the poor segments — apprentices and clerks in stores and factories — were sometimes superior in their practical pioneering spirit to many of the students of the gymnasium. The training camps proved it — they were occupied mostly by the first group, those who by reason of their social and economic status had no other choice than preparing for pioneer realization. Many of the students of the gymnasium originated in the bourgeois or lower middle classes, where the spirit of pioneering realization was pushed aside temporarily for the ambition to study, to get a degree. This youth that was organized as an integral part in the Hechalutz was therefore from a certain point of view also the healthy kernel in the revival movement, but without tumult and lavish banquets. They did their work quietly, with diligence and with stubborn resistance to their parents and their environment. They lived a hard life, for not always did they succeed in finding work; general unemployment was growing continually, and also there was a lack of faith in their ability to work. Of course, the Jewish employers particularly avoided contacting them. Nevertheless, they broke through a path for themselves until they reached their goal — *Aliyah*. In this chapter, which constitutes one of the glorious ones in the history of Hebrew education in Subcarpathian Ruthenia, the emissaries played an important role; the envoys of these youth movements, who appeared from time to time from Poland or from Eretz Israel, did invaluable work. They constituted the element of ferment, for they penetrated into the poorest strata of the population with the most primitive but heart-captivating means.

Another class of youth came from more affluent families, mostly pupils of non-Jewish schools, if their parents were not too Orthodox; but they remained without a high school education. If their parents were ultra-Orthodox, they were dragged along by every blowing wind and their path in life was unstabilized. They realized the narrow-mindedness of their parents, the stifling atmosphere surrounding them, the prejudices, the conventional ills in their social and family life, but they were not in a position to change all this and bring about a revolution. They were influenced by every new stream, by every new idea that came up on the horizon and seemed to them new, attractive, and promising. They were not deeply rooted in their Judaism — only in its formal aspect. As to general culture, their grasp of it was superficial, a hurried acquaintance of petty details. This youth turned to every new wind. They exuded lower middle class provincialism. At first they were usually taken in by communist ideas, which to them meant cosmopolitanism; but soon it was clear to them that this was not the way to satisfy their hidden aspirations. After all, they could not escape their Judaism and shed their own skin. There were some who were hardened in the course of time and made their way to the other extreme and reached the very edge of mixed marriage — mostly the daughters of ultra-Orthodox families. But most of them grew up to be neither one nor the other.

The function of the Zionist youth was to attract these people to the movement. Occasionally the movement acquired from among them some fine members and thereby released hidden powers and very noble traits. This class included particularly some young women who found their way to the Zionist youth movement, where they became a valuable asset and contributed much to society; but attracting them was a difficult and slow process. To this task also the students of the Hebrew gymnasium were mobilized, and very often they had to make use of their personal qualities in addition to the ideological arguments in order to succeed in their work.

It is noteworthy that "the battle of fathers and sons" (or, more correctly, the fathers and daughters) was very sharp. This is also a chapter full of suffering and humiliation, distinguished by heroic acts of quiet resistance of the part of the youth. The sons emancipated themselves more easily because of their substantial share in the economic life in the family. A lad who worked and earned a salary and handed over most of it for the upkeep of his family was automatically freed from the harsh supervision of his father. Not so the girl who sat at home and helped out in the house chores, taking care of the younger brothers and sisters, and was under constant observation. She suffered more keenly when she realized her miserable situation and when she was imbued with an ambition for a better and more beautiful life. These daughters were possessed of energy and a strong character; they broke their chains at once and started out, each in her own manner, on the road to "wicked indulgence" (*"tarbuth raah,"* a term of opprobrium used by the Orthodox). Those finer souls, with stronger sentiments and an understanding for the parents, suffered quietly and were compelled to make use of all sorts of difficult methods to find ways and means for the realization of their secret ambitions. Witness the following: a girl of sixteen from a very devout house made up her mind to reach on her own a certain positinn of independence. Under the guise of learning how to sew, she got employment in the office of a Zionist journal. When this became known to her father he immediately called together his colleagues and for a full day they investigated the traditional law — in this case, there was a suspicion of the loss of virginity, since she worked in a room through which men may have walked. The poor girl was questioned on matters that never entered her mind and could not even understand what the "judges" were driving at with their insinuations. But the incident was enough to instill her with fear, the results of which she felt many years afterwards. This was not an isolated case. An ultra-religious father, upon finding "unworthy" books, would be ready to burn not only the books themselves but also every other object that had come in contact with them.

The thirst for knowledge was stronger than everything—candles in the night were burned secretly, and books were hidden under mattresses. From the social aspect, also, their lot was a difficult one; if in spite of that, they dared meet boys in the streets or in some more distant places, their ears were always alert and their eyes always open to every move and sound, their senses were sharpened to perceive from a distance the men of "darkness," and they could disappear quickly. At their secret meetings with the students of the Hebrew gymnasium, the girls were of course able to pour out their groans and their yearnings, everything that was weighing heavily upon their hearts.

The sons who paralleled the girls in conditions of life were also pitiful. They were not endowed with the same courage and strength of character as the girls and had fewer opportunities for effective contrivances to alleviate their situation. These were condemned to life imprisonment in the Chadarim, yeshivot, and Batei Midrash under the strict supervision of rabbis, overseers, and yeshiva headmasters. These were lads with pale, drawn faces, perfectly fitting the description in Bialik's "Hamatmid." The only opportunity they had for a breath of fresh air was underground contact with the students of the Hebrew gymnasium, when they might receive from them a magazine, brochure, or book.

IV. YEARS OF TRIAL (1932–1938)

With the graduation of the first group of graduates of the Hebrew gymnasium, a period of hard work in the Hebrew education in Subcarpathian Ruthenia came to an end, full of pitfalls, but also crowned with valuable results. This was the time when a period of trial began and the secret of the future was still this: would the first graduates, all fitted out with the best of modern enlightenment and Hebrew knowledge, succeed in their task and would they really fulfill their function as solid foundation stones of all the ideals with which they were educated and in whose name they had come this far? And another more important and crucial question: would the youths coming after them be guided by the light of the torch that was now kindled and held up high with such might and uproar?

What in essence was the value of a few tens of youths for the Jewry of the whole country, whose youths numbered several thousand? And how much could such a meager number accomplish, even if all the wishes and aspirations that were hopefully expected of them during their twelve years of training were to be fulfilled? This question can easily be answered if we carefully consider the character of the whole youth in that country, at least in Subcarpathian Ruthenia or in Mukačevo alone, in order to see the intense ferment that transpired in their ranks and the factors that brought this about. And why the youth in particular? Were the older strata unaffected by this ferment? They were, but it was the youth that were mainly involved. First, it is only natural that the youth is the most aware and responsive to what is going on around it; and second, the history of the country was particularly connected with the history of the youth after World War I. During those very years youth reached its first stage of maturity and could therefore serve as a reliable reflection of all the events and phenomena throughout the country. Herein lies also the special importance of education and more exactly the Hebrew education; for, from this aspect, it was not just one of the different areas of life but the main area, in which were revealed all the lights and shadows in the life of the whole society. Because of this in all the multicolored manifestations of the country, we find a special importance in every direction, no matter how minor, that testifies to an independent attitude and conception of life, and this does not at all depend on quantity. For the quantity that had accumulated up to then was now ready to turn into a new quality, and in that was undeniable value.

Subcarpathian Ruthenia, in which the city of Mukačevo is situated, was long since a sensitive crossroads, a focal point for everything that was developing in the big world, in the East as well as in the West. And indeed from both sides even the least joyous tidings enlivened the hearts, and the discussions among the high school pupils in general, and among the pupils of the eighth class (soon to be graduates of the second round of the Hebrew gymnasium) in particular, all testified to that. Not only the student youth was engaged in discussion. The youth outside the walls of the schools, the one behind the counters of the stores or in the workshops — and their number was not at all negligible — were swept into the stream of debates and the actions that followed in their wake. However, it should be noted that this ferment particularly encompassed the Jewish youth. The non-Jewish one was of different material altogether, his range of interests extremely different; only on very rare occasions were there any points of contact between them.

That is quite understandable. The sweeping world events affected first of all the Jewish youth. The rise of Hitler to power at the beginning of 1933 uncovered many painful wounds in the very body of the people of Israel. There are indeed many sides to this subject, but not every one of these sides directly concerns the non-Jewish youth. In the Hungarian youth for instance — especially the nationalist one — there were awakened the old dreams of the annexation of the region to Hungary. But these dreams were still dim and only in the following years, with the formation of the Rome-Budapest-Berlin Axis, did these dreams take on substance. On the other hand, Ruthenian youth, who also managed during that generation to produce a budding intelligentsia, also were dreaming that their vision of autonomy, promised by the Czech government and not yet put in operation, was soon to be realized. These youth groups were therefore not interested in the rest of the problems involving the rise of Hitler. But the Jewish youth immediately grasped, as indeed they were compelled to grasp, that here they were confronted by a revolutionary change in their lives, in everything that concerned their existence in the Diaspora and therefore everything that was bound up with the development of the rebuilding of Eretz Israel. It is clear that no one could visualize the concrete results that were clearly seen years after and were beyond all expectations.

As is well known, these years were favorable to the flowering of the Zionist movement. They therefore also marked in the life of Subcarpathian Ruthenia's Jewry a great advance in Hebrew education. From all directions endeavors were made to seize new positions. The tragic situation of German Jewry served as a background for everything, even though it was not so obvious. This situation required clarification, historical as well as sociological, and who, if not the youth of the Hebrew gymnasium, was able to grapple effectively with hostile attitudes? The Zionist Congress that happened to be held in Prague attracted also many from the ranks of the Hebrew youth. The activity of the gymnasium graduates was already noticeable in all areas. First, they served as unending reserves for the teaching positions in the public schools; second, as reinforcements in the training groups that were so necessary from all angles; third, they engaged in practical activity toward a Jewish and Zionist public event. The greatest drive on their part was in the direction of winning new souls from among the Jewish youth, who was still standing at some distance, either from indifference or from mistaken opposition to the Zionist movement.

Thus came into existence a group of "The Daring" (Mapilim), which included enlightened and semi-enlightened boys and girls tath for various reasons could not or would not join openly and did not intend to identify themselves fully with one of the particular movements. Thev were sympathetic to the Hashomer Hatzair but kept aloof from the central ideal, Hagshamah, materialization — not because they opposed it in principle but because they knew that in their present circumstances they could not accomplish it. As to engaging in a "filial revolution," they were unable to do it for various objective and subjective reasons. This group would get together every Saturday, arrange walks or discussions in a club, and above all study Hebrew and Zionism enthusiastically. It is clear that the personal contacts were the decisive ones here, and as long as these contacts existed the group also continued to exist; but when this contact was weakened, the existence of the group became a question mark. In any event, this was for many a transition link to Zionism and to the youth movement, leaving a very deep impression upon the soul; and when the time came it brought forth good fruit.

With the opening of the new semester in the year 1933, three new Hebrew schools were opened. Because of lack of funds, only the first grades with one teacher were opened in these places, even though there was room for the next classes and also for additional first classes. In the city of Mukačevo the number of the pupils rose by 25 percent. Many were not accepted because of lack of space. In the public school close to 300 pupils were registered and in the gymnasium 85 pupils were registered, and parallel classes were therefore opened. A noticeable change took place also in the composition of the pupils. The boys and girls from the provincial cities, far and near, increased, and it was therefore necessary to open a dormitory for them. This dormitory marked again additional progress in the Hebrew education. It served as a new cultural center for youth, in whose homes in the outlying villages there would never have been that privilege.

Whoever thought that this continued growth of Hebrew education would finally open the eyes of the Hasidic antagonists to the realization that all the curses and insults not only could do no harm but could actually turn into blessings was surely in error. For all these, headed by the rabbi of Mukačevo, continued their attacks. An opportunity would always present itself, both at the beginning and at the close of the study season, either during a celebration, jubilee, or political assembly. Also exploited were catastrophes such as epidemics, floods, and conflagrations, in order to point to the punishment from Heaven. Such an opportunity, for instance, occurred at the end of 1933, on the occasion of the celebration of the fifteenth anniversary of the existence of the Czechoslovak Republic. When orations were delivered and demands were presented by the national minorities, the Hasidic sect naturally found an opportunity to demonstrate their boundless loyalty to the country, unlike the Zionists. The sermons and proclamations foretold of a hard and unrelenting battle. For the sake of illustration we will quote the full text of one of the proclamations. It speaks for itself.

Society Shomrei Torah of the Holy Community of Mukačevo, May

Aufruf [Proclamation]

Nevertheless if thou warn the righteous man, that the righteous sin not, and he doth not sin, he shall surely live, because he took warning: and thou hast delivered thy soul. (Ezekiel 3:21)

To all Jewish parents, may the Lord keep them and preserve them, who believe in the holy Torah and in the words of our Sages of blessed memory. We are turning to every father and mother and warning them in the name of G-d and His Torah not to fall into the harmful path of the Zionist school or gymnasium, which has been prohibited by world-renowned rabbis, because it is a place from which come out heretics pure and simple who deny the Torah and deride all the commandments of the Lord, may He be blessed. They make a mockery of the words of our Sages of blessed memory and poison the Jewish heart with disbelief, may the Merciful preserve us (masquerade balls, mixed excursions, etc.). The parents will never be able to defend themselves in this world and in the world to come for the grave sin that they have committed against the innocent children by having torn them away from the Torah and belief and having cut them off from the Jewish religion…

We have already once pointed out the great loss that the Jewish home suffers when you allow the children to study in such schools and public institutions that are not under the compulsory education law, because they bring the innocent child to the desecration of the holy Sabbath and heresy, G-d forbid. And how many have already forsaken the Jewish home and caused anguish to their parents, may you be preserved from that, with shame and disgrace, G-d preserve us. Therefore consider carefully now when there is still a little time — later, there will be no use in regretting — lead the little children in the path of our fathers and mothers, and by this merit the Lord, may He be praised, will help us see joy in our children until the coming of the Redeemer, speedily in our own days, Amen.

> Society Shomrei Torah, Mukačevo, may the Lord preserve them, which is under the supervision of the gracious holiness of our lord teacher and master, chief of the court of our holy community here and in the provinces, may he have a long life, Amen

Blessed is the Lord, Mukačevo, on the eve of the holy Sabbath, portion of Balak 5694, according to our reckoning. The court of justice of the holy community of Mukačevo and the province may the Lord preserve them.

Also our hands will strengthen this noble society, and there is not sufficient space upon this sheet to describe the grave heresy, may the Merciful preserve us, of the Zionist houses of iniquity in all their varieties, and all the heretical books that they teach the young boys of the children of Israel and they actually ensnare them to apostasy, denial of G-d, may the Merciful one preserve us. And all this we saw with our own eyes and not those of a stranger, and especially since that which is universally known does not need any proof at all.

Therefore we are coming to warn once more our brethren the children of Israel in our community and in the provinces. Watch out and be careful, and whoever will not be cautious in this, G-d forbid, will loose his religious reliability and will not be appointed to any function of sanctity. And they, the guilty ones will be separated for shame and disgrace, and the one who listens will be delighted and rewarded with all good things forever and we shall be worthy of redemption among all of Israel and the deliverance should soon come, speedily in our own days.

On the eve of the holy Sabbath, portion of Balak 5694, Mukačevo, may the Lord protect it, Amen.

Chaim Eleazar Spira and the associate judges

At the same time that these and similar proclamations appeared, there also appeared announcements that "by order of the rabbinical court, gentile gymnasiums are *kosher*," since they feared being taken to task by the government for dissuading the parents from sending their children to the schools.

When in the year 1934 a typhus epidemic broke out in the city of Mukačevo and in the great misfortune two children, a brother and sister who happened to be students of the Hebrew school, were among those who succumbed to the epidemic, the rabbi found an opportunity to deliver a sermon in the large synagogue and to admonish publicly the bereaved parents upon their sin, saying that with their own hands they had brought upon themselves this punishment. Such cruelty aroused against him even some of his Hasidic followers, who said that this time he went too far. Others spoke openly upon the desecration of the Name on his part. In order to justify himself before the public, he published proclamations that his sermon was delivered with the approval of many parents. But in the meantime it became known that this was not true and that the signatures supposedly gathered for this purpose were forged; each and every person denied in the press that he had ever given his approval. No wonder, then, that more than once during such sermons Zionist youths appeared and caused disturbances with their shouts and that at times things got so far as fist-fights and the throwing of rotten eggs. From the correspondence between the community and the management of the gymnasium during that year we learn that the community demanded forcefully that the gymnasium hand over the names of the pupils who disturbed the sermons of the rabbi on Shabbat Teshuvah (Sabbath of Repentence), on Sabbath Pinchas, and on the Sabbath Chol Hamoed Sukkoth. Since it was not proven at all that the disturbers were necessarily pupils of the Hebrew gymnasium, many of the parents saw in this an intentional defamation of the institution, and they reacted with a sharp protest against the false accusations. Sometimes things would reach the courts and would result in the payment of fines for the benefit of Hebrew education.

In other correspondence that year we find a strange request on the part of the community that the gymnasium turn over within fourteen days the names of the teachers and their certificates of authorization, the list of the texbooks, the names of the pupils, their parents, and their addresses — a request that was not fulfilled. But with this the chapter of the relationships between the community and the Hebrew education had not yet come to an end, for on the side of the community stood organizations, institutions, and societies such as Maginei Degel Hatorah (Defenders of the Banner of the Torah), Shomrei Torah (Guardians of the Torah), and Darkei Teshuvah (Paths of Repentence). If they could not act directly against the gymnasium, they engaged in all sorts of actions against the many adversaries of their rabbi, but this chapter is outside the boundaries of the subject at hand.

In the meantime, the situation in the Jewish quarter became increasingly difficult. The echoes of Germany penetrated here also. The struggle for positions between the Czechs and the Germans soon turned into a battle between Aryans and non-Aryans (read: Jews). The hopeless unemployment, especially in the ranks of the academic youths who after decades of study could not secure even the most insignificant position, was frightening. The situation of the Jewish academic youth was sevenfold more difficult: the systematic displacement of Jews from public positions was one of the signs of the time.

Elections to the Parliament were to be held on May 19, 1935,* and all other problems were put aside. The Jews had now a special interest in the results of the elections. The right-wing camp in the republic increased, and many feared that they would win. Also among the Jewish party there were conflicting political opinions and tactical methods regarding the elections, and that weakened its strength. The Hasidic sect also strengthened its activities and published the following proclamation:

Blessed is the Lord, Chaim Eleazar Spira,
Head of the rabbinical court of the holy community of Mukačevo and the provinces.

Now regarding the election of deputies for the state that everyone is duty bound to consider carefully, many will take it lightly and will be of the opinion either willfully or inadvertently that it does not concern at all the faith of Judaism!

Therefore I find myself compelled to let my voice be heard publicly that according to the religion of our holy Torah it is forbidden to assist in any way the representatives of the Zionists heretics; and an Israelite unbeliever is even more lawless, since they have nominated as their candidate a rebellious son who forsakes the way of the Torah, who denies the faith, seduces and leads astray the young children of Israel in the Hebrew gymnasium from which emanates, as is well known, heresy and disbelief against G-d and His Messiah and against our holy Torah and faith, which we inherited from our

* [See A. M. Rabinowicz: The Jewish Party, pp. 253–346 (Ed.)]

forefathers and our masters, may their merits protect us. It is therefore the duty of everyone to stand up against this breach and protest with self-sacrificing efforts.

The Zionist candidate, the "rebellious son," was Dr. Chaim Kugel, whom everyone expected to be the proper representative of Subcarpathian Ruthenia's Jewry. Indeed, the results of the elections prove that among the Jewish population there began a movement toward national consciousness and a sobering up from conservative-religious leaders. There is no doubt that this progress in Jewish self-consciousness can be attributed largely to the younger set that had already reached maturity and participated in the elections, the great majority of which was on the side of the Zionist movement. Truly the "desert generation" was expiring and the young one was ready to bring about revolutionary changes in the life of Jewry, if only given the opportunity for full physical and spiritual crystallization. That was the result of a Hebrew education during only half a generation. But this time its initiator celebrated his full victory. Dr. Kugel was elected as a deputy to the Parliament.

The Zionist convention of Subcarpathian Ruthenia, which was held in those days in Mukačevo, proved also that behind the veteran forces stood a long line of youth that was ready to gradually take over many of the responsible functions. The national convention of the Hechalutz in the Republic of Czechoslovakia, which was also held in Mukačevo in May 1935, was in the category of a highly important event for the Jewish youth in that country. About 150 representatives of the local branches and about 350 members from all parts of the country took part in it. Also present were representatives of Histadrut, the labor union of Eretz Israel; the World Center of Hechalutz and of Hashomer Hatzair. At this convention the growth of the Hechalutz movement in the Republic of Czechoslovakia was brought out. There were in existence 98 branches that numbered more than 1,500 members. About 700 members were enrolled in 28 training groups spread throughout the country. The ideal of Halutziut, the pioneer spirit, captivated the hearts of the youth and became their life's ideal, and no wonder. For this youth had no prospects of a decent life and no possibility of normal existence in their land of residence. The young heart was crying for activity, yearning for work, and so Halutziut actually became a mass movement and was destined to play an important role in the life of the Jews and win for itself a strong influential position among the youth as well as the adults.

This convention made it clear that the center of gravity of the Zionist movement was situated in Subcarpathian Ruthenia. Fifty-two percent of the Hechalutz branches were there, and among the members that were in training, 59 percent were from Subcarpathian Ruthenia. Indeed, in relation to the number of Jews in other areas of the Republic, from the standpoint of Halutziut, Subcarpathian Ruthenian's Jewry was several times more numerous. Of the 360,000 Jews in the whole of the Republic, 100,000 of them were in Subcarpathian Ruthenia.

These movements were in need of spiritual ideas also, and to that task were dedicated the ideological seminars that were organized from time to time and the center for which was again the institute of the Hebrew gymnasium, with its building, teachers, books, and supplies. In these seminars were held discussions and lectures on such subjects as the labor movement in Eretz Israel, the Histadrut and its institutions, the Zionist movement and its history, the Kibbutz movement, foundations of socialism, fascism, Jewish history and the Jewish problem, culture and literature, labor literature, geography of Eretz Israel, the Jews and the Republic of Czechoslovakia, the national funds, etc. During the seminar, concerts, discussions, and literary contests were conducted. For the dissemination of the ideal of Halutziut they had at their service a wide press in various languages: German, Slovak, Czech, Hungarian, Yiddish, and Hebrew. These magazines were not permanent and continuous, but each issue accomplished its mission at the proper time and the proper place. Single numbers of *Hechalutz* and *Hed Hechalutz* — many of which appeared only in stencil — were prepared with great devotion, and each one embodied personal and collective experiences of the movement or a particular social class. In their pages one could read of the trials and tribulations experienced by these youths, especially those who had to uproot the very foundations of their traditional way of life and start a completely new form of life.

About their material struggle we need not elaborate. They received some slight assistance, thanks to the representation of Subcarpathian Ruthenian's Jewry in Parliament by Dr. Kugel, who made it one of his central aims to work for the welfare of this youth. The problem of the Jewish youth was brought up at every opportunity, and the acuteness of the situation was pointed out every time. Thousands of young men roamed around without work, without a profession, completely indifferent, not even seeking a purpose and content for their existence. In their battle for their physical survival they made use of methods that cannot in any way be approved of. On the one hand it was the unlimited influence of the "wonder-working" rabbi and, on the other hand, the demagoguery by which they were affected as a result of their lack of culture. The only alternative for this youth, which continued to deteriorate and become improverished, was a complete break with their way of life and the acquiring of a productive profession of which they could make use. That necessarily had to go hand in hand with a guiding, directing Hebrew education.

The prewar Hungarian regime endeavored to erect a barrier between the Russian and Jewish intellectual and between the masses so that the former would serve as a means of Hungarization in the country. After the war, the situation was completely changed. Among the Russian population arose an active intelligentsia that was working for the benefit of its people and the country. The aim of the Jews was also to educate an intelligentsia of their own, whose function it would be to guide and direct the masses. The aim was to attain Jewish completeness in spirit and to fight against cultural dualism. If during the last decade the Jewish people lost their youths, who left Judaism and went over to other movements, it was because of the lack of a way out from the dualism. The whole Jewish tragedy was inherent in the effort to alienate the Jew from his people and to put up a barrier between the intelligentsia and the masses. The intelligentsia was seeking an escape from Judaism by means of abstract ideas. Since the schools were the best means for the education of a modern youth, therefore, after many efforts a network of Hebrew schools was established in Subcarpathian Ruthenia, in which students from ninety different sections of the Republic were learning. In the meantime, another Hebrew gymnasium was established in the city of Užhorod, for the time being only for the lower classes.

Dr. Kugel continued in office, and he attempted vigorously to convince the government that there was no other way out, insofar as the Jews were concerned, but the establishment of schools of their own; then no such incidents would occur as had previously, when Ruthenian parents protested to the school administrations against their children being educated by Jewish teachers, whereas Jewish children attended Czech schools whose teachers were non-Jews.

Surely Dr. Kugel would not have been able to continue in office had he not felt the support of the large groups of youth behind him, groups that were brought up in the Hebrew spirit. How this youth was aroused to general Jewish social activity could be seen from one of the conferences in which Jewish students from Subcarpathian Ruthenia were organized. The idea of the conference stemmed from the dissatisfaction of the college students studying in Prague, who looked upon themselves as uprooted from their environment in general and from their Jewish way of life in particular. The Jewish student who was a native of Subcarpathian Ruthenia usually came from various Zionist organizations in his home town, wherein he found some field for activity. However, when he came to Prague for his course of studies in the college, he saw himself as torn from the soil upon which he grew and matured and as not having the ability to become rooted; he felt as if he was suspended in air. It was not because there was no room for Zionist, cultural, and political work but because it was difficult for a native of the eastern part of the country to acclimate himself in the western environment of the capital. We also cannot ignore the fact that the student of Subcarpathian Ruthenia, upon coming to study at the university in Prague, was compelled to compress as much as possible his years of study there, for his material conditions were hard and he lived in the strange city under very difficult circumstances.

It is obvious that here again most of those participating in this conference were graduates of the Hebrew gymnasium. This proved that the seed of this education was not sown in vain. The youth at this conference took upon itself a new and difficult task, namely, to tour during the summer months the Jewish settlements in towns and villages in order to see with their own eyes the condition as it was and to bring to every remote corner the good tidings of the new life. This activity was not to be limited within the framework of official Zionism only, but also was to encourage the participation of non-Zionist Jewish students whose heart still beat for the Jewish people.

With the rise of political tension in Europe in the year 1937, Czechoslovakia was the most sensitive country toward the changes that were sure to come. The head of the government therefore endeavored to correct the errors that were then committed in various fields, and especially to come to a reasonable arrangement with all the minorities living in the Republic. The government knew that the German and Hungarian minorities could not be considered as loyal elements to the country. Only the Ruthenians and the Jews were left, both of whom lived mainly in Subcarpathian Ruthenia. The Ruthenian population was therefore promised a speedy implementation of autonomy, whereas the Jews were promised that this time their rights would be fulfilled in accordance with the provisions of the international treaty. That day was a joyous holiday for Czechoslovak Jewry. First and foremost, the rights in reference to the independence of the Hebrew schools were emphasized, which meant that from then on they would have to be under the patronage of the government. One of the dreams of Carpatho-Ruthenian Jewry was about to be realized when all the Hebrew schools were to receive their full budget from the government. What a revolution would result from this provision throughout the Hebrew education in the country!

Another point not less important for the Hebrew education in the country was the recognition by he government of the justification of the demands concerning social aid for the Hebrew youth. Organizations for social work among the youth were in existence in various forms, but they could not succeed without government aid. Czechoslovak legislation did not know of any social work with youth according to religious tradition. The organizations of this type were built on a national basis. There was social care of Czech, German, Hungarian youth, etc., and these were recognized officially by the government and were supported by it.

But the special conditions of the Jewish inhabitants were responsible for the fact that organizations of this sort were due to the initiative of individuals or organizations that also had other functions. In order to get support for such a cause from the government it had to come only in the official capacity of an express national minority, and of this method both the assimilationists and the Orthodox were reluctant to make use. This right could be fully demanded only by the Jewish party, the party that represented the Jewish national minority. Social aid to the Hebrew youth meant again the expansion of the training groups, the strengthening of the pioneer movements, and in general the all-out propagation of the Zionist ideal among the Jewish youth.

It would seem, then, that this time the ranks of the youth were standing ready for very positive undertakings. Indeed, the various project that the youth took upon itself were many. Beginning with the Jewish National Fund and continuing with projects of contributions for the upbuilding of the land of Israel — whether this was the Miral Hagalilah or the building of K'far Masaryk — the youth always had a hand in it. The new organization Hechalutz Hatzair, which implanted the pioneer ideal in the hearts of young school children, also added to the optimistic Eretz Israel atmosphere and the fever of *Aliyah* was felt everywhere. New circles were added to the Zionist camp, and the Hebrew schools could not contain all the pupils, even though the building of the Hebrew gymnasium had recently been completed according to the plan outlined thirteen years before. True, this time they celebrated the event in privacy, for those that were closer to informed sources knew the seriousness of the situation. In the not-too-distant future the skies were darkened and covered with heavy clouds. The more the head of the government made his optimistic announcements, the greater were the apprehensions and fear concerning the near future.

In 1938 new laws were enacted in order to lighten the burden of that part of the population that was underprivileged, and the Jews again were rejoicing. The head of the government met continually with the representatives of the Jews and confirmed his promises in reference to their demands. Activity was feverish. National Jewry in Subcarpathian Ruthenia made great efforts to bring about uniformity of representation in the institutions of autonomy that were soon to arise. But the discussions were suddenly silenced — they were too late. The whole world seemed to have been covered with a black, blinding cloud, and only one phrase rang out from the chaos: to arms! The days of the Munich-Vienna conferences arrived.

Due to the resolutions of Vienna at the end of 1938, a large part of Subcarpathian Ruthenia and Slovakia was ceded to Hungary, and after awhile the whole state of Czechoslovakia fell apart and the annexation of Subcarpathian Ruthenia became a fact. From then on, the history of the Jews was nothing but a long chain of troubles and persecutions in the style of Hitlerite anti-Semitism, in which its Hungarian disciples were in a certain sense even superior to their teacher.

As to the Hebrew education it seemed at first that the end had come and that its complete extinction had been decreed. The Hebrew public schools, together with the Hebrew gymnasium, were closed down until further notice, and the attitude of the Hungarian military officials toward them was extremely hostile. The teachers and the method of teaching was declared to be contaminated with communism, and that was sufficient to keep away from this magnificent project every person who was concerned for his own fate and the fate of his family. There was at work many an old grudge between the Hungarians and the director of the institution, Dr. Chaim Kugel, whom they considered enemy number one. Also, the assimilationist Jews on the one hand and the Hasidim on the other — because of their stupidity and blindness — derived some satisfaction from all this. But the guardian of Israel did not slumber. This time several courageous Jews came to the aid of the institution, being fearless, and thanks to their economic and social contacts they succeeded in paving their way to the officials. Help was extended also by the Hungarian Zionist Organization in Budapest, which, in spite of its faults and lack of influence, was still able to mobilize public opinion and to create official contacts with the Ministry of Education in the capital. After extended and tiresome negotiations, they agreed on the continuation of the studies in the Hebrew schools with some notable changes in several areas. Not having any choice, they agreed to continue in the struggle.

Even with this achievement, however, Hebrew education was still hard hit. First, the number of pupils was suddenly diminished, since certain areas of Subcarpathian Ruthenia were severed, one part remaining within the boundaries of Czechoslovskia and the other within Hungary. This problem was solved afterwards with the complete annexation to Hungary. Second, the teachers and their quality deteriorated. Many of the teachers who were not citizens of the country left the place and among them at the top of the list was Dr. Kugel himself, whose life was in danger. They were replaced by teachers from Hungary, some of whom had no knowledge of Hebrew at all but were Zionists. This was true in the more fortunate cases, but there were some who came from the ranks of avowed assimilationists. Only two or three teachers were found who knew Hebrew and were also Zionists, and these were students of the rabbinical seminary and were not trained for teaching. The nucleus for the faculty was therefore those left from the previous faculty and the new Zionist camp.

With such a group of teachers it was obviously not possible to continue with the previous curriculum and method of teaching, but besides this the officials interfered in the course of studies and dictated a new curriculum. The main struggle concerned the language of instruction. After a long fight a compromise was reached: the practical subjects were taught in Hebrew, the humanities were taught in Hungarian. The intention was clear. The school itself was interested in just the opposite arrangement. But the officials were apprehensive lest the teaching of humanities such as history, social sciences, and geography in the Hebrew language affect adversely the Hungarian spirit they were interested in inculcating.

The Hebrew language and its literature was taught for the same number of hours in every class as the Hungarian language and its literature. Besides this, it was also allowed to teach "religion" in Hebrew. Religion in the gymnasium meant the Bible, and from this aspect, therefore, the Hebrew schools gained some notable achievements. The Hebrew language continued to be the speaking language of the students, and their Hebrew reading books constituted their spiritual nourishment. This condition was in effect only when the Hungarians first came in. In the following years, with the decree of the "numerus clausus" and afterwards the "numerus nulus" leveled against the Hungarian high schools, the Hebrew schools were forced to admit Jewish pupils into the higher classes who did not know even one word of Hebrew. However, the Hebrew school did this willingly and lovingly. After all, this was its moral and national obligation, to give asylum to these unfortunate pupils who were punished because of the "sin" of their parents. The Hebrew gymnasium opened for them special courses in order to make it easier for them to be instructed in Hebrew.

With the admittance of these pupils, the moral and national standards of the gymnasium also rose, since this time even the most assimilationist circles had to admit that national Judaism was on the right path and foresaw the future. This of course they did hesitatingly, but many of them later became true friends — but alas, again it was too late! They were not in a position to give any material or moral assistance to the Zionist institution, either because they themselves continued to become improverished or because the officials started afterwards to persecute the Zionist Organization, and the Hebrew gymnasium was forced to change its name to "Jewish gymnasium." The faculty and the directors and the Zionist Organization did the best they could to keep within the walls of the gymnasium the Zionist tradition, but this became harder day by day. Self-sacrifice and exposing oneself to physical danger were necessary in order to continue, by means of all sorts of tricks and cunning, to preserve the traditional Hebrew spirit. When the officilas ordered the offices of the Zionist Organization throughout the whole Hungary closed, it was within the building of the gymnasium, under the guise of cultural and sport activities, that youth groups of all kinds and classes continued to meet. More than once did officials and police conduct searches among teachers who were suspected of being active, and they were interrogated about it.

Many "technical" difficulties stood in the way of continuing the project. The main concern of the organization was finding the material means for the upkeep of the institution. The work of Tarbut in Czechoslovakia ceased. The communities that were won over for the ideal of the Hebrew schools were still very few, and needless to say Hungarian Jewry was in this respect unlike Czech Jewry. Other concerns also, such as Hebrew textbooks, that until then had been brought in from Poland or from Eretz Israel, troubled the educators and the public workers. These problems were solved by superhuman efforts and unusual self-sacrifice. The new needs of the time required also the complete reorganization of the aims and very essence of the institution. In a gradual manner they added to the institution workshops for metal and wood handicrafts and art work, in order to equip the pupils with skills and a certain measure of general ability to work, to enable them to adapt themselves more easily to the new forms of life. Around the gymnasium new types of schools were also put up, such as a civil school for girls, since the officials did not agree to allow the lower high school classes to be mixed. This oppressive decree had, however, beneficial results, since this led to the establishment of a separate school for girls which was approved by the Orthodox, who willingly enrolled their daughters there. It was in this form that the Hebrew schools continued to exist.

From the aspect of quality, Hebrew education deteriorated, but in quantity it encompassed wider and wider circles which the former regime had never even considered would follow in this path. Thus did the Hebrew schools fulfill even then an important mission, and from their ranks devoted disciples came up who actually saved them from spiritual extinction; when an opportunity for *Aliyah* presented itself they willingly joined the Zionist camp.

This period did not last long. As the Hitler war spread, the noose became tighter around the neck of Hungarian Jewry, and the first to be involved were those in Subcarpathian Ruthenia, whose Jews were considered "Polish Jews." It all began with orders of expulsion because of lack of statehood and citizenship, since the time of the Hungarian regime, and it ended with the institution of the ghetto and total extermination after the invasion of the Nazi hordes into Hungary. But the Hungarians prepared the soil long before by instituting camps of Jewish labor groups that were a proven means of the extermination of the Jewish people. With the establishment of these camps, first the youth and the middle-aged people were taken away — that is, the most vital element of the people. Jewish-Hebrew education received a direct blow, since teachers and communal workers were also taken away. The period bordering the horrible Holocaust began and it soon engulfed Subcarpathian Ruthenian's Jewry. It ended as swift as lightning, both within the land and outside of its boundaries.

REALISM AND ROMANTICISM: OBSERVATIONS ON THE JEWISH INTELLIGENTSIA OF BOHEMIA AND MORAVIA

by Felix Weltsch

The following study is intended as a contribution to the better understanding of the character of the Jews of Bohemia and Moravia and of the manner in which that character was shaped by historical factors during the early decades of the twentieth century. Our study will deal with a group of Jews who for centuries lived in two provinces in the heart of Europe, midway between north and south, east and west — indeed, midway between Western and Eastern European Jewry, and who, as a result, acquired certain traits typical of their "midway position."

These Jews could look back upon a great past. The names of Avigdor Karo, Löw Ben Bezalel, Yomtov Lipman Heller, Mordecai Maisel, David Oppenheim, Jonathan Eibenschütz, and S.I. Rapoport speak for themselves. The Jews of Bohemia and Moravia had produced a considerable number of creative individuals who had achieved much in scholarship and in the arts. They also played a useful and distinctive — though perhaps not a leading — role in the Zionist movement.

Our attempt at a character study of this distinctive part of the Jewish people, based on the observations and reflections of one who himself was part of that group, must, of necessity, have certain shortcomings. Our approach does not utilize methods of modern sociology, nor is it based on tests administered or on questionnaires filled out. It is founded neither on statistics nor on fact-finding operations — instead, the present study is based on recollections of personalities, situations, and events. It evaluates the achievements, the character traits, and the shortcomings of these personalities, with a liberal admixture of introspection.

I shall take as my thesis the result of my reflections, namely, that the distinctive characteristics of the Jews of Bohemia and Moravia may be attributed to a *delicately balanced blending of romanticism and realism*.

Before I go any further, this statement must be qualified. First of all, this formula about the "blending of romanticism and realism" must not in itself be construed as a distinctive trait of the Jews of Bohemia and Moravia, for with just a little good will we can discover such a blending in all men. Our aim in the present study is to show the manner in which romanticism and realism are blended in the particular case of the group we are discussing. What is important for our present purposes is not the definition of this polarity but the manner in which it occurs. These two concepts serve as a substructure from which we may proceed and which will help us attain a better grasp of the fine nuances involved.

Second, the present study deals with the Jews of Bohemia and Moravia only in a specific historical era. As we ourselves have learned by personal experience, for better or, even more, for worse, groups and peoples change, and their character at any given time depends on the phase of development at which they happen to be at that particular time.

Third, what I have to say here is true to a large extent also of Central European Jews in general, of which Jews of Bohemia and Moravia represent only a specifically modulated group. Just what we mean by these specific modulations, we shall have occasion to point out later on.

Fourth, character evaluation of a group can vary considerably, depending on whether we think of it in terms of its brilliant, exceptional personalities or in terms of the average individuals, or even in terms of a specific intellectual elite. The measure of unpredictable, inexplicable, and incomprehensible components is considerably greater in the character of the genius than in others. But, on the other hand, in evaluating the character of a group, it surely is not out of order to give consideration also to its great minds.

What, then, do we mean when we speak of a blending of romanticism and realism? I use the term romanticism, though I am fully aware how vague it is if used in a sense other than its narrower connotation as a specific trend in the arts. Still, I believe that the term romanticism, conceived in a broader sense, best expresses what I mean. Romanticism for the purposes of the present study is an attitude which does not view and evaluate existence from the standpoint of everyday routine, and which does not rest content within the sphere of the rational and the demonstrable. This, then, clearly implies inclinations toward transcendental objectives. I have described this attitude as "romantic" because this adjective best points up the contrast with realism, and because all such strivings are referred to by this adjective — if not by less complimentary one — by those who, refusing to participate in them, remain enmeshed in the material and economic aspects of their lives.

Realism, on the other hand, denotes the tendency and ability to see the data, i.e., the "givens," of the world as they "really" are, to see them unencumbered by irrational views, emotional distortions, illusions, or delusions. The realist, then, aims at accurate observation; he tests and clarifies; he employs all available technical means in order to gain a better understanding of reality; indeed, he may even change reality, the better to learn what it really is like — that is, he experiments, measures, and calculates. The realist subjects man and human society also to his observation. He observes events from the vantage points of psychology and sociology. Nor does he exempt his own personality. When he comes to his own person, observation turns into introspection and analysis into psychoanalysis.

There is no doubt but that there is a certain contrast between the romantic and the realistic tendencies. But the two are not mutually exclusive. There are fortunate instances in which, instead of canceling one another out, they work to shape and mold each other. This happens wherever realism finds its sphere of activity in the basic material of action, in all the givens which serve man as the raw material from which he shapes his objectives.

Accordingly, one may speak of a realistic romanticism, a blend which is romantic as to its objective but realistic in the pursuit of that objective and familiar with methods and psychological possibilities. Such a blend is found specifically in the creative personalities we are about to discuss. This type of romanticism is not one of fantasy, illusion, meditation, asceticism, neurosis, or nihilism, but one which knows life and takes reality into account. The realistic element in this blend, on the other hand, is not centered on the natural drives or on economic objectives; it is neither positivist nor bureaucratic, but simply provides the foundation for a finer structure of life.

This sort of realism has still another most important aspect. If applied to the human personality, to the ego of the individual himself, it can serve as a means of making possible and promoting an honesty with oneself, a critical attitude toward oneself and an antagonism to illusion. Only a realistic attitude toward one's own self can make possible that unmasking of one's own personality which will uncover hypertrophied economic and political drives, and prepare the way for the truth which will in turn make possible mankind's liberation from the crises in which it now finds itself.

It would be self-deception to think that such an ideal blending of romanticism and realism is the rule rather than the exception. The fact is that it is only an ideal which not more than a few outstanding individuals can approach. In the majority of cases, the realistic component predominates, and the romantic component remains suppressed or repressed, well concealed beneath an armor of skepticism and self-ridicule. Only in exceptional individuals does the romantic component occasionally burst into flame.

The foregoing has a bearing on the preponderantly critical attitude of the Jews of Bohemia and Moravia, their acute observation, their predilection for psychological explanations, this critique of self which frequently ran to self-mockery, and also their critical attitude toward their own group and their own religion.

In some individuals the repression of the romantic tendency is so strong as to make them inimical to imaginativeness and unaffected greatness and become submerged in a certain provincial pettiness. The elements of freedom and detachment, which are originally inherent in the basic romantic trend, merely suffice to cause such individuals not to accept life naively as the nonromantic does, but to view it from afar in a posture of caution, irony, and unproductiveness.

Such is the development which this polarity may set off in lesser men. But how fine the fruit it may bring forth in greater personalties. There was Gustav Mahler, a Jew from Kaliště, a brilliant musician whose creative work appears to us as a massive breakthrough of romanticism, produced with the help of a conscious and thoroughly realistic mastery of all the musical media, an approach which his enemies decried as typically Jewish. The romantic element in his music is expressed not only in his choice of texts and themes — German romanticism and Chinese lyricism — but also in the religious depth of his *Weltgefühl.*

Another sort of blending of romanticism and realism is shown in the works of Franz Kafka, the Prague poet who, after his untimely death, gradually gained recognition as one of the foremost literary spokesman of our era. His stories are characterized by a kind of realism which could be described as a "dreamlike realism," a representation of unreal happenings in realistic terms. The strange, unearthly, and supernatural antagonists of man, the unapproachable personages of the "Court of Justice" and of the "Castle" live and work in highly realistic settings such as offices, taverns, and attics. Transcendence is transposed throughout into disgusting or ludicrous reality. The crime for which Kafka's heroes are condemned and die is not a real crime such as is familiar to human society: it is metaphysical, existential, and romantic in character, but the judges and executioners are portrayed by way of the realistic medium of satire. The major theme of Kafka's work is man's unfathomable relationship with God, but his way of shaping this theme is that of humor. This humor, of course, is not meant to amuse the reader; it is a very somber humor, a realistic medium of portrayal which, by that objective observation of which humor alone is capable, makes the incomprehensible conceivable.*

In the case of the works of Max Brod it can be said that there is hardly any among them, poetic or philosophical, that does not have as its theme the contrast between romanticism and realism in the sense in which these concepts are used in the present study. In his novel *Tycho Brahe's Weg zu Gott* ("Tycho Brahe's Way to God"), the two main characters, Tycho Brahe and Johannes Kepler, are actually representatives of these contrasts: Kepler stands for romanticism, Tycho for realism. In his *Reubeni, Fuerst der Juden* ("Reubeni, Prince of the Jews"), Reubeni is the realist and Shelomo Molcho the romantic. In the novel *Das grosse Wagnis* ("The Great Venture") Brod attempts to carry a nonromantic way of life *ad absurdum.* Certainly Brod's familiar definition of Judaism in *Heidentum, Christentum, Judentum* ("Paganism, Christianity, Judaism") as a

---

* See my volume: *Religion und Humor im Leben und Werk Franz Kafkas.*

Diesseitswunder ("this-worldly miracle") in itself implies a synthesis of romanticism and realism. Finally, the basic purpose of his philosophical work *Diesseits und Jenseits* ("This World and the Hereafter") is to explain that, his recognition of the trancendency and absolute perfection of God notwithstanding, the reality of evil cannot be argued away. Brod therefore attempts to localize the dichotomy within God Himself, whose nature contains not only the infinite essence of perfection (as in the romantic view) but also the element of growth through time, with all the attendant imperfections which Brod's realistic eye cannot overlook.

Franz Werfel, another poet whom Prague Jewry could claim as its own, was a romantic through and through, overflowing with emotion and love, intoxicated with devout humility — and yet he had a sharp eye for reality which worked to shape the plots of his novels with operatic splendor and in ingenious and sweeping architecture.

Egon Erwin Kisch, the son of an old Jewish family of Prague, rushed through the world to write romantic reports on realistic everyday life; and the masterpiece of Joseph Popper-Lynkeus, who was born in the Bohemian town of Kolín, bears the highly descriptive title *Phantasien eines Realisten* ("Fantasies of a Realist").

Let us turn to some men of science and learning. Sigmund Freud, who was born in Příbor (Freiberg), Moravia, and grew up to become one of the greatest psychologists of the century and a creative personality of absolute veracity, penetrated into the world of dreams, the world of the unconscious. By way of analysis through association, he conquered this great romantic kingdom for the conscious mind, but at the same time he stripped it of its illusions by uncovering the very real drives and the mechanism of symbols which direct the strange happenings in the dream world and the enigmatic aberrations of the human soul. While he trancended our conscious, he did away with romanticism in the sphere of the unconscious. Indeed, he carried his zeal to sweep away all illusion so far that he proceeded with a maximum degree of realism even on his work on religion, the true sphere of trancendence, to the extent that he gave his book the title *The Future of an Illusion*.

The opposite path was taken by Edmund Husserl, the great son of the town of Prostějov (Prossnitz). His slogan, summarizing the essence of his phenomenology without which the development of modern philosophy would be inconceivable, was "*zu den Sachen*" —

"to the business at hand." But it was by way of this realism that Husserl discovered a surrealistic world of eternal truths and values.

In this connection, mention should also be made of Hugo Bergmann, whose philosophy likewise shows the typical blending with which we are concerned here — an extremely clear and objective view of the problems of logic and epistemology which drives to the root of things conscientiously and unencumbered by illusion. Side by side with it, or perhaps in the midst of it, there is a transcendental core of genuine religious experience from which Bergmann gained the strength to accept calmly and humbly the limitations of the possibilities of philosophical inquiry.

The personality of Hugo Bergmann brings us to those young Zionists whose leader he was and who had a significant role in the development of the character of Bohemian and Moravian Jewry in the early twentieth century. Among them were leading personalities in the Zionist students' organization of Prague, including Leo Hermann, Robert Weltsch, Hans Kohn, Sigmund Katznelson, and Viktor Kellner, in addition to Bergmann himself.

These young men sought the content of their lives outside the sphere in which the life of the preceding generation had unfolded, outside the natural framework of material and economic interests, family, synagogue, business, religious community, and organizational life. Their main ambition was not to train for a specific occupation but revolved around a broader objective, namely, the future of the community in the sense of a complete change in the status of Jewry and hence also in the objectives of the Jew as an individual. What they had in view was a departure from the conventional paths, a passing beyond the realities of life, a type of transcendentalism, as it were. Their slogan, which summarized their aims, was "the rebirth of the Jewish personality" and signified a break between the world of the fathers and that of the sons. Indeed, in many instances the fathers would regard the strange paths of their sons as unreasonable, if not madness; others, with slightly more understanding, would dismiss it all as "romanticism."

The idea which had taken hold of these young men was Zionism. It had originated not with them but in neighboring Vienna, the city of Theodor Herzl. To be sure, Zionism was a romantic idea, but it soon became something more — a movement working with political methods, propaganda, diplomacy, and all the realistic machinery of democratic politics such as congresses, committees, sessions, newspapers, brochures, fund-raising campaigns, emissaries, negotiations, and resolutions — and thus Zionism was constantly in danger of sliding into the conventional, familiar grooves of tendencies to power politics, self-assertion, catch phrases, and the myth of racial superiority.

The antidote against this danger is realism and antagonism to illusion; above all, that sort of realism which makes for a critical attitude toward, and an unmasking of, one's own personality, as well as an adequate dose of skepticism, psychology, and the moral resolve to start the work of rebirth with one's own self. All this applies also to the "rebirth of the Jewish personality." In this case Husserl's realistic appeal "to the business at hand" means, first and foremost, "to one's own self."

It is certainly not our intention to say that this, the most basic of all moral impulses, was a decisive factor in the development of the character of the Jews in Bohemia and Moravia. That would be an idealistic distortion of reality. But perhaps we are within our rights to say that this was the direction in which the leading personalities of this group, at their best, sought to influence the Jews of that period and that they achieved some success — which, in this field, is saying a great deal.

Before turning to a study of the personalities that made up the various groups of Bohemian and Moravian Jewry, let us inquire into the circumstances that influenced the behavior of the young people of that period. What was the origin of those elements of romanticism and realism which came to a unique synthesis in the Jews of Bohemia and Moravia, and what caused the synthesis to take the form it assumed?

The development of a given group or community may be influenced by any of following factors: heredity, meaning all those tendencies which the individual inherits from parents and ancestors; environment, meaning the natural, geological, economic, and political conditions under which the individual or group lives; the great realm of the unconscious — habit, training, tradition; knowledge, particularly the awareness of being part of a general development taking place through time; a sense of continuity; a sense of history; open-mindedness vis-à-vis the world and ideas; the ability of the conscious to follow up reality in the direction of infinity and universality; and religious consciousness.

As to the romantic component, today we probably lack the knowledge needed to determine whether and to what extent it is influenced by hereditary factors. But we know that the unconscious and traditional realities play a significant role in it, and that, without a doubt, its main source is a sense of history and religious consciousness. Indeed, it may be said that the religious position of that generation was the most important factor in the genesis of the romantic component. The religious position of that generation was entirely different from that of the generation which had gone before and which had lived in a metaphysical sphere safeguarded, to a greater or lesser degree, by tradition. The harsh lot of that older generation among the "host peoples" was counterbalanced by their carefully regulated relationship to the World to Come as expressed in daily prayers, in the celebration of the Jewish festivals, and in the observance of the commandments. All this was reality which did not even admit of a need for "romanticism." This is how things had stood through many centuries. Then the 19th century brought a massive upheaval. Enlightenment, scientific thought, closer contacts with non-Jewish neighbors, and economic and social advancement — all led to a weakening of religious belief. But it was only the content that was destroyed; the need and, more important, the transcendental horizon, that heritage of centuries, remained alive in the emotions, in the subconscious, and in tradition. Exposed and liberated, in this religious consciousness was now search of new content.

This upheaval did not take place all in one generation. It developed gradually. But it was in the generation which is our present subject that the vacuum first made itself clearly felt. To be sure, religion had already lost its former power in the previous generation, but at the time it still had sufficient force to prevent the formation of a vacuum. The fathers still observed some of the commandments and attended synagogue. Their faith was no longer complete, but childhood memories still exerted a powerful pull, filling in their religious sphere. Franz Kafka clearly described this difference between the generations in his diary, where he recorded his visit to the synagogue with his father. To the fathers, religious observance was a conscious state whose emptiness they still did not realize at that point; to the sons, it had become an agitating vacuum. The power of the concrete religious bond had declined, but the pull of religious need remained, and sought the kind of fulfillemnt which clearly lay beyond the sphere of occupational life and outside the normal course which the development of Jewish life had taken in the years that had gone before. It was a need which the fathers had not felt.

It was no surprise that, in their search, the eyes of the younger generation should turn to the past. That which had been lost had come from the past; hence it was to the past that one had to turn to find it. The awareness that a whole code of laws had been lost is most clearly expressed in a number of Kafka's stories and sketches. Jewish religion, to a very considerable extent, consists of a sense of history, a profound knowledge of the unity of the sequence of events in the history of the generations of the Jewish people, and the conviction that history had its beginning in the Book of Genesis and moves toward a definite goal, the messianic era. Despite terrible recurrent setbacks and calamities, the Jew knows that there is meaning and unity in his turbulent history. This sense of history has proved stronger than concrete forms of religious observance, and this sense of history, too — which is composed of loyalty to the past and a sense of obligation to the future — set about the task of filling the religious vacuum.

The form in which this occurred, and the content which was supplied, varied with the specific conditions prevailing in the group concerned, with the nature of the memories that still remained from the past, and above all with the specific historical juncture at which the vacuum had first made itself felt. This consideration helps explain the many ways and forms which rebirth took in the various Jewish communities.

In the case of Russian Jewry the renascence of the language, which had been kept alive by prayer and by study of the Talmud, caused the language and its literature to take central place in the process of secularization. Thus the Jews of Russia cherished the romantic concept of the rebirth of the language of their fathers. In the case of the Jews of Central Europe, the renascence took place in the sphere of the sense of history as such. The crucial change which marked the new generation there was the degree of awareness of its relationship with the past. This relationship had presented neither a task nor a problem to the generation that had gone before; it had simply been taken for granted. But it occupied a place of paramount importance in the consciousness of the new generation. This was a distinctive feature of the Central European Jewish youth of that period: amidst a gradual, barely noticeable slipping away on the part of the older generation from its ties with the past, the return to the past on the part of the younger generation assumed the dimensions of an internal revolution. The new path which suddenly opened before the eyes of that youth was one of return, and since that generation by then was far removed from the past, the return took on romantic colors.

At this point we must not lose sight of the one factor which, though at least in part outside the domain of Jewish history, could not fail to be one of profound psychological influence, namely, the role of the city of Prague, the spiritual and political center of the Jews of Bohemia and Moravia.

Few cities were as apt to awaken a sense of history and romanticism in the beholder as was Prague. Let us consider what impressions their walks through the romantic old parts of the city must have left with the young people who had been born and raised there or who had come there for their studies. There were the splendid mansions which, though long since occupied by offices and janitors, evoked dreams of a glorious past; the strangely meandering streets which lost themselves in dark, mysterious corners; the quiet old courtyards which not even the washing hung out by the wives of artisans could deprive of their old aristocratic air; the multitude of churches in which two styles of romantic architecture vied with one another; and, finally, Saint Vitus's Cathedral atop the Hradčany, the architectural pinnacle of the city in which this rivalry between Gothic and Baroque culminated in a surprising and meaningful harmony. A rich garland of legends, which flourished until the very end, clustered around the Jewish landmarks of the city, the *Altneuschul*, the ancient Jewish cemetery, and the legends of the great Rabbi Löw. It was typical of this city that the bylaws set down for the Burial Brotherhood centuries before by the *Maharal*, that personality who had become a legendary figure not only for the Jews but for the other inhabitants of Prague as well, remained in force as long as the city's Jewish community was in existence. The romantic aura of Prague reached out far into Bohemia, Moravia, and even into Austria. It inspired poets, artists, and sculptors — Jewish, German, and Czech alike — so that it would have been surprising indeed if it had had no effect on those young Jews who came to the city at that point in history with open minds and receptive hearts.

These factors, which fostered the spirit of romanticism in the young people, were rooted in the religious sphere, in a sense of history, in tradition, in the unconscious, in the environment, and in the epoch in which that historical development took place. But there was also an economic factor.

The fact is that there was not only a religious vacuum which made itself felt in the young generation but also an economic vacuum. Most of these young people, including the ones who eventually became famous writers, musicians, artists, scholars, physicians, and scientists, were the sons of Jewish businessmen. We should not think that these merchants and storekeepers were as wealthy as many of their counterparts in Germany were at the time. This is important to remember, for the difference — which on the surface appears to be one in quantity only — resulted in a considerable divergence in mentality between the Czech Jews and those of the German Reich.

This fact is brought out in a highly interesting manner in the biography published by the widow of the philosopher Ernst Cassirer. Although she came from a very wealthy Bohemian Jewish family, she writes, she was amazed when she first went to visit her fiancé's family in Berlin and saw the aura of economic security and the standard of living maintained by the wealthy Jews of the German capital. In our own day we still note with amazement the natural sense of economic security with which Cassirer could embark on his career, untroubled by thoughts of his future livelihood or of the future of the Jewish people. Cassirer lived to learn that his confidence was unwarranted, but at the time that sense of confidence was widespread and had a profound influence on the character of the young generation.

The fathers of the young sons of Bohemia and Moravia, on the other hand, could not even be described as wealthy. They definitely had financial problems, but nevertheless their standard of living was such that they could allow their sons to become "something better" instead of having them start out as apprentices and commercial travelers, as they themselves had done. The sons became doctors, lawyers, or, if worst came to worst, bank clerks. But many of these young men were not content with this. Filled with romantic ideals, they saw no purpose in simply continuing the economic careers of their elders — hence the "economic vacuum." These members of the younger generation became writers, scholars, journalists, scientists, and also Zionists. The things which the older generation had taken for granted — entering the family business, marrying well, and making money — held no charms for them. The young man who felt that he was endowed with a special talent had the chance to cultivate that gift. By the same token, those who were troubled by the religious vacuum and had a sense of historical obligation searched for a link with the past of their people. All these circumstances made for romanticism.

Let us now turn to the conditions which fostered the realism that was equally typical of the Jews of Bohemia and Moravia. There was one sociological factor which, while it was not the only factor, clearly played an important part in training the younger generation to become realists. It was the circumstance that the Jews of Bohemia and Moravia were a people amidst several others. Here again we see a considerable difference between the situation of the Jews in Bohemia and Moravia, on the one hand, and that of the Jews in Germany and interior Austria on the other, a difference which certainly must have had a considerable influence in the formation of the character of both these Jewries. The Jews of Germany lived *in the midst* of the German people. In some respects, it is true they might have constituted a foreign body, but still they may be said to have dwelt within the people of the country in which they lived. There is no doubt that it was more difficult for the German Jews to become aware of themselves than it was for the Jews of Bohemia and Moravia who, living as they did as an "intermediate" class, were "fated by destiny to see clearly."

There is no doubt but that a life lived amidst several peoples tends to make for a realistic approach. It should be remembered, too, that the Jews of Bohemia and Moravia not only lived amidst, but also midway between, the religions, social tendencies, and political parties of other peoples. Being observant, they noted what was going on around them. They saw not only the stage on which the struggles took place but also could see — and, indeed, of necessity had to see — what went on behind the scenes. As a result, they became adept at social criticism and psychology. A group of individuals which is in a position to observe a variety of political parties and politicians in operation without participating in these activities and without even being part of these peoples has every chance of getting to know human weaknesses and seeing through illusions.

The Jews of Bohemia and Moravia learned to do just that, and eventually they grew so adept at it that they came to practice social criticism and psychology on themselves as well. It was in this manner that the group which lived in the middle of Europe, midway between

German and Czechs, Catholics and Protestants, clericalists and freethinkers, capitalists and socialists, dynasty and subjects, achieved a realistic outlook on communal life.

We have already touched on the desirable effects of this type of realism. Given favorable circumstances, it can make for a proper evaluation of the possibilities and ways of human behavior, and result in the exposure of the artifices of our natural and assertive drives which exploit the intellect for selfish objectives. Most important of all, this sort of realism can show the way to honesty with oneself and to the ability to unmask the hidden recesses of one's own personality. To be sure, this path does not offer absolute security. Realism and the ability to take a critical view of one's environment do not in themselves constitute a guarantee that one will become honest also with oneself, but they do afford chance in that direction. In view of the possible results of this effort at self-refinement, even such remote possibilities must be given due consideration.

At the same time, we must not lose sight of the fact that the sort of realism created in this fashion also has its weak points. It may lead to an overcautious view of all enterprise and change, to a suspicion of anything that smacks of adventure, daring, or even romanticism. In short, it may give rise to an attitude of cautious, fainthearted skepticism not only toward developments outside but in many cases also toward one's own self.

Another danger inherent in this realistic view is that the individual adopts an overly psychological approach to things. In many instances, the individual may think that he understands a development or a relationship because he has constantly remained in the position of the objective observer. But then he has failed to see that there are certain strata which can be properly evaluated only if one observes them not merely from the outside as an objective psychologist but from within as well. It must be admitted that the practice of automatically taking the position of outside observer is dangerous, and also that it has not always been avoided by many members of the groups discussed in the present study. Indeed, criticism on this count may be legitimately leveled even at this study itself.

However, the Jews of Bohemia lived not only midway between peoples and political parties but also midway between cultures. Thəy took part in two different ethnic cultures, and their position as observers among the nations was not so objective that it would have prevented them from becoming aware, and even enamored, of the true value of the cultural achievements that became apparent behind the political struggles among the peoples. Their intermediate position made the Jews of Bohemia and Moravia not only critical but also — and fortunately — openminded. As a result, the young Jews opened their hearts and minds to the offerings of the German philosophers and poets as well as to those of the Czech musicians and thinkers. Anyone able to recall that era knows the stamp which Buber and Avenarius, Weininger and Wyneken, Masaryk and Fichte, and many others left upon the thinking of that generation of Jews.

There is no doubt but that this attitude of open-mindedness toward the cultures that surrounded them left its mark on the Jews of Bohemia. However, it was not an unmixed blessing. Here again we see the problem of finding the proper balance between loyalty to one's own heritage on the one hand and open-mindedness to that of others on the other. There is no set formula for achieving the ideal balance between the two. It is only possible to discern the negative results that ensue when openness toward alien cultures becomes so great that one loses one's own individuality in the process, and to recognize that it would be just as bad to shut oneself off from the enriching and stimulating influence of other cultures and to remain in self-centered isolation.

Our lives unfold in time as well as in space. We owe loyalty to time, that is to our own past. But we have an obligation also to space, to the world in which we live. He who forgets himself and merges into space is a traitor to time. But he who turns inward betrays thereby the world of which he is a part. While we certainly cannot claim that the Jews of Bohemia and Moravia were entirely successful in avoiding both these errors, we may say that there were among them some individuals who, by the example of their own lives, showed proper way to the others.

ON THE SO-CALLED JEWISH SPIRIT

by Jan Ehrenwald

Author's Note: The article below is a condensation of six lectures given to the B'nai B'rith lodge *Fides* in Bratislava from 1932 to 1937. They were published by Ludo Sturc, Kreis Verlag, Bratislava, 1938, under the title *Ueber den Sogenannten Juedischen Geist.* So far as I know, they are the only surviving mementos of the proceedings of the lodge fter the ransacking of its premises by the Hlinka Guard in the same year. The book was subsequently confiscated and burned by the Nazis.

The lectures reflect the forebodings and anxieties that swept the Jewish communities of Czechoslovakia in the years prior to the Nazi holocaust. At the same time, they are another example of the age-old Jewish quest for spiritual identity and self-respect in the face of overwhelming threats to Jewish survival. The reader may note the author's studied avoidance of giving offense to the authorities; his attempts to sound like a spokesman for "His Majesty's loyal Opposition"; his repetitive use of allusions and circumlocutions, made necessary by the prevailing climate of persecution.

Shortly before its publication, the author sent the book to Sigmund Freud, who was at that time still living in Vienna.

Freud's response, in a heretofore unpublished letter, is appended to the article. Both the condensation of the book and the letter are given here in the author's translation. The essays mentioned by Freud were subsequently published in the book *Moses and Monotheism.* It was to be Freud's last.

For the assimilated Western Jew of our time, the encounter with anti-Semitism seems to be the usual introduction to the problem of Judaism. This is by no means a matter of coincidence. For many

Jews it is the very condemnation and negation of Jewishness which brings home to them the experience of their historic, religious, or social identity. It is forced on them by the growing host of sneering, hostile, vindictive adversaries, emerging seemingly without a warning from the lunatic fringe of our culture. It is this hostile encounter which compels the assimilated Jew to come to terms with his Jewishness, to reevaluate his position, and to make whatever decision is called for in the circumstances. The fact is that long before growing aware of being Jewish, he was brought face to face with it in the distorting mirror held out before him by those whose vision of hate had been responsible for the distortion in the first place.

What, then, is the reason for all that hate? What are its root causes and ultimate determining factors?

Clearly, the question can be—and indeed has been—approached from racial, socioeconomic, cultural, and psychological angles. Yet whatever way we view it, we have to realize that Judaism has its historic origin in a compelling spiritual experience. In trying to lay bare the primary, spiritual roots of anti-Semitism we must therefore bring into focus that particular state of mind which, at the dawn of Jewish history, gave rise to the first ominous rumblings of resentment against Judaism.

Viewed in historic perspective, it is a resentment which, irrespective of time and place, and regardless of the succession of generations and shifts of geographical locations and national boundary lines, has essentially remained the same throughout the ages. It is this enduring and omnipresent Jewish experience which should alert us to the part played in the origin of anti-Semitism by spiritual factors, over and above those envisaged by theorists of historical materialism.

From all we know, these spiritual origins have to be sought in that fateful moment of history when a raw, illiterate, nomadic tribe made its revolutionary break with the pagan idols, the magic rituals, and the primitive moral codes of the neighboring tribes. It is true that the moment may have lasted for decades, if not for centuries. The revolutionary new departure may have been a rerun of the first faltering attempt by an Egyptian pharaoh to establish a monotheistic creed in his land. But as it happened, it was the Jewish attempt at so doing which was the first one to succeed. It was the Jewish venture in monotheism which proved to be viable enough to survive.

It is difficult for modern man, brought up in the spirit of enlightenment, to appreciate the full historic impact of this state of affairs. Primitive man, living in the twilight of magic and animistic belief, found himself at the mercy of a host of cruel, bloodthirsty idols and divinities. They were irrational and unpredictable in their demands, unbending to his compulsive rites and incantations, implacable in exacting their tribute in human sacrifice and self-sacrifice. Man stranded in such a perplexing universe finds himself caught in a web of his own superstitions, threatened at every move by demoniacal powers beyond his control.

It was at this juncture that the Age of Revelation dawned upon the tribes inhabiting the eastern banks of the Mediterranean. Its message was conveyed by a people possessing a new magic of words, formulating a new hierarchy of symbols and abstractions and an unprecedented universal code of ethics which transcended the parochial concerns of tribal lore. It was a code of ethics which flew in the face of the irrational taboos, injunctions, and prohibitions of this people's neighbors. Its impact upon the minds of men was truly revolutionary. The twilight lifted; objects, events, responsibilities, and values came into new focus. Primordial fears were dissipated, together with a gamut of irrational taboos and injunctions. All power, meaning, and purpose were traced back to the one single source from which it came: to the One and Only God who revealed Himself to Moses in the Burning Bush, to the giver of universal moral laws, binding to all mankind. In contrast to the countless idols and graven images of their polytheistic neighbors, the Children of Israel enunciated a set of commandments which was to rule the lives and conduct of all men for all times.

It is not surprising that such a discovery, or indeed such a revelation, imparted a sense of divine mission to the Children of Israel. It filled them with boundless national pride, if not arrogance. They were the Chosen People, the beloved children of the Lord. They felt imbued with His spirit of holiness. They felt that they themselves had become the high priests and guardians of a congeries of sacred and inviolable taboos. They were raised above ordinary human stature to become holy and tabooed themselves. In turn, Yahweh made His covenant with them, pledged to protect His children against their enemies. It was He who led them out of the land of bondage and set them free. It was He who made the prophecy come true: "And the land of Judah should become a terror unto Egypt; everyone that maketh mention thereof shall be afraid in himself."

It goes without saying that such a divinely inspired, ecstatic yet overbearing and self-righteous attitude could not but antagonize those who were witnessing such a spectacle. Israel's neighbors — in biblical times as well as in succeeding times of the *galuth* — resisted their claims. They regarded them as a challenge to claims and aspirations of their own. They felt the commandment "I am the Lord thy God.... Thou shalt have no other gods before Me" to be a provocation and a denial of their tribal or national identities.

The Old Testament as well as the Mishnah and the Talmud are replete with intemperate attacks against the worshipers of pagan idols, against their foolhardy customs and superstitious beliefs. Little wonder that the reproach of godlessness had already in early pre-Christian times been leveled against Jewry. The Greeks called the Jews *atheoi*, the people who refused to pay homage to the gods of other peoples. To men of Greek or Roman antiquity, with their pantheon of easygoing anthropomorphic and zoomorphic divinities, residing on fog-shrouded mountain peaks or in sunlit olive groves, the austere, unimaginative, abstract theology of the Galileans was utterly beyond comprehension. To them it amounted to the banishment of the living gods from their Olympian abode and indeed from the face of the earth, the seven seas, and the heavens above them. The Jews, on the other hand, had nothing but contempt for the fanciful tales, the tomfoolery, and the low moral standards of the Gentiles.

Yet from the vantage point of the contemporary observer, the intransigent attitude of early Judaism is thoroughly understandable. Nothing is more apt to provoke intemperate reactions than an ideological position that one has just left behind. What has been barely overcome and relinquished becomes the subject of disdain and disapprobation. By the same token, a newly acquired truth is likely to unite its adherents in the most determined and fanatical defense of their position. The new monotheistic creed was a truth of precisely this order. It was a truth that reduced all riddles of cosmology, all problems of theology and moral conduct to one single all-encompassing metaphysical formula of uprecedented boldness. It was a spiritual position which indeed called for an all-out defense against atavistic throwbacks to primitive paganism and idolatry.

This is how the one overarching spiritual accomplishment of an otherwise insignificant nomadic tribe in the ancient Palestinian landscape brought it from the outset into a fateful psychological conflict with the Gentiles. It was an accomplishment that was to become the decisive criterion for their growing separation and alienation from peoples committed to a spiritual outlook and a set of values different from their own.

To be sure, all this happened so long ago that it may seem idle to give it another thought. Still, the self-imposed segregation of the Jew in the service of a carefully nurtured, preserved, and, if necessary, fanatically defended doctrinal position has become one of the indispensable prerequisites of his self-assertion and of his personal and cultural identity. Indeed, it served as the principal guarantee for the continuity of Jewry in the historic perspective. It is the preservation of these spiritual values which helped to tide their custodians over the loss of their homeland and the vicissitudes of two millennia in the Diaspora: rootlessness, defamation, and persecution. Evidently, what spared Jewry the fate of the Assyrians, the Babylonians, or the Egyptians was their continued commitment to a central idea, and it is one of the tragic corollaries of this commitment that it became one more reason for their growing separation and alienation from the other nations.

Whole libraries have been filled with books pondering the position of Jewry on the world scene. Is it a racial, a religious, a national, or a political entity — or simply a socioeconomic minority group? None of the definitions has gained general acceptance. But there is one thing which can be concluded from the very divergence in opinions: once Jewry as a national entity had lost its fixed territorial attachment, its cultural and linguistic unity and cohesion, the Jews emerged as a new mutation of *Homo sapiens*, as it were. They made the first faltering steps toward establishing a novel, indeed unprecedented, mode of existence outside the historically sanctioned tribal or national frame of reference, without the aid of a biological or culturally preexisting mold. Whether by accident or by design, the new experience in effect became a pioneering experiment attesting to, living by, and demonstrating the value and viability of a new detribalized, supranational mode of existence. It amounted to an attempt at developing an adaptional technique transcending geographical, linguistic, and political boundaries as well as institutionalized political and socioeconomic ties.

As with all new mutations, the life expectancy of the novel detribalized breed of men was dubious at the beginning. But their very survival proves a point. It suggests that man of the new supranational variety is indeed capable of holding his own as a hitherto untested *Lebensmacht*, or Power of Life, as Professor Hans Kohn has put it. In fact, despite the continued claims of the rival forces of Jewish conservatism and orthodoxy, the new mutant has succeeded in evolving precisely that type of political conscience and ideology which is needed for the new "experimental" pattern of a nationally uncommitted detribalized adaption to life.

This is how it has come to pass that the Jew of the *galuth*, released from the individual's traditional commitment to one nation, one state, or one particular tribal divinity or patron saint, has once more become the carrier of a new spiritual dispensation. Having lost (or thrown overboard) the ideological prerequisites for adaptation to an old or obsolescent form of life, the Jew finds himself in the avant-garde of all those who have set the acquirement of a new supranational mode of existence as their goal.

This new breed of man cannot, and will not, join hands with those who are substituting the Moloch of the State for the fallen idols of a past era. He stands aloof from their pagan ceremonies, once more drenched in the blood of human victims sacrificed to the "greater glory" of long-defunct cannibalistic gods of war. Although he may have been among the combatants who shed their blood in defense of their homeland or on the battlefield of clashing political ideologies, he refuses to go along with those who seek to drum up support for their own brand of a traditional self-seeking nationalism. The Jew, committed to this outlook, has realized — he was destined to realize it sooner than many others — that human life and cultural values can indeed evolve and thrive outside the nationalistic frame of reference. This does not mean that he is bent on denying the values of old. Indeed, he holds that they are included in the new ones, as the nations of this earth comprise all mankind, or as all regions of the earth are encompassed by our planet.

It is obvious, however, that it is precisely this fateful spiritual posture of Jewry — the very core of its being and what it happens to stand for — which the partisans of a narrow nationalistic position are apt to mistake for an act of defiance, for a sinister plot or open aggression against all nationalistic concerns and aspirations. It is also fully consistent with this state of affairs that every sign and symbol, big and small, featured on the Jewish scale of values, is taken for an open negation of the values mapped out on the nationalistic side of the scale. Indeed, in view of the absolute value claimed for the nationalistic position, values outside its ken are necessarily considered as *anti*-values, destructive of values, as evil incarnate. This is how Hitler put it his *Mein Kampf:* "No — the Jew possesses no powers to create cultural values since he is lacking, and indeed always has lacked, the idealism needed for a true progressive development of man. This is why his intellect will never be constructive — only destructive. . . . He is the archetype of the force which always wills the evil and always produces the good." After this oblique compliment Hitler goes on to say: "Progress of mankind is accomplished *in spite* of him not *through* him." This accusation is well on the way to becoming an article of faith and an acid test of the new national socialistic ideology of our day.

Hitler's disciple and fellow campaigner Gregor Strasser hailed this mentality as "that way of German thinking in politics, economy, theater, and sports which is based on the sole consideration of what is of benefit to the nation." In a similar vein, Count Reventlow, the National Socialist leader, once pointed out: "All that is the essential in German nature, its best manifestations and impulses, are the targets of Jewish aggression and destruction. . . . The Jew runs counter to the welfare and organic growth of German nature and must therefore be stopped in his tracks. The *sacro-egoismo* of the German people clearly demands the elimination of the Jew from German life."

Hans Blueher, one of the spiritual interpreters of national socialism frankly reproaches the Jews for having put the "natural laws of nationalistic ethics *under* those of God," that is, they subordinated them to the command of a universalistic supranational moral code. And he recalls the First Commandment: "Thou shalt have no other gods before Me."

Here is, once again, the age-old grievance against Judaism: it has deposed the pagan gods of old and put the monotheistic creed in their place. It is charged with *Sakralraub:* with the rape and violation of all things sacred. The Jews' indifference to the fetishes and graven images worshiped by a new pagan generation is held against them as a major crime.

What kind of spectacle, what waking nightmare, is being acted out here before our eyes? Is it Judaism which is being dragged before the court of justice, or is it the spirit of universal humanistic enlightenment, which until yesterday had been considered as the highest attainment of Western man? Has all that suddenly been exposed as a fallacy, or have our adversaries raised the so-called Jewish spirit on such a lofty pedestal merely by default?

It is idle to speculate on this point. But one thing seems to be perfectly clear: the new accusations hark back to the age-old charges against the Jew as the iconoclast, the violator and destroyer of the taboos and fetishes of a divided and fragmented pagan world. The cleavage between the One and Only God and the multitude of counterfeit divinities pitted against Him has come out in the open again. The difference between then and now — between the past and present — merely lies in the fact that the blood of human sacrifices is no longer spilled on the rockhewn altar stones of a past era but on the newly erected places of worship dedicated to the Moloch of war and nationalism. On one side there are lined up the reincarnations of the fetishes of old. On the other side: the Non-Nation, the Non-People, or Super Nation, as Alfred Döblin put it — the mute witness to an all-encompassing messianic idea which has in effect been wrongly claimed — or denounced — as an exclusively Jewish accomplishment.

Still, the past seems to be catching up with the present: we are witnessing the same labor pangs now as then; we are caught up in the same spiritual crisis; and, by the same token, now as then, Judaism meets with the same hostile response — the reproach of iconoclastic, if not blasphemic, rationalism: "the Children of Israel rising against Christian-nationalistic values."

What seems to be taking place at this juncture is the consummation of Jewish destiny as a consistent and inexorable course of historic events. The Jewish people, having left behind an obsolete tribal form of existence and finding themselves in the avant-garde of the new form, are becoming increasingly aware of the dangers attached to the newly emerging or, rather, reemerging, archetype of an uncompromising tribal nationalism. This dawning insight anticipates a new historic departure which, I trust, will one day be shared by others who follow in their footsteps.

But once again, as happened before in Jewish history, Jewry itself is wary of its own unsought-for messianic mission. Indeed its historic assignment may not have registered consciously on the Jewish mind. But hatred seems to have sharpened the perceptions of our adversaries, past and present. They are keenly aware of the dangerous insight stirring in the Jewish soul, and they have vowed to crush it, to stamp it out, to nip it in the bud wherever they find it: in the Jews themselves or in their ideological dupes and fellow travelers, who have become carriers of the purported infection.

The fact is that even a cursory glance at the local Czechoslovak — and for that matter, the Austro-Hungarian or German — scene shows that the Jews hold no brief on the humanistic, detribalized, supranational tradition. This is equally true for Germany of both the old and the new Weimarian vintage. Lessing, Goethe, Thomas or Heinrich Mann can hardly be described as *Gesinnungs Juden* — or fellow travelers of Heine or Stefan or Arnold Zweig. The so-called Jewish spirit, as defined by the ideologists of national socialism, is in effect a Judeo-Christian, "Nazarean" attitude in Nietzsche's sense. It is an attitude bearing in good measure the brunt of the pagan onslaught. At the same time it has a close ideological affinity with the universal humanistic tradition of Comenius and Tomáš Masaryk, or of men like Karel Čapek or František Langer. It is a reflection of the singular confusion of the value system held by our adversaries when they see fit to condemn summarily all values that run counter to those of their own making. They are consistent, however, in one respect: theirs is certainly the photographic negative of a more than merely provincial, tribal, or nationalistic set of values.

All these remarks are little more than faltering attempts to restore the tarnished image and self-image of today's Western Jew, and to remove from it the distortions made in its currently circulated ghoulish caricature. You may also note that so far I have only touched upon general characteristics of the so-called Jewish spirit, which may or may not be valid in the broad historic perspective. But you may well ask at this point: What about the specifics? What are the political and spiritual realities of Jewry in today's world?

The question plainly goes beyond the scope of these reflections. Yet it points to more than a merely academic problem. It calls attention to the urgent need to make a major existential decision for each of us, whatever, his position in the community. We have to decide which one of the diverse currents and undercurrents stirring in today's Judaism is the true carrier of the "Jewish spirit." Which one can claim to be the rightful inheritor and owner of the genuine ring from among the three sons in Lessing's celebrated parable?

Orthodox Jewry, the custodian of ancient tradition and of the letters of the law, is certainly the first in line for such a consideration. Orthodoxy represents what has remained stable and indeed immutable amidst the kaleidoscopic changes of Jewish history. It stands for turning inside and recoiling from outside. It represents a commitment to the static versus the dynamic principle of Judaism, if not for the principle of stagnation amidst the winds and tides of change in the world at large. Yet for this very reason orthodoxy has become the guarantor of Jewish survival, an unremitting source of rejuvenation and reactivation of forces lying dormant in its core. Alfred Döblin compared Jewish orthodoxy with encapsulated forms or spores of certain microbes which are capable of withstanding the rigors of even the most cruel and inhospitable physical environment. Yet the role of orthodoxy is by no means confined to preserving its past heritage. Its dream of a messianic mission is oriented toward the future. It is a vision of things to come which the Orthodox Jew, despite his self-righteous claim of belonging to the Chosen People, cannot but share with others who likewise pin their hopes on salvation and the coming of utopia.

Needless to say, Jewish assimilation is the diametrical opposite of the Orthodox position. It represents the Jew ready to blend with virtually all colors of the spectrum of cultural values he has encountered in his way through history: German, French, American, Hungarian, Czech, Slovak — as the case may be. He is open to, and capable of making his own, the values and ideals of any and every host nation with whom he happens to live. In doing so, he may emerge from the process either spiritually enriched or emotionally depleted, but in any case with an altered image of himself.

This is how the Jew of the pre-Hitler period literally immersed himself, body and soul, in his adopted culture. He became a German citizen of the Jewish faith, committed to German values and ideals. He was Jewish only as far as entries in his birth certificate or other vital statistics were concerned. This situation has been lucidly summed up in Arnold Zweig's study *Bilanz der Deutschen Judenheit*. It shows the intimate meshing and interpenetration of the German and Jewish genius and thereby lends a semblance of justification to the "accusations" leveled against Jewish influence on — or indeed Jewish contributions to — the German cultural heritage. The fact is that both the Jewish and German experience have emerged invigorated from this spiritual partnership. A spectacular array of cultural, scientific, and economic achievements by German Jews is a matter of historic record, even though some of it had to be paid for by some flaws of character in those involved in the transaction. The same is true for the mutual inspiration and cross-fertilization of the Jewish and French, or English, or Hungarian, cultural heritage.

The vicissitudes of Jewish assimilation to the Czech — or, to a lesser degree, to the Slovak — culture follow much the same pattern. Jewish assimilation in Bohemia and Moravia was a happy marriage with the wholesome, industrious, law-abiding, yet placid and easygoing spirit of the local populace, even though many of its accomplishments had come down to them through the medium of the old Austro-Hungarian tradition. The fact that men of the caliber of Sigmund Freud, Gustav Mahler, Franz Kafka, Karl Kraus, and Max Brod have likewise sprung from the same source shows that it was capable of also bringing forth figures towering high above the standard of middle-class respectability and petty-bourgeois materialistic values.

It is for others more competent than myself to point to the accomplishments of Jews who have left their mark on the Czech cultural scene. Only such names as Karel Poláček, František Langer, Otokar Fischer, and Vladimír Weinberger may be mentioned in the present context. In the "gentile" department of the Czech Hall of Fame you find men of the stature of Karel Čapek, Ferdinand Peroutka, and Emanuel Rádl who, just owing to their spiritual closeness to what our enemies tend to decry as the Jewish spirit, are the representatives of the true humanistic outlook, indeed of the spirit of the Western world. Their spiritual affinity is obviously due to more than mere geographic proximity. It is derived from the wellsprings of a common dedication to shared democratic and humanistic ideals.

Jewish assimilation to Slovak cultural values has been hampered by the competing claims of the politically, culturally, and economically more advanced, and consequently more influential, Hungarian tradition. Yet here, again, there is growing evidence that the pattern of cultural interpenetration and *rapprochement* is being repeated in a new key on the Slovak cultural scene. The Slovak patriotism of a new Jewish generation, educated in the Slovak language and reared in the Slovak cultural orbit, speaks for itself. So does the literary work of the late Dr. Hugo Roth or the wholly "Slovakized" Géjza Vámoš.

It goes without saying, however, that both deliberate segregation and excessive assimilation have their dangers. The German example shows that, as in a chemical action, the growing and extended intimacy of contact may lead to increasing friction and ultimate explosive discharge of resentment. This can already be discerned in the faltering attempts at assimilation in Slovakia, with the Jews playing the role of Jacob assiduously wooing Rachel and laboring in the services of Laban.

The other extreme is represented by the far-reaching segregation of the Orthodox Polish Jew from the culture of his host country. It shows at the same time that in the presence of an uncompromisingly hostile attitude by the majority, any ideological position taken by the suppressed minority makes no difference. The case for or against assimilation or segregation has already been decided without a hearing by those in authority.

Another fateful dichotomy is represented by the Zionist position, pitted against an essentially humanistic, supranational, messianic Judaism. It is true that the latter trend has never been wholly taken over by the mainstream of Jewish spiritual life, but Max Brod and Felix Weltsch have sought to bring about a reconciliation of the two opposing points of view by advocating Zionism of a new humanistic variety. Yet it may be well to recall at this point that even Theodor Herzl was never an advocate of a narrow nationalistic position. Nor was, incidentally, Tomáš G. Masaryk, the chief architect of Czechoslovak statehood and national identity. He, too, was anxious to integrate nationalistic aspirations with an overarching set of humanistic and humanitarian ideas. In one of his books dealing with this issue, he quotes the Slovak poet Ján Kollár as saying: "Whenever you address a man as Slav — be ready to receive 'Man' as his answer."

"National humanism" as advocated by Max Brod and Felix Weltsch is, however, only one of the many facets of contemporary Zionism. Indeed, Zionism, in our day, includes the whole spectrum of Jewish hopes and political aspirations, from an actively self-assertive Jewish *Realpolitik* to a wide variety of political partisanships and factionalisms, shading from the radical extreme to a frankly utopian, idealistic position. The emergence of so many splinter groups in Jewish political, cultural, and religious life has often been deplored as counterproductive. But it may well be that it is precisely the inner tensions and polarities generated by this multiplicity of currents and crosscurrents which are responsible for the ongoing dynamism of Jewish spiritual life.

All these political and religious alternatives are merely a few among many others which are competing for the pride of place in Jewish spiritual life today. Together they go into making the diversity of an essentially universalistic outlook that is characteristic of Judaism as a whole. But I noted that all its underlying dichotomies are derived from the original Jewish encounter with the One and Only God (and the corresponding set of universalistic values), as opposed to the shiftless spiritual promiscuity of the pagan world. The repercussions of this fateful encounter have endured in Jewish history up to our day. This is a basic fact of Jewish life which should help each individual Jew to maintain his self-respect in the present crisis. It should help him to do so even though our adversaries may hold that spiritual positions and universal human values are nothing but empty slogans invented to fool the man on the street and to camouflage the self-seeking interests of cynical pressure groups and manipulators of public opinion. Yet Freudian psychology can easily expose such explanations for what they are: attempts to attribute one's own repudiated attitudes to the enemy; they are attempts at "projection."

But it is fair to say that not all accusations leveled against us are of this order. There is indeed some truth in the charge that the "so-called Jewish spirit" essentially amounts to a detribalized, supranational, nationally uncommitted ideology, derived as it is from the discovery of the One and Only God of all creation. Yet the traumatic experience of the two millennia of the Diaspora has raised this experience to the level of a compelling new political insight, to the insight that, in the final reckoning, it is universal humanistic values — transgressing national, ethnic, racial, and religious boundaries — which will carry the day. Whether he likes it or not, the Jew of the Diaspora seems to be destined to be in the vanguard of this inexorable historic development and to pay for it in terms of his abject or creative suffering, as the case may be. But I submit that this, too, is by no means an exclusive Jewish predicament. It is a universal human experience, transcending particular ethnic, social, and religious boundaries, though it is thrown into sharper perspective by the Jewish example.

* * * * *

Wien IX Berggasse 19.
14 December 1937.
Geehrter Herr Doctor:

I have to accompany my thanks for sending me your valuable little book with a few remarks of my own. I wish to do this not only because you obviously appreciate psychoanalysis, and have also made several friendly references to my own person, but above all because it contains so much that must appear valid and important to the Jewish reader.

Several years ago, I set out to deal with the question as to how the Jew had acquired his characteristic personality makeup [den ihm eigentümlichen Charakter] — I started as usual at the very beginning. I have indeed gone far in the field. I was surprised to find that already the first, as it were embryonic, experience of the people decidedly influenced its history up to our day: the influence of the man Moses and the Exodus from Egypt. The effect of these experiences is comparable to a veritable early infantile trauma in the life of a neurotic individual. There is, in the first place, the turning toward the *here* and *now* of one's outlook on the world [Diesseitigung der Lebensauffassung]; the overcoming of magic mentality; the renunciation of mysticism, both of which can be traced back to Moses, if not — though not quite with the historically desirable certitude — to an even older time. Two essays in this year's *Imago* contain at least one part of my results. The most important pieces I had to hold back. I should be pleased if you would take cognizance of these articles.

With friendly regards,
Ihr Ergebener
Freud.

The reader familiar with Freud's last literary masterpiece will notice that his premises, as well as his conclusions, are at considerable variance with those of the present writer. Freud's letter is thus a moving testimony to his tolerance with other people's opinions, which had not been in evidence in his younger years. J.E.

5. Art

JEWISH ARTISTS IN THE HISTORIC LANDS

by Hana Volavková

The history of Jewish artists in Bohemia and Moravia spans some two hundred years only, and yet included are personalities of uncommon significance prominent among Czech, and indeed world-renowned, artists. In Oto Gutfreund's work and in the efforts of his generation, who were born in the eighties of the past century, the most prominent era of Jewish culture in Bohemia culminates. For the purposes of this essay we might define that period as from art nouveau to cubism — whatever preceded in fine arts belongs to placid local history; whatever followed is branded by political events and thus defies most generally accepted and established criteria of style.

Objective esthetic judgment is overshadowed by human destinies and by the fate of individual works, most of which found their way into public collections from liquidated Jewish households — Kars and Guttmann and Bindeles and Pereles. Other works are preserved, some in hastily made photographs shortly before their authors were deported to concentration camps (Wiesner's pictures, for example); others, such as the drawings of children and of Fritta, paid for with life itself, were incorporated into public collections in the Jewish Museum* and in the theater section of the National Museum only after the Terezín concentration camp was liberated.[1]

* In order to avoid any misunderstanding in the text, the Jewish Museum in Prague is referred to instead of the Jewish State Museum in Prague.

The history of Jewish artists on Czechoslovak soil should conclude somewhere here. However — and this may amount to a dubious vindication — Jewish wartime subject matter so profoundly marked the past fifteen years of Czechoslovakia's culture that it cannot be passed over in this study.

In the postwar period the relationship and attitude toward Jewish themes changed fundamentally. The negative Jewish types devised in Czech literature of the nineteenth century and at the outset of the twentieth were followed suddenly by a greater gallery of positive representations. In addition, books, films, and pictures covering Jewish topics are among the most mature works, valued for their initiative and invention. Concurrently with these themes others, still broader in aspect, began once more to filter into Czech art. Through the more universal themes art became aware of its existentialist point of departure, and painting and sculpture could engage in competition with the conventionality of the fifties.[2]

Frequent queries as to what might have been responsible for this outstanding success usually elicited the reply that although Jewish subject matter per se makes nothing easier, it does offer, says Karfik, "an amazing continuity of evolution plus considerable cohesion. Also, it has contrived a whole gamut of styles...." Thus if an artist. makes up his mind to join this world he is compelled to adopt a precise spot in the tradition.

Tradition

Old-time Jewish memorabilia of fine arts from Bohemia, Moravia, and Slovakia bear true witness to a certain type of tradition. For the most part they show traits of artisanship but all betray acute eagerness to pinpoint the intrinsic character of their objects and to endow them with a razor-sharp, albeit grotesque, pitch.[3] Such may derive from a latent perception of life which, in times of enduring social crisis and spiritual insecurity, leads toward some incisive form of expression. This is thought to be precisely one of the specific traits of Jewish art.

Within this environment originates and is anchored the first interesting memorial of Jewish art in Bohemia, a collection of twenty pictures, once the property of Prague's burial brotherhood (Hevra Kadisha). (See illustrations 1, 2, 3.) The artist is unknown. The date of inception, as indicated, is 1773, but the collection as a whole underwent such frequent restoration that the date may indicate only the intended plan and stipulation of the iconographic program. The pictures once adorned the main office of the burial brotherhood. They formed a frieze and hence, so to speak, substituted for a mural. The commissioned painter (or painters) were instructed to portray, faithfully and accurately, every activity of the brotherhood, as well as each of its notable members of the day. Several painters succeeded — in the spirit of a period that created novel burgher heroes — in imbuing the faces with almost portraitlike features. Thus there appears to be, for instance, a faithful likeness of Jonas Jeiteles, a well-known physician of Prague, who is shown paying his last visit to a dying patient. Other pictures of the cycle show the employees of the brotherhood engaged in washing the dead, sewing the shrouds, digging graves, nailing the coffin; others portray the brotherhood members dutifully attending funeral processions and collective annual meetings. These painters were not particularly troubled by their relatively complex task. They probably could turn to the French and Dutch engravings of J. B. Piccart and J. E. Grave. They may also have acquired engravings made of some paintings by Pietro Longhi, the Italian protagonist of the genre pictures. Indeed, we must presume that some scenes of the brotherhood series derive, in a sense, from engravings made of Hogarth's works.[4]

With the older, home-bred tradition of anonymous artisans who executed commissions by Jewish patrons or institutions and the new generations of no longer anonymous, expertly trained Jewish artists, the Academy of Fine Arts, established in Prague in 1800, should have normally produced a sharp divide. Nothing of the sort happened. Josef Bergler, an advocate of the classicism of Raphael Mengs, became the academy's director, and throughout his long tutorship many disciples attended the academy. The school register of 1830 lists 354 students, but only 6 of them were Jews. Abraham Devidels, of Prague, enrolled at the academy in 1802 but left it in 1805. He had only been fifteen at the time of his enrollment and nothing of his work was ever found. The same applies to Jonas Bondi, who also enrolled at the academy at the age of fifteen, in 1808.

During the second decade of Bergler's directorship a generation studied at the academy whose work preempts Prague's romanticism by being a bizarre synthesis of the one-time classicism and historical romanticism. Josef Führich became representative of the trend; he enrolled in 1818 with Josef Navrátil, who continues to be a much-valued and live scion of Czech art. Concurrently enrolled with them were Šimon Jacob Arkeles, a portraitist, and — a year later — Leopold Pollak (1819), a genre painter; in 1827 Isák Jeiteles Schöpel, a landscape and portrait painter, enrolled and in 1829, Ignác Josef Porges, who proceeded to become a specialist in the honest portrait.[5]

The first Jewish students at the academy did not begin to assert themselves before the eighteen-thirties, when a romantic interest in Jewish subject matter and Jewish memorabilia showed itself.[6/7]

The Jewish students at the academy indulged in Jewish themes on a modest scale only. Šimon Jacob Arkeles, the oldest of them (born in 1803 in Prague, died there in 1875) drew (for Wolf Pascheles, the publisher, in the second half of the thirties) portraits of Prague's chief rabbi, Samuel Landau, and of Mordecai Benito of Mikulov, the chief rabbi of Moravia. Ignác Josef Porges provided the portrait of Rabbi Salomon Judah Rapoport in 1843, and Isák Jeiteles Schöpel (1811–1855), son of a secondhand clothes dealer in the Prague ghetto, made a drawing in 1855 of the Old-New Synagogue's interior, but with the catafalque of Emperor Francis I added. This, too, was a work commissioned purely for the occasion. (Karel Henning reproduced it in a lithograph by Antonín Wach.)

Antonín Mánes guided his students to the Old Jewish Cemetery and the Old-New Synagogue, deeming them the most ancient and most romantic areas of Prague, and his son Josef Mánes sought in the ghetto — and, specifically, in the Old-New Synagogue — the enchantment of both the antiquity and the Orient; the Jewish portraitists were not attracted by that type of romanticism.[8]

Least romantic of all was Ignác Josef Porges (1812–1890). (See illustration 4.) His eagle eye approximated the lens of a camera, and in effect he did at times make his living at daguerreotyping and photography. An ardent lover of truth, it was with great reluctance that he embellished his female models even a little. (He liked to use colorful wraps — Indian scarves.) Portraits of young men were set in landscapes, painted skillfully; those of older men he preferred in the actual sanctum of their study, and there he was most at home. Toman said of Porges that he selected "motley Jewish types clad in outlandish garments," and Jiřík wrote of him, in 1930, that Porges demonstrated "an oriental penchant for colorful imagery." Nothing of the sort approaches the truth. Porges is virtual fanatic of the sober, down-to-earth, microscopic realism, quite common in Prague in those times.[9]

Realism

The creative curve of Czech art is apparent, in the second half of the nineteenth century, in a romantic molding of the national idea. Artists subscribing to this trend discover the people, the land, and they embody, in allegory, national myths. A representative of the first generation is Josef Mánes, and of the second Mikuláš Aleš. In between, of course, the realists are active in Prague: Karel Purkyně, Soběslav Pinkas, and Viktor Barvitius[10] — the great Neruda-Purkyně controversy over art's mission is on. Neruda, the romanticist, calls for historical subjects to honor national obligations. Purkyně emphasizes that such didactic art is subservient art. What a pity that the three realists were not allowed to bring their élan to fruition!

If several more Jewish painters were united into a coherent stream and the basic tendencies of their art were outlined in a scheme, we might say — though not without stretching the point quite a bit — that, as far as it is in their power, they do pursue realism, although more often than not they are sidetracked by its secondary elements.

The first movement in support of realism actually provides a humorous page in the annals of art. It is premature, for it falls into the thirties and forties of the nineteenth century, when the true followers of realism were still babes in arms. The protagonists of this crusade are now almost forgotten "heroes" — Leopold Pollak and Itzig Jeiteles. The former (1806–1880) earned great popularity in the first half of the nineteenth century by introducing into Prague's exhibition of 1835 the sugary genre painting derived from Italian environment. But by some mistake this type of genre painting, which may have left an imprint even on the art of Josef Navrátil, the Czech classic, was labeled by one theory — realism.[11]

In 1841 an article signed "SZ" in the magazine *Prag*, a supplement to the publication *West und Ost*, outlined the theory of the "realism." Its author was Julius Seidlitz (real name Itzig Jeiteles, 1814–1857). [See vol. I, The Jews of Czechoslovakia, pp. 510 and 512.] The essay, published with a review of the exhibition in 1841, is unique, considering the ambiance which was prevalent in Prague in those days. It is a polemic against classicism — which was still much appreciated in Prague — and, for all practical purposes, also against romanticism, still a novelty in Prague. Also, Jeiteles mentions Mengs in it for the first time, and contemptuously. He advocated realism — with the aid of genre.

But of course Jeiteles maintains in the essay some really progressive criteria as well. Twenty years later Karel Purkyně will fight for these same tenets — also in vain. Jeiteles stressed the almost iconoclastic view that technique and color constituted the real substance of a painting.[12] In Prague in 1841 these are daring words, for had not Antonín Müller, a far more erudite critic and a professor of esthetics, asserted only in 1840 that the opposite was true — namely, that a painting's sublime goal was to make people forget the colors? The solitary attempt of Jeiteles was destined to fall into oblivion. Still, in the sixties Purkyně will repeat every one of Jeiteles's advanced beliefs regarding color and the importance of seventeenth-century Dutch art — though all in vain. He, too, must still fight for color versus line and for realistic subjects as opposed to historical themes.

The handful of Jewish students at Prague's academy naturally could not join the first Czech realists and their heroic struggle, for they had enrolled only in the early forties, at the same time as Josef Mánes. Among the portraitists we think primarily of Ignác Josef Pereles and Josef Bindeles, and among landscape painters of Methuselah Wehli.

The work of Josef Bindeles (1826–1914) is least known. Ignác Josef Pereles (1823–1893), on the other hand, left many works. (See illustration 5.) In the portrait collection of the Jewish Museum in Prague he is represented by ten female likenesses: young ladies, old ladies, ladies with fans, ladies adorned with cameos, ladies wearing wigs or holding roses. Rather conventional yet pleasing portraits, done in a gray, discreet — if vague — palette.

Methuselah Wehli, or Wehle (1824–1889), studied landscape painting under Max Haushofer and remained a steadfast contributor to Prague's picture exhibitions. Drawings of the Old Jewish Cemetery, which date mostly from the 1860s, plus several oils of identical subjects, are at the Jewish Museum in Prague. Wehli instills some fantastic atmosphere into the cemetery and the adjacent area. He knows this corner of Jewish Prague in and out. He is not as austere as František Havránek, nor does he enliven the cemetery with oriental action, like Jaroslav Čermák. He confronts the architecture of the synagogue, the diminutive architecture of the grave , and the twisted trees with a stray cat. Wehli was once much appreciated by the younger generation of painters of Prague, Antonín Waldhauser among others. Wehli's broad brushstrokes probably struck them as very modernistic. Today, he is another forgotten man.

Natives of Brno were more attracted to the academy of Vienna: among the sculptors, Bedřich Salamon Beer (born in 1846, died in Paris in 1912); among painters, Eugen Jettel (born in 1845 in Janovice near Rýmařov in Moravia, died in 1901 in Italy).[13] Jettel is an accomplished landscape painter, a late adherent of the Barbizon school; he lived in Paris for almost twenty years but exhibited in Vienna quite often, and his oils figured in shows of contemporary art. He was esteemed in Prague as well. Whenever Aleš came to Vienna he always scanned Jettel's landscapes with the meticulous interest of a trained expert. He seems to have been taken by Jettel's colors, the dark hues of his palette. They inspired Aleš's early oils — all of which were painted in Suchdol near Prague, while Aleš was the guest of Alexander Brandeis.

Alexander Brandeis (1848–1898) has a niche in Czech letters as patron and customer of Mikuláš Aleš, and George Kars introduced him to art literature for the same reason.[14] "Old Brandeis was the type of grandseigneur," relates Kars. "His interest in art was outspokenly idealistic, which did not hinder his being a bon vivant on a grand scale nor his fanatical dedication to luxury."

Probably a charmer, Brandeis could impel those around him to share in his predilections. One of Aleš's notebooks might very well be called "Brandeis-inspired."[15] Aleš simply had to go to the ghetto again and again to draw there; he had to study the gravestones at the Old Jewish Cemetery and from motifs gathered there compose, among others, ex libris vignettes for his benefactor and for his brother-in-law as well. Aside from the manifold commissions, Alexander Brandeis provided his protégé with enough money and peace of mind to make possible his creation of cartoons for the epic cycle he called "Vlast" (the Fatherland), and to enter the contest for decorating the National Theater in Prague with it — which contest he won.

Art Nouveau (*Secession*)

The decorating of the National Theater was concluded, roughly, in the 1880s. The generation of artists that was entering the lists in the following decade subscribed to quite different goals: their program was to come to grips with the evolution in current foreign art, and they aspired to opportunities permitting them to make individual contributions. At the fin-de-siècle the initiatives generating reactions mushroomed: pleinair, illusionism, impressionism, symbolism, and the secession or art nouveau — it was one big jumble. New teachers and professors at the Academy of Fine Arts and the newly founded School of Arts and Crafts advocated some of the trends. Other styles, secession among them, had yet to be tackled by that generation. Jakob Schikaneder, once a schoolmate of Aleš, and Jiří Jílovský deserve to be called representatives of the pleinair school. Maximilian Pirner of the academy, teacher of Richard Pollak and Adolf Wiesner, stands for symbolism. Emil Orlik, a painter, still more outstanding in graphic arts, developed into an eminent promoter and representative of the art nouveau, and Hugo Steiner-Prag also became a brilliant book illustrator. Applied graphic arts — posters, book covers — assume a leading role in the nineties; and free graphic arts play practically a greater role than painting proper.

The Prague of the nineties is strictly divided: here is the Czech, there is the German sphere. Wiesner and Pollak count as Czechs, Orlik and Hugo Steiner-Prag as Germans.

New Czech artistic aspiration found their organizing focus in the Mánes Society of Artists, established as early as 1884. Its organ *Volné Směry* (Free Trends) engaged in an increasingly virulent struggle for Czech art's orientation toward Paris — and France.

Aside from the Mánes, in which Adolf Wiesner and Richard Pollak were active since its inception, a second new institution originated, namely, the Modern Gallery. Founded in 1901–1902 by two autographed imperial patents, the Modern Gallery started out, from the cradle, with two sectors: the Czech and the German, with the following goal: "to give the artists of both nationalities the opportunity to develop their ability in a friendly competition." Among the initial purchases of the German sector was a collection of Orlik's graphic work, pictures by Eugen Kahler (who settled permanently in Bavaria, near Munich), and one by Walter Bondy, his *Woman Resting*.

In this generation the oldest artist is Richard Pollak-Karlín (1867–1945). (See illustration 8.) He and his Viennese wife, Hilda Pollak, also a painter (1874–1945), perished together in the Terezín concentration camp. Through part of their work both artists are ranged among the symbolists.[16] Richard Pollak was a portraitist.

In the Jewish Museum are ten of his portraits, covering the period between 1892 and 1920. From about the turn of the century Pollak places his models skillfully into interiors, and he combines the two elements after the fashion of intimists. There had been a time when he was classified rigidly among the realists (thus Jiřík in 1909).

Pollak was among the original members of the Mánes Society; every annual exhibition featured some of his work. He took part in the Paris exhibition of 1900. where an honorable mention was awarded him. He then moved to Vienna, traveled extensively, and returned to Prague in 1920. That year, he and his wife had their last exhibition in the Krasoumná jednota (Fine Arts Union). Judging by the prices quoted there the artist valued his "multicolored moods" far more than his portraits.

The somewhat younger Adolf Wiesner (1871–1942) died in Terezín. (See illustration 6.) His wife, Helena Wiesner, also a painter, was a daughter of the previously mentioned Alexander Brandeis of Suchdol. A pupil of Pirner, Wiesner also belonged to Professor Hynais's initial circle. He studied in Dresden and Munich. His first exhibit, in 1896, was a picture called *Anniversary*, which the Modern Gallery bought. Wiesner was a dedicated member of the Mánes, as well as one of the first. He drew the very first cover — 1897 — for the *Volné Směry* art magazine and also a poster for the society's first exhibition in the Salon Topič.

Among the eleven portraits in the Jewish Museum from the years 1898–1917, the *Family Portrait of the Old Couple* (1901) stands out. It shows the timely influence of Max Švabinský. Of Wiesner's larger compositions *Woman with Child on Horseback* should be mentioned. The same motif — though signifying something different — crops up later at František Kupka.

To be sure, Wiesner's drawings and pastels — incorporated in the collection of graphic works of the National Gallery — show his affinity to Luděk Marold, for instance, in the drawing made in Paris in 1908, or in the one entitled *Lady with a Dog*, made in the nineties in Prague.

Hugo Steiner-Prag's starting point was similar (born in 1880, he died in 1945 in New York). (See illustration 7.) He is the youngest of that generation. Since his tender years he had known how to make use of authentic graphic techniques, including lithography, which he applied in the poster for Joshua Winternitz in 1899. Despite brisk beginnings in the vein of Marold, Steiner focused his efforts, and indeed his life, onto the artistic appearance of a book. The typographical arrangement, the flyleaf, the binding, all is soberly conceived. In Leipzig, where he became professor of graphic arts and book production, Steiner acquired a significant position in the field.

The leading personality among these artists is Emil Orlik (born in 1870 in Prague, died in 1932 in Berlin). (See illustrations 9, 10,11, and 12.) In 1892 and 1893 Orlik studied with Prof. Heinrich Knirr in Munich as did — somewhat later — George Kars, and still later, around 1910, Walter Trier (born in 1890 in Prague), a successful illustrator of Erich Kästner and others.

In 1894 Orlik went to Prague to stay for a time, but he traveled frequently during this period — to England (1898), to Japan (1900–1901), to Vienna (1903–1904), at which juncture he painted his *Finis Ghetto*. His studio on the Smetanka had a sweeping view of the city, which Orlik rendered in various media — in oil as in a grayish-beige lithograph. In his obituary for Orlik, Hugo Steiner-Prag said that that canvas was a great discovery for representing everyday, non-historical Prague.[17] It was a warranted evaluation. Orlik was one of those Prague artists who know how to put their finger on their city's commonplace atmosphere. The picture initiated a notable series of works that culminated later in Slaviček's famous view of Prague from the Letná. Certainly Orlik is a figure painter rather than a landscapist. His ingrained domain is the inner city, the demolished ghetto houses, the tiny yards of the Dlouhá třída bathed in sunlight, or the corner of old Platnéřská ulice at night, with the chestnut vendor on the pavement below and the prostitute in the upper window. Orlik's woodcuts and etchings of Prague's hucksters in wine cellars, of the used-clothes peddlers going from house to house, of his bright, Degas-inspired *Tailor Shop* — all show him as possibly the only follower of Viktor Barvitius's tradition of the sixties. Orlik was also a knowledgeable colleague of Zdenka Braunerová — in short, of any and all who loved Prague and had sketched there around 1900. He learned not only from French artists — Corot, Manet, and, in particular, Degas — he learned in Japan as well. This knowledge he generously imparted in numerous lectures and made use of in his subjects and technique. His color lithographs gleam with silver dust, and he prints in gold with great artistry. He even derives constructive elements from gold, thus superseding the floral design that formerly framed his interiors and plans for theatrical settings. Orlik composed settings for Max Reinhardt in pure secession style. Exteriors, too, he now saw in simplified parallel lines: witness his *Hunt in the Forest* or *Gathering Firewood;* there the surface is tidily divided and the lines form their own space. Orlik was also fortunate in stylizing Slovakia's countryside. His *Reapers* surpasses the genre-minded realism of Jóža Úprka, and his Slovak pines are truly Japanized.

Orlik left a vast collection of portraits, heads known and unknown. Gradually he recorded every personality of his time, every contemporary painter, musician, physicist. Anybody of importance is to be found in that vast portrait gallery, from Zemlinski to Trotski, from Einstein the physicist to Einstein the violinist. And in stately graphic technique, in mezzotint, for example, he portrayed the great men of the past, from Michelangelo to Kant.

Orlik could enjoy his well-deserved success in his lifetime. In 1905 he became a professor in Berlin, where Leo Haas (born in 1901 in Opava) was among his students; but it is also true that for quite a long time Czech criticism could make neither head nor tail of his art. The oncoming avant-garde generation hated him. In 1911 Josef Čapek saw Orlik's work as an example of bad, superficial art. "Incompetent hands," he says, "producing the shallowest painting imaginable." In his verdict, Orlik is a pompous character, fond of displaying a frivolous suavity of a languid wit.[18]

Not even the posthumous exhibition of Orlik's oils (1934) in Feigl's gallery in Prague would basically change that position. True, the brilliant skill of Orlik the draftsman, his chic and elegance, as well as the refined handling of color and line, all that had to be acknowledged — but the inhibitions in face of the secession persisted in the critics. And yet, the vogue carrying secession to favor was in, and Orlik was its noble representative. In Prague only Vojtěch Volavka recognized Orlik as being on a par with Gustav Klimt of Vienna.[19] Today Orlik is considered part of Austria's secession.[20] In works dealing with modern art he is still classified as a mere — if clever — academician (thus Walter Mehring 1965).[21] Nevertheless, Orlik's real recognition — especially his younger years, while he was at home in the circle of Prague's artists — is probably not too far away.

Avant-garde

The succeeding group of artists, who were only slightly younger than the preceding, that is, more or less the same age, already counts as avant-garde. There are Alfred Justitz (1879–1934) (see illustration

21), George Kars (1880–1945) (see illustrations 13, 23), Bedřich Feigl (1884–1965) (see illustration 22), and also Max Horb, Emil Artur Pittermann-Longen (1885–1936) (see illustration 14), and Oto Gutfreund (1889–1927).

This generation was beset with doubts and confusion, which George Kars pertinently and most vividly brought to light in an unpublished interview, saying: "And so I used to sit in Heinrich Knirr's private school in Munich, always drawing — that is, if I didn't happen to sit in the tavern of the Café Stefany with schoolmates sporting long hair and fluttering ties. Herman Haller was there, and also Paul Klee. Both very gifted. But of course, Klee was way over our heads with his views on life and art. Even then he envisaged new possibilities of development. Even then he predicted and foresaw an art apart from the bounds of tradition."

Kars was well aware of the trends which modern art would follow. At the same time, he knew where his own art was headed. Kars appreciates Klee intellectually without, however, subscribing to his tenets. That premise of a "pristine existence, unsullied by the slimy mud of reality" is alien to Kars. Where Klee sees subtlety, Kars is irresistibly attracted to robustness. Where Klee searches for the soul of a leaf of grass or the scheme of the circulation of sap in the tree, Kars seeks the tree as such.

Then came my studies with Stuck [Kars continues to reminisce]. To be in the class of the Renaissance master was a rare distinction, but, alas, his art did not appeal to me even then. Via Liebermann, the paragon of all artistic Prague of the period and of Bedřich Feigl in particular — I was smitten with yearning for France's impressionists and for Gauguin and van Gogh. The switch from German impressionism [Kars remained in Munich until 1905] to the French [he went to live in France in 1908] discomfited me. My assurance was shaken. And the least understandable fact was that it was van Dongen and Matisse that swept me off my feet most of all. And life, real life complemented every blessed thing. To the French, art is not anything transcendental. [When František Kupka went to Paris in 1895, he experienced the same liberating impact.]

Well, the cafés were the headquarters of two opposing camps. In the Café du Dome, Wilhelm Uhde wielded the scepter; at the Chez Amie on Montmartre, Picasso pontificated. Daytime, one lived in the cafés — but every night meant drawing. Once more we were students and, together with Marquet, we drew from live models. In Munich we had instruction in Renaissance palaces and people addressed us "Sir" — in Paris it was school-benches again. There, in France, I had an interesting confrontation with the genius of impressionist painting. It came from two directions. Juan Gris, Braque, and Lipschitz thought that art could be mastered with logarithms. They enlisted a collaborator, a young man called Rincée. He was a mathematician endowed with enough sensibility to try to talk them out of that method of searching for art. Nonetheless, years later he believed himself to be the father of cubism. To other artists, like Suzanne Valadon, Utter, her husband, and to Utrillo, their son [they became Kars's friends] painting meant serious and devoted work. In 1909 I exhibited in the Salon d'Automne. Quite some guts on my part, considering I was a foreigner. The pictures struck people as being too modern, but they respected them.

Kanudo, d'Annunzio's friend, the discoverer of Chagall, editor of *Ma Joie* magazine, appreciated Kars at that time.

Kars's annotations underscore the three dominant trends in contemporary art, among which Czech avant-garde, too, had to find its bearings. They were cubism, fauvism, and expressionism. In retrospect, Kars comments almost jokingly on all those past discussions and arguments trying to decide which trend was the best. Czech avant-garde, however, unflinchingly uncompromising from the very outset, became increasingly dogmatic as time went on. Artists unable to conform to that inflexible attitude artistically sooner or later left the movement or came to hover on its outskirts, in the sphere of corollary participants and observers. This goes for Kars as much as for Bedřich Feigl who, just prior to World War I, when the first center of contemporary avant-garde art formed in Prague, was its intellectual head.

The movement grew from very slender beginnings — virtually from the schoolroom. At the Academy of Fine Arts, in the studios of Professors Thiele and Bukovac, congregated Filla, Horb, Nowak, Špála, Kubín, Bedřich Feigl, and Pittermann-Longen.

"We used to stand at our easels at the academy... rather browbeaten and crestfallen by the misguided, irrelevant leadership, but brimming with courage and eagerness; then again we were alternately bewildered and hopeful of the perspectives that opened for our future life," says Filla in his essay "Edward Munch and Our Generation," in *Volné Směry* (1938).

Most of the future group Osma (The Eight) took part, in 1906, in the academy's student exhibition. F. X. Šalda, the greatest and most authoritative critic of that time — "the pope" of the modern movement, as the *Umělecký měsičník* (Art's Monthly), organ of the second artistic center, the Skupina výtvarných umělců (Group of artists), was to scoff in 1912 — wrote subsequently of that exhibit: "With these boys, a quite novel type of painter has entered the arts, quite different from their predecessors. These people wear neither grease-drenched ten-gallon hats, nor unfurled ties... nor do they dish out would-be puns or witticisms.... They do not loll about in cafés..... They are workmen, laborers of veracity, almost sternly matter of fact. They are more like explorers or scientists than artistic bohemians."

On April 18, 1907, the first exhibition of the Osma opened in a first-floor apartment of Královdvorská ulice no. 16. Its major contributors were Feigl and Pittermann-Longen. The whole enterprise was financed by Willi Nowak, a close friend of these artists, who for the venture sacrificed compensation money he had collected for a gunshot wound in the knee. The catalogue of the exhibition consisted of one single sheet of paper featuring the words "Výstava 8 — Kunstausstellung" (Exhibition of 8 — Art Exhibit).

However, only seven artists were represented. Kars had been invited to participate, but by then (1906–1907) he had moved to Spain and allegedly refused. Horb was asked to join since he entertained valuable friendships — with Max Brod, among others, who actually reviewed the exhibit in the foreign press. Of the second exhibition of the Osma (held in June and July 1908) Zdeněk Kratochvíl wrote in 1917 in *Kmen* (The Treetrunk), in an article entitled "Mánes and Its Group": "The public repined, spat, grumbled loudly and demanded refund of admission money."

Some crisp drawings by Emil Artur Pittermann-Longen, made in Špála manner, may be included in that early period (Pittermann-Longen was born in Pardubice, in 1885, and died in 1936 in Benešov). The drawings are in the Collection of Graphic Works of the National Gallery. In them Pittermann-Longen appears as highly talented and hopeful, influenced in the composition of his *Funeral* by Edward Munch, whose exhibition in Prague, in 1905, left a mark on one and all of the Osma group. More of Pittermann-Longen's drawings are kept in the one-time Resistance Monument on the Vítkov Mountain. They record scenes from a French battlefield of World War I. But Pittermann-Longen soon abandoned painting to become actor and dramatist at the Revolutionary Theater, and also adaptor of foreign plays.

*Oto Gutfreund**

The year 1909 marks a signal event in Prague's art world: the exhibition of E. A. Bourdelle. (See illustrations 15, 16, 17, 18, 19, 20.) The artist put in a personal appearance, and Mařatka, his pupil, arranged a meeting with Oto Gutfreund, who was then studying at the Umělecko-průmyslová škola (School of Arts and Crafts), where he had enrolled in 1906. That fall Gutfreund entered Bourdelle's studio and private school, the Grande Chaumière, in Paris. Gutfreund's Paris sojourn disconcerted him. In his diary we find the following entry in 1910: "I don't ever want to follow contemporary examples; I don't ever want to see exhibits of mediocre sculptors; and I don't want to work for exhibitions. My model will be nature, my goal antiquity and the Gothic."

But only a year later, in 1911, in Prague, Gutfreund propagates the creative problematics of cubism even in sculpture. In the context of world events, this is a unique phenomenon and one not adequately valued even today.[22]

The one-time admirer of Bourdelle thus is catapulted, virtually overnight, to the helm of Prague's avant-garde movement. Gutfreund's masterpiece of 1911 is the sculpture called *Anguish*. The figure seems to cower, to retreat into itself. It, too, issues from an interpretation of life that bears marks of Munch's philosophy. Indeed, Gutfreund's sculpture is closely akin to Munch's famous *Shriek*. This bizarre work, a true symbol of its time, presages the same agony that we find in Kafka's prose writings. It is existentialism coming long before existentialism, it is an augury of innermost drama but also apprehension of the unknown and of the future. We are unable to name in Czech art, and perhaps not even in that of the world at large, a work of so many comparable portents.

Every one of Gutfreund's early sculptures belongs to the specific Czech school called, today, cuboexpressionism. Their essence — as in his *Anguish* — lies again in the capacity to lend immediacy to man's stamina and willpower through plastic form. Gutfreund expressed the theoretical facet in an article "Two Annotations on Donatello," published in *Umělecký měsíčník* (Art's Monthly, vol. II). There Gutfreund comes to grips with the Renaissance in a highly

* Born in 1889 in Dvůr Králove, died in 1927 in Prague.

responsible manner. The conclusion of the article stipulates a sculptor's ideal: "to incorporate the abstract in a concrete form which, to the beholder, relapses into abstraction."

Gutfreund's work grew from these theoretical foundations. Actually, he was the first sculptor to expound the principles of pre-cubism in its Czech cuboexpressionistic version.[23] Gutfreund's absolute primacy is challenged solely by Picasso's *Head*, a sculpture dating from 1910. It is impossible to say whether Gutfreund had seen the work, quite unique among Picasso's sculptures. The path Gutfreund followed was unquestionably independent of Picasso, and the conclusions he arrived at analyze the complete range of problems from the viewpoint of plasticity and content on a broad basis that endures as one point of departure in the evolution of cubist sculpture.

In the context of sculpture at large, Gutfreund's reliefs of 1911 may figure as sole examples of analytic cubism in the progress of modern plastic art, for Lipschitz conceived his first cubistic sculpture only in 1913–1914.

Very likely Gutfreund's pre-World War I work has not come down to us complete, and the loss is compounded by the misfortune that befell the artist during that war. Following the assassination in Sarajevo, Gutfreund went to Paris — with Filla. He joined the Czech company Nazdar (Hellol) and fought at the front line, but in December 1915 some altercation caused by a string of misunderstandings landed him in a concentration camp. There he vegetated until the end of hostilities. According to the memoirs of V. V. Štech, Gutfreund attempted to produce some small sculptures there, made from wooden slats. His *Woman Sitting* (1917) may be one of them; it conveys the most elemental problematics of construction, a construction stripped to the core. Not a trace of the anthropomorphic is left in it: all that remains is a pristine plastic and spatial composition consisting of form elements. These elements represent the prophetic parallel, felt by a genius, to contemporary problematics. The flimsy slats of ersatz material, making do, stimulated the expression of something that had rankled in Gutfreund's subconscious since 1913 and 1914. Obviously he returns to that material in 1919 for the very same reason when he resumes work in Paris. *Still Life* and *The Head* testify to it, even as does the idea of a distinctive architecture of forms which he elaborates. The balanced counterpoint of geometrical blocks may be understood as the classical conclusion of Gutfreund's cubism. The absence of circumstances conducive to creating, and possibly also a lack of strength, prevented further elaboration.

That is how M. Lamač and Jiří Padrta, two most progressive Czech critics, evaluate Gutfreund's work. The young generation puts up a fierce fight for the recognition due to him. But only some exhibitions of the sixties promoted Gutfreund's name at the world forum. The first of these, entitled "Paris-Prague," took place in Paris in 1966. However, French critics declined to acknowledge Gutfreund's creative impetus as having been instrumental in the evolution of the original cubism; indeed, they denounced the notion that he was not paraphrasing French cubism. A few months after that exhibition, however, Charles S. Spencer published an extensive study in London's literary review, *The Jewish Quarterly*, where he called Gutfreund the guiding spirit of the avant-garde. He also maintained that future exhibitions of the artist who perished tragically would establish his long overdue international repute.

Since then exhibitions of Gutfreund's collected works have truly traveled all over the world. His sculptures are now being bought for collections of modern art, to document that Gutfreund is among the very first artists who initiated modern, avant-garde sculpture.

Between the Two Wars

Oto Gutfreund remained a sculptor of genius in his post-World War I work, as witness his terracotta polychrome portraits and some of the small sculptures, gripping in their well-expressed Chaplinesque sadness. Gutfreund's monumental work of the twenties, commissioned by the State and by various other authorities, does bear some vestiges of officialdom, yet it is not to be compared to the run-of-the-mill sculpture of the somewhat older Rudolf Saudek (born in 1880 in Kolín, died in 1962) or of that by Karel Vogel (born in 1897 in Č. Budějovice). Indeed, a most important place must be accorded to Gutfreund in Czech sculpture as being both the direct and indirect teacher of coming generations. No, Gutfreund cannot be sidestepped or passed over, for he is the founder of the Czech school of sculpture.

Czechoslovak architecture of the thirties has attained a very respectable standing. Its representatives, among whom we find many Jewish architects, have contrived an all-embracing conception of architectural work and a harmonious synthesis and interaction of functional, technical, and social considerations.[24] They have often succeeded in outstandingly integrating architecture with its environment and in expressing, even through the exterior, the perfectly planned interior. One example of such pleasing and historically notable design is the sanatorium in Vyšné Hágy (Tatra Mountains) built in 1937 by F. A. Libra and Jiří Kann (who soon after perished with his entire family in a concentration camp).

Between the two wars, modern painting found greater response than in the past — a number of collectors sprang up (Dr. Oscar Federer in Ostrava, Armand Grosz in Prague), but while a differentiation of taste and opinion flourished, the capacity to react to truly avant-garde currents declined astonishingly. One proof is the scant reaction in Prague to František Kupka's art, so highly valued today. Between the two wars his only friend in Prague was Jindřich Waldes, and although Prague was very well informed of what was going on in the world, the creative give-and-take toward novel happenings of any kind remained minimal. In the main Prague mostly emulated Paris, yet preponderantly through prewar lenses.

A typical example of compounded positive and negative attributes is that of Alfred Justitz. In his lectures he appears as a fighter for purchases of modern art, but his own work betrays every possible influence. In effect he is an amalgam of each of his predilections in painting, and according to these leanings his life's work can be segmented. To pigeonhole it, however, offers some difficulties .Just before his death in 1931 Justitz is classified as belonging to cubism, the trend he really professed in his later years.[25] Later, however, Václav Nebeský (1937) puts him into one group with Coubine, Kars, and — of all people — Zrzavý.[26] Why? Perhaps because Justitz exhibited with Zrzavý and with Josef Čapek at the first post-World War I exhibition of the Trvdošíjní (The Stubborn Ones) in 1919. Justitz later joined the Mánes Society where the entire once revolutionary but now grown sensible avant-garde congregated. Equally uncertain as Justitz's position on the map of Czech art is his place between Czechs and Germans. In the Modern Gallery it is the German section that buys his pictures, but it was Vítězslav Nezval who took leave of the dead artist in a poem published as a posthumous monograph (1935).[27] Aside from Gutfreund, Justitz is the only Jewish artist to whom Czech art literature has paid a like tribute.

Another association of artists emerged in Prague in 1929. It was called Prager Sezession, and it gathered the remaining adherents of the defunct avant-garde. Bedřich Feigl is among the active founding members, Kars is among the corresponding ones. Around 1933 Otto Flatter, a Moravian and a student at the academy of Vienna, exhibited with the new group. He has made a name for himself as conservator and now lives in London. Karel Vogel, too, was among the members. The society's program stated as the common denominator of every member's aspiration: "aconservatism." In Otto Flatter's words, "aconservatism" may be taken to mean that "living art is timeless."

German provincial circles remonstrated against the Prager Sezession, alleging that Prague had no room for a German organization. Their objections were countered by citing Palacký, the emperor, but also T. G. Masaryk, to affirm that the culture-saturated soil of Prague should and must combine the supreme accomplishments of both nationalities inhabiting the land. The new society wanted to promote "a perceptive competition along with solidarity with the Czech colleagues." The Prager Sezession arranged nine exhibitions in all. It petered out around 1937. Among its achievements was reintroducing Prague to Paul Klee's watercolors. At the time Klee taught at the Bauhaus (Dessau).

The newly established gallery of Dr. Hugo Feigl — brother of Bedřich Feigl — collaborated closely with the Prager Sezession. Its activity in the thirties — when the name was changed to Gallery Europe — is admirable. Dr.Feigl shows old and modern masters in small exquisite exhibits. He acquaints Prague with German expressionists — long overlooked there — he introduced Chagall, and stages two exhibitions for Bedřich Feigl, too. Vincent Kramář, then custodian of the Old Art collection, a theoretician of cubism, wrote a comprehensive introduction to the first exhibit in 1932. He recapitulated the story of the avant-garde and then, utterly discreetly, relegated Bedřich Feigl to the outer limits of the movement. He did acknowledge every positive facet of Feigl's art, analyzed affectionately its Liebermannesque residue, lauded Feigl's adopting van Gogh's iconography approved of Munch's influence, still palpable in 1920, yet he was unable to deny Feigl's clinging to traditional optical views, and the fact that he was no cubist, since he had often derided his former friends for their indiscriminate adherence to Picasso and Braque. Feigl's artistic career thereupon waned in his brother's gallery and from the vantage point of the Prager Sezession as well. He did exhibit landscapes — *Jerusalem, The Valley of Gideon, The*

Valley of Kidron — and he traveled extensively, though hardly because of longing for exotic scenery but rather out of a desire to render scrupulously biblical scenes, such as *Rebecca at the Well* or *The Finding of Moses.*

In the annals of Jewish art in Czechoslovakia, Feigl occupies a position apart. He alone tackles Jewish biblical themes. Some remote kinship with Jiří Langer's literary efforts is detectable. Feigl's watchword became the aphorism "A Jew is rather a Rembrandt than a Raphael."

World War Two

The only innovators are Nemeš and Bauernfreund, both students of Willi Nowak, both exhibiting in Feigl's gallery and in the Prager Sezession.[28] They belong to the new generation organized only in the forties. By then the two had long been emigrés. Their colleague, the somewhat younger Peter Kien — also a pupil of Willi Nowak — continued to paint in the ghetto of Terezín. Born in 1919, he died in Oswięczim. František Zelenka's last works also originated in Terezín. Zelenka died in 1945, on the death march from Oswięczim. He belongs to the younger generation of artists working for the theater — as did Karel Šourek and Adolf Hoffmeister.[29] In the Osvobozené divadlo (Liberated Theater), where he worked before Bedřich Feuerstein, Wachsman, or Muzika, Zelenka created settings for such classics as *North against South*, *The Golem*, *Don Juan & Co.*, *Caesar*, *Robin Hood* — all between 1930 and 1932. His career in the theater was initiated, in 1926, by an invitation of K. H. Hilar, the famed director of the National Theater in Prague — a rare distinction in itself. With his infallible instinct, Hilar discerned Zelenka's talent, tempered by the esthetic potentialities of cubism and constructivism and completely free from dogmatism. Zelenka knew how to make the two styles, so to speak, carefree in order to have them meet the requirements of the theater. His sense of humor in creative art parallels that of Voskovec and Werich in dialogue. Zelenka's settings tell the truth jocularly. In them and in his costumes he incarnates the young years of the First Republic, its cultural thrust, its avant-garde zeal, its buoyance and — sometimes — also its flightiness.

A true theatrical artist, Zelenka knew all leading actors through and through. He invented costumes for these stars as if he were the most accomplished tailor or couturier. He clothed Miss Pačová,

Elena Hálková, Mrs. Vrchlická, and Světla Svozilová just as he did Messrs. Pollert or Rubík. Conversant with their figures in the nude, he draped ever-new creations over them, whether historical costumes or modern gowns were called for; the same for the settings. Corbusier's subtleties of iron chairs would reappear on Zelenka's stage in humorous versions. Zelenka laughed until 1939. He still laughed in 1941, when — still in Prague and working under the most diverse pseudonyms — he created settings for some of Shakespeare's comedies for the city theater at Vinohrady. From 1942 he worked in the Jewish Museum in Prague and created an impressive installation of the museum collection in cooperation with Dr. Josef Polák, the art historian.

Then came Terezín. Even there Zelenka continued to work, even there he continued to laugh. But then came the end of 1943, and 1944 began. Some drawings from that period testify to Zelenka's knack to reveal, in a shortcut, the nature of the flimsy yet impassable bars of the ghetto; to tell what he knows of the ghetto barracks, of the fraudulent trumpery of attics to be shown to foreign commissions, and of the secret Council of the Elders. The drawing *The Die Is Cast* seems to be the last. It is terrifying, yet as simple as some of the children's drawings that we have come to call "Children's Drawings from Terezín."

With one transport that came to Terezín from Vienna came Frieda Brandeis, a graduate of the Bauhaus, who had studied with Klee, Kandinsky, Istler, and Walter Gropius. Applying the Bauhaus method, she began to teach the children of the Terezín ghetto. These drawings, retrieved quite by chance from waste paper and taken to Prague after the liberation of the ghetto, became an overwhelming denunciation of the fascist régime and an almost equally overpowering artistic sensation. The little authors of the drawings were creating, without a shred of ambition, to become part of the history of art. Hunger appears in the likeness of a cook; War in the guise of an execution; Happiness takes the form of a fruit stall; and Ideal is represented by a hospital bed. Return Home has the shape of an arrow pointing toward Prague. These children experienced their existence, defeated, broken in the bud, in an exemplary way; and that is the second dimension, the true dimension of these drawings which the onlooker perceives.[30] Something similar has happened with the oils of Robert Guttmann, who died in Lodz in 1942. (See illustration 24.) Once Guttmann was a type that people in Prague used to laugh at. The war taught him to paint large forms with an almost childlike naïveté. What the children of Terezín created in the ghetto, Robert Guttmann produced while still in Prague. He thus became the pathetic bard of the once-more-ghettoed wartime Jewish Prague. The force of ingenuous art could once more speak up, and it succeeded in conveying the virtually ineffable dejection, anguish, and humiliation — and also the human dignity strenuously held on to.

Here perhaps we may seek the answers to debates conducted in Terezín amidst the war. At issue was who had best portrayed the ghetto's cruel lot. Was it Kien, was it Fritta, Fleischmann, Ungar, or Haas? All had to face new experiences and an incredible reality. "Transport!" That word — that had changed its meaning so utterly. How many times did these artists endeavor to portray a transport of those arriving and of those leaving. How many times did they narrate the individual stages of the so-called life in Terezín: its streets, its crammed-full shacks. How many times did they render its typical inmates: old women, blind people, children, youngsters in love and at play, preparing concerts or a theater production. Though they mustered every accessible artistic means, though they applied slight deformations and symbols — their work yet forever remained in the initial stage. Bedřich Fritta (real name Taussig, 1907–1944) — went to Terezín as an accomplished artist, trained on Theodor Heine's satire; Peter Kien, the sensitive and cultivated disciple of the delicate Willi Nowak; Otto Ungar (1901–1945), the expert landscapist. Fritta is best in drawings having his own rank of people as the butts — i.e., when caricaturing prominent persons. His friend Leo Haas (1901) reveals, in his sharp drawings, the incredible horror of Terezín and the transports to the East. Kien clings to his impartiality and culture, and Ungar almost falls in love with the enchanting surroundings of Terezín. The multitalented Karel Fleischmann (born in Klatovy in 1897, died in 1944) wrestled with his subject matter most valiantly and honestly of all (see illustration 25), and still everything remained a sketch, a comment, a mere annotation. Except for Fleischmann, who was a physician by profession, the above-named worked in the technical office of the ghetto where some inevitable hygienic installations were on the drafting board. Fritta, the group leader, made technical designs with ruler and compasses. The total horror of the situation lurks in those accurate, technical lines and circles; it is disclosed there with a greater insistence than in the definitive picture where he sought adequate symbols. To express these new realities, even such abstract media would have sufficed.

* * *

A Prayer for the Dead

The total enormity, the consummate absurdity and senselessness of that mass vegetating and of the subsequent mass extermination is incorporated in the truly monstrous, yet multimeaningful metal sculpture of Aleš Veselý (born 1935), entitled *Kaddish*.[31] It is repeated in the not yet executed model for the Memorial at the Terezín cemetery. On eight thin, spindly, 25-ft.-high, atrociously ugly legs, welded and soldered out of what seem to be human bones, sits a birdlike nest full of holes; it is 20 feet wide, 10 feet deep. From it protrude spikes and bodkins on all sides. The sculpture has mutations: in front of a leafy tree it will be less forbidding — as if a conciliation were possible. Towering high on the river bank, the sculpture seems to exude warning signals. Its most terrifying impression arises in confrontation with human dimensions — with architecture. Then the inhumanity of the work becomes crushing. It is as if Veselý had known the satanic treatise of Walter Jacobi — Heidrich's assistant — dealing with the Aryan cultural integration of Europe — an integration built of Jewish bones. And yet the work originated only between August 1967 and May 1968. (See illustration 26.)

For this reason, perhaps, the one-time incentives of Terezín could mature in this monument into a complete work of art.

The history of Jewish artists from Bohemia and Moravia ends with a Kaddish. But it also begins with one.

NOTES

1. This could happen due to the circumspection of several Jewish art historians, for instance, Dr. Josef Polák (died 1945). Compare Hildegard Brenner: *Die Kunstpolitik des Nationalsozialismus*, Rowohlt Verlag Reinbeck bei Hamburg, 1963, and Hana Volavková: *Příběh židovského muzea v Praze* (The Story of the Jewish Museum in Prague), English, 1964, Prague, Artia; German, 1965, Prague, Artia; Czech, 1966, Odeon.

2. From the many studies dealing with this question, quoted at random: Eduard Goldstücker in the *Orientace* magazine, 1968, no. 2, p. 15, "Today's art most forceful in quantity and quality, is inspired by Kafka... Medek, Tichý, Hoffmeister, Mařanová, Oravec, Hladík... a long, abundant string of names." Vladimír Karfik: "Two Poles of Tradition" (Dva póly tradice), in *Orientace*, 1969, no. 6, p. 84; numerous studies by Růžena Grebeníčková, who underscored the stamp of initiative in Jiří Weil's prose works; the Richard Weiner commemorative program, arranged at Strahov in the Memorial Hall of Literature on January 26, 1965, as well as a number of articles published as contributions to the discussion.
3. Reproductions of all significant objects, see *Příběh židovského muzea....* Part of a quite exceptional series are two glass goblets of 1783 and the ornamentation of a publication by Israel Landau: Abraham Farizola: *Geographie*, 1793, illustrated by etchers of the Balzer family in Prague. For details on these neomanneristic illustrations, see Ruth Kestenberg-Gladstein: *Neuere Geschichte der Juden in den böhmischen Ländern*, I. T. Tübingen, 1969, pp. 149 ff.
4. Reproductions of all works of the authors mentioned, see any Jewish encyclopedia under Chalices, The Seder, Funeral brotherhood, etc. (The picture by W. Hogarth is in the Tate Gallery, London.) For reproductions of portraits of Jonas Jeiteles, after etchings by Balzer, see Kestenberg-Gladstein, loc. cit.
5. The latest to mention the Jewish students at the academy of painting in Prague is F. X Jiřík: *Vývoj malířství českého v XIX stol.* (Development of Czech Painting in the 19th Century), Prague, 1909, publ. by Jednota výtvarných umělců, and idem: *Miniatura a drobná podobizna v Čechách* (Miniatures and Small Portraits in Bohemia), Prague, Štenc, 1930. P. Toman took over and often enlarged Jiřík's data: *Slovník čsl. výtvarných umělců*, I. vyd. Praha 1962/27, II. vyd. Praha 1934, III. vyd. Praha 1955 (Dictionary of Czechoslovak Artists, 1st ed. 1926/1927, 2nd. ed. 1934, 3rd ed. 1955, Prague). For the general atmosphere at the Academy of Fine Arts in Prague around 1800, see E. Petrová: *František Tkadlík*, Prague.
6. L. A. Mayer: *Bibliography of Jewish Art*, ed. Otto Kurz, Jerusalem, 1967. He dates the era of modern Jewish art from 1830.
7. A selection of these memorabilia was concentrated in the exhibition and reproduced in the catalogue *Stará Praha* (Old Prague), Prague, 1947, Židovské muzeum (The Jewish Museum), by Hana Volavková. Supplements on the work of Antonín Mánes were published by Eva Reithartová in *Antonín Mánes*, Prague, 1967, Odeon, catalogue, 180–186, 580, 586.
8. Hana Volavková: *The Old-New Synagogue in the Steps of Josef Mánes*, Prague, 1955, and *Jewish Studies*, pp. 62–70.

9. Hana Volavková: "*Grafické portrétní dokumenty pražského ghetta z počátku 19 století*" (Graphic Portrait Documents of the Prague Ghetto from the Beginning of the 19th Century), *Hollar*, XXVIII, Prague, 1956; Hana Volavková: "*Machkův portrét S. J. Rappoporta*," (The Portrait of Machek by S. J. Rappoport), *Umění*, XXVII, Prague, 1964.
10. Emil Filla: "*Purkyně a česká tradice umělecká*" (Purkyně and the Czech Tradition in Art), written in 1924–1925, published by Emil Filla in *O výtvarném umění* (About Fine Arts), Prague, 1942, pp. 47–48.
11. Leopold Pollak, of Loděnice near Rakovník, once enjoying greater esteem than Führich and even Navrátil, has vanished from Czech and Austrian history of art completely. We are citing him in the history of Jewish artists rather for sociological than artistic reasons.
12. His namesake Ignác Jeiteles recommends in the second volume of his *Ästhetisches Lexikon* (Dictionary of Esthetics), 1859, primarily purity of design and only then a meticulous study of the color pattern. Ignác Jeiteles, too, stipulates a scale of values:
    1. Historical painting and portraits
    2. Landscape and animal pictures
    3. Genre painting
    4. Still life
    5. Painting of architectural objects.

    How little these Central European esthetes knew about the contemporary French painting. Jeiteles enumerated them thus: David, Regnault, Vincent, Gérard, Guerin, Vernet, Isabey. Not a word about Delacroix, not to mention Daumier, Courbet, and other grand phenomena of French art.
13. Literature dealing with the preceding and, notably, succeeding artists; see also Thieme-Becker: *Allgemeines Lexikon der bildenden Künstler* (General Encyclopedia of Artists, vol. I, XXVIII (1907–1934).
14. See, for instance, catalogue of the sales exhibition of drawings: *George Kars*, München, 1968, Galerie Ketterer, where in a biographical sketch of Kars we find mention of Brandeis and a list of all of Kars's exhibitions up to 1954, together with an enumeration of writings on Kars up to 1958.
15. The notebooks of Aleš and his entire correspondence with Alexander Brandeis and his daughter are now housed in the Alois Jirásek and Mikuláš Aleš Museum in Prague; the correspondence with V. Brožík is still owned by descendants of Alexander Brandeis who live in Prague.
16. Adolf Donath (see vol. I, *The Jews of Czechoslovakia*, pp. 479, 511, 514); Internationale Kunstwelt (The International Art World), 1935, published in the early twenties by the *Jahrbuch für Kunstsammler* (Yearbook for Art Collectors) in Frankfurt on Main. Five Yearbooks

were published in all, the last in 1925. Donath knew how to enlist considerable authorities for his venture. Upon his return to Czechoslovakia and during the Hitler period, he restored the disrupted relations and commented on various exhibitions. (See also below, note 19.)

17. Hugo Steiner-Prag in the magazine *Hollar*, Year VIII, 1936. Even on the occasion of Orlik's posthumous exhibition, the reporter denies in the magazine *Forum*, IV, of 1934 any kinship of Orlik's work with Prague. Of course, here the late oils were at issue.
18. *Umělecký měsíčník* (Art's Monthly), I, 1911–1912, p. 182, on the occasion of a report on the exhibition by the Deutsch-Böhmischer Küstlerbund (German-Bohemian Artists Union), organized by the Krasoumná Jednota pro Čechy (Beaux-Arts Union) in Prague, 1911.
19. Catalogue of the exhibition of oils by Emil Orlik in 1934, in the gallery of Dr. Hugo Feigl. The German publication with Donath's preface was not obtainable.
20. Hans H. Hofstätter: *Geschichte der europäischen Jugendstilmalerei* (History of the European *Jugend*-style Painting), Köln, 1963, DuMont-Schauberger.
21. W. Mehring: *Verrufene Malerei* (Infamous Painting), Munich, 1965, Wilhelm Heyne.
22. Miroslav Lamač: *Ohniska české výtvarné avantgardy*, 1905–1918 (Focal Points of Czech Creative Avant-garde, 1905–1918); Jiří Padrta: *Ohniska české výtvarné avantgardy*, 1905–1918 (Theory of Czech Creative Avant-garde, 1905–1918). Both works were lent to this author in manuscript, for which sincere thanks are extended to the owners.
23. *Umělecký měsíčník* (Art's Monthly), II, 1912–1913, p. 136, and *Art*, pp. 101, 240; also *Umělecký měsíčník*, I, 1911–1912, p. 140.
24. Some of their successful works are published in the magazine *Forum* vols. I (1931) to VIII (1938): in vol. I, for instance, the department store Bárta by B. Schwarz; in vol. III (1933) the interiors of E. Mühlstein and W. Fürst, and of Kurt Spielman; in vol. IV (1934) interiors of Otto and Karl Kohn and the synagogue of Leopold Ehrmann.
25. František Kovárna: *Současné malířství* (Contemporary Painting), Prague, Orbis, 1932, p. 146.
26. V. M. Nebeský: *L'art moderne tchécoslovaque* (Czech Modern Art) (1905–1933), Paris, 1937, p. 110.
27. *Alfred Justitz*, Prague, 1935, Melantrich, Edition Prameny (Sources) (authors Vl. Novotný, Kamil Novotný, and Jaroslav Pečírka). Emil Gutfreund: *Dětství Oty Gutfreunda* (The Childhood of O. Gutfreund); Josef Císařovský: *Oto Gutfreund*, Prague, 1962.

28. Accompanying text by Johannes Urzidil, who in the magazine *Forum*, as well as in various catalogues of exhibitions, listed almost every Jewish artist who exhibited and made a name for himself in the thirties. His gifted pen could elucidate remarkable beginners such as Bauernfreund and Nemeš — as well as Karel Vogel, Kars, Feigl, and Justitz.

    In the thirties, a whole group of theoreticians and historians of art came to the fore — men who had returned to Czechoslovakia after long years: Emil Utitz (1893–1956), founder of the modern esthetics, Adolf Donath, and Leopold Kreitner (1892–1969), reporter of the daily *Prager Presse* and coorganizer of many outstanding ventures such as the Slovak exhibition, the Saint Wenceslas exhibition, the Saint Wenceslas jubilee of 1929, and the author of studies on the beginnings of the Czech baroque art and of several other works that today remain inaccessible (one of which is *Intellektueller und Kunst* [The Intellectual and Art], Prague, 1936, Orbis). During World War II Kreitner emigrated, worked and taught in Johannesburg as a professor until 1962, and then moved to Taormina (Sicily), where he died.

    Dr. Joseph Polák worked in Slovakia as director of the museum of Košice; he wrote on Slovak art as its first historian in the Czech language in a book called *Slovensko*, published in the *Dějepis výtvarného umění v ČSR* (History of Art in Czechoslovakia), Prague, 1935, Sfinx. Polák moreover collected and classified the material for a great Slovak exhibition in Prague, in 1937 — Umění na Slovensku (Art in Slovakia).

    Of the others, Richard Messer must be named; Richard Weiner and Josef Kodíček also worked with the avant-garde.

    In the thirties Edith Hoffmann began her work. She is a highly esteemed collaborator and correspondent of the magazine *Weltkunst* (World Art) to this day.

29. In memoriam František Zelenka, in the magazine *Architekt*, vol. V, p. 319. Sylva Marešová: "František Zelenka," in the magazine *Acta scenographica* 1965–1966, vol. VI, book I, p. 15. A. Wenigová filed her thesis at the university on František Zelenka in 1969 (not yet published).

30. Children's drawings "Na zastávce smrti" (Threshold of death), Terezín, 1942–1944, Prague, 1959, edited by Hana Volavková, epilogue by Jiří Weil. Catalogue of drawings and introduction by Olga Herbenová. Published also in English, Italian, German, and many other foreign languages. The theme was filmed under the title *Motýli tady nežijí* (No Butterflies Live Here).

31. Studied at the Academy of Art in Prague, 1952–1958. Collaborated in several installation projects of the Jewish Museum in Prague until

1960, and there came to know the vast material from Terezín. Exhibited independently in Prague, 1963–1970; in Liberec, 1965; in Vienna, 1969. Represented in public collections in Czechoslovakia, Naples, and Paris, in the Bibliothèque Nationale.

* * *

ACKNOWLEDGMENT

The Society for the History of Czechoslovak Jews expresses thanks and gratitude to the National Gallery in Prague and to the Jewish State Museum in Prague for reproduction rights.

1. "Making of a Coffin," artist unknown. Oil painting, 22 x 44 inches; from a set of 20, painted between 1773 and 1836 for the burial society in Prague (Hevra Kadisha). Owner: Jewish Museum, Prague

2. “Sewing of a Shroud,” artist unknown. Oil painting, 22 x 44 inches; from a set of 20, painted between 1773 and 1836 for the burial society in Prague (Hevra Kadisha). Owner: Jewish Museum, Prague

3. "Washing of Hands before Leaving Burial Ground," artist unknown. Oil painting, 22 x 44 inches; from a set of 20, painted between 1773 and 1836 for the burial society in Prague (Hevra Kadisha). Owner: Jewish Museum, Prague

4. "Portrait of a Jewish Old Man," Ignác Porges. Aquarelle, 8 x 10 inches, oval; 1837. Owner: Regina Mirsky-Tauber, Prague

5. "Portrait of a Lady with a Flower," Ignác Pereles. Oil painting, 27 x 34 inches; 1862. Owner: Jewish Museum, Prague

6. First cover for art magazine *Volné Směry*, Adolf Wiesner. 1897

7. Placard of Josua Winternitz store, Hugo Steiner-Prag. Lithograph, 1899

8. "Portrait of a Lady," Richard Pollak-Karlín. Oil painting, 34 x 36 inches; 1900. Owner: Jewish Museum, Prague

9. "To Attend the Sick," Emil Orlík. Charcoal, pencil and pen, 8 x 13 inches; 1896. Owner: Graphical Collection of National Gallery, Prague

10. "Tailor Shop," Emil Orlík. Colored woodcut, 10 x 18 inches; 1897. Owner: Graphical Collection of National Gallery, Prague

11. "Lady in a Long Coat (Old Vienna)," Emil Orlík. Woodcut, 15 x 22 inches; 1903. Owner: Graphical Collection of National Gallery, Prague

12. "Evening Mood in Japan," Emil Orlík. Mezzotint, 6 x 8 inches; 1901. Owner: Graphical Collection of National Gallery, Prague

13. "Family of Farmers," George Kars. Drawing with pen and pencil, 9 x 12; 1915. Owner: Graphical Collection of National Gallery, Prague

14. "Countryside," Artur Pittermann-Longen. Drawing with brush, 16 x 23; 1908. Owner: Graphical Collection of National Gallery, Prague

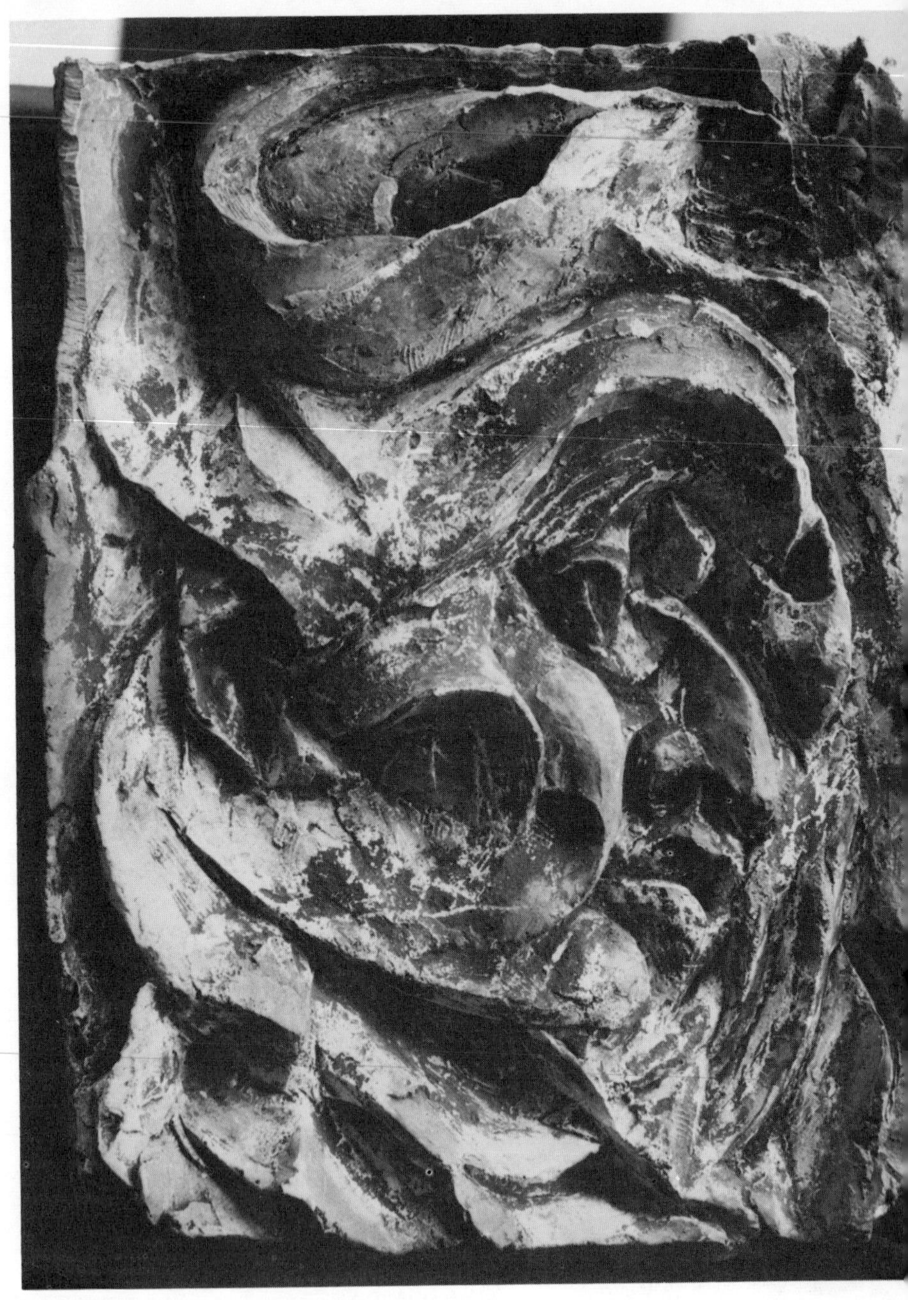

15. "Portrait of Father" (fourth version), Oto Gutfreund. 1911. Owner: National Gallery, Prague

16. "Anguish," Oto Gutfreund. 1911. Owner: National Gallery, Prague

17. "The Head," Oto Gutfreund. Wood; 1919. Owner: National Gallery, Prague

18. "The Head," Oto Gutfreund. Plaster of paris; 1919. Owner: National Gallery, Prague

19. "Self-portrait," Oto Gutfreund. Polychrome terra-cotta; 1919

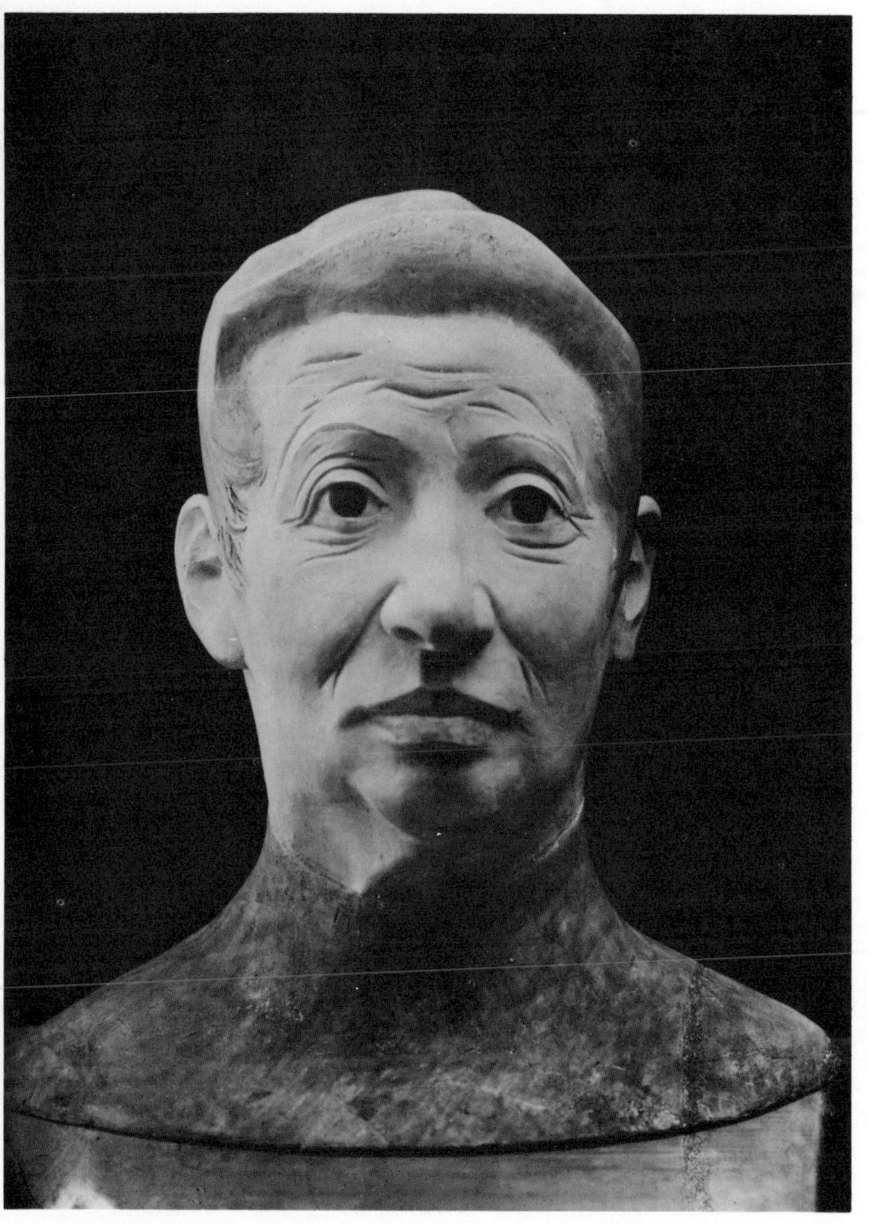

20. “Portrait of Mother,” Oto Gutfreund. Polychrome terra-cotta; 1920

21. "Still Life," Alfred Justitz. Pencil drawing, 8 x 10 inches; 1918. Owner: Graphical Collection of National Gallery, Prague

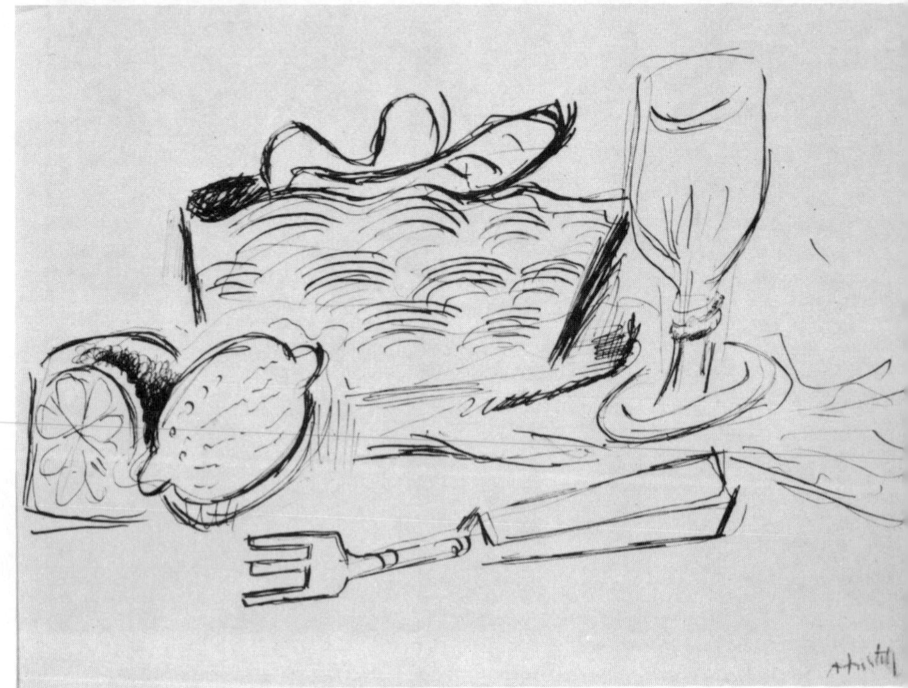

22. "Indian Embroiderer," Bedřich Feigl. Drawing, india ink, 16 x 20 inches;1926. Owner: Graphical Collection of National Gallery, Prague

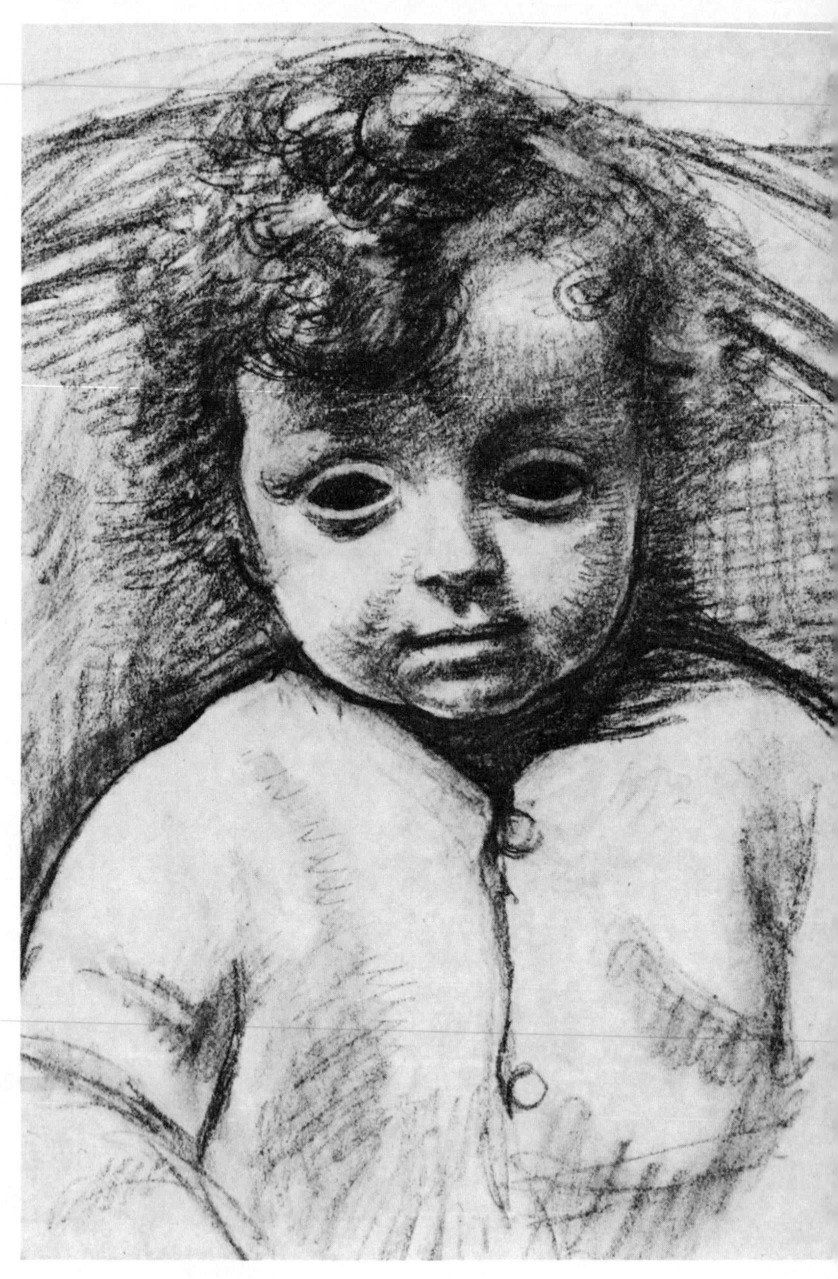

23. "Son of Václav Nebesky," George Kars. Charcoal drawing; 1920. Owner: Graphical Collection of National Gallery, Prague

24. "Family," Robert Guttmann. Oil painting; 1941. Owner: Jewish Museum, Prague

25. "Terezín," Karel Fleischmann. Pen drawing; 1943

26. "Kaddish," Aleš Veselý. Metal sculpture, 25 feet high; 1968

JEWISH ART IN SLOVAKIA: A PERSONAL RECOLLECTION

by Frank Reichenthal

To write about Jewish art in Slovakia is a rather problematic undertaking. For one thing, the cultural and political history of Slovakia was entirely different from that of Bohemia. Slovakia was never a political entity before 1918. It was not even a separate province. It was simply an integral part of Hungary. Before the Hungarian eruption of more than a thousand years ago, it was part of a Slav empire. But the Hungarian overlordship made the development of a national Slovak culture impossible. Under Hungarian rule there were no Slovak schools. The Hungarian schools assimilated the would-be Slovak intelligentsia, and thus left the masses leaderless. Only the 19th century changed the situation. Influenced by the nationalistic tendencies of the time, some intellectuals of Slovak parentage tried to infuse a national consciousness into the people. These new leaders were dedicated individuals, but to fill the vacuum of a thousand years with a national culture was not an easy task.

It was nothing less than a miracle that within two decades after the establishment of Czechoslovakia, the Slovak people were able to build a national culture on the foundations laid by these dedicated leaders. The beginnings were hard, especially with regard to art.

Art is not a flower blooming in hidden, shadowy, provincial places. It thrives in the climate of big centers, to which all artists gravitate, and where all the cultural, educational, economic, and similar institutions, as well as the seat of government, are. For Slovakia, until 1918, this center was Budapest, the capital of Hungary. There were, of course, always a few obscure painters and sculptors in provincial cities. But they were not there because of their Slovak, Rumanian, or any other origin but because they were more or less amateurs, unfit to compete for recognition in the capital. The fact is that many of the great Hungarian artists were born to Slovak parents: Lászlo Mednyánszky, Ede Ballo, Gyula Benczur, János Kmetty, György Konecsný, and so on. But they lived in Budapest and were thoroughly assimilated Hungarians.

The establishment of Slovakia as part of the Czechoslovak Republic changed all that abruptly. Bratislava, formerly an insignificant provincial town, suddenly became a district capital. Even smaller cities like Košice or Turčianský Sv. Martin developed into important cultural centers. Artistic contact with Prague, the nation's capital, was negligible at first. Only in the early 1920s, when the first art students went to Prague for their artistic education, was a livelier contact established.

Jewish art, in general, hardly existed before the middle of the 19th century. The reasons are simple and well known: the strict religious tradition and the social segregation of the Jews. However, after the chains of tradition were loosened, Jewish talent broke through like an avalanche. The beginning of the 20th century saw not only Jewish participation but effective Jewish leadership in all fields of cultural endeavor, including art. It would be futile to search out which of the Jewish artists were born in the territory of Slovakia. We can only consider those who kept in touch with their birthplace after the establishment of the new state. The situation changed with the younger generation who were studying or embarking upon their artistic career about that time. Their connection with the new state and its cultural life was an intense and natural one.

Let us now turn to the individual artists and discuss them briefly in a chronological order.

Dominic Skutecky was dean of the Jewish artists in Slovakia. Partly for artistic, partly for family reasons, he lived in Slovakia. He had been an established and recognized artist in Budapest long before 1918. In reality Budapest was his artistic home. When he decided to stay on in Slovakia after the political changeover it was simply because he wanted to remain where he had spent most of his life. He painted almost exclusively the people of the mining area where his home and studio were located. To remain in Slovakia may have been a natural decision for Skutecky, but to make himself part of the new situation as an artist was not a simple matter.

The Slovak provincial painters began to organize and take stock. The historical change had thrust upon them a new importance and pride. In reality, however, what was at stake was not so much the question of position and national pride as that of greater material gains. Most of the organizers were narrow-minded provincial people for whom Skutecky constituted a problem. It was only natural that in such a situation Slovak nationality carried more weight than artistic ability. If one was a Slovak, one was an exponent of the new national culture. Provincialism thus suddenly became something of a distinction. The fact that the Slovak artists had not been able to join the mainstream of Hungarian art was now regarded as an imposed or voluntary suffering for the artists' Slovak nationality, rather than an indication of lack of ability.

The new Slovak organizers did not know what to do with Skutecky. As an artist he was far superior to them, but his nationality was questionable, and this was ample reason to cast him aside. Some were inclined to accept him because of his established name, but the majority reserved decision.

Dr. Bela Tilkovsky, today one of the leading art historians in Czechoslovakia, wrote his doctoral thesis about Skutecky, characterizing him as one of the fathers of Slovak art. On the other hand, the author of a recent history of Slovak art, Dr. Marian Váross, while not exactly forgetting Skutecky, deals with him in a reference which is ridiculously brief compared with those he gives to lesser painters of the time. It would thus seem that in retrospect Skutecky was not considered as an integral part of Slovak art.

Skutecky's art was deeply influenced by the Hungarian Mihály Munkácsy, and thus indirectly by the Piloty school of Munich. His warm colors appear against a deep brown background. He achieved his greatest success with his paintings of metal-workers. The play of the artificial red and yellow light was an ideal subject for this technique of working from a brown background. These paintings were extremely effective. One of my own childhood recollections is of standing before a painting of a burning furnace in the National Gallery in Budapest and admiring the play of light on the figures and surroundings. Little did I realize then that the "Fauves" were already on the way out, and that Skutecky's art and his brilliant technique were relics of the 19th century.

Many Jewish artists, even in later years, found themselves in the same predicament as Skutecky, and had to experience the same agonizing tensions and face the same choices. The artist's identification with nationality has seemingly very little to do with his participation in the artistic life of Slovakia. However, these facts must be mentioned because they shed light on the work, life, and development of some of the Jewish artists to be discussed.

Andor Boruth's position was very similar to that of Skutecky. Both were equally known and enjoyed established reputations. Both participated in all important exhibitions in Budapest. Boruth, too, had his domicile in Slovakia and stayed there after the establishment of the Republic. True, his decision to remain was based on personal considerations. He inherited a partnership in the health resort of Tatranská Poliana, his hometown, and lived there for practical reasons.

Boruth was first and foremost a portrait painter. He found his rich clientele among those who had come to Poliana for health reasons and in search of recreation, and ended up by having their portraits painted. There is no question that as an artist he was far superior to most of his contemporaries in Slovakia. But, like Skutecky, he was somehow cast aside. Apart from his portraits he found his subject in the environment in which he lived — the people and the landscape of the Tatra Mountains. In Vaross's history of Slovak art, tinted by the prevailing political and nationalistic sentiments, Boruth, too, is denied the place due to him. Ironically, he fared even worse in a recent history of Hungarian art: his name is mentioned only as one in a group of fifty without any special comment about his art. Hungarian artists who remained in Slovakia were discounted in Hungary, but because of their Hungarian background they were never really accepted for their true value in Slovakia.

Boruth's art, too, had its roots in the 19th century. In his later years he absorbed some aspects of the Impressionistic technique, but the real substance of his outlook was derived from Munkácsy and the Munich Academy. His portraits are conventional in technique and composition, except for his self-portraits of the 1930s and 1940s, in which he was able to overcome the shackles of convention. His brush became freer, his lights sharper and more expressive. His most convincing works are his spontaneous sketches done without posing and preparation. These really show a masterly freshness.

Skutecky may have been the more original talent, but compared with Boruth he was an unchanging conservative. For that matter, the same thing can be said of the Hungarian and Slovak art of that period in general. Even the boldest Hungarian artist of that time, József Rippl-Rónai, did not go in his probings beyond a very timid Fauvism. It is in this light that we must look upon and judge these artists.

Just before, during, and after the First World War a few innovators tried to integrate new post-Impressionistic and Cubistic elements into their art, but the Hungarian counterrevolution of 1919 drove most of these artists into emigration. As early as 1911 they had formed a group called "The Eight," five of whom were Jews, but only one, Bertalan Pór, had come from the territory of Slovakia. Pór threw in his lot with the Communist Revolution after the First World War. He became a member of the party directorium and was named professor at the Academy of Arts. Before the revolution he had painted mostly portraits in an Expressionistic style with gray and brown tonality. Behind the bold brush strokes one could see the shadows of Munkácsy and László Pál. To me it seems that these masterfully painted, deeply felt, expressive human images of his friends, family, and himself were the best work he ever did.

During the revolutionary period his work became bombastic and theatrical, full of forced grandiosity. From then on his paintings were always in part political manifestos, which, by their very nature, have to be somewhat pathetic. After the fall of Béla Kun's short-lived Communist régime, Pór had to leave Hungary. He returned to his hometown, Sliač, into the bosom of his very well-to-do family. There he was safe in every sense. The persecuting hand of the Horthy régime could not reach him in Czechoslovakia, and he had no worries about his livelihood either. He became a Czechoslovak citizen, but as an artist he was — and remained — a stranger. After a year or two he went to Paris and later to Moscow. He tried to achieve a certain simplicity of approach, but even in his Paris years political theories and considerations were too much in his way. He tried the impossible: to combine the dictum of socialist realism with a glaze of modern art. In his paintings of this period he tried to unite nature, man, and animal. Unfortunately, for reasons already mentioned, the simplicity for which he strove was seldom achieved. The result was often a pathetic emptiness.

From time to time, the School for Applied Art in Bratislava (on whose teaching staff I served) exhibited works of modern artists. In 1935 we gave a showing of Pór's art. The years in Paris showed their influence. The paintings were smaller in size, and I could see the striving for a certain intimacy. But, unfortunately, superficial political and social overtones combined to burden his work. One felt somehow that he was afraid to paint simply for the sake of painting itself. Between the two world wars he returned nearly every year to Slovakia but was never considered in any way part of Slovakia's cultural life. Shortly after the Communist takeover after the Second World War he returned to Budapest. He was warmly welcomed by the Communist régime, and his services as an old Marxist were finally rewarded. He became the government's grand old man, but his art, or whatever was left of it, had to pay for it. Shortly before his death, in 1959, the Czechoslovak Communist government honored him with a retrospective exhibition. He was a potentially great artist torn between politics and art, and naturally in a competition of this kind his art had to suffer.

Nándor Katona belonged to the same generation as Pór. He came from the Slovak region of Spiš. He was the follower of the early Impressionists and never changed his style or subject matter. From beginning to end he painted the Tatra Mountains around his birthplace, in all seasons: the velvety snow in the winter, the thaw of the spring, the colors of fall and summer. This is all that he painted, year after year, over and over, in all moods and changes. Thus, it was inevitable that after the establishment of the Republic he had to return to the landscape he loved and understood.

A graphic artist who came to Slovakia as a political immigrant after the overthrow of the Hungarian Revolution was Eugen Krón. The then director of the East Slovak Museum in Košice, Dr. Josef Polák, was a kindhearted man and a great admirer of art and artists. He was instrumental in making possible Krón's permanent stay by encouraging him to open a private school for graphic arts in the museum. The school was very successful until the middle 1920s. Many Slovak artists who later were to become well known took their first steps in Krón's school. Koloman Sokol, who later became one of the leading graphic artists of Czechoslovakia, was one of his pupils. Krón was a professional lithographer and a brilliant technician. His sojourn in Košice was very fruitful, not only because of his influence as a teacher on the development of the graphic arts in Slovakia but also for his own artistic development. Although most of his work had a tendency to be overliterary, his artistic culture and taste overcame this handicap, especially in his cityscapes of Košice and other eastern Slovak cities.

A group of Jewish artists who began their careers shortly after the First World War included two sculptors, four painters, and one graphic artist. The graphic artist, David Lang, was a native of Nové Mesto nad Váhom. He had no formal training and drew under the influence of Schiele, Kokoschka, and other German Expressionists. He also did etchings and lithographs. His subject matter was figurative, mostly portraits. His work had a certain expressiveness but lacked technical skill. He lived mainly outside of Slovakia and never had any artistic connection with it.

The work of the sculptor Pavol Bán was, from beginning to end, unimaginatively naturalistic. His best sculptures were portraits done in his younger years, especially the ones made of his family: his son as a little boy and his mother.

It was not simple for an artist to make a living and support a family. It is therefore merely a statement of fact and not criticism when we characterize Bán as a sculptor who was as much a businessman as an artist. He was ready to serve anybody, without reservation. His studio often resembled a factory which mass-produced portraits of leading personalities. He was a good technician and draftsman. His draftsmanship showed itself mostly in his plaquettes. His low reliefs, which are more or less plastic drawings, show him at his best. His more ambitious work unfortunately belongs more to the commercial category. On some of this latter work he cooperated with other sculptors, in which case the others mostly supplied the connections and Bán did the work. He was never able to overcome the conventional. A different point of view, a belief in art as such, instead of his being a sculptor only in a technical sense, might have made all the difference in his work.

Besides Bán, the only other Jewish sculptor in Slovakia, or rather from Slovakia, was Artur Fleischmann. Fleischmann was educated and lived in Vienna but belonged to the organization of Hungarian artists in Bratislava, where his family lived. He visited the city of his birth very often. From time to time he had commissions in Bratislava and he exhibited regularly. His studio was always in Vienna, and naturally, most of his work — especially the more monumental — is in Austria today. He strove for a certain simplicity and decorativeness and loved most of all to work with ceramic materials.

Originally he had studied medicine but, as in many similar cases, art prevailed. The reason for such a dualism in Jewish families is obvious: Jewish parents wanted their children to have the security of a respectable profession, and art was not thought to belong to this category. As soon as he was able to stand on his own feet as a sculptor, Fleischmann gave up medicine. He was a man of high principles and purpose. He did not cut himself off from the new trends in art. By aligning himself with the post-Impressionistic school, especially that of Maillol, he rejected everything picturesque. Sculpture had to be derived from the massiveness of the block — this, to him, was the fundamental principle of sculpture. Sometimes Fleischmann even adhered too slavishly to this idea, which made his work somewhat formalistic and decorative. His work had so much calmness and peace that he was a natural choice for modern churches, which often gave him commissions. After Hitler invaded Austria he left for Australia, where he continued his artistic work successfully.

Arthur Szalatnai, an architect by profession, painted watercolors from time to time and exhibited with a group of Hungarian artists and later with a group of Slovak painters. After the war he changed his name to Slatinský. He painted mostly flowers and sometimes the old streets of Bratislava. When architects paint they have usually a tendency to be hard in design and drab in color. Slatinský was able to divorce his painting from all architectural influence. His colors are light and shiny and the forms loose in the best tradition of aquarelle painting.

Géjza Schiller, a very talented and progressive painter, went to Košice, like Krón, as a homeless immigrant from Hungary following the short-lived revolution. Even in his poverty he worked feverishly, as if he knew that he had only a few more years to live. His influence on the development of Slovak art would have been much greater if he could have spent his few remaining years in Košice, but his misery forced him to leave for Nagybánya in Rumania, where there was an old art colony and where he had some relatives. However, even the few years he spent in Košice left a mark on the art scene. Today his name is hardly mentioned on either side of the border. Even in the Hungarian history of art I could not find his name, and in the Slovak one only the fact that he had lived for about three years in Košice and had died in Nagybánya was recorded. I remember seeing some paintings of his after the Second World War and being shocked that a man of such talent and conception, whose art had been more advanced in the early 1920s than nearly anything done in Slovakia in the 1930s or 1940s, should have been so completely overlooked.

The last of this group, Arnold Weiss-Kubinčan, was very little known outside the region where he worked and resided. He was born in Dolný Kubin, and studied at the School for Decorative Art in Budapest. He served during the First World War in the Hungarian Army and went home to Dolný Kubin after the war. He tried his luck in Berlin for a while, but finally returned for good to his native land and city. His work in the postwar years was confused, and he was unable to find his way in the bewilderment of the new trends. Possibly Kokoschka was the most decisive influence on his development, but he could never lose the shallow decorativeness resulting from his education at the School for Decorative Art. His friendship with Miloš Bazovský influenced them both. From Bazovský he took elements of Slovak folk art which, in turn, were based on the style of the Moravian artist Ján Hála. Bazovský, on the other hand, learned something from Kubinčan about the new ways and tendencies of Western art, but being potentially the greater artist, Bazovský prevailed while Kubinčan faded away. After the anti-Fascist uprising in Slovakia in 1944 was put down, he was deported and killed.

Imro Weiner (who after the Second World War called himself Weiner-Král' — Král' being the name he had used in the underground movement in France during the German occupation) came from a Jewish middle-class family in the Žilina region. He studied in Budapest, Prague, and Germany. His beginnings can be characterized as mildly Expressionistic. In the 1920s he published an album of lithographs with genrelike scenes of Slovak small-town life. A certain social comment made them heavily literary, because the subject seemed more important than the artistic expression. His tendency for literariness accompanied him throughout his career, and sometimes it dominated his work entirely. Under the influence of the then well-known social commentators in art, such as George Grosz, Otto Dix, Franz Masereel, and others, his painting and graphic work became, to a certain degree, satirical. One could hardly escape the impression that in everything he did he wanted to prove, more than anything else, his faithfulness to the principles of social thinking. The result was that in most of this work the social comment of the subject matter overwhelmed the artistic elements.

I met Weiner when he came with Irene Blüh, then his wife, to Bratislava in the late 1920s. They opened a bookstore which served many purposes, as I can clearly see today. It provided the Weiners with a fairly secure livelihood, it propagated left-wing literature, and at the same time it was a gathering place for the leftists. All intellectuals, especially artists who considered themselves modern, had to belong to the group around the bookstore. I myself was one of them. In the 1930s friendship with František Malý — who taught textile design at the School of Applied Art — brought Weiner under the influence of the Surrealist movement. From then on Weiner's paintings became harder and harder, and even more literal. The surrealists mixed elements of reality in an unreal way to achieve a dreamlike quality. Weiner was never able to accomplish anything like that, however hard he tried. He simply used surrealist elements to underline a certain social tendency or meaning by putting in one single painting a sequence of events. His pictures reminded me of the prints, which were to be seen in nearly every house in the early 20th century, showing the stages of a man's life — from birth through manhood to death. Weiner turned more and more to subjects illustrating the life of Slovak peasants. In nearly all of his paintings from 1934 on, one found the wooden houses, the mountains, a dominant figure, and then — somewhere — smaller ones, showing different stages of the life of the main figure.

Later, Weiner borrowed elements from the early Renaissance. Even the golden background was not neglected. As mentioned, he spent the war years in France, probably in Paris, and the Parisian atmosphere, as it always does, softened somewhat the stiffness of Weiner's style. He exchanged the hard pre-Renaissance forms and colors for those of the Impressionists, or sometimes those of the Pointillists. But he stuck to his old subject matter, the Slovak peasant. In the 1930s he joined the Umelecká Beseda, a group of artists which had a liberal — one could even say international — character; not only the Slovak artists but all the Czech artists living in Slovakia belonged to it. On the other hand there were also reactionaries, anti-Semites, and even Nazis in the Beseda, but up to 1937 the majority, even though it was sometimes a shaky one, was held by the liberals because of a coalition of those members who either artistically or politically opposed the conservatives. Only the Nazi occupation was able to change the equilibrium.

The following incident, although it has no direct bearing on an artistic evaluation of the events, may serve to illustrate the situation in which Jewish artists found themselves. After the Nazi occupation of the Sudetenland we had, I recall, a membership conference of the Umelecká Beseda. We knew that the right wing was preparing an assault on the liberals. But we did not know that our defeat was a foregone conclusion. Some of the modernists, foreseeing the future or sympathizing politically with the nearing events, deserted the ship. They solved the problem by simply not appearing at the meeting. Others, seeing the writing on the wall, voted outright with the conservatives.

We were outvoted, and the "ins" were out and the "outs" were in. The next exhibition already had an entirely different character from the previous ones, and because the jury was in the hands of conservatives we had no influence on the selection of the paintings to be exhibited. The opening day was a surprise for everybody, a surprise worse even than had been anticipated. A Czech artist exhibited clearly anti-Semitic drawings with openly Nazi tendencies. But what surprised me most was that everybody took it more or less calmly, and nobody thought of doing something about it. The only thing to do, after my protests were brushed aside, was to turn to the Zionist Youth Organization. Next day, a group of Jewish boys solved the problem: they went to the exhibition, took the drawings from the wall, and smashed them to pieces. Although everybody knew who had committed the "vandalism" its perpetrators were never caught — and that was the beginning and the end of it.

After the consolidation of the Communist régime, when the no-nonsense socialistic realism was proclaimed as the only way to paint, Weiner complied. I have no firsthand knowledge of his achievements as a social realist, but I saw a catalogue of an exhibition in which an art critic, in his foreword, made a few disparaging remarks about the futile attempts of Weiner in that direction. The artistic element in Weiner's work, the critic said, simply disappeared under the pressure of the subject. But what most amazed me in that catalogue was a reproduction of a crucifixion by Weiner. To be frank, the painting in itself was very unappealing. Weiner acted as if he had never known what a Jew was all the time I knew him, and here, suddenly, Christ was shown as a poor man in civilian clothes with a yellow Star of David on his shirt. The tragedy of out six million martyrs, including many of Weiner's own relatives, must have reminded him that a good many of his glorified Slovak peasants helped to accomplish the genocide and tried, even after the war, to destroy everything that was left, including our cemeteries.

I would not be objective if I did not recognize that Weiner is a highly intelligent painter, whose knowledge of art history, draftsmanship, and great technical ability have made him one of the most influential artists in Slovakia. Whatever path he chose to follow, his mind was always open to the new trends and preoccupied with the problems of European art. When he rejected most of the new tendencies, he did it knowingly. True, he did this more often for political than for artistic reasons and when I saw his work done during the war years in Paris I had high hopes that his whole artistic conception would loosen up — the tendency was there. Unfortunately, the artistic part in him again had to suffer under the burden of the political element.

The Jewish artists who began their studies after the First World War, and had their start in the middle and late 1920s, were in a better position than their elders. In their formative years they breathed the new, changed political air. It was not that they had no problems, but the problems — not being the result of sudden, bewildering political and social upheavals — could be faced clearly. The young people from a Slovak environment spoke Slovak and went to Prague for their higher education; those from the Hungarian-speaking part of the country had the choice of going either to Budapest and assimilating there or turning to Prague, accepting the new environment and situation, and finding a place for themselves in it.

Ludo Feld, who studied in Košice in Krón's school, continued his studies at the Academy of Arts in Budapest under Gyula Rudnay. Then he returned to Košice, his hometown. His very realistic drawings and etchings mirrored the influence of both his masters. But unfortunately his work did not arouse much interest outside his hometown. He still lives and works there.

So far as I can remember, all the artists in that period came from the territory which had formerly belonged to Hungary. There are only three who must be mentioned here, two from Komárno and one from Šamorín, and all of them very talented. One, George Rauscher, studied in Budapest under Rudnay. He worked mostly outside Slovakia, and despite his nominal membership in a Hungarian association, the Jókay Egyesület in Komárno, he never had any connection with artistic life in Slovakia and had practically no influence on it. To study in Budapest was a natural choice for him. Fairly well-to-do, the son of a doctor, and almost entirely detached from Jewish traditions, he embraced the Catholic religion and had no difficulties in being accepted in the Academy of Budapest.

Under my influence and the influence of the times in which he lived, Rauscher's subject matter began to change. His parents and mine lived in the same city, and we both spent the summers in Komárno. I had at the time a few exhibitions already behind me in Vienna, Budapest, and Prague, and thus I was, in the eyes of the upcoming young artists like Rauscher, the grand old man, although I was hardly more than thirty years old. Rauscher's real strength was always the portrait. He developed a somewhat sentimental, elegant style, light colors and pleasingly flowing lines and forms; combined with an immense ability to achieve likeness, all this made him the ideal portraitist of delicate women.

I remember that my judgment of his art was somewhat clouded and negatively influenced by certain factors not directly connected with art. For example, his weakness for social recognition many times led him to compromise with the artistic conception. In Berlin, where we were together in the late 1920s, he painted a few wonderful covers for the magazine *Sport im Bild.* He was happy and carefree then, but his very promising career was brought to a sudden and tragic end. He was only in his early thirties when, without any prior warning, he contracted acute tuberculosis and succumbed. On his deathbed Rauscher returned to the faith of his fathers.

Rauscher's life was tragic not only because of his abrupt death but because two desires were fighting constantly in his heart: the desire for social elegance and achievement and a longing for artistic fulfillment. He was a fascinating individual and a young man endowed with grace and beauty, the like of which I have never seen since. His charm and love of life were simply irresistible, but his forced march of living exhausted him both mentally and physically to such an extent that very little was left for purely artistic achievement. Years later I was surprised to find his name not mentioned in either the Hungarian or the Slovak history of art.

Another artist of that period was Géza Szobel. He, too, came from Komárno, where his parents settled when he was a young boy. At the age of sixteen he quit high school because he wanted to be an artist. He tried to gain admittance to the Academy of Arts in Budapest, but in vain. He was too young, too immature artistically, and above all a Jew. At that time very few Jews were accepted to institutions of higher learning in Hungary. For a while he studied at an improvised art school provided by the Jewish community just for young people like him. Then he returned home and went on to Prague, where he studied at the so-called Ukrainian Academy, led by Russian immigrants. The school was fairly free and intellectually inspiring. Many good artists had their beginnings there, and Szobel was one of them. His first paintings had a certain crudity: a mixture of Matisse-like contours filled with unimaginative colors, large canvases looking rather empty. Life was not easy for the poor boy who had only one ambition: to make some kind of a living in order to prove to his family that his artistic ambitions were not in vain. He especially wanted to impress his mother, who viewed her son's ambition somewhat skeptically.

Szobel went to Berlin and tried to make some money with illustrations. He did not succeed. All his work was crude and lacking in technical perfection. The great turn in his life came when he married a lovely French girl who taught at the French Lyceum in Prague. In the middle 1930s his wife was transferred to Paris. Szobel went with her, and his life changed completely. First of all, the search for the daily bread ended. Then the atmosphere of Paris entirely changed his outlook. The hard lines and meaningless colors were replaced by a kind of poetic vision.

I saw very little of his work in 1937 and 1938 but what I did see surprised me. During the Second World War, in Paris, Szobel was mobilized in the Czechoslovak Army and was evacuated from Dunkirk to England. The few Czechoslovak artists and writers in London were more or less under the protection of the Czechoslovak government-in-exile. This meant that they could concentrate on their work, carefree and unhampered. Szobel's paintings and illustrations which I saw from that period had a dramatic and poetic ring, which I never expected from him. Frankly, I was touched and surprised and full of admiration when, in 1947, I visited his studio in Paris. By then he had achieved recognition and had exhibited with the best artists of the old generation and of his own. The once-crude Szobel had developed into a poet of colors and lines. It was the greatest and most beautiful transformation over a few years I ever saw.

The next time I went to Paris was in 1959. In the meantime, Szobel's artistic development had proceeded apace. He had had one-man shows in the great galleries with excellent reviews. The collectors were beginning to buy his paintings, not only in Paris but all over the world. When I returned again in 1964, my first visit was to Szobel's studio. It was one of the greatest shocks of my life to hear from his grief-stricken wife that only a few months earlier he had died of a heart attack while driving to his last exhibition. It was a sad sight to see that little woman, his wife, among the large paintings turned to the walls of the half-empty studio.

Except for his wife, none of his family witnessed the artistic achievement of his last ten years — all his relatives were killed in Hitler's gas chambers. Szobel was never attracted to Jewish subject matter, but among his paintings after the war I saw one showing a praying Jew. The picture surprised me with its deep feeling and quality. He probably painted it under the stress of deep emotions, perhaps in memory of his parents and family, who were very religious and who could not be with him to see his success.

Blanka Tauber, the only Jewish woman artist in Slovakia, survived the concentration camps and lives in Israel. She lost her parents and most members of her family in the death camps. She came from Šamorin, not far from Bratislava, from a very religious family. The deeply ethical principles implanted in her heart in that environment were later transformed into a predominantly humanitarian outlook. She became a vegetarian and an ardent socialist, but she never wanted anything from the movement except to serve it and to work to uplift the downtrodden. She was not a fighter, she was a believer. The experiences in the death camp in Germany only strengthened her in her belief. Naturally, a sensitive woman such as she had to wake up sooner or later. After her return from the concentration camp she left Czechoslovakia and went to Budapest, where she intended to stay for good. She had the opportunity to observe the political machinations from close range. The purges which took the life and liberty of some of her innocent friends opened her eyes. She was thoroughly disillusioned.

At about that time the State of Israel was reborn. It was only natural that Blanka Tauber, with her background and her personality, her enthusiastic longing for new involvements, should embrace the idea of the new state not only as a new homeland but as a symbol of new beliefs. She lives now in Israel and, as these pages were written, had had a successful exhibition in New York at the Herzl Institute.

Blanka Tauber studied in Prague and in Paris with André Lhote, under whose influence she experimented with a kind of tamed Cubism which Lhote himself practiced. But after awhile she felt impelled to search for a new style. She returned to Czechoslovakia, trying to find her own way. A version of Cézannish colors with Expressionistic forms became the elements of her developing style, and even when her subject matter was not Jewish one sensed all through her work something like an accompanying Jewish melody.

In Israel she went through very trying times, as nearly every newcomer in the first two years of the new state did, with very little to eat, nowhere to live, and hardly any privacy for work. She worked wherever she could get work. The turn in her fortunes came when she met the director of the Tel Aviv Museum, Eugene Krón, who had himself come from Budapest. Krón was very helpful in establishing her as an artist. Through his influence she got the Dizengoff Prize, and after that things began to look up. She built herself a studio in the art colony in Safed with very little money and much sweat and blood. There she works and exhibits in the summer; in the winter she lives in Tel Aviv. The increasing prosperity of the country and the developing tourism benefit the artists in Israel, Blanka Tauber among them. I do not know anyone more deserving.

Her art never changed basically — it only deepened. On visiting her exhibition in New York I was surprised to see signs of timid probings, of experimentations. Unfortunately, I did not find them too successful. Her figural painting never achieves the poetic quality of some of her pastel landscapes, especially from the years between '50 and '60. The softness of the pastel, congenial to her character, is much better suited to her than the more rigid oil paint. The soft, brilliant colors, embedded in dark blue, brown, green, and black in her best pastel landscapes, are the ones which best express that which she wishes to express.

To a younger generation of artists belong Eugene Nevan, Jakub Bauernfreund, and André Nemeš. All three developed about the same time, and all three studied at the Academy in Prague. Two of them, Bauernfreund and Nemeš, were very good friends, both in an artistic and a human sense. Both studied under Novak, who was an excellent pedagogue and a man of deep understanding. He himself never went further than the Impressionists but encouraged his students to experiment and search for self-expression. He had a great influence on nearly all the Slovak artists of that generation. One can imagine what qualities he must have possessed when one considers that, although he taught in the German section of the academy, many Slovaks chose him as their teacher. Nemeš and Bauernfreund were his most beloved pupils. He not only taught them but also did everything in his power to help them in every other way.

I cannot forgo recounting here a certain recollection. When Nemeš came to Prague, he began to study philosophy, but he was a very facile draftsman and his style was suitable for swift newspaper illustrations. Up to 1931, I myself — whether I was in Berlin, Paris or Prague — never stopped working for the daily or periodical press. It was not an ideal solution, but I had well-paid jobs which made me independent. Through my connections I was able to secure for Nemeš a few jobs with newspapers in Prague. Everbody took a liking to the talented, quiet boy, for whom these jobs meant quite a lot financially. He had already studied at the academy, after giving up philosophy. One day Nemeš quit, and I could not understand it since I knew that he badly needed the money. He explained to me that doing that kind of work was incompatible with dedicating one's life to art. Perhaps Professor Novak, too, had something to do with the decision.

After the Nazi takeover both Bauernfreund and Nemeš left the country — Bauernfreund for London and Nemeš for Sweden. Bauernfreund is today a recognized artist in England, and Nemeš is professor at the academy in Oslo. Artistically, Nemeš was the more forceful one. Both began with Cubistic still lifes and compositions. Bauernfreund later developed more illustrative tendencies with a kind of romantic, symbolistic subject matter. Nemeš stuck to his guns. His art rests today on the same principles as in his early years, but instead of a classic kind of Cubism, his later work is based on reevaluated, freer versions of the same concepts.

The third artist of the group, Eugene Nevan, was only four years old when the Czechoslovak Republic was born. He came from the deep Slovak part of the country, from Liptov. Consequently, he did not have the same problems as most of us before him. He was educated and raised in the new Republic. He, too, originally studied something other than art. He wanted to be a physician and studied at the Prague medical school. He tried to combine his desire to be an artist with the practical career of a doctor. As usual, it did not work — something had to give. Finally, he quit medical school and devoted himself entirely to his studies at the Academy of Art. His art changed very little from the beginning to the end. He transformed influences from Matisse and the Fauves into a somewhat more realistic style of form and color.

His subjects were mostly quiet people sitting around in quiet rooms. No emotions, no searching for deeper meanings of life. He belonged to a little group of Slovak artists who lived in Prague and did not return to Slovakia even after Slovakia was declared an independent country. I do not know how he survived during the war years — probably most of the people did not even know that he was a Jew, or perhaps some of his friends helped him. So far as I remember, he tried his hand only once at a subject outside of his quiet, bourgeois scenes. He painted Lidice. That painting, of course, dictated a different technique because of the emotions involved. He had to borrow heavily from the Expressionists. It was not the same Nevan. He must have felt it, too, because he never repeated his excursion into strange territory. His art has never had even a trace of Jewishness, either theoretically or spiritually.

Armin Stern is a special case. It is impossible to put him chronologically where he belongs because he did not live in Czechoslovakia — except during a few visits to his family in Galanta, where he was born — until his involuntary return home in 1933. Nobody knew about him as an artist until then. He studied in Paris and in Frankfurt, where he married and established himself. He had a good reputation there and was very well known.

In 1933 the coming to power of Hitler forced him out of Germany, and he went home and opened a studio in Bratislava. He spoke not a word of Slovak, and even Hungarian, his mother tongue, he spoke with a thick German accent. Through his connections he was able to carve out a fair living for himself. One has to understand one thing: in artistic groupings, sometimes quite untalented people have established interests and occupy positions of seniority similar to those in a union; a newcomer, even if his abilities are far greater than anybody else's in the group, has to play second fiddle and sit on the back bench. This was the case with Stern. Even with his established name, he had to fight for a small place in Bratislava. One could see in every one of his paintings that Cézanne was his idol, but Cézanne's loose forms became stiffened and more realistic in Stern's hand. His colors had the bluishness but not the warmth of those of his master. Grays and greenish tones predominated. Stern was one of the very few artists of reputation who must be considered as Jewish, not only because he was born a Jew but also because of his deep involvement with Jewish tradition, and because he tried to give expression to his Jewish feelings in his art.

Unfortunately, Hitler caught up with him again. In 1939 Czechoslovakia fell apart, and Slovakia came under indirect German rule. Stern had to look again for a new place for his family. Luckily, he had some relatives in America and so he was able to emigrate to the United States, where he died during the war. He did not have the time to make a name for himself in his new country. He painted mainly portraits, one of which — the portrait of President Eduard Beneš of Czechoslovakia — was reproduced during the war on the cover of the *Sunday Times Magazine*. Nevertheless, Stern got the same short shrift from the Slovak art historians as the artists previously mentioned.

Among the artists who studied just before or during the war and then made their appearance in the reestablished Czechoslovak Republic, there was only one with whom I had direct contact in 1946 in my capacity as president of the statewide Art Association in Slovakia. His name was Stefan Reiner. He was the lone survivor of his family, and as such he had to take over the family bakery business in Lučenec to prevent the state from expropriating it. He was very unhappy in the small provincial town, having to spend most of his time with something he was not only not interested in but did not even know very much about. At his request I arranged for him to be accepted in the Art Association, and from then on he took part in official exhibitions of Slovak artists. In 1948, when I was finally able to emigrate to America, I told him that he, too, should think about leaving for some other place if he wished to save his artistic independence.

I do not know whether or not it was upon my advice, but he left Czechoslovakia and went to Israel. When I saw him again in Israel in 1959 I was amazed. He had been a boyish-looking youth — now I saw before me a veritable athlete of a man. He had changed his name to Alexander and began his career as a night watchman in an orange grove. As part of his salary a big house was put at his disposal. The house was divided by a wide corridor, on one side of which he had made himself a comfortable studio; on the other, his wife, whom he had married in Israel, had set up a ceramics workshop.

After a time, Reiner was freed of his watchman's job but was able to keep the house for his wife and two children. He obtained a teaching position which provided him with an income on which to live. Great as the change was in the man, his development as an artist was even greater. In barely ten years he had matured from a beginner into a truly great artist. This was really a most happy surprise, remembering as I did his dry, colorless probings in the early postwar years. His new paintings were sometimes turbulent but all of them showed great dramatic expressiveness and artistic ability. The lines and forms were flowing, the colors sometimes subdued or even gray, sometimes vividly gay, but always held together in the frame of the composition in the best abstract sense. Such a development can only be the result of freedom — freedom in every sense of the word.

With this the story of Jewish art and artists in Slovakia, as known to me, has reached its end. I know of no Jewish artists after Reiner's generation. Maybe there are some, but I do not know about them. There are very few Jews left in Slovakia, and one can hardly count on the appearance of a new generation of Jewish artists.

In conclusion it seems appropriate to sum up the influence of these Jewish artists on the development of Slovak art in general. This influence was much greater than is generally assumed. The reasons are very simple: Jews, being cosmopolitan by nature and susceptible to new ideas, exercised a fermenting influence on the provincialness of Slovak art, especially in the early years of the Czechoslovak Republic. I, myself, simply by being the oldest Jewish artist and having steady contact with Slovak art and artists, had a considerable influence. My art, while neither extreme nor revolutionary in itself, nevertheless stirred up many Slovak artists who, at that time, were as yet untouched by the new winds of 20th century art. The same can be said about Imro Weiner, whose influence, for similar reasons, was a very positive one. Even a lesser artist, such as Weiss-Kubinčan, had a stimulating influence, as indicated above, on Bazovský and others who are considered today the founding fathers of Slovak national art. Subsequently, when some young Slovak artists, having studied in Prague, returned to Slovakia with their radical artistic views, the whole scene changed. But by then the seeds had already been sown by the early Jewish artists.

Since we were examining *Jewish* art in Slovakia, one more relevant question remains to be answered: How Jewish, in spirit or in theme, was the art produced by the Jewish artists in Slovakia? The answer must be that, with a few exceptions, it was not Jewish at all. Only

Lang, Stern, Blanka Tauber, and the author of this essay occupied themselves with Jewish subjects.

BIOGRAPHICAL NOTES ON ARTISTS MENTIONED IN THE ARTICLE

BÁN, Pavol. Born 1892, in Trenčianske Teplice. Studied at the Academy of Arts in Budapest. Worked in Bratislava. Died in 1964.

BAUERNFREUND, Jakub. Born 1904, in Zborov near Bardejov. Studied at the Academy in Prague under Willy Nowak. The German occupation forced him to emigrate. He lives in London.

BAZOVSKY, Miloš. Born 1899, in Tužany nad Váhom. Studied at the Academy of Arts in Budapest, and in Prague under Bukovac.

BORUTH, Andor. Born 1873, in Satoraljaujhely. Studied under Hollosy in Munich, and in the *Masterklass* of Benczur at the Academy of Arts in Budapest.

BUS (FINSTERBUSCH), Maximillian. Born 1909, in Štitnik, Slovakia. Studied at the School for Applied Arts in Prague. Theatrical designer. Lives in Košice.

CÉZANNE, Paul. Born 1839, in Aix-en-Provence. It is one of the oddities of our time that Cézanne, who gave direction to the art of the late 19th and early 20th centuries, was rejected by the École des Beaux Artes. As a pupil he was not acceptable, but he became the master of generations of artists who came after him.

DIX, Otto. Born 1894, in Unterhaus near Gera, Germany. Studied in the *Masterklasses* at the Academy of Dresden under Feldbauer and Gussmann. One of the leading German artists of the school called New Objectivity. Was persecuted by the Nazis. Now professor at the academy in Düsseldorf.

FELD, Ludo. Born 1904 in Košice, where he lives today.

FLEISCHMANN, Artur. Born 1890, in Bratislava. Studied and lived in Vienna. Emigrated to Australia.

GROSS, Hugo. Born 1894, near Trenčin, where he lived and worked.

GROSZ, George. Born 1893, in Berlin, where he died after the Second World War. During the Nazi era he lived on the Riviera and in New York. He became famous for his satirical drawings of German militarism and petty-bourgeois life.

HAHN, Karol. Born 1922, in Budapest. After the Second World War he lived in Bratislava, where he was successful with his graphic art. His present whereabouts are unknown.

HÁLA, Ján. Born 1890, in Blatná, Moravia. After 1923 he lived in Vážec, Slovakia. Studied at the Academy in Prague under Pirner. Contributed much to the development of a special Slovak style.

KATONA (KLEINBERGER), Nándor. Born 1864, in Spišká Nová Ves. Studied under Greguss, Lotz, and Székely in Budapest and later under Laurens and B. Konstant in Paris. Died in the late 1920s in Budapest.

KOKOSCHKA, Oskar. Born 1886, in Proechlarn a.d. Donau. Studied in the class of W. Loeffler at the School for Applied Arts in Vienna. One of the best-known German artists. During World War I he lived in exile. Now works in Salzburg, Austria.

KRÓN, Eugen, Born 1882, in Sobranec. Worked as a lithographer in Budapest and studied in the evening classes at the Academy under V. Olgyai. Since 1940 active in Stockholm, Sweden.

LANG, David. Born 1896, in Nové Mesto nad Váhom. Lives in the United States.

LHOTE, André. Self-taught; exhibited with the *Indépendants* in the first grouping of the revolutionary Paris school. He was more important as a teacher and theoretician than as an artist.

MAILLOL, Aristide. Born 1861, in Banyols sur Mer, France. He is considered the leading sculptor of the time. He was opposed to Rodin's Impressionistic style in sculpture.

MASEREEL, Franz. Born 1889, in Blankenberghe, Belgium. Studied at the Art School in Ghent under Jean Deloin. Lived in Paris. One of the more important graphic artists of the century. Belonged to the circle around Barbusse and Romain Rolland.

MATISSE, Henri. Born 1869, in Le Cateau. Died 1954, in Nice. One of the founders of the Fauves. Leading artist of the 20th century. His main concern was to reduce painting to the two dimensions of canvas.

MUNKÁCSY, Mihály. Born 1844, in Mukačevo. Studied at the Academies of Arts of Budapest and Vienna, and later in Munich and Dusseldörf. He was the most famous Hungarian artist of his time. Lived mostly in Paris. Many of his paintings are in the United States.

NEMEŠ, André. Born 1909, in Pécsvárad, Hungary. Studied at the Academy in Prague as a pupil of Willy Novak. Lives in Sweden.

NEVAN, Eugene. Born 1914, in Liptovský Sväty Mikulaš, Slovakia. Pupil of Willy Nowak at the Academy in Prague. Now professor at the Pedagogic Faculty of the University of Bratislava.

NOWAK, Willy. Born 1886, in Mnísek, Bohemia. Studied under Fratišek Thile at the Academy in Prague, where he became a professor in 1929.

PÁL, László. Born 1846, in Zám, Hungary. Died 1879, in Carentou, France. Studied in Vienna, Düsseldorf, and Paris. A friend and collaborator of Munkácsy. Had great influence on Hungarian landscape painting.

PILOTY, Karl. Born 1826, in Munich. His importance lies not in his oversized historical paintings but in his pedagogical activities. A whole generation of artists went to Munich to his art classes at the academy.

PÓR, Bertalan. Born 1880, in Bábaszék, Hungary. He was an infant when his parents moved to Sliač, Slovakia. Studied in Budapest, Munich, and Paris. Died in Budapest, 1960.

RAUSCHER, George. Born 1902, in Dorog, Hungary. His parents moved shortly after his birth to Komárno. He died there in 1930. Studied at the Academy of Arts in Budapest under Rudnay.

REINER (ALEXANDER), Stefan. Born 1922, in Lučenec. A student of the Academy of Prague. Now lives in Israel.

RIPPL-RÓNAI, József. Born 1861, in Kaposvár, Hungary. Studied in Munich and in Paris under Munkácsy. In Paris he associated himself with the revolutionary Fauve movement and is considered a founder of modern art in Hungary. Died 1927, in Kaposvár.

ROTTMAN, Mozart. Born 1874, in Ungvár (Užhorod). After the Second World War settled in the United States.

RUDNAY, Gyula. Born in 1878, in Pelsöc, Hungary. Was a student of Hollosy in Munich. Continued at the Julian Academy in Paris. Was professor at the Academy of Arts in Budapest.

SALVENDI, Frida. Born 1887, in Bratislava. Lived in Vienna. Once or twice exhibited in Bratislava.

SCHIELE, Egon. Born 1890, in Tuln a.d. Donau, Austria. Died in Vienna, 1918. Despite his untimely death he was one of the most influential artists of the 20th century.

SCHILLER, Géjza. Born 1890, in Nagybánya, where he died in 1926.

SIPOS, Béla. Born 1894, in Košice, Slovakia, where he still lives. Studied at the University in Budapest.

SKUTECKY, Dominic. Born in 1848, in Kisgajár, Hungary. Educated in Banská Bystrica, where he died in 1921.

SOKOL, Koloman. Born 1902, in Liptovský Sväty Mikulaš. The most important Slovakian graphic artist. Lives in the United States.

STERN, Armin. Born 1882, in Galanta, Slovakia. Studied under Franz Stuck in Munich. Died in 1944 in New York.

SZALATNAI (SLATINSKY), Arthur. Born 1891, in Slatina. Studied at the University of Budapest.

SZOBEL, Géza. Born 1905, in Slovakia. Studied in Prague. Lived in Paris and died there in 1963.

TAUBER, Blanka. Born 1912, in Šamorin, Slovakia. Studied in Prague and under André Lhote in Paris. Lives in Israel.

WEINER (-KRÁL'), Imro. Born 1901, in Považská Bystrica. Studied architecture at the University of Brno. He continued his artistic studies in Berlin and Paris. Lives in Bratislava.

WEISS-KUBINČAN, Arnold. Born 1898, in Dolný Kubin. Lived in Turčiansky Sväty Martin. Was killed in 1944 by the Nazis.

27. "Portrait of the Chief Rabbi Akiba Sofer/Schreiber," Armin Stern. Oil on canvas, 80 x 105 cm. Gallery of Bratislava

28. "Preparation for Dinner," Dominic Skutecky. Slovakian National Gallery, Bratislava

29. "My Mother,"
Imro Weiner-Král'.
Oil, 54 x 65 cm; 1967

30. "Jewish Street,"
Imro Weiner-Král'.
1964

31. "Reading of the Torah," Géza Szobel. 1932

32. "Trees in the Garden," Blanka Tauber. Oil

33. "Noah," Frank Reichenthal. Herzlia Museum, Israel

34. "Kiddush," Frank Reichenthal. Collection of S. Rosenfeld, Israel

35. "Sabbath Candles," Frank Reichenthal. Private collection, Toronto

THE OLD-NEW SYNAGOGUE IN PRAGUE: ITS ARCHITECTURAL HISTORY

by Zdenka Münzer

In the 9th century — as we know from literature — commercial routes led from France to Russia via Prague. Caravans of Jewish tradesmen traveling along these roads were establishing halts and settlements that later developed into religious communities — for example, in Regensburg, in Mainz, and in Prague.

A more distinct picture of Prague emerged only during restoration work on the Pinkas Synagogue. Potsherds revealed that building was in progress at the synagogue's site as early as the 9th century and continued up to the 11th century. That area, in fact, represents one of the oldest settled parts of Prague. Hana Volavková elaborates on the extent and exact location of this most ancient district of Prague and concludes that two Jewish settlements existed, both originating between the 9th and the 11th centuries. Jews coming from the East founded the older of them around the Old School, and Jews coming from the West settled around the Pinkas Synagogue. The two communities were surrounded by groups of indigenous inhabitants, flocking close to the churches of the Holy Spirit, St. Gastulus, St. Clement, and St. Peter. Directly between the two Jewish colonies and along the road connecting them, foreign — mostly German — traders had settled.

During that earliest period Jewish newcomers were allowed to buy land freely and to settle anywhere on uninhabited tracts. Christian traders from the West settled on the western outskirts of a community that was growing in the vicinity of St. Valentine and St. Peter.

Jewish newcomers from the West originally established themselves at the western boundaries of this Christian community, in the

36. Postage stamp issued in Prague in 1968, commemorating the 700-year-old Old-New Synagogue of Prague

neighborhood of the church of St. Valentine. By the 13th century, however, their numbers had grown so considerably that they also populated a large area toward the east; yet no compact community developed, for the western and eastern parts were divided by a Christian settlement located in the area of the present Old Jewish Cemetery.

This anomaly is explained by the fact that in 1215 an ordinance of the Lateran Council deprived the Jews of equality as citizens, and thereby of the right to buy land freely and to build houses. After that Jews were permitted to buy only such property as was offered to them. Also at that time the international trade route shifted somewhat farther away from the often-inundated banks of the Vltava River, toward today's Old Town Square. Accordingly, the Jews were "offered" depreciated lots of diminishing value and importance.

It was Přemysl Otakar II who realized the financial and economic assets which a prospering Jewish community contributed to the land. He invited Jews to come there and granted them greater advantages than they enjoyed elsewhere in Europe.

The two segments of the Jewish settlement became united, and the equality denied them through the decrees of the Lateran Council was reestablished. But alas only temporarily, for after Přemysl Otakar II's death the validity of these decrees was reasserted, and once again Jews were forbidden to acquire real estate. Only rarely was permission granted them to build synagogues, and then only according to methods determined by the Royal Exchequer.

The relationship at that time of Jews to the land where they had lived as equal citizens — even if only temporarily — found clear expression in the writings of Abraham Chládek, dubbed "the Ancient of Bohemia," and of Rabbi Yitzhak. In the works of both scholars we find Slavic — and even Czech — annotations instead of Hebrew words, and also phrases like "as one says in the language of our kingdom," or "as we say..."

Roman Jakobson deduces from these statements that in those days the Jews of Prague communicated in Czech. It probably applied more to Jews hailing from the East; the Jews who came from the West distinguished themselves and their era in Prague's annals in another sphere — they constructed the Old-New Synagogue.

In contemplating the seemingly plain, small building, only a fraction of the innumerable visitors — visitors coming from all over the world — realize that the Old-New Synagogue is among the most ancient jewels of early Gothic style in Europe, around which a sizable literature has already accumulated.

Among the first to write about the synagogue was J. S. Schaller, the first Czech topographer of the 18th century. He used as a point of departure an inscription found on the tombstone of Sarah, wife of Joseph, at the Old Jewish Cemetery in Prague; this tombstone is said to have been erected in 606 C.E., which proves that Jews not only lived in Prague prior to the advent of the Slavs in Bohemia but even had their own synagogue.

J. M. Schotky, a somewhat more recent German topographer (1794–1849), is the author of a largely uncritical and also unreliable compilation. He doubts Schaller's information; yet he cannot be taken to task for putting the origins of the Old-New Synagogue between 1150 and 1200 or for defining it as a Gothic structure with still-detectable Byzantine influences. No systematic historiography expatiating on the development of artistic creation existed at the time. What were available were, at best, enumerations and descriptions of individual works whose mutual correlation and style analysis remained unheeded.

In 1855 a book was published in Prague — and subsequently widely read — written jointly by D. J. Poděbrad, custodian of the Old Jewish Cemetery, and B. Forges, a Jewish teacher. The authors devote great love and reverence to the history of Prague's ghetto, but are completely lacking in criticism. They put the origin of the Old-New Synagogue at 502 C.E., on the strength of an erroneously interpreted and later discarded line of poetry. They give as the reason for calling the synagogue "Old-New" its reconstruction following a conflagration occurring soon after 1142, or around 1316.

Only in the 19th century did the history of art — by then an independent discipline with a meticulously defined goal, though it has been considerably transformed today — permit the tackling of the synagogue with the appropriate groundwork at hand. No longer could individual works of art be considered isolated phenomena devoid of interrelations with external and internal cultural factors. Like other branches of science — spiritual and natural — the history of art strives to fathom the principle of its evolution and to discern in a single work of art the specific links forming the chain of development.

At that juncture K. Schnaase and F. Kügler, both Germans, attempted a systematic exposition of the unfolding of various styles on the basis of cultural and historical considerations. With this development history of art began to assume valid scientific foundations. The two authors concur in placing the origin of the Old-New Synagogue in the 13th century, notwithstanding Schnaase's concession that the Jewish builders were highly conservative and that Christian architects chose unusually austere forms — probably out of cnnsideration — even at a later date. The details, as well as the salient character of the structure, do not admit of a more recent starting date than the close of the 13th century.

B. Grueber, a German architect and professor who taught at the German Technical University in Prague (1844–1874), had a thorough knowledge of early Bohemian Gothic structures and was well equipped to draw comparisons. He diverges only slightly from Schnaase; and Kügler by putting the origin of the Old-New Synagogue early in the second half of the 13th century.

J. Brániš, one of the first Czech art historians, opted for a somewhat earlier period, i.e., the second quarter of the 13th century. More recently V. Birnbaum, in comparing the synagogue with the buildings of the convent of the Blessed Agnes, puts its inception at the time of Václav I (reigned 1230–1253). But E. Poche assigns it to the subsequent period, i.e., the reign of Přemysl Otakar II (1253–1278).

In explaining hall churches with two naves, A. Grotte takes as his example the Romanesque synagogue in Worms, which he dates 1034; evolution leads from that to the Gothic synagogue in Regensburg. But this evolution — interrupted by pogroms and the oppression of Jews during the Crusades — was resumed only two hundred years later in Prague. Grotte is inclined to agree with Grueber's dating, notably because of the propitious living condition of Jews in Bohemia during the reign of Přemysl Otakar II. According to Grotte, the earlier constructions in Worms and Regensburg served as models for the synagogue in Prague.

Toward the close of the past century, the German art historian J. Neuwirth went to teach at the University of Prague. He had studied the history of Czech art for many years. Based on intelligence from Czech historiographers who, in the first half of the 14th century, speak only of "the synagogue" without differentiating between an old and a new synagogue, Neuwirth deduces that at that time only one single synagogue had ever existed in Prague. Only following the fire in the Jewish city in 1338 was there erected a new synagogue, and needs dictated completion by 1350, for in that year the Jews were prohibited to construct synagogues. A 1342 entry in Prague's archives mentions a house that was "*contra novum synagogam Judaeorum*."

In his elegy describing the horrors of the 1389 pogrom Abigdor Karo speaks of people penetrating "into the old and the new synagogue." Neuwirth understands the old synagogue to be the *Altschul* (so called in German) and the new one to be today's Old-New Synagogue, for during restoration work on the latter, an inscription was found both at the eastern and at the western walls containing the date 5141, which is 1381 C.E.

Since the present Old-New Synagogue was known as the "new one" in the reign of John of Luxembourg — to differentiate it from an undoubtedly more ancient "old" synagogue — Karo's designation becomes intelligible: the new synagogue was erected in King John's time, which also explains its purely Gothic character. Since the Jews of Prague entertained lively intercourse with the Jews of Regensburg, Neuwirth infers structual influences from there.

K. Guth takes exception to Neuwirth's opinion; he judges the archival annotation of 1342 to be nothing more than an entry meaning something like "in this year the synagogue had already been built and was called 'the new' because it was more recent than the so-called old synagogue." The designation "old-new" allegedly refers rather to the circumstance of the synagogue's terrain. As to the particulars of style, Guth finds parallels in the church of Santa Barbara of the convent of the Blessed Agnes, "where an equally naturalistic elaboration of foliage can be observed as well as an identical technique..." Accordingly, Guth fixes the inception of the synagogue in the second half of the 13th century.

However, he was unable to convince Neuwirth, whose dating was also accepted by R. Krautheimer. Indeed, Krautheimer's work is the very first comprehensive treatment of synagogal architecture. He explains the name "old-new" as follows: originally there existed an old synagogue somewhere in Prague; a new synagogue was then built somewhere else in the city and this one came to be known as "Altneuschule" — but only centuries later, after a third, still newer synagogue, "the new Neuschule" (new New School), was constructed. This explanation is the most plausible of all so far offered.

Nonetheless, Krautheimer clearly lacked the necessary erudition in Czech medieval art and its evolution to determine the dates of Prague's Old-New Synagogue. Seeking parallels to the plastic ornamentation of the portal and the aron, he found them in German structures of the 13th century, in Marburg and Strasbourg, and on the synagogue in Miltenberg. The foliage of the consoles and that of the capitals in Prague's Old-New Synagogue seem to Krautheimer to be rather schematic; the naturalistic forms from which Gothic foliage issued are forgotten. Here, Krautheimer alleges, we have the foliage of the 13th century, such as we encounter in the apsis of the *Barfüsserkirche* (the Church of the Barefooted) in Erfurt, dating from 1316. Krautheimer also assigns the use of octagonal piers to the same period. Older forms found in the synagogue which point to the middle of the 13th century are not conclusive — to determine a date the most recent forms are decisive, and here they point indisputably to the first quarter of the 14th century. This would mean that the Old-New Synagogue was started after the fire in 1316.

Oscar Schürer mentions the synagogue only very briefly. He assigns it to the middle of the 14th century, quite undisturbed by the affinity of its architectural forms with early Gothic, since the spatial dimensions of the synagogue correspond to other Prague structures of the 14th century — for example, to that of the Týn Church, which was written about before the synagogue. The name "Old-New" — so Schürer claims — is the result of a decree providing that the new synagogue had to be erected on the same spot as the old one. However, the pertinent decree was never found.

Most recent literature assigns the origins of the Old-New Synagogue to the 13th century, give or take a few years. E. Poche speaks of "some time around 1270" and Hana Volavková cites the years 1270-1290.

DESCRIPTION OF THE SYNAGOGUE

The Old-New Synagogue consists of a main building which is freestanding and a few adjacent, more recent annexes. The main structure is a rectangle, 15 meters (approximately 50 feet) long, and 9 meters (approximately 27 feet) wide, built of rough stone, originally whitewashed. The longer walls are each supported by two buttresses, the shorter walls each by one. On the northern side these buttresses are of brick. All are relatively low and crowned by half-pitched roofs.

The smooth walls are pierced by narrow, deep-set, bevel-cut, pointed windows innocent of all tracery. On both the western and the eastern side high brick gables of triangular shape are soaring, and surmount the windows. The western gable is articulated by eight concave cells, ascending perpendicularly; its circumference is adorned by battlements. The triangular area of the eastern gable is divided by five blind arcades. These gables, originating around 1500, were partially changed in the course of the restoration work that was done in the years 1921–1927, for a different material was then used.

The intentionally plain and inconspicuous exterior of the structure contrasts with the lavishly decorated interior. A splendidly articulated entrance in the western part of the south wall leads to the synagogue. The jambs are articulated by simple early Gothic moldings, running without interruption all the way up to the apex. A three-quarter pilaster placed on a platelike base, and ending in an elongated chalice-shaped capital, forms the outward edge of the portal. The exterior members of the archivolte is encrusted with finely chiseled beads.

The interior of the synagogue is divided into two naves by two octagonal piers placed parallel to the long axis, resting on upward sloping, tapering octagonal pediments, 2 1/2 feet (approximately 75 cm) high. From these piers — in fact from eight consoles fastened to them — there lead both groins to half-round wall pilasters and also ribs of identical profiles as the groins; they are supported by wall corbels, thus giving rise to a quinquepartite rib vault. The ribs converge in a central keystone. The wall pilasters are half-round and reach up to the cnrdon frieze, running at about one-third of the structure's height.

Both the northern and the southern wall are pierced in each vault-bay by two pointed windows with plain sloping jambs, the western wall by only one. In the eastern wall the windows are round and end in segments dating from the 17th century.

It remains to mention the decor of the individual parts. The most elaborate entrance, the southern, has jambs richly articulated by moldings. On each side a three-quarter pilaster stands on its own base and has its own chalicelike capital plastically ornamented with grape leaves. All consoles and corbels of the synagogue are decorated with foliage. On the consoles, the foliage is articulated only negligibly: grape and oak leaves are arranged in two, sometimes three, successive alternating tiers that seldom overlap or are superimposed. The consoles on the two piers resemble one another closely — both in form and in decoration — and the wall corbels always support the fifth rib of the vault cell.

Corner pilaster strips — four of them — support elongated chalice capitals; the pilaster strips in the southeast corner and the capital of the northeast pilaster have two tiers of grape leaves, one above the other, for decoration; the pilaster capital of the southwest corner is covered by minute oak leaves on stalks bearing interspersed acorns. The last pilaster capital in the northwest corner supports trefoiled, deeply undercut leaves. The pilasters supporting vault ribs also have chalicelike capitals decorated with somewhat livelier and more variegated foliage.

The decorative elements mentioned here should suffice for a comparative and timely analysis of the structure. Minute detail would only encumber the present study needlessly.

Of the original interior equipment, all that remains are plain stone benches, now wood-clad, which stretch along the north and south walls, and parts of the Holy Ark on the eastern wall. This aron or Torah shrine, is aedicula-shaped, that is, it has a triangular gable supported by a plinth and by two columns. It is reached by five stone steps. The space between the columns holds the shrine for the scrolls and is enclosed today by decoratively wrought bronze doors dating from the 19th century. The aron's architecture is in the Renaissance style of the 16th century, when the original ark seems to have been reconstructed. The two sandstone parapets alongside the steps — on whose right-hand side stands a stone pulpit for the reader — are presumably in the original location. Their ends are formed on both sides by supports decorated with tracery in relief.

Two half-columns that form the aedicula proper, and whose shafts are adorned with grapes and acanthus leaves in relief, are placed on pediments forming consoles in the shape of volutes.

The tympanon of the Holy Ark, now the summit of the aron, derives indubitably from the original structure. Its edges feature oak leaves with a flower ball, and the tympanon itself is adorned with grape leaves and grapes growing out of a single tree trunk, similar to the tympanon of the southern entrance hall.

Of other equipment in the synagogue there remains the interesting and artistically valuable almenar, i.e., a platform occupying the entire space between the two piers; it carries a high, wrought-iron grille of the early Renaissance.

The building became surrounded by recesses and annexes, added at various times for different purposes. They are, in fact, narrow, low passages reaching merely to the bottom of the windows and are pierced only by doors or windows and covered by pent roofs. The oldest of the corridors of the synagogue proper is about 4 meters (5 yards) wide and runs along the southern wall; the original entrance was on the north side of the part which overlapped the main building in a westerly direction. The two south entrances are more recent. Next to these, there used to be an entrance at the eastern end; now it is transformed into a window. The steps, however, that once led to that entrance still exist. The pointed tunnel-vault of the passage rests on crude grates fortified by pyramidlike consoles, two of which lean on the southern wall of the main structure and the remaining two on the supporting piers. At first there was an oculus in the western wall; the pointed window that provides light for the hallway today was pierced only in the 16th century. At the eastern wall of the corridor a lectern for the reader is found below the last step. To the right stretches a plain stone bench; to the left, there is a sort of free-standing ark perching on a high socle, topped on each side by tympanons of Renaissance disposition and profiles, with metopes in the corners. Closer to the entrance to the synagogue proper a second, similar annex has been built, having its own ceiling and a window with Renaissance sandstone jambs; it is decorated with rather powerful but primitively profiled volutes.

The purpose of these annexes eluded all knowledge until the explanation was found in an archival annotation of the Ministry of Interior: at the beginning of the 18th century the alcoves or corridors were treasuries in which the taxes imposed upon the Jewish city were deposited.

In that part of the corridor with the pulpit for the reader, just below the steps and the benches, morning services were apparently observed for those inhabitants of the Jewish city who had to leave early in the day to attend to their occupations and thus could not take part in the services proper.

This corridor, closest in style to that of the main structure — as testified to by architectural details — was built shortly following the completion of the chief structure: the massive character and poor articulation of the entire hallway betokens the fact. In effect, the corridor was the entrance hall to the synagogue and may have served other purposes as well.

Considerably later a narrow passage was added to the synagogue's western side; it is vaulted by two cross-rib bays, between each of which there is another bay featuring a tunnel vault with lunetts, situated next to the buttress of the main structure. In each of these vaulted bays is a square window of varying width, and beneath each window is a segmented niche. Since this room is connected with the synagogue proper by small windows that taper off sharply, it is conceivable that prior to the erection of the new, northern annexe this passage served as the women's section. On the western exterior wall and above the last window, a Hebrew inscription says, in translation: this women's synagogue was newly erected from scratch in 1732. Thus we have the annex accurately dated.

The origins of the northern annex of the synagogue — the present women's section — belong to a yet later period. This annex is a long room about 3 meters (10 feet) wide, stretching along the northern wall of the main building, which it exceeds in the west by approximately 2 meters (6 feet) and in the east by approximately 1½ meters (4 feet). This room is roofed by a tunnel vault, and the windows are surmounted by lunettes. The gently sloping pent roof reaches just below the jambs of the windows in the main structure. Again, this women's section is connected with the main synagogue by narrow windows whose width varies here between 56 and 96 cm (between 2 and 3 feet), whereas in the men's section the windows measure between 121 and 135 cm (7 and 8 feet). The windows are about 1 meter (3 feet) above ground so that the women in their room — admittedly only those sitting close to the windows — may follow the services in the men's section.

Prior to the erection of this structure there was nothing at the northern side, for even during restoration work no trace of any previous construction was unearthed. Hence we must presume that the annex of the western side served as the original women's section and was later enlarged or replaced by the northern annex, whose entire character points to its having been conceived only in the second half of the 18th century.

THE OLD-NEW SYNAGOGUE AND ITS RELATION TO THE DEVELOPMENT OF ARCHITECTURE IN BOHEMIA

Evidently the architectural form of the Old-New Synagogue diverges from the common type of Gothic structures in Bohemia. Thus the question arises as to what served as the model for a building having two equally high aisles.

The Jews living in the Diaspora have not evolved for their synagogues any specific architectural form to meet every requirement. The synagogue as such originated when the sacrifice in the Temple — up to then the culmination of religious rite — was abolished. The Temple of Jerusalem could not have differed greatly from that seat of God, the Temple of antiquity, to which only the high priest had access, the populace being allowed to enter only the precincts or the courtyard where the sacrifice was offered at the altar. With the elimination of that rite the Temple disappeared, and the synagogue took its place as a locality where Jews gathered, prayed, and listened to the Scriptures and, mainly, learned to know them. Even in Jesus' time a theological school was attached to every synagogue. This gave purpose and was the reason for an elevated position for the interpreter of the Bible — in order that he might be seen and heard by all participants; it also required a shrine in which the scrolls would be deposited. This position with its purpose demanded no specific architectural form: any room sufficed in whose center a raised dais could be erected and a cabinet placed at the wall to house the Scrolls. Krautheimer's assumption — that initially community buildings or spacious and appropriate rooms within the community, where all its members could congregate, were thus used — surely is not far from the truth.

But later, Jews in communities where the non-Jewish population was in the majority felt the necessity of having their own buildings. The oldest synagogues on Delos, dating from the 2nd century B.C.E., and those of late antiquity excavated in Galilee all show a rectangular room with columns on three sides, with the southern side featuring several entrances. Some of these synagogues have tribunes. The ancient columnated hall was plainly the model for these structures, the chief difference being that the row of columns runs only on three sides. In the single instance of the synagogue of Alexandria, razed in 116 C.E., we know that two rows of columns ran along all four walls; in the center of that synagogue was the almemar. Even as these synagogues of the late antiquity were like basilicas both in form and decoration, they resembled them in purpose as well: they were public buildings in which the most diverse community matters were attended to. Their religious objective is revealed in the 2nd and 3rd centuries C.E. by a consistent orientation toward Jerusalem: the entrance front always faces east. In these synagogues the aron was movable and could be carried from place to place.

In the 4th century C.E. the Talmud prohibited eating, drinking, sleeping, and making business deals on the premises, thereby emphasizing the synagogue's religious destiny. About 500 C.E. the forms of the Jewish cult became stabilized, and they have later been merely enriched by new prayers and songs. Maimonides, in the 12th century, was the chief opponent of any further individual change in the religious service, and thus the development was terminated at the outset of the 13th century. The aron got its firm place next to the eastern wall, pointing toward Jerusalem. Still, it remains partly eclipsed by the almemar, where the Scriptures are read and interpreted. The almemar remains the center of gravity and focal point of the entire space. Even today, in the more northerly parts of Europe, mainly in Germany, Poland, and Bohemia where Jews have settled, the synagogue is not primarily a house of prayer but first and foremost a place for congregating, an auditorium and a school — from which the designation "Schul" stems (German-Yiddish for school). The synagogue is also the place where Jews are judged, where decisions and ordinances of the community and of the state are handed down to them, and where they negotiate covenants among themselves.

No specific precepts exist even today on how a synagogue should be constructed. Each community with at least ten adult males should establish a house of prayer; often it is located in some spacious room of a private dwelling where the ark for the Scrolls and a small rostrum for the reader have been placed. If the community decides to build its own synagogue, it must be careful to have the aron face east. Also, the structure should be higher than the surrounding houses and the floor should be below street level — for the word of God sounds from the nether depth. These last two regulations have been circumvented of old: if the terrain does not permit of attaining the required height, a mast reaching higher than the neighboring houses is affixed to the rooftop. If for any reason the floor level cannot be lowered either the area in front of the aron is hollowed out or the entrance is arranged so as to have several steps leading upward, in order to oblige people to descend a few steps before entering the house of prayer.

As in antiquity, the Jews of the Middle Ages sought the architectural models for their synagogues in their environment. Selection was limited in medieval times. A Christian church could not be contemplated as a model for two reasons: (a) the asacral purposes of the synagogue and the more-or-less asacral cult demanded a different formation for the space; (b) more important, the sacral Christian space could not be emulated, for both religious and psychological reasons. Accordingly, the choice had to fall on representative profane structures — the city halls, palace halls, and chapter houses of convents and monasteries, the refectories and dormitories of which were either simple square rooms or, later, a space divided in the center by one single column or pillar. From the 12th to the 16th centuries it was a space divided by two central supports in two aisles. Of the medieval synagogues still in existence the one in Speyer, dating from the close of the 11th century, has the form of a plain hall with a truncated apsis in the east and a flat ceiling. In the years 1145 to 1241 the first synagogue in Frankfurt was built. The last known synagogue of this type, in use up to the 17th century, is that in Rufach, erected around 1300. The second type, a square construction supported by one central pillar, was applied only in the women's synagogue in Worms, in 1213. Otherwise, all known medieval synagogues and notably the three oldest — the one in Worms, dating from the end of the 12th century, that in Regensburg of the first half of the 13th century, and the only truly preserved synagogue in Prague of the second half of the 13th century — each has two aisles.

The two-aisled space is a form mentioned nowhere within the scope of European history of art up to the 12th century. Now we begin to encounter it frequently: the chapter houses, the refectories and the dormitories of monasteries, the double-aisled parts of cloisters (Walkenried), the city halls and castle halls in Germany and France — all feature this arrangement almost exclusively. Enlart cites a whole array of two-aisled chapter houses divided by pillars in 12th-century France — Fontfroid, Mortemer, Flarau, Vaucelles,

Vézelay — and for good measure adds a number of other structures divided by columns. Krautheimer names the following asacral buildings in Germany: prior to 1160, the refectory in Klosterode; in the second half of the 12th century, the refectory of the Michelstein monastery; around 1166, the ground floor of Castle Dankwarderode and, somewhat later, Goslar. Wartburg, Walkenried, and Maulbronn date from the 13th century. Sacral constructions of similar disposition are of later date and they involve mostly smaller chapels of lesser consequence and chapels in castles. Churches of mendicant religious orders adopted this plan in the 14th century.

Shortage of space necessitates our skipping a general outline of medieval architecture in Bohemia and directing attention to the evolution of two-aisled spaces, to which the Old-New Synagogue also belongs. Not many of them from the time of early Gothic style are preserved in Bohemia. The first such space known is the Romanesque crypt in Louka, Moravia, which is vaulted onto a central pillar; the monastery there was founded in 1190. The second is the chapter house in Vyšší Brod. The chapter houses of Osek and Tišnov originated after 1221, and the chapter house of Zlatá Koruna was built later than 1263 — and all three are divided by two piers into two aisles. Probably only the sacristy of the baroque-adapted monastery-churches of St. Thomas, on the Malá Strana in Prague, and that of St. James in the Old Town there, both vaulted onto the central pillar, stem from the beginning of the 14th century. The early Gothic disposition of space in castle halls that were not preserved has been insufficiently explored and studied as yet. It seems, however, that the hall in Zvíkov was also two-aisled. Of course, the type of synagogue at that time was not derived solely from these Czech two-aisled constructions, particularly since there was considerable intercourse with other countries at that juncture. Buildings that were akin should be mentioned once more, notably those in neighboring Germany — but again this would lead too far afield.

Anyone who enters the Old-New Synagogue will be stunned by two peculiar octagonal piers dividing the synagogue's space into two aisles. Krautheimer finds the first octagonal piers in Germany to derive from the 14th century only — they are those of Erfurt, dated 1316. Scanning Czech structures we find octagonal piers of earlier origin, for example those on the exterior galleries and below the raised gallery in the chapel of the Písek and Zvíkov castles, in the chapter house of the Cistercian Convent in Tišnov, and in the crypt of the church in Třebíč. All these constructions date from the 13th century. Octagonal piers are, moreover, found in the monastery church in Louka, and they date from the Romanesque period. In the 14th century, octagonal piers are rare on the whole, but in the 15th and 16th centuries they appear very frequently, with ribs issuing directly from them to extend without interruption up to the summit of the vault — as in Louny and in the City Hall in Tábor. Yet to maintain that they did not occur in Germany prior to the first third of the 14th century is erroneous. The crypt below the St. George choir of the Bamberg Cathedral, which Dehio puts in the first third of the 13th century, and the vault of the chapter house and the dormitory of the early Gothic Heiligenkreuz Monastery in Austria, too, rest on octagonal piers. An analogy to the unembellished, half-round, and rather sturdy pilaster strips supporting relatively small capitals, from which issue all ribs of the vault as well as of the wall arches, is found only in the St. Francis Chapel of the Blessed Agnes Convent in Prague. Pilaster strips of the 14th century — in contrast to early Gothic ones — are very slim, may often be clustered, and carry comparatively far larger capitals. Such are found in the Saint Mary church Na Slupi, in Prague.

Attention should be paid also to the eggform consoles embellished by the floral decorations described above, as well as to consoles adorned by only three slightly concave, indented, square prisms, which broaden as they ascend. In form and decor they greatly remind one of the consoles in the Old-New Synagogue; we find them only in the chapter house and the chapel of the Guardian Angel Church in Zlatá Koruna. In that chapel we also find a small portal whose soffit profiles parallel the soffits of the Old-New Synagogue's portal. The outer member, formed by a three-quarter pilaster, rests on its own base and ends in its own capital, which is plastically ornamented. In turn, these two are closely related to the small portal leading to the sacristy in Vyšší Brod. This one and the portal in Zlatá Koruna are located in the parts constructed during the reign of Přemysl Otakar II. The cornice encircling the entire synagogue at one third of its height is by no means unique. Indeed, we find it in every synagogue, for its purpose is to hold the lighting fixtures, and its form is adapted to that end.

The peculiar form of ribs — analogous to the ribs in the Old-New Synagogue — we find again in constructions originating in the reigns of Václav I (1230–1253) and his successor, Přemysl Otakar II (1253–1278).

The distinct details to which we have sought analogies from articulations of the wall or possibly of the bay of the vault. Looking closely at the Old-New Synagogue's wall we notice immediately that it cannot be compared to the 14th century structures we have described. The large surfaces of the walls are but scantily articulated by plain, half-rounded pilasters and by a cornice running all around the synagogue; beneath it the walls remain innocent of any articulation whatever. The massive character of the walls is not at all nullified by the low, narrow windows with simple, sloping jambs. These walls are reminiscent mostly of the convent buildings of the Blessed Agnes in Prague. A similarity can be found also in the quinquepartite vault bays articulated by wedge-profiled groins and ribs. Indubitably, the quinquepartite vault represents a reduced form of the very early sexpartite vault, for which we have no analogy in Bohemia. Closest to such vault, both chronologically and geographically, are the early Gothic quinquepartite-vaulted lateral aisles of the Magdeburg Cathedral.

In reviewing structures with recognizable analogies to some of the specific architectural details of the Old-New Synagogue, we find that they belong — without exception — to the time of Václav I or to the early part of Přemysl Otakar II's reign. It is hardly possible for a structure systematically applying every early Gothic element, and assigned to the sixties of the 13th century, at the latest, to have been built as much as a half-century later — or even later still, according to some scholars. The entire space created by the given elements matches the period indicated: everywhere we see a great attempt to give the building a constructive framework, everywhere we sense the zeal to liberate from the substance the hidden, latent forces. But this zeal must still wrestle with the Romanesque tradition of molding space, in which substance was not negated but rather subordinated to a higher organic and rhythmical order.

Our dating is also based upon the character of the Old-New Synagogue's entrance hall. Before us stretches a long, rectangular passage with a pointed tunnel vault resting on strong, sloping arches; there is no Gothic rib vault, which at that period was already to be found on every structure of consequence. On the building proper we could convince ourselves that this hall was a subsequent annex. Owing to the strong influence of Romanesque tradition, it could not possibly have been devised later than in the second half of the 13th century, a fact leading of necessity to the conclusion that the synagogue proper can be but little later.

Another criterion for dating the Old-New Synagogue is its sculptural decoration. The 13th century saw a mighty efflorescence of the plastic arts. The sculptor, until then creating by merely giving objects he had seen the form of ornament, turned his attention to nature and its living, actual forms; he derived enchantment from them and began to represent them with the zest of visual experience. That this evolution traveled the customary road from France via Germany to Bohemia means that it took what was the self-evident avenue for our art at that time.

In Prague's church of Santa Barbara and in other parts of the Blessed Agnes Convent we encounter almost every element of plastic decoration noted subsequently in the Old-New Synagogue: keystones and capitals, as well as consoles, featuring rich floral decoration. The finely worked, vivid foliage nevertheless discloses that here we have the very outset of the development: the stonecutter obviously had seen a lot, but, thus far had worked independently only little. He was trying everything conducive to close communication with nature, yet many a time he slipped back into Romanesque ornamentation and schematism and reverted to the sketchy flatness of the period.

The synagogue's plastic decorations seem to have been grievously damaged and later replaced during its restoration in the 19th century, so that today we should speak of *copies* of the original decor. Either the leaves are cut off or whole capitals have been newly made, modeled after the old fragments. Only in the four corners of the synagogue, below the cordon ledge, did the consoles retain — almost — their erstwhile likeness; but, alas, they suffered great damage. Despite that, we can differentiate two trends vying for primacy. The stonecutter who cut several of the capitals, keystones, and — notably — the decorations of the tympanon and tabernacle is already and completely a Gothic artist. He displays a fine sense of reality and nature and has created some vibrantly plastic foliage, winding slender stalks around the core of the corbels. In decorating a keystone or a tympanon, he has separated the decor from the flat surface so as to leave the latter as a ground on top of which the new pierced, plastic surface discloses merely fractions of the base. The work differs from that of a second stonecutter whose decoration covers the surface completely, in the true sense of the word. The first stonecutter, then, had forgotten Romanesque schematism and had become wholly permeated by Gothic experience.

Yes, another stonecutter had been at work in the synagogue. The consoles of both piers and a number of consoles of the wall pilasters at the south and west walls were created by him. This presumed second stonecutter — of course, we cannot be quite certain of our facts in either this or the preceding instance, and so do not know whether there might have been only one artist who was having a hard time ridding himself of Romanesque schematism — this presumed second stonecutter repeatedly simply placed flat, lifeless, elongated, and barely articulated leaves around the core of the capital. (Note the second wall pilaster from the west at the south wall.) On two other capitals, he arranged two tiers of similar small leaves, one above the other — for example, in the middle wall pilaster at the south side. Finally, he managed somewhat more amply articulated leaves that faced one another, so that their lobes intermingle and even intersect. This is found on several consoles on piers and others supporting the fifth vault rib. Yet nowhere did he detach the decoration from the surface plane of the base, whether it was formed by the core of a capital, of a console, or of a keystone. Nowhere do his leaves live or move, nowhere do they thrust out from the surface; the artist's chisel knew no depth. Conversely, the more advanced stonecutter sees no schema, not even vestiges of rigid plans — he sees real, live, growing plants, winding and climbing, curling around stalks, filling out the areas in keystones and capitals, and he lets them protrude, regardless of whether the core may be registered as the constructive element or disappears beneath the plants.

The plastic decoration of the less-progressive stonecutter, with his marked bent for schematic work, is reminiscent of the older parts of the Blessed Agnes Convent, and notably of its St. Francis Church, as well as of the decoration found in the regrettably undated apsis of the diocese church in Nymburk and of the north wing of the transept at the Strahov Monastery; on occasion we are even reminded of the Romanesque portal at the church in Vince.

Searching for analogies to the work executed by the more-advanced stonecutter we must go to the Santa Barbara Chapel of the Blessed Agnes Convent and, most importantly, out of Prague to Vyšší Brod; here, on the small portal leading from the transept of the cathedral to the sacristy, a tympanon, which is filled out vibrantly by plant decoration that emulates nature by jutting out plastically from the relief, shows some truly fine stone carving. From among woolly clouds the hand of the Lord emerges, which is equally naturalistically conceived and elaborated. Placing this tympanon next to that of the Old-New Synagogue we see that neither the dates of the works' inception nor the biographical dates of the artists could have been too far apart. The only difference is that in the tympanon of the synagogue, the four rods, growing symmetrically out of one single vine stem overgrown by luxuriant leaves and grapes, are linked together by a symbolic flame and are, if possible, still more finely worked, still more meticulously observed than in Vyšší Brod, and disclose a yet greater delight in and love for the greatest artist extant: nature.

The Vyšši Brod Monastery is dated accurately. It was founded in 1259 by Peter Vok, Master of Rožmberk, who, upon his death in 1262, was buried there. At that time, the apsis of the church with its side chapels, the hereto attached part of the transept, and the small portal had been completed. Construction of the other parts of the church continued in the sixties of the 15th century. Here belongs also the small portal of the aforementioned chapel of the Guardian Angels in the nearby convent of Zlatá Koruna, probably built prior to 1263, which in style is like the Vyšší Brod structures. There we find a tympanon decorated identically with that of the aron in the Old-New Synagogue. The realistic foliage — ivy, in this case — forms an openwork area jutting forth from the base. The entire character of this portal is related to the one of the Old-New Synagogue and to that in Vyšší Brod as well.

The plastic decor of each architectural part of the synagogue reaffirms what we found when we compared the architecture proper: namely, that the synagogue does correspond in style, conception, and execution with the level of development achieved by plastic vegetative decorating in Bohemia during Přemysl Otakar II's time. Consequently, it is not warranted to assign the construction of the Old-New Synagogue to a different period. It manifestly originated in the sixties of the 13th century and most likely just in the middle of that decade.

Our method of dating, derived solely from artistic elements and their historic evolution, is firmly compatible, nonetheless, with both history and political circumstances. Every synagogue erected within the time and territory of the Diaspora reveals to us that Jews were building their temples only in periods when oppression and persecution were at a somewhat lower ebb, when anxiety and fear for bare life could be relegated to the background. This, of course, is quite logical. History teaches that the reign of Přemysl Otakar II was just such a happy period for the Jews of Prague, and not alone for them but for Jews settled everywhere in Bohemia; the synagogue in Cheb — now demolished — was also built at the time. Cheb was then under the jurisdiction of the king of Bohemia.

The assurance at that time of statutory protection from other inhabitants for Jews in the Czech lands was based upon the Privilege promulgated in the German Empire by Frederick II in 1244. A similar Patent of Přemysl Otakar II followed in Bohemia in 1254. It determined precisely the relationship of Jews and Christians in terms of both business and social life. The Patent protected Jewish cemeteries and schools. Jews were exempt from city jurisdiction and subordinated directly to the king or his officials: the so-called *Judex Judaeorum* was established, according to which both civil and criminal matters were adjudicated in the synagogues. In litigations between Christians and Jews the king himself, or his highest chamberlain, would conduct the trial. In court proceedings, Jews and Christians enjoyed identical rights; sentences were meted out against transgressions perpetrated by Christians against Jews. The exemption of Jews from city jurisdiction gave them the impetus to organize their own community. Commercial and monetary matters were also arranged very advantageously for the Jews. All in all, the Patent provided far-reaching freedoms and great earning possibilities for the Jews, and this brought about an eminent flowering of the Jewish community and most likely was the incentive for erecting the costly synagogue.

WHY THE NAME "OLD-NEW"?

It remains to try to explain the name of the synagogue. Conjectures expressed in literature allege that the name is not a translation of the German *altneu* but rather of the Hebrew *Al tenai*, which means "on condition" or temporarily. The explanation for this is that the Jews, trusting in their eventual return to Palestine, wanted to emphasize that this synagogue was a hallowed place only until the Temple of Jerusalem was rebuilt in the newly regained homeland. But if this is the true explanation, then every synagogue erected in the Diaspora should have been named thus. Moreover, that designation would have been written differently from the way it actually was written. It is therefore more plausible to surmise the existence in Prague of an old synagogue, and a second *schul*, or school, built entire centuries later, which was called "new." When still later a third synagogue came into being, the second synagogue got its name "old-new" to differentiate it from the third or newest.

The question cannot be resolved by pure conjecture. An attempt has to be made to ascertain whether historic accounts can elucidate where the "old synagogue" had been and when the "new" synagogue had acquired the name "old-new"; closely allied to that is the question of which was the third — the latest — synagogue, and when it was built.

To assume that the Old-New Synagogue as we know it today is a reconstruction of a yet-older synagogue once standing on the same spot is highly controversial. True, Kosmas tells us of a synagogue existing in Prague in 1124 and also of the burning down of a synagogue there in 1142 — but how do we know that that synagogue was in the Jewish city at all? We might prove that the Old-New Synagogue in its present aspect originated in the initial period of Přemysl Otakar II's reign and that except for trifling changes — namely, at the gables and on occasion of repairs of ribs and of the aron — changes have taken place since. That the "old" synagogue had stood there and that the scene of the fire was left to lie fallow for more than a hundred years seems very doubtful. No subsequent fire or destruction of the synagogue has been reported nor any occurrence in the ghetto that might have brought about such a catastrophe. As a result we have to believe that the present-day "Old-New Synagogue" was, originally, the new one.

The first annotation concerning the old synagogue is found in an account of 1315, which tells us of houses... *versus antiquam synagogam Judaeorum sitas*... This account — quoted by Neuwirth, too — does not specify any circumstance of the synagogue. However, the name "old" does imply the existence even then of some other, newer synagogue — in contrast, that is, to the present-day "Old-New" Synagogue which had already been erected as well. According to the Selichoth of Abigdor Karo — we shall discuss it later on — the synagogue existed in 1389.

V. V. Tomek tells us of a synagogue existing in 1401; he calls it *"antiqua apud sanctum spiritum."* It is the first explicit designation of that "school" thought to have been located on the spot and in the district where the so-called Temple stands today — a district which available sources often refer to as "at the old Jewish school." We find this reference supplementing several names in the "Description of Prague's Jews, their wives, children, relatives, and retainers — devoid of the protective documents promulgated on June 8, 1545..." Similarly, we often find this term to describe the district in the *Liber Judaeorum albus* and in the *Liber contractum Antiquae Urbis Pragensis*, attending entries recording purchases and sales of houses, and in various contracts. In referring to the years 1348–1378, Tomek divides the Jewish city — which he calls either Subiudea (lower) or Jewish Quarter or Jewish Street (platea Judaeorum) or sometimes simply "in the Jews" (inter Judaeos) — into two parts which are separated from one another, and he calls the individual sections "the Old Jewish School" and "the Jewish District Proper."

Teige describes events occurring around the Old School — as the entire district had indubitably been called — as follows: "Today, after the reconstruction of 1868, no ancient vestiges remain. Consequently, it is impossible to adjudge when and where the Synagogue had been founded. It seems to have existed already during the massacre of 1389. It burnt down in 1516 and was newly vaulted by 1536. It was reportedly elongated in 1622. Then, following an Imperial Order, it was closed down in 1693 and reopened only ten years later. Subsequent to its sack in 1744, it was restored with moneys provided by the Jewish Mayor Israel Frankl Spiro in 1750, only to burn down again on May 16, 1754."

Writing about the *Old School*, D. J. Podiebrad mentions services held there until 1837, observing partially Portuguese rites. This ostensibly corroborates the tradition of an Oriental colony, whose cult contrasted with the remaining Jewish community, having existed in Prague. Local synagogal customs allegedly remained unheeded in the synagogue. Podiebrad finds substantiation for his assertion, among others, in the fact that the "Old School District" had been severed from the other part of the Jewish city by Christian houses. The arrival of Portuguese Jews is not assigned to the close of the 15th century, since, according to Abigdor Karo, the synagogue already existed in 1389, but is presumed to have occurred during the era of Hostivít (843–873), who is reported to have welcomed immigrants whose mores and customs differed from those of the indigenous population. This certainly appears to be a bold interptetation. The small community of Portuguese Jews reportedly moved on again in 1538. For the rest, Podiebrad describes the vicissitudes of the synagogue much as Teige does, except that according to an inscription from the synagogue's present-day walls which he cites, the reconstruction was undertaken in 1604 and the elongation in 1622.

František Ruth describes the Dušní Street (Street of the Holy Spirit) and speaks of a *former* Old School, said to have been erected by Jews who had come from Portugal in the 12th century. When it burned down in 1389, private Jewish dwellings were built on the site, and only later was a synagogue again constructed, one that also burned down, in 1516. Around 1605 the "old" school was rebuilt but burned down in 1754. It was completely reconstructed in 1868, after the plans of Professor Nyklas in Moorish style.

J. Prokeš writes of how the Jews had fought for this old synagogue when, in the nineties of the 17th century, the Jewish city was to have been truncated. The district first considered for destruction was the one near the Old Jewish School — surrounded as it was by Christian houses. With it, the Old School was to have been abolished as well.

On April 25, 1690, the Jewish elders, in soliciting the preservation of that synagogue, wrote that there was a wide gap between it and the Christian dwellings adjacent to the Church of the Holy Spirit. The custodians of the Old Synagogue submit ed almost simultaneously — on May 20, 1690 — a supplication to the emperor to grant permission to use the synagogue, which had been shut down the preceding February. They argued that it was the most ancient synagogue in Prague, built of stone and roofed by tiles that had been miraculously spared in the fire that had raged in 1689. The applicants asked that this old synagogue be included among the six synagogues granted to the Jews by the emperor. The Jews' struggle for the old synagogue lasted until June 1703, when it was indeed reopened and thus safeguarded from devastation, at least for a while. References to that synagogue as the oldest persisted, as even then the tradition seems to have lived on.

More ancient reports about the inception of that old synagogue were not found. The synagogue, which burnt to the ground in 1142, may have been a wooden predecessor of the old synagogue. However, this supposition cannot be substantiated at all.

From all these data we can nevertheless glean nothing quite definite about the founding of that old "school" that would enlighten us on the matter of the Old-New Synagogue. The assumption remains that the synagogue in Dušní Street was indeed that *old* synagogue.

Let us then tackle the *new* synagogue. In 1342, a report — Neuwirth quotes it, too — speaks of a house "...*sita in Subiudea contra novam Synagogam Judaeorum*..." Another report of 1363 also tells of a house "...*sitam inter Judaeis prope Novam scolam*..." Nothing more can be deduced from either report than that at the time a "school" existed and was called "new," which in no way meant that it had been erected recently. All during the 16th century a "new" school is talked of — and surely a synagogue erected in the 14th century would not have remained "new" for two or three centuries. The designation "new" expresses a stabilized, ingrained name and not the actual state or condition. That same manuscript mentions a similar annotation from 1402 "...*penes novam synagogam Judaeorum ex una*..." and one from 1404 "...*penes novam synagogam dictorum Judaeorum*..."

V. V. Tomek, referring to the years 1348–1378, speaks of the "new Jewish School" in Rabbi Street; this was inevitably the Old-New Synagogue, since it did stand in the street formerly so called. Elsewhere Tomek says: "Apart from this main street, running from west to east, from the gate opposite St. Valentine up to the Holy Spirit gate, the chief center of the Jews in Prague was a narrow square with the main 'school' in the center, which was then still called 'the new school,' facts to the contrary notwithstanding." Judging by the description of the locale, none other than today's Old-New Synagogue was meant.

Abigdor Karo, who died in 1439 and thus was, most likely, an eyewitness of the 1389 massacre, writes in his elegy describing the horrors of that bloodshed: "Maniacs penetrated into the old and the new synagogue...," by which he apparently means the old synagogue in Dušní Street and the present Old-New Synagogue. Nothing supports Gruen's opinion that the Old-New Synagogue then comprised two prayer-rooms, one old and one new.

In the library of the Jewish Community in Prague is a German translation — printed in Hebrew characters — of a Selichoth. According to its frontispiece, it was published by "Chanoch, sexton in the Old-New School" and was printed by the sons of printer Jacob Bak during the reign of Emperor Ferdinand. M. Steinschneider notes, under index entry No. 2911, another translation of that Selichoth by Jacob ben Elia Levi of Teplice, also published by

Chanoch, sexton in the Old-New Synagogue and printed by Moses ben Bezalel in 1602. Under entry 2912, Steinschneider mentions a second edition of that translation. Translator and publisher remain the same; only the printer changes. This time, the sons of printer Jacob Bak do the printing and indicate no precise date other then the "reign of Emperor Ferdinand," without even saying whether Ferdinand I or Ferdinand II is meant. Accordingly, the time between 1620 and 1657 comes into consideration, the period in which the two rulers reigned. But we are satisfied with the second (1602) edition of the first book published, which names in its frontispiece Chanoch as sexton of the Old-New School, for this is the earliest date for this appellation that has been ascertained. Zunz also cites the edition of 1602 and labels the other as undated. The regulations (tekanos) posted in the Old-New Synagogue, the updated rules of Rabbi Löw of 1591, speak of the "Old-New Synagogue" in a Hebrew abbreviation, ANS. However, this designation is certainly a supplement of subsequent rules, and as a result cannot be considered here.

A document in the archives of the Ministry of the Interior, listed under the symbol I 4/5, speaks, in 1642, of "the Churchwardens of the Old Newschool."

In the responses of Jair Chaim Bachrach (Worms, 1628–1702), we read that his father's seat in the so-called Old-New Synagogue in Prague was at the south wall, close to the aron.

In the manuscript containing entries on debts, purchases, and sales of Jewish houses in Prague, only as late as 1634 do we find references to the Old-New Synagogue for the first time. In that year there is an entry saying that "Gutkind Gans, a Jew...had bought unto himself... part of a house between the houses of Rabbi Enoch Winternitz in Jewish street... located behind the Old-New School."

Another entry records that Rabbi Joachim Prostějovský had bought two parts of the corner house next to the house of Mayer Epstein, "across from the Jewish Old-New School." That entry was made in the *Liber Judaeorum albus*, Folio 239, on October 22, 1635. Also on page 239 the same house is described as "the corner house adjacent to the house of Mayer Epstein." In the second volume of the same manuscript, on September 7, 1671, a house is described as being "at the corner off the Old-New School."

The instances cited here reveal that by 1602 the synagogue had already been called Old-New, or rather (in German) "Altneuschul" (sometimes it was spelled in two words, "Alte Neuschul"). Up to then people always spoke either of the "new school" or the "old school." The German terminology, in particular, shows that the synagogue which was up to that date called "Neuschul," i.e., New School, had bestowed upon it the second attribute of "old" only after the erection of the "new Neuschul" (New Newschool), and so became the "Old-New School."

This change of appellation's having occurred only in the 17th century warrants the supposition that what came to be called New School was one of the truly new synagogues erected during the lifetime of Mordecai Maisl. Precisely which synagogue it was is difficult to determine today. In 1599 one Isaac Wechsler died. He had established a synagogue in his own house — No. 113–V — and that synagogue, too, was called "new" (Neuschul).

The Gal-Ed mentions one Jacob, son of Isaac, deceased in 1595, as donor of Torahs and paraments to the "New School." Hock's German text, referring to the same gift, names the Old-New Synagogue erroneously as its recipient.

Whether Wechsler's synagogue was the "New School" or whether — as S. H. Lieben believes — it was the already-built Maisl synagogue has not been ascertained as yet. In his "Inscriptions on gravestones at the Old Jewish Cemetery in Prague," K. Lieben cites one Abraham, son of Israel, dubbed Isserle, deceased in 1628, who had been reader in the New School and "a good ambassador of those who sent him from the Old School." This doubtlessly refers to a new synagogue built at the close of the 16th century, yet leaves the question of which synagogue was the new one unresolved, for in 1899 it vanished without trace along with other synagogues of Prague.

In summary, we see that in 1124 somewhere in Prague a synagogue existed that was destroyed by fire in 1142. Whether there had been other synagogues in Prague prior to or simultaneously with that one is not known. In the 12th century or at the outset of the 13th century a synagogue was erected not far from the church of the Holy Spirit in the Dušní Street, which was subsequently called "the old school." Of its early history we know merely that the Jews thought it to be the oldest synagogue in Prague built of stone. At the beginning of Přemysl Otakar II's reign, i.e., in the sixties of the 13th century, a second synagogue (the present "Old-New School") was built; to differentiate it from the other, the old synagogue, it was named "new." At the end of the 16th century or at the beginning of the 17th century another "new" synagogue was constructed, and the former "new" synagogue came to be known in German as the "Alte Neuschul," or "the Old-New School" — a name that was later spelled in one word. This synagogue became the *Altneuschul.* That this renaming was not the consequence of any reconstruction we have been able to demonstrate by means of the architecture per se. Nor were any historical documents found showing that the renaming occurred prior to the beginning of the 17th century.

BIBLIOGRAPHY

Foges, B. and Podiebrad, D. J., *Altertümer der Prager Josefstadt* (Antiquities of Prague's Josefov). Prague, 1862.

Grotte, A., *Deutsche, böhmische, und polnische Synagogentypen* (German, Bohemian and Polish Types of Synagogues). Berlin, 1915.

Krautheimer, R., *Mittelalterliche Synagogen* (The Synagogues in the Middle Ages). Berlin, 1927.

Lion, L. and Lukas, L., *Das Prager Ghetto* (The Ghetto of Prague). Prague, 1959.

Schürer, O., *Prag, Kultur, Kunst, Geschichte* (Prague, Culture, Art, and History). Wien, Leipzig, 1930.

Steinherz, S., *Die Einwanderung der Juden in Böhmen; die Juden in Prag* (The Emigration of Jews to Bohemia; The Jews in Prague). Prague, 1927.

Vilímová, M., *Seven Hundred Years of the Old-New Synagogue*, Judaica Bohemiae, Prague, 1969.*

Wischnitzer, R., *The Architecture of the European Synagogues.* Philadelphia, 1964.

* [Reached the author after her study had been set in type (Ed.)]

THE *ALTSCHUL* SYNAGOGUE OF MIKULOV [1]

by Richard Teltscher

The *Altschul* Synagogue of Mikulov* is an outstanding example of Moravian synagogue architecture. Its excellence lies not only in its rich yet delicate decorations, but also in its fine and elegant proportions and constructional elements. It is also of great interest when one considers its history and style in relation to other stone synagogues of the region and beyond.

One of the most important types of sixteenth- and seventeenth-century synagogue construction is found in Central and Eastern Europe, chiefly in western Russia, Poland, and Moravia. This is the massive, often fortresslike, stone synagogue, as opposed to the tall wooden synagogue which was typical of the heavily forested areas of Poland and western Russia.

The stone synagogues were usually erected in urban centers where Jewish communities were protected by a powerful nobleman, and they were often intended to serve not only as houses of prayer and study, but also as strongholds in times of trouble, when they afforded sanctuary. Their plain exteriors also served to ward off envy and religious intolerance, but by contrast the interiors were all the more richly decorated.

They shared a common layout: the interior space was divided by columns into aisles covered by vaulting and domes. The dome as an architectural feature originated in Byzantium, and to this extent this synagogue architecture shows Near Eastern influence. The most distinctive feature of the interiors is that the central nave, as distinct from Byzantine type, is not larger, but rather smaller than the aisles on the sides.

* [The *Altschul* Synagogue of Mikulov is also known as of Nikolsburg (Ed.)]

The central nave forms a raised platform or dais, over which rises a vaulted or domed canopy, supported by four columns or piers — one at each corner, and forming the *Bimah*. The *Bimah* is not a separate construction but is joined integrally to the main roof structure by supporting pendentives of the adjacent domes or vaulting covering the surrounding aisles. The *Bimah*, from which the Scriptures are read to the congregation, is the central — though not necessarily the largest — part of the synagogue. This is in contrast to the houses of worship of other faiths, such as mosques and churches, where the central part is reserved for worshipers.

Owing to the position of the *Bimah*, the layout of this type of synagogue is centripetal and not central, as is usual in other houses of worship. From the functional viewpoint this is an original Jewish architectonic conception which arose out of technical considerations, and as such is rather rare. In other places of worship, spaces usually have a longitudinal center of gravity — as is the case in Gothic cathedrals — or a central one, as in the Pazzi Chapel in Florence. In fact no other type of architecture is based on this centripetal concept, with the possible exception of the modern experimental theater-in-the-round, where the center, while it is the focus of attention, is not greatly stressed architecturally.

According to an inscription, the synagogue in Mikulov was built in 1550. Razed in 1719 by a fire which destroyed all but one of seven hundred houses, it was reopened in 1723. It has been generally assumed that its present appearance dates from its reconstruction after the fire. However, there are a number of indications that the original layout of 1550 may have survived the fire and have been incorporated into the rebuilt synagogue.

The main hall of the synagogue is in the shape of a rectangle — almost a square — 32 feet, 9 inches by 38 feet. Instead of four pillars supporting the ceiling, as is common in other synagogues, there is only one central support. This, however, does not take the weight of the heavy roof structure. The four columns are close together, standing on the same platform and bearing a small baldachin, forming the *Bimah*. From the central *Bimah* four arches reach the peripheric masonry, and it is the latter which supports the weight of the roof structure. Each bay thus created is roofed by a hemispheric dome on pendentives of the same type as was used by Brunelleschi in the Pazzi Chapel (1420). Therefore this type of construction may have been in use in Moravia as early as 1550.

The domes and arches are decorated with elegant eighteenth-century stucco work. This stucco work and the sumptuous Ark, splendidly decorated in the manner of a Baroque altar, are the only features that can be dated with certainty as belonging to the eighteenth century. The windows of the outer walls do not have Baroque shapes.

The four slender central columns have capitals decorated in the Renaissance style. Their proportions also indicate that they could well be the original columns, since if they had been badly cracked in the fire they most probably would have been replaced by slender Baroque pillars. It is highly probable that the solid brick construction of the domes was not affected by the collapse of the roof timbers and that the total damage was not so great as to necessitate complete reconstruction.

There are strong indications of Italian influence in the total design. The good proportions of the constructive elements, especially of the four columns, which are unusually slim and elegant, are in striking contrast to the heavy and sometimes clumsy pillars of synagogues located farther east.

The relatively small size of the central area between the four supports, compared with the hall as a whole, makes for unity of space and harmony of spatial relationships, avoiding the monotonous division of the main hall into equal areas found in Polish synagogues. Furthermore, the Pazzi-style domes and the whole Renaissance conception of the interior strongly supports the theory of Italian influence, which is borne out also by the elaborate style of other parts of the building, particularly by the columns and arches which form a loggia of essentially Italian design. A wall which filled in the empty spaces had to be removed before this charming feature was rediscovered some twenty-five years ago.

The question of Italian influence in the style of the synagogue must be studied in the wider context of the dissemination of the Italian Renaissance. In the early part of the sixteenth century, Italian influence was beginning to spread abroad from its centers in Rome, Venice, and Florence. The increase of trade and prosperity was followed by a greater interest in the arts on the part of the wealthier classes in the rest of Europe, as it had been in Italy. Starting with Francis I of France, art patrons throughout Europe began to import and employ leading architects and artists from Italy. This was certainly the case in Vienna at that time, and Mikulov, situated very close to the

Austrian capital, has numerous historic links with it. It is not improbable that the prosperous Jewish community of Mikulov, flourishing as it did under the protection and patronage of the House of Dietrichstein, copied the wealthy Christian merchants and nobles of the times and employed Italian or Italian-trained architects for the building of its synagogue.

Unfortunately, there are no historical documents to support this view, but the internal evidence gives strong indications to this effect. It would be interesting and worthwhile to apply modern methods to the study of construction of the Mikulov *Altschul* synagogue. It would be a complicated task, but it is the only possible way of establishing with certainty the architectural origins of this the most elegant of Moravian synagogues.[2]

NOTES

1. The remarkable synagogue in his hometown of Mikulov (Nikolsburg) has always been of great interest to the writer, who, being intimately concerned with setting up of the Jewish Museum there, was in a position to initiate further studies of the building by a number of architects. The first of these was Dr. H. Blum, whose work was published on the occasion of the museum's opening, and this was followed by a study by Professor D. Dostal, which was privately communicated to the writer. These two studies formed, to a considerable extent, the basis for the preceding article, which greatly benefited also from observations by Professor T. Kurent. Thanks are also due to Miss P. Holliman, A.R.I.B.A., for her assistance, and last but not least to the writer's daughter-in-law, Mrs. R.H.M. Teltscher, M.A.

   The generally accepted theory among writers on the subject of synagogue architecture in Europe is that influences in the development of style moved from the East to the West. If this were the case, the synagogue of Mikulov, which forms the subject of this paper, would be based on Polish examples. After considerable study of the subject in collaboration with the above-named architects, the writer reached the conclusion that here the trend was in the opposite direction — that is to say, from West to East. This conclusion is borne out by the construction dates of a number of synagogues in Moravia and Poland. all of which are later than that of the Mikulov synagogue.

2. Excerpt from letter of Dr. Richard Telscher, March 17, 1964, concerning the condition of the Mikulov Synagogue: "Earlier this year the synagogue was in a poor state of repair and therefore was not in use. Part of the building was in danger of collapsing. It is understood, however, that moves are afoot locally to have the synagogue saved by the Commission on Historic Shrines."

BIBLIOGRAPHY

1. G. Loukomski, *Jewish Art in European Synagogues*, London, 1947, Hutchinson & Co., Ltd.
2. Jahrbuch der Gesellschaft für Geschichte der Juden in der Tschechoslovakischen Republik (paper by the author of 3), Prof. Samuel Steinherz, ed., Prague, 1935. Taussig & Taussig.
3. Alfred Grotte, Deutsche, böhmische und polnische Synagogentypen. Berlin, 1915, Der Zirkel Architektur Verlag G.m.b.H.
4. Pamatnik (Gedenkbuch) Židovského ústředního musea pro Moravsko-Slezko, Prof. Dr. Alfred Engel, ed. (Paper "Die Altschulsynagoge in Nikolsburg-Kunstgeschichtliche Studie und Zustandbericht" by Dr. Heinrich Blum), Mikulov (Nikolsburg), 1936.
5. Mitteilungen der Gesellschaft zur Erforschung jüdischer Kunstdenkmäler I. Frankfurt-am-Main 1900.
6. Prof. D. Dostál, Das Jüdische Landesmuseum in Nikolsburg, Brno, 1937 (private communication).
7. Prof. Tine Kurent, private communication on synagogue architecture, Ljubljana, 1956.
8. *Jüdisches Lexicon*, Jüdischer Verlag, Berlin, 1929 (article on Lublin).
9. *Encyclopedia Judaica*, Berlin, 1934, Verlag Eschkol, A.G., (article on Lutsk).
10. Die Juden und die Judengemeinden Mährens, Hugo Gold, Brno. 1929, Jüdischer Buch- und Kunstverlag.

37. Exterior view of *Altschul* Synagogue of Mikulov, showing loggia before restoration (bottom right-hand corner)

38. Interior of *Altschul* Synagogue of Mikulov, general view with *Bimah*

39. *Altschul* Synagogue of Mikulov, two of the ceiling domes

40. *Altschul* Synagogue of Mikulov, ceiling as seen from the center of *Bimah*

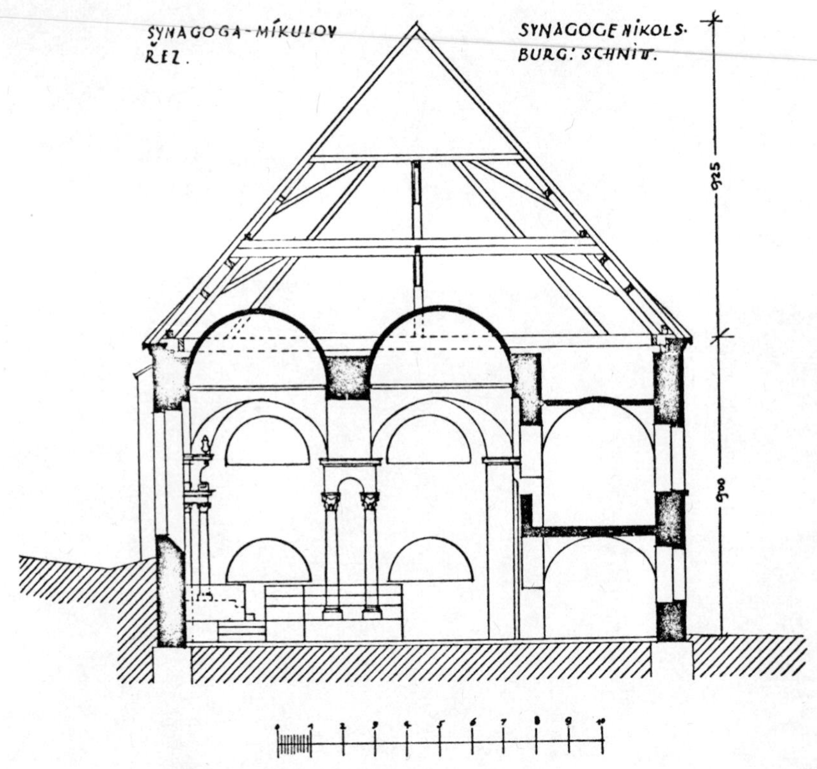

41. *Altschul* Synagogue of Mikulov, cross-section

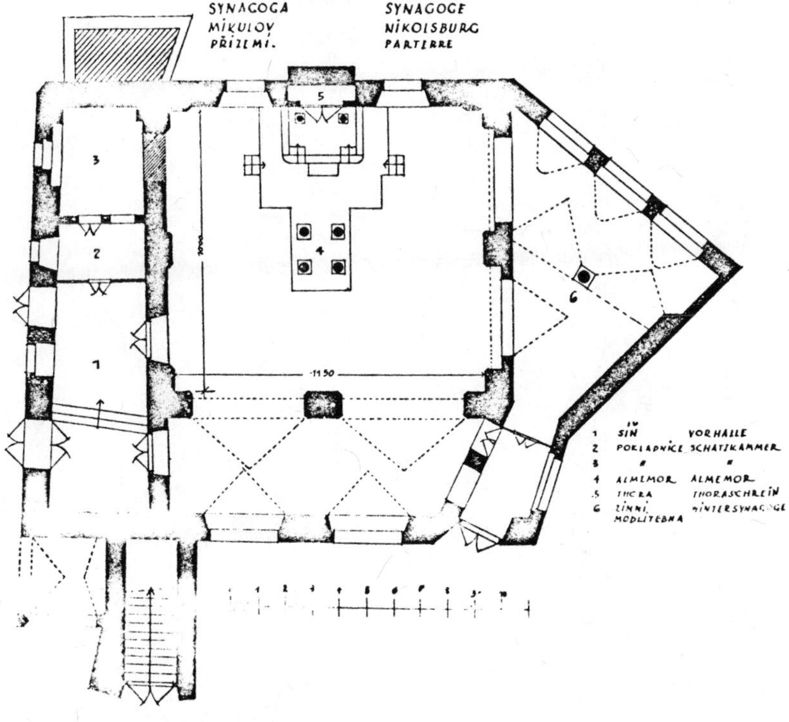

42. *Altschul* Synagogue of Mikulov, ground floor plan

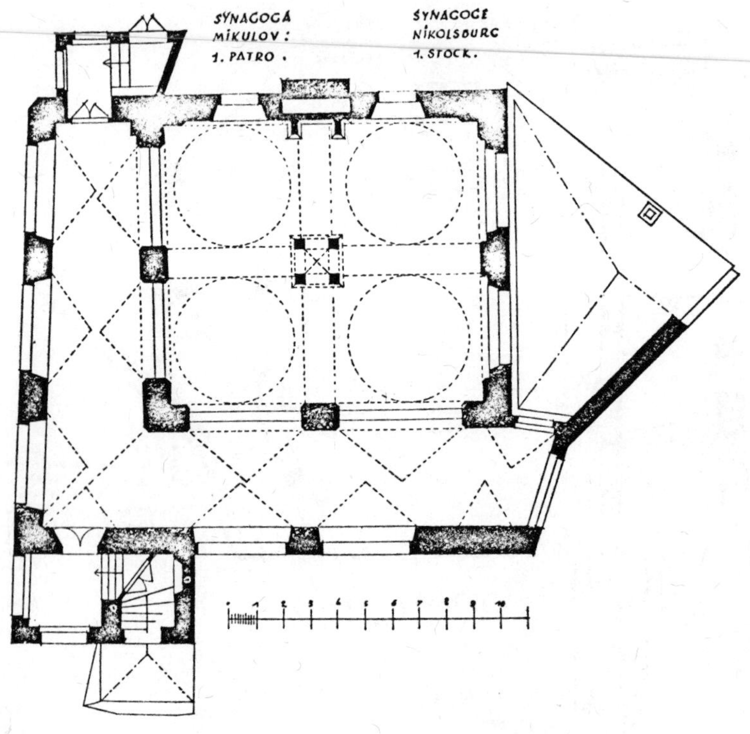

43. *Altschul* Synagogue of Mikulov, first floor plan

44. Podivín Synagogue, Moravia

45. Kroměříž Synagogue, Moravia

THE YIDDISH THEATER IN CZECHOSLOVAKIA

by S. J. Harendorf

Prior to 1918 the Yiddish theater was unknown in the territory which later formed the Czechoslovak Republic. One of the reasons for its absence in Bohemia and Moravia was that culturally and linguistically the Jews in these provinces were closer to the Czech and German population than to the Yiddish-speaking Jewish groups. However, the Jews of Slovakia and Subcarpathian Ruthenia included Yiddish-speaking residents.

It should be pointed out that there were also external factors which tended to discourage interest in the Yiddish theater as well as in other Yiddish cultural activities, such as Yiddish literature and journalism. Most important among these was the pressure exerted prior to 1918 by the Austrian authorities on the Jews of Bohemia and Moravia to adopt German culture and the efforts at Magyarization tha were made in Slovakia.

With the establishment of the Czechoslovak Republic this situation changed. The authorities made every effort to draw the Jews from German and Magyar cultures alike. Recognizing the Jewish community as a minority group with cultural and educational institutions of its own, the state encouraged all endeavors to accord to Hebrew and to Yiddish a prominent place in the life of its Jewry. Soon there were Hebrew and Yiddish schools, newspapers, and cultural societies throughout the Czechoslovak Republic.

Unfortunately, nobody took the initiative to create a Yiddish theater in the country. But as the news spread of the great successes throughout Europe of the Vilna Troupe, the *Yiddishe Kunsttheater* (art theater) in New York, and another *Kunsttheater* in Moscow and elsewhere, it was inevitable that someone in Czechoslovakia would contact such troupes in nearby countries in order to bring them to the Republic.

The first group, which was headed by Zacharia Franzos, Jacob Mestel, and Shelomo Prisament, consisted of fourteen members (nine men and five women); it arrived in Bratislava from Vienna in the fall of 1920. Lacking the money to hire a theater or even a hall with a stage, they performed on an improvised stage in a Jewish restaurant. Their repertory consisted mainly of plays with a Jewish historical or nationalistic note like *Shulamit*, *The Sacrifice of Isaac*, and *Bar Kokhba* by Abraham Goldfaden, *The Wild Man* by Jacob Gordin, and *The Golem of Prague*, a musical composed by Shelomo Prisament.

Since the players were all foreigners, they had to report to the Czechoslovak police upon arrival in order to obtain permits to perform. When Zacharia Franzos, who knew neither Czech nor Slovak, was asked what kind of language Yiddish was, he replied that it was somewhat akin to Hebrew. As a result, the troupe received permission to perform plays "in Yiddish, which is similar to Hebrew." Hence, when the authorities asked him the name of his company, Franzos thought it best to give it a Hebrew name *HaOr*, meaning "The Light." This was the first time that a Yiddish theater company performed under a Hebrew designation.

HaOr toured Czechoslovakia for three weeks, playing not only in Bratislava but also in other cities and towns, including Nitra, Trnava, Spišská, Nová Ves, Žilina, Košice, Prešov, and Sabinov. Trouble started when *HaOr* crossed into Subcarpathian Ruthenia and announced plans to make Mukačevo (Munkács) its first stop. The Hassidic *Rebbes* of Mukačevo and Belz, the two largest Jewish communities of the region, were united in their opposition to performances of a Yiddish theater in Mukačevo. It is interesting to note that Rabbi Haim Eleazar Schapiro, the rabbi of Mukačevo, had never taken the same active stand against performances by Magyar companies in his city, although it was commonly known that 90 percent of their audiences were Jews. But he attacked the Yiddish theater even more bitterly than he did the Zionist movement and the Hebrew-speaking schools of his province, insisting that the Yiddish theater would lead Jewish youth into immorality. For reasons best known to himself, he failed to see the same danger in the Magyar theater.

When *HaOr* arrivcd in Mukačevo and hired the Municipal Theater, the rabbi proclaimed a *herem* (ban) on the theater. The Zionists, concerned lest this might set a precedent for bans on their own institutions by the anti-Zionist rabbi, countered with a campaign promoting attendance at the performances. Insisting that a ban of this sort was not in accordance with the law of the land, they urged the actors not to be intimidated by a rabbi but to go ahead with the show as planned. However, the leaders of *HaOr* did not wish to see the troupe become an object of controversy between the rabbi and the Zionist movement, and therefore left Mukačevo, playing instead in Užhorod, Hust, Jasina, and Sevluš.

HaOr disbanded in the spring of 1922, primarily for economic reasons, and most of the members returned to Vienna. While it was short-lived, this company earned the lasting credit for having prepared the way in Slovakia and Subcarpathian Ruthenia for many other theater groups that were to delight Jewish audiences in the years to follow.

Two years later, in 1924, a new Yiddish theater troupe appeared in Slovakia and Subcarpathian Ruthenia under the name of *HaBima* ("The Stage"), not to be confused with the famous Hebrew company of the same name. It so happened that Zacharia Franzos, formerly with *HaOr*, was the licensee of the new group, which consisted of twenty-one members. *HaBima*, which existed until the Nazi occupation of Czechoslovakia, performed not only in the eastern part of the Republic but also in Bohemia and Moravia in the west. Concentrating on dramas, comedies, and operettas of better quality, *HaBima* was praised not only by Jewish audiences but also in Czech and Slovak circles. The Czech and Slovaks regarded this theater company as an important factor in diverting the Jewish population from their German- or Magyar-oriented cultural interests. As a result, the director of *HaBima*, supported by Zionist and other Jewish communal leaders, succeeded in obtaining annual subsidies from the municipal council of Nitra, Trnava, Žilina, and other cities in S]ovakia. While the amounts involved were by no means substantial, the fact that the company had gained official recognition for its cultural and educational activities served to raise considerably the spirit of *HaBima*. Annual subsidies were also granted by a number of cities and towns in Subcarpathian Ruthenia, with the city councils of Mukačevo and Užhorod voting annual amounts of 5,000 korunas ($218) each for this purpose.

The poor Jewish peasants would scrimp and save, often going without bread, to be able to purchase tickets. Carriages loaded with peasant families would come from far-off villages to the cities where the performances were given, and those who lacked money to buy their tickets would bring flour, eggs, or a goose to be sold in town in order to obtain the needed money.

During the following years, many Yiddish theater companies came to the Republic for guest performances. The most famous of these was the Vilna Troupe, which visited the country in 1925.

As has been noted, certain cultural and linguistic factors delayed the development of interest in the Yiddish drama in the western part of the Republic, so that at first the Yiddish theater was seen mainly in Slovakia and Subcarpathian Ruthenia. The late spring would be the slack season for theater groups in those regions, for immediately after Passover there began the *sefira*, the seven-week mourning period extending until Shavuot. Those two provinces were strongholds of traditional Judaism, which forbade all public entertainment during *sefira*. Therefore the Yiddish theater troups utilized this free time for guest performances in Bohemia and Moravia, where the Jewish public took a more liberal attitude toward observance of the *sefira* period. Thus, in the late spring of 1925 Yiddish theater groups visited cities like Brno, Hodonín, Mikulov, Kyjov, Prostějov, Znojmo, Jihlava, Boskovice, Pohorelice, Mor. Ostrava, Opava, Bohumín, Č. Těšín, Uh. Brod, and Uh. Hradiště.

Unlike the Jews in the eastern provinces, those in Bohemia and Moravia had to be "sold" on the Yiddish theater. In Slovakia and Subcarpathian Ruthenia, it was sufficient for the company to announce the date of its performance; but in the west, particularly in smaller communities, good attendance depended largely on the amount of canvassing done, mostly by the actors and actresses themselves. This was one of the reasons why Yiddish theater troupes did not visit the western part of the Republic very often: the proceeds from those performances, as a rule, were not proportionate to the amount of effort and energy expended by the players before they ever set foot on the stage. Still, even in the western regions, the Yiddish theater achieved some striking successes.

HaBima was not the first company to come to Moravia. Soon after the First World War, a German theatrical agent named Krátký, having heard of the financial successes of Yiddish stage performances all over Europe, sent his impresario to Vienna to select a Yiddish troupe for appearances in Moravia and Bohemia. The agreement between the agent and the company provided for a 50–50 split of the net profit remaining after travel and all other expenses had been paid. The first performance in Moravia took place in May 1921 in the hall of the *Deutsches Haus* ("German House") in Brno. At that time, there were in Brno a large number of Jewish students from Poland, Romania, and Slovakia who, because of the Jewish quota, were not admitted to the universities of their native countries, and who were thus compelled to enroll in schools in Brno. It was expected that these young people from the east would be prominent in the audiences of the Yiddish companies. Unfortunately, the poor selection and presentation of plays greatly disappointed those who had expected drama on a higher cultural level in a city such as Brno. After only four performances, the six men and two women of the ensemble had to close the show and leave the city.

Despite this failure, the agent did not give up but took the company to a number of smaller communities in Moravia, where they toured with some measure of success for two months. Leaving Moravia, the players arrived in Prague in July 1921. There they reserved the *Kleine Buehne* (which was affiliated with the city's "New German Theater") for five performances. This was strongly criticized by the Zionist leaders in Prague, for that time in particular had been one of bitter strife between the Czechs and the Germans. Despite the fact that the Yiddish theater company certainly had no connection with either side and that it had chosen the German hall simply because the agent and the impresario had happened to be Germans, the Jews of Prague boycotted the performances, and the Prague venture ended a dismal failure. The same happened in Plzeň, where the agent also hired a hall in the *Deutsches Haus* of the city.

In general, it can be said that the lack of success of the Yiddish theater in Bohemia and Moravia was due, in part, to the fact that the Jews in the western regions of the Republic were accustomed to drama and acting on a high level by both the Czech and German theaters. The Yiddish plays tended to be crudely performed and revolved mostly around Jewish life in the small communities of Eastern Europe, which was mostly unfamiliar to the Jews in the west. The situation was better in the famous spas of Karlový Vary (Karlsbad), Mariánské Lázně (Marienbad) and Františkový Lázně (Franzensbad), where Yiddish plays were patronized by visitors who came from all over the world during the summer months.

Some of the very factors which resulted in failure of the theater in the west were the reasons for its success in the eastern parts of the Republic. Between 1921 and 1938, Yiddish companies performed in only twelve Moravian and twelve Bohemian towns (the spas included), but they visited thirty-eight Slovak towns and ten in Subcarpathian Ruthenia.

Despite its shortcomings, Yiddish theater in Czechoslovakia made an important contribution to Jewish life and culture. It acquainted the Jews of the Republic with the social and cultural conditions under which their brethren lived in Eastern Europe, and it made familiar to them the names of the great Yiddish playwrights, such as S. Anski, Abraham Goldfaden, David Pinski, Leo Kobrin, Perez Hirschbein, Sholem Asch, and Jacob Gordin. Unfortunately, the Yiddish theater in Czechoslovakia lived only for seventeen years, coming to an abrupt end with the Nazi occupation of the country.

BIBLIOGRAPHY

S. J. Harendorf: *Teater Karavannen* ("Theater Caravans"), with a foreword by Dr. Aron Steinberg. London, 1955 (in Yiddish).

JEWISH CEMETERIES IN SLOVAKIA

by Eugen Bárkány

Among the oldest Jewish cemeteries in Slovakia, and indeed in the whole of Central Europe, is the one in Trnava. Its history reflects the fate of Jewish gravestones in the area. On a trumped-up charge of ritual murder the Jews were exiled from the city in 1539, and King Ferdinand ruled that henceforward no Jews might live in the vicinity. The Jews left the city by a gate in the direction of Sered, after which the citizens of Trnava walled up the gate with gravestones from the Jewish cemetery. For more than three hundred years not one Jew lived in Trnava.

About 1862 part of the city's fortifications, with the so-called Gate of Sered and its tower, must have been removed because they were in a dangerous condition, and nine of these gravestones were found, all very well preserved. The Hebrew inscriptions with their translations were published in *Archeologický věstník*, Vol. 6, Prague, 1867, p. 104. Their dates were 1340, 1377, 1390, 1391, and 1394—all older than the gravestones in the old cemetery of Prague. But the stones no longer exist. In 1863 the Jewish community purchased the stones from the city and set them in the walls of the old cemetery; later the walls and the stones in them were crushed to make a foundation for new graves.

Another old Jewish cemetery was in the small town of Huncovce on the banks of the river Poprad. The cemetery was partly washed away by the river, and contemporary tourists can see gravestones under the water. A like fate befell the Jewish cemetery at Námestovo, about a third of whihc was inundated by the construction of a dam.

In Bratislava most of the old cemetery disappeared during a large urban development between 1939 and 1945, and only a small part with twenty-six graves remains. Here lies Chasan Sofer, rabbi of Bratislava (Pressburg) 1806–1839, as well as several other important rabbis. The graves are in an underground mausoleum which is covered with a platform of concrete. About a thousand of these gravestones, mainly of the sixteenth and seventeenth centuries, have been carelessly scattered near the enclosure of the Orthodox Jewish cemetery of Bratislava.

The old cemetery of Lipjany, situated in a forest about two kilometers from the village, has traces of walls, but not one tombstone remains; they were used some years ago in the construction of a nearby railway.

The Jewish cemeteries of Slovakia are variously situated. Some are in towns or villages, as in Liptovský Mikuláš, Nové Mesto nad Váhom, Martin (destroyed in 1964), Rajec, Hanušovce, Giraltovce, and so on. Permission to establish a cemetery within an urban area depended on the arbitrariness of the landlord who would collect the rent for the land. In towns and villages with large German populations, like Bratislava, Trnava, Trenčín, and Levoča, the Jewish cemeteries had to be far from the town, and this was also true of towns which were the seats of bishops, like Spišské Podhradie.

Nearly every Jewish cemetery had a stone wall, and beside the entrance was "Zidduk Hadin," a kind of chapel. Several are situated in forests (Červený Kameň), a few at the foot of rocks or of castle ruins (Beckov), and many on the slopes of mountains or hills. The gravestones, nearly equal in height, are arranged in rows, and differ only in sculptural work. Sometimes the effect of equal height was spoiled by higher stones, some of which were made out of Swedish granite in the last century, often at great expense. It is no accident that these most striking monuments were destroyed in the Second World War.

The gravestones were arranged in two rows, usually with an orientation from north to south, the head always to the east. The placing of male and female graves depended on the individual community. In several cemeteries they are buried separately, the males in a group on one side, the females on the other. In other places they are buried in separate parallel rows, Finally, there are some cemeteries in which this distinction did not exist and burials were made without regard to sex, all being buried in one place together; this was true in the most progressive communities. But examples can be found where different manners of burial have been used in the same cemetery, reflecting changes in thinking wrought by time. Sometimes, however, it is impossible to recognize the orientation of graves, perhaps because of the shape of a cemetery or because of its location on a steep slope.

In several cemeteries the graves of Kohanites are in a separate place. Similarly, boys under thirteen and girls under twelve are buried in separate groups. The graves of suicides are in a remote place by the wall.

The language of the epitaphs changed in the course of time. In the Middle Ages only Hebrew inscriptions were used, but by the second half of the eighteenth century a stone might have a text in another language in addition to the Hebrew epitaph — usually German, Hungarian, or Slovakian. Some Jewish communities to this day prohibit the use of non-Hebrew language or alphabet for the writing of epitaphs, perhaps because of the reform movement which developed in the nineteenth century.

By Jewish law and practice exhumation was prohibited, and for this reason in some of the older and smaller cemeteries there are a good many strata of burials. The old cemetery in Prague has twelve layers of graves, and the cemetery of Stupava is of this kind. Such a burial is only possible if a thick layer of earth covers each preceding grave, and this explains the uneven terrain of some cemeteries and the numbers of gravestones on a single grave.

The style, form, and decorative motifs of the gravestones are remarkable. The oldest were simple shapeless slabs, chiefly of sandstone, though some were of limestone or gray or white marble, or, recently, Swedish granite. Gradually the rough slabs were squared off, but the only decoration was the epitaph on the front, the back having only a rude carving. From this developed a new type with the arc of a circle on top, sometimes reaching semicircular form but still having the epitaph as the only decoration. This was the typical Romanesque stone, not one of which remains in Slovakia (a well-known one may be seen at Worms in Germany).

Gradually decoration developed, and Gothic and Renaissance forms and ornamentation appeared on gravestones. Incised inscriptions gave way to the more expensive and more effective raised letters, the stone having a groove around the edge in the Renaissance manner. Only a few stones in the Gothic stylere main, in Trstina,

Holič, Stupava, Huncovce, and Bratislava; stones in the Renaissance style may be found in Bratislava and Ilava, and there are some examples in Nové Mesto nad Váhom, Beckov, Senica, and Šaštin.

The majority of stones in Slovakia are in the Baroque style. The tombstone of Sečovce, of 1741, is remarkable, very simple at the top with a raised floral arrangement on the face. There are very handsome stones of the period at Rozhanovce, but the ones at Bratislava are even more so. In some cemeteries in Slovakia can be found stones — there are some at Stupava — with spiral columns and typical upper parts. Those of Vrbové, Sobotište, Námestovo, and Dolný Kubin are masterpieces of Baroque art.

There are also tombstones in the Rococo and Empire styles. The stones of the eighteenth and nineteenth centuries have a gable supported by two pillars and are richly decorated with herbal ornamentation.

As stated above, both form and ornament developed during the Baroque period, changing greatly the size and features of the gravestones. The semicircular top was replaced by different forms of arcs, volutes, or shells, sometimes decorated with balls or a cornice or gable supported by spiral pillars. The borders might have a grooved outline, but not always. The seventeenth and eighteenth centuries saw the culmination of the development of the art of Jewish stone carving.

With the change of shape of the stones came a change in the relief decoration. The carved decoration is on the upper part, sometimes covering two-thirds of the surface; rarely was there any on the lower part of the stone, which held the inscription in bulging letters and dominated the whole monument.

Although there were Jewish communities in Bratislava and Trnava in the thirteenth and fourteenth centuries, very few gravestones of the fourteenth century have been preserved. On the oldest stones found, the inscriptions are now illegible. The epitaphs have either peeled off, or after having been long covered with moss the Hebrew letters have disappeared. The epitaphs usually begin with the word SNASZ, meaning "in the year"; after that is an abbreviation of the word LPAK-LPAK KUTN, which means "the small number of years," i.e., the millennium number is by Jewish custom omitted. The numbers have points for the marking of time on different parts of the stone — sometimes on the upper part of a free surface, sometimes on the lower part of a cornice, but often in the last sentence of the epitaph on the lower part of the monument.

The elements of decoration can be divided into two parts: figural (animals and — rarely — human figures) and floral, herbal, and geometric decoration. It may be mentioned that, in decoration as in style, the expression of Jewish art on gravestones was much influenced by the artistic environment, so remarkable in all branches of Slovak folk art. The style and shape of stones architecturally were influenced by the development of styles in Central Europe, which set its mark not only on the Jewish gravestones in Slovakia but on the whole life of the country. Although the Jewish stone carvers, largely unknown, maintained the features of artistic work used by Jews, some of their work mirrored the rich tradition of Slovak folk art, most notably ceramics, wood carving, and embroidery. The stones show a variety of acroteria, some features of the Empire mansard roof, and attic balustrades in combination with other marks of contemporary style; the decoration shows the use of domestic ornaments which express religious and social motifs of the Jewish people.

Animals used as figurative ornaments offer a rich and varied theme. In obedience to the Commandments the depiction of the human figure is indeed rare, despite the influence of several of the ghetto rabbis. There are only two stones in all Slovakia with scenes from the life of man; one is in Pečovská Nová Ves, dated 1872; in the upper part it shows Jacob reclining with his head on a rock, dreaming that angels are moving on a ladder reaching up to heaven. The other is in Námestovo; the upper part of this stone shows two men carrying a coffin among pots of flowers.

A number of motifs, however, depict human hands, a Kohanite symbol that appears in several different arrangements. The hands are often parallel, whether vertical or horizontal, but sometimes they are shown within a frame. The symbol on the stones of the Levites, another important group, is related to that of the Kohanites — it is a jug, and this was used by the Levites for the ceremonial washing of hands. The Levite pours water on the hands of the Kohanite. The jugs sometimes stand alone, sometimes in a dish, sometimes with the cover half open, either vertical or slightly sloping; from several jugs water, flows, symbolizing mortality.

The Chevra Kadisha in Senica had two jugs, one from the Habans pottery works and the other from the Holič factory; they are now in the Slovak National Museum in Bratislava. The decoration on one, which is dated 1776, shows members of Chevra Kadisha visiting someone who is sick in bed. The gaps are filled with floral ornament. The other, dated 1734, shows a corpse being carried on a bier. There is floral ornament here, too, and also a horse, probably symbolizing the fact that the cemetery was far from the city.

Animals are depicted in a rich variety of motifs. There are couchant lions guarding something, alone or in pairs, deer, roe, bears, rams, eagles, doves, serpents, and crayfish. All originate in two sources. An animal carved on a monument may have a name identical with that of the deceased (for example, Löwe, a lion); the picture is in a medallion, like a coat-of-arms. The lion, however, was often used as a symbol on the Ark of the Covenant, supporting and guarding the stone slabs of the Commandments. Indeed, the lion is frequently found as a symbol in the religious art of the Jews.

Some of the other animals denote family names, all German: a wolf, a bear for Bär, a deer for Hirsch, and occasionally an eagle for Adler; all are in medallions with a raised edge, and they sometimes support a shield with the letters JD ("Here rest") or VD ("Here lies"). The symbols of a trade or profession were also added, and sometimes symbols show a biblical connection with the deceased's own name.

Later on the heraldic changed into the symbolic, thus creating a second large group. A decoration like a coat-of-arms no longer satisfied the artist, who now sought to express a definite idea in a monument. Such works are frequently found in Poland, and Jewish gravestones near the Polish border have more varied and symbolic decoration. A tree trunk, sometimes broken, symbolizes a catastrophe overtaking a man in his youth. An overturned flowerpot, with a broken flower or twig, is a reminder of the dead. An open book indicates a man of science or a cantor. Birds and candlesticks often appear on the gravestones of women, crowns and stars on the monuments of scientists. A bird with a flowering twig in her beak signifies death in youth. This symbol is a specific expression in Jewish art. The later Jewish gravestones show the widening of the rich Jewish art and poetry.

A great variety of ornamental motifs without figures are found, engraved or in relief, on the stones of southern Slovakia: all kinds of flowers; a candlestick, five or seven-branched (especially for women); elaborately carved grapevines signifying the fertile land of Israel; meander on drapery; and so on. In Poland the number of children of the deceased is indicated by birds, in Slovakia by the number of branches on a candlestick.

In Zborov, Bardejov, and several other cemeteries many of the monuments are colored, but this is a Polish influence, and evenl in these the patterns of folk art are used. The colors are mainly bue, yellow, red, and green, but sometimes one finds a rich polychrome. The most outstanding of these are the monuments of rabbis, and they are painted black or gold. There are extraordinary double monuments. A few stones remind us of those in Orava in the north of Slovakia.

Who made the Jewish gravestones? The simple inscriptions of the earlier periods were made by skillful pupils of yeshivot, several of whom became stone carvers. In the second half of the nineteenth century the art of the gravestones ceased to be valued. Stone carving as an art, executed with pious and dutiful love, was replaced by stones made in advance for stock.

The gravestones of the Jewish cemeteries in Slovakia are the only remaining monuments of the former intensive life of the Jewish people in this part of Europe, except for a few remaining synagogues. Besides their artistic value, the epitaphs make them remarkable as historical documents.

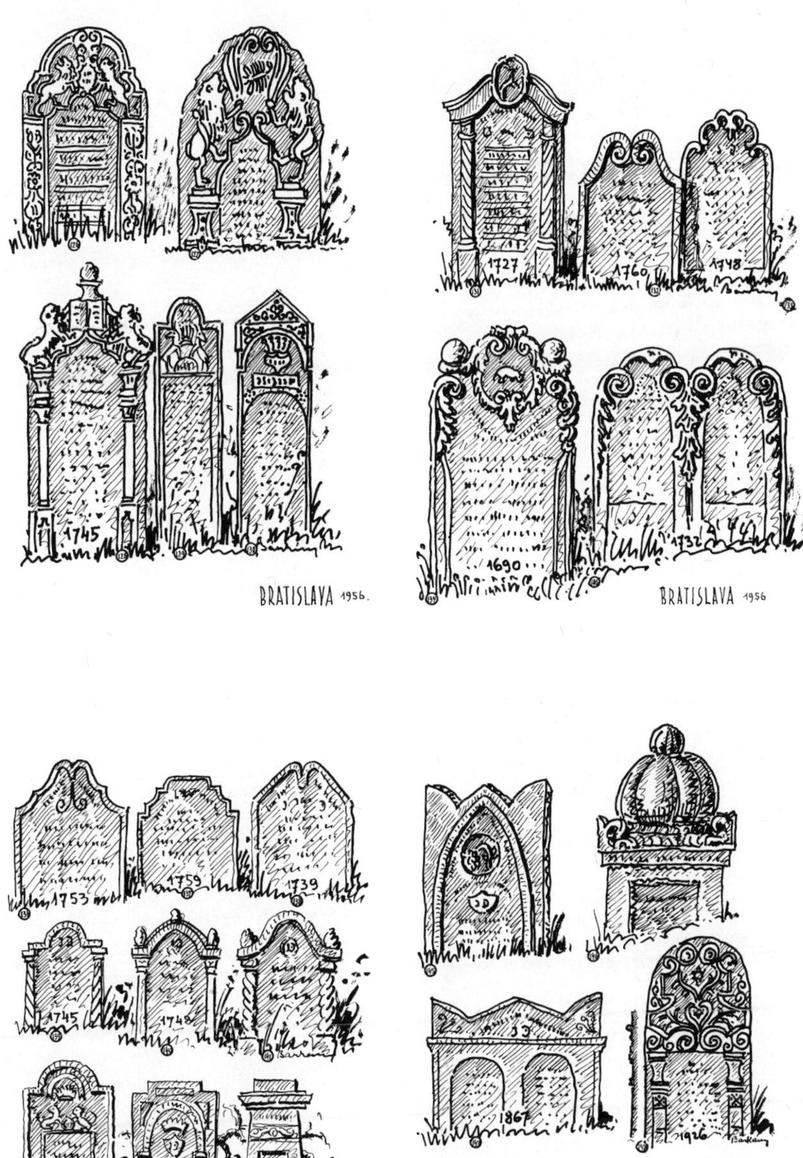

46.–53. Jewish gravestones in Slovakia

NOVÉ MESTO n V. 1956

TRNAVA 1957

VRBOVÉ 1956

BYTČA 1957

DUNAJSKÁ STREDA 1957.

PEZINOK 1956.

MALACKY 1956

SEREĎ 1956.

BECKOV 1956.
TRENČÍN 1956.
MIKULÁŠ 1957.
MARTIN 1957

1848
1850
1830
1906
TRSTENÁ 1957

1849
1849
1852
TVRDOŠŠÍN 1957

1814
1838
1820
1820
NÁMESTOVO 1957

1845
1846
DOLNÝ KUBÍN 1957.

KOŠICE 1953
HUNCOVCE 1954

MICHALOVCE 1953
BARDEJOV 1954.

VRANOV 1954

VELKÉ KAPUŠANY 1954.

BREZOVICA 1954

STROPKOV 1955.

ZBOROV 1954

SEČOVCE 1955.

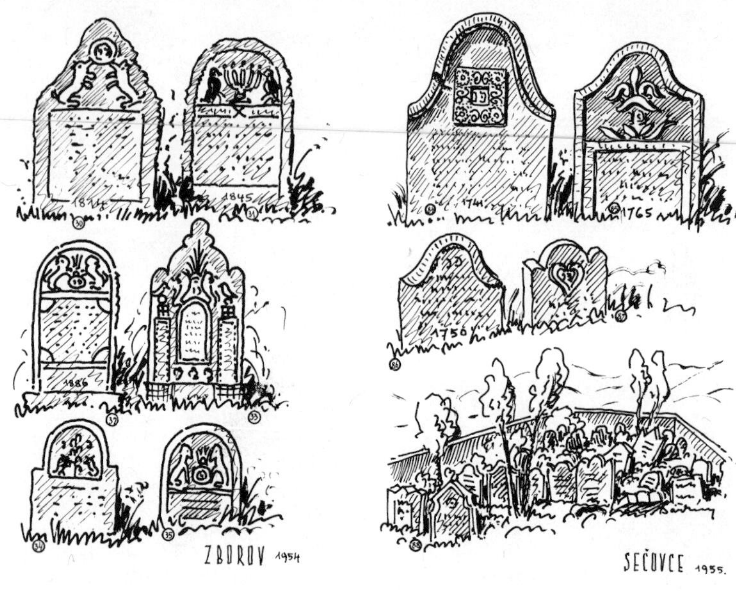

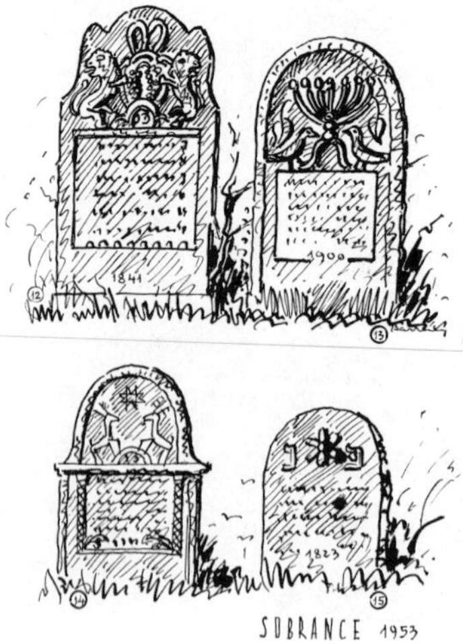

SOBRANCE 1953

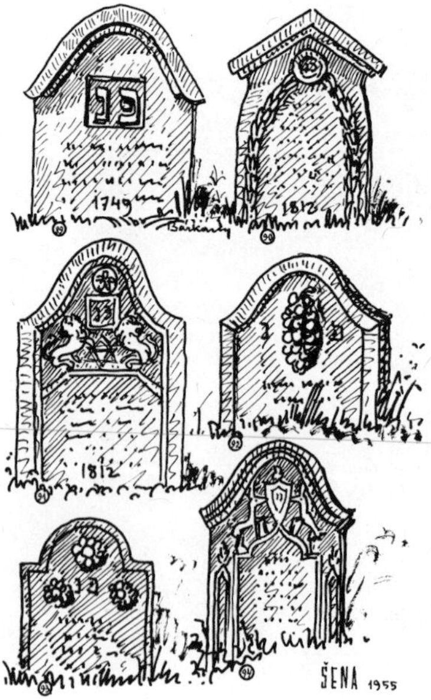

ŠENA 1955

6. Transition

REFUGEES TO AND FROM CZECHOSLOVAKIA

by Kurt R. Grossmann

Czechoslovakia Receives Refugees from Germany

When on January 30, 1933, Adolf Hitler became the Chancellor of the German *Reich*, a new refugee movement was created. Among the various European countries to which refugees from Germany turned in the years 1933–36, Czechoslovakia played an important role as a reception center. This democratic country, the only one in Central and Eastern Europe, tried to remain true to its ideals by granting aid and asylum to the refugees from Nazi persecution. Several thousands of political refugees came to Czechoslovakia and were able to live there, though often under poor conditions, because the critical economic situation prevailing in Europe at the time did not permit the integration of the refugees into the economy of the country. For this reason, the refugees in Czechoslovakia received financial support from relief committees, which helped some of them move on to overseas countries, or, at least, to reach some other temporary asylum.

In contrast to most of the other European reception countries for refugees, Czechoslovakia did not require a visa from those who possessed a valid German passport. Naturally, many refugees crossed the border illegally. Since the boundary between Germany and Czechoslovakia was 1,100 miles long, the illegal crossing could be made with ease in the regions of the Bavarian Forest or the Krkonoše Mountains. If the refugees were recognized and registered by one of the refugee committees in Prague, with which the Police Commissariat cooperated, they were granted residence permits in accordance with prevailing regulations and could obtain "stateless" passports. This provision proved helpful, especially after the Munich episode, when thousands upon thousands of refugees carried the famous "pink" passport. Czechoslovakia was the only European country which granted residence permits to refugees who were vouched for by one of the accredited relief committees. This recommendation was submitted by the present writer shortly after his arrival from Berlin in Prague in March 1933, and accepted by the Czechoslovak authorities in March 1933. Each refugee accepted by a relief committee received a registration certificate (*Evidenzbogen*) that he had to submit to a central registration office in which all relief committees were represented. After he had gone through clearance, the Police Commissariat accepted him as a *bona fide* refugee. Needless to say, the existing legislation pertaining to foreigners was also applicable to the refugees. Some were expelled on account of their political, e.g., Communist activities, or other pursuits considered detrimental to the welfare of the State.

In the province of Moravia, the authorities were not as accommodating as they were in Prague (Bohemia). After the occupation of Austria by Hitler especially, when many refugees came from Austria, Brno, the capital of Moravia, sought to effect a more stringent enforcement of police regulations to limit the number of refugees allowed to settle there temporarily.

While arrest of refugees was the exception in Prague, many were apprehended in Moravia and ordered to leave. The Foreign Office in Prague under Dr. Eduard Beneš, and later under Dr. Kamil Krofta, continued to champion the cause of asylum for the refugees; the Ministry of the Interior, however, under the agrarian Milan Hodža, was not always guided by the spirit of Beneš, who had said: "We take pride in offering a refuge to German refugees, just as the United States, Great Britain and France once could pride themselves on offering asylum to the persecuted."

Assistance by the Community and the Population at Large

When the first refugees from Germany — most of them political refugees — arrived in Prague, no refugee relief committee was in operation. However, on February 28, 1933, the League for Human

Rights of Czechoslovakia, at the suggestion of its vice president, Dr. Frederic Bill, issued a public appeal. This was the first such appeal to meet the impending refugee problem, and it appeared on March 1, 1933, in various newspapers. It led to the establishment of the non-sectarian Democratic Refugee Relief Committee.

Among the personalities who joined the Democratic Refugee Relief Committee was Marie Schmolka, who was very active in Jewish affairs and other humanitarian causes. A few weeks later she resigned, because she had been appointed to head the refugee relief work of the Jewish Congregation in Prague.*

In the beginning the political refugees outnumbered the refugees from racial persecution, and consequently various political relief committees came into being. There was the Social Democratic Relief Committee, connected with the German Social Democratic Party in Czechoslovakia, as well as with the exiled Social Democratic Party of Germany (SOPADE), and the free trade unions. The Union of White-Collar Employees in Prague set up its own refugee relief committee serving members of its counterpart in Germany. The Šalda Committee, named after F. X. Šalda, a Czech writer, was formed by Czech intellectuals who sympathized with the Communist cause. Since many Communists came to Prague where the authorities were more lenient as long as they did not discover any non-approved group activities, the Communists founded their own refugee aid committee, the Central Association to Aid Refugees. In addition, there was the Jewish Community and the Democratic Refugee Relief Committee, which had the support of the Freemasons' Lodges and liberal German-speaking Czechoslovak citizens.

At the suggestion of the Czech Government, all of these relief committees merged to form the National Coordinating Committee of which Marie Schmolka was named Chairman, and this writer Executive Secretary.

In the first few years the relief committees had to support the refugees, find lodgings for them, arrange for medical care, clothe them, and help them emigrate to other countries. In some cases it became necessary for the committees to intercede with the police on behalf of certain individuals. There were also special projects organized for the children of the refugees. All these functions neces-

* [See Polak, The Zionist Women's Movement, pp. 137–147; Yahil, Social Work in the Historic Lands, pp. 393–400 (Ed.)]

sitated the raising of substantial funds. As far as the Jewish refugees were concerned, it was not difficult to find the necessary means, but after the Munich Agreement, in 1938, the situation changed. It is estimated that the six refugee relief committees spent a total of 25,-000,000 Czech *Koruny* (approximately $800,000), at the exchange rate of 30 *Koruny* = $1, 65 per cent of which was used by the Jewish communities. This total does not include the amounts granted by the British Government after Munich (see pp. 574–575).*

The Middle Thirties

In July 1936, Sir Neill Malcolm, a retired British general who had just succeeded James MacDonald as League of Nations High Commissioner for the Refugees from Germany, convened the members of the League of Nations in a conference to adopt a refugee statute. At this Conference the National Coordinating Committee of Czechoslovakia submitted a memorandum describing the situation of its refugees. The memorandum stressed the fact that the refugees, like any other foreigners coming to Czechoslovakia, were subject to the Czechoslovak Law of March 28, 1935, and to the Executive Order of July 25, 1935, covering the admittance of foreigners. Any foreigner intending to stay in Czechoslovakia longer than two months was obligated to apply for a residence permit, which was then granted or denied by the district government concerned. Refugees who did not possess a passport had to apply for one within the first six days after arrival. All aliens had to register with the police within the first twenty-four hours after arrival. However, this regulation was relaxed by special arrangement of the Police Commissariat with the refugee relief committees. In 1935, a total of 37,000 passport applications from foreigners were submitted, but of these, only 6 per cent came from refugees. Of 2,220 refugees, only 10 per cent held valid passports.

The memorandum further pointed out that in its report on the refugee problem, the Committee for Constitutional and Juridical Questions of the Czechoslovak Parliament had referred to the existence of more stringent alien regulations in other European countries, and suggested the adoption of similar rules in Czechoslovakia. It should be noted, however, that on October 5th, 1934, the Govern-

* [See Brada, Emigration to Palestine, pp. 589–598. (Ed.)]

ment made it clear that none of the refugees expelled by Czechoslovakia would be returned to Germany. Thus, while the right to asylum for the refugees was never incorporated into Czechoslovak law, it received a mrasure of recognition from the Government.

The memorandum also contained statistical information on the situation of the refugees. According to a census of April 1, 1936, conducted by all relief committees, a total of 973 refugees were receiving financial assistance, amounting to an average of 6.40 Czech *Koruny* (or approximately 21 cents) per day. Up to that time the committees had raised a total amount of approximately 8,000,000 Czech *Koruny* (or $260,000) from private sources for a total of 8,000 relief cases, including countless transients, for whom transportation had to be paid. A total of 3,600 refugees were transferred to other countries with the help of the Committee. Fifty-five per cent of these elected to remain in these countries, while 45 per cent stated that it was their intention to move on to some other country.

The memorandum warned that increasing difficulties could be expected in the future, and that substantial funds would be required to deal with a multitude of new problems.

Of the 973 refugees, there were 661 men, 216 women, and 96 children. Of the men, 229 were skilled and unskilled workers, 152 were white-collar workers, 83 businessmen, and 114 professional people. Of the women, 91 were housewives, while 125 had some occupation or profession. The overwhelming majority of refugees were between 20 and 50 years old. Only three men and three women were over 60; 49 men and 11 women were between 50 and 60; and 240 men and 104 women were between 30 and 40 years of age.

The memorandum submitted to the High Commissioner for Refugees proposed the issuance of internationally recognized passports and amnesties for all refugees who had been expelled from Czechoslovakia, the application of the *jus soli* principle in the case of children born to refugees, the granting of work permits to all refugees, special protection for the young and the old, freedom of movement (as was eventually stated in Article 13 of the Universal Declaration of Human Rights), and last, but not least, assistance to refugees in finding countries where they could reside permanently. All combined efforts led to the Provisional Arrangement of July 4, 1936, safeguarding the status of refugees coming from Germany. This was replaced by the Convention of February 10, 1938, which included, in accordance with a decision of the Council of the League of Nations of May 10, 1938, refugees "from the country which formerly constituted Austria."

The Provisional Arrangement, as well as the Convention, accepted some of the submitted suggestions as to the safeguarding of the right of asylum; the prevention of expulsion, especially to Germany; and facilitating the issuance of travel-documents. However, the proposals concerning permission to work and integration into the social system of the country of asylum were not adopted, although a promise was made to the effect that they would be dealt with at a later date.

Those years brought still another serious problem, namely, that of the "Fifth Column" adherents versus the German refugees. This problem was most acute in Czechoslovakia, whose German minority group had become increasingly powerful, and allied to a great extent with the German National Socialist movement. The Gestapo sent spies into Prague and other parts of Czechoslovakia, and Nazi gangs threatened the lives of prominent political refugees. A number of refugees were kidnapped, and some, including Professor Theodor Lessing, were murdered by Gestapo infiltrators.

March and September 1938

After Adolf Hitler's speech on February 28, 1938, before a wildly applauding *Reichstag*, and the ensuing occupation of Austria on March 11, 1938, the relief committees in Prague shifted their work from relief to emigration aid. There began an intensive search for overseas countries which would accept refugees. Not only the refugees from Germany and Austria, but also many Czechoslovak Jews frantically applied for visas to distant lands. The Democratic Refugee Committee helped a number of them to secure visas to Bolivia. After the crisis of September 1938, feverish attempts were made to send the refugees to France, England, Sweden and Norway, while at the same time migration of those who possessed visas to overseas countries such as the United States, Canada, South America, and Australia was accelerated. HICEM, under the leadership of Marie Schmolka attempted to send the refugees to Palestine.

The Nazi occupation of Austria created two new problems. First, there was now a new refugee wave from Austria. Most of the Austrian refugees who poured into Czechoslovakia went to Bratislava and Brno, but Prague, too, had a considerable influx. Secondly, Austria could no longer be used as a transit country for refugees en route to Switzerland or France, and from there to other countries. Prior to March 1938, numerous refugees had traveled by railway, via Linz (Austria), Buchs, and Basle (Switzerland). Now the refugees had to go by air via Zurich, which meant an additional financial burden. In part, the problem was met by selling Czech *Koruny* at "black market" exchange rates. The refugees — mostly Jews — gave their Czech *Koruny* to the relief committees and received the counter-value in dollars outside of Czechoslovakia.

After Munich

There was no organized anti-Semitic movement in Bohemia during the Masaryk and Beneš administrations.

The shameful Munich Pact, however, brought about a basic change in the situation. Within twenty days, the whole Sudeten territory had to be turned over to Germany. A domestic refugee situation was created, affecting about 70,000 Czechs, 11,000 Germans (mostly German Social Democrats) and 17,000 Jews. The news from Munich stunned the Jews, the anti-Nazi Germans in the Sudetenland and the Czechs, who had made it their responsibility to keep this territory for the Republic. According to Sir John Hope Simpson's report "Refugees from Former Czechoslovakia," there were, on October 1, 1938, at least 5,000 refugees from Germany and Austria in Czechoslovakia. The vicious propaganda from the Sudeten area and from the *Reich* had first disturbed and then disrupted the neighborly relationship between Czechoslovakia and Germany, and created fears among the refugees from the *Reich* and the Jews in Czechoslovakia.

The sudden occupation of the Sudeten districts by Germany according to the Munich Agreement drove new masses of refugees in the direction of Prague, consisting of Sudeten Germans loyal to the Republic, Czechs and Jews. The Czechoslovak Government, beset as it was with problems, feared the creation of an unduly large German minority within its new frontiers. With an economically important part of the country amputated, the presence of thousands of homeless fugitives added to the prevailing general political and economic confusion. The pressure in Prague for living accommodations and food supplies was so great that Sir Neill Malcolm, the High Commissioner for Refugees, reported after visiting Prague that speedy action was necessary to save many thousands from starvation.

The chaotic condition that prevailed in Czechoslovakia made it clear that everything had to be done to get the refugees to other countries. The question of a country of permanent residence would have to wait until later. At that time the National Coordinating Committee, to which the Committee for Austrian Refugees had been added, assumed a role of major importance in the rescue operations. However, a rereading of the minutes of the meetings of the Committee for the period from September 1938 to March 1939 reveals that disputes on controversial principles among the various groups continued despite the crucial nature of the situation, mainly with the Communists who rejected any criticism. Among the topics weie guarantees regarding the right of asylum, an issue which the Communists jeopardized for political reasons.

Unfortunately, at the time the Communists wielded considerable influence in the National Coordinating Committee. The fact that the High Commissioner for the Refugees from Germany had delegated to Prague Rudolph Katz, a card-carrying member of the Communist Party, who had come from Paris, made it easy for the Communists to "run the show." Cooperation with the Communists in the refugee efforts had met with many difficulties as far back as 1936, the period of the famous Moscow trials.* But, now in the emergency period, the question was raised openly as to why Russia should not receive those refugees who were members of the Communist Party. This debate went on for quite some time. The Communists opposed this proposal by insisting that the "Democratic countries" were responsible for the situation, and therefore were obligated to rescue and care for the refugees. In retrospect, it is of historical interest to learn the official Russian position with regard to an inquiry made by the High Commissioner at the request of the present writer as to whether Russia would accept such refugees. The High Commissioner subsequently forwarded to me the answer he had received from Ivan Maisky, the Russian Ambassador in London. The reply dated December 2, 1938, reads as follows:

* *The Moscow Trials, Stalin and German Communism*, Harvard University Press, Cambridge, 1948.

My Dear Sir Neill:

On the 2nd November last you raised with me the question of whether the Soviet Government would be prepared to receive a certain number of refugees who were under your care as High Commissioner of the League of Nations for Refugees coming from Germany, and who had fled their country on account of the persecution of the German regime, having found a temporary home in Czechoslovakia, France, Belgium, etc.

You explained to me that about nine-tenths of these refugees are Jews, and that their economic existence in the aforementioned countries is extremely precarious. And in order to alleviate their sufferings, you suggested that the Soviet Government should allow the entry into the U.S.S.R. of a certain number of these refugees, and especially those belonging to two groups: (a) highly qualified specialists such as engineers, doctors, architects, agriculturists, and (b) people who by virtue of their previous experience are most suited for working on the land and in farming.

As I mentioned during our conversation, I was not then in a position to give an immediate answer to your question, but I promised to submit the matter to the consideration of my Government.

I have now been advised of the attitude of the authorities of the U.S.S.R. with regard to my enquiry, which is that the Soviet Government is prepared in principle to allow the entry into the U.S.S.R. of a certain number of refugees of the above mentioned type, but each case will be considered individually on its own merits.

Full details will, therefore, have to be furnished by each applicant particularly with regard to his other qualifications and training. Application forms will be supplied by the Soviet Consulates in the respective countries to applicants upon request, and these forms when completed, will be transmitted to the U.S.S.R. authorities for consideration.

(signed) I. Maisky.

In this letter the Russian Ambassador mentions nothing about granting unconditional admission even to that small group of Nazi victims who were in dire peril in December 1938. Only individual applications, he insisted, would be considered, each case on its own merits. But as far as available information indicates, the Soviet Union did not give refuge either in 1936 or 1938 to so much as one Hitler victim, excepting Communist Party functionaries. This was the case despite the fact that a considerable percentage of the 1,180 political refugees to be rescued from Czechoslovakia were Communists or Communist sympathizers.

Marie Schmolka and Dr. Chaim Hoffman (now Chaim Yahil, a

high official of the Israeli Foreign Office) expressed their dissatisfaction with the attitude of the Communists, who considered themselves the last recourse. Thereupon certain reforms were introduced, such as agreement that the Katz Committee would have to consult with the Coordinating Committee, and that the distribution of visas would be effected on an equitable basis. Mrs. Schmolka, for all prctaical purposes, became head of the office, with a few Communist case workers to help her.

The next serious problem arose when Czechoslovak authorities demanded "a solution of the refugee problem" within eleven days, by the beginning of December 1938. This deadline could not be met due to the scarcity of available visas. Visas for Great Britain were being given on an individual basis only. Futhermore, many refugees applied for visas to more than one country at the same time, the visas they did not need could not be used for some other prospective immgirant. When on March 15, 1939, the rest of Czechoslovakia was occupied by the German army, the catastrophe of the refugees from Germany and Austria and of the Jewish citizens of Czechoslovakia entered its second phase.

The Emigration of Czechoslovak Jews

On March 15, 1939, Lord Simon, Britain's Chancellor of the Exchequer, rose to inform a hushed House of Commons that the British Government had instructed the British Embassy in Prague to arrange "as quickly as possible for the departure of endangered persons [refugees] already in possession of British visas."

In the brief respite before the occupation of Bohemia and Moravia, efforts had been made to place the settlement and emigration of refugees at least on a sound financial basis. After the invasion of the Sudeten Territory by Nazi Germany, the British Government loaned to the Prague Government £10,000,000 (approximately $40,000,000), part of which was to be used for assistance to refugees. In December 1938, negotiations took place between the Czech, British and French Governments for further financial assistance. The resulting agreement placed at the disposal of the Prague Government another £16,000,000 (about $55,000,000), half of which was an outright gift and the other half a loan. Of the £8,000,000 loaned, £6,000,000 had to be repaid to Great Britain on account of the earlier loan of £10,000.000. The remaining £4,000,000 was to be considered as another gift, with the proviso that these £4,000 000 and an equal sum would be used for relief and resettlement of refugees. These financial arrangements were made by Britain and France to compensate the refugees, as it were, for the fate that befell them as a result of the Munich Agreement.*

The financial arrangements, however, had not yet been completed when Germany established the Protectorate of Bohemia and Moravia. The £4,000,000, which could now not be transmitted to Prague, were held at the Bank of England and made available to help resettle refugees in the countries where they would find permanent homes. In his study, entitled *Refugees*, Sir John Hope Simpson relates that emigration after the German occupation of Bohemia and Moravia was brought to a standstill.

Emigration for political suspects was only possible by illegal means, as permits to leave the country legally, even for those who had obtained visas for foreign countries, had to be endorsed by the Gestapo. Some escaped over the Polish border individually and in small groups. When the Deputy High Commissioner of the League of Nations visited Katowice on March 31 [1939] he found that refugees were crossing at the rate of about thirty a day. All classes were represented among them — Austrian and German Jews and politicals, Sudeten Jews and politicals, Jewish refugees with means from the new Protectorate, and a growing number of Czech politicals. The Deputy High Commissioner was assured in Warsaw that the Government would suspend measures of expulsion in respect of illegal entrants until a representative of the British Committee had time to make a selection of persons suitable for temporary emigration to the United Kingdom. In the meantime, the Poles were anxious to be assured that no refugee Jews would remain in Poland (pp. 578–579).

In the interval between September 1938 and the German occupation of Bohemia and Moravia in March 1939, there was a considerable amount of emigration. Many left for the United States, South America and other countries, where they had relatives and others to receive them. A group of 550 refugees from Austria and Germany, who had found asylum earlier in Czechoslovakia, left in January for various Central American countries and other groups were expected to follow. Plans for emigration to Paraguay, Palestine and Canada were prepared, and there was substantial migration, assisted and

* [Cf. Brada, Emigration to Palestine, pp. 596–597 (Ed.)]

unassisted, to various countries in Europe that could serve as transit points.

Of those known to have left the country, between September 1938 and May 1939, a total of 7,100 went to Great Britain. Of these, 3,800 came from Czechoslovakia; another 3,300 came via Poland. Of these, about 1,000 later settled in Canada, where an advance group was sent to prepare the ground. A good many found refuge in France. Trade unions and allied organizations, as well as the Matteotti Fund* arranged for the emigration of a certain number of Social Democrats and other refugees from the Sudeten territory to various Northern European countries. Belgium took 240 refugees (of whom 58 eventually proceeded to Canada), Sweden 319, and Holland 70. Others went to Norway and Finland. It was expected that while many would be able to remain in the Scandinavian countries, some, with the help of the British Fund, would emigrate to America.

When the Germans occupied Bohemia and Moravia, more than 117,000 Jews were added to the roster of victims of Nazi persecution. Within the year following the Munich Pact and the outbreak of World War II, a total of 35,000 Jews left the Protectorate. But more than 80,000 were still in Czechoslovakia after the first shots were fired.

Hitler's program for the mass emigration of Jews was begun after the annexation of Austria. Adolf Eichmann was charged with the administration of the "Center for the Emigration of Austrian Jews." When Eichmann came to Prague on July 6, 1939, he applied the methods he had previously employed in Vienna and established a "system of indirect rule," through Jewish units. As stated in the court judgment against Eichmann:

> ... Thus the Jews of Bohemia and Moravia also caught in the trap. The accused moved from Vienna to Prague, together with [Eichmann's] superior, Stahlecker, and he was given the task of setting up in Prague an Emigration Center like the one in Vienna. We have heard from Dr. Paul Meretz (März), who was then chairman of the Czech Zionist Organization, about the activity of this Center during the short period from its establishment to the outbreak of the War. Here, too, great pressure was

---

* This Fund, established by the International Trade Movement (Internationaler Gewerkschaftsbund), with offices in Paris, aided Trade Union refugees. It was named after the Italian Socialist Giacomo Matteotti, who was murdered by Italian Fascists in 1924.

exercised upon the Jews to emigrate to other countries, legally or illegally. After paying taxes (the *Reichsfluchtsteuer* and the "Jewish" tax), the emigrant also had to pay the full value of the household effects he was permitted to take with him. He also had to hand over his apartment, and was compelled to give the power of attorney to a Bank with regard to the rest of his property, so that he left the country stripped of all his possessions, with the exception of baggage weighting a few kilograms.

Of approximately 357,000 Jews — the total for the whole of Czechoslovakia — only 17.5 per cent survived.

Slovakia

At the time of the census of 1930, 136,737 of the 356,830 Jews living in the whole of Czechoslovakia were residing in Slovakia. The change in Slovakia, with its own national ambitions to secede from the Masaryk-Beneš Republic, became manifest after the signing of the Munich Pact when the advocates of Slovak autonomy, the Slovenská L'udová Strana (The Slovak Peoples' Party) came to power. From then on the policy of autonomous Slovakia was guided by extremist leaders who outlawed not only the Communists but also the Social Democrats and the Slovak National Party. Only the German and Magyar minorities were granted the right to form parties along ethnic lines. In her study entitled *The Destruction of Slovak Jewry* (Yad Vashem Archives, p. viii), Livia Rothkirchen stated that the autonomous government of Slovakia "declared from the very beginning that it considered it its task to implement the solution of the Jewish problem in a way similar to that pursued in Germany." The Slovak leaders felt that such an inhuman approach would greatly strengthen their position and gain them the support of the *Reich*.

After the Vienna Award, which forced Slovakia to cede part of its lands to Hungary, the situation took a turn for the worse. Looking for a scapegoat, the Slovaks accused the Jews of having helped bring about the Magyar annexation of Slovak territory by speaking Magyar and disseminating Hungarian culture. There was an outbreak of anti-Jewish propaganda, thinly disguised by nationalist slogans.

On March 14, 1939, the activities of the separatist leaders bore fruit, when Dr. Jozef Tiso became President of the "Independent" State of Slovakia and the notorious Professor Vojtech Tuka Prime Minister, while Dr. Ferdinand Durčanský was named Foreign

Minister. By virtue of a Treaty of Protection, Slovakia became a satellite of the German *Reich.*

The very first months of Slovakia's independence saw the implementation of restrictive measures against the Jews, especially in the economic field. They were expelled from the free professions. Land owned by Jews was confiscated and turned over to Aryan trustees. The year 1940 brought still more discriminatory legislation.*

In the beginning, emigration was still encouraged, with Jews owning no property finding it least difficult to leave the country. At the same time Slovakia served as a transit country for Jews from neighboring countries en route to Palestine.†

According to a census in Slovakia taken on December 15, 1940, following the cession of territories to Hungary with a "loss" of 40,000 Jews, the number of Jews had dropped to 88,951, representing 3.3 per cent of the entiie Slovak population of 2,653,654, an indication that approximately 8,000 Jews had been able to emigrate. These figures are much smaller than corresponding statistics for Bohemia and Moravia but larger than those for Subcarpathian Ruthenia, where 102,542 Jews had resided before Hitler had truncated the Czechoslovak Republic and this area had been annexed by Hungary. Only a small number of Jews were able to escape from Subcarpathian Ruthenia.

Emigration Via Poland

In a memorandum dated May 15, 1939, submitted by the Democratic Relief Committee, describing the tragedy of the refugees from Czechoslovakia, it was stated that they had only two alternatives: either legal emigration with the consent of the Nazi authorities, or illegal emigration via Poland.

No political refugee, no Jewish refugee from the *Reich,* dared to make use of the German offer of help to leave the country. The *Manchester Guardian* of May 5, 1939, carried an article by one of its special correspondents on the plight of the thousands of refugees in flight, all seeking to get to Poland and from there to a country where they would be able to reside at least temporarily. "Some day the story of escape of men and women from Czechoslovakia marked

* [Cf. vol. I, Rothkirchen, pp. 116–118 (Ed.)]

† [Cf. Polak, Zionist Women's Movement, pp. 137–147 (Ed.)]

by the Gestapo as Hitler's enemies will become one of the most exciting chapters in our European history books," the article begins.

The *Manchester Guardian*, one of the staunchest supporters of the refugees at the time, did not exaggerate in its account. The flight of the refugees from Czechoslovakia is a story of agonizing attempts to cross the border only to be turned back by pitiless Polish guards, of the imprisonment of more than 1,100 refugees in Moravská Ostrava, of human targets provided by hundreds caught while running for their lives, and of helpless human beings hiding in ditches flooded with water, pleading for entry with the Polish frontier guards, some of whom turned out to be sufficiently humane to let the victims of persecution pass.

By the early spring of 1939, 1,400 refugees, including Jews, Czechs, and victims of political persecution, had converged on the Polish cities of Katowice, Cracow, and Warsaw. There were a number of unpleasant incidents between Czechs and German-speaking refugees, since the Czechs did not differentiate between anti-Hitler Germans and others. The Jewish communities of the three cities mentioned assisted all refugees regardless of their religious beliefs or political views, according to that report. An exemplary job was being done by the Bund (Jewish Worker's Organization). Refugees traveling on foot in the direction of Těšín reported that even before reaching the city they had been met by young members of the Bund who conducted them to safety via routes circumventing the tough police guards operating in the region. The *Manchester Guardian* tells of refugees unable to walk who were carried to safety on the backs of Polish workers.

The majority of refugees did not reach Warsaw but remained in Katowice or Cracow. "The long waiting period for visas wore on their nerves." Of all their cruel sufferings, this needless waiting was the worst. Many of the refugees were in a state of hysteria.

During the months of April and May 1939, these refugee islands of some 500 in Cracow and 500 to 600 in Katowice grew by 100 to 120 persons each week. Crowded together in mass shelters, these victims of tragedy waited. At the outbreak of World War II, 600 of them, who still had not found a permanent refuge, set out on an unbelievable attempt to reach Rumania. To this day, no one knows whether they reached their destination.

BIBLIOGRAPHY

Books

Hitler's Ten Year War on the Jews. Institute of Jewish Affairs of the American Jewish Congress. New York, 1934, pp. 52 ff.

European Jewry Ten Years After the War. An Account of the Development and the Present Status of the Decimated Jewish Communities of Europe. Institute of Jewish Affairs of the World Jewish Congress, 1956, p. 85 ff.

Rothkirchen, Livia, *The Destruction of Slovak Jewry*, A Documentary History, from the Yad Vashem Archives, Yad Vashem Martyrs' Memorial Authority, vol. III, 1962, pp. xi ff.

Simpson, Sir John Hope, *Refugees: A Review of the Situation since September 1938*, The Royal Institute of International Affairs, August 1939, pp. 35 ff.

Tartakower, Arieh, and Grossmann, Kurt R., *The Jewish Refugee*, Institute of Jewish Affairs of the American Jewish Congress and World Jewish Congress, 1944, pp. 302 ff. and pp. 485 ff.

Pamphlets, Memoranda, Articles

Bodensick, Heinrich, "Das Dritte Reich und die Lage der Juden in der Tschechoslowakei nach München." *Vierteljahrshefte für Zeitgeschichte*, vol. 9, no. 3, July, 1961, Deutsche Verlagsanstalt, Stuttgart, pp. 249–261.

Die Deutsche Emigration in der Tschechoslowakei. National Coordinating Committee, 1933, 9 pp., Memorandum submitted to the Prague Press.

Grossmann, Kurt R., *Fünf Jahre Not, Flucht, Rettung, Prague, Demokratische Flüchtlingsfürsorge* 1938, 44 pp.

———, *Memorandum zur Lage der Flüchtlinge in der Tschechoslowakei* (typescript), 20 pp., December 1938, British Museum, London, NW 9, 100 d. 37.

———, *Die Tragödie der Emigration in der Tschechoslowakei.* May 15, 1939, 17 pp. Typescript.

———, "Das schwierigste Flüchtlingsproblem," *Sozialistische Warte*, Paris, 1938, Internationaler Sozialistischer Kampfbund.

———, "Refugees in Peril," *Manchester Guardian*, March 27, 1939.

———, "Die Flüchtlinge in Prag," *Pariser Tageszeitung*, March 16, 1939.

———, "Der kochende Kessel ohne Ventil," *Die Zukunft*, Paris, March 24, 1939.

Hiller, Kurt, "Prag," *Sozialistische Warte*, February 17, 1939. Internationaler Sozialistischer Kampfbund.

Judgment against Eichmann, English translation, pp. 63, 65.

Memorandum zur Deutschen Flüchtlingsfrage in der Č.S.R. Published by Č.S.R. National Committee for German Refugees, 1936, 13 pp.

Minutes of meetings of the National Coordinating Committee in Czechoslovakia during the period from December 22, 1938 to March 1, 1939 and typescript report by Rolf Bader of Demokratische Flüchtlingsfürsorge, Prag.

Reports from Poland (typescript). Concerning the period from March 16 to June 1939 by various authors, including Willi Kressmann, former District Mayor of Berlin.

In Memoriam Marie Schmolka. Maria Schmolka Society, London, September 1944, 36 pp. Contributions by Jan Masaryk, Rebecca D. Sieff, Dr. Frederick Thieberger, Dr. Felix Weltsch, Max Brod, Irma Polak, Dr. Joseph Popper, *et al.*

Schütz, Otto, *Flüchtlingshilfe in Brünn, 1933-1939*. Written in German, typescript, 3 pages. An account of the selfless work for Jewish and non-Jewish refugees from Germany and especially Austria.

"Refugees in Flight." (By a Special Correspondent), Manchester Guardian, May 5, 1939.

REFUGEES IN PRAGUE, 1933–1938

by Manfred George

In contrast to many countries — and the hardly cordial reception vouchsafed to them all too often — people fleeing from Hitler's persecution were welcomed affably in Czechoslovakia, for the most part at least. From 1933 till the day she was overrun by the hordes of barbarism and betrayed by the majority of Sudeten Germans settled within her borders, Czechoslovakia was a haven and host to many Jewish and non-Jewish refugees.

This article can only outline a few random facts and names. Yet they will show how potent Hitler's loss and Czechoslovakia's gain were, if only foı five years. The brief annotations here recorded are from the author's notebooks. They do not presume to be more than pointers. To describe comprehensively the nature of the Hitler refugees and their activities in Czechoslovakia would require a more-inclusive study.*

This writer was among the early refugees. Once he had cleared the Krkonoše (Riesengebirge) Mountains and with luck had avoided the frontier patrols, he found himself in Trutnov (Trautenau) and on the threshold of a singular phase of his existence. Disregarding the relatively impecunious state of affairs it was, all in all, among most fruitful periods of his life.

With a towel and a cake of soap — picked up in Trutnov and wrapped in a newspaper — as the only luggage, he traveled to Prague to see the manager of the *Prager Montagsblatt* ("Prague's Monday Gazette") who — although himself a Sudeten German — was anti-

* [See K. R. Grossmann, Refugees to and from Czechoslovakia, pp, 565–581 (Ed.)].

Nazi and a sworn enemy of Konrad Henlein, the Sudeten quisling. A job offer resulted from the interview. The time was September 1933.

This was my second flight from Germany. During the first, in the preceding May, while working in Berlin as the *Prager Montagsblatt's* correspondent, I met Egon Fischer von Seekamm, its owner, in Zurich. I went back to the Reich temporarily, but once my wife and children were safely out of the land I set out for Hain in Silesia, with nothing except two sandwiches in my pocket, to climb over the Krkonoše (Riesengebirge) ridge to exile.

During those initial years of Hitler's era, the refugees — preponderantly intellectuals and men persecuted for political reasons — found a truly interesting new environment in Prague. Czech, Jewish, and leftist Sudeten German circles vied in initiating them into the unique, grandiose, spiritual atmosphere, the bilingual world of the Czech capital, with its stimulating — indeed, exciting — mixture of cultures. Jewish and non-Jewish groups extended aid to any and all. The Petscheks, the Weinmanns, and other leading Jewish families helped wherever possible. Refugee committees mushroomed, among them the Democratic Refugee Welfare, with Kurt R. Grossmann at its head, and the Šalda Committee.* No refugee will forget the two great Jewish women Hanna Steiner and Marie Schmolka,† who overextended their forces in order to enable the organizations they directed to proffer the most effective assistance humanly possible.

Some of Prague's Jews who represented foreign countries as consuls also helped, wherever their diplomatic authority permitted. Tribute is due to Consul Fuchs, representing Ecuador, Consul Lederer, for Bolivia, and Consul Engel, acting for the United States. In 1938 Engel provided me with a United States visa in a matter of twenty-four hours — as I sat in the Café Nizza I had read in the still-moist extra edition about Hitler's invasion of Austria, and I had stormed to him forthwith. In this connection, it was strange that very few Jews in Germany, and also in other countries, availed themselves of the then-open United States immigration quotas up to 1938.

I knew Prague. In 1919, after the First World War had ended, I was

---

* See Grossmann's Refugees to and from Czechoslovakia, p. 567.

† Both women were prominent Zionists, but Marie Schmolka was also very active in the International Women's League for Peace and Freedom.

the first German journalist accorded an extensive interview with President Tomáš G. Masaryk. Sitting for fully two hours at a window of his study at the Hradčany Castle, with the afternoon sun streaming in, we discussed politics — and even more exhaustively Goethe and Tolstoy and the complex problem of German-Czech conciliation. The *Prager Presse*, a government-subsidized German daily, filled its entire front page with that interview.

So now I was again in Masaryk's country. I worked for the Czechoslovak press — published in either Czech or German — and was a correspondent for Swiss and other papers.

Prague's world of journalism was simply grand — and how many truly great Jewish faculties were at work there to produce some of the most outstanding papers in existence. At the *Prager Presse* there was Arne Laurin, editor-in-chief and confidant of both Masaryk and, later, Beneš — a brilliant politician. Paul Eisner was also there — an essayist par excellence. The paper *Bohemia* had Gustav Kauder as chief editor, one of the foremost Ullstein-bred journalists and also an escapee from Hitler's Germany. When the Nazis invaded Czechoslovakia in March 1939 he committed suicide.

In an ancient former convent and its many-nooked rooms men such as Franz Bacher and Ferdinand Demel worked — the latter published the *Europress* in Frankfurt in the postwar period. There was the *Prager Tagblatt*, a model of journalism, with Rudolf Keller as its magnificent writer of editorials and Bruno Blau (called "The Doctor") its editor-in-chief. The unique Rudi Thomas was its live wire and stimulant; he, too, chose death when the Nazi boots first trod Prague's pavements. Here was Max Brod, the prolific writer of conversation pieces (*feuilletons*) and the paper's most famous theater critic.

Yes, indeed, journalism at its best had many distinguished representatives on the *Prager Tagblatt*. The room Thomas had abandoned was occupied for many years by Johannes Burckhard — refugee, poet, and author. He was the son of a high state official of Saxony and was known by his pen name, Ossip Kalenter; on the *Tagblatt* he worked as manuscript reader.

At the time socialist papers were almost everywhere. Prague's *Sozialdemokrat* was led by Dr. Emil Strauss, who succumbed later in Hitler's concentration camps. Emil Franzel, who was for a long time the postwar Socialist party's educational director, with his friend Wenzel Jaksch (who in the postwar period played a leading role among the Sudeten refugees), tried to give the paper a new direction toward their *volks-sozialische* ideas. Franzel and Jaksch had close contacts with Otto Strasser of the "Black Front," an opposition party to Hitler's "establishment party." The *Montagsblatt's* chief, Fischer von Seekamm, mentioned above, had his brother-in-law Franz Glaser as number two man; he was a drama critic and international journalist and later worked in Berne. Emigrés such as myself worked eagerly with all of them, as did Dr. Fritz Weiss, the psychoanalyst, and Ludwig Wronkow, the cartoonist. Wronkow's wife, Sonja, the ballad singer, opened the Malý Bar (Little Barroom) in Prague's old city. Leo Baum — son of Oscar Baum, the blind poet — worked for the *Prager Abend-Zeitung*. He subsequently went to Israel and perished there when the King David Hotel in Jerusalem was bombed. A no less distinguished paper was the *Börsenkurier*, a leader in the economic field, directed by Robert Lam.

Various emigrants founded new publications. Heinz Pol and Hermann Zucker worked at the anti-Nazi humor magazine *Simplicats*, to which both the great Czech satirist Adolf Hofmeister and cartoonist Erich Godal of Berlin contributed splendid caricatures; this magazine (financed by Dr. Ludwig Nathan) had a lifespan of only nine months. The *Arbeiter Illustrierte*, a leftist emigré creation (Communist), had on its staff F. C. Weiskopf, who later became Czechoslovakia's first ambassador to Peking. He was assisted by his Berlin-born and -bred wife, Alix Wedding, an author of children's books. Last but not least the *Arbeiter Illustrierte* had on its staff John Heartfield, famous for his political montages. His brother Wieland Herzfelde, the founder of the noted Malik-Verlag publishing house, had also come to Prague, where he continued his publishing house under a different name.

Here let me mention the German Communists who had found asylum in Prague and now met their Czechoslovak counterparts face to face. They stood for the "popular-front" idea. Back rooms of restaurants were the meeting places for emigrés such as Max Seydewitz* and Wilhelm Koenen, to name only two of the rather more important ones, with friends from the Czech camp such as E. E. Kisch — dubbed the "Raving Reporter" — and André Simon, alias

---

* Seydewitz continued during the Prague years to belong to the S.A.P. (Socialist Workers party), which he had founded in October 1931, though his sympathies grew more and more toward the Communists. See *Mit dem Gesicht nach Deutschland* by Em. Mathias, edited by Werner Link. Eine Dokumentation, published in Düsseldorf, Germany.

Otto Katz, who much later (in fact, just a week prior to Stalin's death) became the hapless victim of Stalinist persecution.

Still other emigrés founded the *Prager Mittag;* Wolfgang Bretholz, son of the eminent historian of Brno, became its editor-in-chief; Fritz Cassirer (of the family of philosophers), and A. Spann (subsequently with *The Herald Tribune*), and K. E. Winter were on the administrative staff. Later, Julius Hollos assumed the position of chief editor.

The *Weltbühne*, too, was an emigré publication, the continuation of its Berlin predecessor. Siegfried Jacobsohn's widow — publisher of the famed Doolittle books — became its director for one year, Willi Schlamm (and later Hermann Budzislawski), its chief editor. A strange fate was in store for Schlamm and Budzislawski: both came to America and both subsequently returned to Germany — to land in diametrically opposite political camps: one rightist, the other Communist.*

It would, of course, be wrong to indulge in constant comparisons between Jews, non-Jews, native Germans, Austrians, Czechoslovaks, and so on.† The Jewish contingent among those named in this presentation is, however, overwhelming. Many of them had settled in neighboring countries and returned to the Czechoslovak homeland as victims of Nazi persecution.

Indigenous and immigrant artists abounded in Prague in those years. Arnold Marlé, Fritz Valk, Ewald Schindler (the son-in-law of Arthur Nikisch), Walter Taub (son of the social democratic leader Siegfried Taub), Inge Waern (the Swedish Jewess), Marion Wünsche, Ferdinand Hart (the Golem of Duvivier's French movie version of the old legend, shot in the Barrandov studios) — they all enriched the theater and films. In one picture Ernst Reicher incited the mob — consisting mostly of refugee-extras who thus earned a few crowns — to unvarnished passion in a riot scene against Hitler.

Among the conductors towered George Schick and George Szell — to reap triumphs later in America — and Franz Allers, who was active at the City Theater in Aussig (Ústí n/Labem) and often came to Prague. He later was the leading conductor of *My Fair Lady*, the Shaw-inspired musical, and as such famous throughout the world.

---

* Compare Kurt R. Grossmann: Emigration — Die Geschichte der Hitlerflüchtlinge 1933–1945, Europäscher Verlagsanstalt, Frankfurt a/M, pp. 37 ff.

† The nonsectarian League for Human Rights published for about two years a German-language magazine, *Aufruf*, under the splendid editorship of Dr. Friedrich Bill, a Praguer and contributor to the *Prager Tagblatt*.

The multitude of native Jewish and non-Jewish writers, such as Max Brod, Rudolf Fuchs, Bruno Adler, Leo Perutz, and later Johannes Urzidil — still pervaded by shades of Franz Kafka and Gustav Meyrink — now was swelled by a broad and representative group of Nazi-oppressed intellectuals: Alfred Wolfenstein, Heinz Liepmann, Kurt Kersten, Julius Bab, Stefan Heym, Hans Sahl, Roda Roda, Arnold Hahn, Robert Jungk, Robert Lantz (of the cinema), Frank Warschauer, Anton Kuh, Wilhelm Sternfeld, Willi Haas, Bruno Fürst (dubbed "Memory-Fürst"), Emil Faktor, Georg Lukacz, and Theodor Lessing, whom the Nazis murdered insidiously in Marienbad on August 30, 1933. Eugene Hollos, who became a reader of the Mercy publishing house of Moravská Ostrava, often came to Prague to visit. Oskar Maria Graf, with a group of his friends, had his headquarters in Brno. Josef Löbl, the great doctor and journalist, returned to his native Františkovy Lázně (Franzensbad), and Doc Loewy of Karlovy Vary (Carlsbad) founded a puppet theater there and later moved it to Israel with him.

Zionist-oriented writers were welcomed to the alert *Selbstwehr* by Felix Weltsch, its brilliant head; and for several years *The Jewish Review* could be published, a high-principled, internationally circulated monthly, a notable fighter against Hitler and for Israel. On the occasion of a journey for the United Jewish Appeal, this writer founded *The Jewish Review* in Mukačevo, Subcarpathian Ruthenia, assisted by two stout-hearted printers, Goldstein and Deutsch.

Many intellectuals among the emigrés found the doors of the Czech press open to them; they could write for the *České Slovo*, the *Lidové Noviny* — the leading dailies — or the weekly *Přítomnost*, and others. The cafés and hotels, established sanctuaries of Prague's intelligentsia, now became the home of the refugees as well. In the Café Continental, Gustav, the headwaiter, ruled — and extended credit, too; the Urban Café was the daytime haven and the Juliš the nighttime one. Political huddles, meetings, and trysts would take place in the various hotels — the Eden, Ambassador, Alcron, Šroubek, Zlatá Husa — or in restaurants, preferably Piskáček's or the Savarin.

Communication and "the grapevine" linked Karlovy Vary (Carlsbad), Prague, and Brno and fanned out to Vienna and Paris or went — underground — to Berlin. The literary output of Prague, written in both Czech and German, offered unceasing stimulation. Jewish life flourished, and to every professing emigré it offered an inexhaustible font of spiritual, and frequently actual, sustenance. Indeed, practically no one was lonely in Prague — except those refugees vegetating on the modest financial aid the various committees could provide! Hospitable doors were often opened to the refugees. Those seeking solitude and reflection found both in the Old-New Synagogue (*Altneuschul*) or at the unforgettable ancient Jewish cemetery. In that city, the past emanates enduringly from her houses and palaces, her churches and temples. The scene of a frequently violent history envelops the stranger, permeates his thinking; and tradition and modern life are interwined there. Here indeed is the theater of an uninterrupted struggle for the meaning, or national and international portent, of freedom and progress. Three cultures — Czech, German, and Jewish — share Prague's background.

A truly meaningful life opened before the refugee—a life, of course, with ever-novel shadows gathering on the horizon. Will anyone ever forget the day of Tomáš Masaryk's death, the forlorn start of the Beneš government, the deepening storm-auguries of Nazism, the conspiratorial cabals in the Sudetenland and, subsequently, the first harbingers of the approaching catastrophe — the airraid tests in the darkened city?

To the escapees from Hitler, Prague became a junction where, thanks to the magnanimous lenience of the Czechoslovak authorities, the friendship and amity of the city's elite, and the circumspect and spontaneous readiness of the Jewish community and society, they could not only live but could also fight against the common foe — their own and hospitable Czechoslovakia's.

The Czechs, and the Czechoslovak Jews in particular, were fully aware of the happenings beyond the frontiers. This knowledge fostered solidarity with the emigrés, and more often than not the nationals placed the refugees on a par with their own class or social level, thereby sparing them the humiliations that were frequently visited on refugees in other countries.

Let me reiterate that these are but scant reminiscences of mine. Each event here recorded might be amplified by some remembered vivid episode; each street of Prague has its history and tells an odd and thrilling story of men and humaneness. One thing is certain: this one-time refugee and his friends in Prague, many of whom became refugees themselves later on and are probably forgotten or even dead by now, will always recall those five years spent in Prague, in that almost-last outpost of democracy of the thirties.

EMIGRATION TO PALESTINE

by Fini Brada

Centuries before the founding of the Czechoslovak Republic, there had been Jews who left Slovakia, Bohemia, Moravia and Subcarpathian Ruthenia to live in the Holy Land. The very religious considered it a blessing to be able to settle and die in Eretz Israel. Supported by funds raised by their home communities or by various organizations, they built synagogues and living quarters. To this day there are in Jerusalem "Hungarian Houses" and "Mukačevo Houses," which are still occupied by descendants of settlers from Subcarpathian Ruthenia.*

With the issuance of the Balfour Declaration (1917) and the proclamation of the Palestine Mandate (1922), however, emigrants began to come to the Holy Land not so much for the purpose of ending their days there as in order to work toward the rebuilding of the Jewish National Home.

Almost immediately after the establishment of the State of Czechoslovakia, a "Central Palestine Emigration Office" was set up in Prague by the Zionist Organization in response to pressure from many young Zionists and transient refugees who were anxious to go to Palestine. Due to the fact that little was known about living and working conditions in Palestine and no visa system had been worked out, the Emigration Office could not begin organized operations until March 1920. But even before that date, the Office, with the help of Davis Trietsch, a prominent Zionist then residing in Czechoslovakia, had begun to assemble important data and to register prospective emigrants to Eretz Israel.

---

* [See Hirschler, The History of Agudath Israel in Slovakia, pp. 155–172 (Ed.)]

At a meeting of HaPo'el HaTzai'r and Tze'ire Tziyon held in Prague in March 1920, with a number of delegates from Palestine participating, a detailed program was worked out.* In April 1920, the Central Emigration Department (*Va'ad Ha'Aliya*) of these groups in Berlin sent a representative to Czechoslovakia who set up additional Palestine Emigration Offices in Moravská Ostrava (now Ostrava), Bratislava, and Mukačevo. The task of unifying the activities of these new offices and maintaining contact with similar organizations in other countries fell to the Palestine Emigration Office in Prague.

The Palestine Emigration Offices in Czechoslovakia found themselves faced with a huge case load, consisting not so much of Czechoslovak Jews seeking to settle in Palestine as of thousands of refugees who streamed into Czechoslovakia during the year 1920 from Poland, Rumania, and Hungary seeking entry into Palestine. Most of these refugees had neither the official documents nor the means to reach their destination on their own. Besides, many lacked the qualifications required for the task of rebuilding the Jewish Homeland. The Palestine Emigration Offices had to select those who were not only willing to go to Palestine, but would prove useful there. It was on the recommendation of the Palestine Emigration Offices that the Palestine authorities granted immigration certificates.

In September 1920, Samuel Landman, political secretary at Zionist Headquarters in London, visited Czechoslovakia on his journey to the various Palestine emigration centers in Europe. His presence was the occasion for a conference held in Moravská Ostrava that October, at which representatives from all the Palestine Emigration Offices of Europe met to formulate plans to unify their activities.

After the Palestine Administration had passed official regulations pertaining to immigration, the Palestine Emigration Offices began to issue "certificates" (visas) to prospective emigrants who were without financial means. Within a period of two years, a total of fifty such certificates were issued in Czechoslovakia. During the period from 1920 to July 1921, a total of 4,112 emigrants to Palestine were processed by the Palestine Emigration Offices of Czechoslovakia.

In 1921, these early immigrants established in Palestine the Histadrut 'Ole Czechoslovakia (Federation of Immigrants from

* [Cf. O. Rabinowicz, pp. 19–136 (Ed.)]

Czechoslovakia). This group, renamed Hit'ahdut 'Ole Czechoslovakia (Union of Immigrants from Czechoslovakia) in 1938, is still in existence in the State of Israel today.

In 1920 'Avoda,' a Palestine settlement society, was founded in Prague. That same year saw the establishment of the Halutz Association, which prepared and organized young Zionists for settlement in Palestine. Also in 1920, the first group of *'olim* from the Bar Kochba students' organization* left Czechoslovakia for Palestine. After a period of agricultural training in Hefziba, a small settlement near Hadera, this group built its own settlement, also named Hefziba, at the foot of Mount Gilboa.

The second organized group of young people to leave Czechoslovakia for Palestine belonged to the Blau-Weiss ("Blue-White") youth organization. This group, known as K'vutza Biberach, after the German town of Biberach where they had received their agricultural training prior to embarking for Palestine, eventually formed the core of the settlement of Sarid near 'Afule. At the same time, most members of the Prague Girls' Club also left for Palestine.

In view of the increasing demand, it was soon decided to set up agricultural and industrial training centers in Czechoslovakia rather than have the settlers receive their preparatory instruction in Palestine itself or in countries in transit. The first organization to establish such centers in Czechoslovakia was the Halutz Association which was founded at the Second Territorial Zionist Conference in 1921. By the end of that year, this organization had one hundred members in its various training centers.

As a result of the growing interest in settlement in Palestine on the one hand, and various political developments within the Zionist movement on the other, each Zionist party with a youth organization undertook to establish a training center of its own. Thus, by 1926, HaShomer, the Socialist Zionist youth movement, with a membership of some 1,800, had established its first settlement, K'vutza Shomriya in Palestine, and the Mizrahi HeHalutz, the religious Zionist youth organization in Czechoslovakia, had also formed a settlement in Eretz Israel. In 1930, the Revisionist B'rith Trumpeldor (Betar) founded its first training center in Slovakia.

Unfortunately, not all of the Jews in Czechoslovakia who decided to settle in Palestine were able to do so. In view of British restrictions

* [Cf. A. M. Rabinowicz, vol. I, pp. 193–200 (Ed.)]

on Jewish immigration to the Holy Land, first priority for the limited number of certificates available had to be given to the Jews of Poland, Rumania, and Germany who were increasingly menaced by anti-Semitism; Czechoslovakia was still considered a place of peace and safety for Jews. Hence during the period from 1920 until the Nazi occupation of Czechoslovakia, no more than 5,895 certificates wece issued to Czechoslovak Jews. It should be noted, however, that in addition to these "legal" immigrants, there were considerable numbers of young men and women who went to Palestine merely to visit, but decided to stay there. Many of the young people who participated in the Maccabi Festivals held in Palestine in 1933 and 1935 did not return to Czechoslovakia.* Other visitors sometimes decided to forfeit the deposit required of tourists and stayed to join one of the settlements.

In 1937, the Central Palestine Emigration Office in Prague attempted to obtain a number of special certificates required for immigration into Palestine under Youth 'Aliya. However, the request was refused because all available certificates of this type were being allocated to Germany and Austria.

Hitler's annexation of the Sudeten area forewarned the Jews of Czechoslovakia of impending disaster. By the fall of 1938, Youth 'Aliya camps had been set up all over Czechoslovakia, not under that official designation, but within the existing organizations of Makkabi HaTza'ir (Youth Maccabi), the Blue White, HaShomer HaTza'ir, and HaPo'el HaMizrahi.

In May 1939, a Youth 'Aliya school was established in Prague by the Zionist Organization. Consisting of four homeroom units with an enrollment of twenty children each, this training center offered a program of general and Jewish history, Bible, mathematics, nature studies, and Palestinography. After the outbreak of World War II four months later, four additional classroom units were added to the school. Similar Youth 'Aliya centers were also established in Slovakia and Subcarpathian Ruthenia.

The first Youth 'Aliya group, consisting of 150 boys and girls, left Czechoslovakia in September 1938. The second group left after Hitler's entry on April 2, 1939. In view of the fact that a total of no more than 350 Youth 'Aliya certificates had been allo-

* [See Pick, Sports, pp. 185–228 (Ed.)]

cated to the Palestine Emigration Office in Prague, Czechoslovak Youth 'Aliya leaders had to explore possibilities for the temporary settlement of youngsters in countries other than Palestine.* Unfortunately, due to lack of time for proper organization, not much could be accomplished along these lines. During the final months before the outbreak of World War II, only thirty-six boys and girls were transferred to England, and no more than thirty-five to Denmark. These youngsters were given agricultural training at *hakhshara* farms in the two countries. Eventually most of them succeeded in reaching Palestine.

Apart from these groups, some 100 young people who had gone to Palestine from Czechoslovakia with their parents joined Youth 'Aliya centers in Palestine.

By 1942, a total of approximately 520 boys and girls had received training through the Czechoslovak Youth 'Aliya Department, and subsequently settled in groups in various villages and settlements.

In 1938 and 1939, the Va'ad Le'umi and the Jewish Agency initiated a special project for the rescue of children from Czechoslovakia, whereby families in Palestine were requested to take into their homes Czechoslovak refugee children between the ages of eight and fifteen. A total of eighty-three boys and girls were taken to Palestine through this project. It must be pointed out that most of the families who accepted these children were themselves from Czechoslovakia, and many were either relatives or friends of the parents the children had left behind. A number of such families undertook to pay for the education of the newcomers, with the Social Department of the Va'ad Le'umi acting as guardian. When they reached the age of fifteen, the children were transferred to institutions run by Youth 'Aliya.

In 1939, special certificates were issued to young men and women in Czechoslovakia who had completed their final secondary school examinations and had registered for studies at institutions of higher learning in Palestine. A total of 137 students from Bohemia and Moravia, and another 65 from Slovakia availed themselves of this opportunity to enter Palestine without the usual visa difficulties. Among the students from Prague were several who had originally

---

* [Cf. Grossmann, p. 576 (Ed.)]

come from Subcarpathian Ruthenia and had been pursuing their studies at the universities in Prague. Of these students, 108 enrolled at the Hebrew University, 24 at the Jerusalem Conservatory, 39 at the Haifa Technion, and 11 at various *yeshivot*.

"ILLEGAL" IMMIGRATION

In view of the few certificates for immigration allocated to Czechoslovakia, and the closed-door policy of all countries, it soon became apparent that the approaching avalanche of Nazidom would force those who desired to emigrate to take desperate actions. As long as there was hope in Zionist circles that negotiations with the British authorities would result in increased numbers of certificates, "illegal" means of emigration were not considered practical or advisable. In this period, only the New Zionist Organization (Revisionists) and their youth organization B'rith Trumpeldor (Betar), which was not affiliated with the Zionist Organization, began organizing "illegal" transports from Czechoslovakia to Palestine. Soon, however, He-Halutz also began to organize "illegal" transports.

Participants in these transports were not only Czechoslovak citizens; Jewish refugees who had escaped from Germany and Austria and were staying in Czechoslovakia were also included. In many instances, the Czechoslovak police authorities cooperated in issuing to "stateless" refugees in Czechoslovakia temporary passports valid for travel abroad to enable them to pass through Europe unmolested on the way to Palestine.

These transports, as a rule, left from Bratislava, sailing down the Danube River. Taking this route made it possible for them to pass Hungary and Rumania without transit visas, since the Danube is an international body of water. At Constanta on the Black Sea they embarked for Palestine, where they were received by the organization which had arranged their particular transport. As is well known, many such transports were prevented by the British authorities from landing on Palestinian soil, and a great number of Czechoslovaks were among the "illegals" who were interned on Cyprus and Mauritius.* Still, some 6,000 Jews from Czechoslovakia succeeded in reaching Palestine by this means.

---

* [See Zwergbaum, From Internment in Bratislava and Detention in Mauritius to Freedom, pp. 599–654 (Ed.)]

THE "TRANSFER OF FUNDS" AGREEMENT

As the danger of war drew closer, the Palestine Emigration Office, administered by Jakob Edelstein, could no longer cope with the mushrooming demand for Palestine visas and certificates. To help meet the urgent need, the Jewish Agency, in 1939, allotted to the Czechoslovak Palestine Emigration Office 600 Halutz certificates and 1,070 other certificates distributed among the categories listed below:

1. Businessmen	400
2. Relatives of residents in Palestine and professional persons	68
3. Rabbis	18
4. Students	137
5. Youth	350
6. Children	77
7. WIZO and Women Workers' Council	20
Total	1,070

On the basis of these certificates, the Czechoslovak government gave permissionfor the transfer of a total of £500,000 ($2,500,000) to Palestine.

The background of this "transfer of funds" agreement is of some interest. As early as 1938, representatives of the Jewish Agency, seeing that the transfer of personal funds by emigrants had been blocked by the Národní banka which functioned as the State Bank of Czechoslovakia, began negotiations with the Czechoslovak government in Prague about possibilities of a barter transfer of property. Just as the two parties were about to come to an agreement, the Munich Pact was signed, ceding the Sudeten territory to Germany. Under the circumstances, it was feared that the government of Czechoslovakia would break off its negotiations with the Jewish Agency. These fears proved unjustified, however. There were still in the government men of good will who were anxious to help the Jews solve their emigration problems, and, even more important, with thousands of Jewish families moving into Prague from the Sudeten area, the Czech government was ready to agree to anything that might relieve it of the refugee burden. The £500,000 which were transferred to Palestine were part of a loan of £8,000,000 which the British government had just then extended to the government of Czechoslovakia. Under the terms of the agreement between the

Jewish Agency and the representatives of the Czechoslovak government, the £500,000 were to be used for the resettlement of Jews from Czechoslovakia in Palestine. In return, the Jews leaving Czechoslovakia turned over an equivalent amount in personal funds to the Národní banka of Czechoslovakia. The agreement, confirmed in writing by Dr. Josef Kalfus, the Minister of Finance in a letter to Dr. František Friedmann, the Jewish Agency representative in Prague, further stipulated that 2,500 Jews would have to leave Czechoslovakia by the end of June 1939.

Then, on March 15, 1939, Hitler's armies marched into Prague, and the loan of £8,000,000 was frozen in London. However, thanks in large measure to the untiring efforts of Leo Herrmann, a former member of the Bar Kochba group who was then in London representing the Jewish Agency, the British Parliament passed a special bill authorizing the transfer of £500,000 from the original amount earmarked for Czechoslovakia.

Unfortunately, by the time the money finally arrived in Jerusalem, the war had begun in Europe, and since there were no boats available in the ports of embarkation, the prospective emigrants for whom the funds had been set aside were stranded in Prague. Transports could leave only whenever the Jewish Agency managed to charter a boat. This slowed up emigration considerably, extending the operation well into the middle of 1940.

The £500,000 forwarded to Palestine under the transfer agreement were distributed among the arrivals as follows:

Businessmen	£275,000
Students	20,000
Immigrants without Certificates	45,000
Youth 'Aliya	50,000
Children's 'Aliya	3,840
Financing of auxiliary settlements	7,785
Middle-class settlements	4,000
Middle-class settlement of Nira	1,400
Loan funds for existing settlements of immigrants from Czechoslovakia	2,500
Loan fund for settlements of immigrants from Czechoslovakia to be established	
Gaston	600
Ma'anit	500
BaNiv	100

Loans for industries to be established by immigrants from Czechoslovakia	2,500
General Loan and Relief Fund	4,500
Fund to assist former Czechoslovak Zionist functionaries	2,500
Fund for Veteran Zionists	2,500
Keren Hayesod (Palestine Foundation Fund)	30,000
Keren Kayemet (Jewish National Fund)	20,000

When Slovakia broke away from the State of Czechoslovakia, the Zionists of Slovakia succeeded in effecting a special barter transfer in the value of £40,000. By this arrangement the emigrants paid the cash value of their merchandise to the Slovak State Bank and received the equivalent in Jerusalem.

The Jewish Agency allotted certificates as follows to the Palestine Emigration Office in Bratislava:

For Zionist functionaries	10
Agricultural workers	13
Businessmen	28
Students	56
Schools of WIZO and Women Workers' Council	24
Total	131

An amount of £4,000 was set aside by the Slovak government for students emigrating to Palestine from Slovakia.

Despite the almost insuperable difficulties, a total of 17,000 Jews from Czechoslovakia settled in Palestine prior to the establishment of the State of Israel. An additional 18,000 have arrived there since the founding of the State. It is generally agreed that these 35,000 immigrants from Czechoslovakia made an impressive contribution to the new society that is taking shape in the Jewish Homeland.

BIBLIOGRAPHY

Reports of the Executive of the Zionist Organization to the Zionist Congresses XII–XIX.

Jüdische Jugendblätter Prague, 1921–1924.

David Paul Merez (Maerz), "HaHa'avara Heczechit — Hatzala Bish 'at Tzara" (The Czech "Transfer" — Rescue in the Hour of Need), in *Prag Uyerushalayim* (Prague and Jerusalem) *Volume in Memory of Leo Herrmann*, Jerusalem, pp. 160–179.

Yehoshua Halevy, *Toldot Betar Czechoslovakia* (History of Czechoslovak Betar), Tel-Aviv, 1960 ("'Aliya' by All Means," pp. 158–165).

Sefer Ma'apilim (Book of the Courageous), edited by Moshe Bassok, Jerusalem, 1947.

John and David Kimche, *The Secret Roads*, London, 1954.

Ira A. Hirschmann, *Life Line to a Promised Land*, New York, 1946.

M. J. Ben-Gavriel, *Palästina und Israel*, Part of *Weltgeschichte der Gegenwart* (*World History of Present Time*) vol. I, Berne and Munich, 1919.

Hugo Bergmann, *Kibbutz Galuyot*, in *Jüdischer Almanach der Selbstwehr*, Prague, 1935/36.

Fini Brada, *The Czechoslovak Immigration to Palestine*, published by The Czechoslovak Settlers' Association, Tel-Aviv, 1919.

Britschgi-Schimmer, *Die Umschichtung der Jüdischen Einwanderer aus Deutschland zu städtischen Berufen in Palästina* (*The Retraining of Jewish Immigrants from Germany in Preparation for Urban Jobs*), published by the Jewish Agency for Palestine, 1936.

Gil Benjamin and M. Sikron, *Die Jüdische Bevölkerung, gemäss Alter, Geschlecht und Geburtsland, zwischen 1931 und 1954* (*The Jewish Population, According to Age, Sex, and Country of Origin between 1931 and 1954*), edited by The Central Bureau of Statistics, Jerusalem, 1955.

Gil Benjamin, *Dreissig Jahre Einwanderung nach Israel von 1919–49* (*Thirty-Years Immigration to Israel, from 1919 to 1949*), edited by the Immigration Department of the Jewish Agency, 1949.

"Dapim" (Pages) Report on Twenty Years of Youth 'Aliya, 1949.

Five Years of Youth 'Aliya, Volume of Essays, edited by the Jewish Agency, Jerusalem, 1919.

Jüdisches Lexicon, vols. I–V (*Jewish Encyclopedia*), Berlin, 1929.

James G. MacDonald, *My Mission in Israel 1948–1951*, New York 1951.

Report of the Jewish Agency, *Documents to the 22nd Zionist Congress*, 1946.

Abraham A. Weinberg, *Migration and Belonging*, The Hague, 1919.

Felix Weltsch, editor: *Prag Uyerushalayim* (*Prague and Jerusalem*), *Essays in Memory of Leo Herrmann*, Jerusalem, (undated) (Hebrew).

Aaron Zwergbaum, *Exile in Mauritius*, reprint from *Yad VaShem Studies on the Jewish Catastrophe and Resistance, IV*, Jerusalem, 1960.

W. Preuss, *Das Genossenschaftswesen in der Welt und in Israel* (*Cooperotives in the World and in Israel*), Berlin, 1958.

L. F. R. Williams, *The State of Israel*, London, 1957.

FROM INTERNMENT IN BRATISLAVA AND DETENTION IN MAURITIUS TO FREEDOM

THE STORY OF THE CZECHOSLOVAK REFUGEES OF THE ATLANTIC (1939–1945)

by Aaron Zwergbaum

1. *Preface*

September 4, 1970, was the thirtieth anniversary of the beginning of the odyssey of a group of 318 Jews from Czechoslovakia — while it did not last as long as the tribulations of the hero of Greek mythology, its duration of six years was long enough. A substantial difference between the ancient odyssey and this modern one is in regard to the happy ending: Odysseus returned to the island of his birth, Ithaca; the great majority of the Czechoslovak refugees found a new and permanent home in what was then Palestine. For most of its members their wanderings had begun before September 4, because they had been interned for nine months before they could leave the territory of Czechoslovakia. The fate of this group — detention in Bratislava, "illegal immigration" to Palestine, deportation to Mauritius, enforced stay in a detention camp on this tropical island, struggle for freedom, and final liberation — is a unique chapter in the checkered history of Czechoslovak Jewry and as such is worthy of being recorded and preserved. The time to undertake this task is now, when most members of the group are still alive and documents and other written material are still available. To the best knowledge of the present writer this subject has not yet been treated in a comprehensive and systematic way. Several short articles on the deportation of the refugees of the S.S. *Atlantic* — of whom the

Czechoslovak group formed a part — and on their detention in Mauritius have appeared at different times.[1] An extensive study in Hebrew and English — *Exile in Mauritius*, by this author — was published by Yad Vashem in 1960.[2] However, all these writings dealt with the Mauritius story in general rather than with the Czechoslovak group in particular. Furthermore, nothing has been as yet published on the important prelude, the internment in Bratislava, nor have the special position and problems of the Czechoslovak group in Mauritius adequately been described and explained.

Therefore, this article can claim to be the first monograph on what may be called the longest and most exotic chapter of the Aliya Bet[3] from Czechoslovakia. As far as sources are concerned, the author has used not only those articles that have been published on the Mauritius case,[4] including of course his own, but also the extensive files on Mauritius deposited with the Central Zionist Archives of Jerusalem[5] containing a number of important documents, as well as the material in the archives of Yad Vashem in Jerusalem. Supplementary information was gleaned from *The Camp News*, published in Mauritius in 1941 and 1942, and from the *Sefer Hamaapilim*,[6] which deals with "illegal immigration" in general. Further sources were the author's diaries, surveys, and annual reports covering the internment in Bratislava, the Aliya Bet and the detainment in Mauritius. They have the advantage of being almost contemporary testimonies, because they were written in Mauritius a short time after the happenings described therein. Furthermore, numerous former members of the Czechoslovak group of Mauritius were interviewed, particularly on matters of which the author had no personal experience — such as service in the Czechoslovak Army in World War II.[7]

2. *Aliya Bet*

Although as early as 1934 the S.S. *Velos* arrived at the shores of Palestine with 350 Halutzim from Poland and ushered in the Haapala — illegal immigration — with the consent of and under the auspices of the Zionist authorities, the Zionist Organization of Czechoslovakia (where the need for emigration to Palestine was not felt as strongly as in Eastern Europe) was averse to "illegal" transport organized either by the Czechoslovak Revisionist movement* or

---

* [See O. K. Rabinowicz, Czechoslovak Zionism, pp. 99–108 (Ed.)]

by private persons. After Munich this policy was changed under a double pressure and challenge: the infamous White Paper of Malcolm MacDonald (1939), which severely restricted Jewish immigration to Palestine, and, in particular, the distress of the Jewish refugees from the Sudeten and the Jewish emergency in the Protectorate and the Slovak state. The Zionist institutions began quite openly to organize aliya, which was illegal under the immigration regulations issued by the Palestine government — but those again were inconsistent with, and repugnant to, the letter and the spirit of the Palestine Mandate.

The Zionist authorities treated this Aliya Bet like regular immigration; it was highly selective, demanding (at least of younger people) Hakshara (agricultural training), a certain knowledge of Hebrew, affiliation to a Zionist body, good health, and so on. There was a rather low age limit, and the passage money was fixed on the principle that the well-to-do should pay not only for themselves but also for those without means.[8]

The first Aliya Bet transport arranged by institutions of the Zionist Organization and implemented in Czechoslovakia augured well for the future: it left Brno on April 4, 1939, avoided interception by the British, and reached Palestine as early as April 22.[9] Its members could disperse in the country without being apprehended and imprisoned as "uncertified immigrants." A second transport was to follow soon. However, it was not as favored by fate as its predecessor. This "Maccabi-Hehalutz Transport," as it was called at the first stage, will be the subject of this study.[10]

As its name indicates, the transport consisted of two main groups: members of the Maccabi (about 40 per cent) and members of the Hehalutz (about 60 per cent). The latter were subdivided into the youth movements (Hashomer Hatzair, Techelet Lavan, Netzach, Maccabi Hatzair) and in Stam (unaffiliated) Halutzim, some of whom hailed from Podkarpatská Rus and had lived for some time in the Hehalutz homes of Prague and Brno. By and large the Maccabim were the older and the Halutzim the younger element. The average age was twenty-seven; people over fifty were a rare exception, and the children in the transport could be counted on the fingers of one hand. Women were in a minority of about 40 per cent. About two-thirds came from Bohemia and Moravia, one-third from the eastern half of Czechoslovakia.

As to its social and economic composition, the transport was made up of quite different elements: destitute Halutzim and children of rich parents who had found their way into the pioneering youth movements; once-prosperous businessmen; quite a few members of the professions — doctors, lawyers, engineers; numerous white-collar workers; and many young people whom the German occupation had compelled to discontinue their studies. Some people were what in Zionist parlance were called *umgeschichtet* — they had learned a trade or craft, though not always thoroughly.

Since the members of the transport had been carefully picked from various points of view — in particular with regard to their usefulness for Palestine — the Maccabi-Hehalutz Transport was in a sense an elite, at least in comparison with some "private transports" launched from Czechoslovakia in 1938 and 1939. Some participants had enjoyed a good Jewish and Zionist education — there were a few graduates of the Hebrew *Gymnasium* of Mukačevo — and most of them had been active Zionists; but some of the younger people were more than half assimilated. In spite of this great diversity, strong bonds linked them together: the common fate, the common enemy, and the common aim. Before the transport, which numbered 318 persons, could leave Prague for Bratislava, its members had to undergo nerve-racking experiences. First, they had to produce many documents from the authorities of the Protectorate* and their German masters and to pay numerous and onerous rates and taxes; then they had to report personally to the dreaded Gestapo-staffed Central Office for Jewish Emigration in Prague-Střešovice. Some people passed without difficulty, others were subjected to various indignities. The worst, however, was the endless waiting from one term to another, the false alarms followed by postponements when one had the feeling that time was running out and that a trap was closing around the Jews of the Protectorate.

When at last the hour of departure came, it was heart-rending to take leave of family and friends, to put on a brave face, and to conceal the fear that it would be a farewell forever, as indeed it was in most cases.[11] That the Germans permitted able-bodied Jews to leave their territory in wartime, knowing full well that the visas for Peru and Paraguay that figured in the passports were fakes and that

* [The western part of Czechoslovakia is known as the Protectorate: Bohemia and Moravia-Silesia occupied by Germany after the Munich accord. (Ed.)]

Palestine was the destination, appears today, almost even more than it did then, a veritable miracle. Perhaps they thought that the reinforcement in manpower delivered to the British by the transport would be more than outweighed by the troubles the Arabs were expected to start because of the large influx of Jews.[12]

3. *Life in the Slobodáreň*

In the north of Bratislava, not far from the railroad station, the municipality had erected a tall and rather ugly structure called Slobodáreňi a noclaháreň — a sort of cheap hotel and boardinghouse especially for single people. It served as accommodation and place of internment for the various "illegal transports" of Jewish refugees to Palestine during their short stay in the Slovak capital. The members of the Maccabi-Hehalutz Transport of Prague, however, were to live there for almost nine months.

It should be said at the outset that not all of them stayed at the Slobodárni, as it was called, all the time. The Halutzim who were affiliated with the Mizrachi preferred to be at the Patronka, the second internment camp in Bratislava — a conglomeration of huts and barracks which had formerly served as an ammunition factory — because only kosher food was issued there;[13] in the course of time a few members of the transport received immigration certificates and could leave for Palestine legally via Hungary. Others who were natives of that country or of Slovakia despaired of the prospects of the transport when its fortunes were at the lowest ebb and returned to their domiciles. On the other hand, in the course of these nine months a few people who had been granted individual exit permits from the Protectorate joined the transport. These additions and "defections" almost cancelled each other out, and when the transport left in September 1940 it had almost exactly the same number of members as when it had arrived in December 1939.

Living conditions in the Slobodárňa were very bad. The internees had to pay 5 korunas per head per night for accommodations of the worst sort. The rooms and halls reserved for their use — some of them underground without daylight — were terribly overcrowded. Two women had to share one bed; men slept on planks or on very poor mattresses. Washing and toilet facilities were inadequate, and the central heating worked only a few hours a day, a great hardship in the exceptionally rigorous winter of 1939–1940. The food, which was alternately provided by the kitchen of the Slobodárňa and restaurants like Reismann's, turned from bad to worse — quite naturally, because the price paid for it had to be reduced drastically from 29 korunas at the beginning to 9 korunas at the end. While the inmates of the Slobodárňa received rather large quantities of badly prepared meat at first, there were times later when only a generous bread ration stood between them and the pangs of hunger. A limited number of people got kosher food, which was somewhat better than the ordinary fare.

The total bill for the Slobodárňa (accommodations, food, guards, and so on) amounted to approximately 1,500,000 korunas. This considerable sum was provided out of the funds of the Maccabi-Hehalutz Organization in Prague and, when these had become exhausted, by the Jewish community of that city. Thanks to the indefatigable efforts and the skill of its treasurer, Dr. Franta Friedmann, the numerous financial difficulties which arose and often threatened the very existence of the transport were always somehow solved.[14] The Slobodárňa was in fact a prison and the Hlinkova Garda,* the mainstay of the puppet Slovak state, served as prison guards.

The detachment of the guard stationed in the Slobodárňa — and also the one in the Patronka — were commanded by Plukovník (Colonel) Imrich Vašina, an "old fighter" of the Hlinka party.† Vašina was indeed what he proudly used to call himself, a "človek z l'ùdu," a man of the people, but in the worst sense of this term: uneducated but shrewd, overbearing and suffering from inferiority complexes, an opportunist and drunkard, and utterly corrupt. The latter trait was, of course, rather an advantage for those in his clutches, because with money many things could be arranged. However, it would be unfair to say that he was always brutal, and sometimes he even showed himself to be good-natured, in a primitive way.[15] The men under his command, the guards, were mostly taken from the dregs of Slovak society; they had put on their black uniform not out of conviction but in order to earn easy money. Their daily pay — which was borne by the transport — amounted to 68 korunas, apart from what was called "refreshments." The monthly

---

* [The storm troops of the Hlinka Guard (Ed.)]

† [Slovak People's party (of Hlinka); Hlinkova Slovenská Ludová Strana (HSL'S). (Ed.)]

income of the Plukovník was estimated at 10,000 korunas. It was a terrible defenseless feeling to be in the hands of such men and to depend on their whims. Nevertheless, the Hlinka Guard, as it was in 1940, was infinitely preferable to German SS or SA.

Owing to the overcrowding, the problems of food and washing and cleaning and the like took much time; the problem was how to spend the rest of the day usefully. Some people — like the leaders of the transport, doctors, nurses, teachers, and so on — were fully occupied; others devoted much time to studies, in particular Hebrew and English. Many Hebrew courses for beginners and advanced students were held; a special Rosh Tarbut organized lectures and provided reading material; a few homemade plays were performed — no mean achievement in view of the terrible lack of space. While some people understood very well how to organize their lives and to spend their time profitably, others were too nervous to concentrate on studies and sought relaxation in card playing, in particular bridge. Twice a day the inmates of the Slobodárňa were permitted to breathe some fresh air in the small courtyard — of course, under the supervision of the Hlinka Guard. These breaks were the highlights of the day because only there could men and women meet; there also the eagerly expected mail was distributed. Because of the censorship a postcard from Prague or Brno to Bratislava took as long as a week. It was possible to play volleyball in the courtyard. This became the favorite sport of the Slobodárňa. On occasion, longer outings — usually to the Patronka — took place, provided one of the guards graciously consented to serve as escort.

A typical, but neither pleasant nor productive, pastime was discussion of the current political and military situation which, during the nine months, grew from bad to worse and at the end looked desperate. When the transport arrived in Bratislava, the "phony war" was still going on; when it left, the Battle of Britain had just begun. The main occupation in the Slobodárňa was waiting and preparing for the departure, and there will be more about this in the following section.

The attitude of the Jews of Bratislava toward the internees was beyond praise. Not only did individuals extend brotherly help to the inmates of the Slobodárňa whom they happened to know personally, but the Jewish community as such did its utmost to ameliorate the position of the members of the transport and also of the people in the Patronka. These latter were in an even worse predicament because they were not so well organized and had no Dr. Franta Friedmann to care for them. It was not only the material help that mattered but also the manifestation of Jewish solidarity, the feeling that other Jews were thinking of them, that gave great comfort to the inmates of the Slobodárňa, who had recently left behind their loved ones and whose future was uncertain.[16] It should be mentioned here that thanks to the guarantees of Jewish bodies and also individuals, at certain periods leave passes could be obtained for a limited time. However, they were revocable and were indeed often suddenly canceled without any apparent reason.[17]

During the nine months between arrival and departure, the position of the Jews of Bratislava and of Slovakia in general deteriorated very much. After the fall of France the infamous trio Tiso-Tuka-Mach embarked on a radical anti-Semitic course. The Slovak state, which from the very beginning had been dependent on, and directed by, Nazi Germany, became a complete — and perhaps the most faithful — satellite of the Reich. Developments which in Germany had taken years and in the Protectorate months occurred in Slovakia in the course of a few weeks. "Aryanization" of businesses, the elimination of Jews from schools, severe restriction of movement, the interdiction of coffeehouses, places of entertainment, and so on came almost overnight. Many Jews of Bratislava who a short while before had generously helped the refugees themselves became destitute. The assistance rendered by the local Jewish community to the inmates of the Slobodárňa is to be appreciated the more as it was given at a time when the Slovak Jews had indeed enough troubles of their own.[18]

4. *Waiting for the Ship*

The position of the Maccabi-Hehalutz Transport in Slovakia was utterly unstable and precarious. The Slovak transit visa had been granted for a few days only, and the transport was to depart at the end of December 1939 at the latest. The original plan was that after a few days' stay in the Slobodárňa it would be joined by a group of Halutzim from Berlin and leave. This project did not materialize; when the Danube became icebound at the beginning of January — earlier than usual — it was clear that for this reason alone departure was unthinkable before the lapse of several weeks. Consequently, the permit for the sojourn in Bratislava had to be renewed from time to time — either tacitly by bribing police officials, or openly by a prolongation of the visa. Both cost a lot of money. It may be said that in the last analysis it was Slovak corruption which the refugees had to thank for the extension of their stay in Bratislava and their rescue and survival. Beginning in May 1940 the Slovak authorities began to fix terms for the departure of the transport and to threaten that, unless it left on time, its members would be sent back to the Protectorate. June 17, 1940, a sad enough day anyway because of the capitulation of France, was most critical for the refugees. They were ordered to pack their belongings and told by the grinning guards that they would be taken to the German frontier, which meant a Nazi concentration camp. At the last moment money again averted the worst, but it became abundantly clear that the situation was untenable and that it was imperative to get away as quickly as possible.

The episode of the *Vojvoda Misič* and *Princezna Elena* in April 1940 bode ill for the people of the Slobodárňa, a few of whom had been allowed to join a Slovak Aliya Bet transport which was to leave on these two Danube steamers. After spending a fortnight on board, the passengers were ordered to disembark, and the whole project came to nothing. There existed two versions of the reasons for this failure: according to the first, the Yugoslav authorities, apparently at the instigation of the British, did not permit the transit; according to the second, it was the Germans who prevented the ships from sailing; even more important, no seagoing ships were available. In June hopes rose again because the *Pencho*, an ancient, rickety paddle steamer, actually left Bratislava with an illegal transport which had been organized by the Revisionists. In August, when the disbandment of the Maccabi-Hehalutz Transport was earnestly considered and the possibility of sending its members to Hakshara in Hungary and Slovakia was being explored, a miracle happened: it became known that the inmates of the Slobodárňa — and also of the Patronka — were to be joined to a mass transport arranged with the consent (and probably also with the assistance) of the Germans by Kommerzialrat Storfer of Vienna.[19]

It is clear that this waiting, with its ups and downs of high hopes and bitter disappointments, was trying and nerve-racking for everybody and in particular for the leaders of the transport. Here a few words should be said about its organization, which was conceived in Prague and remained substantially unchanged until the transport got to Mauritius.

The transport was organized on semimilitary lines into Kvutzot, consisting as far as possible of people belonging together either by common experience — e.g., those who had been together on Hakshara, like the groups of Medlánky and Požáry, named after the place where they had undergone agricultural training — or by affiliation to the same youth movement or by membership in a joint scheme. Here the "Meshek Minimum" should be remembered; it was organized as a group of the Maccabim by Dr. Erwin Samstag, a veteran Zionist of Znojmo, and was intended to form in Eretz Israel an independent economic unit on a mixed basis — partly collectivistic, partly individualistic — according to the lofty principles of Popper-Lynkeus,* which, however, had not so far been put to a practical test.[20] There were six plugot (companies), consisting of several kvutzot each: 1 and 2, Maccabi; 3, Hashomer Hatzair; 4, Maccabi Hatzair; 5, Hakshara Meurevet (mixed) West; and 6, Hakshara Meurevet East. Their heads, the rashej plugot, formed a vaad (committee) which was to advise the leaders of the transport who had been appointed by the Maccabi and the Hehalutz in Prague. Head of the transport (Transportleiter) was Gustl Trieger of the Hehalutz, an experienced youth leader, who was assisted by the other members of the Transportleitung, consisting of Dr. Pavel Strahovský (Steinhauer) and Willy Gansel (both Hehalutz) and Eli Friedmann (Maccabi). Apart from this central committee, certain people were put in charge of special tasks like sanitation or cultural activities (the writer of these lines) without belonging to the Transportleitung proper.

The task of the Transportleitung became less and less enviable the longer the transport was delayed and the more impatient its members grew. In order to maintain discipline and to bolster the morale of the transport, for the avoidance of panic, and in deference to the wishes of the Aliya Bet headquarters in Geneva (with whom they were in almost daily telephone contact), the Transportleitung had to put off the members of the transport with promises of an imminent departure. They could not reveal the full truth — as far as it was known to themselves. This truth was ugly enough. The Aliya Bet headquarters — which later became known as the Mossad — could not get the ships for transporting the emigrants on the Danube and over the sea. The British were buying up vessels that were potential carriers of illegal immigrants, and they let it be known that even if

* [Joseph Popper (his nom de plume was Lynkeus) was a cosmopolitan, scientific writer, Kolín, 1838–1921. (Ed.)]

ships were hired or bought, they would place in their way insurmountable difficulties.

Although these delays and postponements were absolutely beyond the control of the Transportleitung, it was only human that the members of the transport, in their nervousness and apprehension, began to put the blame on their own leaders, charging them with inefficiency and "softness" toward Geneva. In July a "palace revolution" broke out; the Transportleitung was deposed and replaced by a new one consisting of Dr. Pavel Horetzky (Hehalutz) and Mr. Leo Leschner (Maccabi), who at fifty was one of the oldest members of the transport.[21] The new leaders took the wise precaution of letting each member sign a declaration of loyalty, which indeed was honored.

Just as the former Transportleitung cannot in fairness be blamed for the procrastination and delays, the new one cannot be credited with the ultimate success of the departure, which was due to a singular and happy coincidence: the Germans were going to repatriate *Volksdeutsche** from Bessarabia, which had been ceded by Rumania to Russia. They were to be transported to the Reich on Danube steamers. This was, of course, a one-way traffic and the steamers would have gone down the river empty. Thus the human cargo of the Jews was welcome because the exorbitant price paid for their voyage was enough to cover also the fare of the German repatriates.

It should be added that the conduct of Geneva (Zvi Yechiel, Nathan Schwalb, and Moshe Auerbuch), which exasperated the members of the transport, appears today in a different light: they were not free agents but worked against heavy odds and encountered obstacles which were often indeed insurmountable. In any case, when the seventeenth year of the State of Israel was proclaimed "Year of Illegal Immigration" (see note 12), the former inmates of the Slobodárňa did not join in the lavish praise bestowed on the Mossad for its feats in organizing and carrying out Aliya Bet (which indeed, in many other cases, was well deserved). They remembered that it was Storfer to whom they owed their escape from the clutches of the Nazis and their Slovak satellites and even more to Oskar Krasniansky,[22] the Bratislava representative of the Maccabi-Hehalutz and the Jewish community of Prague, who had persuaded a rather reluctant Storfer to join the Slobodárňa to his huge transport; and also to Dr. Jakuboci of the Bratislava police, chief of its Aliens'

* [Native Germans (Ed.)]

Department, who added some pressure to this persuasion because he wanted to aid the refugees and, quite understandably, also get rid of them.

The month of August saw preparations for the departure both on the part of the Transportleitung — which acquired stores and various pieces of equipment, from cooking kettles and medicines to books for the ship's library — and individuals and kvutzot, many of whom intended to live as communes, a form of life which proved to be well adapted to the conditions of the ship.

There occurred again some delay, until at last two ships that belonged to the Donaudampfschiffahrtsgesellschaft of Vienna arrived: the *Uranus*, with a Hehalutz transport from Germany, and the *Helios*, which was destined to carry the remnants of the Jewish community of Gdansk (Danzig), more than five hundred people, headed by their young chief rabbi, Dr. Meir Bieler, with many elderly people and some children. The inmates of the Slobodárňa would have preferred to be assigned to the *Uranus* with her more congenial company, but a Zionist Court of Arbitration decided, and quite rightly so, that the Patronka should embark on that ship and the Slobodárňa on the *Helios*, in order to equalize the composition of both transports and to make them viable. Otherwise one ship would consist almost entirely of young men and women and the other mostly of elderly people and children.

September 3, 1940, was the definite date of departure. Vašina made a great farewell speech. Its keynote was "Já som človek" (I am a human being), and its almost philosemitic contents were wholly inconsistent with his behavior during the past few weeks. The refugees had to undergo a customs examination which was utterly arbitrary: some officials confiscated things like chocolate, coffee, and soap which others let pass without any difficulties. There was a last-minute hitch; it appeared that the Peruvian or Paraguyan visas were missing in the passports of a few people, especially those who had not come to the Slobodárňa with the main body of the transport but joined it later from the Protectorate or a few days before departure from Slovakia. The captain of the *Helios*, though knowing perfectly well that Palestine was the destination, insisted with true Nazi regard for pseudolegality that the visas be provided. They were, though not by very orthodox means, with the active help of the Slovak police.

It should be added that Storfer had agreed to pay the fare for the voyage on the Danube for the whole transport, the people from

Danzig and Czechoslovakia no less than the Viennese, who formed the great majority of his own transport, while the seagoing ships were chartered out of funds collected in the Protectorate, whose national bank permitted their transfer to foreign countries.[23] The welcome given to the ex-internees of the Slobodárňa by the Danzig people on board the *Helios* was rather cool; small wonder, because the ship was crowded enough even before this addition of more than three hundred passengers. Little did the Danzigers imagine that within two years many of their girls would marry young men of the Prague transport. With the help of the "Hagana" which had been set up, organized, and equipped in the Slobodárňa, order was established soon; the little space available was equitably allocated, and every person and every group arranged themselves on board the ship as best they could. It was an odd and disagreeable feeling to sail under the swastika flag. But on the other hand, the very fact that the steamers were German guaranteed that seagoing ships were available; otherwise no one would have taken the Jewish refugees on board.

On the morning of September 4 the *Uranus* and the *Helios* left Bratislava; a few days later they were joined by two more ships, the *Schoenbrunn* and the *Melk*.[24]

5. *The Adventures of the S.S. Atlantic*

The voyage was by no means one of the pleasure trips for which the *Helios* was originally designed. The ship was overcrowded, washing facilities were inadequate, and the food was neither good nor ample. The weather, however, was glorious. The convoy passed Budapest, Belgrade, the Iron Gate, and Turnu Severin without incident. On September 7 the refugees were met by a shocking sight between Ruse, on the Bulgarian bank of the river, and Giurgiu, on the Rumanian side: the *Pencho* was anchoring in midstream because she was not permitted to call at a port nor to continue her voyage, being unseaworthy.[25] The passengers of the *Helios* volunteered part of their rations for the *Pencho*, where food had become very scarce. The convoy arrived at Tulcea, in the Danube delta, exactly one week after the departure from Bratislava.

Three days later, on September 14 — the third anniversary of the death of T.G. Masaryk, as many people remembered — the passengers of the *Helios* embarked on the *Atlantic*, one of the three ships that were waiting in the harbor. So did the people of the *Schoenbrunn*, most of them Viennese Jews, and some of the former inmates of the Patronka. The *Atlantic* was an old and decrepit Greek freighter belonging to Mr. Avgerinos of Athens but flying the Panama flag. It had been adapted for the transport of human beings in a way that was not only primitive but also utterly inadequate; the few cabins and tiers of wooden bunks set up in the holds did not suffice and therefore every square foot in the gangways and on deck was occupied by refugees, some of whom had so little space that for more than two months they could not stretch their limbs and sleep properly. The sanitary conditions were terrible: people had to wait in long queues for one hour or more to use the primitive latrines in the stern.

Three kitchens doled out poor food: soup at noon, tea twice a day, and in the evening as far as possible, a small ration of cheese, vegetables, and the like. The bread ration was 250 grams (less than 10 ounces) a day in "good times," but frequently it had to be reduced to 150 grams of moldy biscuits and even less. The Czechoslovaks were in a better position than the rest because they could at least in the beginning, supplement these rations by the provisions they had acquired in Bratislava.

Owing to the poor sanitation and food the *Atlantic* became a fertile ground for maladies and epidemics. Twelve people died of typhoid on board the ship or after its arrival in Palestine, one of them a young girl of the Maccabi-Hehalutz Transport.[26] It was, first and foremost, thanks to the "Hagana" of the Czechoslovaks that order was brought out of chaos. The "Hagana" was reinforced by young people from other transports, especially the Viennese, but it remained predominantly Czechoslovak. It carried out the commands of the "Transport Committee"[27] and was responsible for order and security on the ship. Its task was very difficult and not always popular.

Soon a distinct pattern of life and routine developed on the *Atlantic:* medical services and special facilities for the children were set up, a number of minyanim came into being and even a lending library began to operate. The ship sailed from Tulcea on October 7, 1940, and arrived in Istanbul on the eve of the Day of Atonement. The local Jewish community sent 1,500 loaves of white bread and other provisions to the refugees, who were deeply moved and greatly encouraged by this tangible expression of Jewish solidarity.

After the holiday the ship passed the Dardanelles, anchored for some time at Mytilene (Lesbos), and after short stops at the Aegean islands of Samos and Ios arrived at Iraklion (Candia) on Crete on

October 16. There the refugees were caught by the outbreak of the Greek-Italian war. Once again a miracle happened: in spite of the emergency they were given food and fuel, enjoying again the brotherly help of fellow Jews, first of the small community of Crete, afterwards of an aid committee in Athens.

When the *Atlantic* seemed to be ready to sail, a new difficulty arose. The crew — which apart from some honorable exceptions was composed of the scum of the Levant — was afraid of leaving Crete. In order to prevent the departure they resorted to sabotage and burnt or threw into the sea a great part of the precious coal. The captain refused to continue the voyage and thus the Transport Committee took over and deposed him. Members of the "Hagana" worked as engineers and stokers, and with the help of a few members of the crew who had remained loyal[28] the *Atlantic* sailed from Crete on November 8, 1940.[29]

However, very soon the effects of the sabotage made themselves felt. When the coal began to run out, the Transport Committee reluctantly decided to change the course of the ship and to sail to Cyprus. Even for this much shorter distance the coal did not suffice, and so the *Atlantic* became the scene of weird operations resembling those described in Jules Verne's famous novel *Around the World in Eighty Days*. The ship was stripped of every piece of wood that was not absolutely vital: masts, chairs, planks, and even beds served as fuel, and the *Atlantic* became a strange metal skeleton floating slowly on the sea. When even this substitute fuel was almost completely used up and the ship was in acute danger of becoming a plaything of the waves and foundering in the next storm, on November 12 the coast of Cyprus emerged on the horizon. The *Atlantic* was dragged by British tugs into the harbor of Limassol.

The joy of the refugees was indescribable; not only had they been saved from mortal danger, they were now under the protection of the British flag. They were however somewhat disappointed to learn that they would not get the needed food and fuel free of charge but would have to pay £480 for them. Since many passengers had no cash, they paid their share with valuables, including wedding rings.[30]

On November 23 the *Atlantic* sailed from Cyprus under the escort of a British warship. Twenty-four hours later the refugees saw the sun rising over Mount Carmel. Deeply moved and extremely happy, they sang the Hatikvah. In Haifa harbor they saw a luxury liner, the *Patria*, and were told by the policemen and officials who had come on board that they would soon be transferred to this ship and kept there for some time in quarantine, like the passengers of the *Milos* and the *Pacific*, who were already on board the *Patria*.

The transshipment started in the early hours of November 25. Only a few dozen people had left the *Atlantic* when a loud explosion was heard; the *Patria* capsized and went to the bottom of the harbor. The sea was covered with wreckage and hundreds of people struggling with the waves. It had been intended to sabotage the engines of the ships in order to prevent the deportation of the "illegal immigrants" and this scheme succeeded only too well. The death toll of the *Patria* was more than 220.[31]

A few days later it was officially announced that persons rescued from the *Patria* would be permitted to remain in Palestine. The passengers of the *Atlantic* thought that this amnesty also applied to them. Shortly afterwards the disembarkation took place: women and married men were transferred to the reception camp of Atlit, while single men were taken first to Acre but joined the rest of the refugees at Atlit after a few days.

6. *The Deportation*

On the evening of December 8 the refugees of the *Atlantic*, whose huts in the camp of Atlit were separated by sentries and fences from those persons rescued from the *Patria*, were ordered to pack their luggage and to prepare for departure. They were not told their destination but were assured that they would be taken to a "good place." The representatives of the refugees — and especially those of the Maccabi-Hehalutz Transport — resolved to offer passive resistance: it was decided that the refugees should sleep naked, refuse to get up, and remain in their huts. The idea was that in face of such resistance — particularly on the part of the women — the British would not enforce the deportation order and that the Yishuv would come to the aid of the refugees. More than these considerations, however, the refugees were motivated by the feeling that their honor as Jews and human beings forbade them to acquiesce in an expulsion from the Jewish homeland.

In the night the camp was surrounded by a large force of the Palestine Police and also by the military. When on the morning of the 9th of Kislev (December 9) the refugees did not obey the order to get up and dress, the police proceeded to clear the huts by force, starting with the center of the resistance, several huts with young men of the Maccabi-Hehalutz Transport. They used their heavy truncheons indiscriminately and blood flowed freely. The refugees were dragged from their huts, and as they were naked, blankets were thrown over them. They were hauled to waiting trucks like so many sacks of flour. Only after a large number of huts had been cleared in this way and the ground was strewn with wounded did the hopeless passive resistance cease.

While the first batches left the camp virtually naked, covered only with gray blankets with the initials PP,[32] later groups took some luggage with them. Some of the soldiers who escorted the refugees could not disguise their embarrassment and disgust at the "glorious victory" that the high commissioner of Palestine, Sir Harold MacMichael, had won over naked and defenseless Jews.

In the port of Haifa the refugees were subjected to a customs examination, in the course of which a variety of innocuous objects, such as shaving kits, forks and spoons, fountain pens, and even watches and spectacles, were confiscated — or, to put it more exactly, stolen.[33] Shocked, stunned, and dejected, but feeling that they had done their duty, the refugees were taken on board two big Dutch liners, the *Nieuw Zeeland* and the *Johan de Witt*. They were much depressed by what seemed to them the failure of the Yishuv to come to their aid and to prevent the deportation, or at least to make an attempt to prevent it. They did not know of the protest strikes that had taken place in the country and of the declaration issued by the Jewish Agency expressing the Yishuv's indignation at the deportation and promising that "the Jewish Agency will spare no effort to achieve the redemption of the refugees from life in exile and their return to the homeland." This promise was kept.

The voyage to Mauritius via the Suez Canal and Aden and around East Africa lasted seventeen days. The deportees were treated badly, in particular at the beginning, when the two liners formed part of a big convoy protected by British warships. Some guards, constables of the Palestine Police, behaved very brutally. On the *Nieuw Zeeland*, which carried the majority of the Czechoslovaks, men and women were compelled to use the same open latrines together and only at the end of the voyage were curtains provided. During the first days the refugees were kept in the holds of the ships, which were unbearably hot. On the *Nieuw Zeeland* the men's hair was cropped close — not for hygienic reasons but in order to annoy and humiliate them.

They were not permitted to celebrate the festival of Chanuccah because the police commander asserted that this holiday was already over; no calendar or testimony of the rabbis could induce him to cancel this absurd order. It is only fair to remark that his opposite number on the *Johan de Witt* even put candles at the disposal of the refugees in order to enable them to celebrate the festival of lights.

Toward the end of the voyage the deportees were treated better and even permitted to sleep on deck, quite a relief in the tropical climate. The food was good and plentiful, and the refugees ate more at breakfast than they had eaten in three days on the *Atlantic*. Most touching and encouraging was the friendly and kindly attitude of the Dutch and Malay crew, who distributed clothing among those men who were dressed solely in the blanket in which they had left Atlit. They were also helped by fellow deportees who had brought some luggage with them.

On December 26, 1940, the two ships dropped anchor in the harbor of Port Louis, the capital of Mauritius. The disembarkation started immediately after Christmas and took two days. When the refugees were driven in buses to their destination, natives lined the road, greeting and cheering them. It was not clear whether they extended this unexpected welcome because they regarded the refugees as enemies of their British masters or simply because they sympathized with them in their plight. On December 28, 1940, the iron gates of Central Prison at Beau Bassin closed behind the last refugee.

7. *The Island and People of Mauritius*

Mauritius is situated in the Southern Hemisphere, in the tropical zone — 20 degrees south latitude — some five hundred miles east of Madagascar. Discovered by the Portuguese in the sixteenth century, it was occupied by the Dutch and used as a naval base. They called it Mauritius after the Stadhouder of the Netherlands, Prince Maurice of Nassau.

In 1715 the French took possession of the island, settled, and developed it rapidly, thanks to the outstanding abilities of the first French governor, François Mahé de Labourdonnais, who established a thriving agriculture and — most important for the future of the island — introduced sugarcane. French rule was terminated in 1810 when the British occupied Mauritius during the Napoleonic Wars, but the French have left a distinct mark on the culture and the institutions of the island, which even today, after 155 years of British rule, has in many respects remained "Île de France," the name given it by the French colonizers.

The owners of estates, professional people, managers, and officials of French extraction, numbering about fifteen thousand persons, still form the upper class of Mauritian society. They are mostly conservative and strongly Catholic; they seem to have preserved something of the outlook and way of life of France prior to 1789. The one thousand or so British have not struck roots in the island: they are mainly members of the Colonial Service and representatives of commercial firms.

In the West Indies and elsewhere the name "Creole" is used for people of pure European descent; in Mauritius, this term is applied to a mixed race of Negroes, mulattoes, and their offspring, the descendants of the former slaves and slaveholders, many of whom have attained a considerable degree of French culture. The majority of the present population consists of the sons and grandsons of Indian immigrants. After the abolition of slavery in Mauritius in 1832, agricultural laborers were brought to the island mainly from southern India. Today the Indians are conspicuous not only in agriculture but also in commerce and in the professions. Some twenty thousand Chinese play a part in the economy of Mauritius similar to that of the Jews in Eastern Europe in former times.

In brief, the population of Mauritius is a motley mixture of many races, languages, and creeds — the Indians alone use at least half a dozen quite different languages and are sharply divided into Hindus and Moslems. Creole, a French patois based on the Breton dialect and mixed with Malagasy elements, is the common language of all Mauritians.

This small island of 805 square miles was once of great strategic and commercial importance, hence its proud Latin designation, "Stella Clavisque Maris Indici" — star and key of the Indian Ocean. After the opening of the Suez Canal the importance of Mauritius declined but has risen again in the last few years because Mauritius has become a busy junction of international airlines.

Mauritius exports about half a million tons of excellent sugar a year. Although almost anything can grow in the rich volcanic soil of the island and bananas, aloe (sisal), coconuts, and pineapples are produced on a large scale, sugarcane has remained the main crop of Mauritius and the production of sugar her main industry.

Compared with other tropical countries the climate of Mauritius is not bad, but the humidity, rather than high temperatures, make it very difficult for Europeans. The scenery of Mauritius is very beautiful; there are rugged mountain peaks, dark woods, charming blue bays, and everywhere the lush tropical vegetation.

Mauritius is famous for three things (apart from the sugar): as the native habitat of the dodo, an enormous bird resembling a swan, discovered and very soon completely exterminated by the Dutch; as the scene of the idyllic, sentimental novel of the eighteenth century by French novelist Bernardin de Saint-Pierre, *Paul et Virginie;* and last but not least as the country that issued the stamp that is probably the most valued in the word of philately: the 1847 2d. "blue Mauritius." [34] [35]

8. *The Detainment Camp of Beau Bassin*

In Mauritius, even more than on the *Atlantic* and on the deportation ships, the Maccabi-Hehalutz Transport was part of a larger community rather than a separate entity and shared the fate of the detainees as a whole. Therefore, what will be said about life in the detainment camp in the following applies also to the Czech group,* as it was officially styled and will be also called here for the sake of simplicity and brevity. The Czech group, of course, also had problems and aspirations of its own and those will be dealt with separately, wherever necessary.[36] H.M. Central Prison at Beau Bassin is situated about five miles from the capital, Port Louis, and is 750 feet above sea level. The prison compound of about twelve acres is surrounded by a fifteen-foot-high wall of stone. In the center of this compound are two huge "blocks," three-storied structures some one hundred yards long, each of which contains cells for about four hundred prisoners. In their vicinity are auxiliary buildings for stores, administration, workshops, and so on. While parts of this "men's section" of the camp date from the time of Napoleon I, the adjoining "women's section" — some thirty tin huts — had been erected especially for the newcomers from Palestine; it was likewise surrounded by walls on all sides.

Several acres of vegetable gardens and orchards with papayas, mangoes, bananas, and pineapples outside the walls also belonged

* "Czech group" is used interchangeably to mean the same as "Czechoslovak group."

to the camp area. In the course of time part of them were set aside as a recreation ground. The camp hospital, some five hundred yards distant from the camp proper, also belonged to the detainment area.

At the time of their arrival the refugees numbered 1,580 persons — 849 men, 635 women, and 96 children. This number was steadily decreasing, since deaths by far exceeded births and since, in the course of the years, 212 volunteers — more than half from the Czech group — joined the Allied forces. At the end of 1943 the detainees, as they were officially called, numbered 1,422 persons, and in the last report submitted by the commander of the camp to the governor of Mauritius, a total of 1,371 — among them 208 Czechoslovaks — was given.[37] At the time of their liberation in August 1945 the detainees numbered 1,310. Ten persons were, for individual and special reasons, released before the liquidation of the camp.

The highest authority in the camp was the commandant of the detainment area; he had a deputy called the assistant commander. The staff of the camp consisted of thirteen supervisors: four in the men's section — all of them former officers of the Palestine Police — and nine women supervisors, Englishwomen and French Mauritians. There were also seventy-three special constables, commanded by two sergeants and a sergeant-major, all natives. After some time their number was substantially reduced. Some refugees, who were infected by the ideology from which they fled, thought it an insult to be guarded by nonwhites but, as a matter of fact, the Creole and Indian constables were unobtrusive and well behaved. The camp staff also numbered a few civilians, like Mr. Renie, the quartermaster.

Practically all members of the Czech group lived in Block A, except for the doctors, who lived in huts similar to those in the women's section. The accommodation in cells — which were never locked by the authorities and where formerly criminals had served long terms of imprisonment — offensive as it seemed, was a blessing in disguise because it offered the detainees some sorely needed privacy. The women, on the other hand, were condemned to live in crowds of twenty or thirty in large huts, unless they were lucky enough to be accommodated in partitioned structures, where four or five lived in one compartment. In summer these huts of corrugated iron were unbearably hot, and in the rainy season the heavy tropical downpours made a terrible noise beating on the tin roofs.

Each cell was about nine feet by twelve; the window was provided with iron bars and a shutter but had no windowpanes. The furniture consisted of a hammock and a shelf; only some of the cells could boast a locker. In the course of time most detainees supplemented this niggardly allocation with simple furniture, like chairs, tables, and so on, made by themselves or bought from the joiners of the camp. Only the huts had electric light; the cells were lit by kerosene lamps bought and operated by the detainees at their own expense. The few double cells on the ground floor of Block A were allocated to older people.

The régime in the camp was not intentionally brutal or irritating but some of its aspects tended to embitter the detainees and make their lives quite needlessly more miserable than circumstances warranted. The detainees had to apply to the commandant for almost everything, large or small. No grounds were given for a refusal and an appeal was impracticable. The number of persons to be present at weddings, circumcision ceremonies, and even funerals was arbitrarily and quite senselessly restricted. During the first few months the local newspaper was forbidden in the camp. As late as in 1943 the authorities prohibited listening to the BBC broadcasts in Polish and Czech. It was more than strange that radio emissions from London were considered dangerous in a British colony!

The whole system of police escorts for individuals and groups — e.g., school excursions — that left the camp was most annoying. In the latter stages of the detention, matters improved in this respect. The repeated requests on part of Jewish institutions to admit Jewish delegations to the camp met with an adamant refusal, and every obstacle was placed in the way of private persons desirous of visiting their relatives or friends in the camp. Such visits can be counted on the fingers of one hand. The first was made by a doctor who served in the Royal Navy and succeeded in obtaining permission to see his friends from Czechoslovakia.[38] The visit took place under the conditions laid down in the prison regulations, in the presence of supervisors and with the conversation being held in English.

Apart from the general censorship in Mauritius — a matter of course in wartime — there existed a special censorship in the camp, designed to prevent the leakage of news regarded as undesirable by the camp authorities. Cables and letters were frequently delayed or mutilated or even disappeared completely, without any possibility of redress.

The detainees found themselves under the authority of the commandant also in what they regarded as their own affairs. One example will illustrate this point: in 1943, the Czech group unanimously approved a scheme for dividing up a certain sum which had been sent by the Czechoslovak Consulate in Cape Town for distribution among destitute Czechoslovak nationals. The commandant refused to confirm the scheme, although all people concerned had reached full agreement, and he delayed the distribution of the sorely needed subsidy for many months.[39] The authorities insisted on distributing themselves the consignments of medicine, clothing, and so on sent by Jewish institutions, according to their predilections and not in compliance with the instructions of the senders and the wishes of the detainees. In the last years of detainment these gifts were sent to the address of the Zionist Association or to specified groups or individuals rather than to the inmates of the camp in general, and that put some check on the authorities.

A glaring example of unjustified interference was that of the Camp Fund set up by a special enactment of the Legislative Council of Mauritius;[40] its object was to finance schemes and activities for the benefit of the detainees, e.g., the supply of textbooks for the school, the purchase of equipment for sport and games, and so on. The main source of income for the Camp Fund — apart from the profits from the canteen and the workshops — was a 5 per cent deduction from the remittances which many detainees received from abroad.[41] The authorities did not permit the detainees, on whose money, after all, the fund was based, to have a say in its administration. The inevitable result was that the fund, and in particular the 5 per cent deduction, became most unpopular, and it wascontended that the authorities used the fund to pay for necessities that they ought to have provided out of the regular budget of the camp, which at the end of the detention period reached the sum of 1,300,000 rupees (almost £100,000) a year.

During the first few months Colonel Dickens commanded the camp; in January 1945 Major George Tuach was put in charge. Between these two short periods Captain H.J. Armitage was commandant. His authority, though considerable, was far from unlimited; in many matters he was dependent on the consent instructions of the colonial secretary, Mr. J.M. Moody,[42] the governor of Mauritius, or the colonial secretary in London. Captain Armitage's character showed many inconsistent traits. Though generally polite, he took revenge for any real or imaginary insult and showed remarkable patience in waiting for the right moment. He was very clever, and his diplomatic skill could, less charitably, be called a proclivity to intrigue and double-crossing. He was evasive and therefore a most difficult partner in negotiations, generous in making promises but utterly unreliable in keeping them. He had initiative and was interested in improvements to the camp, particularly in those that could be photographed or otherwise used for publicity. The relations between Captain Armitage and the detainees became increasingly strained, and toward the end of his term he was universally detested, by the Czechoslovak group perhaps even more than by the rest of the camp.

The assistant commander, Superintendent H.H. Hargreaves, on the other hand, was very popular. This officer of the Palestine Police did not conceal his sympathy for the detainees and Zionism. Utterly correct in discharging his duties, he found ways and means to alleviate the position of the detainees.[43] The relations with the supervisors, Sergeants Thomson and Hipperson, were quite good, as was the case with most of the women supervisors, headed by Mrs. Gilbert and Mrs. Armitage. At the beginning nobody was permitted to leave the detainment area, except on special occasions like school excursions. At the end of 1941 "outings on parole" were introduced: every detainee was permitted to leave the camp for four to five hours — at the beginning once every two or three months, later once every four or five weeks. This short leave was normally used for outings to the main towns: Port Louis, Rose Hill, and Curepipe. Other "privileges" were attendance at cinema performances at Beau Bassin and outings to the seaside (Albion, Flic en Flaq), both with police escorts.

In August 1943 all these "privileges" were suddenly canceled, the camp was completely sealed off from the rest of the island, and the work of the few experts employed outside the camp was discontinued. General "security reasons" served as the pretext for this measure; the true reason was the appearance of Japanese submarines near Mauritius. Some vessels were sunk and the supply situation of the island adversely affected. In order to show the population that something was being done, the authorities decided to pursue the line of least resistance and to take measures against the Jewish detainees, who were neither in a position nor inclined to conspire with the Japanese against the British.

While the population had in the beginning been friendly it was now no more than indifferent. Rumors were circulating on the island that certain goods were no longer available because they were being delivered in large quantities to the detainment camp. These rumors were either completely unfounded or at least vastly exaggerated, although of course the presence of the detainees on a small island was bound to affect the supply situation. There was now a community of interests: both the Mauritians and the detainees wanted — though for different reasons — the exile of the Jews in Mauritius to end as soon as possible.

The authorities did not look with favor on social contacts between the detainees and natives. Requests of Mauritians that certain detainees be permitted to give them lessons were frequently turned down. Nevertheless, bonds of friendship were formed between members of various Mauritian communities and detainees. Apart from the above-mentioned tension at the time of the supply difficulties, relations between the Jewish refugees and the natives of the island were not bad, and therefore the Mauritians are today in general well remembered by the ex-detainees.

As a sort of compensation for the abolition of the "privileges" in 1943 a "holiday camp" was set up on the eastern coast near Flaq, where batches of sixty people at a time could enjoy a week of better food, marvelous scenery, the seaside, and relative freedom and quiet.

The régime improved during the last few months of the detention, after permission to return to Palestine had been granted. The detainees were given passes for a whole day's outing, so that they were able to admire the various sights of the island such as the Botanical Garden of Pamplemousses — reputed to be one of the finest in the world — or to climb the Pouce, the highest mountain of the island. These relaxations had no detrimental results whatsoever — and this proved that had it been desired, the camp could have been administered from the outset more liberally without prejudice to discipline or security and that the detainees could have been spared many superfluous hardships.

9. *Family Life, Health, Food, and Clothing*

Particularly irksome was the strict separation between men and women that was enforced by the authorities, and it was only after a bitter and protracted struggle that some form of family life was introduced. At the beginning the walls and sentries prevented contact between the sexes in general and between husbands and wives in particular. Men could enter the women's section — and vice versa — only on production of a special pass, which was given to a very restricted class of persons — for example, doctors — or in special cases. This separation was in the first months enforced rigidly and even cruelly. There were cases of husbands not being permitted to visit sick wives; and one man died — and not suddenly — without being allowed to see his wife before his death.[44]

As a poor substitute for family life the women were permitted to come to a special restricted area of the men's section several times a week for two hours and to meet their menfolk there under the watchful eyes of numerous constables. This arbitrary separation of married couples was perhaps the main grievance of the detainees. In the beginning of 1942 the authorities decided to alleviate the situation in a most peculiar way: permission was granted to set up tents in a certain section of the recreation ground, and these tents offered privacy to couples — but everybody knew who had entered a tent and for what purpose. One cannot blame the relatively few people who availed themselves of this opportunity; the majority of the detainees detested "Tents Alley" and saw in it a studied insult and also an example of the hypocrisy in sexual matters which rightly or wrongly is regarded as typically English.

On May 25, 1942, the commandant announced that it had been decided in principle to permit "family life" and asked the detainees to submit suggestions as to how to put this decision into effect. Various proposals and counterproposals were made, until on July 11, 1942, a scheme that had been worked out by the commandant and most reluctantly and hesitantly approved by the majority of the detainees was put into operation: married women received passes entitling them to be in the men's section (and the cells of their husbands) from 11 A.M. to 6 P.M. (later from 9 A.M. to 9 P.M.).

After the introduction of family life many weddings took place — thirty in 1943 alone. At first the marriage was religious only, but beginning in February 1943 a civil marriage — which alone was valid under local law — could be contracted before the civil state officer of Rose Hill; thus practically all couples were married twice, once before Rabbi Dr. Bieler "according to the Law of Moses and Israel" and a second time in accordance with the Code Napoléon, which is still in force in Mauritius. From 1943 to 1945 some sixty children were born in the camp. Mothers with babies were allocated special huts and had more living space than other women. Some babies got malaria, but in general they did not suffer from the climate and developed into sturdy little boys and girls.

The quantity and quality of the food doled out to the detainees by the camp authorities varied but it was never plentiful or good. Much, of course, depended on the general supply situation of the island. The average daily cost of feeding a detainee rose from 48 cents a day in 1941 to 1.02 rupees in 1944, but this increase reflected rising prices rather than an improvement in the food. Although food is comparatively cheap in Mauritius, a daily budget of 10 cents or even 22 cents was not sufficient. Between the "diet scale,"[45] which did not look too bad on paper, and reality was a wide gap. First, to many items on the diet scale the proviso "if available" was attached, and more often than not such things were not obtainable. Second, the vegetables on the scale were mostly tropical, which the majority of the detainees were unable to eat and therefore they did not get the calories and vitamins which these vegetables were supposed to furnish. Third, the preparation of the food was not satisfactory because the equipment of the kitchens[46] was primitive, the conditions of work there difficult, and some of the cooks unskilled. The quantity of many rations was insufficient; for many months only 200 grams of bread were allocated and for some time this ration was reduced to a mere 100 grams a day. Even cornmeal, which many people refused to eat, was not always available in sufficient quantity. Since the rations supplied by the authorities were inadequate it was a necessity rather than a luxury to supplement them with food bought in the canteen of the camp or elsewhere. Those who had no money for improving their diet suffered from malnutrition and went hungry.

If the food was inadequate, the care — or lack of care — for clothing was scandalous indeed. If the detainees had been dependent solely on what they got from the authorities, they would have gone half naked.[47] The main source of clothing was what little had remained of the contents of the luggage and the consignments of clothing sent by Jewish organizations in the United States, Australia, and in particular South Africa. The tropical climate of Mauritius had one advantage: during most months of the year a minimum of clothing was sufficient: shorts and shirts for the men and light summer frocks for the women.

A few years after the termination of World War II the Health Department of Mauritius succeeded in wiping out malaria completely, but in 1940 through 1945 only parts of the island were free from this scourge and Beau Bassin was not among them. By January 1941 a large number of the inmates of the camp had contracted malaria, and the percentage suffering from this disease approached 50 per cent at the end of the detainment. Immediately after the arrival of the deportees a terrible epidemic of typhoid broke out, to which nearly fifty persons succumbed.[48] It is only fair to remark that this disease originated on the *Atlantic* and not in Mauritius. According to a memorandum submitted by the refugee doctors in 1944,[49] about 15 per cent of the detainees were afflicted with chronic dysentery, about 50 per cent were suffering from various forms of avitaminosis, and ailments of the heart and blood vessels were giving cause for anxiety. An average of 10 per cent of the camp inmates were sick in the camp hospital, and some of them hardly ever left it during the whole term of the detention.

The post of chief medical officer of the camp was competently filled by Dr. René Lavoipierre, a French Mauritian, a good, experienced, and well-mannered doctor. He was assisted by some local physicians and in particular by the refugee doctors,[50] who in the beginning did their responsible and exacting work gratis and later on got a symbolic salary of about three dollars a month. The camp hospital was staffed by native personnel and by nurses and warders from among the detainees who had received or improved their training in special courses held in the camp. Operations were performed in public hospitals like those of Mocca and Port Louis. In general, medical treatment was not bad; that so many people had to undergo medical treatment so frequently was, however, very bad.

A total of 124 detainees (among them four members of the Czech group) died in the camp of Beau Bassin. They were laid to rest in the Jewish section of the Cemetery of Saint Martin, one mile from the camp. A Hevra Kadisha was founded, and suitable arrangements were made for decent burials, the erection of tombstones, the planting of trees on the cemetery, and so on. Before leaving the island the detainees placed the cemetery under the protection of their friend, the Anglican bishop of Mauritius.[51]

10. *Economic, Social, and Cultural Life*

Very soon three different classes emerged among the detainees: the "capitalists," who received money from abroad (and a monthly remittance of as little as ten dollars sufficed to qualify one for this designation); the workers in the workshops and offices who, from the beginning, received a small amount of pocket money termed "wages"; and the rest of the detainees. Thanks to the initiative of the third group various economic enterprises were launched, such as laundries; workshops for the manufacture of candies, jam, bags, corsets, belts; and, of course, coffee bars. Barbers, tailors, and teachers offered their services, as did those employed in the camp workshops — like tinsmiths and carpenters — who executed private orders against payment, in addition to the work performed by them free of charge for the camp as a whole.[52]

It was characteristic of the economy of the camp that it operated on a system of very low figures, as evidenced by the following examples: 10 cents[53] in 1942 could buy a cup of coffee and a cake or ten bananas or fourteen cigarettes or one hour's private lesson in English or Hebrew or a haircut. In the course of time the prices for goods rose more than the fees for services. The majority of noncapitalists were under the necessity to work, because the authorities failed to provide them with sufficient food and clothing. This, however, was a blessing in disguise: those who worked, and especially those who worked a lot, were better able to stand up to the enervating and demoralizing influence of camp life. Detainees who did not receive remittances from abroad and did not earn a certain minimum were given pocket money — first not very tactfully called "alms-money" — in the amount of 2.50 rupees, out of a special subsidy sent for this purpose by the South African Jewish Board of Deputies.

The attitude of the detainees to the British was ambivalent. On the one hand, it was the British who expelled them from Palestine and were keeping them on this faraway tropical island, subject to restrictions both serious and petty. On the other hand, the British bore the brunt of the war against Hitler and for more than one year stood alone against this archenemy of the Jewish people. Therefore, in their struggle for freedom the detainees used some restraint, feeling that though adversaries on this front, the British were their allies on a more important one.

The detainees were single-minded: their principal object was to get away. Most of them wanted to return to Palestine, but even the small minority which had another country in mind did not oppose the demand of the spokesmen of the camp: collective return to Palestine. This quest for freedom was indeed a "magnificent obsession."

The camp was a fertile ground for rumors of every sort, about the detainees themselves and about other matters. Gossip was widespread; people were living in closest contact, and everybody knew everything about everybody else. This interest in the doings of others had also positive aspects: social life was intensive, and married couples used to invite each other and single friends to their "homes" — the cell of the husband. Birthdays were celebrated with great enjoyment and — relatively speaking — lavishly. It was as if the inmates of the camp seized every opportunity of putting some color and light into their drab existence.

Some people were acutely depressed by the walls, the guards, and the whole prison atmosphere; others suffered intensely from the lack of privacy. Particularly difficult in this respect was the position of the women who were living in large and crowded huts. Younger people suffered more from the futility of camp life than older ones. A few detainees broke down under the stress, strain, and frustration of their life and became demoralized, cynical, and apathetic. Most, however, succeeded in adjusting themselves to the conditions of their existence and quite a few proved their mettle in adversity: the community in general and the Czech group in particular could boast a considerable number of devoted and fearless leaders, dedicated workers for the common good.

German was the common language of the camp and served as the medium of cultural activities, although there were some exceptions like vocal newspapers and lectures in Hebrew, a memorial meeting on the anniversary of the death of T.G. Masaryk conducted in Czech, and the camp revue, which for the benefit of guests from outside the camp was performed in English.

The Camp News was published from January 15, 1941, to May 15, 1942. It brought general news, in particular on the war, as well as announcements and information concerning the camp.[54] After the paper had ceased publication, the news bulletins of the BBC were the chief source of information, and those who knew French and English read the local newspapers *Le Mauricien* and *Advance*. The New York refugees' paper, *Der Aufbau*, enjoyed great popularity. *The Czechoslovak*, published in London, was eagerly read by many members of the Czechoslovak group and so were Hebrew newspapers from Palestine and the Jewish weeklies sent from South Africa.

There were two libraries in the camp, both much used by the detainees: the camp library, whose first stock of books in English and French was put as its disposal the police library of Port Louis, and the Zionist library, set up by the Zionist Association, which lent books not only on Jewish but also on general subjects in Hebrew, Yiddish, German, French, and English, which were received in large quantities from Eretz Israel, South Africa, and other countries.

A "popular university" was established early in 1941. Its numerous lectures covered a wide range of subjects, from mathematics and the geography of Africa to philosophy and Jewish law. Though it ceased to function after one year, a number of courses were continued in other frameworks. There was great interest even in difficult subjects like "Kant and Hassidism." Those with a good command of English could enjoy the weekly talks with prominent members of the British colony, such as the Anglican bishop Hugh Otter Barry, the director of education, Mr. E.W.F. Ward, and Professor Hunt Cook.[55]

Concerts were arranged quite frequently. Choirs were formed, and the camp band gained an excellent reputation throughout the island; it often played outside the camp on official or festive occasions. When in June 1941 the opera *La Boheme*, by Puccini, was performed in Rose Hill — a special performance was given for the detainees and their escorts — the camp's musicians formed part of the orchestra. Various plays were performed by amateurs in the recreation hall of the camp, puppet shows entertained young and old alike, plays were produced for children and by children, and so on.

Sports activities and competitions were greatly encouraged by the camp authorities. There were football and volleyball teams; some people specialized in athletics, others in gymnastics. However, in course of time the active interest in sports declined considerably because people realized that in the tropical climate and in the absence of sufficient food, strenuous exercise was not advisable. The camp school was set up and operated thanks to the devotion of a small band of volunteers, some of them former professional teachers, some amateur pedagogues. The teachers worked under difficult conditions because the school was badly accommodated and ill-equipped, and there were virtually no textbooks for the children. Religion, Hebrew, Jewish history, and geography of Palestine were included in the school curriculum, whose aim was to educate the children for a life of productive work in Eretz Israel. The children liked to go to school; the hours they spent there were the most enjoyable of the day and more interesting than the monotonous camp routine.

A great many people were eager to study: first of all, languages —

Hebrew, English, French, and even Arabic — but also other subjects, practical, such as bookkeeping, and theoretical, such as philosophy. Learning was also a device for keeping the mental equilibrium and balance, a means of killing time, a preparation for Eretz Israel, and even a fashion, albeit a very useful one. With the help of the Anglican bishop and Dean Dawson, troops of Boy Scouts and Girl Guides were set up.[56] Not only the essence of scoutcraft but also the uniforms, badges, stripes, and tests gave much delight to the children and helped to fill the time after school hours — which the home was unable to do for the simple reason that a home in the normal sense of this term did not exist in the camp. The percentage of strictly observant Jews in the Czech group was much smaller than the camp average of about 20 per cent. Therefore, those Czechoslovaks who were synagogue-goers — and most were on the High Holidays — frequented the "liberal synagogue," headed by the former Chief Rabbi of Danzig, Dr. Bieler, rather than the Orthodox one. Jewish tradition was respected in the camp. Saturday was the official day of rest and a real Shabbat atmosphere was felt in the camp.

11. *The Czechoslovak Group in the Camp*

The Czechoslovak group numbered at the beginning some 20 per cent of the camp inmates and after the departure of the volunteers[57] much less, but its weight and impact were much greater than its numbers warranted. In the camp administration, so far as it was staffed by detainees, several Czechs held, comparatively speaking, key positions.[58] The more important economic enterprises were largely initiated or run by members of the Czechoslovak group.[59] Among the experts who were for some time allowed to work outside the camp, mainly for the war effort, the Czechs were again represented far beyond their percentage.[60] Also in the workshops of the camp, from the blacksmiths to the shoemakers, the Czechs numbered more than their 20 per cent. Before the volunteers left, about 50 per cent of the doctors, nurses, and warders belonged to the group and so did one-half to two-thirds of the teachers of the camp school.[61] Also, in the cultural life of the camp the Czechs were well represented, both as to numbers and to quality.[62]

Leaders of the Czechoslovak group stood in the forefront of the struggle for freedom — or were the chief troublemakers, as the commandant put it. The first contact with Jewish bodies abroad was established by the author[63] on behalf of the Czechoslovak group, and from its midst came the initiative for the founding of the Zionist Association of Mauritius, to which all its members, without exception, became affiliated.

The causes of the great, and in some cases even preponderant, influence of the Czechoslovak group are obvious: the members of the Maccabi-Hehalutz Transport from Prague were on the average much younger, stronger, and healthier than the rest of the detainees. They had been under Nazi rule a much shorter time, and their power of resistance was not yet sapped, as was the case with many members of the other groups, particularly those who had undergone the dreadful experience of a German concentration camp. Comparatively speaking, more Czechs than other detainees knew English or French, more were skilled in a useful trade or profession. It must be admitted that in particular some younger and more assimilated members of the Czechoslovak group were too conscious of these advantages, looked down on their fellow detainees, and displayed a misplaced and galling arrogance. This haughty and overbearing behavior of a minority was, rightly, resented. By a part of the camp, however, the Czechs were equally disliked because of their positive qualities — their dynamism, their radicalism in public affairs — which disturbed the inertia and got on the nerves of people who wanted to be left in peace and who in the depths of their hearts were not entirely averse to a life with no responsibilities and few worries about the next day.

In the beginning there was a distinct undercurrent of tension between the "Prager," as they often were called, and the others. But the position was improving from month to month and from year to year; on the one hand, the Czechs found out that among the Viennese and the Danzigers there were many men and women of outstanding qualities and also excellent Zionists; the assimilated elements among the Czech group became imbued with feelings of Jewish consciousness and solidarity which they had lacked. Their fellow detainees again learned to appreciate the great services which numerous Czechs were rendering to the whole camp rather than to their particular group. The common adversary — the camp authorities, the common struggle for freedom, and also the common framework and activities of the Zionist Association did very much to lower and finally to remove the intergroup barriers; but the most important single factor in this respect was no doubt the "mixed marriages" contracted between Czechs and members of other groups — mostly, though by no means exclusively, by young men from Czechoslovakia and young women from Danzig.

Before going into the special status and problems of the Czech group it is necessary to summarize the legal position of the detainees as a whole.[64] The passengers of the *Atlantic* were deported by virtue of the Defence (Entry Prohibition) Regulations of 1940,[65] whose sections 2 and 3 laid down that the high commissioner of Palestine might order any person deported from Palestine to a British possession "if he was satisfied that such person had entered, or attempted to enter, Palestine without being authorized to do so." According to the Defense (Immigration) Regulations of 1940[66] a "prohibited immigrant" was criminally responsible even if "on board a vessel which is found in the territorial waters of Palestine, whether such vessel came into these waters voluntarily or not." This precisely was the case with the refugees of the *Atlantic*, who were taken to Palestine under British escort. Therefore, the legal advisor of the Jewish Agency was obliged to write to the detainees: "It appears that so far as the legal aspect of the question is concerned, the deportation order of the high commissioner is valid and cannot be challenged in court."[67] However, this legality of the deportation was purely formal. It was legal only within the framework of a policy and legislation which themselves were illegal.[68]

The government of Palestine published a statement on the deportation on November 20, 1940, which said among other things that "the ultimate disposal of the refugees will be a matter of consideration at the end of the war, but it is not proposed that they shall remain in the colony to which they are sent or that they should go to Palestine." This banishment from Palestine in perpetuity was upheld until 1944, when as a result of countless representations of Jewish organizations to which the detainees had addressed themselves, Colonel Oliver Stanley, secretary of state for the colonies, stated in the House of Commons on May 16, 1944: "After the war His Majesty's government will be prepared to consider individual applications from Mauritius refugees for immigration certificates to Palestine under any immigration quotas which may be available, on equal terms with others who wish to enter the country." This meant that the Mauritius detainees would no more be discriminated against, a great improvement, but nevertheless a far cry from the demand of the detainees: collective and unconditional return to Palestine. The final decision to take them back to Eretz Israel will be dealt with in the penultimate section of this article.

The legal position of the detainees in Mauritius herself was governed by a special European Detainees Control Ordinance 1940, but the detainees had no means of knowing its text or contents. They were intentionally kept in the dark about their legal status. The rules governing their life were the prison regulations of Mauritius with some modifications, small in the beginning, more substantial later. From the régime in the camp one might infer that their status resembled that of civil prisoners,[69] but on the other hand they did not enjoy certain privileges of that class, for example, free mail, and their camp was never visited by a representative of the International Red Cross. The leaders of the Czech group — and also the Polish group, for that matter — demanded from the outset that their members, being nationals of a country that was occupied by the Nazis but had in London a government-in-exile recognized by the British, should be treated as Allies rather than as enemy aliens. This demand was, however, not met and the attitude of the authorities in this matter did not change throughout the whole period of detention: they did not care at all about the citizenship of the detainees, and the Czechoslovaks were treated in exactly the same way as German enemy subjects. The authorities adhered, as it were, to the principle of "equality of lack of rights." Even those Czechoslovaks who had enlisted in, and been accepted by, the Czechoslovak armed forces — or later the Jewish Brigade group — did not enjoy any preferential treatment while waiting in the camp for transport.

The struggle for a special status for the Czechoslovaks caused some resentment in the camp, quite wrongly, because it was both natural and legitimate that every group, like every individual, try everything to improve their legal and actual position. Others in the place of the Czechoslovaks would have done exactly the same. Indeed, they were later imitated by the Austrians, likewise unsuccessfully, once the Allies had declared that they regarded Austria as an enemy-occupied territory rather than as a part of Germany.

If the camp authorities, and the British in general, did not have the slightest regard for the Czechoslovak nationality of the refugees, they were recognized and aided as citizens by the Czechoslovak government in London. They were fortunate in belonging to the jurisdiction of the Czechoslovak Consulate General in Cape Town and in having there one of their own people during the second half of the detention. The consul, Mr. Antonín Blahovský, a man of progressive views and a faithful follower of Dr. Beneš, had many friends among the Jews of Cape Town and was a Zionist sympathizer. He showed great understanding for the plight of the refugees and did everything in his power to alleviate it. In 1943 he invited one of the detainees, Mrs. Franziska Berger, an experienced office worker, to serve as secretary to the consulate, and she was the first of some ten civilians who were released from the camp before the liberation. Mrs. Berger made very good use of the opportunity provided by her appointment and also of the connection which she established with various South African Jewish bodies. It was thanks to her indefatigable efforts[70] and to the intercession of Mr. Blahovský with the Czechoslovak government in London that the Czech group received substantial material aid and that its members were granted new Czechoslovak passports. Although for the time being they were of no practical use, their possession strengthened the morale of the refugees, giving them a certain legal status. After Mr. Blahovský had relinquished his post, his successor, Mr. Fr. Pospíšil, carried on the good work. The attitude of the Consulate General in Cape Town and of the government in London did not change after the desertion of a part of the volunteers,[71] although one could hardly have blamed them if they had withdrawn or reduced their help.[72]

The monthly allowance of £75 remitted by the Consulate General was distributed among the group so that a single person received on the average three rupees and a couple double the amount, with increments for the children. From the medicines and various materials sent by the consulate the whole camp benefited indirectly, because of a general improvement of the medical treatment and sanitation. There was a steady flow of correspondence between the Czech group and the consulate, and the very existence of this exchange of letters was greatly appreciated by the detainees, who in their isolation valued contact with the outside world — and official quarters in particular — more than anything else.

The Polish government in London — which had an honorary consul in Port Louis — did something for the Polish citizens among the detainees, and at a latter stage even the so-called Free Austrian Committee (consisting almost exclusively of Jews) got in touch with the Austrian group; but it should be put on record that the assistance — moral, material, and political — given by the Czechoslovak authorities on all levels was by far the greatest. In this respect the

Czechoslovak group undoubtedly had a privileged position in the camp.

12. *The War Volunteers*

The Czech group could be justly proud of the war record of its members: the overwhelming majority of those who were eligible for military service volunteered and much more than half of the able-bodied men actually carried arms in the war against the Nazis.

Only a few weeks after the arrival in Mauritius, the authorities were approached with the urgent request to permit Czechoslovak citizens to join the Czechoslovak forces. Those eager to volunteer were not only prompted by the desire to get away from the camp, but primarily by the conviction that it was the sacred duty of every Jew to fight against Hitler, and by an understandable and honorable loyalty to their country of origin. The authorities, instead of welcoming and encouraging this movement, showed a very lukewarm attitude and even placed obstacles in the way of its leaders, Ing. Kovács and Dr. Enoch, who had succeeded in contacting the Czechoslovak government in London in this matter. At last the offer was accepted and the volunteers underwent medical examination, in which some of them were rejected as not being up to the required high standard of medical fitness. Those found fit for service had to wait many months for transport until, on April 16, 1942, a group of eighty-six volunteers could leave Mauritius: the four reserve officers among them were sent to England while the NCOs and enlisted men were shipped to the Czechoslovak forces in the Middle East and assigned to its units in Tobruk, Egypt, and Palestine. The volunteers went away with very bitter feelings because until the last moment they were treated exactly like all other detainees and could not derive any privileges — material or moral — from their enlistment. It was a matter of special indignation that the married men among them had to remain separated from their wives because "family life" was introduced only a few months after their departure.

In Britain, Palestine, and also in South Africa, where they stayed some weeks in transit, the volunteers told the truth about the camp, refuting the rosy official propaganda. It may be safely assumed that the information activities of the volunteers — who, of course, contacted the proper Jewish institutions — contributed very much to creating a pressure of public opinion, thanks to which the régime in the camp was later somewhat relaxed. On the other hand, it is obvious that these activities did not endear the volunteers — or the Czech group, for that matter — to the authorities in Port Louis and London.

Toward the end of 1942 the camp was shocked and dismayed to learn that about 30 per cent of the Mauritius volunteers in the Czechoslovak forces in the Middle East had deserted in Palestine and remained in that country. The motives of the deserters varied from case to case, but according to what the author could gather after a lapse of two decades, the main factors were three: first and foremost, it was the fear of remaining banned from Palestine. Desertion then and there seemed to be the only chance to effect their aliya.[73] After all, the high commissioner had expressly declared that the deportees would not be allowed to go to Palestine after the war.[74] Second, but to a lesser degree, it was the anti-Semitism which existed in the Czechoslovak Army — in spite of the fact that almost three-quarters of the members of its forces in the west were Jews — especially among the regular army officers who formed its backbone. Third, it was the influence of friends, for example, members of the same youth movements or kibbutzim, who persuaded the ex-detainees to carry out their original plans — to take part in building Eretz Israel and to throw in their lot with the Yishuv in its incipient struggle for statehood. Fear of the front was not among these motives: the overwhelming majority later took part in the Israel War of Independence, and some even joined the Palestinian units of the British Army a short time after they had absented themselves from the Czechoslovak forces.

Practically all members of the Czechoslovak group in the camp condemned the desertions both on moral grounds — one must not break a voluntarily taken oath of allegiance and leave the ranks of an army which was going to fight Hitler — and also because they felt that the desertions would be exploited against the detainees and the Czech group in particular. And indeed they were: the authorities used them as an argument against the demands of the detainees and in general, as a means to blacken their reputation.[75] However, those primarily concerned — the Czechoslovak government — took a more lenient view of the matter; on the one hand, few if any attempts were made to trace the deserters and, on the other, a second batch of twenty-five volunteers were accepted. They left the camp on July 18, 1944, all of them for England,[76] where they were incorporated into the Czechoslovak Armored Brigade.[77] [78]

Of the fifty-six volunteers from all groups of the camp who joined the Jewish Brigade group and left the camp on March 12, 1945, a substantial part were Czech, especially married men who had been hesitant to join up.

The episode of the Mauritian contingent to the Jewish Brigade deserves special mention, although as a matter of course it did not concern the Czech group alone but the camp as a whole. In August 1944 Moshe Shertok (later Sharett) — who, it will be remembered, was in charge of the volunteer war effort of the Yishuv — sent a cable to the author in his capacity as secretary of the Zionist Association, inquiring how many men between eighteen and forty years of age would be prepared to serve in Palestinian Jewish units if they were permitted to do so. The reply was ninety-five, that is, the majority of those eligible. When in September 1944 the Jewish Brigade was set up, it was expressly stated that not only Palestinian Jews but also the refugees recently liberated from the camps in Italy and the Mauritius detainees could join it. This news caused great joy in the camp: the Zionist demand that the Jews be given a chance to fight against Hitler in their own name and under their own flag was finally met. It was most important for the detainees that they were put on an equal footing with the Jews in Palestine, and this was interpreted as an indication that they would be permitted to return to Eretz Israel.

It should be added that a few months after the return of the detainees, the volunteers of the Jewish Brigade — who, after joining the main body of the "Chajil," as it was called by the soldiers, had seen service in Egypt, Italy, Holland, and Belgium — arrived in Eretz Israel and were demobilized. It is noteworthy that the great majority of the soldiers who had joined the Czechoslovak Army from Mauritius went to Israel after their demobilization.[79]

13. *Public Affairs*

The detainees were organized by the authorities into five "national groups": Czech, Austrian, Danzig, Polish, and mixed (stateless, etc.). Every group was headed by two group leaders — a man and a woman — who together formed the Detainment Area Committee, which elected from its midst a chairman representing all the detainees before the authorities.[80] This so-called self-government was fictitious, since all power remained in the hands of the authorities. The Detainment Area Committee (whose name was afterwards changed to Advisory Committee) was to serve as window dressing and rubber stamp. After the abolition of the "privileges" in 1943 even this pretense of a restricted autonomy ended: the "advisors" resigned and in their stead an Actions Committee was elected, composed mostly of people who were *persona non grata* with the authorities — a recommendation in the eyes of their electors.[81] The committee's slogan was "Noncooperation," and it saw as its principal task "fighting for our liberation." The tension between the committee and the authorities climaxed in a hunger strike of the camp on June 5, 1944, which was proclaimed in protest of a refusal by the authorities to negotiate with the committee. It was an external event, "D-Day," the Allied landing in Normandy on June 6, that directed the attention of the detainees to quite another area and reduced the tension. Some time later, when the authorities had made some concessions, a new camp committee was elected and cooperation restored, though on a smaller scale than previously.

The commandant in general did not resort to outright lies in his reports on the camp; he used the more subtle and dangerous methods of *suppressio veri* and *suggestio falsi;* quite exceptional things, if they were positive, were described as normal and typical, while serious shortcomings were glossed over or not mentioned at all. Captain Armitage was an expert in composing utterly misleading reports from details that were correct in themselves. Therefore, the representatives of the camp saw the necessity to rectify these misrepresentations and to give a true picture of the situation in the camp. Their line was to stress the principal aspect involved in the Mauritius case, to make it a political issue, to convince the Jewish institutions that their prestige and honor were at stake. It was indeed soon understood that the detention of Jewish refugees in Mauritius was a fundamental issue, and a short time after the deportation the first steps were taken to bring about the liberation of the detainees and their return to Eretz Israel.[82]

In 1942 the Jewish Agency demanded officially that the Mauritius detainees receive immigration certificates under the White Paper quota; this request was rejected but submitted again and again, and Dr. Weizmann himself approached the Colonial Office several times in behalf of the Mauritius detainees. The Mauritius case was not only aired repeatedly in the House of Commons[83] but also in the U.S. Congress, when Mr. James A. Wright included in his speech in the House of Representatives on February 18, 1944, a sharp declaration on Mauritius from the pen of Dr. Abba Hillel Silver.

The ninth of Kislev, the anniversary of their deportation, was annually marked by the detainees by a complete cessation of work and by a day-long fast, as an expression of protest and of their unflinching resolution to return to Palestine.

Although the various groups and the camp as a whole maintained some contact with bodies abroad, what might be called "foreign relations" was essentially the province of the Zionist Association of Mauritius,* which was recognized by the Jewish institutions as the authorized spokesman for the camp. It was founded in May 1941 and was active in every field of Zionist endeavor: the ZAM commemorated important anniversaries of the Zionist calendar like Herzl Day, organized lectures on a variety of Zionist and Jewish subjects, maintained and financed Hebrew courses, kept contact with Jewish bodies abroad, and led the struggle of the detainees for repatriation to Eretz Israel. One of its most important ventures was the "vocal newspaper." *The South African Jewish Chronicle* and *The Zionist Record*, which reached the island about one month after publication in South Africa, *Haaretz* and *Davar*, and Jewish newspapers from Britain and the United States served as material for the "vocal newspaper," which was arranged about twenty times a year. Each was attended by the majority of the detainees, who learned from it about the events in Eretz Israel and in the Jewish world, and also about the efforts made in behalf of the exiles, because each "issue" of the "vocal newspaper" was preceded by excerpts from important letters received and sent by the ZAM.

The work of the ZAM was done on a purely voluntary basis; all offices were honorary.[84] Expenditure was covered by membership fees (five cents a month) and by special drives, if need arose. The income from these sources reached 685 rupees (about $150) during the last year; more than half was spent on postage for the 177 letters and 32 cables sent by the ZAM during that year. These figures show the great extent of the correspondence with Zionist and Jewish bodies and personalities in many countries, in particular Eretz Israel, Great Britain, and South Africa. The closest contact was with the latter country: the Zionist Federation in Johannesburg, the South African

* [The Zionist Association of Mauritius (ZAM) (Ed.)]

Jewish Board of Deputies, and its special Mauritius Committee. The detainees enjoyed the protection of the Jewish institutions of South Africa and received most valuable help from them. Even more important than its practical aspect was the very fact that such help was given and the manner in which it was extended. The brotherly Jewish solidarity shown by South African Jewry greatly encouraged the detainees and sustained their morale.

Since the ZAM spearheaded the detainees' struggle for freedom, the relations between the ZAM and the authorities, though outwardly correct, were far from being good. It was said that the detainment area commandant liked the ZAM just as much as the Mandatory government of Palestine liked the Jewish Agency.

14. *The Liberation*

On February 21, 1945, the following official announcement was made: "His Majesty's government in the United Kingdom and the government of Palestine have decided that the Jewish refugees now in Mauritius be allowed to enter Palestine when the necessary arrangements have been made. No promise can be made when this will be, as transport difficulties are formidable and delay may be unavoidable."

The joy of the detainees was indescribable. There was a procession with torches headed by the volunteers for the Jewish Brigade group in uniform, and special thanksgiving services were held in the synagogues. It transpired that it had been one of the first official acts of the new high commissioner of Palestine, Lord Gort, to propose the return of the deportees.[85]

It was not only lack of shipping space which caused a long delay, but acts of God beyond human control: in March 1945 an epidemic of polio broke out in the island, one of the worst ever recorded in medical history.[86] There were five cases in the camp: two light, two serious, and one fatal. The departure had been imminent but had to be postponed lest the detainees carry the terrible disease to Palestine. In 1945 the island was visited by a plague which is typical of this zone: three cyclones — the last in April — devastated the island. Owing to the general dislocation of life caused by the storms, the departure had to be postponed again. The first cyclone was the worst: it killed some twenty people, flattened whole villages, destroyed a large part of the crops, and lifted locomotives off the rails.

Thanks to the stone walls surrounding the camp, no detainee was killed or wounded, but several sheds were destroyed and some huts in the women's section badly damaged.

The ZAM, in accordance with instructions received from the Jewish Agency, registered those who wanted to remain in Palestine for good, and those who intended to proceed from there to some other country. Eighty-one per cent of the detainees declared that they wished to remain in Eretz Israel permanently, 4 per cent admitted that for family reasons or on other grounds they intended to go elsewhere, and 15 per cent had not yet made up their minds (most of them eventually settled in Palestine). Only 20 per cent registered for "repatriation" to Czechoslovakia.

On June 23 Dr. Menachem Schumert, who had been requested by the Jewish Agency to take charge of the medical side of the transport to Palestine, arrived in the camp and was joyously welcomed by the detainees. About one month later he was joined by Dr. Aaron Biezienski and a few nurses. It was on August 12 that the longed-for departure took place: the detainees embarked in Port Louis on a big liner, the *Franconia*. They took with them their personal belongings which, in general, were poor enough, in camp-made boxes and chests. The duration of the voyage via Mombasa and Suez was seventeen days. It was not very comfortable because the ship also carried many hundreds of troops. One woman died during the voyage and a little girl was born and named Franconia. In Suez a team of workers of the Immigration and Absorption Departments of the Jewish Agency came on board; it had been decided to spare the refugees the stay in the reception camp of Atlit, of which they had such bad memories, and to make all arrangements on board the ship.

The *Franconia* arrived in Haifa on August 26 and the returnees were met and welcomed by Dr. Dov Joseph on behalf of the Jewish Agency. They disembarked quickly and all formalities were met within a few hours. Some of them went to kibbutzim, others to relatives, and about four hundred families were sent to the houses which had been built for them by the Jewish Agency. A number of ex-detainees could rest in convalescent homes and recuperate there from malaria and other maladies. Those who had declared that they wanted to, got to other countries, including Czechoslovakia, and were accommodated by the British in a transit camp near Rafiah; but most of them were soon permitted to leave it and wait for their departure in Jerusalem or elsewhere. The whole

Yishuv rejoiced that the Mauritius affair had ended with the redemption of the exiles,[87] the ex-detainees were profoundly happy with their liberation and homecoming.

15. *Epilogue*

More than thirty years have passed since the Maccabi-Hehalutz Transport of Prague was launched and a quarter of a century since the odyssey was ended by the aliya of the majority and by what was called repatriation to Czechoslovakia of a minority. It may be of interest to note the present position of the former members of this transport in Israel and abroad. No written records are available; therefore, much of what will be said is a matter of general impression and conjecture rather than of precise facts and figures. There is no association of members of the former Czech group — or of the Mauritius ex-detainees in general, for that matter — which would register and retail information. However, the bonds created by the common fate and experience are still very strong, and wherever ex-detainees live in great numbers they meet in informal circles where information on mutual acquaintances is exchanged. The conventions of the Mauritius ex-detainees held at Nahariya in 1950, in Ramat Gan in 1955, and in Tel Aviv in 1962 and 1965, as well as similar occasions such as a reception given in honor of the prime minister of Mauritius in the Sheraton Hotel of Tel Aviv in July 1963, served not only as rendezvous of the former group members but also as a sort of clearinghouse for news. From pieces of information obtained in this way the following pattern and picture emerge.

By and large the former members of the Czechoslovak group have become well integrated and firmly established in the life of Israel, socially, economically, and to a lesser degree culturally. It is true that few, if any, outstanding personalities known to the general public can be found among them, but, on the other hand, misfits and what in Israel are known as "social cases" are likewise almost completely absent. The majority of them belong to the middle class of the country. Some of them have become well-to-do but hardly anybody really rich. There are successful businessmen and small manufacturers, good doctors, lawyers, engineers, and other members of the professions, either in public employment or in private practice, and quite a number of officials and clerks. Like Czechoslovak Jews in general they enjoy a good reputation for efficiency and reliability. It is interest ing to note that none of them plays a major — nor even a minor — part in the political life of the country, although by virtue of their arrival before the establishment of the state they are regarded as *Vatikim* — old-timers. Apart from very few exceptions they have become what in the United States are called "solid citizens."

So far as their geographical distribution is concerned, they may be found all over the country, from Kiriat Shmoneh in the north to Eilat in the far south. There are certain territorial concentrations: in the big cities of Tel Aviv, Haifa, and to a smaller degree Jerusalem, as well as Ramat Gan, Bat Yam, Cholon, Nahariya, and the "Krayot," the townships in the Haifa Bay — the last-mentioned places owing to the fact that it was there that the Jewish Agency had apartments or houses prepared for them after their arrival in 1945. In this connection it should be said that by the standards of that time, if not by the present ones, the Jewish Agency went out of its way to provide the returnees with housing. Also the Hitachduth Oley Czechoslovakia, the Association of Czechoslovak Settlers, tried to assist the members of the Czechoslovak group from Mauritius, the first considerable influx of countrymen after the end of the war in Europe. A special loan fund was set up for them by means of voluntary contributions among the members of the Hitachduth, most of whom had arrived in the country as recently as 1939 or 1940.

The integration of the ex-detainees was facilitated by three significant circumstances: they were mostly young, able-bodied people willing to do any work; second, they had come to Palestine freely and voluntarily, having rejected the alternative of "repatriation" to Czechoslovakia; and, finally, the detention in Mauritius had in a certain sense been a very good school for Eretz Israel: they had not come to the Promised Land from the fleshpots of Egypt, but after long wanderings in the desert. Compared to their recent experience Eretz Israel was, in spite of all difficulties and hardships, a very comfortable place. Although their number in the kibbutzim is larger than the percentage of the members of collective settlements in the general population would warrant (some 4 per cent), it is nevertheless rather low, approximately thirty. That is somewhat astonishing, if one remembers that about 60 per cent of the Prague Transport had belonged to the Hehalutz and that about 25 per cent had been members of pioneering youth movements, some of them leaders of long standing. While the imprisonment, the privations, and the struggle for freedom in Mauritius had been a good education for Eretz Israel in general, as mentioned above, the experience of the enforced collectivism of the camp militated against any collective framework. After their involuntary association with too many people for too long a time, most ex-detainees set too great a store at privacy to be desirous of joining a collective settlement, whose régime and pattern of life were in the forties much stricter than they are now.

Incidentally, it is rather interesting that while a few people who had never been trained for the kibbutz became — and have remained — happy members of agricultural settlements, some — though by no means all — leaders of the Halutzic Youth Movements never joined a kibbutz, or, if they did, left it very soon. A case in point is the Hashomer Hatzair, which is regarded as the most radical and consistent of these movements: of all its members in the Czechoslovak group only one has remained in a kibbutz (Haogen). "Mauritians" may be found in greater numbers in two kibbutzim: Kfar Ruppin in the Beisan Valley and Neot Mordechai in the Hule Region.

The former Czechoslovak group played an honorable part in the Israel War of Independence: most of the younger men saw active service, some were wounded, and three made the supreme sacrifice for the nascent State of Israel.[88] Among the "Haganah Volunteers" who were trained in Czechoslovakia and emigrated with the express purpose of joining the Israel Army were also some former Czechoslovak volunteers from Mauritius. The children born in Mauritius have grown up and are now young adults. They are rather proud of their exotic origin because being born in Mauritius is a unique distinction even in Israel, whose inhabitants hail from practically all countries of the world. However, they are hardly interested in their Czechoslovak descent. They share this indifference to the Diaspora roots of their parents with the great majority of the Sabras, the native-born Israelis.[89]

While former nationals or residents of Austria received from that country compensation for their imprisonment in Mauritius, although only a small one, by virtue of a special provision in the Austrian law for indemnifying the victims of the Nazis, former Czechoslovak citizens have not received anything at all on this account, either from Germany, Britain, or, of course, Czechoslovakia. As these lines are being written it is by no means sure whether certain hopes pinned on the amendments to the German laws on restitution and indemnification will be vindicated and some compensation be paid for the detainment in Mauritius. Only minor claims to *Haftentschaedigung* were partly met: some people received compensation for the internment in Bratislava, while part of these claims are still pending. A number of people received a small sum for the "illegal aliyah" from Europe to Palestine, but so far no former Czechoslovak citizen has received anything for the detention in Mauritius.

A small number of former members of the Czech group are living in countries other than Israel and Czechoslovakia, mostly in the United States, Canada, Australia, or Great Britain, having arrived there either via Czechoslovakia and the Czechoslovak Army or from Israel; in the latter case they are what in Israel is rather disparagingly termed *Yordim*, because they were either attracted by real or imagined economic opportunities or invited by relatives.

The number of former Mauritius detainees still living in Czechoslovakia may be estimated at two to three dozen — several left the country for Israel in the wake of the Russian occupation of Czechoslovakia in 1968. During the Stalinist era in that country their contact with friends and relatives in Israel was almost nonexistent.[90] After the "thaw" in Czechoslovakia not only were letters exchanged quite freely but also some former detainees went to Israel for a visit and were warmly welcomed by former fellow prisoners. They reported that the greater part of the ex-Mauritians in Czechoslovakia were quite well off, at least by the standards of that country, and were working as doctors, officials, clerks, and the like. Whether all of them are feeling happy there is another question. In any case it is certain that those who went to Israel at the beginning of the sixties and then after the end of the Dubček régime did so not only because they were afraid of future developments in Czechoslovakia but were mainly prompted by the desire to live a full Jewish life in Israel and, in particular, to ensure the Jewish survival of their children.

NOTES

1. See, for example, "The Mauritius Case" by Dr. Y. Freudenheim in *Haaretz* of August 31, 1945, and a number of short articles and notes in a special "Mauritius Supplement" published by the Israel daily *Yediot Hayom* of August 26, 1955.
2. See *Yad Vashem Studies on the European Jewish Catastrophe and Resistance*, IV, Jerusalem, 1960, pp. 190–257 (English edition).

3. See the section which follows.
4. The famous book of Jacob Wassermann, *Der Fall Maurizius*, has nothing in common with this case but the name.
5. The Central Zionist Archives will hereafter be indicated as CZA.
6. *Sefer Hamaapilim*, edited by Moshe Basok and published by the World Zionist Organization in Jerusalem, 1947, pp. 273–301.
7. The author wishes to put on record his indebtedness in particular to the following people: Gustav Trieger, Dr. Pavel Strahovsky (Steinhauer), Hansi Steiner, Franzi Schlesinger, Dr. Seev Goshen (Goldberger), O. Karmil (Krasniansky), and Shimon Polák.
8. The author paid 11,000 korunas (at that time about $300, according to the official rate of exchange) — somewhat more than the average price.
9. Its 308 members sailed from the Yugoslav port of Sušak on the *Colorado* and were transshipped on the high seas to the *Atrata*. The landing took place near Shefayim.
10. After World War II, when most inmates of the DP camps wanted to go to Palestine and the number of certificates was utterly inadequate, Aliya Bet reached large proportions. From its inception until the establishment of the State of Israel, no fewer than 136 ships took 115,000 *maapilim* to Eretz Israel. Tens of thousands of them, including many Czechoslovak Jews, could reach it only after internment in Cyprus.
11. The background of the Aliya Bet from Czechoslovakia — including the atmosphere in and around Brno before the German occupation and after — the organization of a transport, and its departure and voyage are vividly and faithfully described in the book *Patria* by Dr. G. A. Steiner, published by Am Oved, Tel Aviv, 1964 (in Hebrew).
12. Aliya Bet in general was commemorated in numerous speeches and articles in the seventeenth year of the independence of Israel (April 1964 to April 1965), which was proclaimed "Year of Haapalah" (illegal immigration).
13. They did not rejoin the main group but sailed on the *Pacific*, were transferred to the *Patria*, and thus escaped deportation to Mauritius.
14. Sometimes they were caused not so much by lack of funds as by lack of cooperation and good will on the part of the official Slovak travel agency, Želka, which served as intermediary for the transfer of monies from Prague.
15. Afterwards he rose in the Fascist hierarchy: he was appointed commandant of the big Jewish labor camp of Sered and became a member of the Slovak Parliament. After the liberation of Czechoslovakia, he was sentenced to a thirty-year prison term.
16. In March the inmates of the Slobodárňa had an opportunity of showing in a small and symbolic way their gratitude to their friends

and benefactors: they volunteered to remove snow from public places after learning that local Jews were going to be ordered to do this heavy work.

17. Among the numerous persons who helped the refugees, two at least should be singled out for special mention: Dr. Oskar Neumann, chairman of the Zionist Organization and of the "Židovská Ústredňa" — now retired in Tel Aviv and president of the Hitachduth Oley Czechoslovakia; and Mrs. Gisi Fleischmann of the HICEM, who was murdered by the Nazis.
18. Developments in Slovakia and the various stages of the catastrophe that befell Slovak Jewry are described the Dr. O. Neumann's book *Im Schatten des Todes*, Olamenu, Tel Aviv, 1956. Valuable documentation may be found in "Tragedia Slovenských Židov" — Dokumentačná Akcia pri USŽNO, Bratislava, 1949. Rothkirchen, L., *The Destruction of Slovak Jewry: A Documentary History* (Yad Vashem, Jerusalem, 1961). Hebrew and English.
19. The name of Storfer's firm was *Ueberseetransporte* but his transports were better known under the designation *Rothgasse*, after the street in Vienna where his offices were situated.
20. The deportation to Mauritius meant the end of this scheme.
21. Dr. Horetzky is now employed by the Library of Congress in Washington, D. C., and Mr. Leschner died in Haifa in 1969.
22. After World War II Mr. Krasniansky (now Karmil), able organizer and skillful negotiator, became chairman of the Zionist Federation of Czechoslovakia. He is now an official of the Israel Ministry of Agriculture and lives in Tel Aviv.
23. See a letter of October 16, 1940, from the committee of the *Milos* to the Jewish Aid Committee in Athens (ZCA).
24. The passengers of the *Schoenbrunn* — more than six hundred — were later transshipped to the *Atlantic* and deported to Mauritius, apart from a minority which was transferred to the ill-fated *Patria*, like the whole company of the *Uranus* and the *Melk*. It is this latter group, a "Fleschtransport" from Brno, whose fate is described in the aforementioned book *Patria*, by Dr. G. A. Steiner.
25. After many adventures the *Pencho* finally reached the Dodecanese but was wrecked in a storm. Her passengers were later transferred to the camp of Ferramonti in southern Italy. They were liberated by the Allies and went to Israel in 1944. See B. Kalischer, "Vom Konzentrationslager nach Palaestina," Tel Aviv, 1945; and Jehoshua Levy, "Habajta! Arba Shanim Baderekh Lezion," Tel Aviv, no date.
26. Marietta Heinemann.
27. This was composed of Dr. P. Horetzky and L. Leschner (Prague), Dr. Bieler and E. Hirsch (Danzig), and S. Weiss and W. Schenkel

(Vienna). The dominant personality was no doubt the energetic and purposeful Dr. Horetzky.

28. On the other hand, the whole crew of the *Milos* and in particular her captain remained loyal and cooperative. See *Patria*, by Dr. G. A. Steiner.
29. It was mainly thanks to the expert knowledge and leadership of Ing. E. Kovăcs, a former pilot officer in the Czechoslovak Army, that the refugees succeeded in running the ship.
30. They gave little attention to an ominous prophecy in the *Cyprus Post* of November 21: "It may well be that these wandering Jews and other refugees will not be permitted even to weep at the Wailing Wall. They will be compelled to go even farther in their tragic odyssey."
31. For details about the *Patria*, including the causes and the background of the catastrophe, see *Sefer Hamaapilim*, pp. 235–271, and the final chapters of *Patria*, by Dr. G. A. Steiner.
32. Palestine Police.
33. In April 1945 the government of Palestine offered a lump sum of £3,000 in settlement of all claims for damage sustained in the course of, or owing to, the deportation. Apart from the losses suffered at the "customs examination," a considerable part of the luggage, which had remained at Atlit, was collected by the authorities and forwarded to Mauritius but did not reach its destination. Out of this £3,000, every detainee received 18 per cent of the claim he had filed after his arrival in the camp in Mauritius. The detainees contented themselves with this insufficient compensation because they were afraid that a refusal to accept this settlement would delay their liberation.
34. A few words on developments in Mauritius during the twenty years that have elapsed since the liberation of the detainees: Malaria, from which they suffered so much, was completely wiped out shortly after World War II. Mortality, therefore, dropped from 25.5 per thousand in 1945 to a mere 8.2 in 1965. This achievement contributed to a veritable population explosion: the number of inhabitants of the island rose during these two decades from 417,000 to 735,000. This increase has posed an economic problem of the first magnitude.

    Mauritius has traveled a long way from its original status as a Crown Colony. After a conference held in London in 1961, the Executive Council of the island was transformed into a responsible government (headed by Dr. Rangoolam of the Labor party) and only matters of defense, internal security, and external relations remained within the jurisdiction of the governor. While the almost exclusively Indian Labor party aimed at full independence, the Mauritius party, representing the non-Indian elements (some 34 per cent of the population), which were afraid of Indian domination, preferred internal autonomy and a continuation of the British presence. The first view prevailed, and in 1968 Mauritius became a fully independent state.

In May 1965, after a visit of the British Colonial Secretary Anthony Greenwood, there occurred intercommunal clashes with numerous casualities, including fatalities. British troops had to be flown in from Aden to restore order. However, from the proclamation of independence to the end of 1969, the situation has remained quiet.

35. The Mauritian prime minister and other members of the government of the island visited Israel in the years 1962 to 1965 and also got in touch with former ex-detainees. In 1969 the Knesset received a parliamentary mission from Mauritius, composed of representatives both of the government parties and of the opposition.

Several students from Mauritius are studying at the Hebrew University and other Israel institutions of higher learning. Trade between the two countries has developed quite satisfactorily. All this proves that the relations between Israel and Mauritius are really friendly.

36. See in particular the sections on "The Czechoslovak Group in the Camps" and "War Volunteers."
37. See "Interim Report on the Detainment Camp for the Period October 1, 1943, to September 30, 1944," Government Printer, Port Louis, Mauritius, 1945 (CZA).
38. His name was Dr. Kurt Neumann (now in Sydney), and he was primarily interested in his colleagues from the "Spolek Sionistických Akademiků" of Brno.
39. See the memorandum of the Actions Committee of October 15, 1943, submitted to the Colonial Office in London and containing various grievances (CZA).
40. European Detainees Control (Amendment) Ordinance 1940.
41. The 5 per cent deduction amounted in 1944 to almost 30,000 rupees (about $6,000).
42. Mr. Moddy visited the State of Israel several times and professed great sympathy with the Zionist cause which, however, had not been apparent at the time of the detainment, nor had it been when he was civil secretary of Palestine prior to his appointment in Mauritius.
43. Mr. Hargreaves returned with the detainees to Palestine and is still well remembered by the residents of Hadera, where he commanded the local police station. In his letter of greeting sent to the ex-detainees' meeting in October 1955 he wrote, among other things: "I shall never forget the long years we spent together on the island, nor the human values I learnt from you. I had seen Zionism at

work in Palestine for years. You taught me its spirit and for that I am grateful. I only wish it had been possible for me to have stayed among you to share the joys and dangers in the creation of your new state."

44. The case of Shmuel Feier, mentioned in the petition of married couples drawn up by Dr. O. Freudenheim and submitted on June 14, 1942.
45. The diet scale in the middle of 1944 was as follows (in grams): weekly rations — beef 125, corned beef 125, fish 300, pickled beef 75, salt fish 75, butter 60; daily rations — sugar 115, batata or other potato substitute 300, bread 375, wheat or maize flour 60, jam 60, vegetables 500.
46. There were five kitchens in the camp: for men, for women, for children, the hospital kitchen, and a kosher kitchen for about three hundred people.
47. For details, see the author's *Exile in Mauritius*, the chapter on "Food and Clothing," p. 36.
48. It should be noted that only two of them belonged to the Czech group, because its members had been vaccinated against typhoid before embarking on their journey, while most of the others had not.
49. Attached to the petition of the Actions Committee to the camp authorities and the British government, dated 15.5.1944 (CZA).
50. Of the nine doctors who worked in the beginning, four were Czech (Dr. Kumerman, Dr. Steinhauer-Strahovský, Dr. Abeles, and Dr. Lederer). In the course of time five doctors joined up, retired, or died, so that in 1945 only three were practicing, among them Dr. Lederer.
51. When in 1955 the ex-detainees in Israel learned that the cemetery was in need of repair, they collected a sum of money among themselves and sent it to Mauritius. The cemetery was thoroughly restored in 1958, thanks to a subsidy on the part of the South African Jewish Board of Deputies and the generosity of a few individuals, among them the French Mauritians Pierre de Comarmond and J. Desmarais, who volunteered professional and other services, and Christian d'Unienville.
52. For details about various economic enterprises, as well as on the assistance rendered by the Czechoslovak authorities, see the section on "The Czechoslovak Group in the Camp."
53. There was a saying in the camp that its monetary unit was not the rupee but the cent. The legal tender in Mauritius is the rupee (about $0.21), divided into 100 cents.
54. The editors — H. Weiss (Austrian group) and G. Ardo (Czechoslovak group) — tried to give expression to the feelings of the detainees,

and their uncompromising stand was one of the main reasons why the paper was closed down.

55. These talks were characterized as follows in the article of Dr. Freudenheim mentioned in note 1: "These personages helped to satisfy our spiritual needs, showing a profound understanding of our situation and genuine sympathy with our fate. These friends from among the Gentiles and their exceptional kindness will always be well remembered by us."
56. There were Czechs among the leaders and instructors, such as Mr. Ezra Horn and Mrs. Hansi Steiner, but not among the scouts and guides themselves, because the few children of the Czechoslovak group were much too young to join.
57. See the section on "War Volunteers."
58. For example, Mr. E. Braun in the men's camp Supervisor's Office and Mrs. Hansi Steiner in its counterpart in the women's camp; Mr. Erwin Fuchs and Dr. Ludvik Schmerler in the stores: and Mr. Paul Loewy in the Paymaster's Office.
59. Mention should be made here of Mrs. Ilse Loewy's manufacture of handbags and ladies' underwear and of the camp shop, which produced and even exported toys and other articles; its cofounder and manager was Mr. Leo Leschner. Mrs. Lilly Spitzer was in charge of the showroom in which the products of the camp were displayed to customers. More for export (to the stores of Mauritius and even to South Africa) than for the consumption of the camp was the work of Mrs. Rose Hillel (artificial flowers), Lilly Holdengraeber (brassieres), and Mrs. Ali Oesterreicher (handbags). This list does not lay claim to completeness.
60. The engineers Bedřich Steiner and Norbert Presser (wireless), Willy Gansel and Uri Spitzer (Royal Navy workshops), Hans Metzker (butcher), Egon Rosenblatt and Ezra Horn (camp garage), and so on.
61. The first headmaster, Mr. Ota Panzer, and the second, Dr. Rudolf Goldberger, who succeeded him after he had joined up with the second batch of volunteers, were both members of the Czech group.
62. The head of the camp band, Fritz ("Papa") Haas, was undoubtedly one of the most popular figures in the whole camp; Beda Maier was a very good painter; Fritz Haendel was a gifted amateur in many fields.
63. By means of a letter sent to the Maccabi, Cape Town, in January 1941 and published in *The South African Jewish Chronicle.*
64. For details, see the author's *Exile in Mauritius*, pp. 27–31.
65. *Palestine Gazette Supplement II*, 1940, p. 1401.
66. Ibid., p. 465.

67. Letter of Dr. Bernard (Dov) Joseph—at present Minister of Justice of Israel—to the Zionist Association of Mauritius, May 25, 1944 (CZA).
68. For details about the illegality of the various regulations made for the implementation of the White Paper, see: *Law and Policy under the Palestine Mandate*, by J. Stoyanowsky, The Jewish Yearbook for International Law, Rubin Mass, Jerusalem, 1948, pp. 42–86.
69. As a matter of fact, their food and accommodation were much worse than those of a German family detained as civil internees near the camp hospital.
70. Mrs. Berger (now Schlesinger) went to Palestine at the end of 1945 and worked until 1951 with the Czechoslovak Consulate General in Jerusalem. Also in this capacity she proved very helpful to her former fellow detainees and other Jews from Czechoslovakia.
71. See the following section.
72. The nature of this help is illustrated by the following two letters sent by the Consulate General in Cape Town, the first to the camp commandant—incidentally showing a well-founded distrust in the camp authorities; the second to the present writer:

I

"Cape Town
"May 19, 1943

"I have the honor to inform you that upon the instance of the Czechoslovak Red Cross Society, London, the Czechoslovak Ministry for Social Welfare has arranged for a monthly remittance of £75 being made to you, which money is destined for those Czechoslovak citizens, detainees in Mauritius, who are in need of help. You are requested kindly to use the services of Dr. Zwergbaum in this connection, who is best informed of the needs and requirements of the members of the Czechoslovak group of detainees.

"It is understood that this additional support, destined for destitute Czechoslovak detainees, will in no way impair, or interfere with, the regular allowances granted to all detainees alike. Copy of this letter is being sent to Dr. Zwergbaum."

II

"Cape Town
"August 10, 1942

"I beg to inform you that upon the instructions of the Czechoslovak government, London, I have applied for an export permit for 300 vitamin capsules A & D, 4 gallons of Lysol and 3 gallons of absolute alcohol.

"As soon as this is issued I shall arrange the dispatch of the consignment through Messrs, Thomas Cook & Son, free of any charge for you, if possible, and advise you by cable. Hoping that it will arrive safely, Yours, etc."

73. A member of a kibbutz, a veteran of the Palmach when asked the reason for his desertion, simply said: "I did not want to leave Eretz Israel for a second time and perhaps forever."
74. See the preceding section.
75. See the statement of the Secretary of State for the Colonies in the House of Commons made on March 16, 1944.
76. Their leaders were Ota Panzer and Dr. Pavel Horetzky.
77. Also the volunteers of the first batch were, with very few exceptions, ultimately transferred to Britain and took part in the invasion of the Continent, in particular the siege of Dunkirk.
78. The volunteers had to deplore four fatalities: Honza Oplatka and Dolfa Treulich lost their young lives in a plane crash, K. Blumental fell in France, and Gustl Spazier died under tragic circumstances connected with the war.
79. The Polish citizens, for understandable reasons, were not very keen on joining the Polish Army; only 8 detainees volunteered for the Polish forces in the Middle East and left the island on April 3, 1943. Together with the second batch of the Czechoslovak volunteers, 25 detainees who had joined the British Auxiliary Pioneer Corps also embarked. This was the only unit that could be joined by enemy nationals such as the Austrians. Of the 212 detainees who in the course of the detention joined up, much more than half were members of the Czech group. Even if one takes into consideration that the percentage of young men in this group was much higher than in the others, it still may be said that the Czech war record was by far the best.
80. The Czechoslovak group leaders were, at first, Mr. F. Haendel and Mrs. E. Gansel and afterwards Erwin Fuchs, Dr. Enoch, and Karel Poláček. The post of camp chairman was always filled by an Austrian, as representative of the strongest group.
81. The most prominent members of the Actions Committee were the "radicals"—Rabbi Dr. M. Bieler and Mr. G. Ardo — and the "moderates"—Ing. Kraemer and Karel Poláček. Because of this difference in approach, the Actions Committee was often divided in itself.
82. Significant of the attitude of the Jewish Agency was a letter sent by Moshe Shertok (Sharett) dated August 16, 1942, and saying: "We have never forgotten you, not for one day. The efforts in your behalf

have been unremitting and will continue. One day, when we meet, as we shall, we will no doubt hear a moving story, but we shall also have a story to tell" (CZA).

83. For example, by the Members of Parliament Miss Eleanor Rathbone, Mr. Martin, Mr. Hammersley, and Reverend Sorensen.
84. The first chairman of the ZAM, Dr. Jiří Kraus, was a member of the Czechoslovak group. He was succeeded by Rabbi Dr. M. Bieler and Dr. B. Soberski (both Danzig). The author was secretary of the ZAM from its founding until its dissolution on board the *Franconia* in August 1945. Other Czechoslovak members of the board of the ZAM were Leo Leschner (treasurer), Dr. R. Goldberger, Mr. P. Schwarz, and Mrs. Ilka Samstag.
85. Lord Gort showed sympathy and understanding for the aspirations of the Yishuv, but his term of office was short; he resigned after less than two years, perhaps for reasons of health, perhaps in protest against Bevin's Palestine policy.
86. See Professor Seddon: "Poliomyelitis in Mauritius," Government Printer, Port Louis, Mauritius, 1945.
87. The *Davar* of August 26 gave expression to these feelings: "This morning all hearts in Eretz Israel are throbbing in unison, the expression of gloom has been removed for a while from all Jewish faces: the deportees have returned from Mauritius. A great injustice, one of the greatest wrongs done to the Jewish people during this war, without sense and foundation, has been righted."
88. Erich Gross, Benzion Šmilovič, and Erich Tramer.
89. In 1964 the foundation was laid for the third generation of "Czechoslovak Mauritians": Mr. Dan Trieger, who was born during the internment in Bratislava and arrived in Mauritius as a baby in arms, married Miss Judith Maier, born in Mauritius. This wedding was, of course, attended by many members of the former Czech group, particularly those living in or near Haifa.
90. A notable exception was the former group leader Mr. Karel Poláček, who kept up a steady and most interesting correspondence at a time when this was, rightly or wrongly, considered too risky by most people.

    In recognition of the valuable work he had done for the community in Mauritius, Mr. Poláček was invited to Israel by some fifty members of the former Czech group, who covered the costs of his stay and of the plane ticket from Athens to Lydda to Athens by means of a subscription among themselves. The visit took place in March and April 1967, and Mr. Poláček, at that time seventy-eight years of age, enjoyed tremendously sightseeing in Israel and meeting again many of his friends.

NOTE ON AUTHORS

Eugen BÁRKÁNY (1886–1967); graduated Technical College in Budapest, Hungary; architect and builder, his best-known work: modern synagogue in Kežmarok, Slovakia; Cofounder of the Jewish Museum in Prešov, Slovakia.

Fini BRADA M.A. (1896–1968); publicist, social worker; member executive WIZO, ČSR, active Poalei Zion, delegate several Zionist Congresses; in Israel since 1938: Hitachduth Olei Czechoslovakia, secretary women's section Jerusalem Labor Council, director Dept. Social Welfare, Jerusalem Municipality; author of *Women in Society; The Integration of the Czechoslovak Immigration in Palestine.*

John Wolfgang BRÜGEL, Ph.D. (Prague); Czechoslovak civil servant 1929–1946, private secretary to member of the Czechoslovak government Dr. Ludwig Czech, 1930–1938; since 1946 writer in London, author of many studies in contemporary history and international law; author of the biography *Ludwig Czech* (1960) and the standard work *Tschechen und Deutsche, 1918–1938* (1957)

Jan EHRENWALD, M.D. (Prague); practiced in Bratislava 1931–1939; emigrated to England 1939–1946; since then in U.S.A.; author of *Telepathy and Medical Psychology, New Dimensions of Deep Analysis; From Medicine Man to Freud; Neurosis in the Family; Psychotherapy: Myth and Method,* as well as over 100 articles in the field of neuropsychiatry and psychoanalysis, and parapsychology.

Meir (Marcel) FÄRBER; journalist; coeditor of the daily *Yediot Hadashot* (Tel-Aviv); author of several books in Hebrew and German; Israel correspondent of a number of Jewish periodicals in the Diaspora; Chairman, Economic Advisory Board for Immigrants of the B'nai B'rith Grand Lodge.

Manfred GEORGE, Dr. jur. (1893–1965); author of several books, newspaperman, Editor-in-Chief of the weekly *Aufbau* in New York; contributed many studies in leading European and American publications.

Seev GOSHEN (*Rud. Goldberger*) Dr. jur. (Prague); Bath Jerusalem, 1947–49, Davar correspondent in Prague; cofounder of kibbutz Neoth Mordechai; assistant lecturer at Haifa University.

Kurt R. GROSSMANN; former secretary general of German League for Human Rights; after 1933 active in refugee relief and rescue work in Prague (Demokratische Flüchtlingsfürsorge) and (World Jewish Congress and Jewish Agency for Israel); published, with Prof. Arieh Tartakower, in 1944, *The Jewish Refugee* (Institute of Jewish Affairs) and numerous other essays and pamphlets on the same problem; his last work *Emigration, Die Geschichte der Hitler-Flücht!inge 1933–1945*, Europäische Verlagsanstalt, Frankfurt, won wide acclaim.

Samuel Jacob HARENDORF (1900–1969); journalist; founder of Jewish World News Agency (IWNA) and of the first *Yiddish Folksblatt* (1925) in Munkačevo; correspondent for Yiddish newspapers in New York, Buenos Aires, Tel-Aviv, Johannesburg, etc.; author of *The King of Lampodusa*, 1944, *Hannah Szenes* and other plays, and the book *Theatre-Caravans*, 1955.

Gertrude HIRSCHLER; writer, translator, editor; has translations into English of numerous works of Jewish religious and historical literature, including *The Psalms*, by Samson Raphael Hirsch; associated with Herzl Press, New York, as Assistant Editor of the *Encyclopedia of Zionism and Israel*.

Egon HOSTOVSKY; author, novelist; literary consultant to the Czechoslovak government; spent World War II in U.S.; returned to Czechoslovakia, 1945; joined diplomatic corps, Chargé d'Affaires, Norway; resigned after Communist takeover, returned to U.S.

Zdenka MÜNZER, Ph.D. (Prague); formerly librarian in the United Nations, at present time on the staff of the Metropolitan Museum of Art in New York; publications: *The Altneuschul in Prague*, *Agnes Monastery in Prague*, *Great Moravian Architecture of the Ninth Century*, papers on early medieval art.

Joseph C. PICK; executive, Moldavia-Generali Insurance Company Ltd., Prague; delegate, Czechoslovak Union of Transport Insurers to International Marine and Aviation Conventions in Europe, 1927–1939; consultant, U.S. War Department, and Harvard University, 1942–1944; technical advisor, International Civil Aviation Conference, Chicago, 1944; licensed insurance broker, marine and aviation adjuster, 1945–1967; active in Maccabi movement since its inception in Bohemia.

Irma POLAK; born in Czechoslovakia, lived since 1941 in Israel; prominent in Zionist women's work in Czechoslovakia; Vice-pres. of WIZO, hon. Secretary of Histadrut Tarbut; hon. member of World WIZO, etc.; writer on economic and consumer matters.

Theodore K. RABB, Ph.D.; Associate Professor of History, Princeton University; formerly taught at Stanford, Northwestern, Harvard, and Johns Hopkins Universities; author of various articles and books on sixteenth and seventeenth century European history.

Aharon Moshe (Kurt) RABINOWICZ, Ph.D.; formerly editor, *Palestine Digest;* Secretary to Research Council of Israel, Prime Minister's Office; Secretary, Faculty of Law, Hebrew University, Jerusalem; published articles and essays on problems of Human Rights and International Relations.

Oskar K. RABINOWICZ, Ph.D. (Prague) (1902–1969); Zionist historian, lecturer, and author of many books; Coeditor of *The Jews of Czechoslovakia* and the *Encyclopedia Judaica*, Jerusalem; Cofounder-Director of The Society for the History of Czechoslovak Jews, New York.

Frank REICHENTHAL (1895–1971); painter, studied art in the Academies of Budapest and Petrograd (Leningrad); 1932–1938 Chief of the Department for Decorative Art at the State School of Applied Arts in Bratislava; 1946–1947 President of the Slovak Artists Association; participated in many art shows in Czechoslovakia, Israel, U.S.A., and other countries; 1948 immigrated to U.S.A.

Cecil ROTH, Ph.D. (1899–1970); Anglo-Jewry's major historian, reader in postbiblical studies at Oxford, Chief Editor of *Encyclopedia Judaica*, Jerusalem; fellow of the Royal Historical Society (England); author of many important historical books.

Aryeh SOLE, graduated from Hebrew gymnasium (Mukačevo); teacher of Judaic studies since 1937; now at Teachers' Seminary, Natania, Israel; published articles on literature and education.

Hugo STRANSKY, Ph.D.; ordained, Rabbinerseminar, Berlin; formerly Rabbi, Náchod, Žilina (Czechoslovakia); Jewish Chief Chaplain of the Czechoslovak Armed Forces and of the Czechoslovak Brigade under Allied Command, World War II; Chief Minister, Melbourne Hebrew Congregation (Australia); presently Rabbi, Congregation Beth Hillel, New York; writer, lecturer in rabbinics and history.

Richard TELTSCHER, Dr. jur. (Vienna); Editor, *Archiv für jüdische Familienforschung*, Vienna; Founding Member B'nai B'rith Lodge "Massada," Vienna; Founder and Life President, Central Jewish Museum for Moravia-Silesia, Mikulov; Member, Jewish Historical Society of England.

Hana VOLAVKOVÁ (née Frankensteinová) Ph.D., (Prague); Director emeritus Jewish State Museum, Prague; writer, author of many publications on Jewish Museum and Czech art.

Felix WELTSCH, Ph.D. (Prague) (1884–1964); Librarian, author; Director of University Library, Prague; wrote numerous works and essays on philosophy and Zionism.

Chaim YAHIL, Dr. res. pol. (formerly H. Hoffmann); Secretary of Hechalutz in Czechoslovakia, member of Presidium of Poale-Zion, Director of Jewish Welfare Centre and Social Institute of Jewish Communities, Prague; from 1939 in Palestine with Histadruth; 1945–49 head of Palestinian mission to Jewish D. P. camps in Germany, joined Israel's diplomatic service; Ambassador to Sweden, Norway, and Iceland, Director-General of Israel Foreign Ministry until 1964; since 1965 Chairman of Israel Broadcasting Authority.

Aharon ZWERGBAUM, Dr. jur., (Brno); honorary Secretary of Zionist Association of Mauritius; with the Executive of the World Zionist Organization (Jewish Agency) Jerusalem since 1945, now its legal advisor on organizational matters; published articles on historic, Zionist, and legal subjects.

NAME INDEX*

The roman numeral indicates in which volume of *The Jews of Czechoslovakia* the page reference is to be found.

Complied by Zdenka Münzer.

SUBJECT INDEX*

The roman numeral indicates in which volume of *The Jews of Czechoslovakia* the page reference is to be found.

* *Complied by Zdenka Münzer.*